AN EXPLORER'S GUIDE

# Blue Ridge & Smoky Mountains

AN EXPLORER'S GUIDE

# Blue Ridge & Smoky Mountains

Jim Hargan

*with photographs by the author*

FOURTH EDITION

The Countryman Press * Woodstock, Vermont

Interior photographs by the author unless otherwise specified

Maps by Erin Greb Cartography, © The Countryman Press
Text and cover design by Bodenweber Design
Composition by PerfecType, Nashville, TN

Explorer's Guide Blue Ridge & Smoky Mountains
978-0-88150-968-7

Published by The Countryman Press, P.O. Box 748, Woodstock, VT 05091

Distributed by W. W. Norton & Company, Inc., 500 Fifth Avenue, New York, NY 10110

Printed in the United States of America

10 9 8 7 6 5 4 3 2

# EXPLORE WITH US!

Welcome to the 4th Edition of The Blue Ridge & Smoky Mountains: An Explorer's Guide, the definitive guide to the tallest mountains in the East. It's the perfect companion for exploring the Great Smoky Mountains National Park, the Blue Ridge Parkway, and all the ridges in between. Here, you'll find thorough coverage for both sides of the Tennessee–North Carolina state line, with detailed listings on the best sight-seeing, outdoor activities, restaurants, shopping, and bed-and-breakfasts. Like all Explorer's Guides, this book is an old-fashioned, classic traveler's guide, where an experienced and knowledgeable expert helps you find your way around in a new area or explore some fascinating corners of a familiar one.

## WHAT'S WHERE

In the beginning of the book you'll find an alphabetical listing of special highlights and important information that you may want to reference quickly. You'll find advice on everything from Area Codes to Wildlife.

## LODGING

We've selected lodging places for inclusion in this book based on their merit alone; we do not charge innkeepers for inclusion. Prices: Please don't hold us, or the respective innkeepers, responsible for the rates listed as of press time in late 2011. Changes are inevitable. At the time of this writing, the state and local room tax ranged from 6 to 11 percent.

## RESTAURANTS

In most chapters please note the distinction between Eating Out and Dining Out. By their nature, restaurants included in Eating Out are generally inexpensive. A range of prices is included for each entry.

## KEY TO SYMBOLS

- ✎ Child-friendly. The crayon denotes a family-friendly place or event that welcomes young children. Most bed-and-breakfasts prohibit children under 12.
- ♿ Handicapped access. The wheelchair icon denotes a place with full Americans with Disabilities Act (ADA) standard access, still distressingly rare in these remote areas.
- ☂ Rainy day. The umbrella icon points out places where you can entertain yourself but still stay dry in bad weather.
- 🐾 Pets. The dog's paw icon identifies lodgings that allow pets—still the exception to the rule. Accommodations that accept pets may still charge an extra fee or restrict pets to certain areas, as well as require advance notice.

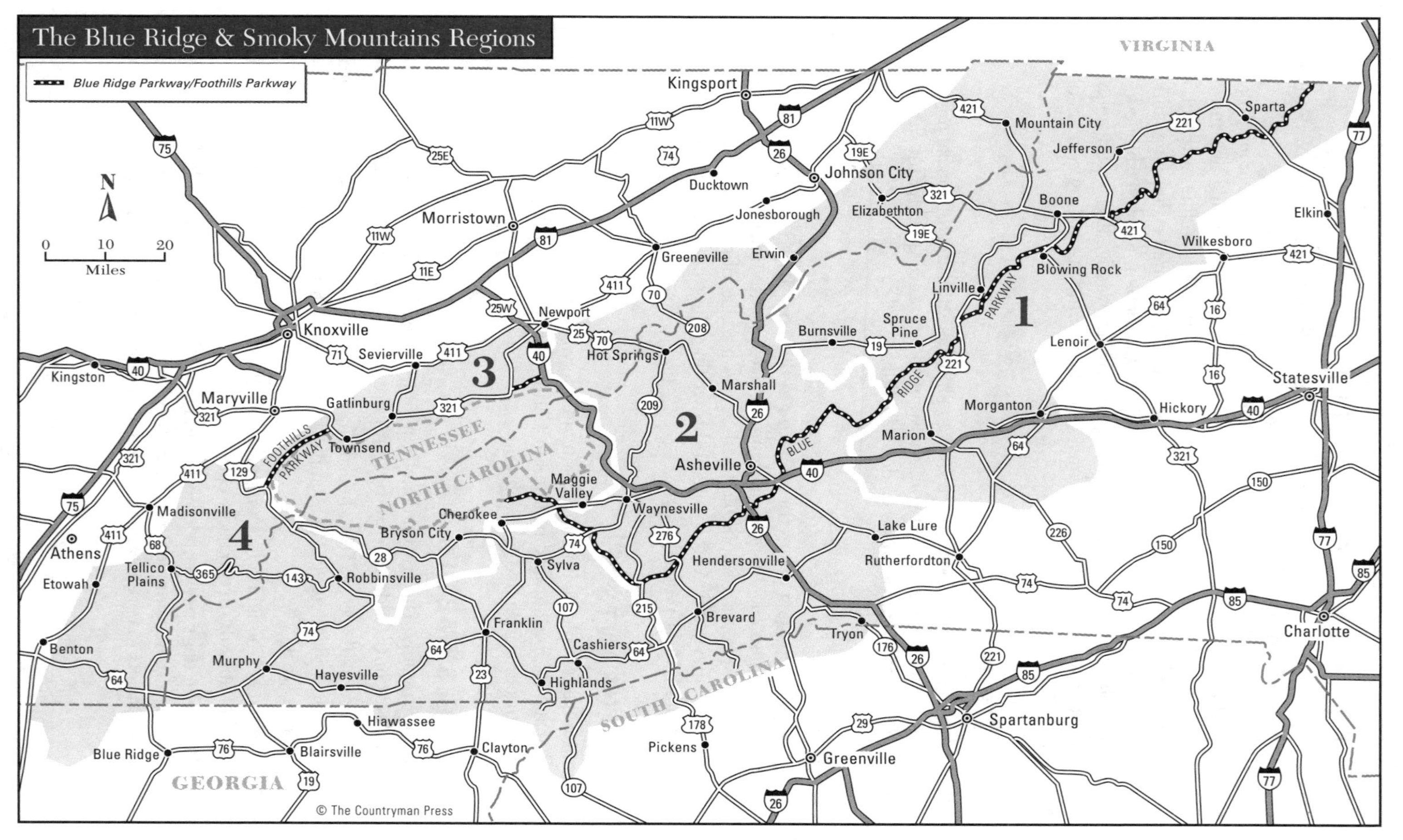
The Blue Ridge & Smoky Mountains Regions
Blue Ridge Parkway/Foothills Parkway
N
0 10 20
Miles
VIRGINIA
TENNESSEE
NORTH CAROLINA
SOUTH CAROLINA
GEORGIA
1
2
3
4
BLUE RIDGE PARKWAY
FOOTHILLS PARKWAY
Kingsport
Johnson City
Ducktown
Jonesborough
Elizabethton
Morristown
Greeneville
Erwin
Mountain City
Jefferson
Sparta
Elkin
Boone
Wilkesboro
Blowing Rock
Linville
Spruce Pine
Burnsville
Lenoir
Statesville
Hickory
Morganton
Marion
Knoxville
Kingston
Maryville
Sevierville
Gatlinburg
Townsend
Newport
Hot Springs
Marshall
Asheville
Maggie Valley
Waynesville
Cherokee
Bryson City
Sylva
Madisonville
Athens
Tellico Plains
Etowah
Robbinsville
Lake Lure
Rutherfordton
Hendersonville
Brevard
Tryon
Franklin
Cashiers
Highlands
Benton
Murphy
Hayesville
Hiawassee
Blue Ridge
Blairsville
Clayton
Pickens
Greenville
Spartanburg
Charlotte
© The Countryman Press

# CONTENTS

# MAPS

# INTRODUCTION

Some travel experiences are for passive enjoyment, for being gently led from meal to pastime to meal. Not so the Smokies. The Smokies and the Blue Ridge are for involvement—for finding the perfect little inn with broad views from an antique-furnished room, for discovering the wonderful meal superbly prepared at an unpretentious roadhouse, for digging up the odd little corner, the unforgettable museum, the remarkable site. The Smokies and the Blue Ridge are for exploring.

And this is a guide for explorers. It is a guide for finding your way down a winding mountain road to a beautiful river, a quiet log cabin, or a wide view. This guide seeks out the memorable, the unique, and the worthwhile—whether it be a place to visit, a place to shop, a place to eat, or a place to stay. It excludes the ordinary or routine places—after all, there are plenty of those back home. And, unlike many guides, it doesn't charge fees or accept advertising. This is a collection of personal recommendations.

This guide centers on two of the most popular national park lands in the nation: the Great Smoky Mountains National Park and the Blue Ridge Parkway. In doing so it covers the 40 highest peaks of the East, the most biodiverse forests in temperate North America, scores of waterfalls, and hundreds of panoramic views. However, this guide goes well beyond the boundaries of the national parks to cover all of the surrounding mountains and forests, the small towns and the settled valleys. In it you'll find tidy county seats, brick-front downtowns little changed in half a century, artist colonies hidden away in remote valleys, and well-tended farms and old log cabins that welcome overnight visitors. You'll find the homes of Carl Sandburg and Daniel Boone, the summer estate of an aristocratic South Carolina governor, and the log cabin of a frontiersman North Carolina governor. And you'll find lots of outdoor activities as well—whitewater sports, horseback riding, still-water boating, fishing, rock climbing, snow skiing, and golf.

Specifically, this guide covers the most rugged areas of the South's two great mountain ranges, the Blue Ridge and the Smokies/Unakas. The Blue Ridge, with its long series of gray cliffs facing toward the distant Atlantic, defines the eastern edge of the region. A set of mile-high ridges defines the western edge, variously named (from south to north) the Unicoi Mountains, the Great Smoky Mountains, the Bald Mountains, the Unaka Mountains, the Yellow Mountains, and the Stone Mountains. Together, these are called the Unakas (you-NAY-kuhs) by geologists, and the Smokies by ordinary folk; this book splits the difference and calls them the Smokies/Unakas.

This guide divides this 10,000-square-mile area (larger than New Jersey) into 21 chapters. Each chapter takes in a coherent area with a good range of sites, activities, and places to stay. The chapters are grouped into four broad areas, each a major region worthy of a long trip. The Great Smoky Mountains National Park gets four chapters to itself, making up one entire part of the book. The Blue Ridge Parkway, over 250 miles long and very skinny, also gets four chapters, spread throughout the first half of the book; these chapters always have "Blue Ridge Parkway" in their titles. The remaining chapters cover the areas in between the two great national parks—frequently as rugged, as wildly beautiful, and as entertaining as the parks themselves.

This guide gains strength from being part of an established series known for its high standards—the Countryman Press's *Explorer's Guide* series. As part of this series, the Smokies and the Blue Ridge share a format polished from long experience and honed to the needs of adventurous travelers. Each chapter covers an area that can be conveniently explored from any of its listed inns. The chapters start with an overview, then follow with general descriptions of exploring the scenery (*Exploring the Area*), the major areas of natural scenic beauty (*Wild Places*), and the major settled places (*Villages*); the titled paragraphs let you go straight to the parts that interest you. After that, the chapters get down to specifics: sites and attractions worth a visit (*To See*); outdoor activities (*To Do*); the most interesting and unique of the area's best lodging (*Lodging*); places to get good, fresh food prepared from scratch (*Where to Eat*); places with regular evening entertainment (*Entertainment*); unique shops and worthwhile shopping districts (*Selective Shopping*); and some of the best of the annual festivals (*Special Events*).

Readers experienced with our New England guides will immediately notice that this guide spends a lot more time in the woods, and a lot less time in the towns. Travelers experienced with the American South will see nothing odd in this; in much of the South, the woods are the good part. Yet this guide finds much to recommend in the towns and villages of the Smokies and the Blue Ridge. Most remarkable are the busy, well-tended brick-front downtowns that appear in one country town after another, from Sparta in the far north, to Copperhill 290 miles south. Equally amazing are the artists' colonies spread throughout these hills, from Penland, with its hundred or more studios, to Tellico Plains, with a dozen impressive local crafters. Not surprisingly, good shopping can be found in some unexpected places.

Our author, Jim Hargan, lived deep in the Smokies and the Blue Ridge for 17 years. A travel photographer and writer with a background in geography, he's been involved with the Smokies since vacationing there as a small boy and later attended one of the mountain universities. The Smokies and the Blue Ridge remain one of his core specialties (Great Britain being the other), and he brings his own local insights to these recommendations.

**Appalachians or Alleghenies?** Are these really the Appalachian Mountains? Or are they the Alleghenies? Or perhaps the Alleghenies are farther west and the Appalachians include them: the Great Valley (Knoxville and Chattanooga), the Smokies/Unakas, and the Blue Ridge. All such usages can be found in contemporary writing. So what's the real name of these mountains?

In 1565 French cartographer Jacques Le Moyne published a map of Florida in which he identified a mountain range, far to Florida's north, which he labeled the Montes Apalatchi. Evidently the Apalachee Indians of the Florida Panhandle had boasted to Le Moyne that they owned these mountains, an obvious tall tale. At any rate, both Le Moyne and his Florida informants had been referring to the Georgia Blue Ridge, not the entire mountain chain that stretches from Alabama to Nova Scotia. However, five years later Gerard Mercator repeated the name Montes Apalatchi on his landmark map, the term stuck, and the mountains became known as the Appalachians.

If only the story was that simple. The fact was, the name Appalachian was a silly one and nobody liked it. By the late 1700s it had died out in favor of the Allegheny Mountains, and the term *Appalachian* disappeared from use. By the mid-19th century, only antiquarians knew the meaning of the term *Appalachian.*

And that is exactly where it came from. In 1861, Swiss geographer Arnold Guyot revived the term and applied it to "the Appalachian Mountain System," which he identified as consisting of the eastern mountains (the Blue Ridge and Smokies/Unakas), the Great Valley of Tennessee (Knoxville and Chattanooga), and a plateau escarpment farther west whose heavily dissected edge has a mountainous look. The mountain people disliked Guyot's new terms (if they ever heard of them), and continued to use *Allegheny* well into the 20th century. Indeed, one of North Carolina's mountain counties is named Alleghany, an alternate spelling. But it was no use. Twentieth-century geographers followed Guyot's lead and ignored common usage, even taking the liberty of moving the term *Allegheny* westward from the Blue Ridge to the plateau escarpment. Sociologists followed, professing to discover a unified social and cultural region in Guyot's Appalachian Mountain System. They dubbed this purported region Appalachia, a place they described as characterized by social atavism and extreme poverty, "a strange land inhabited by a peculiar people," as one writer put it. No wonder terms remain confusing.

With all this, readers will be pleased to learn that both the names Blue Ridge and Smoky Mountains are authentic early terms, in common usage by the mid-18th century. Cherokee names still abound, and some, such as Nantahala (nan-ta-HAY-la) and Unaka (you-NAY-ka) retain their original pronunciation.

**About This Book.** Unlike many other guidebooks, Explorer's Guides are not collections of paid advertising. No entry has been charged a fee or allowed to supply copy. Rather, these entries are the personal recommendations of the author, a geographer, travel specialist, and long-time resident of the Smokies and Blue Ridge.

This guide does all it can to include phone numbers, addresses, e-mails, websites, and prices. Prices, however, quickly slip out of date. Use them for comparison, with each other and your budget. Make a little adjustment in your head; these prices were quoted to the author in the summer of 2011.

This book uses icons to denote entries with special characteristics:

✐ The crayon denotes a family-friendly place that welcomes young children. Most b&bs prohibit children under twelve; those that welcome them will sport display the crayon.

🐾 The dog paw shows that the place allows pets—very, very unusual among small inns and bed & breakfasts. An establishment with a dog-paw icon might still charge an extra fee or restrict pets to certain units or areas.

♿ The wheelchair icon indicates places with full Americans with Disabilities Act (ADA) standard access.

Here are a few notes about the organization of this book:

*Exploring the Area*—The one thing you can always rely on in the Smokies and the Blue Ridge is some first-rate sightseeing. This section orients you to an area's scenic qualities while steering you toward the best of the roads and trails.

*Wild Places*—In the Smokies and the Blue Ridge, settled areas can be widely separated islands in a sea of trees—"Ploughed Spaces" in an area where wild lands are the norm. This section describes, in broad terms, the qualities of the giant wild tracts of publicly accessible lands, and follows this with the best of the parks and picnic areas. (New visitors should note that picnicking is an excellent alternative in a land where restaurants are far apart and may not be very good.)

*Villages*—Of course, the American South doesn't really have villages in the New England sense. More typical is a small county seat with a courthouse and a brick-front downtown, a tiny urban island surrounded by many miles of dispersed farms and houses. The mountains are no different. This section describes all places with well-defined centers that a visitor might want to visit or stumble into by accident, plus a few dispersed settlements that have notable sites mentioned elsewhere in the text.

*To See*—Worthwhile destinations are listed here. To be included, a place must be unique and interesting in some mountainy way—the sort of thing you traveled here to see. After all, there are plenty of water slides and miniature golf places back home. Listed places must be reasonably authentic, and not exploitative to either the mountain folk or their own customers. You won't find any salted gem mines or "hillbilly hoedowns" in these pages (but there are several authentic local gem mines and mountain music venues).

*To Do*—These entries list outdoor activities, for those who get antsy with too much relaxing. This book tries to include all outdoor sports that are quiet and non-invasive, as well as some golf courses and ski slopes.

*Lodging*—This book lists only independent, local establishments with high standards of comfort, cleanliness, and hospitality. Not all worthy establishments can be listed; this guide tries to give a good selection of different types of places, emphasizing character and uniqueness. Unless noted, listed lodgings have private baths for all rooms. We make a special effort to find places that are disabled accessible, family friendly, and/or pet friendly, but we are not always able to find such places in each chapter.

*Where to Eat*—This section emphasizes food made fresh from scratch, using fresh ingredients. It lists places in two categories: casual, inexpensive places in *Eating Out,* and formal, expensive places in *Dining Out.* In *Eating Out,* the occasional catered (premade) side is allowed if the price is right and the atmosphere nice; in *Dining Out,* catered or precooked food is unforgivable.

*Entertainment*—The Smokies are not noted for their lively nightclub scene (always excepting the city of Asheville). This section lists places that have authentic mountain music and bluegrass ("mountain music" being the old-time folk music on which bluegrass is based), as well as summer theater, regular classical music schedules, and some miscellaneous neat stuff.

*Selective Shopping*—As with other entries, this section emphasizes the unique and unusual. Rather than a complete listing, it's typically a few suggestions to help get you started in the right direction. You'll find a lot of craft galleries listed, as this region is a major center of the Fine Crafts movement.

*Special events*—Again, this is not a complete listing, but rather a selection of some of the most worthwhile annual events and festivals.

# WHAT'S WHERE IN THE SMOKIES AND THE BLUE RIDGE MOUNTAINS

**AIRPORTS AND AIRLINES** There are five airports with scheduled passenger service in or near this region, with at least some jet service. Most visitors will want to fly into either Asheville Regional Airport or Knoxville's McGhee Tyson Airport. However, there are some exceptions: Greenville-Spartanburg, South Carolina, is the closest to Cashiers/ Highlands (see "The Blue Ridge: Cashiers and Highlands"); Chattanooga is closest to Copperhill and Murphy (see "The Southern Unicois: Murphy and the Copper Basin"); and the Tri-Cities of Johnson City, Bristol, and Kingsport, Tennessee, (see "The Mountains of Northern Tennessee) are closest to the northernmost counties (see "Behind the Blue Ridge: Boone & Banner Elk"). Bargain-hunters should consider flying into the nearest major hubs (either Charlotte or Atlanta) and driving from there into the mountains (typically two to four hours). In any case, expect to rent a car; these mountains have virtually no regional or local bus service.

**AMTRAK** (www.amtrak.com) There is no passenger train service to these mountains; not even Chattanooga gets a choo-choo these days. The closest approach is at Greenville and Spartanburg, South Carolina, about 45 minutes south of Asheville, where the Crescent stops twice a day on its travels between New York and New Orleans.

**AMUSEMENT PARKS** This book does not cover amusement or theme parks, as a modern intrusion from the outside having nothing to do with mountain wilderness or culture. However, there are several such parks within this region, of varying quality. For those who like such things, look for amusement parks outside the main gates of the Great Smoky Mountains National Park, at Gatlinburg and Pigeon Forge, Tennessee, and at Cherokee and Maggie Valley, North Carolina. Pigeon Forge's Dollywood being the largest and best of this bunch. Afficionados of Wild West attractions will find two to choose from, at Boone and Maggie Valley (completely rebuilt and modernized in 2007). The Wild West attraction in Boone features a historic steam locomotive that was in local, commercial use through most of the first half of the 20th century.

**ANTIQUES** Antique lovers used to the rich selections in the Virginia Blue

Ridge and the mountains of New England may find this region disappointing. Truth is, most of these valleys were unspeakably poor until the 1950s and '60s, and folks did not buy a lot of fancy furniture. However, this is a good area to look for old farm implements; animal-drawn plowing did not die out in most of these valleys until the 1960s and '70s. What's more, the tradition of handmade furniture has never died out, and you can find pieces ranging from centuries old to newly made.

**APPLES** Cherokees introduced apple growing to the Smokies and the Blue Ridge in the early 18th century, having picked it up from the Creeks (who had learned it from Spanish missions in La Florida). While English settlers dismissed apple horticulture as impractical in the cold mountain climate, the Cherokees learned to grow trees in special valleys turned warm by persistent air inversions. Nineteenth-century mountain folk took up the Cherokee techniques in a big way, creating the beginnings of a mountain apple industry. Today, the Brevard area has the largest commercial orchards (see "The Blue Ridge: Hendersonville & Brevard"), while a fine heritage orchard is open to the public at Altapass, along the Blue Ridge Parkway (see "The Blue Ridge Parkway: Blowing Rock & Grandfather Mountain," To See). U-pick-ems are a common sight in the Brevard area; look to pick apples from late August through early October.

**ARTISTS AND ART GALLERIES** In the 1920s and '30s, folk crafts were widely seen as a way of bringing hard cash into the remote mountain coves. Folk art schools and guilds, founded in that era to support the economic development of poor mountain families, today survive as centers of the Fine Crafts Movement, dominated by university-educated artists building on mountain traditions. Major schools survive at Penland, Gatlinburg, Tennessee, and Brasstown, while the Highlands' Crafts Guild promotes craft artists from its headquarters in Asheville. There are a number of craft communities as well, and these are described in the relevant chapters.

**BALDS, GRASSY** While most of these mountains are covered in dense forest, an occasional grassy meadow will cling to a high ridgeline. Known as "grassy balds," these high meadows furnish wide panoramas across swaths of wildflowers, framed in the spring by bushes purple with Catawba rhododendrons and orange with flame azaleas. These balds may be as small as a few dozen acres, but may also sweep for miles along a high ridge. Their origin is unclear. Grassy balds were far more common in the 19th century, when a hundred thousand cattle grazed along the crest of the Great Smoky Mountains every summer. Left ungrazed, these great fields have been returning to forest since the start of the 20th century. The grassy balds may have been created by the Cherokees, burnt out to create wildlife habitats for hunting. Or they may have been formed by grazing elk and buffalo in the 16th through 18th centuries, and then maintained by cattle after the elk and buffalo had been hunted to extinction. The largest surviving grassy balds are in the Roan Highlands (see "Behind the Blue Ridge: Spruce Pine & Burnsville," Exploring the Area). The huge grassy meadows of the adjacent Shining Rock and Middle Prong Wildernesses are entirely different, having been caused by early 20th-century clear-cut wildfires that were so massive that the forests have yet to return (see "The Blue Ridge Parkway

Approaches the Smokies," Wild Places).

**BALDS, ROCKY** Unlike grassy balds, rocky balds are a completely natural phenomenon. Common to the Blue Ridge, a rocky bald consists of a broad expanse of smoothly curving, exposed bedrock, elevated at any possible angle from dead flat to totally vertical. A typical rocky bald will extend from 1 to 5 acres, with the bare rock covered by patches of moss and an occasional dwarf pine. The rock looks like granite, but isn't; it's schist, a metamorphosed granite whose peculiar geology causes this unusual formation. Along the Blue Ridge, this ancient schist has been compressed under immense pressure for most of the last quarter billion years, only to be raised up and exposed by erosion during the last 50 million years or so. This great relief of pressure has allowed the rock to expand like a spring, in the stateliest of slow motion, exfoliating in thinly compressed layers. This exfoliation is just fast enough to slough off soil as it forms, leaving the bedrock smooth and bare. Needless to say, rocky balds furnish some of the most dramatic views anywhere. One of the most impressive sights along the Blue Ridge is an entire dome of rock exposed in this way, such as Stone Mountain (see "The Blue Ridge Parkway Enters North Carolina," Wild Places) and Looking Glass Rock (see "The Blue Ridge Parkway Approaches the Smokies," To See).

**BARBEQUE** People who've heard of the wondrous qualities of North Carolina barbeque will be unpleasantly surprised to learn that this rich and varied tradition seldom extends into the mountains. Instead of the piquant, slow-cooked Piedmont barbeque with its vinegar/cayenne baste and its coleslaw made fresh with the barbeque sauce, mountain visitors are more likely to find gas-grilled meat smothered with a ketchupy tomato sauce, and sweet, mayonnaisey cole slaw dipped from tubs. Good barbeque, slow-cooked over wood, does exist in the mountains, and we highlight it whenever we find it.

**BED & BREAKFASTS** A rare sight 30 years ago, bed & breakfasts are now found in every part of the Smokies and the Blue Ridge except Cherokee. They are generally price-competitive with local motels, and a lot nicer. Small and friendly, a bed & breakfast is a good way to relax and meet the locals. A typical mountain bed & breakfast will have a wide porch with rocking chairs and a view over a garden, a great room with comfortable sofas and chairs grouped around a wood fire, a friendly group of guests who swap experiences over a luxurious breakfast or an evening glass of wine, and a gregarious host who never seems to tire of meeting new people and giving a helping hand to visitors.

By the way, you might want to check the Internet for a bed & breakfast web page before calling for a reservation. Nearly all of them have one, and most show photos of the individual rooms.

**BICYCLING** The Smokies and the Blue Ridge offer wonderful opportunities for bicyclists. Back roads, increasingly paved, have wonderful scenery and light traffic, with a down side of narrow, shoulderless lanes and the occasional mean farm dog. The premiere road biking experience is the **Blue Ridge Parkway**, where the scenery is nonstop and wide shoulders, gentle curves, and frequent pullovers reduce traffic problems. The huge tracts of national forest land found throughout this region offer many miles of trail biking, mainly down old logging roads. Finally, a few places offer dedicated bicycle trails, most notably the Nantahala National Forest's **Tsali Recreation Area** (see "Bryson City and the Southwest Quadrant," *Wild Places*). For those who don't travel with their bicycles, this book lists bicycle rentals in most areas.

**BUGS** First the good news. The Smokies and the Blue Ridge are largely free of swarming black flies, midges, and mosquitoes—the kind that form clouds around your face and fill your nose when you try to breathe. What's more, flies and roaches are less of a nuisance here than in warmer parts of the South. This is not to say that these mountains are free of all pests. You are likely to get **chiggers**—microscopic larvae buried in your skin—any time you sit on the ground in even slightly warm weather. **Ticks** are very common, and likely to jump on you whenever you brush against a plant in warm weather. Chigger bites itch like crazy, and can last for weeks if you have an allergic reaction. Ticks spread diseases, some of them crippling. Your best defense against both chiggers and ticks is to wear long sleeves and pants and spray insect repellant around your neck, belt, and cuffs.

**BUS SERVICE** (www.greyhound.com) This region's major scheduled passenger bus route, a Greyhound line, runs from Winston-Salem to Asheville, then across the mountains to Knoxville,

**BERRY PICKING**

Wild berries are available for the picking throughout the public lands of the Smokies and the Blue Ridge. Old fields and grassy balds offer wild **strawberries** in June, then **blackberries** starting in mid-July, with **blueberries** in the high grassy balds in August. Wild strawberries, tiny and intensely flavored, hide low among the grasses in old fields. Blackberries grow on thorny canes in old fields, and are full of chiggers. Blueberries grow on low, woody bushes on grassy and rocky balds, and like the cool, wet weather above 4,000 feet. There are lots of other edible berries; look for a ranger-led talk in a national park or forest. You can collect up to a gallon of each type of berry per day without a permit in the national park and forest lands—free fun that kids love.

Tennessee, stopping in Waynesville along the way. A second line follows the Great Valley southward from Virginia to Knoxville, stopping in the Tennessee towns of Bristol, Johnson City, and Greeneville. A third line runs from Winston-Salem through Wilkesboro to Boone.

**CAMPING** Campgrounds are found in abundance throughout this region. The national parks and forests contain scores of public campgrounds, generally cheap and scenic but frequently without hookups. (The popular campgrounds within the Great Smoky Mountains National Park don't even have showers.) While many of the public campgrounds stay booked up all summer, you can always find a good site in a remote, beautiful little national forest campground down a gravel road somewhere; ask a ranger at the nearest district station (listed in this book). Private campgrounds are the best bet for RV'ers who want electricity and running water.

**CANOEING AND KAYAKING** This region has abundant whitewater and still water, with suitable streams in nearly every chapter. Famous whitewater streams include the **Ocoee**, site of the 1996 Summer Olympics; the **Nantahala**, well known as a training ground for Olympic medalists; and the **Chattooga**, made famous in the novel *Deliverance.* Two other rivers, the **New River** and the **French Broad River**, offer excellent areas for long, scenic canoe trips, perfect for overnight camping. Places to hire canoes and kayaks, join a whitewater rafting party, or have your boat shuttled to a drop-off point, are noted throughout this book.

**CHEROKEES** (www.cherokee-nc.com). This entire region was the core home of the Cherokees, centering on the fertile valleys of the Little Tennessee River south of the Great Smoky Mountains. The Cherokees lived in villages ranging from a half-dozen to maybe a hundred houses, made of logs, and surrounded by cultivated fields. These were organized along clan lines, similar to the Scottish Highlands but without the constant warfare; the Cherokee villages shared a traditional legal code, enforced through consensus and the leadership of chiefs. Until the wars of the late 18th century, the Cherokees had three major settlement areas: an area of villages in the South Carolina upstate, a second area in the deep mountains to the immediate south of the Smokies, and a third area (called the Overhill area) at the foot of the mountains in Tennessee. The more northern mountains, around present-day Burnsville and Boone, were kept as a hunting ground.

In the late 18th century, the Cherokee tried to defeat the European invaders in battle, with disastrous consequences. After that, tribal consensus swung toward working within the invaders' legal system. Led by wealthy, Europeanized chiefs, the tribe formed itself into a quasiautonomous legal entity known as the Cherokee Nation, located in northern Georgia, southeastern Tennessee, and the westernmost corner of the North Carolina Mountains. In 1838, President Andrew Jackson's administration expelled the Cherokee Nation to Oklahoma, forcing the Cherokees into a deadly winter march known as The Trail of Tears.

About 600 Cherokees remained in the deep coves of the Smokies, and their descendants still live, work, and thrive in these mountains. The Eastern Band of the Cherokee Nation, some 10,000 strong, inhabits a sizeable reservation, properly called the Qualla Boundary, located on the North

Carolina side of the Great Smoky Mountains National Park.

**CHILDREN, ESPECIALLY FOR** The author spent many a summer as a child in these mountains, and vividly remembers the things he found the most fun: splashing in mountain streams, exploring the forests, picking berries, visiting log cabins, sifting for rubies, and climbing around on rocky crags with dramatic views. Whitewater rafting hadn't been invented yet, otherwise that would have made the list as well. Rustic cabins were a lot neater than motel rooms, especially on cool, rainy days when we played board games by the wood fire. Home-cooked suppers at our cabins were more fun for us than eating out, and picnics in a national park were more fun than burgers in a tourist town. Museums could be patience-testers, but log cabins and pioneer log farms were endlessly fascinating—particularly those with farm animals, or grist mills that worked. We liked to walk down short, easy trails, particularly to cliffs or waterfalls; or just get out of the car and run around. We gained these tastes as small children, and retained them as teenagers; perhaps if we had first seen the mountains at age 14 we would have been too cool for any of this.

This region is jammed with child-appropriate, family-friendly stuff. The text makes a serious effort to mention anything that will challenge a child's patience, endurance, or safety, making it easy to judge what's right for your kids. Please note that most bed & breakfasts do not accept children under 12; the text notes those who do with a family-friendly icon.

**THE CIVILIAN CONSERVATION CORPS (CCC)** When President Franklin D. Roosevelt founded the Civilian Conservation Corps (CCC) in 1933, he meant it to attack two of the Great Depression's problems at once. The first, and most visible, was a veritable army of unemployed, and unemployable, older teenage men. The second, hidden from city folks' view but just as serious, was tens of millions of acres of land destroyed by exploitative forestry—now abandoned and covered with tinder-dry waste. He formed the veritable army into an actual one, run by the U.S. Army (and spied upon by a suspicious Nazi government) that fanned out through America's ruined forests to restore them.

Today we are reaping the harvest that Roosevelt and his CCC army sowed. The CCC restoration efforts have provided us with the luxuriously deep forests that now blanket the mountains of the Virginias. The CCC also provided us with some of our finest architecture. Combining standard plans, local materials, hand craftsmanship, and lots of imagination, these classic structures—ranging from camp offices and workers' cabins to picnic shelters and hiking paths—present a coherent style of notable simplicity and beauty. This book will highlight surviving CCC recreation areas wherever it finds them, and you can be assured of finding both beauty and thoughtful quality at these spots.

**COTTAGE RENTALS** Cottage rentals have long been a tradition in these mountains, and have become increasingly popular in recent years. In some places, small compounds of log cabins, recently built in traditional styles and luxuriously furnished, have been springing up faster than chain motels. A rental cabin can be a pleasant retreat for a couple, with its ample space, separate living room, and porch; for a family with kids, it can also be a major money saver, allowing breakfasts and dinners at home with picnic lunches on the road. This book includes a selection of good cabin compounds throughout the region. Many of these cottages can be rented for only a night or two; others require rental periods up to a week.

**DRY COUNTIES** These mountain regions are a patchwork of local liquor laws. Both North Carolina and Tennessee allow local options on beer, wine, and liquor sales, and North Carolina still has a socialized liquor control system. Depending on where you are, you may be able to buy wine and beer but not liquor, liquor but not wine or beer, wine or beer in a store but not a restaurant, or in a restaurant but not a store—or all sales may be banned outright. That is, except for golf clubs, tennis clubs, or hotels and restaurants within 3 miles of the Blue Ridge Parkway. This book tries to include whether wine is available at a fine dining spot, but it's best to check in advance.

**EMERGENCIES** There is nothing more frightening that having a serious medical emergency, and not knowing where the nearest emergency room is. For this reason, each chapter introduction includes the location of the nearest emergency room.

**FALL FOLIAGE** The Smokies and the Blue Ridge have one of America's outstanding autumn color displays—the result of a large variety of species, spread over a large range of elevations and habitats. Look for color to begin in early October and reach its peak in the middle of the month. From then on, colors will last until the first strong wind, generally in the third or fourth week of October. In most years, color is nearly gone by early November. But not all; with recent warming, the mountains have seen several years when color began as late as early November. If you are coming for the color, you can check out the views on webcams on these sites:

- www.nature.nps.gov/air/WebCams/, listing two webcams within the Great Smoky Mountains National Park and showing elevations between 5,000 feet and 1,000 feet.
- webcam.srs.fs.fed.us/webcams/shining.php, a National Forest Service webcam pointed at the Shining Rock Wilderness, and showing elevations from 6,000 feet to 3,000 feet.
- www.raysweather.com, the mountain's best weather site, displays a number of private webcams in the Boone area.

**FISHING** This region is a wonderful place for fly-fishing, and this book tries to include contact information for guides. You will need a state fishing license everywhere but within the Cherokee Reservation, where you will need a tribal license instead.

**HIGHWAYS AND ROADS** This region is crossed by **I-40** from east to west, and by **I-26** from north to south; they intersect at Asheville. (Parts of I-26 north of Asheville are marked "Future I-26"; these are expressway segments slated for major upgrades in the coming years.)

Apart from interstates and U.S. highways, this book follows a welter of road types. State highways are designated as "NC 80" or "TN 70." Although these are supposed to be main through-highways, some are no better than local roads with fancy signs, and three of them in North Carolina are gravel surfaced (NC 281, NC 197, and NC 90). Local roads have names in Tennessee, Georgia, and South Carolina, but four-digit numbers in North Carolina. National Park Service roads always have names. National Forest Service roads have numbers such as "FS 712"; please note that many Forest Service roads are not passable for passenger autos.

The mountains being what they are, this book frequently recommends touring on gravel-surfaced roads. These are roads that have been improved by pounding in a mixture of gravel and rock dust, the rock dust acting as a sort of temporary cement. Gravel roads form potholes and washboard-like ridges if not graded once or twice a year, a condition most apt to occur on Forest Service roads. The text will highlight known problems. In general, if a road starts looking too rough for you, don't hesitate to turn around and go back.

**HIGHWAYS AND ROADS IN NORTH CAROLINA** Unlike other states, North Carolina has no local roads. All of its rural roads are state roads, from the largest freeway down to the roughest dirt rut. The state's Department of Transportation (known as NCDOT, or NickDot) distinguishes "state highways" from "state roads." **State highways** are considered major thoroughfares, with regular state highway signs and two- or three-digit numbers, such as NC 90 or NC 197. **State roads** have four-digit numbers, sometimes marked on stop signs with those little home address stick-on numbers, but more often found on the standard green street signs now used everywhere in America. In this book, state roads are denoted as, for example, SSR 1300 or SSR 1407, the "SSR" standing for state secondary road. This guide tries very hard to get the state road numbers right, because—unlike road names—they are almost always present at intersections. However, don't expect locals to direct you to an SSR number; no one in North Carolina pays attention to them.

**HIKING** Sooner or later, nearly everyone gets out of their car and walks through the woods. The Smokies and the Blue Ridge are laced with footpaths, up creeks and along ridges. There are thousands of miles of walking trails to choose from, with good choices in every chapter of this book. The *Exploring the Area* section contains a suggestion or two, very reward-

ing and not particularly difficult. Other sections will mention still more trails, each with a brief indication of the type of scenery, as well as its difficulty and length.

**HORSEBACK RIDING** Most parts of this region have at least one horseback riding stable. Some offer trail rides on their own property, while others outfit longer expeditions on national forest lands. Nearly every chapter lists at least one stable. In addition, there are several listed accommodations that offer stabling for people who travel with their horses.

**HUNTING** The main hunting season runs from **September through January**. Remember that hunting is allowed in all national forest lands, including the sixteen wilderness areas; you should always wear hunter orange anytime you enter these areas during the season. If you wish to avoid hunting areas altogether, you should stay in the 3 national parks and the 11 state parks (which, fortunately, offer plenty of outdoor opportunity). Hunting is also prohibited on Sunday in the state of North Carolina, making that a good day to enjoy God's creation (but wear hunter orange anyway, just in case).

**INFORMATION** As much as we like to be encyclopedic in our coverage, we admit that there is nothing like fresh, local information. Each chapter of this book lists the relevant chambers of commerce, along with their toll-free numbers and web page. We also describe the local tourist information center, so you can drop by and talk to someone friendly and in the know.

**LAKES** There are no natural lakes in this region. All of the lakes in the Smokies and the Blue Ridge are manmade, mostly for hydropower. Typically, the lake drowns a gorge-like mountain valley, twisting upstream for miles through roadless areas into steep-sided woodlands, poking little inlets up side valleys. In many cases the shores are national forest lands, with no restrictions on boat-side camping. However, other lakes are privately owned—and this may include the lake's surface as well as the surrounding shore. This book will point out interesting opportunities as they arise, as well as give contact information for lake-oriented fishing guides.

**LOG CABINS** While most of us associate log cabins with the first generations of settlers, log construction continued in the mountains into the early 20th century. This was not a matter of isolation or tradition, so much as saving money; logs were free, while milled studs required scarce dollars. The Great Smoky Mountains National Park displays a superbly crafted log cabin built by its owner in 1902 (see "Cherokee and the Southeast Quadrant," *To See*).

In these parts, all vernacular log cabins were built with planked logs—that is, logs that had their vertical sides hewn flat. Planking reduced rot by allowing rain water to run straight down, rather than bead up on the underside of a round log. While barns frequently used round logs, a round log cabin is invariably modern.

This book will sometimes describe a log cabin in terms of its cribs. A crib is the rectangle made when the logs are fitted together; doors and windows are then cut out of the cribs. The simplest cabins had one crib, covered with a roof. Larger cabins had two cribs, and the cribs could be placed together to form a two-room cabin, separated by a chimney (a rare form in the South), or (most commonly) separated by a roofed central breezeway, or dogtrot.

Log cabins were an important part of mountain life—but today, all the log cabins you will see will be carefully restored museum pieces, or else abandoned hulks. Not so with log barns; keep an eye peeled for log barns still in use along any back road, and particularly in the areas covered by part 1.

**LOST** Even with the best maps you are likely to get lost once you stray from a main highway. On these twisting roads, even the sharpest explorers will lose their sense of direction. Your best defense is a compass—one of those round ones you stick on your dashboard. Pay attention to it along several twists, and take an average. This will at least tell you if you are going generally toward your destination or away from it. And relax. How bad can it be? Getting lost is an adventure, not a disaster.

**MAPS: ROAD MAPS** (www .delorme.com). Really good road maps can be a problem in the mountains. Main highways are easy enough to follow, but back roads are a twisty maze, frequently with no regular names. Once you start exploring a back road, your folding highway map won't help you much. GPS helps less than you would think, and sometimes it makes things worse; those computer maps tend to confuse logging roads, farm tracks, and an occasional planner's fantasy with actual roads you can drive on. **DeLorme's** great paper atlases are my favorite navigational aid, as they show all the back roads as well as the shapes of the mountains, giving extra clues for your party's navigator to analyze. Unfortunately, you'll have to buy four individual state volumes to cover the entire Smoky Mountain and Blue Ridge area; this will give you a bonus (possibly unneeded and unwanted) of incredibly detailed coverage of the entire Mid-South from the Atlantic seaboard to the Mississippi River. But, whatever map you use, be prepared to get lost every once in a while.

**MAPS: USGS TOPOS** Of course, no serious outdoors enthusiast will step away from the parking lot without a U.S. Geological Survey topographic map, showing every detail of mountain slope at 2.66 inches to the mile. Unfortunately, the Geological Survey hasn't gotten around to updating some of these mountain topos since the Great Depression; the mountain slopes haven't changed much, but don't expect anything else to be very accurate. Both DeLorme (www .delorme.com) and National Geographic (shop.nationalgeographic .com) sell continuously stitched together topographic maps for computers that'll work with many GPS devices, and two websites (mytopo .com and terraserver.microsoft.com) let you download and print topos for free.

**MOUNTAINTOPS** Nearly all of the Smokies and the Blue Ridge are covered in dense forest. You can walk for miles along a high ridgeline without ever having a view. Of course, the forests are a prime attraction of these mountains, endlessly varied and with more tree species than Europe. However, the occasional overwhelmingly dramatic panorama is certainly welcome, the more so if you don't have to hike all day to find it. The best views are from **balds**, great sweeps of open grass or rocky ground. Other views are intentionally created and maintained by the National Park Service, within the Great Smoky Mountains National Park or along the Blue Ridge Parkway. This book highlights the best of the views, both roadside and from the easier paths.

**MUSIC** This guide tries to find and describe worthwhile music venues throughout the region. These range from rural dance halls, to weekend bluegrass jams, to large-scale classical music festivals. Mountain music is featured most often, along with bluegrass—the local favorite, more popular than Nashville-style country. Classical music is found near the universities, along with jazz, and the town of Brevard hosts a major classical music festival every summer (see "The Blue Ridge: Hendersonville & Brevard," *Entertainment*).

**MUSIC, MOUNTAIN** Mountain music isn't bluegrass, and it definitely isn't country. Mountain music is the music people knew before radios came along, the music they used to play deep in the coves and hollows. Mountain music was already a fast-disappearing anachronism when Mars Hill native Bascom Lamar Lunsford started his vast collection of mountain folk music in the closing years of the 19th century. Today, the music collected by Lunsford and others represents a carefully preserved folk tradition, still popular and readily available throughout this region. This book cites mountain music venues wherever it can.

**PETS** Only a few bed & breakfasts will allow pets, and these are highlighted in the text. You will have better luck with a cottage rental, which fortunately are very common in this area, but verify in advance that your pet will be welcome. Of the places that allow pets, many charge an extra fee or restrict pets to special units. The Great Smoky Mountains National Park is notoriously pet hostile, prohibiting pets on all hiking trails with no exceptions, and requiring dogs to be kept on leashes at all times anywhere else.

**PUBLIC LANDS: THE NATIONAL PARK SERVICE** (www.nps.gov) The National Park Service,a bureau of the U.S. Department of the Interior, maintains three properties in this region: The Great Smoky Mountains National Park, The Blue Ridge Parkway, and Carl Sandburg Home National Historic Site. Each has its own management style. **The Great Smoky Mountains National Park**—the only designated "national park" of the three and the most visited such park in America—has always been maintained as a wilderness park with the emphasis on hiking, camping, picnicking and fishing. **The Blue Ridge Parkway** (the most visited property managed by the National Park Service) is more purely recreational, with hotels and restaurants along its length. **The Carl Sandburg Home**, small and little visited, faithfully preserves the great poet's historic ante-bellum estate the way he knew it—including an active goat farm. However, all three share one major characteristic with each other and every other NPS property. They are all preserves, each safeguarding a precious resource for the future. All prohibit hunting, gathering plants, rockhounding, and picking wildflowers.

**PUBLIC LANDS: THE NATIONAL FOREST SERVICE** People frequently confuse the National Forest Service with the National Park Service—yet the two agencies couldn't be more different. While the National Park Service preserves our finest natural and historic lands, the National Forest Service—part of the Department of Agriculture—manages forest lands for sustainable exploitation. The National Forest Service logs many of its tracts, getting much of its operating revenues from timber sales. It allows hunting on virtually all of its lands, including congressionally declared wildernesses. The actual type of use given to any tract of national forest land—logging, recreation, preservation—is set by a plan that is revised every eight years.

This region has five national forests, any one of which dwarfs the local national parks in size: the **Cherokee National Forest** in Tennessee, the **Chattahoochee National Forest** in Georgia, the **Sumter National Forest** in South Carolina, the **Nantahala National Forest** in the southern half of the North Carolina Mountains, and the **Pisgah National Forest** in the northern half of the North Carolina Mountains. Nearly every chapter in this book includes huge tracts of national forest land, some with many wonderful things to do and see.

**ROCKHOUNDING** Eons ago, columns of molten magma broke into veins throughout the mountain bedrock, crystallizing out quartz, garnets, rubies, sapphires, beryl, and gold along with the granite. None of these valuable minerals have been found in large quantities, although optimists formed small commercial mines in the 19th century. Instead, the mountains have always been mined for the cruder minerals associated with such magmatic intrusion: granite, feldspar, mica, and kaolin are all still mined. In past decades, rockhounds have loved the old abandoned feldspar and mica mines for the occasional precious stone or valuable specimen found in the tailings. Today, few if any sites allow such casual and dangerous trespassing. Instead, entrepreneurs offer sites where tourists can sift for rubies, selling buckets of "pay dirt" salted with cheap foreign stones (which they will cut for you, for a fee). There are, however several authentic ruby mines, as well as an excellent placer gold mine, that offer unsalted dirt from on-site, and these are cited in the text.

**SKIING** Many people think that the southern Smokies and Blue Ridge are too far south for skiing. They're right; snow seldom sticks around more than a week or so at even the highest elevations, and cold rain is a lot more common than fleecy blizzards. However, a number of ski slopes stay in business using manufactured snow. Mostly the result of a speculative boom in the 1960s (during a series of cold winters), some of these slopes are old and unpleasant, while others keep themselves up. None is particularly fancy. Winter skiing is not really an environmentally friendly sport, as it carves great scars on hillsides and breaks the winter silence with the sideshow roar of diesel generators and massive snow-blowers. However, this book lists several of the better slopes, for those so inclined.

**SIX-THOUSAND-FOOT PEAKS** (tehcc.org/hiking/challenges/south-beyond-6000/). $10 for a patch, plus a lot of walking. Most of the East's mountains stay below 4,000 feet. Of those that rise higher, a handful reach the mile-high mark, and only 41 top 6,000 feet, commonly referred to by hikers as "6'ers." Of these 41 6'ers, 40 are within this region, including the 1st through 16th tallest peaks. (The 17th tallest peak in the East, Mount Washington, is located in New Hampshire.) Bagging 6'ers is beginning to catch on as a hobby, akin to bagging Scottish Munros or Coloradan 14'ers, only easier. If you are looking for a reason to choose one mountain walk over another, bagging 6'ers will lead you to a lot of really great places, and the **Tennessee Eastman Hiking and Canoeing Club** will give (well, sell) you a neat patch. This guide points out the location of all 40 of the 6'ers.

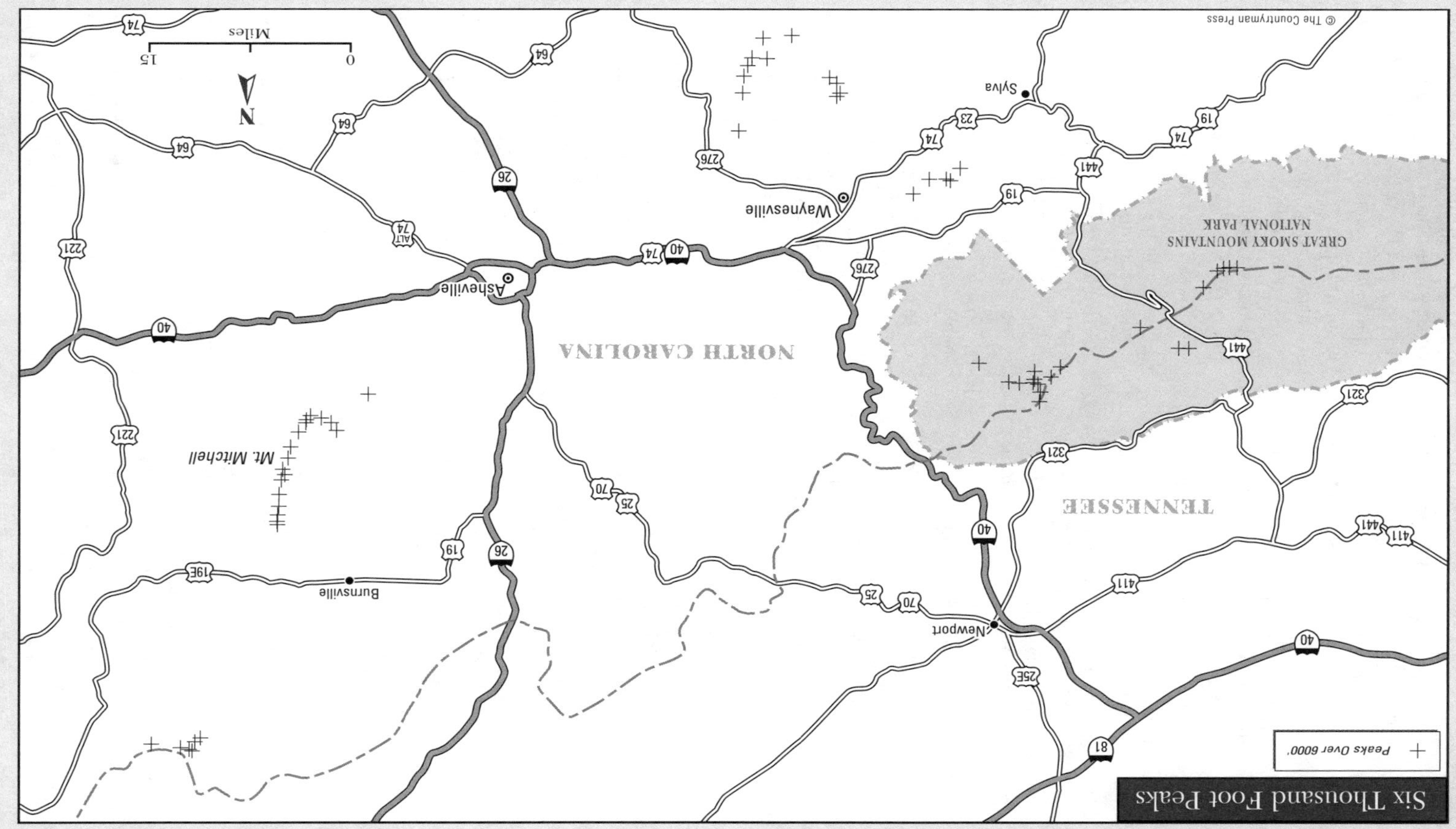
Six Thousand Foot Peaks
Peaks Over 6000'
TENNESSEE
NORTH CAROLINA
GREAT SMOKY MOUNTAINS
NATIONAL PARK
Mt. Mitchell
Burnsville
Asheville
Waynesville
Sylva
Newport
N
0
15
Miles
© The Countryman Press

**WALKING** Frequently the best way to enjoy the mountains is to get out and walk around. Each chapter of this Explorer's Guide offers a few good walks, mainly short and easy, that highlight major features of the locale. This listing is by no means encyclopedic; rather, it's more by the way of a sampler, oriented toward the rushed traveler who doesn't have time to spend on a long, hard hike. There are numerous specialized hiking guides for the enthusiast, starting with Backcountry Publications' *50 Hikes in the Mountains of North Carolina,* and *50 Hikes in the Mountains of Tennessee*—a hundred hikes to get you started.

**WATERFALLS** Erosion—50 million years' worth—has not yet smoothed away all the rock ledges in these mountain valleys. Waterfalls abound throughout this region, ranging from 6 feet high to over 400 feet high. Many require difficult hikes down gorges, but some can be reached down an easy path, and a few can be viewed from the roadside. The text highlights dozens of these waterfalls, with something in nearly every chapter.

**WEATHER** These mountains have long been a summer retreat because of their famously cool weather—but your results may vary. In general, temperatures are cooler farther north, and at higher elevations. Lower elevations are hotter, as are places farther south. The lowest elevations and hottest temperatures are along the base of the Smokies in Tennessee, where 90-degree temperatures are common in August. Temperatures are lower on the North Carolina side, with 90 degrees a regular event along the low elevations of the Little Tennessee and the Tuckaseegee, and a rarity on the 4,000-foot crest of the Blue Ridge near Cashiers and Highlands. Asheville suffers from air inversions, and can be quite hot. North of Asheville, temperatures seldom reach 90, and the mile-high peaks—Roan Mountain, Mount Mitchell—are nearly always cool. To sum up: escape the heat by going uphill and north. Expect hot weather below 2,000 feet.

There is life after summer. The hot weather can start in mid-June, but normally waits politely for the Fourth of July weekend; it can linger into September, but normally departs by late August. Spring and fall are cool, with highs between 40 and 65 degrees, and lows occasionally dipping below freezing. Consistent freezing weather starts sometime in November, with most days having highs between 25 and 35 degrees. Snow can happen any time between October and April, with January through March getting the worst (or best) of it. January snows are fluffy and clean, while April snows are a soggy mess.

**WILDERNESS** Maybe only God can make a tree, but only the U.S. Congress can create a wilderness. Under the Wilderness Act of 1964, Congress sets aside large, contiguous tracts of Federal land as perpetual wilderness preserves. Each of the tracts remains under the management of its original agency, but is managed under rules that prohibit all logging, all mechanization, and all roads. There are 16 congressionally declared wildernesses in this book, totaling 185,000 acres (289 square miles), all of which are managed by the National Forest Service and allow hunting. Typically, these are the most rugged, remote, and beautiful areas of the mountains—very special places. This book describes every congressionally declared wilderness area within its area, and helps you find its trailheads and its best walks.

**WILDFLOWERS** Wildflower season starts late in the mountains, with daffodils finally starting to decorate winter roadsides in mid-April. By mid-May all the trees are in leaf and the spring wildflowers are underway in earnest. The high grassy balds become colorful by the end of May, with the rhododendrons and azaleas bursting out in mid-June. At that time, natural rhododendron "gardens" in the mile-high grassy balds become dotted with clouds of purple, framing the wonderful views. Color fades slowly into August, then bursts out again in mid-September as the goldenrods and asters make one last fine show under the turning leaves. These will last until late October, when the last of the blooms fade and winter returns.

**WILDLIFE** Bears, of course. People are sometimes surprised to learn that bears are common enough to be hunted in parts of our national forests (and a bear hunt is a massive enterprise, resembling a military search-and-destroy mission). Bears are common enough that you might walk up onto one by accident in the backcountry; treat it as very, very dangerous, and get away without showing panic or fear. The infamous begging bears of the Great Smoky Mountains National Park are less of a pest now than in the past, but are still to be regarded as dangerous.

Wildlife is common, but timid. The author has seen, on his small rural property, foxes, deer, groundhogs, rabbits, skunks, turkeys, a bobcat, and a bear—a pretty typical cross section. Deer are very common, particularly in the national parks. Rangers offer regular wildlife walks in all the national parks and forests, with schedules available at park offices and websites.

# EXPLORATION THEMES

As a general-purpose guidebook, this *Explorer's Guide* is organized by region—but with no expectation than anyone is going to be reading it from start to finish. Far from it! You'll want to skip right to the good stuff. Following are some lists of the best of the good stuff, grouped by topic, so you can find just what you want.

## FINE CRAFTS

This book includes one of the Fine Craft Movement's major centers in the United States—arguably the places where the Fine Craft Movement was invented. Here's a list of the major spots.

**Mayland: Penland School of Crafts** (see "Behind the Blue Ridge: Spruce Pine & Burnsville," *To See*). This craft school has been catering to professional artists and serious amateurs since the 1920s, from its campus near Spruce Pine; it has made the remote Mayland Valley (which includes the county seats of Burnsville and Newland as well as Spruce Pine) into a national leader in the Fine Crafts Movement.

**Mayland: Toe River Crafts** (see "Behind the Blue Ridge: Spruce Pine & Burnsville," *To See*). This modest building holds the cooperative gallery for the large and respected Celo fine crafts community, on NC 80 south of Micaville in the Mayland Valley.

**Mayland: Mount Mitchell Crafts Fair** (see "Behind the Blue Ridge: Spruce Pine & Burnsville," *Special Events*). This major crafts festival, held every August since 1956 in the Burnsville town square, attracts over two hundred craft artists.

**Craft Fair of the Southern Highlands** (see "The City of Asheville," *Special Events*). Held annually since 1948 by the nonprofit Southern Appalachian Craft Guild, this July and October event fills Asheville's Thomas Wolfe Auditorium with the work of member craft artists, plus demonstrations and traditional music.

**Asheville's River Arts District** (see "The City of Asheville," *To See*). Asheville's large and exciting arts community—dominated, as you would expect here, by fine craft artists—has taken over its red-brick riverside industrial district and turned it into something wonderful.

**Downtown Waynesville** (see "The Blue Ridge Parkway Approaches the Smokies," *Villages*). There are a dozen galleries and studios of local fine crafters in Waynesville's three-block-long downtown.

**The Museum of North Carolina Handicrafts** (see "The Blue Ridge Parkway Approaches the Smokies," *To See*). This Waynesville museum, in an historic farmhouse on the south end of town, features authentic mountain crafts rather than modern artistic interpretations.

**Country Workshops** (see "North of Asheville: The Bald Mountains," *To See*). This organization features fine woodworking seminars in a remote mountain cove, north of Marshall, North Carolina.

**The Glades Craft Community at Gatlinburg** (see "Gatlinburg and the Northeast Quadrant," *To See*). Eighty crafters display their own wares from their own studios, just blocks from downtown Gatlinburg.

**Arrowmont School** (see "Gatlinburg and the Northeast Quadrant," *To Do*). Downtown Gatlinburg grew up around this venerable crafts school, founded in 1926, with gardens and galleries open to the public.

**Qualla Arts and Crafts Mutual** (see "Cherokee and the Southeast Quadrant," *To See*). This tribe-sponsored cooperative features authentic, handmade Cherokee crafts.

**Dillsboro** (see "Near the Park: Sylva & Dillsboro," *Villages*). Very nearly a ghost town as late as 1975, Dillsboro has since become a large and active gallery and studio district of local craft artists.

**John C. Campbell Folk School** (see "The Southern Unicois: Murphy & the Copper Basin," *To See*). Founded in 1925, this large farm-like school has long sought to preserve traditional mountain crafts through intensive six-day courses.

## QUAINT VILLAGES

During the last 30 years, the traditional small town has undergone a major revival—not only here, but throughout the South. This book describes all of the small towns in its area; here are a few of the most attractive.

**West Jefferson** (see "The Blue Ridge Parkway Enters North Carolina," *Villages*). This attractive small town has a historic brick-front downtown with some interesting shops, plus a park with its long-gone railroad in the block behind it.

**Blowing Rock** (see "The Blue Ridge Parkway: Blowing Rock & Grandfather Mountain," *Villages*). This tony resort village has straddled the Blue Ridge's crest since the 1890s, and is filled with historic architecture as well as fine shopping and dining.

**Burnsville** (see "Behind the Blue Ridge: Spruce Pine & Burnsville," *Villages*). This pretty town has an active and expanding downtown that straggles down from its immaculately kept square, and seems to add a new art or crafts store every year.

**Mountain City** (see "The Mountains of Northern Tennessee," *Villages*). This Victorian town on a hill commands the beautiful and little-visited mountains of Tennessee's northeastern corner.

**Elizabethton** (see "The Mountains of Northern Tennessee," *Villages*). This mill town has an exceptionally attractive and historic downtown that centers on an 1889 covered bridge in a riverside park.

**Morganton** Furniture money has given Morganton a bustling, active downtown, centered on its beautiful antebellum courthouse.

**Weaverville** (see "The Blue Ridge Parkway Circles Asheville," *Villages*). Weaverville's two-block downtown has a number of good restaurants, and the surrounding residential areas are handsome, historic, and have several nice bed & breakfasts.

**Black Mountain** (see "The Blue Ridge Parkway Circles Asheville," *Villages*). This handsome town is becoming known for its arts community and attractive downtown, and is becoming a fashionable second home center as a result. **Montreat**, the beautiful and historic retreat village, is only 2 miles away.

**Waynesville** (see "The Blue Ridge Parkway Approaches the Smokies," *Villages*). This handsome county seat has a fine old downtown filled with shops and galleries.

**Saluda** (see "The Blue Ridge: Chimney Rock & Saluda," *Villages*). This handsome little railroad-siding village gets nicer every year, with excellent shopping and restaurants.

**Brevard** (see "The Blue Ridge: Hendersonville & Brevard," *Villages*). The seat of remote, mountainous Transylvania County has three blocks of attractive red brick buildings around its historic courthouse, with good shopping and art galleries.

**Bryson City** (see "Bryson City and the Southwest Quadrant," *Villages*). This is the place of choice for visiting the national park. From the WWI U.S. infantryman "doughboy" statue in front of the Old Courthouse to its restored and active passenger train depot, this mountain town is charm personified, and its food and lodging choices are top notch.

**Sylva and Dillsboro** (see "Near the Park: Sylva & Dillsboro," *Villages*). These adjacent towns are another first-rate base of operation for visiting the Smokies, with good food and lodging. They also have superior shopping in their historic cores, to say nothing of a hilltop county courthouse visible from the Blue Ridge Parkway, many miles away.

**Highlands** (see "The Blue Ridge: Cashiers & Highlands," *Villages*). Perhaps the least spoilt resort in the Blue Ridge, Highlands has a five-block downtown that dates from the 1880s and straddles the Blue Ridge at an elevation of 4,100 feet.

**Murphy** (see "The Southern Unicois: Murphy & the Copper Basin," *Villages*). This handsome county seat centers on its grand marble courthouse, then slides downhill to Hiwassee Lake.

## MUSIC

**Alleghany County Fiddler's Convention** (see "The Blue Ridge Parkway Enters North Carolina," *Special Events*). One of the South's premiere country fiddle competitions is held in late July at the Alleghany County Fairgrounds outside Sparta. A month earlier at the same venue, there's a major quilter's meet, with more mountain music and bluegrass.

**Young's Mountain Music** (see "Behind the Blue Ridge: Spruce Pine & Burnsville," *Entertainment*). Located between Burnsville and Spruce Pine in the

Mayland Valley, Young's is noted as a venue for authentic, old-time Appalachian music from serious local musicians.

**Old Fort Mountain Music** (see "Beneath the Blue Ridge: The Catawba River Valley," *Entertainment*). Watch the musicians practice in the EMS parking lot, then stroll inside for the free weekly concert, every Friday night.

**Folkmoot USA** (see "The Blue Ridge Parkway Approaches the Smokies," *Special Events*). This nationally important folk dance celebration brings a dozen national dance troupes to venues all over the western mountain area, but most especially to its headquarters in Waynesville.

**Brevard Music Festival** (see "The Blue Ridge: Hendersonville & Brevard," *Entertainment*). This two-month festival offers classical music in a mountain amphitheater, performed by seasoned musicians leading elite students.

**Appalachian Music at the Rocky Branch Community Center** (see "Townsend, Cades Cove, & the Northwest Quadrant," *Entertainment*). Every Friday night, year-round, local bluegrass and traditional musician come here to share music, far removed from the tourist venues.

## LONG-DISTANCE PATHS

In the 1930s the Appalachian Trail opened as the first modern long-distance footpath in the world, with hundreds of miles of path within this book's region. Now it has been joined by a host of descendants forming giant loops through the Blue Ridge and Smoky Mountains. At last, hikers can experience the sort of multi-week hike common in the West, on a wide choice of trails, and not even need a car shuttle.

**The Appalachian Trail** (www.appalachiantrail.org; e-mail: info@atconf.org; 304-535-6331, 799 Washington St., Harpers Ferry, WV, 25425). Blazed in the 1930s as the world's first long-distance recreational foot path, the Appalachian Trail stretches for well over 2,000 miles along the East's wildest and toughest mountains, from Georgia to Maine. Although officially part of the National Park System (as a National Scenic Trail), the Appalachian Trail is mainly a private volunteer effort, blazed and maintained by 31 hiking clubs that make up the Appalachian Trail Conservancy.

This book covers 365 miles of the trail, including the ultra-popular stretch through the Great Smoky Mountains National Park. Various chapters include rewarding day hikes along bits of the trail. It follows the trail south to north, the more common direction for through-hikers (as they can start earlier in Georgia than they can in Maine). Here are the sections, in south-to-north order:

- "Franklin & the Nantahala Mountains"
- "The Northern Unicois: Robbinsville & Tellico Plains"
- "Bryson City & the Southwest Quadrant"
- "Cherokee & the Southeast Quadrant"
- "North of Asheville: The Bald Mountains"
- "The Mountains of Northern Tennessee"

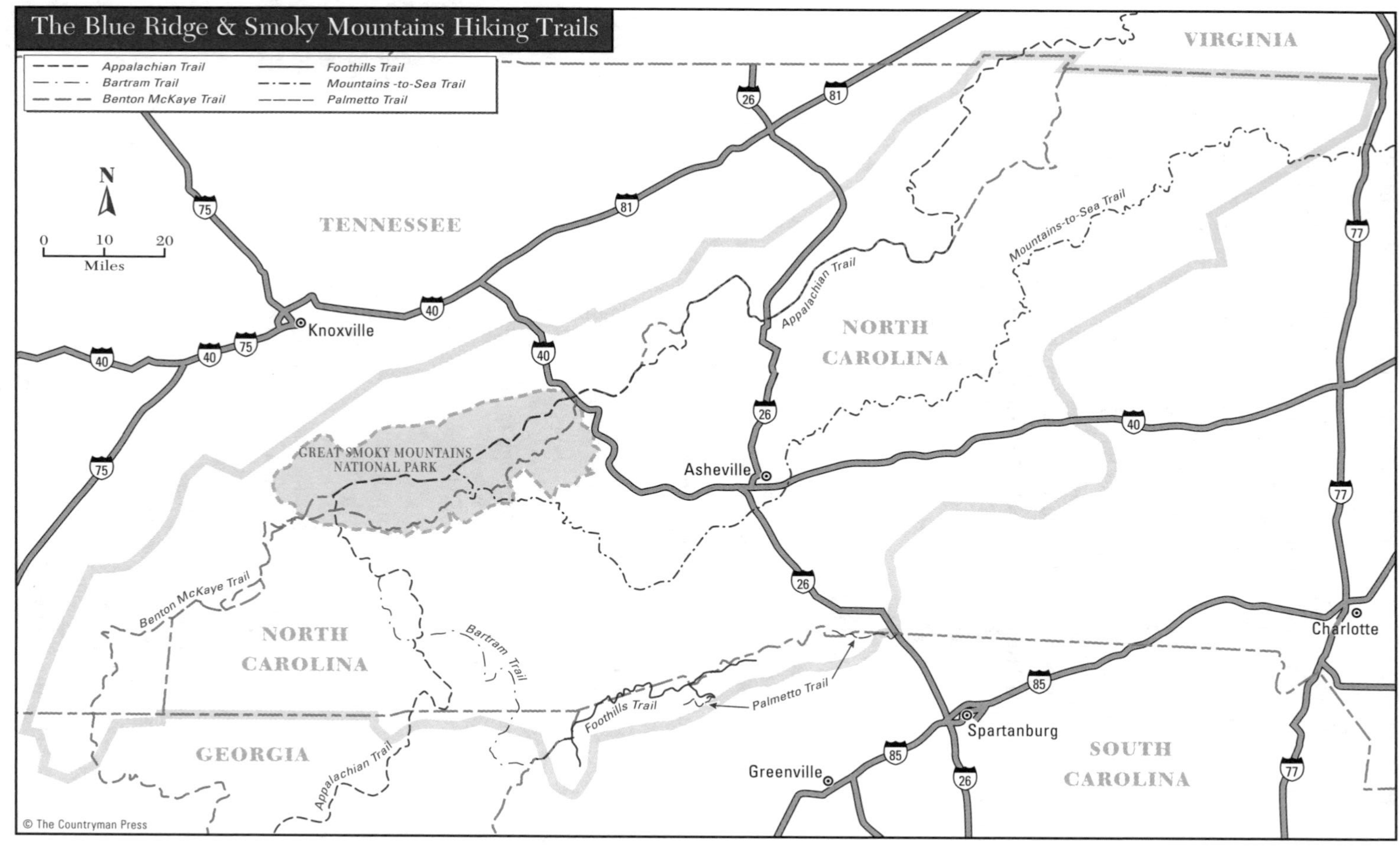
The Blue Ridge & Smoky Mountains Hiking Trails
Appalachian Trail
Bartram Trail
Benton McKaye Trail
Foothills Trail
Mountains -to-Sea Trail
Palmetto Trail
N
0 10 20
Miles
TENNESSEE
VIRGINIA
NORTH CAROLINA
NORTH CAROLINA
GEORGIA
SOUTH CAROLINA
GREAT SMOKY MOUNTAINS NATIONAL PARK
Knoxville
Asheville
Charlotte
Spartanburg
Greenville
Appalachian Trail
Mountains-to-Sea Trail
Benton McKaye Trail
Bartram Trail
Foothills Trail
Palmetto Trail
Appalachian Trail
75
81
26
40
77
85
© The Countryman Press

**The Mountains-to-Sea Trail** Founded in 1973 by an act of the North Carolina State Legislature, this 935-mile trail forms the backbone of the North Carolina Trails System. It runs from Kitty Hawk on the Outer Banks, across the state's coastal plains and Piedmont, to end deep in the Great Smoky Mountains National Park at **Clingman's Dome**. The actual foot bed is about half complete, with the missing ("undesignated") sections being concentrated in the heavily farmed and settled plains and Piedmont. The state government provides planning and administrative support, as well as land and easement purchases, but volunteers actually build and maintain the pathway.

Within the Blue Ridge and Smoky Mountains, the Mountains-to-Sea Trail is over 340 miles long, of which all but 6 miles is either completed or under construction. It roughly follows the course of the Blue Ridge Parkway, sometimes closely and sometimes very far away. This book describes each section in turn, from west to east—the most common direction for through-hikers, as this reduces the amount of ascent by 6,640 feet. These are, in west-to-east order:

- "Cherokee & the Southeast Quadrant"
- "The Blue Ridge Parkway Approaches the Smokies"
- "The Blue Ridge Parkway Circles Asheville"
- "Beneath the Blue Ridge: The Catawba River Valley"
- "The Blue Ridge Parkway: Blowing Rock & Grandfather Mountain"
- "The Blue Ridge Parkway Enters North Carolina"

**The Bartram Trail** The 100-mile Bartram Trail retraces the steps of famed 18th-century botanist William Bartram. It runs northward from the Chattooga River on the Georgia–South Carolina line to Cheoah Bald. On the way it intersects the **Appalachian Trail** twice, making a fine loop in the **Nantahala Mountains**. It also links the **Foothills Trail** with the Appalachian Trail, allowing an extended exploration of the most remote sections of the Blue Ridge, far from the Blue Ridge Parkway. In the future it will also link with the **Palmetto Trail**, allowing a continuous hike from South Carolina's Atlantic Coast to, well, just about anywhere. Here's where to find its sections, in order from north to south:

- "The Blue Ridge: Cashiers & Highlands"
- "Franklin & the Nantahala Mountains"
- "The Northern Unicois: Robbinsville & Tellico Plains"

**The Benton MacKaye Trail** The Benton MacKaye Trail spends 190 miles in this book's area, heading northward from Georgia to the **Great Smoky Mountains National Park**. Completed in 2007, this path intentionally provides a more primitive, less traveled alternative to the **Appalachian Trail**, roughly following the route originally proposed for the Appalachian Trail by its founder, Benton MacKaye. On the way, it also provides three big loops via their intersections—a giant loop that encompasses all the mountains of northern Georgia and western North Carolina, and two smaller (but still week-long) loops within the national park. Here are its sections, from south to north:

- "The Southern Unicois: Murphy & the Copper Basin"
- "The Northern Unicois: Robbinsville & Tellico Plains"
- "Bryson City & the Southwest Quadrant"
- "Cherokee & the Southeast Quadrant"

**The Foothills Trail** Created by Duke Power in the 1970s, the well-engineered path leads through the remote **Jocassee Gorges** along the North Carolina–South Carolina border. It provides 80 miles of hiking, and links with the **Bartram Trail** (and through it the **Appalachian Trail**), as well as the largely unfinished **Palmetto Trail**. Here are its sections, from west to east:

- "The Blue Ridge: Cashiers & Highlands"
- "The Blue Ridge: Hendersonville & Brevard"

**The Palmetto Trail** One day in the (hopefully) near future, South Carolina's Palmetto Trail will link the mountains of the Jocassee Gorges and the Blue Wall with the Atlantic Coast near Charleston. While large sections in the coastal plains are completed, only four small, widely separated sections (called "passages") exist in the mountains. These can be found here:

- "The Blue Ridge: Hendersonville & Brevard"
- "The Blue Ridge: Chimney Rock & Saluda"

**The Eastern Continental Trail** (www.nimblewillnomad.com). This informal trail, declared by famed through-hiker Nimblewill Nomad in 1997, links Key West, Florida, with the northernmost tip of Newfoundland, Canada—around 5,400 miles of (sort of) continuous hiking paths. Or, to be a bit more precise, it's 5,035 miles of officially declared and maintained hiking path, linked by 365 miles of road walk. It enters this book's area at the **Cohutta Wilderness** (using the Pinhoti Trail), then follows the **Benton MacKaye Trail** to the **Appalachian Trail** and points north. All in all, the Eastern Continental Trail span is 360 miles within this book's area.

## PARKWAYS

Over the years, no fewer than five highways have been built in this region solely for sightseers. These offer some of the finest scenic drives in America, and are highlighted in this book.

**The Blue Ridge Parkway** (www.nps.gov/blri). Started in 1935 as a public works project, the **Blue Ridge Parkway** spans 469 miles from **Shenandoah National Park** in Virginia to **The Great Smoky Mountains National Park** in North Carolina. Over 250 miles of the parkway cross this book's region, following the crest of the Blue Ridge from theNorth Carolina–Virginia state line to Asheville, then climbing a series of remote mile-high peaks over to the Smokies. Constructed between 1936 and 1989, the parkway was originally intended as a Depression make-work project, with a long-range goal of bringing tourist dollars to the depressed mountain coves of Virginia and North Carolina. By this standard, it's a roaring success; the parkway gets 20 million recreation visitors a year, the most of any National Park Service property, and comparable to New York City and Disneyworld.

Built and operated by the National Park Service, the parkway's typical 1,000-foot width has been carefully and unobtrusively landscaped over its entire length, for a continuously beautiful drive. As designed by its first superintendent, the great landscape architect Stanley Abbott, the parkway is a "string of pearls," with constant, ever-changing scenery punctuated by major sites every 50 or so miles. The effect is subtle, but remarkable. Grassy verges curve into forests, giving views deep into the trees; split-rail fences line pastures and farmlands; forests drop away suddenly to give wide and dramatic mountain views over low stone walls. Bridges, tunnels, and abutments are clad in hand-laid stonework, done by artisans brought in from Europe. Commercial intrusion is virtually nonexistent, and modern buildings a rare sight. The National Park Service furnishes a small number of concession areas, widely spaced, where food and lodging are available.

This book covers the North Carolina half of the parkway in great detail. Our companion volume, *The Shenandoah Valley and the Mountains of the Virginias: An Explorer's Guide,* covers the remainder of the parkway, along with its extension into the **Shenandoah National Park**, the **Skyline Drive**. Coverage is arranged into chapters that discuss the parkway along with all the features within it. If you want to tour the North Carolina section of the parkway straight through, use these four chapters:

- "The Blue Ridge Parkway Enters North Carolina"—in part 1, covering the northernmost 76 miles, ending at US 421 near Boone.
- "The Blue Ridge Parkway: Blowing Rock & Grandfather Mountain"—also in part 1, covering the famed Grandfather Mountain segment, 67 miles from US 421 to NC 80 near Burnsville.
- "The Blue Ridge Parkway Circles Asheville"—in part 2 of this book, covering the tallest mountains in the East, 44 miles from NC 80 to US 25 at Asheville.
- "The Blue Ridge Parkway Approaches the Smokies"—also in part 2, covering the final 54 miles, with the highest roadway elevations and the most dramatic and remote views, from US 25 to the Great Smoky Mountains National Park.

**The Crest of the Blue Ridge Highway** (see "The Blue Ridge Parkway: Blowing Rock & Grandfather Mountain," *To See*). This curious predecessor to the Blue Ridge Parkway may well have been the first scenic recreational highway in America. Started in 1911 and abandoned in 1917, sections still exist and are traced in this entry.

**Newfound Gap Road** Originally built by the states of Tennessee and North Carolina to jumpstart Smoky Mountain tourism in the late 1920s, this highway crossing through the middle of the Great Smoky Mountains National Park remains the center of the park experience. It is described in these two chapters:

- "Gatlinburg & the Northeast Quadrant"
- "Cherokee & the Southeast Quadrant"

**The Foothills Parkway** In the mid-1930s, when Congress placed the Blue Ridge Parkway wholly inside North Carolina, Tennessee's powerful congressional delegation threw a conniption fit. Congress then created the Foothills Parkway to pacify them, a 72-mile recreation highway making a semi-circle outside the Great Smoky Mountains National Park. It never gained any popularity, however, and, while still on the books, only two small sections have ever been completed—its easternmost and westernmost termini, as it turns out. The eastern segment, a mere 5.5 miles long, runs between I-40 and US 321 (see "Gatlinburg and the Northeast Quadrant," *To See*). The western segment runs from US 129 to US 321 near Townsend, following the crest of Chilhowee Mountain for 16.5 miles (see "Townsend, Cades Cove, and the Northwest Quadrant," *Exploring the Area*). In 1984 the National Park Service completed most of a third section, 14.5 miles, but gave it up when they hit a bedrock layer that leaked highly acidic water into local streams. Now the Park Service has redesigned this section and is ever so slowly constructing it, with a completion date vaguely given as between 2017 and 2022. The Park Service has started the paperwork on a fourth section, 14 miles long, that would be located east of Gatlinburg, but this isn't anything like a commitment to build, and could possibly result in its official abandonment. Your GPS may show a fifth section, between Wear Cove and Gatlinburg; this is a phantom road and is not even under planning consideration (for anything other than official abandonment of the project).

**The Cherohala Skyway** (see "The Northern Unicois: Robbinsville & Tellico Plains," *Exploring the Area*). Completed in the late 1990s, the region's newest parkway explores the mile-high peaks of the Unicoi Mountains, between Robbinsville, North Carolina, and Tellico Plains, Tennessee—one of the most remote and untouched sections of the mountains. Its many sharp curves and stunning views make it extremely popular with motorcyclists.

## RAILROADS

Blue Ridge railroads are very special for railroading buffs. Rugged topography, thousands of feet of climbing, and an irregular, unpredictable geology posed special challenges to the railroad builders. Some railroads, such as the narrow gauge Tweetsie, mastered the terrain by conforming to it; others, such as the ultra-modern Clinchfield, blasted through in uncompromising straight lines. The big timber companies built elaborate, but very temporary, railroads throughout these mountains, and some of the old grades survive as modern automobile roads. You can get a good long taste of an old-fashioned mountain railroad on two separate tourist excursion railroads that between them offer three different 25-mile tours.

**The Clinchfield Railroad Loops** (see "The Blue Ridge Parkway: Blowing Rock & Grandfather Mountain," *To See*). The East's last and most modern railroad, this 1909 engineering wonder climbs the cliff face of the Blue Ridge in 5 hairpin curves and 17 tunnels; you can view it from the Blue Ridge Parkway, or get up close on gravel Peppers Creek Road.

**The Swannanoa Grade** (see "Beneath the Blue Ridge: The Catawba River Valley," *Exploring the Area*). The first railroad to penetrate North Carolina's Blue Ridge curves up in three huge loops; you can stand in the middle of a loop and watch a freight train thunder all around you.

**The Saluda Grade** (see "The Blue Ridge: Chimney Rock & Saluda," *To See*). The steepest mainline grade in America is noted for its long history of derailments; it can be readily explored from a nearby back road.

**Little River Road** (see "Townsend, Cades Cove, & the Northwest Quadrant," *Exploring the Area*). This incredibly beautiful drive within the Great Smoky

Mountains National Park sits on top of an early 20th-century railroad bed that had been specifically engineered for the powerful and flexible Shay engine. There's a railroad museum dedicated to the mighty little Shay at the end of the drive, in Townsend.

**The Great Smoky Mountain Railroad, Bryson City Station** (see "Bryson City & the Southwest Quadrant," *To See*). Bryson City's historic passenger station is the center for rail excursions up the Nantahala Gorge in historic, beautifully preserved rolling stock (including bar cars).

**Stumphouse Tunnel** (see "The Blue Ridge: Cashiers & Highlands," *To See*). This local park in South Carolina preserves the entrance to a mile-long tunnel, started in 1850 and never completed, which its owners wrongly thought would open up the Blue Ridge. It may well be the best place to appreciate the speculative bubble and massive over-optimism that greeted the introduction of the railroad.

**The L&N "Etowah Old Line"** (see "The Southern Unicois: Murphy & the Copper Basin," *To See*). Built in the late 19th century by a small Georgia company, it only took 15 years for this wandering mountain line to become bypassed by a modern railroad, and so earn the title "Old Line." Nevertheless it continues to this day, with passenger excursions along the beautiful Hiwassee River Gorge and then up **The Loop**, where the railroad corkscrews out of the gorge to pass over itself, twice. Its northern terminus in Etowah, Tennessee, has a good railroad museum in its restored passenger terminal.

## RECREATION LAKES

The giant hydropower lakes of the Smokies and Blue Ridge send long fingers deep into mountain wilderness. These can be great recreational opportunities—and the dams can be dramatic sites in their own right. Here are a few of the best:

**Lake James** (see "Beneath the Blue Ridge: The Catawba River Valley," *To See*). This huge hydropower lake uses three dams to combine two rivers together; you can see the Blue Ridge from its shores. A large state park, as well as private marinas, gives ready access.

**Fontana Lake** (see "Bryson City and the Southwest Quadrant," *To See*). The largest dam in the East backs up a pretty impressive lake, stretching for 25 miles and with 238 miles of shore. Access is via **Fontana Village** at the dam, and several marinas at its upstream head near **Bryson City**.

**Lake Jocassee** (see "The Blue Ridge: Cashiers & Highlands," *To See*). This large hydropower lake near Cashiers, North Carolina, starts in South Carolina and stretches into North Carolina. It has 75 miles of shoreline, virtually all of it public lands within the **Jocassee Gorges**.

**Glenville Lake (Thorpe Reservoir)** (see "The Blue Ridge: Cashiers & Highlands," *To See*). Another Duke Power hydropower lake, Glenville Lake, located a few miles north of Cashiers, North Carolina, is noted for its excellent mountain views and high elevation.

**Chatuge Lake** (see "Franklin and the Nantahala Mountains," *To See*). This 13-mile-long lake stretches 13 miles south from Hayesville, North Carolina, well into Georgia, with many public boat ramps and two first-rate recreation areas.

**Nantahala Lake** (see "Franklin and the Nantahala Mountains," *To See*). This large, remote lake sits deep amid the 5,000-foot peaks of the Nantahala Mountains, far from any main highway, yet easily reached by paved road and with several good-quality free boat ramps.

**Santeetlah Lake** (see "The Northern Unicois: Robbinsville & Tellico Plains," *To See*). Located just north of Robbinsville, this is the largest of the four Tapoco Lakes owned by the Alcoa Corporation. It offers exceptionally fine views, lots of national forest owned lakeshore, and a choice of boat rentals.

**Hiwassee Lake** (see "The Southern Unicois: Murphy & the Copper Basin," *To See*). This huge lake meanders through the Unicoi foothills for many miles west of Murphy, NC; most of its banks are national forest land.

**Lake Ocoee** (see "The Southern Unicois: Murphy & the Copper Basin," *To See*). This midsize lake, located 20 miles west of Ducktown, Tennessee, is one of the oldest hydropower lakes in the South. It has US 64/74 continuously hugging its north bank for easy access.

## RECREATION STREAMS

There is no finer water recreation than a mountain stream: fishing, rafting, kayaking, canoe camping, searching for waterfalls, or just splashing around in a swimming hole. Even here, however, there are some streams that rank above the others for their outstanding recreational opportunities. This book seeks them out and describes them in turn.

This region is best known for its whitewater rafting and kayaking. It includes the 1996 Summer Olympics whitewater competition site, as well as the training site of several of our American whitewater medalists. Rivers range from Class II (a few easy ripples), through Class III and IV (fun, and risky fun), to Class V (dangerous). Outfitters will put your group into a raft with other customers, put you in the river, and pick you up (typically 6 miles downstream). Some outfitters put a guide in each raft, some in each group of rafts, and some just put you in and let you float—it depends on the difficulty of the river and how much you pay. With few exceptions these are family-friendly excursions, although infants and toddlers are not allowed, and the more violent rivers have higher age restrictions. Most of the outfitters also rent and shuttle kayaks, and offer kayaking lessons.

Two long Class II rivers, the French Broad and the New, offer miles and miles of easy canoeing. This allows a family group to hire a canoe, paddle gently downstream, and camp for the night along the way. A good weekend trip might cover 30 miles of stunning river scenery, quite a contrast to a whitewater 6-mile thrill ride. The New River, more popular of the two, flows gently through rugged wilderness gorges and narrow pastoral valleys, while the French Broad (upstream from Asheville) meanders through a wide farming valley framed by tall peaks. (Downstream from Asheville, the French Broad is Class IV during floods and has claimed several lives.).

**The New River** (see "The Blue Ridge Parkway Enters North Carolina," *Wild Places*). Officially known as "The South Fork of the New River," this National Wild and Scenic River and National Heritage River provides 90 miles of continuous canoe stream through some of the most impressive mountain scenery anywhere.

The state has created camping spots specifically for canoeists as part of its New River State Park.

**The French Broad River** (see "The Blue Ridge: Hendersonville & Brevard," *Wild Places*). An 8-mile section near Marshall, North Carolina, has prime Class III–IV whitewater; the rest of its 210 miles furnishes some good mountain canoeing, although without legal camping spots.

**The Little River** (see "Townsend, Cades Cove, & the Northwest Quadrant," *Wild Places*). Running through the Great Smoky Mountains National Park for 21 miles, this very beautiful river offers fine hiking, fishing, picnicking, and automobile sightseeing, as well as a 4 mile stretch of Class III–IV plus whitewater.

**The Nantahala Gorge** (see "Bryson City and the Southwest Quadrant," *Wild Places*). This may well be the most popular white-water river in the East, with 8 miles of just exactly perfect Class II–III.

**The Tuckaseegee River** (see "Near the Park: Sylva & Dillsboro," *Wild Places*). Located just south of the Great Smoky Mountains National Park, the Tuckaseegee has become a popular float trip that's convenient, exciting, and suitable for small children.

**The Chattooga River** (see "The Blue Ridge: Cashiers & Highlands," *Wild Places*). Declared a Wild and Scenic River by Congress, the Chattooga offers 57 miles of Class III–V rapids as it stretches southward from the Cashiers, North Carolina, area deep into Georgia.

**The Little Tennessee River** (see "Franklin and the Nantahala Mountains," *Wild Places*). This calm valley river near Franklin, North Carolina, is noted for its fishing, canoeing, and beautiful scenery, with 26 miles of banks in state ownership and open to the public.

**The Upper Tellico River** (see "The Northern Unicois: Robbinsville & Tellico Plains," *Wild Places*). One of the most beautiful streams in the Blue Ridge and Smoky Mountains, the upper Tellico River features fishing, picnicking, and camping, as well as 65-foot **Bald River Falls**—all accessible from a paved U.S. Forest Service recreation road.

**The Hiwassee River** (see "The Southern Unicois: Murphy & the Copper Basin," *Wild Places*). This state scenic river is noted for its beauty and its fishing, as well as canoeably mild whitewater. Its banks are completely accessible to hikers from the **John Muir Trail**.

**The Ocoee River** (see "The Southern Unicois: Murphy & the Copper Basin," *Wild Places*) This rough river furnishes Olympic quality whitewater, quite literally; the 1996 Olympic Whitewater competitions were held here. Its banks are almost continuously accessible from US 64/74.

## BEYOND CLASSIFICATION

The unusual and eccentric abound in these mountains. Here are a few of the most distinctive places:

**Grandfather Mountain Highland Games** (see "The Blue Ridge Parkway: Blowing Rock & Grandfather Mountain," *Special Events*). For more than 50 years, this five-day Highlands Festival has celebrated all things Scottish, with bagpiping, athletics, music, and clan tents. With daily attendance in the 40,000 range, it's one of the biggest events of its kind in the South.

**Mast General Store** (see "Behind the Blue Ridge: Boone & Banner Elk," *To See*). The general store in the mountains of western North Carolina, 19th-century Mast General Store still functions as the local community's center even as it caters to tourists and runs a chain of related stores.

**Kona** (see "Behind the Blue Ridge: Spruce Pine & Burnsville," *To See*). By rights this remote mountain village should be famous for its stunning hilltop views. Instead, it's known as the place where, in 1832, pretty little Frankie Silver chopped her husband Charlie up with an axe, burned the pieces in the fireplace, and then hid them in the snow. It's a pretty spot, with a little museum set up by Frankie's descendants.

**Andrews Geyser** (see "Beneath the Blue Ridge: The Catawba River Valley," *To See*). This 30-foot "geyser" sits in a loop of the 1877 Swannanoa Grade railroad, commemorating its completion; it's fed by an uphill lake, whose owner fires it up most days.

**The Microbreweries of Asheville** (see "The City of Asheville," *To See*). With 11 craft breweries in (or near) its urban area, Asheville must set some kind of per capita record. There's even a tour.

**The Asheville Tourists** (see "The City of Asheville," *Entertainment*). No, not *you*. The A-rated Minor League team, a farm team of the Colorado Rockies, has been going strong since 1909 at its large and modern stadium on the south end of downtown.

**The "Christy" Mission and Rocky Top, Tennessee** (see "North of Asheville: The Bald Mountains"). The two popular concepts of mountain life exemplified by these contemporaneous works could hardly be farther apart. Except spatially—they're actually adjacent in the remote mountains above Del Rio, Tennessee.

**Annual Spring Smoky Mountain Wildflower Pilgrimage** (see "Gatlinburg and the Northeast Quadrant," *Special Events*). This may well be the biggest nature event in the Appalachians, as thousands descend upon Gatlinburg's Convention Center for a week of talks and walks.

**Judaculla Rock** (see "Near the Park: Sylva & Dillsboro," *To See*). This large boulder, carved with pictographs, sits in a field in a remote valley south of Cullowhee; scholars remain unable to date it, much less interpret it.

**Highlands Botanical Garden** (see "The Blue Ridge: Cashiers & Highlands," *To See*). This large garden within Highlands, North Carolina, combines a university research center with the Blue Ridge's premiere collection of native plants displayed in their own environments.

**Field of the Wood** (see "The Southern Unicois: Murphy & the Copper Basin"). This "biblical theme park" commemorates the founding of the Church of God of Prophecy at this remote rural site in 1903, with an elaborate complex of monuments, much of it in art deco–styled whitewashed concrete. Definitely impressive.

# AUTHOR'S FAVORITE TRIPS

## A WEEK IN THE MOUNTAINS

This weeklong trip takes you past the author's favorite sites, from south to north. Not surprisingly, it follows the Blue Ridge Parkway for most of the way. This itinerary assumes a weeklong trip bracketed by two weekends, which gives you a travel-there day, seven days in the mountains, and a travel-back day.

**Day One: Townsend and Cades Cove** *Travel there: Your destination is Townsend, for a stay at a modern log cabin. Use I-75, I-81, and/or I-40 to reach the Knoxville, Tennessee, area, where you will pick up I-140 to Maryville. From the end of I-140, take US 29 south 7 miles to US 321, then left 18 miles to Townsend. Day One: visit the Cades Cove and Gatlinburg area at your leisure, then return to your cabin* (see "Townsend, Cades Cove, & the Northwest Quadrant"). Hire a **modern log cabin** for your arrival night and your first night. On your first night, relax on the porch and enjoy the mountain air. Grab some **barbeque**; then have a soak in your whirlpool bath or hot tub. Visit **Cades Cove** early the next morning. When you finish, take the **Little River Road** to **Sugarlands**. If you have any time left, enjoy Tennessee's permanent unofficial state fair, **Gatlinburg**.

**Day Two: Over the Smokies to Bryson City** *Take US 321 east 23 miles to the Gatlinburg Scenic Bypass, then continue straight ahead 18 miles to Newfound Gap; allow 90 minutes for this 41-mile segment. Explore down the Clingmans Dome Spur Road (14 miles round-trip), then continue south 17 miles on the Newfound Gap Road to US 441 in Cherokee. Follow US 441 south 8 miles to US 23/74; go west 7 miles to the Bryson City exit* (see "Bryson City and the Southwest Quadrant," *Villages*). Cross **Newfound Gap** the next morning, and be sure not to miss the side trip to **Clingmans Dome**. Early risers will want to enjoy a dawn drive and a high sunrise. Then visit **Mingus Mill and Oconaluftee Farmstead** on the North Carolina side. Skip through Cherokee for the time being and head to Bryson City for lunch, followed by a **train ride up the Nantahala Gorge**. Stay at one of the excellent bed & breakfast hotels in **Bryson City**, with an evening stroll downtown and local trout dinner at the **Fryemont Inn**.

**Day Three: The Tuckaseegee Valley** *Return to Cherokee the way you came, or follow US 19 east. The Blue Ridge Parkway starts at the north end of town. For Dillsboro, take US 441 south 14 miles, staying on it as it merges with, then leaves, US 74. The Balsam Mountain Inn is just off the Blue Ridge Parkway at Balsam*

*Gap, US 23/74, 13 miles east of Dillsboro* (see "Near the Park: Sylva & Dillsboro," *Villages*). In the morning, visit the **tribal museums in Cherokee**, and be sure to include the tribal craft shop opposite. If you need more shopping, head on over to **Dillsboro** for lunch and a stroll. Otherwise, get on the **Blue Ridge Parkway** and get your fill of Smoky Mountain views. Be sure to take the Heintooga Spur at least as far as Mile High Overlook, and don't miss the spur to **Waterrock Knob**. Whether you choose Dillsboro or the parkway, end your day at the **Balsam Mountain Inn** with a fine dinner and a glass of wine on the porch.

**Day Four: The Highest Mountains on the Blue Ridge Parkway** *From Balsam Gap (US 23/74), take the Blue Ridge Parkway in the direction marked northbound (south by your automobile's compass), 33 miles, to the Pisgah Inn (see "The Blue Ridge Parkway Approaches the Smokies," Exploring the Area).* This is your day for **hiking** as you follow the Blue Ridge Parkway along mile-high ridgelines with panoramic views. Get the Balsam Mountain Inn to pack you a **picnic lunch**. Enjoy the **sunrise** from the Waynesville Overlook, then stretch your legs at **Richland Balsams**. Follow the **Mountains-to-Sea Trail** for wildflower meadows in the South Fork Wilderness, then admire the view from the **Devil's Courthouse**. When you reach US 220, visit the **Cradle of Forestry in America** and **Looking Glass Falls**. Then return to the parkway for dinner and a room at the **Pisgah Inn**.

**Day Five: Asheville** *Follow the Blue Ridge Parkway in the direction marked northbound to US 25, 20 miles, then north 4 miles to the Biltmore Estate; allow one hour for this leg. Downtown Asheville is north of the Biltmore Estate on US 25, 3 miles* (see "The City of Asheville," *Villages*). Enjoy the **sunrise** from the Pisgah Inn, then follow the parkway into **Asheville** for an early start in your exploration of the **Biltmore Estate**. Be sure to take one of the special tours, and leave plenty of energy for poking around the **gardens**. Eat lunch on the estate, and visit the **winery** on your way out. In the afternoon, check into one of the city's many bed & breakfasts, then stroll and shop through downtown's **Battery District**. Be sure to visit the newly renovated **Grove Arcade**, America's first (and most beautiful) mall. Finish with dinner at one of downtown's many wonderful small restaurants.

**Day Six: Up the Parkway to Blowing Rock** *From downtown Asheville, return to the Blue Ridge Parkway by following US 25 south 7 miles. Take the parkway northbound 103 miles to Blowing Rock* (see "The Blue Ridge Parkway: Blowing Rock & Grandfather Mountain," *Villages*). Today it's back to the Blue Ridge Parkway for some wonderful scenery. An early morning start will reward you with a sunrise from **Craggy Gardens;** on the other hand, you'll miss the shrimp and brown gravy over grits at the **Early Girl Cafe** on Wall Street. Oh well, choices can be difficult. If you're lucky enough to be traveling in late June, schedule some time to enjoy the **rhododendron display** at Craggy. Then go on to the Mount Mitchell Spur for a spectacular drive and a short, beautiful walk to the **highest point in the East** (see "The Blue Ridge Parkway Circles Asheville," *To See*). Back on the parkway, be sure to stop at **Altapass Orchards** for views and heritage apples. You can get lunch at Little Switzerland, the orchard snack bar, or Linville Falls, depending how late you're running. But leave plenty of time for the stunningly beautiful **Grandfather Mountain**, perhaps the world's premiere private theme park devoted exclusively to conservation. Stay at one of Blowing Rock's little bed & breakfast inns; be sure to have **dinner at Crippen's**, finished with a cigar and a malt whiskey on the porch.

**Day Seven and Departure Day: Doughton Park** *Continue northbound on the Blue Ridge Parkway. To reach the Glendale Springs Inn, take NC 16 westbound off the parkway. Doughton Park is 22 miles further on the parkway. Travel back: For points north, south, and east: Take NC 16 east 16 miles to a left onto US 421, a superhighway. US 421 reaches I-77 in 25 miles for points north and south; and I-40 at Winston-Salem in another 30 miles, for points east. For points west: Take NC 16 south 55 miles to I-40 at Hickory* (see "The Blue Ridge Parkway Enters North Carolina," *Exploring the Area*). Early risers will want to enjoy a sunrise stroll around the lake on the parkway's **Moses Cone Estate**, just west of town. After breakfast, spend a relaxing morning strolling and shopping in Blowing Rock, and visiting the Moses Cone mansion. After lunch in Blowing Rock, take a leisurely drive up the parkway. Be sure to see the frescos at **Glendale Springs**, but leave late afternoon free to wander the wildflower meadows of **Doughton Park**. Enjoy dinner and a relaxing final night at one of the bed & breakfasts in the Jefferson-Sparta area.

# The Northern Mountains

1

THE BLUE RIDGE PARKWAY
ENTERS NORTH CAROLINA

THE BLUE RIDGE PARKWAY:
BLOWING ROCK
& GRANDFATHER MOUNTAIN

BEHIND THE BLUE RIDGE:
BOONE & BANNER ELK

BEHIND THE BLUE RIDGE:
SPRUCE PINE & BURNSVILLE

THE MOUNTAINS OF
NORTHERN TENNESSEE

BENEATH THE BLUE RIDGE:
THE CATAWBA RIVER VALLEY

# THE NORTHERN MOUNTAINS

At their northern end, the Blue Ridge and the Smokies/Unakas draw together and grow taller, and the high valleys between them become narrow and rugged. The New River drains the northernmost part of this area—a wide, rolling valley that becomes increasingly higher and more rugged toward its south. The first of many mile-high peaks appear at the end of the New River's drainage and the start of the Tennessee River's. From this high watershed all the way south to Georgia, the Tennessee River and its tributaries drain the land west of the Blue Ridge.

Here the Blue Ridge Parkway follows the Blue Ridge on its 469-mile journey from Virginia's Shenandoah National Park to the Great Smoky Mountains National Park in North Carolina. Conceived in the mid-1930s as a work relief project for desperately poor mountain counties, you'll find it a beautifully landscaped route, with roadworks clad in hand-cut stone, stretching through some of the most remote and stunning scenery in the mountains. In this area the parkway follows the actual Blue Ridge very closely. Typical of this old and unusual mountain, the Blue Ridge's eastern slope is a rugged and cliff-like wilderness covered in trees and nearly empty of people, while its western slope is a series of grass-covered hills, with more farms than forests. When the parkway follows the eastern side of the Blue Ridge it slabs across rugged wilderness with wide views, as at Grandfather Mountain. When it follows the western side, it rolls through pastoral countryside with wide meadows, as it does near Linville or Sparta. And when it follows the crest of the Blue Ridge, as it does in Doughton Park, it yields the best of both worlds—rolling ridgeline meadows with wide views over rugged mountains and peaceful little farms.

The main town of this region is Boone, North Carolina, a college town shaded by the 5,000-foot peaks of the Tennessee/New River divide. Boone has 17,100 residents in its own right, while the downtown campus of Appalachian State University adds another 17,000 students during the school year. Only a half dozen miles away, the historic and exclusive resort town of Blowing Rock adds additional sophistication to the region, and ski resorts top the mile-high peaks that surround these two towns. This whole area makes up a small complex of intensely developed vacation lands with a wide choice of first-class services; northward and southward stretch traditional mountain lands, little affected by tourism or its sprawling development. In these surrounding lands, attractive little county seats such as Burnsville, Elizabethton, and Jefferson offer a quieter and more authentic mountain experience.

This area received European settlement much earlier than other southern mountain districts. For one thing, it had no permanent Cherokee settlement, as the Cherokees held it as a sacred hunting reserve. For another, Daniel Boone lived there. Born in 1734 in Pennsylvania, he accompanied his family at age 14 to their new home in North Carolina's upper Piedmont. Daniel grew up as a hunter and frontier explorer; when he married, he moved to a log cabin even farther west, at the edge of Cherokee lands at the base of the Blue Ridge. Not much of a farmer, Daniel spent his time hunting and exploring the wild mountain lands, eventually learning every track between the Yadkin and the Tennessee Valley. Boone used this knowledge to blaze the first road to penetrate the North Carolina Blue Ridge, running near modern-day Boone into Tennessee. An organized group of settlers used this road to enter the Cherokee hunting lands, lease a large area from tribal leaders, and establish the Watauga Colony, forming their own courts and laws at present-day Elizabethton, Tennessee.

# THE BLUE RIDGE PARKWAY ENTERS NORTH CAROLINA

**GUIDANCE** **Alleghany County Chamber of Commerce** (www.sparta-nc.com; e-mail: director@sparta-nc.com; 800-372-5473, 336-372-5473; 58 Main St., P.O. Box 1237, Sparta, NC 28675). Located in Sparta, this tourist information center covers the northern half of this chapter's area. If you are interested in the Glendale Springs or Jefferson areas of this chapter, contact the Ashe County Chamber of Commerce.

**Ashe County Chamber of Commerce & Visitor's Center** (www.ashechamber.com; e-mail: ashechamber@skybest.com; 888-343-2743, 336-246-9550; 1 North Jefferson Avenue, Ste. C/P.O. Box 31, West Jefferson, NC, 28694). Located off the main highway in West Jefferson's red-brick downtown, this visitors center offers help and advice for the Jefferson and Glendale Springs areas.

**GETTING THERE** *By Car* This area is best approached from I-77. If you're coming from the north and aiming for Sparta or the parkway's northern end, leave I-77 at NC 89 (exit 100) and head west; if you are traveling up I-77 from the south, take US 21 (exit 83) instead. To reach the southern end of this region, leave I-77 at exit 78B to take the US 421 expressway westbound, which intersects with the Blue Ridge Parkway in 41 miles. Once you're in this region, your main routes run northeast/southwest, just like the Blue Ridge itself. These routes are the Blue Ridge Parkway, running along the eastern edge of the region, and US 221, running through the center.

*By Air* Charlotte, North Carolina, is probably your best bet. A major regional hub, it's only a hundred miles away, straight up I-77. The Piedmont Triad Airport (between Winston-Salem and Greensboro) also has good service, and is about the same distance away.

*By Bus or Train* This region has no train service or scheduled bus service.

**MEDICAL EMERGENCIES** **Alleghany Memorial Hospital** (www.amhsparta.org; e-mail: info@amhsparta.org; 336-372-5511, fax: 336-372-6032; 233 Doctors St., Sparta, NC, 28675). Located in Sparta, three blocks from downtown's US 21 via NC 18, this not-for profit hospital offers full emergency services from its recently renovated facility.

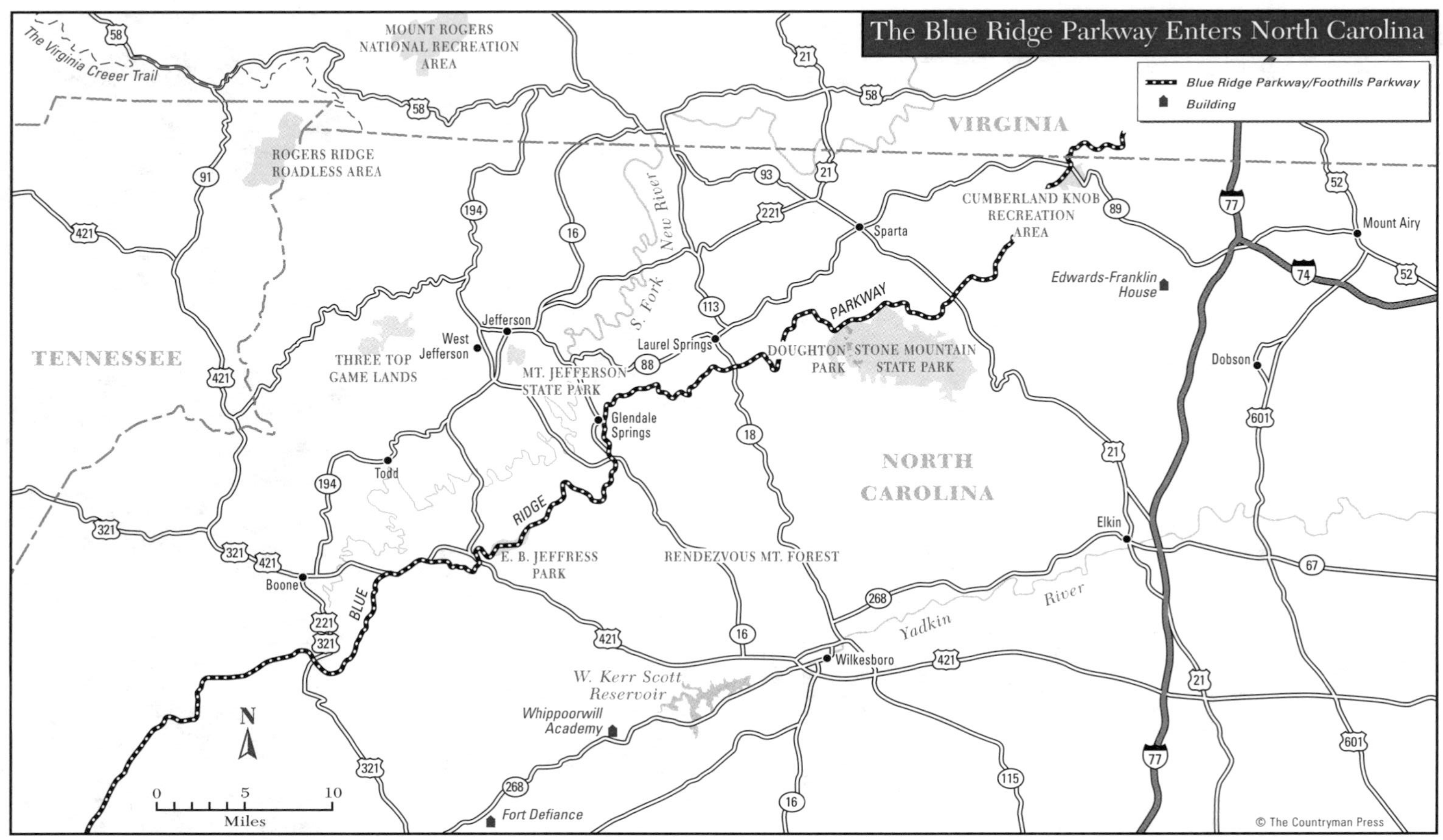
The Blue Ridge Parkway Enters North Carolina
Blue Ridge Parkway/Foothills Parkway
Building
VIRGINIA
TENNESSEE
NORTH CAROLINA
MOUNT ROGERS NATIONAL RECREATION AREA
The Virginia Creeper Trail
ROGERS RIDGE ROADLESS AREA
CUMBERLAND KNOB RECREATION AREA
Edwards-Franklin House
Mount Airy
Sparta
Jefferson
West Jefferson
THREE TOP GAME LANDS
MT. JEFFERSON STATE PARK
Laurel Springs
DOUGHTON PARK
STONE MOUNTAIN STATE PARK
PARKWAY
RIDGE
BLUE
Glendale Springs
Todd
Boone
E. B. JEFFRESS PARK
RENDEZVOUS MT. FOREST
Dobson
Elkin
Wilkesboro
Yadkin River
New River
S. Fork
W. Kerr Scott Reservoir
Whippoorwill Academy
Fort Defiance
0 5 10 Miles
N
© The Countryman Press

**Ashe Memorial Hospital** (www.ashememorial.org; e-mail: info@ashememorial.org; 336-846-7101; 200 Hospital Ave., Jefferson, NC, 28640). This full-service 76-bed hospital with a 24/7 emergency room serves the rural northwest corner of the North Carolina Mountains from its campus at the center of Jefferson.

### *From the Blue Ridge Parkway*

From the Cumberland Knob area in the north, Alleghany Memorial is closest, via US 21. From Doughton Park and the Laurel Springs area, exit onto NC 18 and take it north to Alleghany Memorial. Farther south, exit onto NC 16 north, then take a left onto NC 163 to Ashe Memorial. Finally, if you are at Jeffress Park you want to continue onto the parkway to US 441, then go west to Watauga Medical Center in Boone (see "Behind the Blue Ridge: Boone & Banner Elk").

## ✷ Exploring the Area

This region gains much of its fascination from its rapid contrasts between rough wilderness and gentle farmlands. Its major feature is **The Blue Ridge**, that hard old mountain that runs, nearly unbroken, from Maryland to Georgia. Buried for eons, it's eastern face has been exposed by erosion from streams running into the Atlantic, while its western side remains hidden under younger rocks. These younger rocks form a bowl of prosperous farmland, a northeast by southwest oval that's about 15 miles wide by 30 miles long and known as **The New River Valley**. The **Bald Mountains** rise from the western edge of this valley, reaching heights that typically exceed 4,000 feet and sometimes top 5,000 feet.

Taken together, this landscape breaks into three strips:

- *The Blue Ridge Mountains.* The eastern edge of the Blue Ridge is eroded into steep, jagged mountains, covered in forests. Thin soils over granite guarantee that there will be few farms, even in the narrow valleys. In places the granite forms bare open areas, called **balds;** in one place, **Stone Mountain State Park**, you can find mountain-sized outcrops of solid granite, a remarkable sight.
- *The New River Valley* starts suddenly, at the crest of the Blue Ridge, with an equally sudden transition to pastoral prosperity. Drained by one of the South's great canoe streams, this large area is uniformly scenic. It has the

FARM IN THE NEW RIVER VALLEY

PARKWAY VIEW TOWARD MOUNT JEFFERSON

character of low mountains eroded into gentle valleys, alternating farmland and forest. It holds two pretty little county seats, **Jefferson** and **Sparta**, as well as two state parks, **Mount Jefferson State Natural Area** and **The New River State Park**. The historic village of **Todd**, on its southern end, is particularly pretty.

- *The Stone Mountains* carry the state line along the western edge of this region. On the North Carolina side, they have only one tract of publicly accessible land, the **Three Tops Game Land**. Only back roads cut through these mountains; if you go exploring, take along a good map.

**EXPLORING BY CAR The Blue Ridge Parkway** Although this entire region is scenic enough to be worth a visit, the Blue Ridge Parkway remains by far its most important feature. Here the Blue Ridge is a sharp barrier of hard old rock, a 2,000-foot escarpment facing the Atlantic. When the parkway follows the crest its scenery is wild and its views are long, with deep forests and sharp crags. When the road swerves west, however, it suddenly enters a land of gentle hills, lush meadows, and rich farms.

Start at the northern end of the parkway by taking NC 89 12.1 miles west from I-77's exit 100 to a left onto NC 18; from Sparta, take NC 18 eastward for 14.8 miles. The first site, only a mile from NC 18, is **Cumberland Knob Recreation Area**, with a good view from its visitors center. For the next 12 miles you will be on the first segment of the Blue Ridge Parkway ever built, in 1934; the last segment, **Grandfather Mountain** (see "The Blue Ridge Parkway: Blowing Rock & Grandfather Mountain," *Wild Places*), finally opened in 1987. On this original stretch, look for Fox Hunter's Paradise Overlook with wide views, then a lovely path circling a millpond. The parkway regains the crest just in time for a spectacular view over the edge to **Stone Mountain**; use US 21 to visit this remarkable state park. Brinegar Cabin (MP 238.5) on the left, one of the parkway's most attractive and worthwhile log cabins, marks the beginning of **Doughton Park**, one of the parkway's best features with its beautiful mountain meadow walks and great views.

After Doughton Park there's more farmland, then the Sheets Cabin (MP 252.3), a log cabin built in 1815 and occupied until 1940. The parkway passes the **Northwest Trading Post**, a local crafts shop, then the wonderful views from Jumpinoff Rocks and **The Lump**. Beyond The Lump, the parkway swerves behind the crest for wide views westward over the New River Valley to Mount Jefferson, at **Mount Jefferson Overlook**. The parkway enters **E. B. Jeffress Park** at the **Cascades Overlook** with its fine waterfall walk and log cabin. The final 20 miles of this section pass a series of crest overlooks in both directions; look especially for eastward views from Grandview Overlook (MP 281.4) and westward views from Raven Rocks Overlook (MP 289.5).

**EXPLORING ON FOOT** **Stone Mountain Paths** This large state park has a common boundary with the **Blue Ridge Parkway**, and can be reached by exiting onto US 21 south, then south 4.6 miles to a right onto Stone Mountain Road (SSR 1100), then another 3 miles to the park. Loop trails poke around the interesting back corners of Stone Mountain State Park's **unusual collection of granitic domes**. Formed as one large pluton, or underground dome-shaped magma intrusion, today this exposed granite mound rises up to 1,000 feet above its valley floor, appearing as a series of bare rock monadnocks broken by rugged little stream valleys. Even though these peaks aren't very high by North Carolina standards, their steep sides and rocky terrain can make the paths difficult and tiring. The most popular (and difficult) trail is the 4.5-mile loop that climbs **Stone Mountain** itself—the easternmost and largest of the three monadnocks. Starting at the **Hutchinson Homestead**, the path strolls easily up the grassy valley with great views toward the cliff face of Stone Mountain, then follows a forested stream uphill for a mile or so to the park's most impressive waterfall, **Stone Mountain Falls** From here the path becomes quite difficult, although it's climbing the mountain's easiest side. Surprisingly, the top is forested, but with wide and changing views from the cliff edges that surround the mile-long summit. At the far end of the summit the trail descends exposed rock at an improbably steep grade to reach the parking lot. Another, much easier loop visits the other two monadnocks, Cedar Rock and Wolf Rock—actually two sides of the same summit. Much lower and shorter (although still difficult in places), this loop furnished good scenery and great views. Start the loop from the Stone Mountain Loop Trail, a short distance down from the Hutchinson Homestead; it returns to the parking lot.

BRINEGAR CABIN, IN DOUGHTON PARK

**Doughton Park Walks** Doughton Park is part of the **Blue Ridge Parkway**, with the main entrance at milepost 241. It protects a mile or more of mountain-top meadows, with some wonderful places to walk—beautiful scenery, lots of wildflowers, magnificent views, and much easier than any Blue Ridge mountaintop deserves to be. The walk past the Wildcat Cliffs to Fodderstack Knob, with a trailhead at the lodge, is the most popular, and deservedly so. The cliff-top views at **Wildcat Cliffs** (only a short distance from the parking lot) give a wide sweep down the 2,000-foot escarpment of the Blue Ridge and over the plains of the Piedmont; at the base of the cliffs, a single log cabin breaks the forest. A gentle 1-mile round-trip leads from there to Fodderstack Knob, a rocky bald with the characteristic Japanese garden look framing another wide view. South from the lodge, a path is hardly needed through the wildflower meadows that crown the mountain for a mile—though one exists, just in case. On this long summit you will come across wide and ever-changing views, many wildflowers, rocky outcrops, and dwarfed and twisted trees. The picnic area's access road parallels the summit meadows on their western downhill side, allowing picnickers to stroll up from their tables into the meadows at any point. For those who want a longer walk, the mile Bluff Mountain Trail starts at the Brinegar Cabin and follows the Blue Ridge Crest (including the summit meadows) to Basin Cove Overlook—a good walk for those who can arrange a car shuttle.

**Mount Jefferson** Summit This mile-long walk along the summit of 4,600-foot Mount Jefferson climbs 350 feet in elevation on its way to two spectacular viewpoints. It starts at the picnic area on the top of the mountain in **Mount Jefferson State Park**, 1 mile outside Jefferson. The trail proceeds along an old road bed at the far end of the picnic area, climbing uphill at a steep 15 percent grade—mercifully, for only 1,000 feet or so—to a viewpoint at the highest point of Mount Jefferson. The trail continues along a high rocky ridge, forested with some very tough old hardwoods, for another half-mile to Luther Rock, a rocky outcrop and cliff with very wide views over Jefferson and northward over the New River Valley. A loop returns through rhododendron tunnels.

**LONG-DISTANCE PATHS** **The Mountains-to-Sea Trail** (www.ncmst.org). The Mountains-to-Sea Trail spends somewhere over 50 miles in this current chapter. As with all following chapters, this description goes west to east—in other words, downhill on this trail that, during its length, loses 6,643 feet in elevation.

This section starts at the parkway's intersection with US 421 and stays within the parkway's lands for the next 45 miles. Although this has been a long road walk for many years, the National Park Service has been very cooperative in approving a new off-the-road trail corridor, a complex procedure nowadays that includes archeological studies. The last such corridor, between NC 16 and NC 18 (a length of 16 miles) opened in 2008, creating 300 miles of continuous, dedicated hiking path. Within **Doughton Park** the trail follows the Blue Ridge Crest through a mile of wildflower meadows, then continues past the park to finally leave the parkway for good at Devil's Garden Overlook. Here it starts its final drop out of the mountains on the backcountry trails of **Stone Mountain State Park**, then passes through **Hutchinson Homestead** to circle the base of Stone Mountain. From here a short walk downhill along a creek leads into the Piedmont, and the end of the mountains of western North Carolina. At this point the trail becomes a road walk and bicycle route for most of its journey to the coast—although the State of North Carolina is actively identifying and purchasing right-of-way, and a number of Piedmont and coastal plain sections are already constructed and certified.

**EXPLORING BY BICYCLE The Virginia Creeper Trail** (www.vacreepertrail.org). Located just to the north of this chapter's area, across the state line into Virginia, lies one of the East's finest bicycle trails, the old bed of the **Virginia Creeper Railroad**. As its name implies, the Virginia Creeper was notorious for its steep grades and sharp curves, its steam engines and **remarkable bridges** (famously photographed by O. Winston Link), and above all its wild mountain scenery. The Creeper starts just 3 miles north of the North Carolina line, at Whitetop, Virginia. From there its excellent quality gravel surface heads downhill at grades up to 7 percent, through rugged mountain wilderness, to Damascus, Virginia—a continuous coast of 18.5 miles. On this section you'll pass through 12.4 miles of a little-visited section of the congressionally declared **Mount Rogers National Recreation Area**. From Damascus it's another 15.6 miles of pleasant valley riding to Abingdon, Virginia, with one last huge bridge over the South Holston Reservoir. To reach the Whitetop terminus from Sparta, take US 21 westward from town center for 2.8 miles to a left onto US 221, then go 0.8 mile to a right onto NC 93, which you follow for 10.8 miles to a left onto US 58 in Virginia. Another 21.9 miles brings you to a left onto SSR 726 (Whitetop Road), with the restored station in 1.4 miles.

You can find more details about the Virginia Creeper Trail and the adjacent Mount Rogers National Recreation area—as well as bike rentals, lodgings, and restaurants in the Damascus area—in this book's companion volume, *The Shenandoah Valley and Mountains of the Virginias.*

## ✷ Villages

**Sparta**. The small county seat of Sparta (pop.: 1,817), 7 miles west of the Blue Ridge Parkway's US 21 exit, serves as the main market town for the northern part of this region. It occupies a high mountain bowl at an elevation of 2,900 feet, surrounded by small mountains (or large hills) with peaks scarcely 500 feet above the valley floor. It is very much a throwback to an earlier era. Its central grid of four blocks by three blocks centers on a three-block brick-front downtown, which still functions as the town's main shopping district. A handsome old courthouse, with an historic jail, sits at the main intersection at the center of town.

**Glendale Springs, Laurel Springs, and Roaring Gap**. These three rural settlements provide services adjacent to the Blue Ridge Parkway.

Just off the Blue Ridge Parkway's NC 16 exit, **Glendale Springs** is a rural settlement best known for the spectacular **fresco of the Last Supper** in its tiny Episcopalian church. Visited by 60,000 people a year, Ben Long's moving 1980 Renaissance-style fresco has generated a small local tourism industry, and something resembling a town has grown up near the church during the last 20 years. You will find a number of places to eat, sleep, shop, and gas up within a mile of the church.

Just 10 miles northeast, the community of **Laurel Springs** provides food and lodging convenient to the Blue Ridge Parkway's exit to NC 18. This is a good headquarters area for nearby **Doughton Park** (named after a congressman who lived here).

**Roaring Gap** sits on the downhill side of the Blue Ridge Parkway off its US 21 exit, convenient to **Stone Mountain State Park**. There is food and lodging here, plus a golf course.

**Jefferson & West Jefferson**. Twenty-five miles north of Boone and far off the beaten tourist paths, these little-developed red-brick sister towns retain their old mountain look and feel. They complement each other; Jefferson, with 1,400 residents, has the government functions and the historic domed courthouse, while West Jefferson, with 1,000 residents, has the downtown main street (called Jefferson Street). Once a railroad depot on the **Virginia Creeper** line, West Jefferson's old-fashioned red-brick downtown is surprisingly interesting with a scattering of galleries representing local artists. **Mount Jefferson** looms above both towns, a state park with magnificent views from four overlooks.

## ✷ Wild Places

**THE GREAT FORESTS** ♿ **Stone Mountain State Park** (www.ncparks.gov/Visit/parks/stmo/main.php; e-mail: stone.mountain@ncmail.net; 336-957-8185; fax: 336-957-3985; 3042 Frank Pkwy., Roaring Gap, NC, 28668). A remarkable **granite dome** sits at the foot of the Blue Ridge Crest, just downhill from the parkway's US 21 exit. Here the mountains drop steeply to a valley 1,500 feet below; from there, an oval dome 2 miles long and 1 mile wide rises 1,000 feet nearly straight up. Erosion has cut the dome into several subpeaks, carved stream valleys into its flanks, and covered much of it with thin soil and thick forest. However, the dome's tallest point remains an isolated monadnock, a 1,000-foot mass of nearly bare rock—Stone Mountain.

Since 1969, when underwear king R. Phillip Hanes donated the core holdings to the state, North Carolina has worked to preserve this formation and enough of the surrounding mountains to form a viable wilderness ecosystem. They now protect 21 square miles of unique Blue Ridge backcountry. Park access is down a back road that separates the dome area from the mountain wall to its north, forming a semi-circle around the strange granitic formations at the park's center. Here you will find ample picnicking, tent and trailer camping, trout fishing, **historic sites**, and a network of **loop trails** exploring the granite dome area—including waterfall paths and views both of and from Stone Mountain. The Blue Ridge slopes towering above the granite dome to its north have only one public footpath, a rugged, rocky path to backpacking camps that carries the **Mountains-to-Sea Trail** down into the Piedmont; the rest of the backcountry remains little-visited wilderness.

DOWNTOWN WEST JEFFERSON

**Three Top Mountain Game Lands** (336-957-4197; 1722 Mail Service Center, Raleigh, NC, 27699). This 2,300-acre tract (about 3.6 square miles) between Todd and Jefferson preserves the impressive 4,800-foot craggy peak known as **Three Top** and its surrounding slopes. The tract's public hiking trails lead through rich forests to wildflower meadows, crags, and views. Apart from some amazing natural scenery and the public's only unrestricted access to the northern Bald Mountains, Three Top offers **aspen forests**, otherwise unknown in North Carolina. The Nature Conservancy started assembling this impressive tract in 1989 from a mosaic of donations, cooperative local owners, and a couple of busted subdivisions. It's currently owned by the North Carolina Wildlife Resources Commission, whose main mission is maintaining public land for hunting and fishing. Trails are unblazed and unmapped; be sure to bring the USGS topographic map (Warrensville quad) and a compass. To find the Three Top Mountain Game Land from NC 194 in **Todd**, head north from Todd on Three Top Road for 8.7 miles. The public access parking lot is on the right, just before a bridge over Three Top Creek.

**Bluff Mountain Preserve (The Nature Conservancy)** (blueridgeheritage.com/attractions-destinations/bluff-mountain; e-mail: BluffMountainPreserve@gmail.com; 336-497-1972; Edwards Road, West Jefferson, NC, 28693). This 2,000-acre, privately owned preserve, located in the same mountain range as the **Three Top Game Lands**, protects an unusual **perched valley**, flat bottomed, yet just below the 4,800-foot peak of Bluff Mountain. The site offers wonderful views from rocky outcrops, and a variety of beautiful and unusual ecosystems—a mature hemlock forest, a dwarf oak forest, rocky bald plant communities, and a rare example of the southern Appalachian fen (a mountain bog), protected in the high valley. Owned and managed by **The Nature Conservancy**, Bluff Mountain **is not open** for casual visits from the public. However, The Nature Conservancy has contracted with a local eco-tourism guide, Kim Hadley, to offer tours. Call or e-mail her for information.

**THE FORESTS NEARBY**

Two other major wild areas are easily reached from this region—and are well worth the effort.

**The Rogers Ridge Roadless Area** sits in Tennessee's Cherokee National Park, immediately adjacent to this region. It features wide mountaintop meadows reaching 4,800 feet high, and a notable waterfall on Gentry Creek. From Mountain City, Tennessee (see "The Mountains of Northern Tennessee," *Villages*), follow TN 91 north for 7.9 miles, to a right turn onto Gentry Creek Road, which becomes gravel FS 122 before it ends at the roadless area in 3.1 miles.

**Mount Rogers National Recreation Area** contains a large area of Blue Ridge high country, just 3 miles north of this region in Virginia's George Washington and Jefferson National Forests; it's 24 miles from Sparta via US 21 and US 58. The center of this huge area is a 12,000-acre oval-shaped island in the sky, consistently above 4,000 feet and with more than a dozen peaks over 5,000 feet, the highest in Virginia. This is the largest stand of high country "balsam" forest in the Blue Ridge, dominated by spruce-fir forests and wide alpine meadows. You can find a full description in this book's companion volume, *The Shenandoah Valley and Mountains of the Virginias.*

**RIVERS The South Fork of the New River, and New River State Park** (ncparks.gov/Visit/parks/neri/main; e-mail: new.river@ncmail.net; 336-982-2587; P.O. Box 48, Jefferson, NC, 28640). The most remarkable thing about the South Fork of the New River is the way it meanders, acting as if it is lazily wandering through a level plain. This is not the case. The New River sits more than 3,100 feet above sea level, just behind the Blue Ridge, and follows the Blue Ridge for nearly 90 miles. Of course, those are meandering river miles; the actual linear distance covered is 29.4 miles. Those distance-tripling meanders reduce the slope of the river to the point where canoes commonly replace kayaks; much of the river is still water, and most of its rapids are a mild Class I. These meanders, despite their flatland behavior, have managed to cut straight down into the hard rock of the Blue Ridge, leaving the river surrounded by cliff-like slopes. Frequently the river will make a sharp 180-degree curve, cutting a gorge that doubles back on itself.

The easy paddling couples with the prime mountain scenery to offer 90 miles of day explorations and overnight adventures. The state sponsors formal canoe launching points at a number of places, and its 1,500-acre **New River State Park** is dedicated to supporting this river as a canoe trail. Private livery services offer shuttles, guided and unguided rentals, and lots of information on river conditions and campsites.

This stretch of river has long enjoyed the reputation as the second oldest river in the world and the oldest in North America—claims repeated by former President Clinton when he declared it a National Heritage River from its banks near Jefferson in 1998. Some have objected to this, claiming that there is no agreed-upon measure of a river's age, and even if there was, it has never been used in a world survey. Well, picky, picky, picky. Those 90 miles of meanders formed when the New River flowed through a flat plain. The meanders cut into the rock as the mountains rose underneath them—in this case the Blue Ridge Mountains, 220 million years old. You do the math.

**RECREATION AREAS Mount Jefferson State Natural Area** (www.ncparks.gov/Visit/parks/moje/main; e-mail: mount.jefferson@ncdenr.gov; 336-246-9653; 1481 Mount Jefferson State Park Rd., West Jefferson, NC, 28694.) This isolated mountain rises just south of Jefferson, its peak 1,400 feet above the wide valleys that surround it. A paved lane climbs the west slope of Mount Jefferson in seven switchbacks, with two overlooks giving broad views over West Jefferson and Bluff Mountain. At the top there is a tree-shaded picnic area, a nature trail, and **walking paths** along the narrow half-mile-long summit to two more overlooks.

**PICNIC AREAS Picnicking on the Blue Ridge Parkway** Picnickers will find a number of good sites along this 75-mile stretch of the parkway. From north to south, these include:

- Cumberland Knob Recreation Area, milepost 217.5.
- Little Glade Mill Pond, MP 230.1, with five tables and a short path by a pond.
- Doughton Park, MP 241.1.
- The Cascades Area, MP 271.9

## ✷ To See

### *Along the Blue Ridge Parkway*

**Cumberland Knob Recreation Area** The 1,000-acre Cumberland Knob Recreation Area was the first segment of the Blue Ridge Parkway opened to the public, being the site of the dedication ceremony in 1935. It's a forested knob located 1 mile south of the Virginia border, adjacent to the parkway's NC 18 exit. It has a visitors center with exhibits, and a very nice picnic area. It has two pleasant trails, a 1 mile stroll to the top of Cumberland Knob (only 2,840 feet, but the highest point in the area), and a more strenuous 2 miles loop down to Gully Creek—the latter an 800-foot return climb, offering mountain views, deep forests, attractive small waterfalls, and a log barn.

**Doughton Park** Originally named "Bluff Mountain," this 6,000-acre Blue Ridge Parkway tract includes 6 miles of the Blue Ridge Crest and the watershed beneath it. Typical of all the Blue Ridge, the Atlantic side is a rugged, broken drop of 2,000 feet, while the western side is little more than rolling hills. The crest is especially notable for its large **wildflower meadows** and its **rocky outcrops** with wide views. Paths link the meadows and the outcrops, forming multiple loops than plummet into the stream basin beneath and climb back out again. At the center is a classic parkway recreation area—picnic area, camping area, store, coffee shop, and a motel-style lodge.

CASCADE FALLS IN THE E. B. JEFFRESS PARK

At the north end is the **Brinegar Cabin** (milepost 238.5), built in 1885 and one of the loveliest log cabins in the region; it's the site of weaving demonstrations during the summer. In 2 miles the parkway enters meadows, with a parking area and path on the left (milepost 240.6). You'll reach the main area of meadows, heaths, rocky outcrops, and grand views in another half-mile; take the road to the lodge on the left. The stunning Fodderstack Trail, with its panoramic view centering on a log cabin far below, starts at the lodge. The meadows follow the ridgeline from the lodge south toward the picnic area, extending for nearly a mile along the crest of the Blue Ridge. Along this stretch the parkway descends the gentle western side of the mountain, staying discreetly out of the wild and windy views. The meadows end at a cliff with the parkway dropping below it to a narrow spine passing more overlooks with impressive views back toward the mountain.

**Jumpinoff Rocks and The Lump** The Jumpinoff Rocks are a set of outcrops that form a rocky bald on the crest of the Blue Ridge, with wide views over the valley far below. The level half-mile walk leads through galax and wildflowers; you'll find it at the Jumpinoff Rocks Overlook (MP 260.3), just north of the parkway's NC 16 exit. Four miles farther south, The Lump (MP 264.4) is a knobby peninsula that projects out from the crest of the Blue Ridge. Covered in meadows and surrounded by 2,000-foot drops, The Lump affords views both wide and spectacular. It's a short walk up a small hill from the overlook parking lot; in the summer, there's a good chance you'll see people flying powered model airplanes from it.

**E. B. Jeffress Park** The 500-acre E. B. Jeffress Park, actually part of the Blue Ridge Parkway, is named after the 1935 North Carolina Department of Roads chief who championed the parkway and insisted that it be a free road instead of a toll road. Located along the parkway just north of its intersection with US 421, it preserves a 2.3-mile stretch of the Blue Ridge Crest with its typically steep plummet on its Atlantic side and gentle swale toward the back. A late-19th-century **log cabin** and a rough log structure used as a church and revival site sit in a flower-studded meadow by the roadside (park at the Thomkins Knob Overlook and follow the path). A half-mile north, the Cascade Picnic Area has well-kept tables with excellent views over the edge of the Blue Ridge toward the Piedmont. However, the park's most popular site is the 1-mile loop path that leads from the picnic area through jungle-like old-growth forests and heavy rhododendrons to **Cascade Falls**, a lacy waterfall over a 50-foot gray outcrop.

**HISTORIC SITES** ✐ **Stone Mountain: Hutchinson Homestead & Garden Creek Church** (www.ncparks.gov/Visit/parks/stmo/main; 336-957-8185; 3042 Frank Parkway, Roaring Gap, NC, 28668). Located within Stone Mountain State Park, these two historic sites present a picture of late-19th-century community life in the Blue Ridge area. **Hutchinson Homestead** is a mid-19th-century farm in scenic meadows underneath the cliffs of Stone Mountain. Preserved for decades as a park maintenance area, it was restored in 1998 to its original form. It has a log cabin, barn, corn crib, meat house, and blacksmith shop, all furnished in period. Stunning views over the meadows to the massive monadnock, Stone Mountain, add to its charm. A mile down the park road, the 1897 Garden Creek Baptist Church gives a rare opportunity to visit an authentic 19th-century country church. Nearly unchanged in over a century, the small crackerbox building is of unpainted clapboards, and has a lovely display of daylilies in early summer. It's still used for Sunday services in warm weather.

HISTORIC CHURCH IN STONE MOUNTAIN STATE PARK

**The Parish of the Holy Communion (The Churches of the Frescoes)** (336-982-3076; fax: 336-982-9870; P.O. Box 177, Glendale Springs, NC, 28629). These two rural parish churches close to the parkway's NC 16 exit at Glendale Springs are noted for their exquisite frescoes in the classic Italian Renaissance manner. These two modest Episcopalian churches are simple wood buildings constructed between 1901 and 1905, still serving congregations in Ashe County. Artist Ben Long created the frescoes between 1971 and 1980, choosing themes that mirrored the annual cycle of Episcopalian liturgy. The larger of the two churches, St. Mary's Church in West Jefferson, has three frescoes, each depicting a stage in the life of Christ: *Mary Great with Child, John the Baptist,* and *The Mystery of Faith.* The tiny Holy Trinity Church in Glendale Springs is decorated with one giant fresco behind the alter—a moving and original interpretation of the Last Supper. These remarkable works of art have become an attraction—or perhaps a pilgrimage site—of great popularity, receiving 60,000 visitors a year.

**Todd National Historic District** (toddnc.org). Located halfway between Boone and Jefferson on NC 194, Todd is a former depot town on a long-defunct mountain railroad that followed the New River to Jefferson and over the mountains to Virginia. A bit of a ghost town, Todd today is a collection of late-19th- and early-20th-century vernacular buildings that somehow manage to preserve the look and feel of an old rural railroad siding village. While most of the buildings are private, the general store is still going strong, and the depot houses a local craft gallery and New River outfitter. The New River comes right up to the town's lower edge and makes one of its unique hairpin turns around a cliff—an interesting site. It was at this point that the railroad started following the New River, and its old grade is now a narrow country lane with sweeping river views; you can rent bicycles at the depot for a lovely riverside jaunt.

THE NEW RIVER FLOWS PAST A FARM

**The Edwards-Franklin House** (surrycounty.pastperfect-online.com; e-mail: surry.history@gmail.com; 336-356-4145; 225 Windsor Park Dr., Dobson, NC 27017). Open the second weekend each month, April–September. Built in 1799, this handsome white wood farmhouse with a full porch and shake roof has its original decorative painting on the doors, mantels and wainscoting. Owned by the Surry County Historical Society, it's 12 miles off the parkway's NC 18 exit at the edge of the Blue Ridge Mountains, in the back road community of Blevins Store. Its location way down a back road gives you a chance to see the Blue Ridge backcountry and the scenic

Fisher River Valley; go .65 miles east on NC 18; then right 5.2 miles on NC 89; then right 5.2 miles on Hidden Valley Road (SSR 1338) following Fisher River; then left onto Haystack Road (SSR 1331).

**CULTURAL SITES** **Northwest Trading Post** (e-mail: NWTP@skybest.com; 336-982-2543; 414 Trading Post Rd., Glendale Springs, NC 28629). This gift shop, looking like an old country store, fronts the Blue Ridge Parkway at milepost 259 near Glendale Springs. Run by the Northwest Development Association as a non-profit to promote local mountain crafts, it features lots of handmade art and craft items, as well as baked goods, from the northwestern counties of North Carolina's Blue Ridge.

**Ashe County Cheese Company** (www.ashecountycheese.com; e-mail: info@ashecountycheese.com; 800-445-1378, 336-246-2501; 106 East Main St., P.O. Box 447, West Jefferson, NC, 28694). The mountain region's only cheese manufacturer has been in business in West Jefferson since 1930. They offer factory tours, fresh cheese for sale, and a gift shop.

**GARDENS AND PARKS** ✐ **Rendezvous Mountain Educational State Forest** (ncesf.org/RMESF/rmesf_about; e-mail: rendezvousmountainESF.DFR@ncdenr.gov; 336-667-5072; 1956 Rendezvous Mountain Rd., Purlear, NC, 28665). Open March–November, Tues.–Sun.; closed December–February. This 3,000-acre mountaintop forest sits in the Blue Ridge Mountains, 12 miles east of the parkway's NC 16 exit. The "educational" part is a 150-acre open-air museum, developed and run by the North Carolina Forest Service (a state agency that promotes sylviculture and good forestry practices). Oriented toward children and families, the museum's four loop paths lead through exhibits on forest ecology and logging practices. Loops include "talking trees" who explain who they are and how they fit in the forest, a fire tower and CCC cabin with fine views, and a logging demonstration with an operating saw mill. Much of the museum area is located on the summit of Rendezvous Mountain, with excellent views from the picnic area. The remainder of the tract preserves a beautiful old-growth oak-hickory forest, with 20 miles of hiking, horseback riding, and mountain-biking trails.

**BIG DAMMED LAKES** **W. Kerr Scott Reservoir** (www.saw.usace.army.mil/wkscott; e-mail: chad.eller@usace.army.mil; 336-921-3390; 499 Reservoir Rd., Wilkesboro, NC, 28697). The U.S. Army Corps of Engineers operates this 1,400-acre lake at the base of the Blue Ridge, 18 miles south of the Blue Ridge Parkway via NC 16. Its earthen dam, built in 1962 for flood control on the Yadkin River, is 150 feet high and 1,750 feet long. The lake itself is surrounded by 2,500 acres of government land, managed for recreation. Roughly a dozen sites offer picnicking, camping, boat ramps and docks, swimming, fishing, and trails, including a 4-mile segment of the **Overmountain Victory Trail** (see "Behind the Blue Ridge: Spruce Pine & Burnsville," *Exploring the Area*). Overall, it's a handsome and well-maintained area.

## ✷ To Do

**WHITEWATER ADVENTURES** ✐ **Rivergirl Fishing Company** (rivergirlfishing.com; e-mail: rivergirl124@skybest.com; 877-623-4744, 336-877-3099 4041 Todd

Railroad Grade Rd., Todd, NC, 28684). Rivergirl Fishing Company is located in the1888 train depot at the historic center of Todd, midway between Boone and Jefferson on NC 194. Rivergirl furnishes fly-fishing lessons, tubing, kayaking, and canoeing on the South Fork of the New River, as well as bicycling on the scenic lanes in the area.

**Zaloos Canoes** (zaloos.com; e-mail: zaloos@skybest.com; 800-535-4027, 336-246-3066; 3874 NC Hwy. 16 South, Jefferson, NC 28640). Located on the South Fork of the New River, at the corner of NC 16 and NC 88 (5 miles east of Jefferson), Zaloos offers tubing and canoe trips (including camping trips) along the New River.

**GOLF** **Old Beau Golf Club** (oldebeau.com; e-mail: tommy.maines@oldebeau.com; 800-752-1634; 729 Olde Beau Blvd., Roaring Gap, NC, 28668). Open all year. Located in Roaring Gap, a short distance off the parkway on US 21, this 18-hole resort course is remarkably scenic, with wide mountain views.

**Jefferson Landing on the New River** (visitjeffersonlanding.com; e-mail: proshop@jeffersonlandingclub.com; 800-292-6274; 148 E. Landing Drive/P.O. Box 110, Jefferson, NC, 28640). Open mid-March–mid-November. Built in 1991, this 18-hole course occupies the site of former farmland and has wide views toward Mount Jefferson, as well as water hazards on 15 holes.

**Mountain Aire** (www.mountainaire.com; e-mail: info@mountainaire.com; 336-877-4716; 1104 Golf Course Rd., West Jefferson, NC, 28694). Open mid-March–mid-December. This 18-hole course, built in 1950 in the remote mountains near Jefferson, offers first-rate scenery.

## ✷ Lodging

### BED & BREAKFAST INNS

**Doughton-Hall Bed & Breakfast** (doughtonhallbandb.com; 336-359-2341; 12668 NC 18 South, Laurel Springs, NC, 28644). Located less than 2 miles from the parkway's NC 18 exit, Doughton-Hall Bed & Breakfast occupies the 1898 National Register listed home of Robert L. Doughton, the powerful congressman who helped write the Social Security Act and who brought the Blue Ridge Parkway to North Carolina. Tucked into a quiet rural location and surrounded by lawns, this red-trimmed Queen Anne house has wide wrap-around porches. A stocked trout stream crosses the property, and guests are welcome to try their luck. Its common areas and four guest rooms are furnished with antiques, and the guest rooms have whirlpool tubs. Guests are greeted with wine and hors d'oeuvres when they arrive, and are given a full breakfast at the time they choose.

**Buffalo Tavern Bed & Breakfast** (www.buffalotavern.com; e-mail: DocAdams@BuffaloTavern.com; 877-615-9678, 336-877-9080; fax: 336-877-9081, 958 West Buffalo Rd., West Jefferson, NC, 28694). Built in the 1870s, this large wooden house in the rural Bluff Mountain area (6 miles west of Jefferson) was a popular 19th-century coaching inn and Prohibition era tavern. Today it's an elegant four-room bed & breakfast, one of the rooms being a large, lavish three-room suite. Its first- and second-story porches offer spacious comfortable seating. Decorated in the country Victorian style, all rooms have down comforters and log fireplaces and come equipped with roomy, 5-star hotel quality, plush Turkish bathrobes. A full country breakfast is served in their *Americana* dining room.

**CABIN RENTALS** **Fall Creek Cabins** (www.fallcreekcabins.com; e-mail: vacation@fallcreekcabins.com; 336-877-3131; P.O. Box 190, Fleetwood, NC, 28626). Seven cedar log cabins sit on 78 acres deep in the Blue Ridge Mountains, not 5 miles from the parkway's intersection with US 421. The property has hiking trails, a trout stream and also a creek with waterfalls. The modern two-story cabins, all individually decorated, have full porches and wood floors, as well as fireplaces and hot tubs; some have mountain views, while others look out on forests or streams.

## ✷ Where to Eat

**EATING OUT** **The Pines Restaurant** (336-372-4148; 577 N. Main St., Sparta, NC, 28675). Open Mon.–Thurs., 7:00 AM–8:30 PM; Fri.–Sat., 7 AM–9 PM; Sun., 7 AM–8 PM. This southern-style eatery on the south edge of Sparta, 7 miles off the parkway on US 21, offers fresh country cooking and hand-chopped barbeque.

## ✷ Special Events

**SUMMER** **Alleghany County Fiddler's Convention** (sparta-nc.com; e-mail: info@sparta-nc.com; 800-372-5473, 336-372-5473; 58 South Main St./P.O. Box 1237, Sparta, NC, 28675). Fri., 5 PM–midnight. Sat., 10 AM–midnight. Third Friday and Saturday in July. Old-time mountain and bluegrass bands come from all over to compete for cash prizes at the county fairgrounds at Sparta. There's also a dance competition.

**Alleghany Quilter's Show & Blue Ridge Mountain Craft Fair** (e-mail: info@sparta-nc.com; 800-372-5473, 336-372-5473; 58 South Main St./P.O. Box 1237, Sparta, NC, 28675). 10 AM–4 PM. Free. Third weekend in July. This Friday and Saturday event features a quilters' meet, held in the *Black Building* at the county fairgrounds in Sparta; a craft show at Crouse Park; and live bluegrass and mountain music performed on Main Street across from the courthouse.

**AUTUMN** **Mountain Heritage Festival** (800-372-5473). This annual street fair in downtown Sparta features live bluegrass and mountain music, craft demonstrations, a hundred or more art and craft booths, and food vendors. Contact the Alleghany County Chamber of Commerce at number shown for annual dates and times.

**Sonker Festival at the Edwards-Franklin House** (www.visitmayberry.com/Edwards-Franklin_House.aspx; e-mail: tourism@visitmayberry.com; 800-948-0949, 336-786-8359; 4132 Haystack Rd. (Edwards-Franklin House), Mount Airy, NC, 27030). 1 PM–5 PM. First Saturday in October. A "sonker" is a deep dish fruit or sweet potato pie. This festival celebrates the sonker with old-time mountain music (and lots of home-cooked sonkers) at Surry County's 18th-century Edwards-Franklin House, at the foot of the Blue Ridge.

# THE BLUE RIDGE PARKWAY: BLOWING ROCK & GRANDFATHER MOUNTAIN

This 67-mile stretch of the Blue Ridge has been attracting summer visitors since the late 19th century. First the resort village of Blowing Rock emerged on the Blue Ridge Crest just south of Boone. Then, 12 miles south along the crest, a mountain family created the summer cottage village of Linville and surrounded it with thousands of acres of wilderness preserve. Wealthy flatlanders started buying up old, hardscrabble farmland in the area, and creating large estates surrounding summer homes—later to become parts of the Blue Ridge Parkway, further preserving the crest scenery. Another 12 miles down, the spectacular Linville Falls attracted more summer cottages; and 12 miles below that, Little Switzerland became a magnet for early-20th-century automobile tourists.

This area also has a tiny, but important, slice of early pioneer history: Daniel Boone lived here as a young man, and here started his career as an explorer and road builder. You can visit a re-creation of his cabin, and follow the first road he built, the predecessor of the Wilderness Road. Other early settlement sites, at or near Boone's cabin, include Tom Dooley's home (the guy who hung down his head and cried), and a Colonial-era farm.

This section of the Blue Ridge Parkway is varied and exciting, with rugged, wild scenery alternating rapidly with more settled and pastoral views. Off the parkway, Blowing Rock remains the main focus of interest. Still a popular resort appealing to the wealthy, it features a good selection of gourmet restaurants, luxurious small bed & breakfasts, and fascinating shopping.

**GUIDANCE** **Blowing Rock Chamber of Commerce** (www.blowingrock.com; e-mail: info@visitblowingrock.com; 877-750-4636, 828-295-4636; 132 Park Ave., Blowing Rock, NC, 28605). This chamber runs a visitors center a half block from downtown, in an old house. Their website is very good.

**GETTING THERE** *By Car* This area is best approached from I-40, running beneath the mountains to their south. From there, US 321 runs north to Blowing Rock (and Boone), and US 221 runs north to Linville.

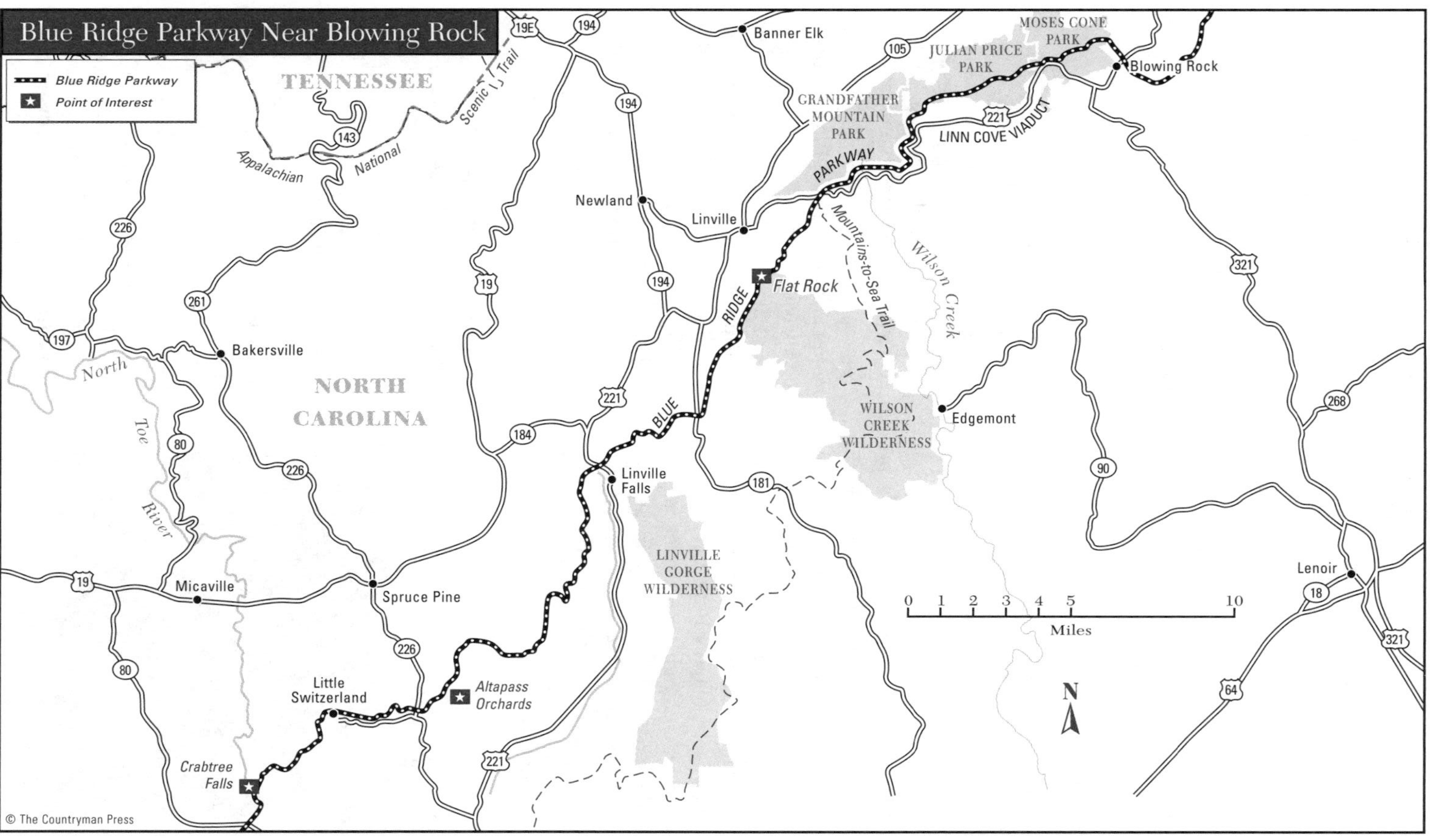
Blue Ridge Parkway Near Blowing Rock
Blue Ridge Parkway
Point of Interest
TENNESSEE
NORTH CAROLINA
Appalachian National Scenic Trail
Banner Elk
Newland
Linville
Blowing Rock
MOSES CONE PARK
JULIAN PRICE PARK
GRANDFATHER MOUNTAIN PARK
LINN COVE VIADUCT
BLUE RIDGE PARKWAY
Flat Rock
Mountains-to-Sea Trail
Wilson Creek
WILSON CREEK WILDERNESS
Edgemont
Linville Falls
LINVILLE GORGE WILDERNESS
Lenoir
Bakersville
Spruce Pine
Micaville
North Toe River
Little Switzerland
Altapass Orchards
Crabtree Falls
0 1 2 3 4 5 10
Miles
N
19E
194
105
221
143
226
261
197
19
194
321
268
184
181
90
18
80
64
© The Countryman Press

*By Air* Charlotte's international hub is the closest airport, 88 miles away via expressway quality US 321. Tri-Cities Airport, in Tennessee (outside Johnson City) is 76 miles away, but the roads you would follow aren't very good.

*By Bus or Rail* There is no scheduled bus service and no railroads in this area.

**MEDICAL EMERGENCIES** In Blowing Rock, or along the northern half of this section of the parkway, Boone's Watauga Medical Center is nearby (see "Behind the Blue Ridge: Boone & Banner Elk"). At the south end of this section of the parkway, Blue Ridge Regional Hospital in Spruce Pine is your best bet (see "Behind the Blue Ridge: Spruce Pine & Burnsville").

## ✷ Exploring the Area

This chapter follows a short section of the Blue Ridge, closely hugged by 67 miles of the Blue Ridge Parkway. As with many other portions of the Blue Ridge, it is steep and cliff-like on its east-facing (Atlantic Ocean) side, carved into deep, rugged mountains with narrow valleys and poor soils. Its west-facing (Tennessee River Valley) side lacks a corresponding drop-off; instead, it rolls downwards into a series of high valleys with rich soils, prosperous farms, and heavy settlement.

This section, however, is unusual, in that the crest and the rich western valleys are separated by a series of increasingly rugged mountains that starts at Blowing Rock and continues well into the next Blue Ridge Parkway chapter (see "The Blue Ridge Parkway Circles Asheville"). In this chapter's area, the barrier ridge reaches its high point at the mile-high crest of **Grandfather Mountain**, topping out at 5,900-foot Calloway Peak. One of the most rugged and impressive mountains in the South, Grandfather Mountain presents a rich mosaic of exposed rock, heath, and deep forest. It's been a privately owned and managed ecological preserve since the 1880s, and is the only privately owned International Biosphere Reserve in the world. You may explore it on foot, and the modest admission fee supports its preservation. The breathtaking **Linn Cove Viaduct** carries the Parkway high over Grandfather Mountain's most delicate environments.

LINN COVE VIADUCT

**EXPLORING BY CAR The Blue Ridge Parkway** This section of the parkway starts at milepost 276, US 421, 11 miles east of Boone, and ends 67 miles later at milepost 344, NC 80, 19 miles south and east of Burnsville.

For the first 15 miles of this section, the parkway circles the civilized outskirts of the small university city of **Boone**. At milepost 285 a sign marks the crossing of the first major road made by **Daniel Boone**, incorrectly labeled "The Wilderness Road" and placed 0.8 mile too far north. You can follow **Boone's Trail** for yourself in the next drive. As you proceed down the parkway, look for good views at the

THE PARKWAY BENEATH GRANDFATHER MOUNTAIN

**Raven Rocks Overlook** (milepost 289). The next major intersection, US 321, leads to **Blowing Rock**, a wonderful resort village that dates from the 1880's, and then on to Boone.

The parkway immediately enters the civilized meadows of **Moses Cone Park**, with its 1890s Neoclassical mansion (now a crafts center) and miles of carriage trails. From there the parkway passes into **Julian Price Park**, with its lovely lake views. Both of these "parks" (all part of the Blue Ridge Parkway) were once great estates of wealthy industrialists, donated by their heirs to the National Park Service. From there, the parkway enters more rugged scenery as it approaches **Grandfather Mountain**, the tallest peak on the Blue Ridge Crest at 5,960 feet. The parkway slabs the high eastern slopes of Grandfather, a wild and impressive drive of wide views and great crags, with viaducts over the most rugged cliffs, and a downhill view over the **Wilson Creek National Wild & Scenic River**. Be on the lookout for the the sweeping S-curves of the quarter-mile long **Linn Cove Viaduct**, one of the most important and innovative structures in recent American bridge-building; there's a visitors center at the western end.

At the western edge of Grandfather Mountain, the parkway has its next major intersection, US 221. Actually, you've been paralleling it since Blowing Rock, and a left turn will take you back. Known as the **Yonalossee Trail**, this highway-in-name-only was built in the 1890s by a local resort owner, who charged for carriage rides along it. The current "highway" is nothing more than a layer of pavement over this old carriage road. To the right, US 221 leads 1 mile to the entrance of **Grandfather Mountain Park**, then on to the village of **Linville** in 3.1 miles from the parkway. At this intersection, **Beacon Heights Overlook** (milepost 305) gives one of the best views of Grandfather Mountain, plus a half-mile walk to another viewpoint. In 3 more miles, the **Flat Rock Parking Area** (milepost 308) marks a short, worthwhile walk to a garden-like rocky bald. The parkway intersects with NC 181 at milepost 312.

Past NC 181, the scenery become more pastoral, passing meadows and farms with pleasant views over split-rail fences. At milepost 316, a spur road to the left leads to the giant **Linville Falls** at the mouth of the **Linville Gorge Wilderness**, one of the deepest and steepest gorges on the Blue Ridge and one of the first wilderness areas created by Congress. Beyond Linville Falls the scenery becomes rugged again. Look for impressive gorge views over the Catawba River to your left, climaxing with the dizzying view from **Chestoa Overlook** at milepost 321, and a 270-degree panorama from **Bear Den Overlook** 2 miles later. After Bear Den, look for your first of many views over the 2-mile-long **Altapass Orchards**, a stunningly beautiful heritage orchard with hayrides, a café and gift shop, and free live music on summer weekends. The historic **Clinchfield Railroad Loops** are visible below, as is the gravel road bed of the 1913 predecessor to the parkway, the **Crest of the Blue Ridge Highway**. At the NC 226 intersection the **Museum of North Carolina Minerals** and services at Spruce Pine are to the right.

From here the parkway parallels the settlement of **Little Switzerland**, then enters another wild and rugged area with fine views in all directions. The parkway passes **Crabtree Falls Recreation Area** at milepost 339, then reaches **Black Mountain Overlook** (milepost 342) for the parkway's best view of **Mount Mitchell**, the tallest peak in the East (see "The Blue Ridge Parkway Circles Asheville," *Wild Places*).

NC 80, the end of this section, is 2 miles farther. It's hard to believe, but you've just spent all day driving 67 miles. The easiest way to get back to Blowing Rock is to return the way you came.

LINVILLE FALLS

**Daniel Boone's Trail, Part I** Born in Pennsylvania around 1734, Daniel Boone spent the first 20 years of his adult life (1753–1773) in this area, at the foot of the Blue Ridge near the Yadkin River at Beaver Creek—just another young, married farmer in a log cabin. And he wasn't even a very good farmer. He spent too much time hunting and exploring in the wild mountain lands north of his cabin. He ranged as far north as Kentucky, and learned every trail and path in between.

This drive (passing through two chapters) closely follows Boone's first road-building effort, known simply as **Boone's Trail**. It is not to be confused with The Wilderness Road, in which Boone acted as an agent for a land company. Boone built Boone's Trail for himself, because he thought he needed such a road and it didn't exist. He built it in 1769, and it led from his cabin to the settlement lands of East Tennessee.

Boone's Trail wasn't a road in any modern sense. It was a footpath, which Boone marked and cleared wide enough to let pack animals pass. Boone had no time or patience for pick and shovel work, so he had to find ground that was already properly sloped and drained; even a short length of difficult terrain could cut off an otherwise good route. Boone couldn't use tricks now common, like slabbing across slopes or building up across marshy areas. Instead, he had to be very clever in finding the best route.

*Start this drive at the* ***Whippoorwill Academy***. You are only a mile from Boone's cabin on Beaver Creek and can visit a faithful reconstruction of it at the Whippoorwill outdoor museum complex. (To see Beaver Creek itself, go a mile east on NC 268.) Now *travel 3.9 miles west on NC 268,* passing the settlement of Ferguson to a *left onto Elk Creek Road (SSR 1162).* **Elk Creek Valley** was already settled in Boone's day, and Boone had friends who lived along it. You'll find this a beautiful drive, with farms squeezed into a narrow valley, hemmed in by steep, forested slopes. *After 7.9 miles you'll turn right onto Fords Road (SSR 1166, becoming SSR 1508),* continuing to follow Elk Creek. After 6.3 miles you will pass the place (on the left) where Boone's road probably left Elk Creek Valley to climb the Blue Ridge. Here Boone's Trail probably passed through a perched valley known as Hodgetown, then followed a ridgeline to Deadmans Gap, then finally followed the high valley of North Fork to the only place where the Blue Ridge is gentle enough for a loaded pack horse to struggle up it: Cooks Gap. Modern automobiles, however, cannot follow this route. *You will continue up Elk Creek (SSR 1508) to a point 7.8 miles from your last turn, and continue on SSR 1508 as it makes a right-angle turn* up a small mountain gap and returns to Elk Creek at the remote settlement of Tripplette.

You are now at the base of the Blue Ridge itself, looming above you on your right. *After 1.4 miles since your turn up the mountain, turn left onto Jakes Mountain Road (SSR 1510) at a T-intersection.* One mile farther on, you start to climb out of Elk Creek Valley on this gravel-surfaced *road.* You will gain 1,000 feet in the next 2.5 miles of road, an average gradient of nearly 8 percent, thanks to modern bulldozers being able to carve a shelf in the wall-like front of the Blue Ridge. Boone had to find a similar gradient in nature; you will quickly appreciate how difficult this was.

As you top the crest, the contrast is startling. The steep climb, deep forests, and cliff-like drop on your right—they all stop, as if someone flipped a switch. You are now in rolling hills, with meadows and wood lots and more than a few signs of suburban growth from the nearby city of **Boone**. *At 2.9 miles from your last turn, you'll reach a T-intersection* with the **Blue Ridge Parkway** visible ahead to your right, and an intersection with your road at milepost 285. If you want to see where Boone's Trail came out, however, you'll want to *turn left onto Little Laurel Road (SSR 1511),* until it reaches **Cooks Gap** and starts to head down the other side, following the roadbed that Boone made.

Boone's Trail continues from here to cross the mountains ahead into Tennessee, and is traced in the next chapter.

**EXPLORING ON FOOT** **Hiking the Grandfather Backcountry** (www.grandfather.com/nature_walks; e-mail: hiking@grandfather.com; 800-468-7325, 828-733-4337; 2050 Blowing Rock Hwy., P.O. Box 129, Linville, NC 28646). Open daily, 8 AM–closing. Free if you start from a public road; you must have admission to start from within Grandfather Mountain Park. The first hike on anyone's adventure list must be the **Daniel Boone Scout Trail**, a National Recreation Trail that runs

**WHERE WAS BOONE'S TRAIL?**

Boone's Trail remained the primary track across the North Carolina Blue Ridge for about 40 years—but, as adequate maps were a hundred years in the future, we don't really know where it went. This is just one of several reconstructions.

Near-contemporary accounts give the crest-out point at Cooks Gap, and his children have described visits to friends up Elk Creek Valley; that gives two endpoints, and accurate topographic maps narrow the possibilities. For instance, no one with any sense would try to take pack horses up the old Cherokee trail that followed Elk Ridge, although the historian who suggested this in 1913 had no way of checking it by maps. But it does open up a question: why would Boone take his trail straight up the cliff face of the Blue Ridge (admittedly by a very clever route), when there was a more gentle alternative a short distance to the east—Deep Gap, now traversed by US 421?

One idea, oft repeated, is that Boone was making this trail for his own use and was simply picking the shortest distance from his cabin. This is at least partially true; when you are on foot and leading horses, saving 15 mountain miles will cut at least a day from your journey. There is another factor, however. Without a work team to move lots of dirt, even a short bit of bad ground can block your trail. We have no way of reconstructing what problems Boone faced when exploring up valleys that appear gentle on modern maps, as a lot can change in 240 years. Nevertheless, if you wish to check out the leading alternative for yourself, here's the route: From Ferguson, turn right onto Mount Pleasant Rd., then go 3.6 miles to a left onto Mount Zion Road. At a fork in 6.2 miles, go right onto Stony Creek Road. In 6 miles, turn right onto US 421, and the Blue Ridge crest is 2.5 miles further. You will probably come away concluding that Boone knew what he was doing when he chose Cooks Gap.

from the peak of Grandfather Mountain through the Grandfather Park backcountry to the Blue Ridge Parkway at Book Fork Parking Area (milepost 300.1). If you start from the parkway you face an uphill climb of 2,000 feet in 2.6 miles, but many hikers find that it's worth it; the trail features high meadows and cliffs with stunning views, through scenery so rugged that the trail uses **cables and ladders** to cross it. The **Nuwati Trail**, also within Grandfather Mountain Park, is an interesting alternative hike, starting at the same parkway trailhead. Nuwati climbs gently and evenly for 1.2 miles to **Storyteller's Rock** for first-rate views over this virgin backcountry. On the return hike, Cragway Trail branches off right to climb 500 feet in a mile to reach the Boone Trail, passing through crags and boulder fields with wide views. The trailhead at the privately owned park's visitors center gives access to another set of trails and starts 1,200 feet higher than the parkway trailhead. From here, the strenuous **Grandfather Trail** leads 2.4 miles along the open, rocky crest to meet up with the Daniel Boone Scout Trail; a car shuttle allows for a truly memorable hike.

**The Tanawha Trail** The **Linn Cove Viaduct** engineers built this 12-mile hiking trail as part of the viaduct project in 1987, and to the same high standards. Staying on the National Park Service's Blue Ridge Parkway properties throughout, this moderately easy path wanders through every type of Blue Ridge scenery, from rough crags to soft meadows. It starts at the **Linn Cove Viaduct Visitor's Center** (milepost 305.1) then passes under the viaduct, giving a close view of the bridge and the ecology it protects. It ascends a boulder wall using stone steps, then passes by a small waterfall on a flagstone path—the headwaters of **Wilson Creek National Wild & Scenic River**. It climbs up to Rough Ridge and crosses its rare and fragile mountain heather ecology on a 200-foot **boardwalk**, with continuous panoramic views off the Blue Ridge, over the viaduct and the Wilson Creek watershed, and into the Piedmont. Beyond, the path goes through New England–style forests and Blue Ridge–style rhododendron tunnels as it approaches **Julian Price Park**, then passes through a long series of old meadows, fields, and apple orchards before ending at **Price Lake** (MP 297). This makes a fine one-day hike if you can arrange to be picked up.

**LONG-DISTANCE PATHS** **The Mountains-to-Sea Trail** This chapter contains a 65-mile segment of North Carolina's 935-mile state trail. Now complete, this section of the trail hits some spectacular and remote backcountry. From NC 181 it dives into the **Wilson Creek Wilderness Study Area**, exploring its waterfall-rich valleys and hopping its ridges, then climbing the face of the Blue Ridge to finally regain the Blue Ridge Parkway and its corridor. As with sections farther south, it now stays on the parkway's property, crossing and recrossing the road—an interesting and (compared with the last few sections) easy walk. It quickly picks up the **Tanawha Trail**—one of the great scenic hikes of the southern mountains—and follows it past **Grandfather Mountain** to **Julian Price Park**. From here it has plenty of opportunity to explore Price Park, then the adjacent **Moses Cone Park**, running directly in front of the Moses Cone House, said to be the second largest in North Carolina (and now a craft center). Beyond Blowing Rock, the path, constructed for the Mountains-to-Sea Trail, stays closer to the parkway, giving good views of the farming scenery south of Boone.

PRICE LAKE, ON THE BLUE RIDGE PARKWAY

## ✴ Villages

**Blowing Rock** This village sits in a shallow bowl just behind the crest of the Blue Ridge, a short distance off the parkway. It's been around since the 1890s, a resort town from the first, and many of the buildings are very historic. The model for **Jan Karon's Mitford**, Blowing Rock's old village center remains attractive and busy, with a four-block downtown and a city park at its center. It has always been a gathering place for the wealthy, so the shopping is excellent, and both quality and prices tend to be high. Parking can be difficult, even in the off-season, and you may find yourself forced to walk a few blocks.

**Linville** Linville was founded as a resort town in the 1890s, about the same time as Blowing Rock; it was the Linville resort that constructed US 221 between the two, the earliest automobile road in the mountains. Linville was conceived as a summer village around the **Eseeola Lodge**, and a collection of historic summer homes still exist at the far end of the lodge. In those days, the resort company controlled the entire valley surrounding Linville, including Grandfather Mountain, and managed it as a wilderness park of great beauty.

**Linville Falls** Twelve miles south of Linville on US 221, and just off the Blue Ridge Parkway, Linville Falls is the third in this series of 19th-century Blue Ridge resorts, and the least successful survivor in the series. Formed on the crest **of the Blue Ridge Highway**, it was expected to be a major tourist stop as visitors took time to visit the **Linville Falls** waterfall. Today it is little more than a name on a crossroads, with a couple of restaurants and handful of motels; a group of interesting stone buildings and a wide scattering of 19th-century summerhouses attest its historic origins. Linville Falls is the most convenient village for both the Linville Falls waterfall and the **Linville Gorge Wilderness**, justly popular for its wild, craggy beauty.

**Little Switzerland** The western end of the abandoned crest **of the Blue Ridge Highway** continued as a toll road to nowhere as late as the mid-1920s. Passing above the cliffs of the Blue Ridge, this early automobile road gave flatlanders easy access to cool summer air and wide views. It still does; and the settlement of Little Switzerland has formed from the people attracted to this high perch. Unlike the other villages in this chapter, Little Switzerland is a linear settlement of a type familiar in the automobile era, stretched along NC 226A (as this section of the crest of the Blue Ridge Highway is now designated) mainly as a series of motels and restaurants. The town center consists of four or five interesting shops gathered around the post office.

## ✴ Wild Places

**THE GREAT FORESTS** 🐾 **Grandfather Mountain Park—The Backcountry** (ncparks.gov/Visit/parks/grmo/main.php, www.grandfather.com; e-mail: hiking@grandfather.com; 800-468-7325, 828-733-4337; 2050 Blowing Rock Hwy., P.O. Box 129, Linville, NC, 28646). Grandfather Mountain possesses over 4,000 acres of primitive backcountry centered on the 5,900-foot central ridge of Grandfather Mountain. Originally a privately owned, admission-charging environmental preserve (and the world's only private International Biosphere Reserve), this unique area is now a state park consisting of all the wild areas beyond the developed core of the Grandfather Mountain tourist attraction.

Viewed from any direction, Grandfather Mountain's most distinctive characteristic is the line of rugged cliffs and bare rock along its main crest and extending down its side ridges. Up close, these become the center of a fantasy landscape of broken rock and sheer drops, with nonstop views that change constantly. These outcrops and boulder fields nurture 16 distinct habitats, creating one of North America's most biologically diverse environments. The park shelters 42 rare and endangered species, with 11 listed as globally imperiled—including the beautiful wildflowers Heller's Blazing Star, Gray's Lily, and Pink-shelled Azalea.

The Grandfather backcountry is open to hikers and campers only. The park maintains a 12-mile system of trails, some in territory so rugged that cables and ladders have been permanently installed. The admission-supported park offers mountaintop trailheads, but hiking up from the bottom is free. The east side route, starting on the Blue Ridge Parkway, is shorter and more popular, while the west side route, starting on NC 105, is a mile longer and 400 feet taller, but leads you past the view of an old man's profile that gave Grandfather Mountain its name. If you pay the full admission, you get to start at the Mile-High Swinging Bridge and take 1,000 feet off your climb; from there, the ladder and cable ascent of the 5,960-foot peak is only a mile away and 600 feet uphill.

The backcountry is only half of this park's story. For details of the "front country"—the main attraction area—see the entry under *To See.*

**RIVERS** **Wilson Creek National Wild & Scenic River** Wilson Creek Wild and Scenic River drains the southeast slope of **Grandfather Mountain**, dropping 4,000 feet in a 23-mile run through the Pisgah National Forest to its end at the upper edge of the Piedmont. It drains a rugged and little-visited watershed, remarkable for its waterfalls, cliffs, and gorges. From the Piedmont, NC 90 winds slowly northward to the heart of this region to end at its center, in the rural community of Edgemont; its last few miles are gravel surfaced, one of three dirt surfaced roads officially classed as "primary highways" by the state of North Carolina. From it, good gravel roads and rough national forest tracks twist uphill in various directions. Blowing Rock, Linville, and Linville Falls are all possible destinations.

Wilson Creek has two halves. The upward half, from Grandfather Mountain to Edgemont, is remote and rugged, with much of the western watershed protected in the **Wilson Creek Wilderness Study Area**. The lower half, starting at the **Mortimer Recreation Area**, is a deep gorge famous for its Class II–V whitewater. Pleasantly enough, a good road (SSR 1328) runs along the bottom of the gorge, making it easy to park, sunbath on a rock, and watch the more vigorous among us kayak through the rapids.

Many of the best sightseeing opportunities are in the 21-square-mile Wilderness Study Area. Containing much of the western half of Wilson Creek's watershed, it's a tangled series of rugged ridges and V-shaped valleys. It has over 30 miles of Forest Service maintained trails (including 10 miles of the **Mountain-to-Sea Trail**), leading to six waterfalls and three clifftop views. Forest Service Road 464, a good gravel road, follows a ridgeline uphill through the center of the study area, starting at NC 90 in Edgemont and ending 11.4 miles later, where NC 181 intersects with the Blue Ridge Parkway. It's a lovely forest drive with several good views and access to a number of good trails, including **Darkside Cliffs Trail** (#272) a nearly level 1-mile round-trip to a cliff view of Grandfather Mountain and the Wilson Creek basin.

**RECREATION AREAS** **Bass Lake** This lovely little lake, in **Moses H. Cone Park**, adjacent to the village of Blowing Rock, is ringed by carriage paths that are wide, flat, and immaculately kept. Popular with joggers, it's a wonderful place to stroll and unwind for those staying in Blowing Rock. It has its own parking lot, a half-mile west of downtown Blowing Rock on US 221. There's a first-rate picnic area just across US 221 from it, run by the North Carolina Department of Motor Vehicles.

**PICNIC AREAS** **Town of Blowing Rock** The village of Blowing Rock offers two convenient and attractive picnic areas. The town park at the center of downtown is convenient for shoppers, and gives nice views of Main Street. **Broyhill Park** has large and lovely gardens as well as a challenging waterfall hike; you'll find the tables at its north end, two blocks west of downtown off US 221, on the left.

**Picnic Areas on** the **Blue Ridge Parkway** On this section, picnic areas are located at **Julian Price Park**, **Linville Falls**, and **Crabtree Falls Recreation Area**, all three of which are large and well kept.

**Mortimer Recreation Area (Wilson Creek Area)** This pretty Pisgah National Forest recreation site is on NC 90 at the rural settlement of Edgemont. It has a nice riverside picnic area, as well as tent camping. It's at the site of a large CCC camp, and marks the head of the scenic **Wilson Creek Gorge**. Two other national forest recreation sites in this remote area also offer picnicking; named Mulberry and Boone's Fork, both are off NC 90 east of Edgemont, along SSR 1368.

## ✳ To See

### *Along the Blue Ridge Parkway*

🐾 **Moses Cone Park** In the 1890s Greensboro, North Carolina, denim manufacturer Moses Cone and his wife, Bertha, started to accumulate a large estate along the crest of the Blue Ridge above the new resort village of Blowing Rock. The pair built a summer home for themselves second only to **Biltmore** in resplendence, with Grecian columns that framed a view that not even the Vanderbilts could command. The Cones converted the tired old farmlands they had purchased into wildflower meadows and laced these meadows with miles of carriage paths. Without any close heirs, they decided to will their estate to their favorite charity, a Greensboro hospital, under the condition that it remain intact, a recreation ground for the American people. In 1949 the hospital did the best thing for meeting the Cones' wishes; they donated it to the National Park Service to become part of the **Blue Ridge Parkway**—the present Moses Cone Park.

This is not a wild place. It is a cultured place, a cultivated place, a place where a man-made landscape of great beauty and richness spreads over thousands of acres. At its base, the lovely **Bass Lake** sits on the edge of Blowing Rock, ringed by carefully planned carriage paths. From it, meadowlands stretch uphill, broken and framed by forests and rhododendrons, woven by carriage paths, to reach the beautiful mansion, simple and elegant, now a **crafts center** run by the Southern Highlands Craft Guild. Crossing the parkway behind the manor, the meadows continue uphill, as the carriage path forks to two **high peak views**—a 3-mile switchback to Flat Top, and a 5-mile spiral to Rich Mountain.

The manor and its craft center get much of the visitor attention, with its shop of fine crafts from throughout the Appalachians, its summer craft demonstrations, and its wide views from a porch well outfitted with rockers. However, the **carriage paths** are the real marvel of the park. Evenly and gently sloped, they wander through the carefully planned landscape in a series of amazing turns and twists, switchbacks, loops, and spirals. They allow a modern walker to meander up the face of the Blue Ridge while hardly breaking a sweat. The paths are also open to horses, which can be hired in Blowing Rock.

**Julian Price Park** Part of the Blue Ridge Parkway, 6.5-square-mile Julian Price Park fills the gap between **Moses Cone Park** and **Grandfather Mountain Park**. It does this in the most literal sense, filling in the mountainous spaces between these two better-known areas; and it does it in a more figurative sense as well, being less civilized than Cone Park, yet not so wild as the wind-swept cliffs of Grandfather Mountain. It is more of a typical Blue Ridge landscape, with fields left from grazing and woods left from logging, crossed by trails that are rough and rolling. The middle of the park is taken up by a rolling plateau, surrounded by slightly taller peaks, containing a pleasant **lake**, a large picnic area framed by split-rail fences, and a campground. The parkway runs close by the edge of the lake and over its stone dam—a popular and scenic stop. From the picnic area, a path runs 2.5 miles (round-trip) along Boones Fork to a pretty 25-foot **waterfall**, from there connecting to a number of rougher backcountry trails.

♿ **Linn Cove Viaduct** One of the most remarkable and important bridges of its era, the Linn Cove Viaduct came about from an environmental dispute between the National Park Service and a local man. Oddly enough (by today's expectations) it was the National Park Service that was trying to destroy the environment in the late 1960s, as it tried to replace its 1930s-era right-of-way (never used) with a much higher route, slashing across the virgin preserve of **Grandfather Mountain** in giant cuts and fills. The local man—Hugh Morton, owner of Grandfather Mountain Park at the time—was determined to protect his century-old wilderness preserve. Although the Park Service believed it had the right to simply condemn Morton's land, they quickly found out that this power did not extend to relocating the right-of-way they had previously seized; yet they refused to budge from their concept of a high mountain slash. Finally the governor of North Carolina forced a compromise, a middle route that would fly over environmentally sensitive areas in great, curving bridges. The longest of these bridges is the Linn Cove Viaduct.

In order to protect sensitive cliff and heath environments, the viaduct's engineers had to invent an entirely new technology. They set their new bridge on towering pillars, installed without a construction road, each one disturbing only a tiny 50-foot circle of land. Every roadway section was precast in concrete and lifted into position; when one section was attached to a pillar the work crews would move onto it to hoist the next section into position, cantilevering out from the pillars. Each roadway section curves slightly to conform to the environmental needs of the land below. The resulting bridge is very beautiful, a soft line winding gently against the wild mountain. This has since become a common technology, found in such structures as Seven Mile Bridge at Key West, Florida. This is where, and why, it was invented.

As you approach from Blowing Rock you will see the viaduct as you get beyond the Rough Ridge Overlook (MP 303); then, a mile later, you'll be on it with no opportunity to stop and admire it. To get a good look, stop at the **Yonalossee Overlook** (MP 303.5), where a roadside path leads to its beginning, and the view you see in postcards. Once you've crossed it, you will reach the Linn Cove Viaduct Visitors Center on the left on the opposite side, with an information desk and exhibits. A disabled accessible trail leads a short distance to an overlook.

♿ **Grandfather Mountain** (www.grandfather.com; e-mail: nature@grandfather.com; 800-468-7325, 828-733-4337; 2050 Blowing Rock Hwy., P.O. Box 129, Linville, NC, 28646). Open daily. Summer: 8 AM–7 PM; winter: 8 AM–5 PM. $15 per adult; $7 per child 4–12. Grandfather Mountain Park describes itself as "a scenic travel attraction"—a theme park where the theme is nature, the environment, and incredible natural beauty. There's a spectacular drive up, a nature center, a first-rate habitat zoo, and a mile-high suspension bridge.The attraction area starts at the park entrance on US 221 (1 mile west of the Blue Ridge Parkway and 2 miles east of Linville), and centers on a 2.2-mile road that climbs 1,000 feet up the mountain in eight tight switchbacks. This section of the Blue Ridge Crest has **spectacular, sheer cliffs** facing west, getting larger as the mountain gets higher. The road gains views of these cliffs on its westward curves (including a clifftop picnic area), while eastward curves wander through lovely forests broken by large rock formations. The road's last half-mile swags steeply up the mountain with wide views over high meadows.

Halfway up is the outstanding **habitat zoo**, open to visitors at no extra charge. Grandfather's large animal enclosures feature native mountain animals in their actual habitats, with the human visitors separated by moats or elevated walks. Animals include black bears, bear cubs, deer, panther, and river otter (with an underwater viewing area), as well as golden eagles and bald eagles. The adjacent nature center presents the history of Grandfather Mountain (both natural and human) in a museum designed by the Smithsonian's former chief of natural history exhibits. It includes a section on Daniel Boone, a display of North Carolina minerals and gems, and an operating real-time weather station. Works of art, rather than dead things, illustrate the flora and fauna of Grandfather: Paul Marchand's artificial wildflowers, songbird woodcarvings by Bill Chrisman, Hugh Morton's photographs of endangered species. There's also a restaurant.

The road ends at almost exactly 1 mile in elevation, in an area of great open views, meadows, spruce-fir forests, cliffs, and strange rock formations. In the middle of it all is the **Mile High Swinging Bridge**, almost 100 yards long, crossing a rocky chasm 80 feet deep. An easy 2.5-mile walk goes through the chasm under the bridge, then through boreal forests and across rocky outcrops to a viewpoint overlooking the Blue Ridge Parkway. A second, more challenging walk leads uphill, using cables and ladders to climb exposed rocks and skirt hoodoos, to the high point of 5,900 feet.

**Flat Rock Overlook** Unlike most of the parkway overlooks, Flat Rock makes you work for your view, with a half-mile circular walk. It's worth it. Flat Rock is a large rocky bald with the beauty of a Japanese garden, its dwarfed pines and azaleas (blooming in May–June) framing 270-degree panoramic views that include Grandfather Mountain.

VIEW FROM FLAT ROCK OVERLOOK

**Linville Falls Recreation Area** The Blue Ridge Parkway has a large recreation area along the Linville River, centering on the tall plunge of **Linville Falls**. As the parkway approaches the river, it enters lovely meadows with split-rail fences. A spur road to the left leads 1.5 miles to the waterfall; just beyond, a side road leads right to the riverside picnic area, where you can get a good view of the parkway crossing the Linville River on a stone-clad arched bridge. The picnic area is nice, and the Linville River Bridge is impressive, but the waterfall is the real attraction.

The falls occur as the Linville River reaches the upper edge of Linville Gorge (see "Beneath the Blue Ridge: The Catawba River Valley," *Wild Places*) and plunges straight down into it. Trails to it spread out in fingers from a visitors center at the end of the spur road to various viewpoints. A path along the Linville River's right bank leads first to a ledge and pool at the top of the waterfall, with a view out over the gorge and a lovely little cascade upstream. Then the path continues to a view toward the falls from the gorge rim and two views over the gorge. A left bank path leads to a rim-top view toward the waterfall, then a drop to the bottom of the gorge for a view from beneath. The shortest walk is a level 1-mile round-trip, while visiting all six overlooks will require about 5 miles of strenuous climbing.

✐ **The Orchard at Altapass** (www.altapassorchard.com; e-mail: billcarson@altapassorchard.com; 888-765-9531, 828-765-9531; P.O. Box 245, Little Switzerland, NC 28749). Open daily, April–November. Admission is free. Weekend music is free. At the turn of the century, the Clinchfield Railroad built an amazing grade up the face of the Blue Ridge, with 17 tunnels in 23 miles of hairpin loops (see below). Above the last loop, the railroad planted an apple orchard that followed the crest of the Blue Ridge for 2 miles. Then, in the 1930s, the Blue Ridge Parkway passed through the middle of the orchard—2 miles of sweeping

ALTAPASS ORCHARDS

views over large apple trees heavy with fruit, one of the great sights of the parkway.

Sixty years later the orchard had suffered from years of neglect, the trees ignored and allowed to grow wild. In 1994 Kit Trubey bought the orchard to restore and preserve it, under the management of her brother and sister-in-law, Bill and Judy Carson. Their plan: restore the orchard, and welcome in the public.

Today it's a wonderful place. The heritage apple trees, nearly a century old, are again healthy and beautiful, framing unimaginable views with bright, red fruit in huge clusters. Hay ride tours wind through the orchard, with orchard storytellers telling the lively history of this important pass. In season, warm weekend afternoons ring with the sounds of local country musicians in free concerts by the apple-packing house. Behind the packing house is a monarch butterfly garden (the staff hand-raises monarchs in a special area of the packing house), an herb garden, and a spring wetland. The packing house holds a remarkable gift shop, with apple products made in the orchard, local honeys and preserves, craft art from local crafters (four of whom have been declared North Carolina Living Treasures), and neat stuff from all over. It also has a small café if you are feeling peckish.

**Museum of North Carolina Minerals** (www.mitchell-county.com/festival/museum.html; 828-765-2761; 79 Parkway Rd. [Blue Ridge Parkway milepost 331], Spruce Pine, NC 28777). Open daily all year, 9 AM–5 PM. This small museum, built of local stone in the shape of a cottage, marks the center of North Carolina's mountain mining industry. Erected in 1953 as a joint project between the parkway and the state of North Carolina, it retained its original exhibits for half a century, becoming more of a fascinating glimpse into the past than an accurate picture of the modern mining industry. It's been recently renovated, however, with interactive displays. You will find the museum by the parkway's exit onto NC 226 at Little Switzerland, at milepost 331.

**Crabtree Falls Recreation Area** This recreation area contains a picnic area, a snack bar and store, and a campground. Its main feature, however, is a 2.5-mile loop trail to **Upper Crabtree Falls**, a very beautiful cascade popular with photographers and valued by waterfall afficionados. It's an easy walk down, but the return walk climbs 500 feet in elevation.

**HISTORIC PLACES** **The Crest of the Blue Ridge Highway** In 1910, North Carolina State Geologist Dr. Joseph Hyde Pratt came up with a wonderful idea—a scenic road following the crest of the Blue Ridge, specifically designed to attract wealthy adventurers driving their newfangled automobiles. This was at a time when farmers struggled down muddy ruts to get their crops to railheads, and through-highways were a starry-eyed dream. Spend state money on a tourist road? However, the toll road would pay for itself, and would bring in out-of-state money to some of the state's poorest areas. The state approved Pratt's plan, dubbed it the "Crest of the Blue Ridge Highway," and built a chunk of it before World War I ended construction.

In a very real sense, the modern Blue Ridge Parkway is the realization of Dr. Pratt's vision. A section of the original "Crest of the Blue Ridge Highway" still survives, closely paralleling the Blue Ridge Parkway from Altapass to Little Switzerland. To follow it, exit the parkway at McKinney Gap (MP 327.7), go under the parkway, and turn right onto SR 1567 to **Altapass Orchards**. This gravel section must look very much like it did in 1913, passing through the heart of the orchards, then continuing (across the parkway) through farmlands. At its end, turn left on NC 226 to return to the parkway; or continue under the parkway and take a right on NC 226A through Little Switzerland, another section of the "Crest" highway.

**Whippoorwill Academy & Village (Tom Dooley Museum)** (www.explorewilkes.com/new/whippoorwill.php; e-mail: whippoorwillvillage@hotmail.com; 336-973-3237; 11929 Hwy. 268 West, P.O. Box 458, Ferguson, NC 28624). Open Sat.–Sun., 3 PM–5 PM; closed January–March. Free (donations appreciated). This open-air museum sits at the base of the Blue Ridge, 20 miles south of the Blue Ridge Parkway via US 421 to Wilkesboro, then west 12 miles on NC 281. It's a collection of late-19th-century buildings that commemorates two famous local boys—Daniel Boone (who lived 2 miles from here), and Tom Dula, better known as "Tom Dooley," the subject of the mountain folk song made popular by the Kingston Trio. Boone lived here as a poor dirt farmer for 20 years before the American Revolution, where he developed the skills as a pathfinder that would make him a leading figure in opening up the American West. (For a detailed account of his early road-building, see *Exploring by Auto.*) Dula's history is less distinguished. A Civil War veteran and a ladies man, Dula was unfortunate enough to have planned to elope with Laura Foster the night she was stabbed through the heart. Even a vigorous defense by North Carolina's popular Civil War governor **Zeb Vance** (see "The Blue Ridge Parkway Circles Asheville," *To See*) didn't save the poor boy from the hangman's noose. The old one-room schoolhouse of unpainted clapboard (called the "Whippoorwill Academy" for its remoteness), authentically furnished downstairs, has a museum to local-boy-made-bad Dula in its loft. Also on site is a general store with period products and locally canned goods, a replica of an 18th-century smokehouse with local art exhibits, a forge and weaving shed, a chapel, and an authentic reconstruction of Boone's cabin, including stones from the chimney.

**Fort Defiance** (fortdefiancenc.org; e-mail: contact@fortdefiancenc.org; 828-758-1671; 1792 Ft. Defiance Dr. on Hwy. 268, Lenoir, NC, 28645). Open April–October, Thurs.–Sat., 10 AM–5 PM; Sun., 1 PM–5 PM. November—March, weekends only or by appointment. Hours subject to change. Not a fort at all, but the 18th-century home of Revolutionary war hero Gen. William Lenoir, this simple, handsome colonial homestead is located on NC 268, the scenic state

FORT DEFIANCE HISTORIC SITE

highway that runs along the foot of the Blue Ridge between US 321 and US 421. Twice a month costumed docents give tours of this authentically furnished house, including 250 items of General Lenoir's. The site is beautiful and the drive well worthwhile for scenic interest; time it right and you can combine it with a visit to the Whippoorwill Academy, just 9 miles east on NC 268.

**GARDENS AND PARKS** **Broyhill Park and Annie Cannon Gardens** This large and attractive town park in central Blowing Rock has informal gardens and a gazebo around a lovely lake. Below the dam lies Annie Cannon Gardens, a native flower garden. Downstream from Cannon Gardens, a hiking path leads steeply downhill to two large and beautiful waterfalls, a worthwhile if strenuous hike (3 miles round-trip, 800-foot climb). A park that any town would be proud of, it's located one block west of downtown.

**The Blowing Rock** (theblowingrock.com; 828-295-7111; Hwy. 321 South/P.O. Box 145, Blowing Rock, NC 28605). Daily, March–December; weekends, January–February. This privately owned attraction features a 1-acre garden and short trails around the rock formation that gave the village of Blowing Rock its name. The views are excellent. A large gift shop is on the premises.

**RAILROADS** **The Clinchfield Railroad Loops** (www.carolina-clinchfield.org; e-mail: arpoteat@blueridge.net; 828-245-3921; P.O. Box 412, Bostic, NC 28018). The Clinchfield Railroad, built in the first decade of the 20th century, climbs the Blue Ridge in an amazing series of loops and tunnels just beneath the **Orchards at Altapass**. The Clinchfield's plan was to link the Atlantic South with the Midwest by attacking the Appalachian barrier head on, using all the techniques of modern engineering. Building north from Marion, the Clinchfield's engineers pushed their road straight up the sheer face of the Blue Ridge; in the 6 linear miles between the bottom and the crest, they built 23 miles of road with 5 hairpin curves and 17 tunnels. Although enormously expensive to build, this superbly engineered road gave the Clinchfield a short, direct route linking Appalachian coal fields directly to markets in the Midwest and ports in the South. The road, now part of the CSX System, remains a heavily used freight line, with 24 trains per day passing along it. The Blue Ridge Parkway parallels it closely for 4 miles, from milepost 327 to milepost 331; look for it from the North Cove Valley Overlook (MP 327.4), Altapass Orchards Overlook (MP 328.4), and Table Rock Overlook (MP 329.8).

For an up-close look, exit the parkway at McKinney Gap (Altapass), then go right on the gravel road to a sharp left and steeply downhill on gravel Pepper Creek Road (SSR 1566). At 0.5 mile from the parkway, the railroad will be 100 feet uphill on your right, just as it approaches its final tunnel. Unfortunately, it's not visible from the road, and the track that reaches it is marked "No Trespassing" with a welded steel sign that could only come from a railroad. In another 0.6 mile, the lane crosses the railroad at the uphill end of its fourth hairpin curve. These views are surprisingly unspectacular; this railroad is so gently graded and curved that any given segment just looks like an ordinary flatland railroad, despite the vertical slopes around it. Remember: this is a heavily used freight line. *Walking on the tracks is **illegal** and **dangerous**.*

**SPECIAL PLACES** ✐ **Linville Caverns** (linvillecaverns.com; e-mail: info@linvillecaverns.com; 800-419-0540; 19929 US 221 North, Marion, NC, 28752). Open daily,

March–November, 9 AM–6 PM; weekends, December–February. Located south of Linville Falls on US 221, this show cave features elaborate dripstone formations along nearly level paths. It's lighted in the most natural way possible, to better show off the subtle colors and shapes of the strange rock formations. The endangered eastern pipistrelle bats, harmless and tiny, are found in this cave. The attractive park-style reception building, made of stone and gray wood, has a nice gift shop.

## ✷ To Do

**WHITEWATER ADVENTURES** **High Mountain Expeditions** (highmountain expeditions.com; e-mail: info@highmountainexpeditions.com; 800-262-9036, 828-898-9786; 1380 Highway 105 South, Boone, NC 28607). Hours vary. Check website or call. Located in downtown Blowing Rock, High Mountain Expeditions furnishes rafting trip—calm, family-oriented floats on the Watauga River, or wild, whitewater trips on the Nolichucky River. They also offer a whole lot of other stuff: caving tours, hiking tours, mountain bike tours, mountain bike rentals, still-water (mountain lake) kayaking tours, and—note this, hikers—shuttle services.

**GOLF** Golfers may think it odd that no courses are listed for the Blowing Rock or Grandfather Mountain area—considering that several are clearly visible from the main road. In fact, there are six golf courses, all of them either largely or completely closed to casual visitors. The single-listed course is some distance south of the ritzily exclusive Blowing Rock area, and there are many more just a short distance north, in the Boone and Banner Elk areas frequented by the hoi polloi.

**Mount Mitchell Golf Club** (mountmitchellgolf.com; e-mail: info@mount mitchellgolfresort.com; 828-675-5454; 11484 Hwy. 80 South, Burnsville, NC 28714). Open April–November. This 18-hole golf course sits at the foot of Mount Mitchell with wide views toward the East's highest peak. It's located just off the NC 80 exit from the Blue Ridge Parkway.

**HORSEBACK RIDING** **Blowing Rock Stables** (828-295-7847) Located on the western edge of the village of Blowing Rock off US 221, this stable offers trail rides through the stunning Moses Cone Park section of the Blue Ridge Parkway.

## ✷ Lodging

**RESORTS** **Westglow Spa** (www.westglow.com; e-mail: info@westglow.com; 800-562-0807, 828-295-4463; 224 Westglow Circle, Blowing Rock, NC 28605). Prices include three meals and all fully staffed spa facilities. Call or visit website for current rates. Located 3 miles west of Blowing Rock on US 221, Westglow is a European-style spa in a beautifully restored 1916 mansion surrounded by 20 landscaped acres. The National Register Classical-style house, with Greek columns framing the front porch, served as the summer home of American impressionist artist Elliott Daingerfield, who named it Westglow. Seven "bedroom suites" are furnished almost entirely in antiques; more modest cottages near the mansion have lower prices. The three meals a day (included in the price) are healthy, balanced, and gourmet, enough so that the restaurant, Elliot's Place, is open to the public for dinner as a fine-dining experience. Spa services, included in the tariff, are both wide ranging and less structured than many American-style spas; a new Life Enhancement Center contains an indoor pool, a wide range of weight and exercise equipment, whirlpools, saunas, hair and nail salon, aerobics studio, and poolside café, with a tennis court nearby.

✐ **Clear Creek Guest Ranch** (www.clearcreekranch.com; e-mail: ccrdude@prodigy.net; 828-675-4510; 100 Clear Creek Rd., Hwy. 80 South, Burnsville, NC 28714). This stunningly beautiful classic dude ranch sits in the shadows of Mount Mitchell, the tallest peak in the east, on a back road at the far southern end of this section of the parkway. The large property has meadows, streams, mountains, and wide, wide views. It also has horses. The tariff includes a full slate of trail rides and ranch activities, both on the ranch and in the adjacent Pisgah National Forest. Accommodations are in log-sided cabins with full front porches, new and immaculately kept, with one to three bedrooms. Hearty ranch meals are served three times a day, family style in the central lodge, or on the trail, or at an outdoors barbeque (including a weekly steak barbeque). The ranch has wide decks spreading downhill from the lodge to surround a pool, as well as a stocked pond. This family-friendly resort offers a full program from children age five and up.

**Eseeola Lodge** (www.eseeola.com; 800-742-6717, 828-733-4311; 175 Linville Ave., P.O. Box 99, Linville, NC 28646). Open May–October. In existence since 1892, the Eseeola remains a summer playground for the wealthy in the village of Linville. It's surrounded by historic homes, the summer homes of its early-20th-century patrons, whose heirs still own the Eseeola. The present lodge, dating from 1926 and on the National Register, has 24 elegant rooms with all amenities. All rooms have private porches, and many have separate living rooms. The rates include breakfast and dinner (coat and tie required) at the lodge's gourmet restaurant; menus change daily, and always include a choice from seven entrées. Guests have access to tennis courts, exercise rooms, and a fishing lake (all at a separate charge), and there's a day camp for the children. Guests also have access to the 18-hole private golf course, little changed since Donald Ross designed it in 1924.

## BED & BREAKFAST INNS

**Crippen's Country Inn** (www.crippens.com; e-mail: sharonwalker@crippens.com; 877-295-3487, 828-295-3487; 239 Sunset Dr., Blowing Rock, NC 28605). Located in a restored turn-of-the-century home, Crippen's offers a European-style experience in the center of Blowing Rock. Located between downtown and US 321 on quiet Sunset Drive, it's a large bungalow-style structure with a full front porch, green clapboarding and shingle gables, and a lovely little garden in the postage-stamp area between the porch and the stone wall bordering the sidewalk. Inside, two front parlors are comfortably furnished with sofas, fireplaces, art on the wall, and coffee table books. The right-hand parlor opens up into a comfortable and intimate bar with a good selection of cognacs and single malts, part of the superb **restaurant** that comes alive in the evening. Upstairs are the rooms, each carefully and comfortably furnished, with modern and antique furniture and quilts on the beds; regular rooms are normal sized, while deluxe rooms are large enough to have roomy sitting areas with sofas. A full breakfast and afternoon wine and cheese are included.

**Gideon Ridge Inn** (gideonridge.com; e-mail: innkeeper@gideonridge.com; 828-295-3644; 202 Gideon Ridge Rd., Blowing Rock, NC 28605). Located just south of Blowing Rock off US 321, Gideon Ridge Inn straddles the Blue Ridge with sweeping views off the edge of the world. This low stone building sits among 5 acres of native gardens, accessible from wide stone terraces. While the terraces, with their wide views framed by gardens, serve as the focal point for the common areas, there is also a large library with a stone fireplace and a breakfast room with original art. Rooms are comfortably furnished with country-style antiques and reproductions; the least expensive rooms are modest upstairs rooms with wide views from dormer windows, but most rooms are larger, with a choice of amenities such as terrace doors, whirpool baths, and fireplaces. Rates include a full breakfast and afternoon tea.

**The Inn at Ragged Gardens** (ragged-gardens.com; e-mail: info@ragged-gardens.com; 828-295-9703; 203 Sunset Dr., Blowing Rock, NC 28605). This elegant bed & breakfast sits on Sunset Drive, a short stroll from downtown Blowing Rock, surrounded by gardens and walled off from the world. It's a large, square manor, clad in shingles, with an oversized porte-cochère topped by a balcony/deck. The large common rooms are elegantly furnished with Edwardian antiques—a spirit carried into the 12 individually decorated rooms, each with a turn-of-the-century theme. Rooms range in size from normal to large; each has a fireplace, goose-down comforter, bathrobes, and seasonal fresh flowers, and the majority have private balconies, whirlpool baths, and sitting areas. Breakfast includes homemade granola and bread, plus a choice of two hot entrées. There's also an evening wine serving with hors d'oeuvres, and two stocked butler's pantries for guests who need munchies.

**Springhaven Inn** (springhaveninn.com; 828-295-6967; e-mail: highl@ecu.edu; Main Street, Blowing Rock, NC 28605). Located at the south edge of downtown Blowing Rock on Main Street, this little bed & breakfast occupies a stagecoach inn built in the earliest days of the village; *Gone with the Wind* author Margaret Mitchell spent summers there in the 1930s. It's a handsome shingle-sided two-story structure with wide porches overlooking Main Street, on a lot surrounded by giant pines. Decorated throughout with antiques, the five rooms all have private baths. Breakfast, typically fruit, muffins or breads, and a breakfast casserole, is included.

**The Alpine Inn** (e-mail: info@alpineinnnc.com; 828-765-5380; P.O. Box 477, Hwy. 226A, Little Switzerland, NC 28749). Located in Little Switzerland on NC 266A just off the Blue Ridge Parkway, the modest Alpine Inn was built in 1929 and once furnished lodgings to the Blue Ridge Parkway workers. Today it is a homey and well-kept low-cost bed & breakfast with 14 rooms, nearly all with breathtaking panoramic views from their balconies.

**CABIN RENTALS** ✐ **Bear Den Creekside Cabins** (bear-den.com; e-mail: info@bear-den.com; 828-765-2888; 600 Bear Den Mountain Rd., Spruce Pine, NC 28777). Open March 1–November 30, with year-round cabin rentals available. Located on a remote stretch of the Blue Ridge Parkway between Linville Falls and Little Switzerland, this set of modern pine log cabins with oak floors is part of a 400-acre camping resort with a lake, a sand beach, canoes, and lots on on-site walking paths. The comfortable and fully furnished cabins—each with full kitchen, fireplace, whirlpool bath, and front porch—are isolated from the camping area, along a creek. There are also some "campin' cabins," described by the owners as "tents with a tin roof."

## ✱ Where to Eat

**EATING OUT** **Storie Street Grille** (www.storiestreetgrille.com; e-mail: dine@storiestreetgrille.com; 828-295-7075; 1167 Main St., Blowing Rock, NC 28605). This downtown Blowing Rock storefront restaurant prides itself on its fresh food prepared from scratch. Soups, sandwiches, and special entrées are prepared to order with imagination and flair—definitely a good Main Street choice.

**Canyons Restaurant** (canyonsbr.com; 828-295-7661; 8960 Valley Blvd. (Hwy. 321), Blowing Rock, NC 28605). Open daily, 11 AM–closing. The cuisine is eclectic, but all dishes are freshly prepared on the premises with the finest ingredients. Seasonally fresh items are offered, so be sure to ask your server what's in. Their Mexican and Southwest dishes will be prepared with your preference of "heat." Good selection of domestic and imported wines and beers.

**The Gamekeepers Restaurant** (www.gamekeeper-nc.com; 828-963-7400; 3005 Shull's Mill Rd., Boone, NC 28607). Located in a remote mountainous area north of Blowing Rock, across from the Yonahlossee Resort, the Gamekeeper occupies a large wooded site, well up from its country road. Its menu puts a modern twist on mountain favorites, featuring game, fish, vegetarian entrées, and fresh seasonal vegetables cooked on a wood-fired grill. The winding drive out is very beautiful, passing through and then along the boundaries of Moses Cone Park; from Blowing Rock, just follow the signs to the Yonalossee Resort.

**Spear's BBQ and Grill** (linvillefalls lodge.com/DINING; e-mail: visit@ linvillefallslodge.com; 800-634-4421, 828-765-2658; 8730 NC Hwy. 183, Linville Falls, NC 28647). Open daily, June–October, noon—9 PM; November–May, Fri.–Sun. only. Located on the grounds of the Linville Falls Lodge, this restaurant was established in 1978 as a small sandwich shop with a walk-up window. Ensuring years saw the addition of an outside covered deck, a new dining room, and conversion to a full-service restaurant and bar. They specialize in barbeque, but are also known for delicious seafood, vegetarian dishes, and fresh baked breads. They boast that they use the best ingredients, buy local as much as possible, and their handmade hushpuppies are a patron favorite. Note that Newland is the nearest town to Linville Falls recognized by GPS.

**Chalet Restaurant at Switzerland Inn** (www.switzerlandinn.com; 800-654-4026, 828-765-2153; e-mail: info @switzerlandinn.com; 86 High Ridge Rd., P.O. Box 399, Little Switzerland, NC 28749). Open daily, 7:30 AM–2:00 PM for breakfast and lunch; 5:30 PM–9:00 PM for dinner. Just off the Blue Ridge Parkway at milepost 334 in Little Switzerland, this restaurant is part of the Switzerland Inn. Nicely decorated, it's mainly noted for its wide panoramic views off the Blue Ridge, which at this point is directly underfoot. A pub/bar is connected to the back. The straightforward menu has a lot of old favorites and some pleasant surprises as well, including local trout smoked on the premises. They have a Friday prime rib and seafood buffet for the all-you-can-eat crowd, and a Saturday outdoor barbeque during the summer (weather permitting).

**DINING OUT Crippen's Country Inn and Restaurant** (www.crippens.com; e-mail: jimmycrippen@crippens.com; 877-295-3487, 828-295-3487; 239 Sunset Dr., P.O. Box 528, Blowing Rock, NC 28605). Dinner only. Open July–October, every day; June, Tues.–Sun.; November–May, Thurs.–Sun. Owner Jimmy Crippen has created one of the finest and most exciting restaurants in the mountains, in this beautifully restored boardinghouse off downtown Blowing Rock. Occupying much of the first floor of this European-style inn, the restaurant features an elegant, yet casual atmosphere perfect for Blowing Rock. A wide front porch welcomes diners, as does a comfortable small bar facing a comfortable parlor sitting area. Past the bar, the roomy dining area has old-fashioned full-length windows and wood floors, simple wood furniture, and fine art on the walls. Each evening's menu is unique, selected from a large repertoire of adventurous, boldly flavored creations. Desserts are decadent, rich combinations of caramel and chocolate and cream and pecans—only part of a dessert menu that also lists ice creams and sorbets made on the premises, fine brandies, single-malt scotches, ports and dessert wines, and fine cigars (smoking on the porch only). Crippen's is located on Sunset Drive, a side street running between downtown Blowing Rock and US 321.

## ✷ Entertainment

### *Blowing Rock*

**Hayes Performing Art Center** (blowingrockstage.com; 828-295-9627; 152 Jamie Fort Rd./P.O. Box 2170, Blowing Rock, NC 28605). This non-profit professional theater company performs four plays (two of them musicals) each summer season.

### *Little Switzerland*

**Geneva Hall** (828-668-7223). The Little Switzerland Town Hall hosts weekly clogging all summer long, just across from the Switzerland Inn.

## ✷ Selective Shopping

### *Blowing Rock*

Blowing Rock's elegant little downtown stretches along four blocks of Bus. US 321, opposite the town park. It's built up from numerous small buildings—old brick fronts, houses, renovated gas stations, even a vacant lot or two—now given over to catering to the needs of the village's well-heeled visitors. Galleries, gift shops, antique shops, and restaurants dominate the street.

**Main Street Gallery/Expressions Craft Guild** (828-295-7839; 960 Main St., Blowing Rock, NC 28605). Located in downtown Blowing Rock in an old stone building across from the post office, this fine craft cooperative features a wide selection of local artists' pottery, jewelry, glass, wood, fiber, and photography. It's owned and managed by its members, and a member should be on the floor willing to talk with you when you drop in.

**Sunset Tees & Hattery** (828-295-9326; 1117 Main St., Blowing Rock, NC 28705). A masculine favorite in downtown Blowing Rock, Sunset Tees features a huge selection of first-rate men's hats in a large room in the back. There's plenty of cowboy hats and baseball caps—but also derbys, bowlers, top hats, berets, jazzy hats, sunday-go-to-meeting hats, leather hats, cloth hats, straw hats, and lots of felt hats. A fun shop.

**Bolick Pottery/Traditions Pottery** (e-mail: sales@traditionspottery.com; 828-295-5099; fax: 828-295-5091; 4443 Bolick Rd., Lenoir, NC 28645). Open Mon.–Sat., 8 AM–5 PM; Sun., 1 PM–5 PM.

Fifth-generation potter Lula Owens Bolick and her husband Glenn moved from Seagrove, North Carolina, to this spot down a back road near Blowing Rock in 1973. They specialize in traditional shapes—mugs, bowls, pitchers, candle holders, tea sets—in colors of gray, oatmeal, and cobalt blue. You'll find their studio 3 miles south of Blowing Rock on US 321, then left on Blackberry Road (SSR 1500) for a half-mile.

### *Little Switzerland*

**Trillium Gallery** (e-mail: latisha@trilliumgalleryonline.com; 828-765-0024; Blue Ridge Parkway milepost 334, Little Switzerland, NC 28749). Seasonal, mid-April through mid-November, Sun.–Thurs. 9–5.; Fri–Sat. 9–6. Located across from the Switzerland Inn, the Trillium Gallery represents a dozen or more local fine crafters, including some associated with the Penland School. You'll find original works of art in pottery, basketry, glass, and jewelry.

**The Barking Rock** (thebarkingrock.com; e-mail: info@thebarkingrock.com; 828-295-8883; 1179 Main St., Blowing Rock, NC 28605). Open Mon.–Sat., 10 AM–6 PM; Sun., 1 PM–5 PM. A pet boutique for your cat and dog travel companions. Treat your pet with gourmet baked goods, unusual dog and cat foods, beds, tableware, toys, clothing, leashes, and collars. They carry apparel, home decor, and gifts for pet owners, too.

## ✷ Special Events

**SPRING Blowing Rock Art in the Park** (www.blowingrock.com/artinthepark; 800-295-7851, 828-295-7851). Open May–October, 10 AM–5 PM, one Saturday a month. This juried art show features a hundred contributors over its six-month run in downtown Blowing Rock's beautiful park.

**SUMMER Grandfather Mountain Highland Games and Gathering of the Clans** (www.gmhg.org; 828-733-1333; fax: 828-733-0092; P.O. Box 1095, Linville, NC 28646). Second weekend in July. For over half a century, the Grandfather Mountain Highland Games have been held on MacRae Meadows at Grandfather Mountain Park. A highly popular five-day event with attendance in the tens of thousands, events include classic Scottish athletics, bagpipe demonstrations and competitions, Highland dancing, a 5-mile footrace and a marathon up Grandfather Mountain, ceilidhs (Celtic jam sessions), Scottish harp, Scottish fiddling, Gaelic song, and sheepherding demonstrations. There are a large number of vendors and clan tents. The games are sponsored by the nonprofit Grandfather Mountain Highland Games, Inc., who uses proceeds to run the games and a scholarship fund.

**Blowing Rock Charity Horse Show** (www.blowingrockequestrian.com; e-mail: info@blowingrockequestrian.com; 828-295-4700; P.O. Box 650, Blowing Rock, NC 28705). Late July to mid-August. Held during the months of June–August, and an annual event since 1923, this horse show consists of two AA-rated Hunter/Jumper shows (at five days each) and one A-rated four-day Saddlebred Show. Although the emphasis is on fun, the first Hunter/Jumper show is a World Champion Hunter Rider event, and the Saddlebred show is part of the American Saddlebred Grand National Series.

**Singing on the Mountain** (800-468-7325, 828-733-4337; 2050 Blowing Rock Hwy., Linville, NC 28646). Open fourth Sunday in June, 8:30 AM–3:00 PM. Free. Held annually since 1924, this all-day gospel sing and church bazaar at the foot of Grandfather Mountain features a dozen gospel groups.

**Grandfather Mountain Amateur & Professional Camera Clinic** (grandfather.com/planning_your_visit/events/clinic1; 800-468-7325, 828-733-2013). Third weekend in August. Free. (Participants must register for free admission to park.) For over half a century, Grandfather Mountain Park has hosted this annual photojournalism convention, open to all serious photographers.

**WINTER** **Blowing Rock Winterfest** (www.blowingrockwinterfest.com; e-mail: info@visitblowingrock.com; 877-295-7851, 828-295-9168). Open mid-January. For a three-day weekend during the coldest part of the year, the village of Blowing Rock celebrates the fun part of winter, with hayrides and hot chocolate, bonfires, a parade, dog sledding, ice sculpting, street musicians, dances, live jazz, live theater, a chili cookoff—and (hopefully) lots of snow.

# BEHIND THE BLUE RIDGE: BOONE & BANNER ELK

On the back of the Blue Ridge, westward from Blowing Rock, the Watauga and New Rivers drain a wide, perched bowl of a valley. Each river runs in a separate direction—the New River northward toward the Ohio River, the Watauga River westward toward the Tennessee River. Nevertheless, their headwaters come within a few hundred yards of each other in a wide, level gap at the center of this region. This location, long a wilderness crossroads, now holds the college town of Boone.

North Carolinian Daniel Boone explored this high, mountainous bowl in the years before the Revolution. He wasn't the first European to do so; he was just the most important. His pa, Squire Boone, had created a prosperous farmstead at the foot of the Blue Ridge, and young Daniel spent his youth poking up every little game trail he could find within a two-week walking distance. Daniel established reasonably good trails up the Blue Ridge into the Watauga lands, and helped European settlers find their way into these Cherokee hunting grounds. The settlers negotiated a private peace with the Cherokee chiefs and settled down the Watauga into Tennessee. Boone went on to blaze more trails, moving on into western Virginia and the empty Kentucky hunting lands.

Today, the town of Boone sits at the center of this rugged valley, a small town with a busy brick-front downtown and a large state university, Appalachian State. Nearby, the settlement of Valle Crucis (Valley Crew-sis) preserves a lively and beautiful historic landscape that mixes farmhouses from Boone's era with general stores from the 1930s. Still farther back, a couple of those 5,000-foot peaks harbor ski slopes—about as snowy and nicely kept as any south of West Virginia.

What you won't find in this chapter is a lot of wilderness and outdoor activity (besides skiing). Fear not. There is a wide variety of nature sightseeing, hiking, fishing, and kayaking nearby, at Blowing Rock and along the Blue Ridge Parkway, only a half-dozen miles from Boone.

**GUIDANCE** The chambers of commerce listed here all have good web sites and helpful visitors centers. Although their information services overlap a great deal, Boone covers the main area, while Banner Elk and Beech Mountain cover the ski slopes. And don't forget to check Blowing Rock; this shopping mecca is only six miles from Boone.

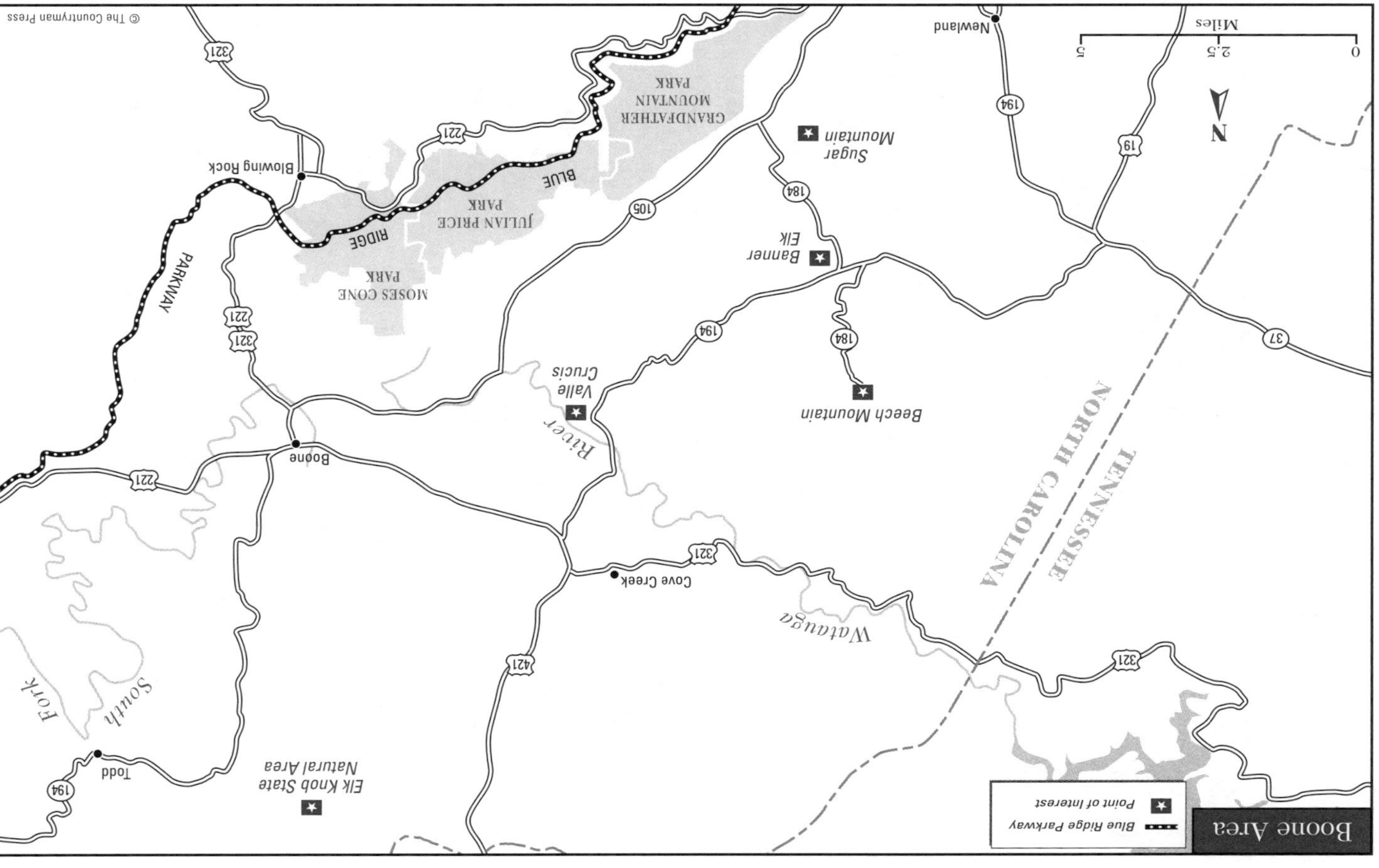

Boone Area
Blue Ridge Parkway
Point of Interest
© The Countryman Press
Todd
South Fork
Elk Knob State Natural Area
Boone
Blowing Rock
BLUE RIDGE PARKWAY
MOSES CONE PARK
JULIAN PRICE PARK
GRANDFATHER MOUNTAIN PARK
Watauga River
Valle Crucis
Cove Creek
Banner Elk
Sugar Mountain
Beech Mountain
Newland
NORTH CAROLINA
TENNESSEE
194
221
321
421
105
184
19
37
N
0
2.5
5
Miles

**Watauga County Tourism Development Authority** (visitboonenc.com; e-mail: wataugatda@gmail.com; 828-266-1345; fax: 828-266-1346; 815 West King St., Ste. 10, Boone, NC 28607). Located in downtown Boone, on a back street, this friendly information desk will help you with the town of Boone and its surrounding area.

**Beech Mountain Chamber of Commerce** (www.beechmtn.com; 828-387-9283; 403A Beech Mountain Pkwy., Beech Mountain, NC 28604). Open Mon.–Fri., 9 AM–4 PM. This small-town chamber welcomes visitors from an office within City Hall—which makes it the highest chamber of commerce in the East, at 5,060 feet. You'll find it at the top of the mountain on the left, on NC 184.

**Avery/Banner Elk Chamber of Commerce** (www.banner-elk.com; e-mail: chamber@averycounty.com; 800-972-2183, 828-898-5605; fax: 828-898-8287; 4501 Tynecastle Hwy., Unit #2, Banner Elk, NC 28604). Open Mon.–Sat., 10 AM–4 PM. Covering all of Avery County (the rural areas west of Valle Crucis), this visitors center is hidden away in the shopping center at the corner of NC 105 and NC 184.

**GETTING THERE** *By Car* The main highways into this region are US 321 and US 421, which converge at Boone. Within the region, NC 105 (a surprisingly unattractive roadway) is the easiest way to drive between Boone and Banner Elk, while US 221 is the easiest route between Boone and Jefferson.

*By Air* You have a choice of two airports, one regional and one international. The closest in miles is Johnson City's Tri-Cities Airport, 70 miles away in Tennessee down some fairly bad two-lane highways. The major international hub at Charlotte, North Carolina, is 96 miles away via US 321—an expressway for all but 6 miles. If you are sensitive to price, check out both, as Johnson City is sometimes cheaper.

*By Bus or Train* Greyhound has recently reestablished regular bus service between Winston-Salem and Boone, stopping at Wilkesboro along the way. There is no rail passenger service.

**MEDICAL EMERGENCIES** **Watauga Medical Center** (apprhs.org; 828-262-4100; 336 Deerfield Rd., Boone, NC 28607). This private, nonprofit regional hospital, with a wide range of surgical and medical specialties, offers 24/7 emergency room services at its main building. It's located 2 miles south of Boone on US 221/321, then a block north on Deerfield Road.

## ✳ Exploring the Area

Boone and Banner Elk sit in a high bowl surrounded by 5,000-foot peaks. The bottom of this bowl is by no means smooth; instead, it is a series of classic Blue Ridge perched valleys, with bottoms commonly reaching 3,000 feet in elevation. The streams that drain the valleys run off in all sorts of directions, ignoring the general trend of the land, showing that some great force, more ancient than they, carved these slopes.

The town of Boone sits in one of these valleys, drained in two different directions: northward Ohio by the New River, and westward toward Tennessee by the Watauga River. Its lowest elevations barely sink below 3,200 feet—higher than most mountain peaks in more northward parts of the Appalachians. From here, the Watauga digs a 500-foot-deep gorge that splits this area in two; then, westward a bit more, the high valleys resume again. At the far western edge of this region, a half-dozen mountains have peaks above 5,000 feet.

These high elevations make this the snowiest area of the North Carolina Blue Ridge. Combine that with high, perched valleys and you have the perfect conditions for winter ski resorts, concentrated in the western area of high peaks. In warmer seasons, the countryside is lush and pastoral, a landscape of small farms with histories that stretch back to the Colonial era, framed by wooded mountain ridges.

**EXPLORING BY CAR NC 194** *Start:* From Boone, take US 221/421 east for 10.9 miles to a left onto US 221, then continue another 8.8 miles to a left onto NC 194.

*Leg #1* (*24.9 miles*): Follow NC 194 back to Boone; in 18.2 miles, NC 194 turns left to combine with US 221/421 and pass through the center of downtown Boone, to turn left onto its own roadway after another 6.7 miles, on the far side of town.

*Leg #2* (*15.9 miles*): Continue on NC 194 for 11.4 miles to a right onto NC 184, then go 4.5 miles to its end at Beech Mountain.

NC 194 passes through the center of this region for 41 miles, from the New River to Boone, then on to Valle Crucis and Banner Elk. It's a very slow and twisty road, but exceptionally pretty, with pastoral vistas over streamside meadows framed by low mountains and dotted with old barns and farm houses. As the road narrows and enters the mountains, it climbs a little valley then switchbacks down to the National Register village of **Todd** (see "The Blue Ridge Parkway Enters North Carolina," *To See*), a tiny collection of historic buildings off the road on the left. On a side lane through Todd, the **New River** makes one of its characteristic 180-degree curves, doubling back on itself around steep mountain slopes. NC 194 twists out of the mountains 11 miles later to combine with US 221/421—and later, US 321—to go through the small town of Boone. History fans should appreciate how these main mountain roads concentrate at a choke point, which by no coincidence at all is a small city's downtown. Boone (named after Daniel but otherwise unrelated to him) is a busy college town, whose old-fashioned downtown is two blocks away from the beautifully landscaped campus of **Appalachian State University**. Here you'll find good restaurants, some interesting shops, and a museum.

Five miles beyond Boone, NC 194 turns off the main highway and once more becomes a mountain road, curving down to the wide meadows of the Watauga River at **Valle Crucis**, passing the **Mast General Store**. The pastoral beauty and historic structures continue for 7 miles past the Mast Store, as the road twists sharply around meadows and up mountain slopes to **Banner Elk**, whose center has some nice shops and a small liberal arts college whose **Mill Pond Picnic Area** is open to the public and very lovely.

On the far side of Banner Elk, this route turns right onto NC 184 to climb **Beech Mountain**, using five switchbacks in 3 miles to rise 1,400 feet above the valley. The road tops out at 5,060 feet above sea level, at the center of the highest village in the East; to the right, Blackberry Ridge Road leads a short distance to superior views. The main road continues through the village to switchback down the back of the mountain, with more good views. You'll find **Ski Beech** down this way, where a summer ride up a ski lift leads to a mile-high panorama. The adventuresome can

MAST GENERAL STORE, VALLE CRUSIS

continue to follow this road to the base of the mountain, ending in a labyrinth of rural roads. Everyone else will want to return to Banner Elk the way they came.

**Daniel Boone's Trail, Part II** This is the second of two parts of a drive that follows the first road Daniel Boone ever built. Known simply as "Boone's Trail," it linked Boone's cabin at the foot of the Blue Ridge, near the present-day **Whippoorwill Academy** (see "The Blue Ridge Parkway: Blowing Rock & Grandfather Mountain," *To See*), to the settled lands drained by the Tennessee River in what is now the State of Tennessee.

When Boone built this road in 1769, however, Tennessee did not exist. The Colony of North Carolina extended across the Blue Ridge Mountains all the way to the Mississippi River—on paper at least. In reality, there were no trails at all across the Blue Ridge. Settlers entered the Tennessee Valley by traveling from Pennsylvania down Virginia's Shenandoah Valley. To get from North Carolina into its western lands, people had to travel north to present-day Roanoke, Virgina, then south again. Boone saw the need, and blazed this trail wide and level enough for pack horses.

For the first part of this drive, see the previous chapter. *This second part starts at the Blue Ridge Parkway's intersection with SSR 1510, marked "Bamboo," at milepost 285.6. Go west 500 feet to a right onto Bamboo Road (SSR 1514), then go 0.25 mile to a left onto Deerfield Road (SSR 1523, becoming SSR 1522).* Boone's Trail is now following a high perched valley now known cheerfully as "Happy Valley," with scenery that alternates between rural farmland and suburban settlement from the nearby town of Boone. Although it doesn't look particularly mountainous, this valley is 3,200 feet above sea level and very prone to heavy snows, even in these warmer times; in Boone's day, winter weather would have been almost sub-arctic up here. *In 3.1 miles, turn right onto US 221/321; then, in 1.2 miles turn left onto NC 105.* You are passing through urban sprawl from the pleasant small city of **Boone**. In fact, Boone's Trail missed the town site, crossing the Eastern Continental Divide 1 mile to its south at Hodges Gap. *Take NC 105 for 1.2 miles to a right onto NC 105 Bypass (SSR 1107), then go 1.9 miles to a left onto US 321/421, then go 0.75 mile to a right onto Linville Creek Road (SSR 1318).* According to 19th-century sources who traveled this road, Boone preferred a track that hugged the lower slopes of Rich Mountain, looming above you on your right; perhaps this avoided wet ground and frequent stream crossings. *In 1.9 miles, turn right at a T-intersection onto Charlie Thompson Road (SSR 1311), then go 1.2 miles to a right onto US 421. In 1.6 miles, turn left onto Tater Hill Road (SSR 1306).* Modern US 421, built in the mid-20th century, follows Boone's Trail remarkably closely. There is no need to settle for "close," however; at the rural hamlet of Silverstone you can pick up Boone's actual road. *In 0.3 mile, in Silverstone, turn right onto Silverstone Road (SSR 1303).* This is a good place to appreciate how Boone's road, typical of its period, avoided both valley floods and mountain climbs by meandering along the base of a mountain, hugging its contours. *In 3 miles turn right onto Slabtown Road (SSR 1302), then go 1.7 miles to a left onto Emory Greer Road (SSR 1301). Reach Zionville in 0.5 mile.* In 1913 the Daughters of the American Revolution erected a monument to Daniel Boone's Road at Zionville; look for it in front of a brick house behind the old general store. *Turn right on Old US 421 (SSR 1233), and go 0.4 miles to US 421 at the Tennessee state line.*

**EXPLORING ON FOOT** 🐾 **Lee & Vivian Reynolds Greenway Trail (The Boone Greenway).** This 7-mile continuous greenway follows the headwaters of the New River just east of Boone. An attractive and well-kept riverside walk, the paved and gravel trails cross the river multiple times on handsome pedestrian bridges to find wildflower fields, river glades, and vistas. Popular with locals and college students, it has plenty of benches for enjoying the view. To find the upstream end take US 321 south 2 miles from downtown Boone to a left turn onto Deerfield Road, then 0.5 mile to trailhead parking on your left.

## * Villages

**Boone** This college town and county seat sits in a high valley straddling the headwaters of the Watauga and the New Rivers. Not that many years ago it was a sleepy mountain town, but the explosive growth of **Appalachian State University** has left Boone bursting at the seams with 17,100 residents, its overflow sprawling down US 321 toward Blowing Rock and NC 105 toward Banner Elk. This is a lot of people for a mountain town that can only be reached down two-lane highways, and traffic can be bad. On the bright side, it has a neat downtown shopping district and plenty of interesting shops and restaurants. The compact university campus sits only two blocks from downtown, paralleling it along a stream and up the opposite mountain slope. The university-sponsored Summer Festival brings a wide variety of performing artists and lecturers into Boone each July.

**Valle Crucis** This rural settlement is nearly unique in the Appalachians—a popular tourist destination that remains unspoiled by success. Pronounced Valley Crewsis, it's a dispersed rural settlement along the Watauga River, its center 9 miles west of Boone on back roads. It has become popular for its lush pastoral scenery, its historic buildings, unique small shops and bed & breakfast inns, and its general store and post office, the famous **Mast General Store**. It has a prosperous look more common to New England than Appalachia, but there's nothing fake about it; this area's been settled since the late 1700s, and surviving buildings date from that earliest period. To find it from Boone, take NC 105 west from Boone 4.75 miles to Broadstone Road (SSR 1112), just over the Watauga River, and turn right. Valle Crucis stretches along Broadstone Road 2.8 miles to **NC 194** and the Mast General Store, generally taken as the center of the village.

**Banner Elk** For many years a quiet little village centered on a small liberal arts college, today Banner Elk is Main Street for the **ski slopes** of Sugar Mountain and Beech Mountain. Banner Elk's original village center sits at the intersection of NC 194 and NC 184 by tiny Lees-McRae College, and this remains the best place to look for shops, cafés, or quaint old bed & breakfasts. It's also the location of **Mill Pond**, a very pretty picnic spot run by the college and open to the public. Modern-day Banner Elk scatters south from its old center along NC 184 for 2.6 miles to the entrance to Sugar Mountain, then beyond another 1.5 miles to the urban sprawl along NC 105.

**Beech Mountain** In all likelihood the highest town in the East, Beech Mountain's town hall sits just barely above 5,000 feet in elevation—and a third of a mile higher into the sky than nearby Boone. This ski village is reached by taking NC 184 north from Banner Elk,and straight up five switchbacks and 1,500 feet. The village sits on a high, flat shelf about 200 feet shy of the summit, a small scattering of modest shops and motels surrounded by condos and second homes. The ski slope starts some distance downhill (toward the back of the mountain) and rises directly behind the town hall, making it easy to watch the skiers from the little town square. In fact, the town government provides a children's sledding slope behind the town hall, complete with artificial snow. The temperature difference is very noticeable, with Beech Mountain being cool and breezy in the warmest of summer weather. Beech Mountain is an isolated mile-high peak surrounded by much lower terrain, so good views are a given from just about anywhere near the village center.

## ✷ Wild Places

**THE GREAT FORESTS** Wild places abound along the Blue Ridge, a scant half-dozen miles to the south of Boone, including some of the most remarkable in the southern Appalachians—the crags and cliffs of **Grandfather Mountain**, the **Blue Ridge Parkway** with its stunning views, and the deep woods and waterfalls of the **Pisgah National Forest**. These are all described in the previous chapter (see "The Blue Ridge Parkway: Blowing Rock & Grandfather Mountain").

Once you've backed away from the Blue Ridge, large public wild places become scarce. Most of the Watauga and New River Valleys have been heavily settled and farmed since the time of Daniel Boone in the late 18th century; the lovely pastoral landscapes are dotted with historic old buildings, but wilderness has long since given way to woodlots. In the western part of this area, the high, wild peaks of the Sugar and Beech Mountains have been converted to ski-oriented tourist attractions and thickly built up, their former wilderness dissected by closely spaced roads and small building lots.

To the north of Boone, tall mountains still retain their wild character. Forests tend to be old and lovely, with rich and diverse ecosystems; the scenery is dotted with beautiful waterfalls, odd little perched valleys, and impressive cliffs. Unfortunately for travelers, virtually all of these wild places are privately owned and closed to the public. To the immediate north of this area, the State of North Carolina owns three tracts of land, two of which are large and being expanded: **Elk Knob State Park** and **Three Top Mountains State Game Lands** near Todd, and The Nature Conservancy's **Bluff Mountain Preserve**, and **Mount Jefferson State**

**Park** near Jefferson (see "The Blue Ridge Parkway Enters North Carolina," *Wild Places*).

**Elk Knob State Park** (ncparks.gov/Visit/parks/elkn/main; e-mail: elk.knob@ncdenr.gov; 828-297-7261; 5564 Meat Camp Rd., Todd, NC 28684). This North Carolina state park sits deep in the Bald Mountains north of Boone; to get there, go east from Boone for 1 mile on US 421 to a left onto NC 194, then 4.2 miles to a left onto Meat Camp Road (SSR 1335, becoming SSR 1340), then 5.3 miles to Pottertown Gap and access on the right. It's not the easiest place to find, but it's worth it. Elk Knob tops out at 5,520 feet, with meadows furnishing wildflower-framed views. Even more interesting: a very large stand of old-growth, and possibly virgin, forest surrounds this peak. At this writing the state is still developing a management plan, and may add land to the 1,200 acres already purchased. You can expect to find, at a minimum, a picnic area, ranger station, and trail to the top with incredible views.

**RIVERS The Watauga and New Rivers** The Watauga River and the New River—both rising from the town of Boone—offer radically different whitewater opportunities. The **New River** (see "The Blue Ridge Parkway Enters North Carolina," *Wild Places*) meanders through a cliff-sided gorge, but with so many twists that its 30 miles of travel is lengthened to 90 miles of riverbed with hardly any rapids. Indeed, it almost qualifies as still water, and most people prefer to travel along it in canoes. It is so stunningly beautiful that it's been declared both a National Wild and Scenic River and a National Heritage River. The **Watauga River** offers shorter and more action-packed runs, with some Class II and III rapids to get your adrenaline running. A third nearby kayaking possibility is **Wilson Creek**, in the Pisgah National Forest below Grandfather Mountain (see "The Blue Ridge Parkway: Blowing Rock & Grandfather Mountain," *Wild Places*), a fairly extreme run with rapids ranging to Class V.

BOONE VIEWED FROM HOWARD KNOB

**PICNIC AREAS Mill Pond Picnic Area** This lovely little picnic area sits at Banner Elk's village center. It's a landmark along NC 184, with a barn-red cottage sitting under great trees by the reflecting surface of the small lake. Its scattered lakeside tables are a great place to picnic, or just sit and relax.

**Howard Knob Park** This 6-acre county park sits high above Boone. Its main feature is a large outcrop and cliff with **stunning views** over Boone and Valle Crucis. Nearly unknown to tourists, it's very popular with locals, and you will frequently see students from nearby **Appalachian State University** studying there while enjoying the view. From downtown Boone, head uphill on Waters Street (away from the university) to its end, then continue steeply uphill on Junaluska Road; when it tops out, go right to Howard's Knob Park.

## ✷ To See

**HISTORIC SITES** ✐ **Mast General Store** (mastgeneralstore.com; e-mail: info@mastgeneralstore.com; 828-963-6511; Hwy. 194, Valle Crucis, NC 28691). Open Mon.–Sat., 7 AM–6 PM; Sun., 1 PM–5 PM. You may have seen various Mast General Stores selling outdoor and gift items in downtown Boone, Hendersonville, Asheville, and Waynesville. Make no mistake; the 19th-century frame store at the center of Valle Crucis is the real Mast General Store and always has been—the primary general store for the community of Valle Crucis since 1882 (when it replaced a smaller structure across the street). This National Register structure is really a collection of white clapboard buildings sort of stuck together, with doorways passing through common walls on the inside. The outside has a false front, plate-glass windows, a wood boardwalk, and a hand-crank gas pump that no longer works. Inside, it combines the items needed by the Valle Crucis community—groceries, mail, fishing licenses, burning permits, and a checkers set by a potbellied stove—with local canned jellies and honeys, barrels of marbles, bulk candy, local arts, outdoor products, and all sorts of other stuff. The Mast family owned it until 1973 and is still involved in its management. Its current owners, John and Faye Cooper, have taken the Mast's long-time formula of "Everything from Cradles to Caskets" and used it to create a general store marketing powerhouse with branches in five mountain towns. However, they've kept the original Mast General Store true to its heritage, one of the few general stores to make it successfully into the 21st century.

✐ **Hickory Ridge Homestead** (www.horninthewest.com/museum.htm; 828-264-2120; 591 Horn in the West Dr., Boone, NC 28607). Summer: Tues.–Sun.,1:00 PM–8:30 PM; spring and fall: Sat., 9 AM–4 PM; and Sun., 1 PM–4 PM; closed winter. This living history museum in Boone recreates a late-18th-century pioneer farmstead. Owned by the Southern Appalachian Historical Association, it preserves two historic log cabins and several outbuildings on an attractive wooded slope near the center of town. The buildings are beautifully and authentically furnished, and have period vegetable and herb gardens. Guides in period clothing explain the pioneer way of life, demonstrate crafts, and perform authentic music. Visitors are invited to participate in activities such as carding and spinning wool, weaving on a 185-year-old loom, candlemaking, or cooking over an open hearth. Hickory Ridge Homestead is located by the **Horn in the West** amphitheater and the **Daniel Boone Gardens**; go east of downtown on US 421 and turn right (south) on Horn in the West Drive. Summer visitors should look into an evening visit followed by a performance of *Horn in the West*—for the same cost as a ticket to *Horn in the West* alone.

**CULTURAL SITES Appalachian State University** (www.appstate.edu; 828-262-2000; Boone, NC 28608). The park-like main campus of Appalachian State University stretches the length of central Boone, along a stream two blocks downhill from downtown. Compact and modern, the 50 or more university buildings squeeze onto a 75-acre site, landscaped with a plentiful number of hardwood trees and rhododendrons. The attractive campus is studded with sculptures and contains several galleries of student and faculty art. On-campus accommodations are available at the tree-shaded, hilltop **Broyhill Inn**, with a first-rate restaurant. A member of the University of North Carolina, ASU has nearly 13,000 students and 175 degree programs.

**Horn in the West** (www.horninthewest.com, 828-262-2120; P.O. Box 295, Boone, NC 28607). Evening performances run June 22–August 11, Tues.–Sun. For over half a century, the Southern Appalachian Historical Association has presented Kermit Hunter's large-scale outdoor musical drama of the early settlement of the Watauga Valley, centering on Daniel Boone and the American Revolution. Held six evenings a week throughout the summer, the performance is preceded by an evening tour of the historically authentic reconstructed pioneer farmstead, Hickory Ridge Homestead—actually an extension of the performance, with period-costumed guides demonstrating the pioneer way of life. It's located on Horn in the West Drive, off US 321, south of Boone.

**The Jones House Community and Cultural Center** (www.joneshousecommunitycenter.org; e-mail: joneshouse@charterinternet.com; 828-262-4576; fax: 828-264-4599; 604 W. King St., Boone, NC 28607). Open Tues.–Fri., noon–5 PM. Free. This 1908 local doctor's home sits incongruously in the center of Boone's brick storefront downtown, a genteel white clapboard mansion with a wide porch overlooking its high lawn toward busy King Street. Today, this National Historical Register structure is owned by the town of Boone and run by the Watauga County Arts Council. While much of this large house is given over to community center uses, several rooms serve as a gallery for local artists, while other rooms are furnished in period. It's definitely worthwhile to take a time out from King Street shopping and pop up for a visit.

JOHN PETERSEN PLAYS A HANDMADE FRETLESS BANJO AT THE HORN IN THE WEST

**The Turchin Center for the Visual Arts** (www.turchincenter.org; e-mail: turchincenter@appstate.edu; 828-262-3017; fax: 828-262-7546; 423 West King St., Boone, NC 28608). Affiliated with Appalachian State University, this arts center occupies the 100-year-old octagonal brick Methodist Church that has long been a prominent downtown landmark. Meant as a center for campus/community interaction, it has a main gallery and six smaller galleries, plus two terraces for displaying sculpture, a lecture hall, and a wing for classrooms and studios.

**GARDENS AND PARKS** **Daniel Boone Gardens** (e-mail: dbgardens@danielboonegardens.org; 828-264-6390; P.O. Box 1705, Boone, NC 28607). Open May–October, 9 AM–6 PM; 9 AM–8 PM on days with *Horn in the West* performances. Closed November–April. Owned and run by the nonprofit Garden Club of North Carolina on land contributed by Horn in the West (Southern Appalachian Historical Association), the Daniel Boone Gardens presents native Appalachian plants in a free-flowing, informal landscape. First open in 1966, the gardens have had more than three decades of growth and improvement, offering season-long displays of every native flower imaginable. The gardens now include a bog garden, a fern garden, a sunken rock garden with a tiny pond, a mountain spring, a reflecting pool, and a meditation garden. The large wrought-iron entrance gate with the initials "DB" was handmade by artist Daniel Boone a descendant of the famous Daniel Boone VI.

## ✷ To Do

**WHITEWATER SPORTS** ✐ **Wahoo's Adventures** (www.wahoosadventures.com; 800-444-7238, 828-262-5774; P.O. Box 3094, Boone, NC 28607). Wahoo's offers a wide range of rafting experiences throughout the Smokies, with branches in Gatlinburg and Ducktown as well as their GHQ in Boone. In the Boone area, they offer gentle family trips on the New River and the Watauga River, and fierce rapid-runners on Wilson Creek, Russell Creek, and the Watauga River Gorge.

**STABLES** **Banner Elk Stables** (828-898-5424; 796 Shomaker Rd., Banner Elk, NC 28604). $15 per hour. Banner Elk Stables offers trail riding along the slopes of Beech Mountain, from their stables at the end of Shomaker Road in Banner Elk.

**BICYCLING** **Magic Cycles** (www.magiccycles.com/main.html; e-mail: info@magiccycles.com; 828-265-2211; 140 South Depot St., #2, Boone, NC 28607). Open Mon.–Sat., 10 AM–6 PM; Sun., 10 AM–4 PM. This full-service bicycle shop, located south of downtown Boone on Faculty Street just off US 321, offers both mountain bike rentals and guided bicycle trips. The Boone area offers a wide variety of bicycle paths and trails, and this is a good place to find out about them all.

**Beech Mountain Biking Trails** (www.beechmountainchamber.com; e-mail: chamber@beechmtn.com; 800-468-5506; 403A Beech Mountain Pkwy., Beech Mountain, NC 28604). The Beech Mountain Bike Club maintains 51 miles of mountain biking trails, which were once a final stage of the Tour DuPont. These trails, with climbs of 1,400 feet in only 3.5 miles, were among Lance Armstrong's favorites on his road to recovery. Beech Mountain offers a wide range of challenges, from casual cruising to advanced cycling. All routes begin at the visitors center, and most trails are through-paved residential areas. Others will take you by Buckeye Lake and the recreation center. Trail maps and more information can be found at www.bikebeechmountain.com.

**ROCK CLIMBING** **Rock Dimensions** (rockdimensions.com; e-mail: info@rockdimensions.com; 888-595-6009, 828-265-3544; 131-B South Depot St., Boone, NC 28607). Tower open spring–fall, noon–5 PM. Guided climbing trips and instruction to a variety of groups and individuals including Boy and Girl Scouts. Outings include rock climbing, caving, traverse zip lines, and multipitch challenges. In addition to utilizing natural sites for the recreational challenges, they also have use of a 35-foot-tall climbing tower located at Footsloggers, a Boone climbing and caving outfitter.

**Rock Climbing Guides** Several of the rafting outfitters also offer guide and/or instruction services for rock climbers. Be sure to check the listings.

**GOLF** **Village of Sugar Mountain Golf Course** (828-898-6464; Sugar Mountain Dr., Banner Elk, NC 28604). Open April–October. This 1974 18-hole course, designed by Duane Francis and Arnold Palmer, sits just beneath the ski slope at Sugar Mountain.

**Willow Creek Public Golf Course** (www.willowvalley-resort.com; e-mail: willowvalley@skybest.com; 828-963-6865; 354 Bairds Creek Rd., Boone, NC 28607). Open May–October. Part of a resort development, this nine-hole course west of Boone off NC 105 features country scenery and well-kept fairways.

**Boone Golf Club** (boonegolfclub.com; 828-264-8760; 433 Fairway Dr., Boone, NC 28607). Open April–October. This 18-hole course, situated just south of Boone on US 321, was designed in 1959 by Ellis Maples.

**Hawksnest Golf Resort** (828-963-6565; 2058 Skyland Dr., Seven Devils, NC 28604). Open April–October. This 4,200-foot-high, 18-hole course offers stunning scenery and lots of dramatic elevation change.

**SKIING** **Ski Beech** (www.skibeech.com; e-mail: info@skibeech.com; 800-438-2093; 1007 Beech Mountain Pkwy., P.O. Box 1118, Beech Mountain, NC 28604). 8:30 AM–10 PM. Located downhill behind the village center, Ski Beech starts with a group of two-story 1960s Alpine vernacular buildings grouped around an outdoor skating rink, with a snack bar and a number of shops. The main lodge is up a set of outdoor wooden stairs—a rambling, '60s-style three-story structure with broad and impressive views from many decks and windows. The whole complex is clean and well-kept, full of adults and families with children; happy little children cover the bunny slope, giggling and screeching. Its run is 3,600 feet with a drop of 750 feet from a summit of 5,505 feet to a base of 4,700 feet, the highest ski elevations in the Smoky Mountains region.

✐ **Sugar Mountain** (www.skisugar.com; e-mail: info@skisugar.com; 800-784-2768, 828-898-4521; P.O. Box 369, Banner Elk, NC 28604). The Sugar Mountain ski lodge is easily accessible from NC 184 in Banner Elk, not that far a distance uphill or off the main road. It's a three-story wood building with gray pressboard paneling in an early 1970s style, perhaps a bit down at the heels but very clean. It is busy with adults and families, but handles crowds well. It has the longest run and the farthest drop in the area—1.5 miles and 1,200 feet from a summit at 5,300 feet to a base at 4,100 feet.

## ✷ Lodging

**HOTELS The Broyhill Inn and Conference Center** (e-mail: explore@broyhillinn.com; 800-951-6048, 828-262-2204; 775 Bodenheimer Dr., Boone, NC 28607). The Broyhill is a full-service 83-room inn and conference center on the attractive campus of Appalachian State University. This modern building of rock-clad concrete with a pitched roof mirroring the surrounding peaks, sits on a park-like hilltop landscaped to appear like a mountaintop meadow. Its charming dining room with a large wood-burning fireplace has sweeping mountain views over a small sculpture garden. Common areas, including the spacious lobby, are roomy and comfortable, with plush chairs and sofas, decorated with local art. A recent renovation has turned the formerly Spartan rooms into the comfortable quarters you'd expect from a high-end business hotel. While standard rooms remain smallish, they are furnished with new, elegant furniture, including a king or two double beds, desk, two phones, a computer data port, and a recliner chair facing the TV. The tariff does not include meals; however, this can be changed by adding a set surcharge.

**The Mast Farm Inn** (www.mastfarminn.com; e-mail: stay@mastfarminn.com; 888-963-5857, 828-963-5857; fax: 828-963-6404; 2543 Broadstone Rd.; P.O. Box 704, Valle Crucis, NC 28691). This popular and respected small country inn at the heart of Valle Crucis has so many historic buildings that it's listed on the National Register as an Historic District. The 1880s farmhouse holds nine comfortable rooms furnished in country antiques. Adjacent historic log cabins and farm outbuildings, original to the site and as old as 1812, have roomy cottage accommodations furnished with mountain country antiques; one and two bedroom floorplans have separate living rooms and wet bars, but no kitchens. The grounds are beautifully landscaped, and the farm house's wide wraparound porch is a perfect place to sit and rock. Their restaurant is noted for its organic gourmet regional cuisine.

**Archers Mountain Inn** (www.archersinn.com; e-mail: theinn@archersinn.com; 888-827-6155, 828-898-9004; 2489 Beech Mountain Pkwy.,

THE MAST FARM INN, VALLE CRUSIS

Banner Elk, NC 28604). Halfway up Beech Mountain, this group of 1970s vintage lodge buildings offers a wide variety of room types (and prices). All rooms are individually decorated with antiques and reproductions, typically in a country or farmhouse style, and all rooms have fireplaces and either a deck or porch. Features available in some rooms include separate sitting areas, kitchens, structural cedar beams, whirlpool baths, feather beds, and private mountain-view porches. A full breakfast is included. The lodge's restaurant, the Jackalope View, is first-rate, and has a weekend jazz bar.

**BED & BREAKFAST INNS Lovill House Inn** (www.lovillhouseinn.com; e-mail: innkeeper@lovillhouseinn.com; 800-849-9466, 828-264-4204; 404 Old Bristol Rd., Boone, NC 28607). Open all year. This inn retains the look and feel of the mountain countryside while sitting on the edge of downtown Boone. Its 11 acres of property has a perennial flower garden, barn, stream, and waterfall, with woodland views on all sides. The 1875 Victorian farmhouse with wraparound porches and rockers, built by one of Boone's most prominent citizens, has hardwood pine and maple floors, and wormy chestnut moldings and doors. Public areas are elegant and roomy, with lovely period antiques. The six en suite rooms are large, with fireplaces (half wood, half gas) and elegant antiques and reproductions. An outbuilding, once a feed store on the 19th-century farm, has been renovated as a self-catering cottage, carrying the same theme of 19th-century country elegance. A full gourmet breakfast is served in the sunny dining room, and a social hour—by the fire in bad weather, on the porch in good—greets guests in the evening.

**The Baird House** (www.bairdhouse.com; e-mail: info@bairdhouse.com; 800-297-1342, 828-297-4055; 1451 Watauga River Rd.; P.O. Box 712, Valle Crucis, NC 28691). This 1790 farmhouse sits above the Watauga River in the lovely rural mountain community of Valle Crucis. Its 16 acres include 500 feet of Watauga River frontage. The Baird House survives in a remarkably pristine condition, a very early example of planked lumber construction (as opposed to log cabins). While the stunning two-story-high porch with its round columns is a bit of dressing up by an early-20th-century judge, the old house's two original cribs and center dogtrot-style hall survive intact—as does the original 18th-century planking on the walls of one of the elegantly furnished common rooms. The guest rooms, ranging in size from normal to large, are furnished with antiques and reproductions typical of prosperous 19th-century farms. Four rooms are in the main house, while three more rooms (one a kitchenette) occupy a renovated 20th-century outbuilding.

**Alta Vista** (www.altavistagallery.com; e-mail: altavista@skybest.com; 828-963-5247; 2839 Broadstone Rd., Valle Crucis, NC 28691). Located upstairs from Valle Crucis' Gallery Alta Vista, this comfy bed & breakfast has large rooms with country antique furniture, beadboard walls and ceilings—and lots of original art on the walls. In fact, having this fine gallery on site is part of the charm of this 1923 brick bungalow in the center of the settlement. Another part of the charm—the large front porch overlooking the Watauga River and the old general store now occupied by the Mast General Store Annex. An upstairs common sitting room serves as the venue for the full hot breakfast, as well as a great place to sit and read.

**Bluestone Lodge** (www.bluestone-lodge.com/Default.htm; 828-963-5177; Bluestone Wild Rd., P.O. Box 736, Valle Crucis, NC 28691). Located down a side lane in Valle Crucis, this four-room bed & breakfast is in a three-story modern home with decks and mountain views on all three floors. The well-landscaped property has an outdoor pool with mountain views, a sunroom, and an indoor hot tub and sauna. Rooms are large and well decorated, each with its own theme. Rates include a full breakfast.

♿ **Azalea Inn** (www.Azalea-Inn.com; e-mail: AzaleaInn@skybest.com; 888-898-2743, 828-898-8195; fax: 828-898-3482; 149 Azalea Circle, P.O. Box 1538, Banner Elk, NC 28604). Open all year. This large 1937 bungalow sits at the very center of the village of Banner Elk, by a stone WPA school built the same year and still in use. A roomy and cheerful house, with country antiques and quilts, has wormy chestnut trim in the front parlor, while three other common rooms offer sunny places to relax. Within the main house are two downstairs rooms, plus one upstairs room with a strange and wonderful attic tunnel sitting area. An addition has more rooms, including one with a whirlpool bath and a full-sized private porch. A detached cottage, over a garage, offers a very high level of self-catering.

🐾 **Banner Elk Inn Bed & Breakfast** (www.bannerelkinn.com; e-mail: bannerelkinn@skybest.com; 888-487-8263, 828-898-6223; fax: 828-898-6224; 407 Main St. East [NC 194W], Banner Elk, NC 28604). Open all year. Built in 1912 as a country church, this large wood house was moved to Banner Elk from a site farther up the mountain to take advantage of the new automobile road—now the Old Toll Road east of town. Beautifully restored, this pink house with green shutters recalls the elegant, comfortable living of a country lawyer or doctor. A breakfast area is flooded with light from large windows; plush chairs face a fire; stained bead-board covers the walls and ceilings. Two standard rooms are ample sized, while a two-bedroom room suite (never offered as separate rooms) offers comfortable quarters for families or couples traveling together. A honeymoon suite, taking up most of the low-ceilinged attic, offers special privacy (and a whirlpool bath) for those willing to take on the extra steep and narrow steps. Pets must be arranged in advance.

## ✴ Where to Eat

**EATING OUT** **Red Onion Cafe** (theredonioncafe.com; 828-264-5470; 227 Hardin St., Boone, NC 28607). Open 11 AM–9 PM, weekdays; 11 AM–10 PM, weekends. This downtown casual restaurant reuses a 1960s-era barbeque as an upmarket sandwich and pasta café. Well decorated and well kept, quiet and comfortable, the Red Onion is a good break from the ordinary. The menu offers a variety of such adventurous fare balanced by familiar favorites within a core of salads, soups, sandwiches, and pasta dishes. Personal-sized pizzas on whole-wheat crusts come with a variety of toppings, from traditional and pesto to southwestern and creole. Desserts are made on the premises.

**Our Daily Bread** (ourdailybread-boone.com; 828-264-0173; 627 West King St., Boone, NC 28607). 8 AM–6 PM, Mon.–Fri.; 9 AM–5 PM, Sat.; closed Sun. This small downtown storefront café in the center of Boone features fresh produce from local farms, lots of choice, and great food prepared from scratch. The menu centers on breakfasts, soups, salads, and sandwiches, with everything done up right. Not just a cup of homemade soup—

three different homemade soups and two chiles, and cream soup made with whipping cream a house specialty. Not just a half-dozen sandwiches—25 different sandwiches, including 12 vegetarian choices, hot dogs, a generous build-your-own, and grilled cheese made with local farm cheese. Their carefully decorated interior is bright and welcoming, with plenty of blond hardwood. Prices are low—all part of the small-town main-street atmosphere.

**Dan'l Boone Inn** (www.danlbooneinn.com; e-mail: info@danlbooneinn.com; 828-264-8657; 130 Hardin St., Boone, NC 28607). Open June–October: 11:30 AM–9 PM, weekdays; 8 AM–9 PM, weekends. November–May: 5 PM–8 PM, weekdays; 8 AM–8 PM, weekends. A popular family eatery since 1959, The Dan'l Boone Inn occupies a large former boarding house at the south edge of downtown Boone. Inside, it's plain and straightforward, with several large rooms paneled in tongue-and-groove pine, floors covered with linoleum. Although seating is at individual tables, all food is brought out in bowls family style. Fried chicken, corn, whipped potatoes (with lumps), green beans (soft, with fatback, southern style), country-fried steak and gravy, cole slaw, a superb country ham on biscuit (the only thing NOT all-you-can-eat), plain biscuits (wonderful!), jelly, baked apples, gravy—all brought out in large bowls, until the oversized tables are filled with food. Beverage, soup or salad, and dessert are also included. You take what you want, and if the bowl goes empty they bring you some more.

**DINING OUT** **The Broyhill Inn** (www.broyhillinn.com; e-mail: info@broyhillinn.com; 800-951-6048, 828-262-2204; fax: 828-262-2946; 775 Bodenheimer Drive, Boone, NC 28607). Open all year. The newly renovated Broyhill Inn, on a hilltop inside Appalachian State University, now sports an elegant dining area off the main lobby. Quiet and pleasant, with simple, attractive decor, it's anchored by a giant hearth with a wood fire and wide views through a glass wall. Breakfasts can be either a buffet or a la carte, while lunches center on an ample buffet, and a Sunday brunch buffet includes an omelette chef. However, dinners are the main event, elegant entrées served with live piano and a crackling wood fire.

**The Jackalope View** (www.archersinn.com/jackalopes; e-mail: theinn@archersinn.com; 888-827-6155, 828-898-9004; 2489 Beech Mountain Pkwy., Beech Mountain, NC 28604). The first thing you notice at the Jackalope View is—the view. Located halfway up Beech Mountain on NC 184, this casual fine-dining restaurant at Archer's Mountain Inn has glass walls and a deck hanging over a 180-degree open south-facing panorama toward Sugar Mountain and the Blue Ridge. However, everything about the Jackalope impresses. Their three wine cellars offer 300 different wines (with a large selection under $25 a bottle), and 28 wines by the glass. The menu presents exotic and original preparation of beef, trout, fresh seafood, and game. Upstairs is a large and comfortable bar, with even more great views, a wide selection of microbrews, and live jazz on weekends.

## ✱ Selective Shopping

### *Boone*

Stretching four long blocks along US 321/421, downtown Boone is a classic turn-of-the-century brick-front, lively and active with interesting shops. The main street is a simple two-lane road with parallel parking, named King Street; behind it on the downhill side is alley-like Howard Street, where most of the off-street parking is to be found; Appalachian State University starts on the next block down. With a 17,000-student university two blocks downhill, parking is very bad and regulations are aggressively enforced. However, there's a trick to it; stop by the Chamber of Commerce on the western end of Howard Avenue and get a permit that lets you park to shop downtown.

**Farmers Hardware** (828-264-8801; 661 West King St., Boone, NC, 28607). This is one of those places you brag about finding, and not just for its classic Main Street storefront, with well-worn hardwood floors, old wood cabinetry, and wide stairs descending downward in the middle of the store. Inside, and to the left, a "housewares department" occupies the former home of the Watauga County Bank, with the sort of kitchenware you normally find only in specialty catalogs, a range of Disney- and Coke-licenced collectables, and a section of wild bird houses and feeders. Inside the old safe (with inspection stickers from 1924 to 1953) are a range of fine decorative items. Then down the stairs, behind the paints section, is another strange and funky selection of pottery and garden decorations.

**The Watauga County Farmers Market.** (wataugacountyfarmers market.org; Boone, NC) May–October, Sat. mornings. Held at the Horn in the West for more than 35 years, the market offers fresh local produce, homemade preserves, honey, baked goods, crafts, and much more. Holiday markets take place from 9 to 1 on the Saturdays before and after Thanksgiving.

**Gallery Alta Vista** (altavistagallery .com; e-mail: altavista@skybest.com; 828-963-5247, 2839 Broadstone Rd., Valle Crucis, NC, 28691). This lovely gallery occupies the parlors and dining room of a large 1923 farmhouse. It features a large selection of realistic and impressionistic watercolors and oils, mainly by local and regional artists, but also by artists from around the nation and the world. It's a good place to browse for fine art original paintings of mountain scenics, as the technical quality and originality are consistently high.

## ✳ Special Events

**SUMMER An Appalachian Summer Festival** (800-841-2787, 828-262-4046). July. Affiliated with Appalachian State University at Boone, the Appalachian Summer Festival fills the July calendar with music, dance, and the visual arts. Music is the main focus, with classical symphonic performances, pop orchestras, jazz, and mountain music, with a mix of regional and national performers. Modern dance and serious theater stud the program, along with lecture series, workshops, and visual art displays. The festival ends with an outdoor fireworks concert featuring a major headliner.

**Firefly Festival** First Saturday in August. Held at the Hickory Ridge Homestead, Boone's annual Firefly Festival includes storytellers, musicians, mountain crafters, and folk artists, with guides dressed as 18th-century pioneers to help things along. It's an afternoon event, sandwiched between the morning Farmer's Market and the evening performance of *Horn in the West,* both on this site, as a fundraiser for this outdoor museum of 18th-century life.

**Lees-McRae Summer Theater** (www.lmc.edu/sites/SummerTheatre; 828-898-8709; fax: 828-898-3467; Lees-McRae College, Banner Elk, NC 28604). June–August. Lees-McRae College, a small liberal arts college in Banner Elk, sponsors this summer theater festival. They typically perform three musicals, each for a five-day run toward the end of a month.

**AUTUMN** **Cove Creek Farm Heritage Days** (Historic Cove Creek High School, Sugar Grove, NC 28679). Mid-September weekend. This annual event celebrates the rich agricultural heritage of the coves and mountains northwest of Boone, known locally as Cove Creek Community. Sponsored by Cove Creek Preservation and Development, a nonprofit organized by residents in 1996 to save the old stone high school, this fundraiser on the high school lawn is patterned after the local agricultural fairs of a hundred years ago. It has mountain music and clogging (under a tent with plenty of seating), all sorts of farm exhibits, farm craft demonstrations, old-time games and activities, a petting zoo, local crafts, and canning judging. The day after the fair, local farms open their doors to strangers for afternoon farm tours; participants get a map and plan their own route, dropping by the farms that interest them.

**Old Boone Streetfest** (828-262-4532). Last weekend in September. This street fair celebrates downtown Boone. It features free concerts on the Jones House lawn and near the Turchin Center, and craft vendors and food on downtown's back street, Howard Street.

**Banner Elk Woolly Worm Festival** Third weekend in September. Held in Banner Elk for the last quarter of a century, this celebration of the furry catepillar draws more than 15,000 people every year. Although there are vendors and food, the main interest centers on the worm races—fifty heats of the worms racing up strings, bringing cash prizes to their owners. When a champion is finally declared, the festival's official forecaster uses its stripes to predict the coming winter weather. It's a fundraiser for local schools, held on the elementary school grounds at the center of the village.

**WINTER** **Cut & Choose Christmas Tree Celebration** (828-264-3061). Mid-November to mid-December. Each Christmas season, 16 or so Watauga County Christmas tree growers organize an old-fashioned family Christmas tree-cutting celebration, holding a special welcome for families coming from the warm flatlands to choose a tree and maybe see some pre-Christmas snow. A brochure describes each farm in detail, telling how to get to it and how you will be welcomed.

# BEHIND THE BLUE RIDGE: SPRUCE PINE & BURNSVILLE

The Toe and the Cane Rivers drain some of the East's tallest mountains. The Black Mountains, whose 10 peaks above 6,000 feet include Mount Mitchell, the highest point in the East, frame this region's eastern edge. The Highlands of Roan, with three peaks above 6,000 feet, loom over its far side, along the Tennessee state line, with miles of mountaintop meadows and hundreds of acres of natural rhododendron gardens. Between these two great ranges lies a broken land of 4,000-foot peaks and 2,000-foot valleys, a land little visited by tourists. Here you'll find the lovely little county seat of Burnsville, gathered around an old town square still dominated by its 170-year-old inn. Away from Burnsville, a rolling pastoral landscape slowly gives way to a difficult and broken country linked to the notorious events of Frankie and Charlie Silver. Here farms give way to mining, and feldspar and granite are dug from giant open pits near the terraced town of Spruce Pine. Here also the famous Clinchfield Railroad cuts straight through mile-high mountains, following the Nolichucky River Gorge out into the plains of Tennessee.

This district is not so much a valley between two ridges as an area of high mountains between two areas of even higher mountains. Nevertheless it does have a certain unity given it by being so hemmed in, and locals have struggled to name it. The U.S. Forest Service once dubbed it "Toecane" after its rivers, but this has never stuck. You are more likely to see it called "Mayland Valley," after the three counties that it contains (Mitchell, Avery, Yancey). Despite being off the beaten track, it has excellent bed & breakfasts and some good restaurants. It also hosts the center of the Fine Crafts Movement in the East. Hundreds of artists maintain studios throughout the area, and Burnsville's beautiful square is lined with galleries.

**GUIDANCE—TOWN AND COUNTRYSIDE** **Yancey County Chamber of Commerce** (www.yanceychamber.com; e-mail: info@yanceychamber.com; 800-948-1632, 828-682-7413; 106 West Main St., Burnsville, NC 28714). The Yancey Chamber of Commerce runs an attractive visitors center in a restored early gas station on the western edge of downtown Burnsville. It has some historic exhibits, and the history museum in the **McElroy House** is immediately behind it.

**Mitchell County Chamber of Commerce** (www.mitchell-county.com; 828-765-9483; fax: 828-765-9034; P.O. Box 858, Spruce Pine, NC 28777). Mitchell County's

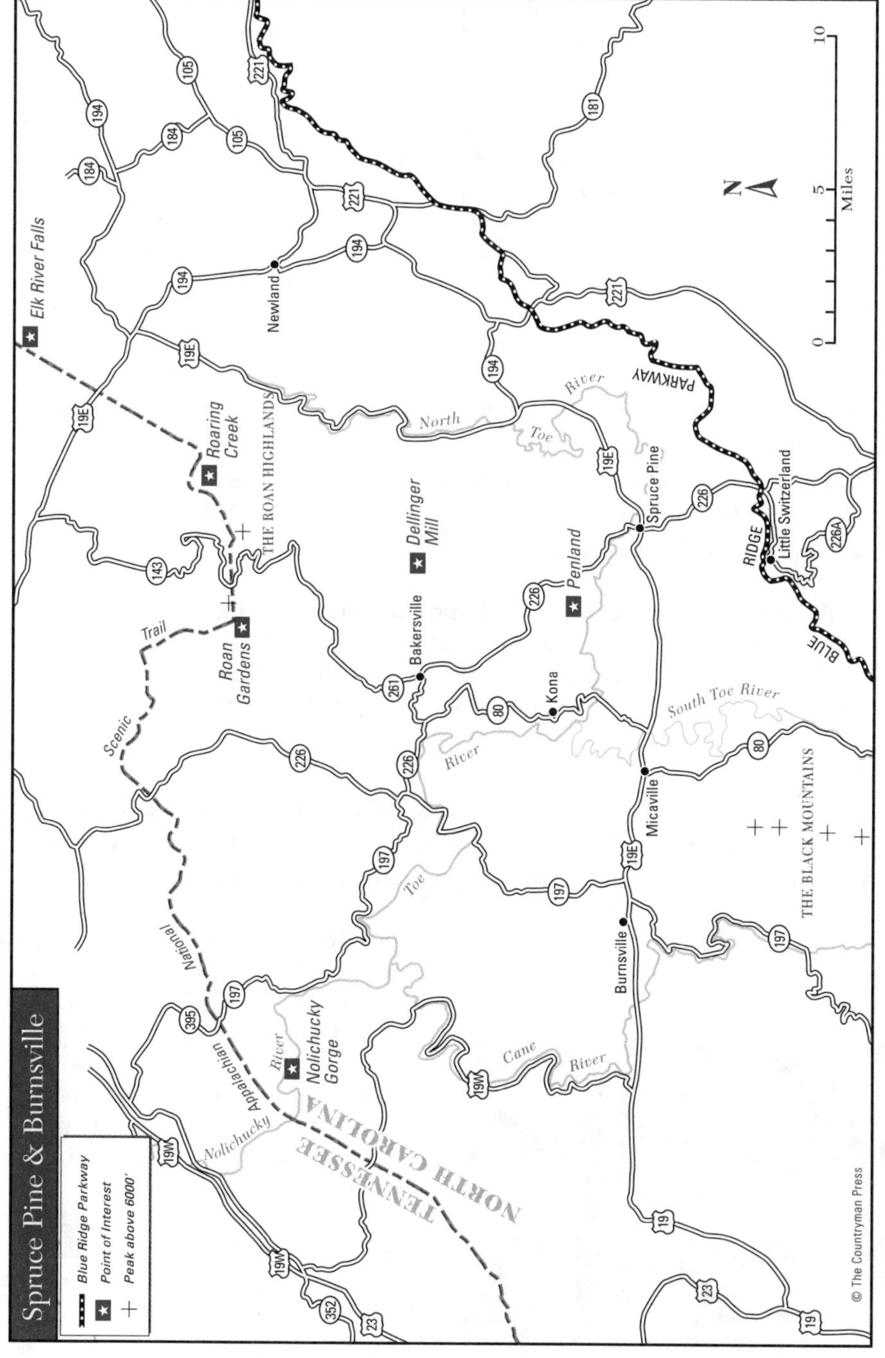
Spruce Pine & Burnsville
Blue Ridge Parkway
Point of Interest
Peak above 6000'
Elk River Falls
Roaring Creek
THE ROAN HIGHLANDS
Dellinger Mill
Penland
Roan Gardens
Nolichucky Gorge
Newland
Bakersville
Kona
Spruce Pine
Little Switzerland
Micaville
Burnsville
THE BLACK MOUNTAINS
North Toe River
South Toe River
Toe River
Cane River
Nolichucky River
Appalachian National Scenic Trail
TENNESSEE
NORTH CAROLINA
BLUE RIDGE PARKWAY
N
0 5 10
Miles
© The Countryman Press

Chamber of Commerce, covering the Spruce Pine and Bakersville areas, maintains an information desk for visitors just off the Blue Ridge Parkway in the Museum of North Carolina Minerals.

**GETTING THERE** *By Car* US 19 (marked as US 19E over much of this segment) runs lengthwise through the Mayland Valley, from Mars Hill, north of Asheville, through Burnsville, Micaville, and Spruce Pine, then into Tennessee near Elizabethton. It is best reached from I-26 at Mars Hill, no matter what direction you are coming from. Once you are in this region, you will want to use US 19/19E as much as possible. Four-laned from Mars Hill to Burnsville, it is the straightest highway in the area and the only one with full width lanes and full-sized shoulders (and that only as far as Spruce Pine). All other roads—even the other primary highways—are narrow and winding. In fact, one of these "primary highways," NC 191, is partially dirt surfaced, one of three such "highways" in the North Carolina Blue Ridge.

*By Air* The closest airports are Asheville Regional, 50 miles to the south, and Tri-Cities Regional at Johnson City, Tennessee, 75 miles to the north.

*By Bus or Train* This region has no bus or passenger train service.

**MEDICAL EMERGENCIES** **Blue Ridge Regional Hospital** (spchospital.org; 828-765-4201, 877-777-8230; 125 Hospital Drive, Spruce Pine, NC 28714). This small regional hospital furnishes the only 24/7 emergency-room service in the region. You'll find it off US 19E on the south edge of Spruce Pine.

## ✷ Exploring the Area

To the south loom the tallest mountains in the East, with 18 peaks over 6,000 feet high, and another 47 peaks that top 5,000 feet; this remarkable range, **The Black Mountains**, is discussed in another chapter (see "The Blue Ridge Parkway Circles Asheville," *Wild Places*). On the north, the Roan and Bald Mountains separate this region from the Tennessee Valley with a series of 19 peaks that exceed 5,000 feet. In between, jumbled ridgelines form rough barriers that rise 2,000 feet above the floors of narrow valleys. Those valleys are farmed in the western half of the region (around Burnsville), with farmers favoring cattle, black burley tobacco, and nursery plants. Active farming tends to fade in the eastern half (toward Spruce Pine), giving way to timber, Christmas tree farms, and mineral mining.

BURNSVILLE TOWN SQUARE

From a practical point of view, however, the most prominent feature isn't a mountain. It's a linear valley, typically a half-mile wide and 2,600 feet above sea level, that runs due east–west across the center of this area. It has no

TOBACCO DRYING IN POSSUM TROT

entrance or exit, however; the Toe and the Cane Rivers flow into it from the south, follow it for a few miles—then carve their way out of it again, forcing a passage northward through the mile-high Bald and Roan Mountains. This valley contains the major towns of Spruce Pine, Micaville, and Burnsville, as well as this area's only highway, US 19/19E, now four-laned (with wonderful views) from I-26 to Burnsville.

**EXPLORING BY CAR NC 80** *Leg #1 (30.6 miles)*: Starting at the Blue Ridge Parkway, follow NC 80 north to its intersection with NC 226 in Bakersville.

*Leg #2 (23 miles)*: After exploring Bakersville, head north on NC 266 for 12.7 miles to the state line in a high gap; continue straight (as the road becomes TN 143) for 10.3 miles to Roan Mountain State Park.

This 54-mile drive features a great deal of beautiful mountain scenery, along with a surprising number of things to do—from exploring craft galleries to wandering through 5,000-foot high wildflower meadows. It starts at the Blue Ridge Parkway's intersection with NC 80, and follows paved state highways north across this region and into Tennessee. From the parkway, NC 80 quickly drops into the lovely South Toe River valley, with fine views over the river to **Mount Mitchell**, the highest peak in the East (see "The Blue Ridge Parkway Circles Asheville," *To See*). From here the highway descends through the scattered rural community of Celo, noted for its **fine crafts**; keep your eyes open for roadside galleries and workshops. It reaches the old railroad town of **Micaville** in 14 miles, with a small engine still parked on an isolated bit of abandoned siding. NC 80 crosses US 19, then quickly reaches the South Toe River and becomes a narrow country lane of astonishing twistiness, coiling past cemeteries and churches, through forests, and into fields with wide mountainy views. A new bridge crosses high above the North Toe River, with views of the historic **Clinchfield Railroad** running through its gorge. Just beyond, country lanes lead 5 miles to the famous craft school and artists' colony at **Penland**. (Side trip: go right on Snow Hill Road, SSR 1170, 2.4 miles to a right on Conley Ridge Road, SSR 1164, the campus being 2 miles farther.) Then NC 80 reaches the attractive village of **Kona**, with excellent views, a neat artist's gallery,

BARN IN A HIGH VALLEY, LICKSKILLIT

and a museum dedicated to the state's most notorious female murderer, **Frankie Silver**, whose husband's parts lie buried in three different graves behind the village's old church. Seven twisty, view-studded miles later, NC 80 ends at the settlement of **Loafers Glory**, named for the gang of old-timers that once gathered in front of its (now defunct) general store.

The second leg starts at the tiny county seat of **Bakersville**, just a few blocks in extent, with a half-block downtown by its old courthouse. **Dellinger Mill**, a 1901 overshot waterwheel still in operation, is 4 miles west. North of Bakersville, the route sweeps through lovely rural valleys, then climbs up to the mile-high **Carvers Gap** deep in the Roan Highlands. At the top, the **Appalachian Trail** leads to the right, following wide mountaintop meadows with incredible panoramic views. To the left, a paved side road leads 2.3 miles to **Roan Gardens**, a 600-acre natural rhododendron garden with wide views from two 6,000-foot peaks. Crossing into Tennessee, the highway becomes TN 143. This is the most spectacular part of the drive, as the highway becomes a narrow ledge carved into the cliff-like side of Roan Mountain, descending steeply with incredible views for 3.5 miles. Tennessee's **Roan Mountain State Park** (see "The Mountains of Northern Tennessee," *Wild Places*), 8.5 miles from Carvers Gap, makes for a good final destination and turnaround point.

**NC 197** *Leg #1* (*25 miles*): From Future I-26 (US 19/23) exit 15 (Barnardsville), follow NC 197 (partly gravel) east to US 19E at Burnsville.

*Leg #2* (*30.3 miles*): Continue north on NC 196 for 27.2 miles to the Tennessee state line, where it becomes TN 395; continue straight for 3.1 miles to Rock Creek Recreation Area.

Like nearby NC 80, NC 197 is remarkably primitive for a road marked as a primary highway. In fact, part of it is gravel surfaced—one of the North Carolina's three unpaved state highways. It gives this drive a certain charm. Its main charms, however, are its many wide river views, fine mountain views, and a remote county seat with surprisingly good shopping.

This 55-mile drive starts at Future I-26, Ashville's main north–south freeway. NC 197 is straight and easy at first, reaching the shrunken mountain town of **Barnardsville** in 6 miles, with the beautiful **Big Ivy** national forest track to the right down Dillingham Road (see "The Blue Ridge Parkway Circles Asheville," *Wild Places*). The pavement gives way to gravel in 4 more miles, as the "highway" switchbacks steeply uphill to reach Cane River Gap, 4,300 feet above sea level. To your right, the National Forest Service's Big Butt Trail allows the adventuresome to hike a 5,000-foot peak every mile for 6 miles, as the path follows a ridge to the **Mountains-to-Sea Trail** at the Blue Ridge Parkway. Beyond Cane River Gap, NC 197, still gravel, descends more switchbacks with good views, for a total of 10 miles of gravel surface. The road finally regains its paved surface and crosses the Cane River, then hugs the river for 11 miles with many lovely views. The first leg ends as NC 197 intersects US 19E in **Burnsville**. This pretty little county seat (left on US 19E, then right at the traffic light) has a handsome town square with very worthwhile craft shopping.

Past Burnsville, the highway climbs Green Mountain, giving good views both north and south, then continues through attractive rural countryside for a half-dozen miles to the wide and beautiful Toe River. From here, the highway will form a complex dance with the Toe River and the mountains that hem it in. First, NC 197 turns right to follow the Toe upstream for 4 miles, with unobstructed views over the river. After crossing the river, it reaches the community of Red Hill (whose general store makes good sandwiches), then turns back on itself to twist and turn 6 miles in the opposite direction, through some very remote and beautiful farmland. It regains the Toe River at Relief, a 10-mile drive but only 5 miles downstream. It then follows the Toe for another mile or so downstream, only to turn sharply right to again twist into the mountains. The highway is not yet done with the river, however, and will regain it—now merged with the Cane River and dubbed the Nolichucky—at Poplar. Look for the U.S. Forest Service's kayak launch site at Poplar; it marks the start of the dramatic **Nolichucky Gorge**. From Poplar, the highway swerves and switchbacks uphill to cross the Unaka Mountains into Tennessee at 3,370-foot Indian Grave Gap. There's a parking lot here, and an **Appalachian Trail** crossing. The gravel road to your right, although marked by the U.S. Forest Service as a scenic highway, was utterly impassable by passenger car when last inspected. **Erwin**, Tennessee, is 7 miles ahead on

GRAVEL LANE IN PIGEON ROOST

TN 395, passing **Rock Creek Recreation Area**, noted for its waterfall walk (see "The Mountains of Northern Tennessee," *Wild Places*). At Erwin, you can get on I-26 and return to Asheville.

**EXPLORING ON FOOT The Roan Highlands** Starting at Carver Gap on NC 216, this walk goes eastward through the wide meadows of the Roan Highlands to the northernmost 6,000-foot summit in the South, Grassy Ridge Bald. This undulating trail is 5 miles round-trip, with 1,000 feet of climbing (a third of it on the way back). Park in the Forest Service picnic area on the left side of the road, and take the **Appalachian Trail** across the road, through a split-rail fence, and into the mountaintop meadows. Both the views and the wind will increase steadily as you climb 300 feet up Round Bald, reaching the first of several 360-degree panoramas from its summit in 0.4 mile. The trail continues down to a small gap, then uphill to Jane Bald (1.1 miles), staying in grassy meadows with wildflowers and wide views the entire way. After a shallow gap, the trail starts on a long climb (600 feet in 0.7 mile) up Grassy Ridge Bald; when the Appalachian Trail slabs off the ridge crest to the left, continue on the side trail along the ridge. After passing through thick rhododendrons, the trail tops out on the 6,200-foot summit, with a full circle view from the top of the world. Return the way you came.

**The Overmountain Victory National Historic Trail** In the Colonial era, a footpath known as Bright's Trace crossed the Roan Highlands through its center at Yellow Gap, following flood-prone Roaring Creek on the eastern side. In September 1780 the frontier militia crossed the mountains on Bright's Trace and united with Piedmont militias in an attack on British forces at Kings Mountain, South Carolina—one of the most important American victories in the Revolution. The surviving segment of Bright's Trace in the Roan Highlands is commemorated as part of the **Overmountain Victory National Historic Trail**.

This walk takes the Overmountain Victory Trail from the end of the motorable Roaring Creek Road (SSR 1132), where a turnaround area offers wide views over the head of Roaring Creek Valley; to find it, follow US 19E north from Spruce Pine for 15 miles, on your left, then another 4.5 miles to the road's end. Now part of the Pisgah National Forest, this area was a private farm until the mid-1990s. It's still covered in meadows, with an apple orchard just below and a bright red barn surrounded by wide fields on the mountaintop opposite. The formal trail follows the gated Forest Service road gently uphill through forests. A much more interesting alternative is to take the informal trail downhill into the fields, then follow it up through wildflower meadows and apple orchards to the barn. Now an **Appalachian Trail** shelter, the barn gives a 180-degree view over Roaring Creek Valley and toward the Blue Ridge beyond; in 1988 the film *Winter People* (with Kurt Rus-

SCHOOL BUS IN JACKS CREEK VALLEY

THE NOLICHUCKY GORGE

sell) was filmed here. To continue, take the blue-blazed trail east, recovering the Overmountain Trail in a couple of hundred yards. The path goes uphill through open woods to Yellow Mountain Gap on the crest of the Roan. Here you will intersect with the Appalachian Trail, in the broad ridgetop meadows so characteristic of the **Roan Highlands**. Head east along the Appalachian Trail, going steeply uphill through wide open meadows, to reach the peak of Little Hump Mountain, with wide views in all directions. Return the way you came. If you go all the way to Little Hump Mountain's main summit, you will walk 5 miles round-trip with a 1,200-foot climb.





### LONG-DISTANCE PATHS

Throughout this chapter, the **Appalachian Trail** closely follows the border between North Carolina and Tennessee; this segment of the trail is described in the next chapter. On the southern edge of this chapter, **the Black Mountains**, with six dozen peaks over 5,000 feet high, present a wide variety of outstanding walks and hikes, centering on **The Mountains-to-Sea Trail** (see "The Blue Ridge Parkway Circles Asheville," *Exploring the Area*).

## ✷ Villages

**Burnsville** This beautiful little village centers around its classic town square. The square is a large, well-kept strolling space with lawns, trees, and flowers centering around its statue of an early-19th-century sea captain (Otway Burns, the town's namesake). Grouped around the square are the county courthouse, city hall, public library, and the town's 170- year-old coaching inn, the **Nu Wray Inn**. These are also several nice restaurants, gift shops, and craft galleries. Parking is free, with overflow parking two blocks west of the square.

**Micaville** This tiny town sits along the South Toe River bypassed by US 19E, halfway between Burnsville and Spruce Pine. It was for many years an important siding on the Yancey Railroad, a spur from the Clinchfield, and it is from those early years that much of Micaville's small center dates. During the 1970s the Yancey Railroad was abandoned so quickly that the tracks were left behind with a pony engine still sitting on them (and there to this day). The old Micaville General Store, attractively restored, is now a craft cooperative, while the Micaville Grille across the street is popular with locals.

**Spruce Pine** This railroad town along the North Toe River has long been supported by mineral mining, particularly feldspar. The mining continues today, with a large strip mine scarring the mountainside immediately above downtown, and another strip mine greeting tourists who approach the town from the west on US

**THE OVERMOUNTAIN VICTORY TRAIL—IS THIS A NATIONAL PARK?**

In 1980 President Jimmy Carter signed a law creating the Overmountain Victory National Historic Trail (nps.gov/ovvi), making it part of the National Trail System and putting it under the auspices of the National Park Service. He did this in order to commemorate the remarkable winter march of the Tennessee Valley militia 200 years earlier, which resulted in the American victory at Kings Mountain, South Carolina, and secured the western frontier for the new nation.

In all this, an important question was left a bit vague: Just what, exactly, is this national historic trail supposed to do? In 2005, 25 years into the planning process, the National Park Service stated that "the Trail is still being fully developed." A quarter-century is a fairly long development period.

So here's the skinny. The Overmountain Victory Trail is supposed to be a 330-mile long-distance hiking trail that parallels, as closely as possible, the actual route taken by the militias. It will start in Abingdon, Virginia, and end in Kings Mountain National Military Park, South Carolina. In doing so, it will create a link between the Blue Ridge's most important long-distance paths, the Appalachian Trail at Roan Mountain and the Mountains-to-Sea Trail at Linville Gorge Wilderness. But don't hold your breath. The National Park Service has created no planning corridor and has appropriated no money for purchasing right-of-way. And it doesn't expect to. It relies wholly on other people to create the trail segments, and limits itself to putting up nice signs along them. The National Park Service hopes that these trail segments will line up correctly someday, but has no specifics on how to bring this about. After more than 30 years of trying, they've managed to post signs along 60 miles of trail, nearly all in short, highly isolated segments. It is remarkably hard to find out where these trails are located, as the National Park Service publishes no guide, no map, and no single list of the segments.

Apart from that, the National Park Service has created a Commemorative Motor Route, and this is the only route shown on its official brochure. This route allows the Revolutionary War enthusiast to closely follow the march and locate all of the important points along the way. The park service also publishes a school curriculum and lends its sponsorship to an annual reenactment.

19E. Downtown Spruce Pine consists of two long blocks paralleling the riverside depot (still active with freight trains), with a lower level facing the depot and an upper level one story above that. There are a number of interesting shops on both levels, and plenty of free parking by the depot.

**Bakersville** The seat of Mitchell County, Bakersville is a tiny town with a scant one-block downtown next to its old courthouse. Located on NC 216 10 miles north of its much larger sibling, Spruce Pine, Bakersville is best known for the large number of fine craft artists who live in the surrounding valleys.





## ✷ Wild Places

**THE GREAT FORESTS** **The Roan Highlands** The 15,000 protected acres of the Highlands of Roan contain the largest concentration of grassy mountaintop balds in the East, 600 acres of natural rhododendron gardens, large tracts of Canadian-style spruce-fir forests, and more rare species that the Great Smoky Mountains National Park. John Fraser discovered the Catawba rhododendron here in 1787, and great early scientists such as Asa Gray and Elisha Mitchell studied its unique environments. Gray called it "without doubt the most beautiful mountain east of the Rockies," while Mitchell wrote, "It is the most beautiful of all the high mountains."

The Roan Highlands consist of a single wall of remote, high mountains along the North Carolina/Tennessee state line, stretching from Hughes Gap (SSR 1330, Buladean Road) eastward to the deep gap that carries US 19E. Most of it is within the Pisgah National Forest, with significant tracts protected by the Southern Appalachians Highlands Conservancy, The Nature Conservancy, and the State of Tennessee. Made up of hard old rocks, the crest of the Roan Highlands stays above 4,000 feet for nearly its entire length, with 5 miles of it more than a mile high. Its three peaks that top 6,000 feet are the last in the Appalachian Mountains until Mount Washington in New Hampshire, 800 miles to the north.

Despite heavy exploitation between 1890 and 1940, the Roan Highlands look much the same today as they did 160 years ago. In 1836, Mitchell wrote, "The top of the Roan may be described as a vast meadow without a tree to obstruct this prospect, where a person may gallop his horse for a mile or two with Carolina at his feet on one side and Tennessee on the other, and a green ocean of mountains rising in tremendous billows immediately around him." Gray rocky crags stick out of the knee-high grasses; wildflowers form carpets whipped by winds that average 25 miles per hour. Most astonishing are the panoramas, frequently extending in a complete circle around the viewer, continuing unbroken for mile after mile. Even the bureaucracy of the U.S. Department of Agriculture is impressed, writing in a 1974 planning document, "There is no other area that offers such extensive panoramic views of the high country of the southern Appalachians. Unique is not, in this sense, misleading."

The Roan Highlands are bordered by two roads (Buladean Road on the west and US 19E on the east), and crossed by one other—NC 216/TN 143, making the climb at mile-high **Carver Gap**. Carver Gap is the Roan's main access point for recreationalists, with a side road leading west to **Roan Gardens** and the **Appalachian Trail** leading east through miles of open

HORSE PULL COMPETITION IN BURNSVILLE

meadows. The crest of the Roan is followed closely by the Appalachian Trail for its entire length, a very difficult through-walk over steep and rocky paths. Side trails tend to be even worse, and the rugged slopes are seldom visited. One notable exception to this is the head of **Appalachian Trail**, extremely scenic and easily reached, the location of a Colonial-era trace that the Overmountain militia followed on their secret march to attack the British at Kings Mountain.

**The Black Mountains** South of Burnsville and Micaville looms the tallest summit in the East, **Mount Mitchell** (see "The Blue Ridge Parkway Circles Asheville," *To See*), one of the ten 6,000-foot peaks in the Black Mountains. The eastern base of the Blacks, rising out of the South Toe River, is almost entirely owned by the Pisgah National Forest. The Blacks typically rise 3,800 feet above the Toe River in a linear distance of 3 miles, creating an unbroken barrier 7 miles long. This great steep slope is banded with forests, each band appropriate for the climate induced by its elevation and topography—the bands occasionally broken by great rock slides at the steepest slopes. While much of the area was logged, the very steepness spared large tracts along these slopes, and some trails climb through old-growth forests. Five paths make the climb up the face of the Blacks, all of them scenic, and all of them difficult all-day slogs. The whole wall of the Blacks can be admired from the South Toe River at **Carolina Hemlocks Recreation Area**, a great swimming hole.

**The Nolichucky Gorge** At the end of their long run, the Toe and the Cane Rivers merge together to become the Nolichucky River, large enough to carve a gorge straight through the high Unaka Mountains. The Pisgah National Forest owns nearly all of the land on both sides of the gorge, as well as the gorge itself. No roads or paths penetrate the bottom of the gorge—just the **Clinchfield Railroad** hugging tight to the riverbank, still under very heavy use as a through goods line (and ludicrously dangerous for walking). A small village, known as Lost Cove, thrived for many years at the bottom of the gorge with no automobile access of any sort—until the railroad ceased passenger service, and its inhabitants had to walk in and out. The upper edge of the gorge can be reached on foot for stunning cliff-top views, though not without difficulty; the easiest route is a Forest Service logging road that runs west from **NC 197** at the state line, dropping 1,000 feet in 6 miles.

Yet more remarkable views can be found from the easily accessible top of Flattop Mountain, a large Pisgah National Forest tract on the west side of the gorge. Here a good gravel road leads to an old farm site near the top of the mountain. The shortest of climbs uphill leads to broad meadows (maintained by the Forest Service for wildlife), stretching for a mile along the rolling top of this table-like mountain. Explore around—it will take a while to find all the vistas from all of the fields. Views include wide panoramas west over the Nolichucky Gorge to the Highlands of Roan, then east toward the Bald Mountains. The marked footpath leads downhill to the remains of Lost Cove village—a very difficult walk by all reputes. The access road to Flattop Mountain, Howell Branch Road (SSR 1415), starts 5.3 miles along US 19W on the North Carolina side of the state line; when you pass through a gate after 1.2 miles you'll be on the gravel Forest Service Road 278 for 3 more miles to its end at a closed gate. This is the old farmstead; the path is uphill to your right.

**RECREATION AREAS** **Elk River Falls Recreation Area** Open all year Located off US 19E near the Tennessee border, this lovely little recreation area offers several picnic tables, a long stretch of Elk River with grassy banks for fishing—and a large waterfall, where this wide and powerful river pours over a 50-foot rock ledge. A short path clambers down to the base of the falls, and a long rocky spur leads out to a fine view.

**PICNIC AREAS** **Ray-Cort Recreation Park, Burnsville** Located in the town of Burnsville, this county park centers on a handsome small mountain stream flowing gently through a tree-shaded draw, with picnic tables scattered along its length. To find it, take the side street north from the town square about five blocks.

**Riverside Park, Spruce Pine** Located across the North Toe River from downtown Spruce Pine, and linked to it by a 410-foot footbridge, Riverside Park offers a shelter and a row of shaded picnic shelters, as well as a paved walking/jogging loop that runs by the river.

## ✷ To See

### HISTORIC SITES

**The McElroy House (Rush Wray Museum of Yancey County History)** (828-682-3671; Burnsville, NC 28714). Located two blocks off Burnsville's town square above the Yancey County Visitor's Center, this large 1840s-era farmhouse is home to the Rush Wray Museum of Yancey County History. It's now a simple and attractive home, but in the ante-bellum era it was the fanciest mansion in this poor, remote corner of the world. During the Civil War it served as the headquarters for the Home Guard, the state forces charged with securing the (largely Unionist) mountain coves and hollows for the Confederacy. Today, its kitchen and living area have been restored to exhibit early mountain farm life, while other exhibits tell about Cane River archeological sites, the Civil War in the Toe and Cane Valleys, and the history and people of the McElroy House. Traditional food and craft demonstrations are made throughout the summer and fall; call for details.

**Dellinger Mill** (spchospital.org; e-mail: jackdellinger@bellsouth.net; 828-688-1009; Cane Creek Rd. [SR 1211], Bakersville, NC 28705). Open 10 AM–5 PM; June–September: every third Sat. October–November: Mon.–Sat. This operating overshot water mill has been grinding corn for the Bakersville area since 1867. Still owned by its original family, the current National Register structure was built of chestnut in 1901, when the original mill was washed out in a flood. All but the flume and mill dam are original to the 1901 structure, including the giant metal overshot wheel and the huge granite mill stones. This is a working mill, producing stone-ground corn throughout the corn harvest season. You'll find it 4 miles east of Bakersville on Cane Creek Road (SSR 1211).

**CULTURAL SITES** **Penland School of Crafts** (www.penland.org; e-mail: info@penland.org; 828-765-2359; fax: 828-765-7389; P.O. Box 37, Penland, NC 28765). Gallery and Visitor's Center: 10 AM–noon and 1 PM–5 PM, Tues.–Sat.; noon–5 PM, Sun.; closed Mon. Campus tours Tuesday and Thursday by appointment. One of the most distinguished craft schools in America, Penland was founded as a weaver's cooperative in 1923, by local schoolteacher Lucy Morgan. Miss Morgan brought in instructors to improve the weavers' skills—and was surprised by the outpouring of interest in professional level craft instruction. In 1929, she formally opened the Penland School to offer regular schedules of instruction.

**KONA, NC (FRANKIE & CHARLIE SILVER)**

Kona resident Frankie Silver (Mrs. Francis Stewart Silver) may not have been the first woman hanged in North Carolina, but she was certainly the most notorious. Three days before Christmas 1832, in her Kona log cabin and with her infant daughter looking on, the petite and pretty 18-year-old chopped husband Charlie into pieces and burned him in the fireplace. The mountain folk song "Ballad of Frankie Silver" (not to be confused with the Delta blues song "Frankie & Johnny") attributed the murder to jealousy—but the real motive was Charlie's brutal abuse. Bestselling author Sharyn McCrumb, whose grandparents lived nearby, has written a fine (and very insightful) novel on the subject, *The Ballad of Frankie Silver.*

Modern-day Kona is a lovely little mountain settlement straddling scenic **NC** 80, 6 miles north of US 19E. Kona occupies a set of meadowy hilltops that drop from the old Baptist church, past the new Baptist church, then straight down to the gorge of the Toe River and the **Clinchfield Railroad** below. The old Baptist church sits by NC 80 surrounded by the Silver Cemetery. The Silver family gives pride of place to their common ancestor, Revolutionary War veteran George Silver, who received the surrounding square mile of land as reward for his service in the Patriot army. However, most tourists are interested in his grandson Charlie's graves—three of them, as they kept finding bits of Charlie hidden in the snow. (After Frankie was hung she was buried behind a tavern near Morganton, now on private land.) The Silver Cemetery is extremely well kept, with banks covered in wildflowers and broad views westward from its grassy top. The old wooden church serves as a museum for the Silver clan, with many interesting exhibits on the notorious murder. The original Silver homestead, built by George in 1806, still stands in the village, on private lands. South of the cemetery is the colorful Mountain Hill Country Gallery, the working studio of painters Pat and Dan Dowd.

By the way, that infant daughter survived, was raised by Frankie's mother, and prospered as much as anyone could in the mountains after the Civil War; she has left more than a hundred known descendants.

Over the years, nine other craft areas have been added: books and paper, clay, drawing, glass, iron, metals, photography, printmaking, and wood.

Then as now, Penland is a serious school for craft professionals and dedicated amateurs. Completely residential, its classes, studios, and student buildings wander over a pastoral 400-acre campus 5 miles northwest of Spruce Pine. Straddling both sides of a twisting country lane, the campus has an informal, slightly shabby look, with buildings of every conceivable 20th-century style. Intense summer programs are one to two weeks in length, while autumn and spring see eight-week in-depth sessions in selected subjects. An old school houses the gallery and visitors center, with excellent rotating displays of affiliated artists. Campus tours are available, by appointment, on Tuesdays and Thursdays.

**Potters of the Roan** (www.pottersoftheroan.com; e-mail: info@pottersoftheroan.com; P.O. Box 554, Bakersville, NC 28705). This cooperative unites 11 potters—all with ties to the Penland School—with studios scattered throughout the mountain valleys surrounding Bakersville. All 11 members open their studios (many of them in extraordinarily scenic locations) to the public. For a brochure giving contact information, a map and directions, and pictures of the work of all 11 potters, contact the cooperative at info@pottersoftheroan.com, or ask the Mitchell County Chamber of Commerce.

**Toe River Crafts** (828-675-4555; Hwy. 80 South, Burnsville, NC 28714). 10 AM–5 PM, Fri.–Sat.; noon–5 PM, Sun. Limited off-season hours. This modest old board-and-batten building, 7 miles south of Micaville on NC 80, is home to a cooperative of local artisans who specialize in a variety of contemporary crafts. Staffed by cooperative members, this gallery features pottery, woodworking, textiles, fibers, glass, paper, metals, toys, photography, prints, watercolors, and needlework.

**GARDENS AND PARKS** 🐾 ♿ **Roan Gardens** Closed in winter. $3 per car. Six hundred acres of natural rhododendron gardens cover two 6,000-foot peaks deep within the Pisgah National Forest. Just off NC 216 on the state line, Roan Mountain Gardens offers a mile of high ridgetop meadows and rhododendron balds, with stunning views. Managed as a park by the U.S. Forest Service (who levies an admissions charge), this site has three major activity areas. First after the entrance station is a ridgetop parking lot with picnic tables; a trail leads right over meadows to the site of a long-gone 1880s hotel, and left uphill to more meadow views. It is here that the **Appalachian Trail** climbs up to its last southern peak above 6,000 feet, Roan High Knob (6,285 feet, 18th highest in the East). A half-mile up the road, a small information booth, toilets, and picnic area on the left mark the center of the gardens. Here a disabled accessible trail loops 0.3 mile through spectacular rhododendrons (blooming mid- to late June), with a platform giving wide views across the Toe River Valley to the Black Mountains. Continuing to the end of the road and the park's third and final picnic area, an easy walking path leads 1.2 miles round-trip to Roan High Bluff, at 6,367 feet the 12th highest summit in the East. Here a platform overlook built over rocky crags gives a clifftop view over the broken mountains of the Toe Valley.

## ✶ To Do

**STABLES** **Springmaid Mountain** (888-297-0725, 828-765-2353; 2171 Henredon Rd., Spruce Pine, NC 28777). These stables offer 1-hour trail rides on their own 400-acre property, south of Spruce Pine near Altapass. Its namesake mountain reflects an early owner, a mattress manufacturer.

**GOLF** **Grassy Creek Golf & Country Club** (828-765-7436; 101 Golf Course Rd., Spruce Pine, NC 28777). Open April–October. This 18-hole course, built in 1957 by Ross Taylor, sits a mile south of Spruce Pine on NC 226, near the Blue Ridge Parkway. You'll find it a hilly course with good views of the surrounding mountains.

**Mountain Glen Golf Course** (828-733-5804; fax: 828-733-5809; Hwy. 194, Newland, NC 28657). This well-kept 18-hole course, located a few miles north of Newland off NC 194, offers surprisingly level fairways and water hazards on 16 holes.

## ✷ Lodging

### COUNTRY INNS AND HOTELS

**Pinebridge Inn** (www.pinebridgeinn.com; 800-365-5059, 828-765-5543; 207 Pinebridge Ave., Spruce Pine, NC 28777). This hotel occupies a 1920s two-story brick high school at the center of Spruce Pine, in a quiet residential neighborhood. Beautifully landscaped and kept, the 44-room hotel is linked with Spruce Pine's terraced downtown by a lighted 400-foot pedestrian bridge across the North Toe River. The hotel's two buildings, separated by a courtyard, are lovely 1920s school-district Gothic, and the rooms retain their high ceilings and large windows. Next door, the former school's former gymnasium, a plain modern structure, houses a recreation center under separate management. Wooded riverside parks, also adjacent, offer walking and jogging paths. The nicely decorated rooms range from normal size to large, and two housekeeping units are available as well. Room rates include a continental breakfast.

**BED & BREAKFAST INNS** **The Terrell House** (www.terrellhousebandb.com; 828-682-4505; 109 Robertson St., Burnsville, NC 28714). Built in the early 1900s as a dormitory for a private girls school, this large old Colonial-style home sits on a quiet residential street in Burnsville. Reminiscent of an old plantation house, it's clad in white clapboard and surrounded by well-kept gardens; white columns hold a two-story roof over its front porch. Common areas include a back garden with a gazebo, a cozy parlor with late Victorian antiques and facing sofas, and a formal dining room where a full breakfast is served on fine china. The six guest rooms are all normal to cozy in size, and are furnished individually in country-style antiques and reproductions.

✐ **The Celo Inn** (celoinn.com; 828-675-5132; 45 Seven Mile Ridge Rd., Burnsville, NC 28714). This five-room bed & breakfast occupies a long two-story log frame building, sitting by the South Toe River, in a grove of old trees. Located in the remote Celo community, about 8 miles south of Burnsville on NC 80 and not far from the Blue Ridge Parkway, the inn is well known and well respected in the small, but national caliber, artists' community that spreads itself through Celo. The inn, a cosponsor of the Burnsville Metric, is particularly welcoming to bicyclers.

✐ **Richmond Inn Bed & Breakfast** (richmondinnbandb.com; e-mail: info@richmondinnbandb.com; 877-765-6993, 828-765-6993; 51 Pine Ave., Spruce Pine, NC 28777). This eight-room bed & breakfast sits on a residential back lane, three blocks uphill from downtown Spruce Pine. It's a large, white clapboard Dutch Colonial house from the mid-20th century, sitting on a high stone terrace with dormers, bay windows, and a wide porch looking out over Spruce Pine to the mountains beyond. Guests share a comfortable parlor, furnished with antiques in a restrained country style. Rooms range from comfortable sized to large, and are individually decorated with antiques. The full breakfast is served in a formal dining room overlooking the garden.

**CABIN RENTALS Laurel Oaks Farm** (e-mail: laureloaks@main.nc.us; 800-528-7356, 828-688-2652; 7334 NC 80, Bakersville, NC 28705). These two cabins sit on a sheep farm in the wooded hills south of Bakersville, on scenic NC 80. One modern and one an old-style log cabin, both of these comfortable, fully equipped cabins have views from their porches. The farm has two trout ponds, on-property walking paths, and a border on the Toe River, as well as a sheep herd and a llama.

## ✷ Where to Eat

**EATING OUT The Garden Deli** (www.garden-deli.com; 828-682-3946; 107 Town Sq., Burnsville, NC 28714). Open 11 AM–2 PM, Mon.–Sat. A Burnsville lunchtime fixture since 1987, the Garden Deli features patio seating shaded by willows and wisterias, overlooking the lovely town square. Inside seating for this year-round café is in a wood-paneled room with bay windows and a large fireplace. The menu consists of soups, salads, and sandwiches, with a selection of fresh-made sides and desserts. Many of the sandwiches are New York deli style, with good quality meat that's sliced thin and piled high. The menu also has specialty items, such as pork barbeque pit-smoked on the premises.

## ✷ Entertainment

### *Burnsville*

**Parkway Playhouse** (www.parkwayplayhouse.com; e-mail: info@parkwayplayhouse.com; 828-682-4285; 202 Green Mountain Dr., P.O. Box 1432, Burnsville, NC 28714). Plays start at 8 PM, most summer weekends. Reservations are required; call on weekday afternoons. Founded in 1947 as a summer outlet for Greensboro University students, the Parkway Playhouse is the state's oldest continuously operating theater. Now a semi-professional company, it features a combination of old Broadway standards, children's plays, and Appalachian-themed plays from its giant barnlike theater down a (well-sign posted) back street in Burnsville.

### *Micaville*

**Young's Mountain Music** (828-765-4365; Hwy. 19E on the Yancey/Mitchell County line. Saturday, from 7 PM. $2 donation. A revered mountain tradition, Young's is noted as a venue for authentic, old-time (pre-bluegrass) Appalachian music from serious local musicians. It features live mountain music and dancing (clogging, two-step line, and square) every Saturday night, with nonalcoholic beverages, a snack bar, and homemade desserts. The large, nondescript building is located just off US 19E, halfway between Burnsville and Spruce Pine on the Yancey-Mitchell county line.

## ✷ Selective Shopping

### *Spruce Pine*

**Twisted Laurel Gallery** (828-765-1562; 333 Locust Ave., Spruce Pine, NC 28777). April–December: 10 AM–5 PM, Tues.–Sat. January–March: 10 AM–5 PM, Fri.–Sat. Established in 1989 by third generation clockmaker Luther Stroup, this downtown Spruce Pine gallery, just across from the railroad depot, features the work of over 130 craft artists, all from the Spruce Pine and Penland area. Beautifully displayed in this large, airy storefront, the art covers just about every medium and style imaginable, with a particularly rich selection of glass art.

**Blue Moon Book Store** (828-766-5000; 271 Oak Ave., Spruce Pine, NC, 28777). 10 AM–6 PM, Mon.–Sat. Located on the upper level of Spruce Pine's terraced downtown, this large storefront bookstore offers a wide selection of regional titles and children's books, used books, art (particularly notecards) by local crafters, and a good café. Blue Moon sponsors a program of music, storytelling, and readings in the store all year long.

## ✷ Special Events

**SPRING** **Spring Studio Tour** First weekend in May. Sponsored by the local nonprofit Toe River Arts Council, this annual event opens more than 50 artists' studios and galleries to the public, spread throughout the Burnsville and Spruce Pine areas.

**Spring Arts Festival** Last Saturday in May. This annual arts festival, held in front of the Yancey County Courthouse in Burnsville, combines local artists, live art demonstrations, and food sponsored by local nonprofits.

**Avery Heritage Fest** First Saturday in June. Held in Newland's beautiful town square, in front of the old Avery County Courthouse, this festival emphasizes genealogy and mountain history, with local history writers, genealogy tents, Civil and Revolutionary War reenactors, and an authentic 19th-century circuit riding preacher. The local church serves up a barbeque lunch.

**SUMMER** **Rhododendron Festival** (www.bakersville.com/rhod.html; e-mail: hensley.bob@gmail.com; P.O. Box 407, Bakersville, NC 28705). Last weekend in July. For more than a half-century, the little mountain town of Bakersville has celebrated the magnificent rhododendron display with a large street fair, including street dancing, a car show, a beauty pageant, and a number of bicycling events.

**Burnsville Fourth of July Celebration** Independence Day. This lively town square celebration includes an all-day band competition, craft booths, local nonprofits selling homemade items and food, fire trucks, a wagon train, and special activities for children.

**Spruce Pine Independence Day Celebration** This downtown street celebration includes square dancing, food, and fireworks. It's preceded by a three-day town-wide sidewalk sale.

**Mount Mitchell Crafts Fair** First weekend in August. Free. This town square crafts fair, founded in 1956, features over 200 local and regional craft artists, selected by the Crafts Fair Selection Committee for quality, originality, and variety. There is ongoing bandstand entertainment that emphasizes mountain music and dance, as well as a number of food vendors.

**AUTUMN** **Overmountain Victory Trail March** Mid- to late September. Every year the Overmountain Victory Trail Association commemorates America's amazing Revolutionary War victory at Kings Mountain, South Carolina, by reenacting the frontier militia's cross-mountain march. The festivities start with a mid-September reenactors' camp at the **Museum of North Carolina Minerals**, in which both British and Patriot sides plot strategies, drill, and practice shooting their black powder muskets. Then a week later (roughly around the anniversary of the events on September 25), the frontier militia marches across the mountains to dinner and encampment at Spruce Pine, followed by a march at the **Orchards at Altapass**.

# THE MOUNTAINS OF NORTHERN TENNESSEE

**GUIDANCE—TOWNS AND COUNTRYSIDE** **Elizabethton-Carter County Chamber of Commerce** (www.tourelizabethton.com; e-mail: director@elizabethtonchamber.com; 423-547-3850; fax: 423-547-3854; 500 Veterans Memorial Pkwy., Elizabethton, TN 37644). The Chamber maintains a welcome center that includes picnic facilities, on the eastern edge of Elizabethton, on US19E/321.

**Unicoi County Chamber of Commerce** (www.unicoicounty.org; e-mail: info@unicoicounty.org; 423-743-3000; fax: 423-743-0942; 100 South Main Ave., P.O. Box 713, Erwin, TN 37650). The Unicoi County Chamber maintains a visitors center and information desk in one of downtown Erwin's restored historic buildings.

**Johnson County Chamber of Commerce** (www.johnsoncountychamber.org; e-mail: info@johnsoncountychamber.org; 423-727-5800; P.O. Box 66, Mountain City, TN 37683). This chamber covers the northernmost third of this chapter's area, and runs a log cabin visitors center in the county seat of Mountain City, on US 421 on the south end of town.

**GUIDANCE—PARKS AND FORESTS** **Watauga Ranger District, Cherokee National Forest** (423-735-1500; P.O. Box 400 [TN 173 north of town center], Unicoi, TN 37692). 8:00 AM–4:30 PM, Mon.–Fri. This large modern office, just east of I-26 off exit 23, has a friendly information desk and bookshop, with full information on the forests in this chapter.

**GETTING THERE** *By Car* I-26, confusingly signposted east–west, provides north–south access to this region with continuous freeway between Charleston, South Carolina, and the Great Valley. I-81, running the length of the Great Valley, links this area with Atlanta and Pennsylvania.

Three important U.S. highways cross the mountainous state line to link this chapter's area with adjacent chapters in North Carolina. US 19E runs from Burnsville and Spruce Pine, North Carolina, to Elizabethton, Tennessee; the Tennessee side is good quality, but the North Carolina side is poor. US 321 links Boone, North Carolina, with Elizabethton, North Carolina; its North Carolina side is also pretty inferior, but still beats US 19E all hollow. Finally, US 421 runs between Boone, North Carolina, and Mountain City, Tennessee, and is good throughout.

*By Air* **Tri-Cities Airport** (www.triflight.com; e-mail: comments@TRIflight.com; 423-325-6000; fax: 423-325-6060; 2525 Hwy. 75, Blountville, TN 37617). The

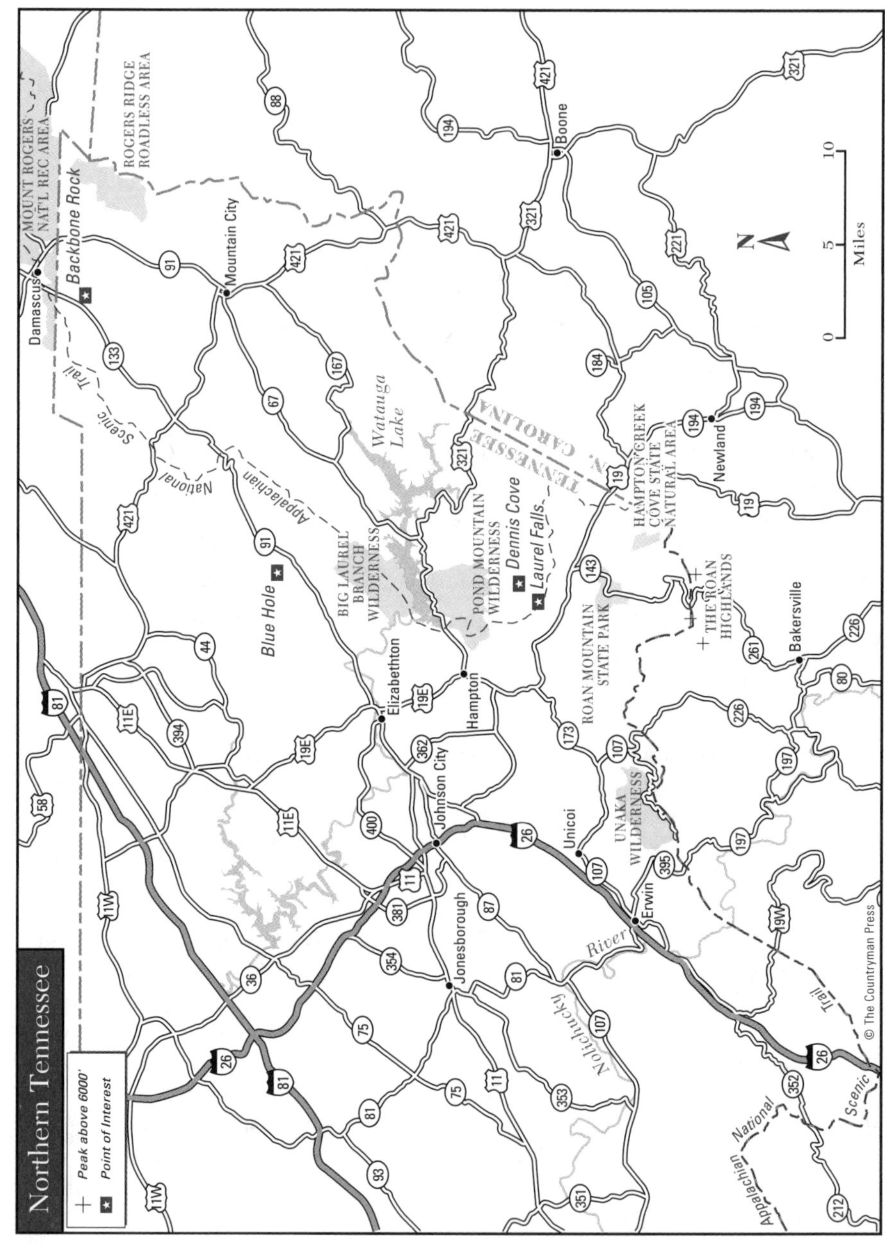


"tri-cities" are Johnson City, Kingsport, and Bristol. Tri-Cities Airport is located in Tennessee's Great Valley in the middle of the triangle formed by the three cities, off I-81's exit 63. This is about 25 miles west of this region, and much farther for any other area of this book. Tri-Cities has four commuter airlines furnishing nonstops to seven different hubs, and it's not uncommon to find good and/or cheap connections to it.

*By Bus or Train* Greyhound Bus service runs to Johnson City, immediately outside this area. There are no passenger trains in eastern Tennessee. (Not even Chattanooga!)

**MEDICAL EMERGENCIES** **Sycamore Shoals Hospital** (www.msha.com/facility.cfm; 423-542-1300; 1501 West Elk Ave., Elizabethton, TN 37643). Elizabethton's 121-bed hospital offers full emergency service from its facility on the west end of town on US 321.

**Unicoi County Memorial Hospital** (www.ucmhnet.org; 423-743-3141; Greenway Circle, Erwin, TN 37650). Erwin's 94-bed hospital is located in town, 1 mile south of downtown via TN 81 (former US 23) and two blocks to the left. It has full emergency services.

**Johnson County Community Hospital** (www.msha.com/jcch.cfm; 423-727-1100; 1901 South Shady St., Mountain City, TN 37683). This new hospital, run by a regional not-for-profit, has a 24/7 emergency department at its campus 2 miles south of Mountain City on US 421.

## ✷ Exploring the Area

**EXPLORING BY CAR** **Wilbur Lake and Watauga Dam Drive** *Start: From Elizabethton, take TN 91 east for 3.4 miles to a right on Blue Springs Road.*

The drive (6.8 miles): Follow Blue Springs Road for 1 mile; then continue straight on Steel Bridge Road for 0.8 mile, where it crosses a steel bridge and becomes Wilbur Dam Road; continue on Wilbur Dam Road to its end in 5.2 miles.

This exceptionally pretty and eventful drive, less than 7 miles long, leads through the Tennessee Valley Authority's (TVA) large and attractive recreation area, which stretches from Wilbur Dam, along the 3-mile length of Wilbur Lake, then over a gap to a hill above Watauga Lake. It starts with a short drive through well-kept farmland, then makes a sharp turn to cross the Watauga River on an historic one lane steel truss bridge. It enters the TVA recreation area in another 1.8 miles, with immediate views on the left of Wilbur Dam. This 1912 concrete structure is 77 feet high; the best view is from the canoe launch at its foot. From Wilbur Dam the road closely follows the banks of narrow Wilbur Lake, with several picnic areas, boat launches, and places to park and fish. The scenery here is particularly beautiful, with cliffs rising out of the opposite shore of the lake and the impressive 50-foot Laurel Branch Waterfall opposite one of the picnic areas. At a fork in this road, the right-hand road follows the river for more picnicking and fishing, while the main road goes left and climbs to Iron Mountain Gap. Here the **Appalachian Trail** crosses the park road; to the right it goes 1 mile to cross the top of **Watauga Dam**, while to the left it enters **Big Laurel Branch Wilderness**. Beyond the gap, the park road drops to **Watauga Lake** at a large and well-kept TVA picnic area, with wide views from a glassed overlook, and a short trail to a view over the 330-foot earthen Watauga Dam.

**EXPLORING ON FOOT** **Laurel Falls on the Appalachian Trail** The trailhead parking is 3 miles up paved Dennis Cove Road (FS 50), which intersects US 321 5 miles south of Elizabethton in the small town of Hampton, marked by a brown recreation sign. This short section of the Appalachian Trail follows an old logging

LAKE WATAUGA FROM THE TVA VISITORS CENTER

railroad grade along the rim of the Laurel Fork Gorge, to end at the lovely Laurel Falls. It is 2.5 miles long with no meaningful elevation change until the steep and difficult plunge down to the foot of the falls; the walk out on the railroad bed is worthwhile in itself. Take the **Appalachian Trail** to the left (north), along a level railroad grade. The trail quickly reaches Laurel Fork, an impressively large and violent stream, noted for its trout fishing. At this point the trail enters the **Pond Mountain Wilderness**, and stays there for the rest of the walk. After 0.7 mile the trail enters a cut, then drops steeply down into a gorge as the old railroad grade ends at a long-vanished trestle. The trail crosses the stream at an impressive footbridge on two rock piers, leading to a ledge in a sheer cliff of exposed quartzite; then the trail rises again to the railroad grade in a flight of 60 stone steps. From this point on the gorge drops away from the level trail very quickly, showing large white quartzite cliffs through the trees. At 1.2 miles the Appalachian Trail plunges steeply off the railroad grade and down into the gorge, reaching Laurel Falls after 265 very difficult stone steps. Alas, there are no views of the falls from the top of this drop, and those determined to see the falls have quite a climb in front of them. Most will find it worth the work. Laurel Fork stair-steps down a 30-foot thickness of plunging quartzite, forming a waterfall about as wide as it is high and framed by gray-white cliffs. Return the way you came.

**Historic Elizabethton Walking Tour** (888-547-3852, 423-547-3850) Elizabethton's Chamber of Commerce (888-547-3852) has established one of the nicest and best-marked historic town walks of the mountains. The short path, starting at the City Hall downtown, wanders past 30 historic buildings and sites along this small town's three-block downtown and along the elegant Doe River. Highlights include elegant southern mansions, lovely riverside parks, an authentic **covered bridge**, and a red 1921 fire engine (not to mention the tallest fir tree in Tennessee, in front

THE APPALACHIAN TRAIL RUNS BENEATH CLIFFS IN THE POND MOUNTAIN WILDERNESS

of one of those mansions). The excellent brochure is available from the Chamber of Commerce, just east of town on US 19E/321.

**LONG-DISTANCE PATHS The Appalachian Trail** This chapter's area contains 113 miles of the Appalachian Trail, starting at the Nolichucky River (1,680 feet), and ending at the Tennessee-Virginia state line. The first 46 miles of this section continue to follow the variously named mountain ridge that forms the Tennessee–North Carolina state line. The trail crosses the Nolichucky on a back road bridge and follows the Nolichucky for about a mile, then gradually climbs the state line mountain (here named the Unaka Mountains), reaching the exceptionally attractive ridgeline meadows at 4,400-foot Beauty Spot after 11 miles, and topping out at 5,180-foot Unaka Mountain, in a spruce-fir forest 2 miles later. It continues along a lower section of the same ridge (now called Iron Mountain), reaching the renowned **Roan Highlands** 40 miles from the Nolichucky, for 9 miles of high altitude forests and meadows, with sweeping views. The price of this spectacular walk is a 2,245-foot climb, starting at 4,040-foot Hughes Gap (accessible from Hughes Gap Road, a rough gravel lane off TN 143) and ending at 6,285-foot Roan High Knob—the last 6,000-foot elevation until New Hampshire. At the end of this stretch, the trail crosses US 19E and turns deep into Tennessee.

A rare farmland walk brings the trail past (without visiting) the **Dennis Cove Waterfalls**, then into the **Pond Mountain Wilderness**, past **Laurel Fork Falls**, leaving the wilderness at US 321 (75 miles from the Nolichucky). Here it slabs above **Watauga Lake** and crosses **Watauga Dam**, then climbs to the crest of linear Iron Mountain. It follows this straight crest, never very far from 3,600 feet, through the **Big Laurel Branch Wilderness** and beyond, staying on the ridge top for 14 miles with some good views along the way. It then zags west to the next linear ridge, Holston Mountain, and follows its 3,600-foot crest to the Virginia state line.

## ✷ Villages

**Elizabethton** Viewed from the main highway, Elizabethton appears to be a modest factory town, a bit on the skids. The usual bypass sprawl, along with an early-20th-century rayon factory, lines US 321, shielding drivers from any accidental views of the Watauga River paralleling the highway. However, Elizabethton holds a secret: turn off the highway, wander into its center, and a charming historic village opens up—a brick-front downtown with a riverfront park, a beautiful white clapboard **covered bridge** reflected in a weir, a line of Victorian and antebellum homes, and a large Veterans Monument in a circle by the old brick courthouse. Elizabethton's center looks as if it would be more at home in New England than in the rural South.

Located at the confluence of the Watauga and Doe Rivers, Elizabethton was one of the earliest trans-mountain settlements south of Virginia. These settlers were well west of any law or government, in Cherokee lands where settlement was prohibited by British law; so they formed the Watauga Association, to establish and enforce laws, and lease land from the Cherokees. The association held its first court under a sycamore tree near the current downtown, a site marked by a section of the original tree (which died in 1987). Guarded by the British army at nearby Fort Watauga and with good fords over two difficult rivers, Elizabethton became an important frontier settlement. The old fort, at **Sycamore Shoals** on the western edge of town, has been reconstructed and now houses a fine local museum.

Elizabethton remained small throughout most of the 19th century, acquiring several antebellum mansions, which still stand today, as well as a fine covered bridge, which still crosses the Doe River in a single 134-foot span. However, the town quickly became a lumbering and factory center when the railroad arrived in the late 1880s. The first railroad was the famous "Tweetsie" Railroad, a narrow gauge that crossed the mountains from **Boone**, North Carolina. In the early 20th century, Elizabethton became a rayon-manufacturing center, with its two early factories finally closing in the 1990s.

**Erwin** Located at the foot of the Unaka Mountains not far from the Tennessee–North Carolina line, Erwin is, and always has been, an industrial town. It is in no way polluted, defaced, or ugly; but neither does it make much of an attempt to put on a pretty face for visitors. Purposely founded as Unicoi County's seat in 1879, Erwin became a small city when, in 1908, the **Clinchfield Railroad** chose it as its major repair yard (a big deal in the days of temperamental steam engines), and later its corporate headquarters. The Clinchfield's bold attempt to slice straight through the heart of the Appalachians was a financial success, and Erwin thrived along with its railroad. During this period, Southern Potteries operated a successful hand-painted china factory in Erwin, turning out the Blue Ridge China now prized by collectors. However, the pottery closed in 1957 (a victim of post-war foreign competition), and the Clinchfield offices closed in 1983 when CSX bought it out. Not that Erwin suffered much from these closures; it had already acquired a new major industry—uranium processing (mainly for naval ships). CSX still maintains a yard in Erwin, servicing the very busy line that the Clinchfield built. Erwin has an attractive, old-fashioned downtown, with several shops that are worth a visit. You will find Erwin just off I-26, the first (or last) town in Tennessee as you travel from (or to) North Carolina.

**Mountain City** This attractive county seat, with a population of 2,400, is the main town for the northern portion of this chapter. It centers on a 3 x 4 gridiron of streets set on a hill between two stream valleys, with an old-fashioned downtown facing TN 91 through its center, and Victorian homes nearby. Modern services, however, have moved south of town along US 421, which bypasses it on its west. A modern-built log cabin on US 421 south of town serves as its visitors center.

## ✷ Wild Places

**THE GREAT FORESTS** **Big Laurel Branch Wilderness** The wilderness is located 6 miles east of Elizabethton via Siam Road, following the signs for Watauga Dam. Cliffs rise straight up out of still lake water; a stream plummets over the edge and falls 50 feet straight down. Such is the dramatic edge of the Big Laurel Branch Wilderness, taking up the southernmost 10 square miles of heavily wooded Iron Mountain (with an additional 8 square miles of the mountain classed as a "roadless area"). Iron Mountain climbs 1,400 feet above the waters of **Lakes Watauga and Wilbur**, then extends northeast, straight and true, with a narrow crest that never swerves. Big Laurel Branch itself is a bowl shaped drainage cut into the southern edge of the mountain, trail-less and inaccessible to all but the most experienced cross-country hikers. However, the **Appalachian Trail** follows Iron Mountain through the wilderness, furnishing good access and a first-rate day hike. You can pick up the trail at **Watauga Dam**, and follow it uphill along the crest for 4.5 miles to a trail shelter, a fairly steady climb of 1,200 feet. The trail passes through a varied and interesting dry hardwood forest, broken by large outcrops and cliffs with dramatic views down to the lake below. The trail shelter, located at the edge of the wilderness area, has a particularly wide and impressive cliff-top view.

**Pond Mountain Wilderness** The wilderness is located 6 miles south of Elizabethton via US 321, on the south side of the highway. Pond Mountain is not a linear mountain like that of the Big Laurel Branch Wilderness; instead, it's a wild jumble of peaks and valleys, ridges that run every which way, valleys perched on high crests, outcrops projecting from deep forests, and gorges cut straight through ridges. From the valley below it doesn't look taller than linear Iron Mountain—but it is, a 2,200-foot climb from nearby **Watauga Lake** to its vaguely crescent-shaped crest. The U.S. Congress has protected nearly 11 square miles of this difficult area as the Pond Mountain Wilderness.

Of the many interesting features of the Pond Mountain Wilderness, the strangest may be the deep gorge carved through its western edge by **Laurel Creek**, a gorge that includes a couple of deep horseshoe curves at the center of the crest line. The Laurel Creek Gorge features an impressive waterfall, sheer cliffs, and some strange rock formations, as well as an historic old railroad bed. **The Appalachian Trail** follows that old rail bed for a fine hike, then curves around to the top of Pond Mountain for some wide views.

**Highlands of Roan** This large area of high, rugged wilderness straddles the Tennessee–North Carolina state line 25 miles south of Elizabethton, via US 19E and TN 143. With three peaks above 6,000 feet and 6 miles of mile-high crest, the Highlands of Roan make up one of the great sights of the southern Appalachians. Nearly 10 miles of the Roan Mountain crest are covered with wide grassy balds and rhododendron heaths; one heath forms a 600-acre natural garden that turns brilliant pink every June. With 23 square miles of protected land, there's plenty to see:

- On the Tennessee side, **Hampton Creek Cove State Natural Area** includes an operating mountain farm that merges with the forests above, its access track leading still higher to the grassy balds along its crest.

ROAN MOUNTAIN IN WINTER, FROM THE APPALACHIAN TRAIL

- Nearby, Tennessee's **Roan Mountain State Park** protects 2,000 acres along the lower slopes, including a reconstructed 19th-century farmstead, the **Dave Miller Homestead**.
- From the state park, TN 143 climbs a dramatic mile-high gap to enter North Carolina, part of the **NC 80 Scenic Drive** (see "Behind the Blue Ridge: Spruce Pine & Burnsville," *Exploring the Area*).
- From that gap, the Appalachian Trail heads east through wide open meadows, on one of the most breathtaking walks in the East.
- Also from that gap, a paved road leads west along the crest to the **Roan Gardens**, a 600-acre rhododendron garden with wide views in North Carolina's Pisgah National Forest.
- Finally, east of the gap is **Roaring Creek Valley**, with stunning views over an apple orchard and a red barn, and a walk along the Revolutionary War–era **Overmountain Victory Trail**. It can be reached on foot from Hampton Creek Cove, or by car via a very long drive south on US 19E well into North Carolina.

**Rogers Ridge Roadless Area** *In Tennessee; from Damascus, take VA 91 (becoming TN 91) south for 6.6 miles to a left onto Gentry Creek* Road *(becoming FR 123); the ridgeline trailhead (FT 192, Rogers Ridge Trail) is 2.2 miles on your left, and the waterfall trail (FT 51, Gentry Creek Trail) is 3 miles on your left*. One of the most rewarding and remote parts of northeast Tennessee, this 4,500-acre roadless area has 11 peaks over 4,000 feet in elevation, wide mountaintop meadows, exceptional wildflowers, the finest waterfall in the area—and almost no visitors. Located 7 miles north of Mountain City to a right onto Gentry Creek Road (FS 122), it's part of Tennessee's Cherokee National Forest. It has two formal trails. The second one (as you drive in) is the more visited, leading up lovely Gentry Creek to **Gentry Creek Falls**. The first trail leads uphill along ridgelines to the extensive meadows on these high peaks. It ends after 3.2 miles, but informal tracks continue along the ridgeline, from one wildflower field to the next. Elevations range as high as 4,980 feet; perhaps if this ridge had the 20 extra feet to reach the magic 5,000-foot line, it would have the high level of protection found to its immediate north in Virginia's Mount Rogers Recreation Area. Instead, it's administered as a National Forest Roadless Area, and protected only by administrative policies at the local level.

**Unaka Mountain Wilderness** The 5,160-foot peak of Unaka Mountain looms above Erwin, Tennessee, its summit clothed in black-green firs and spruces. Downhill from this stretches the Unaka Mountain Wilderness, known for its rugged terrain, steep cliffs, dramatic waterfalls, and wide views from heath balds. It's a surprisingly popular place for hikers, with its beauty outweighing its remoteness and difficulty. One popular trail starts at the wilderness' low point, the **Rock Creek Recreation Area**, and climbs 1,000 feet in a 5-mile round-trip to Rock Creek Falls, a beautiful cliff cascade. Another trail from the same recreation area climbs the exposed backbone of Rattlesnake Ridge to reach the scenic drive after a 2,500-foot climb, and a lot of spectacular views (6 miles round-trip). A third trail is the **Appalachian Trail**, which runs along its crest.

At one time you could drive along Unaka Mountain, almost to the top of the wilderness area, via the Unaka Mountain Scenic Road, a gravel recreation road that links a series of heaths and grassy balds with wide views. The National Forest Service, however, stopped maintaining this road many years ago, and it is no longer passable without a high-clearance, four-wheel-drive vehicle.

**RIVERS** **The Nolichucky River** The Nolichucky forms in North Carolina at the confluence of the Cane and the Toe Rivers, then cuts a dramatic 2,000-foot-deep gorge through the massive mountains on the state line. In this water gap, a wild 12-mile stretch of Class III and IV rapids is flanked by steep, forest-covered lands of the Pigah (North Carolina) and Cherokee (Tennessee) National Forests, with virtually no foot access to the banks. Downstream from Erwin, the Nolichucky continues through beautiful mountain scenery at a much more leisurely pace, suitable for families with small children.

**The Watauga River** Downstream from **Wilbur Dam**, the Class I–II Watauga can be explored by canoe for nearly 21 miles. The first 3 miles are the most popular, with some Class II+ spots, cliff-lined banks, and some beautiful farming scenery. Canoeists out for a day continue to Elizabethton's bankside city park, a distance of 8 miles that becomes gradually more and more urbanized as the town is approached. The entire 21 miles is a scenic mixed bag, first passing Elizabethton's abandoned rayon factories before passing into open countryside, then diving into a beautiful small gorge. This section ends at Boone Lake, just west of this book's area.

**WATERFALLS** **Waterfalls of Dennis Cove** Upstream from **Dennis Cove Recreation Area**, just west of Pond Mountain Wilderness near Elizabethton, stretches a 6-mile-long valley ringed by an oval of low but rugged mountains. This tract of wild national forest land has become known for its waterfalls, with four named falls and any number of unnamed falls. The closest to the recreation area trailheads is *Coon Den Falls,* a 100-foot-tall trickle over a single bare rock. The rest stretch out along the main stream, Laurel Fork, and are reached by the same riverside trail. The first is *Dennis Cove Falls*, a double cascade 30 feet tall, and unusually beautiful. Upstream are more waterfalls, including Firescald Falls and Upper Laurel Fork Falls.

**Gentry Creek Falls** This impressive waterfall is located deep in the **Rogers Ridge Roadless Area**. The trail follows beautiful little **Gentry Creek** for 2.2 miles uphill to the waterfall, climbing 600 feet. There you will find a double waterfall, where the stream twice leaps over vertical sandstone cliffs 30–40 feet high.

**SWIMMING HOLES Blue Hole** One of the region's favorite swimming holes is sited by one of its most impressive waterfalls. Here Mill Creek, not otherwise impressive, gathers up all its energy to thunder over three cliffs in close succession, a total dive of about 100 feet, to a large pool. Above the pool is a sheer rock cliff, which the creek butts up against, then swerves around. From Elizabethton, take NC 91 east for 10.2 miles to a left onto Panhandle Road (becoming FS 56, paved as far as Blue Hole), reaching Blue Hole in another 0.9 mile. The cascades and swimming hole are only a short distance left and downhill from the small (and frequently crowded) parking area. An indistinct path to the left (the only one not heading downhill) goes a short distance to the top of the cliff, for a wide, if somewhat vertiginous, view over the swimming hole and falls.

Adventuresome drivers can continue up Panhandle Road to the mountain top, in another 3.2 miles of steep gravel road. Here, a jeep trail to the right (closed to vehicles) makes for a 1-mile hike to the tower portion of an old fire tower, kept in service as an antenna holder. When inspected there were no posted prohibitions on climbing it—a very long, steep, and exposed stairway to the platform, with amazing views. Panhandle Road continues left along the ridgeline for another 2.8 miles to a 4,000-foot-high primitive camping and picnic area named Low Gap; but, when inspected, the road became nearly impassable by passenger car long before then.

THE BLUE HOLE

**RECREATION AREAS Roan Mountain State Park** (www.state.tn.us/environment/parks/roanmtn; 800-250-8620, 423-772-0190; 1015 Hwy. 143, Roan Mountain, TN 37687). 8:00 AM–4:30 PM, Wed.–Sun.; closed Mon. and Tues. Located 21 miles south of Elizabethton via US 19E and TN 143, this Tennessee state park preserves 3 square miles of the middle slopes of the Roan Highlands. It has an attractive visitors center graced by an old-fashioned overshot wheel, a number of hiking trails, and several good picnic areas. Considered a "resort park," it also has a set of 30 cabins as well as tennis courts and a swimming pool. Roan Mountain is particularly noted for its wide-ranging program of activities, including workshops in traditional mountain crafts, a spring **Naturalists Rally**, and a fall **Naturalists Rally**. The state park is 10 miles from the crest of Roan Mountains and its famous **Gardens** (see "Behind the Blue Ridge: Spruce Pine & Burnsville," *To See*) via TN 143—one of the most spectacular 10 miles in the mountains.

**PICNIC AREAS** **Rock Creek Recreation Area** This attractive picnic and camping area, heavily shaded, sits at the lowermost edge of the **Unaka Mountain Wilderness**, and serves as one of the wilderness' trailheads.

**Shook Branch Recreation Area** This Cherokee National Forest picnic area marks the place where the **Appalachian Trail** crosses US 321, 8 miles southeast of Elizabethton. It's located on **Lake Watauga** with pleasant lake views, as well as access to the **Pond Mountain Wilderness**. As you follow US 321 eastward along the lakeshore, you will find two more lakeside picnic areas in the next 3 miles, plus a boat ramp and a campground.

## ✷ To See

**BIG DAMMED LAKES** **Lake Watauga** This Tennessee Valley Authority (TVA) lake, 6 miles west of Elizabethton, covers just 10 squares miles, but has 100 miles of shoreline—half of it owned by the Cherokee National Forest. With miles of fiddley little indents and coves and lots of forested shoreline, it's a fun lake to explore. It has numerous recreation sites for picnicking, boat launching, and camping, the three largest being along US 321, 21 miles east of Elizabethton. The TVA built Watauga Dam in 1948 for flood control and hydropower. This earthen dam stands 100 yards high and 1,000 feet wide at the top; you can visit the dam by hiking out the Appalachian Trail from Iron Mountain Gap. On the road to the dam, Lake Wilbur Picnic Area gives views of Little Laurel Branch throwing itself out of an adjacent wilderness area and over a 50-foot cliff, into the lake below.

**HISTORIC SITES** **Doe River Covered Bridge** In continuous use since its construction in 1882, this 134-foot wood truss bridge spans the Doe River a block south of downtown Elizabethton. Clad in white clapboard, the bridge looks absurdly elongated and flimsy—but it has survived intact the fierce, deadly floods of 1901 and 1998, when more modern structures were swept away. The secret of its success: its massive trusses, made up of coupled 8 x 8 oak beams that tower 10 feet over the deck. The trusses suspend the deck across the entire width of the river, far above the highest floodwaters. The white clapboard cover exists for one reason only—to protect the wood truss from rot. Without the cover, the beams' slanted joints would pick up rain and snow, rotting away at the points where the strain is greatest. Because of its wood cover, this bridge remains strong enough to survive 120 years and two major floods. It is now closed to vehicles, but open to walkers and bicyclists.

The bridge is flanked by lovely riverside parks on both banks, and framed on its downstream side by a weir that fed a 19th-century millrace. On the Elizabethton side of the river, rows of beautifully kept Victorian houses stretch along the river, facing across the road to the riverside park. A block north is Elizabethton's reviving brick-front downtown, with several antique shops. A walk through the park along the river is a delight, with views that are simply beautiful, particularly in the fall when brilliant colors frame the bridge.

**Sycamore Shoals State Historic Site** (423-543-5808; fax: 423-543-0078; 1651 West Elk Ave., Elizabethton, TN 37643). Park open 8:00 AM–dusk; visitors center open 8:00 AM–4:30 PM, Mon.–Sat.; 1:00 PM–4:30 PM Sun. On the western outskirts of Elizabethton (1 mile west of downtown on US 321), Sycamore Shoals was the center of the Colonial trans-mountain settlement of Watauga. The British built Fort Watauga here in the early 1770s to control a frontier that was supposedly closed to white settlement; however, white settlement had already begun, and the settlers relied on the fort for safety. Sycamore Shoals became one of the most important frontier sites of the Revolutionary period. It was here that the private Transylvania Corporation, made up of North Carolina land speculators, bought Kentucky and eastern Tennessee from a group of Cherokee chiefs; years later, it was here that settlers sheltered from Cherokee attacks during the Revolution; and it was here that the Overmountain Boys mustered for their successful march to Kings Mountain, South Carolina, to defeat a loyalist army poised to harry the mountain settlements. Today Sycamore Shoals is a small, well-kept state park centered around a reconstruction of Fort Watauga, and a small museum with a number of rotating local displays. In mid-July, an outdoor drama featuring local amateur actors tells the story of the Watauga settlement. Sycamore Shoals offers a full calendar of activities, including some very imaginative ones (September's Flint Knapping Day comes to mind). It has good day-use facilities, including a picnic area and a riverside jogging path.

**The Carter Mansion** (elizabethton.org/about/h_places; 423-543-6140; 1013 Broad St., Elizabethton, TN, 37643). Tours daily May to August; arrange at Sycamore Shoals State Historic Site. The oldest frame house in Tennessee, the Carter Mansion was built by John Carter, a leader of the Watauga Association, in

THE DOE RIVER COVERED BRIDGE IN ELIZABETHTON

1780. Astonishingly, over 90 percent of the interior of this modest frontier "mansion" date from the original 1780 construction. This includes the hand-carved paneling, the crown molding and the chair rails—and it definitely includes the two landscape paintings over the fireplaces, executed directly on the wall paneling. It also includes the plumbing; there isn't any, and never has been! Last occupied in 1966, the State of Tennessee acquired it in 1973 with 4.6 acres of land, and restored it to its original appearance in 1978. The Carter Mansion is located at the end of Broad Street (US 321); go straight through the traffic light at US 19E and continue for one block. (The contact information is for Sycamore Shoals, which administers the site.)

**The Dave Miller Farmstead** Open Memorial Day–Labor Day, 9 AM–5 PM, Wed.–Sun. Free. This lovely early-20th-century farmstead, immaculate white with stylish little gable dormers over its front porch, is the successor to two pioneer log cabins, the homes of the Millers since 1870. The first cabin was on land leased from Roan Mountain's land baron, General John Wilder; the Millers bought their farm from the general in 1904, and built the second cabin. The present house succeeded it, the home of later generations of Millers. Now it's an open-air museum, demonstrating a turn-of-the-century mountain farmstead. You'll find it adjacent to Roan Mountain State Park, on TN 143, 3 miles south of the village of Roan Mountain. Try to stop by on a summer's Saturday between noon and 2 PM, when artists and musicians are present.

**CULTURAL SITES** **Unicoi County Heritage Museum** (423-743-9449). Open daily, May–October, 1 PM–5 PM. Free. Unicoi County's Heritage Museum is located in the 1903 Superintendent's Residence of the U.S. Fish Hatchery, off US 23's exit 19 between Erwin and Unicoi, a grand Victorian-style farmhouse with a wraparound porch. Nine of its ten rooms are open to the public. Railroad buffs will head immediately to the Railroad Room on the second floor, with exhibits on the old Clinchfield Railroad. The Clinchfield was (and remains) one of the greatest lines in the East, running straight through the Appalachians like a hot wire through butter; formerly an independent company headquartered in Erwin, it's now a heavily used main line for the CSX. In the next room is a reconstruction of Erwin's Main Street, from about the period when the fish hatchery (and the Clinchfield) was built. Other rooms display home-canned and preserved food; another type of preserve—artifacts of nature, including a stuffed bear (killed by accident); period furniture; local arts and crafts; turn-of-the-century costumes; and just a lot of neat stuff. Individual rooms are sponsored by local civic organizations. A one-room log schoolhouse sits outside (moved in from Greasy Cove), and a nature trail is on the property.

**GARDENS AND PARKS** **Hampton Creek Cove State Natural Area** (423-323-4993; 804 Rock City Rd., Kingsport, TN 37664). Unique among the State of Tennessee's 60 natural areas, Hampton Creek Cove contains a working farm, still run by the family that has farmed this land for the last century. A state-owned part of the 15,000-acre Highlands of Roan, Hampton Creek demonstrates mountain farming practices that conserve natural ecosystems and improve biodiversity. A track runs uphill through the farmlands and into the woods above, eventually reaching the famous ridgetop meadows of the Roan at the **Overmountain Victory Trail** (see "Behind the Blue Ridge: Spruce Pine & Burnsville," *Exploring the*

**THE ET & WNC (TWEETSIE RAILROAD)**

Although the initials stood for "East Tennessee and Western North Carolina," to mountain folk they stood for "eat 'taters and wear no clothes." It was also known as the Tweetsie for the peculiar sound made by the whistle of its main steam engine. One of the great legendary lines of the southern Appalachians, the Tweetsie was a narrow gauge railroad originally built to haul iron ore from a mine north of Spruce Pine to Johnson City; eventually it was extended as far as Boone, North Carolina. A friendly, local line that wandered slowly through the mountains, it linked communities in a way that the more serious-minded Clinchfield did not. The Tweetsie's crew (the same men for many years) would take orders from locals along the line and deliver the goods to their door. The Tweetsie survived surprisingly late into the 20th Century, losing its line to Boone in a 1944 flood and closing its last section in 1950. However, in a sense it survives to this day—as the roadbeds of US 19E, NC 194, and NC 105, all major highways. With most of its bed covered by highways, little remains to be seen.

A final note: some readers will associate "Tweetsie Railroad" with a Blowing Rock, NC tourist attraction, a cowboy theme park that features the actual, original steam locomotive from the Tweetsie Railroad. The attraction has beautifully restored the old engine and keeps it in top shape—and it still makes that strange "tweetsie" sound. If you care to visit it, it will carry you in a fine circle to an Olde West town.

*Area*). You will find the natural area at the end of Hampton Creek Road, which starts at the village of Roan Mountain.

**Backbone Rock** You literally can't miss this geological and historic wonder on TN 133, almost at the Virginia state line; the state highway goes right through it, in what is claimed to be the world's shortest tunnel (10 feet long). Backbone Rock is a 50-foot-tall fin of hard quartzite sandstone, standing vertically and blocking the narrow valley of Beaverdam Creek. At the turn of the 20th century it blocked the upstream valley from being logged, so the loggers blasted a hole through it. Then they found that they had made the tunnel too low for their Shay engine's chimney, so they hand-chiseled a chimney shaped slot in its roof. And that's where the state highway runs today. Tennessee's Cherokee National Forest owns the site and manages it as a recreation area and picnic area. There's a boardwalk and steps to the top of Backbone Rock with some pretty nifty views, and a path to the **waterfall** formed where Beaverdam Creek flows over the formation. From Mountain City, take US 421 north for 10.4 miles, then turn right on TN 133 and go 9.6 miles.

## ✴ To Do

**WHITEWATER ADVENTURES** There are good choices for whitewater excursions in this area. The Nolichucky enters Tennessee by passing through a deep wilderness gorge, a wild 12-mile stretch of Class III and IV rapids. Downstream from Erwin, the Nolichucky continues through beautiful mountain scenery at a much more leisurely pace, suitable for families with small children. Finally, the Watauga River near Elizabethton has an attractive 9-mile stretch of water with Class I–III rapids.

**Cherokee Adventures, Inc.** (www.cherokeeadventures.com; 800-445-7238, 423-743-7733; 2000 Jonesborough Rd., Erwin, TN 37650). This Erwin outfitter specializes in fully guided trips on the Nolichucky River—wild rides on the Nolichucky Gorge, or gentle, scenic floats farther downstream. Most floats include lunch. They also offer mountain bike tours and a roping school.

**B-Cliff Whitewater Rafting** (800-592-2262, 423-542-2262; 390 Wilbur Dam Rd., Elizabethton, TN 37643). Open Memorial Day–Labor Day. B-Cliff offers whitewater rafting and kayaking on the Watauga River 5 miles east of Elizabethton.

**Nantahala Outdoor Center at Erwin,** Tennessee (e-mail: rafting@noc.com; 800-232-7238, 828-488-2175; fax: 828-488-0301; 4 Jones Branch Rd., Erwin, TN 37650). This major regional company, headquartered in Bryson City, NC (see "North of Asheville: The Bald Mountains," *To Do*), maintains an outpost at the head of the Nolichucky Gorge 4 miles south of Erwin—a base for trips through the Nolichucky Gorge.

**USA Raft** (e-mail: rafting@noc.com; 800-872-7238, 828-488-2175; 2 Jones Branch Rd., Erwin, TN 37650). This West Virginia whitewater rafting chain operates an outpost at the mouth of the Nolichucky Gorge, 4 miles south of Erwin.

**STILL-WATER BOATING** **Watauga Kayaking** (423-542-6777; Elizabethton, TN 37643). Watauga Kayaking offers calm-water lake and river tours on area waters, including Lake Watauga, for a quiet and peaceful enjoyment of nature. They also rent kayaks for calm-water use.

**GOLF** **Elizabethton Municipal Golf Course** (423-542-8051; Golf Club Rd., Elizabethton, TN 37643). This fairly hilly 18-hole, par-72 course overlooks the Watauga River on the west side of the City of Elizabethton, off US 321.

**Buffalo Valley Golf Course** (423-743-5021; 90 Country Club Dr., Unicoi, TN 37692). Eight miles north of Erwin, this 18-hole public course sits on the level floor of the oddly riverless valley that stretches north from Erwin to Johnson City. It's in an attractive rural location, convenient to the US 23 freeway that's destined to become I-26 someday.

## ✷ Lodging

### BED & BREAKFAST INNS

**Iron Mountain Inn** (ironmountaininn.com; 423-768-2446; 138 Moreland Dr., Butler, TN 37640). Open all year. This modern log structure, purpose-built as an inn, sits on 140 acres in the Iron Mountains, 12 miles south of Mountain City. It has a porch and a deck with views, a great room with a fireplace, and a library. Its four rooms, individually decorated and themed, have handmade quilts and whirlpool baths; two rooms have steam showers, and three have private balconies. Guests are treated to afternoon refreshments as well as a three-course breakfast, and the cookie jar is always full. Dinner and picnic lunches are available with 24-hour notice (and a fee). Pets and small children require prior arrangement.

**Doe River Inn** (www.doeriverinn.com; 423-543-1444; 217 Academy St., Elizabethton, TN 37643). This 1894 Victorian house faces the Doe River in Elizabethton's historic district, within sight of the covered bridge. Built on the site of the original ford over the Doe River, it was once known as "The Crossover." Today's inn has two rooms, each elegantly furnished with antiques and with its own bath. Common rooms, also furnished in high Victorian style, include a living room, a sun room, and a formal dining room where the full breakfast is served.

**Mountain Harbour Bed & Breakfast** (www.mountainharbour.net; 866-772-9494, 423-772-9494; 9151 Hwy. 19E, Roan Mountain, TN 37687). This four-room bed & breakfast inn is in a farmhouse-style home with stained clapboarding, dormers, and a wraparound porch. The four rooms, ranging in size from cozy to large, are individually furnished in a country antique style, with the largest room having a whirlpool tub and a fireplace. Two rooms are en suite, while two other rooms share a bath.

**Prospect Hill Bed & Breakfast Inn** (www.prospect-hill.com; e-mail: inn@prospect-hill.com; 800-339-5084, 423-727-0139; 801 West Main St. [TN 67], Mountain City, TN 37683). This elaborate 1889 Victorian mansion, built of brick with a wide porch framed by brick arches, sits near the center of Mountain City. The five en suite guest rooms, all individually decorated in period, have fireplaces, whirlpool baths, WiFi, cable TV (and soundproofing), and individual thermostats (heat and air-conditioning). A full breakfast is included. They have a rental cottage, 17 miles north (very near the **Rogers Ridge** area) that welcomes pets and allows children to run around freely; within the inn, pets are not allowed, and children are expected to be quiet and well behaved.

**CABIN RENTALS** ♿ **Roan Mountain State Park Cabins** (800-250-8620, 423-772-0190; 1015 Hwy. 143, Roan Mountain, TN 37687). Open all year. This 2,000-acre state park has 30 rustic cabins available by the day. Each cabin is a modern-built structure in a classic park style with full front porch, living room, full kitchen, and two bedrooms. They are attractively set in a wooded glade, with a stream nearby and a large, well-kept lawn area. Ten cabins are available with phones. Only one cabin is approved for pets.

**Cherokee Forest Mountain Cabins** (www.cabin4me.com; e-mail: owners@cabin4me.com; 866-937-7829; 798 Grindstaff Rd., Butler, TN 37640). Open all year. These two modern log cabins are located at the far northern end of Watauga Lake, on TN 167 near Butler. Both have wide views from their front porches, with wood-finished interiors furnished in a simple, elegant country style. Living areas have cathedral ceilings and fireplaces, and kitchens are full sized.

**Bee Cliff Cabins** (www.beecliffcabins.com; e-mail: beecliffcabins@charter.net; 423-542-6033; 141 Steel Bridge Rd., Elizabethton, TN, 37643). These three cabins are located on a rural stretch of the Watauga River, 5 miles east of Elizabethton. It's a bit like an old-time fish camp; modest log-sided cabins group tightly around a central drive, sharing a common dock on the river. Inside, they are simply and comfortably furnished, wood-walled, with full kitchens.

## ✱ Where to Eat

**EATING OUT Ridgewood Barbeque** (423-538-7543; 900 Elizabethton Hwy., Bluff City, TN 37618). Open for lunch and dinner, Tues.–Sun.; closed Mon. The Proffit family of Bluff City founded this popular pit barbeque in 1948 and still own it today. They run a friendly, family-oriented place, sitting underneath the last of the mountain ridges on the old US 19E (now called Elizabethton Highway), 7 miles north of Elizabethton. They barbeque pork and beef in the two original pits, using their own sauce recipe and slicing it to order. The sides are made fresh as well.

**The Coffee Company** (www.experiencingcoffee.com; 800-358-3709, 423-542-3438; 444 East Elk Ave., Elizabethton, TN 37643). Open for breakfast and lunch. This coffee shop in downtown Elizabethton serves breakfast and lunch along with a full line of coffees roasted on the premises. Breakfasts are limited to muffins and other goodies baked fresh each morning. Lunches are more elaborate, with home made soups, sandwiches, desserts, and a daily special.

## ✱ Entertainment

### *Elizabethton*

**Special Events at Sycamore Shoals** (423-543-5808). This fascinating historic site runs a full slate of events, with something happening every month. Its reconstructed fort hosts several reenactments, including the famous Overmountain March each September 23rd. There is a Native American Festival in June, a fine arts show in July, a Celtic Festival in September, and a quilt show in October.

**The Wataugans Outdoor Drama** (423-543-5808). Tennessee's official outdoor drama and the oldest outdoor drama in the state, "The Wataugans" tells the story of the 18th-century Watauga settlements that brought Europeans into the lands now known as Tennessee. It's held in July at Sycamore Shoals.

**The Elizabethton Twins** (e-mail: etwins@cityofelizabethton.org; 423-547-6441; fax: 423-547-6442; 300 West Mill St., Elizabethton, TN 37643). Elizabethton is one of only two cities in this guide to have its own minor league team (Asheville is the other (see "The City of Asheville," *Entertainment*). A farm team of the Minnesota Twins since 1937, the Elizabethton Twins are part of the rookie level Appalachian League, one of America's last remaining old-time small-town leagues.

## ✱ Selective Shopping

### *Erwin and Unicoi*

**Farmhouse Gallery & Gardens** (farmhousegallery.net; e-mail: info@farmhousegallery.net; 423-743-8799; 21 Covered Bridge Ln., Unicoi, TN 37692). Located north of Unicoi on Erwin Highway, the Farmhouse Gallery features the wildlife art of Johnny Lynch. The gallery is located in a restored log cabin, surrounded by 3 acres of perennial and water gardens and set in a 75-acre preserve. The complex includes an events venue for weddings, meetings, and such.

## ✱ Special Events

SPRING **Peters Hollow Egg Fight** (423-547-3852). Easter. This annual event, held at Sycamore Shoals, started in 1823 when an Easter egg hunt got out of hand. Or maybe it was a competition to see whose hen laid the strongest egg; traditions vary. Some people like to watch, while others join in.

**Fiddlers & Fiddleheads Festival** (423-743-8799). Open late April, 10 AM–9 PM. Free. This annual event at the Johnny Lynch Farmhouse Gallery

& Gardens features music, a vintage car show, antique sales, flower sales, storytelling, and food.

**Roan Mountain (State Park) Spring Naturalists Rally** (423-772-0190). First weekend in May. Roan Mountain State Park sponsors a weekend of nighttime nature lectures and daytime naturalist-led hikes through the early spring wildflowers.

**Unicoi Strawberry Festival** Second weekend in May. This street fair in the small town of Unicoi (5 miles north of Erwin) celebrates the strawberry with live entertainment, a Sunday gospel sing, craft and fair booths, a citywide yard sale, and strawberries.

**SUMMER** **Covered Bridge Celebration** Early June. The town of Elizabethton celebrates its beautiful old covered bridge with a four-day annual festival.

**Annual Rhododendron Festival at Roan Mountain State Park** (423-772-0190). Last weekend in June. This annual festival at Roan Mountain State Park celebrates the peak of the rhododendron display, particularly spectacular in nearby **Roan Mountain Gardens** (see "Behind the Blue Ridge: Spruce Pine & Burnsville," *To See*) (part of the Pisgah National Forest across the line in North Carolina). This two-day event includes old-time mountain music, clogging, crafts, and food. There's another Rhododendron Festival held at about the same time on the other side of the mountain, at **Bakersville** (see "Behind the Blue Ridge: Spruce Pine & Burnsville," *Special Events*). A true festival enthusiast will want to take in both.

**AUTUMN** **Unicoi County Apple Festival** First weekend in October. This two-day street fair takes over Erwin's downtown with 300 craft and food exhibits, live music, and (of course) plenty of apples.

**Shady Valley Cranberry Festival** Second weekend in October. The tiny community of Shady Valley, located 11 miles west of Mountain City on US 421, holds this popular little festival in their schoolyard. There's a bean supper (before World War II this region claimed to be the biggest bean producer in America), a pancake breakfast at the volunteer fire department, a parade to the festival grounds at the school, and day-long craft booths and live bluegrass music. The name commemorates a nearby cranberry bog, a very unusual feature this far south.

# BENEATH THE BLUE RIDGE: THE CATAWBA RIVER VALLEY

In our other chapters the mountains end abruptly, and the Piedmont laps against them like an ocean against a seawall. Not so here. In this chapter's area one of the great rivers of the South, the Catawba River, has carved the front of the Blue Ridge so thoroughly that mountains and Piedmont mix. For the traveler, it's an opportunity to enjoy them both together, as a single entity.

The Catawba rises from the upper slopes of the Blue Ridge 15 miles east of Asheville, near the town of Black Mountain. It then drops steeply to Old Fort and flows eastward into a wide, rolling valley, past the red-brick centers of Marion and Morganton, then out into the Piedmont. The cliffs of the Blue Ridge loom 6 or 8 miles north of the valley bottom; the rugged peaks and clefts of the South Mountains lie the same distance south.

The Catawba Valley has always been the main approach to the Smokies from the thickly settled areas of North Carolina. First wagons, then trains, went up it to reach the rich mountain forests; today, a flood of automobiles and trucks follow I-40 in their path. Before the Civil War, some of those wagons carried the North Carolina Supreme Court to Morganton every summer, escaping the downstate heat; the Supreme Court's graceful little courthouse still sits in the middle of Morganton's old-fashioned downtown. After the war, furniture manufacturers built factories along the rail yards beneath the cliffs of the Blue Ridge, the perfect distance between mountain hardwoods and downstate markets. Today, you will find an axis of urban and industrial development stretching lengthways along the I-40 corridor; however, leave the interstate corridor to the north or south, and the modern development drops away as you climb out of the valley floor and into the mountains.

**GUIDANCE—TOWNS AND COUNTRYSIDE** **Burke County Travel & Tourism Commission** (e-mail: director@discoverburkecounty.com; discoverburkecounty.com; 888-462-2921, 828-433-6793; 110 East Meeting St., Morganton, NC 28655). Open weekdays, 9 AM–4 PM; Sat., 10 AM–1 PM. Headquartered in Morganton's fine Old Courthouse, this small agency is delighted to help walk-in visitors with their visits to the eastern half of the Catawba Valley.

**McDowell County Tourism Development Authority** (www.mcdowellnc.org; 888-233-6111, 828-668-4282; 25 Hwy. 70 West, Old Fort, NC 28762). The

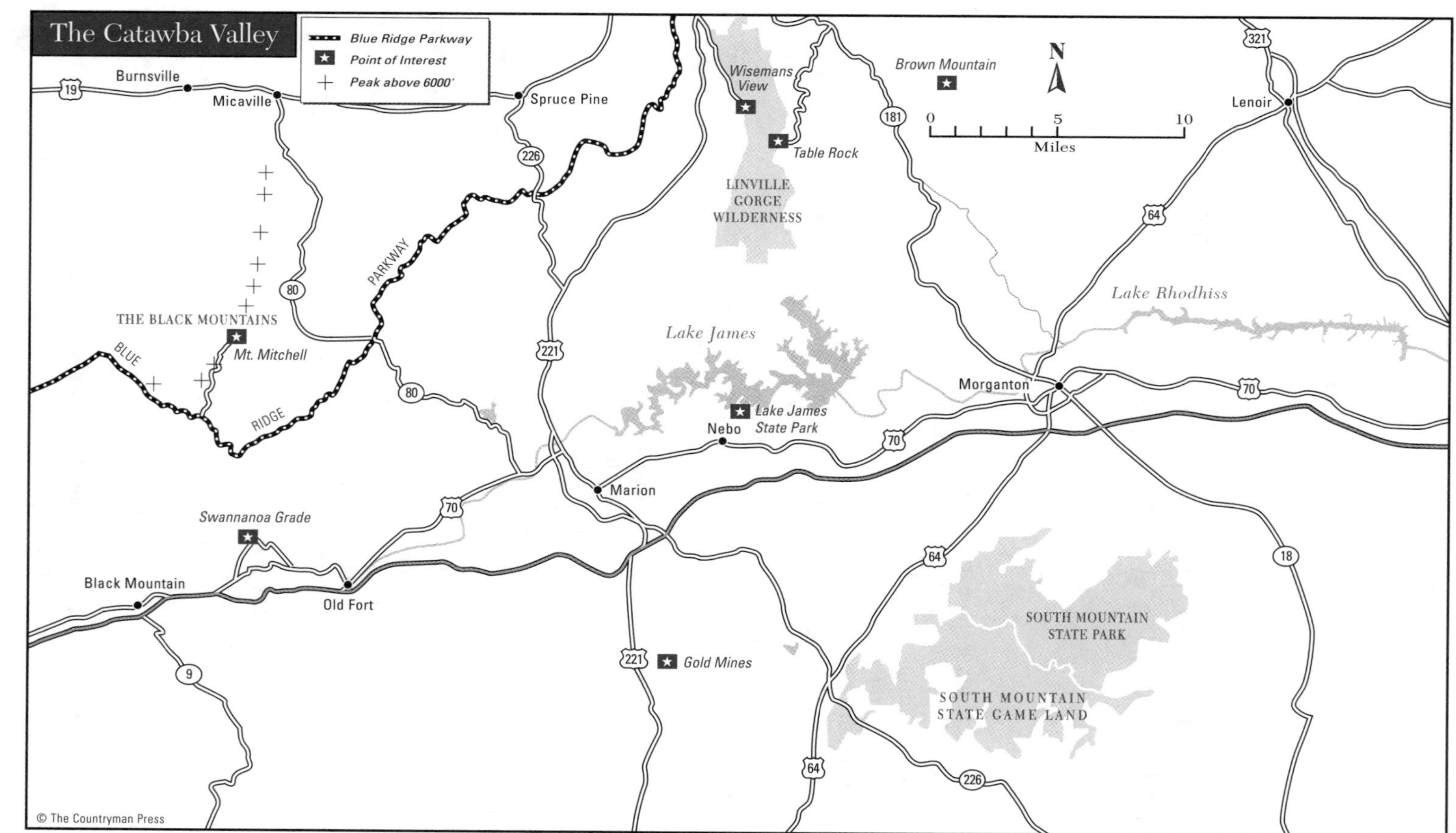
The Catawba Valley
Blue Ridge Parkway
Point of Interest
Peak above 6000'
Burnsville
Micaville
Spruce Pine
Wisemans View
Table Rock
LINVILLE GORGE WILDERNESS
Brown Mountain
N
0
5
10
Miles
Lenoir
Lake Rhodhiss
THE BLACK MOUNTAINS
Mt. Mitchell
BLUE
RIDGE
PARKWAY
Lake James
Lake James State Park
Nebo
Morganton
Marion
Swannanoa Grade
Black Mountain
Old Fort
Gold Mines
SOUTH MOUNTAIN STATE PARK
SOUTH MOUNTAIN STATE GAME LAND
19
226
181
321
64
80
221
70
18
9

McDowell County Tourism Development occupies a large, modern hilltop visitors center by a minor exit on US 221 as it bypasses Marion on its west. Covering the western half of the Catawba Valley, it offers friendly help and advice, a small but interesting display of local art and minerals, and a sweeping view north toward the Blue Ridge.

**Old Fort Chamber of Commerce** (www.oldfortchamber.com; e-mail: chamber @oldfortchamber.com; 828-668-7223; P.O. Box 1447, Old Fort, NC 28762). Open 10 AM–4 PM, Tues.–Sat. The town of Old Fort's local chamber offers visitor help and guidance from the railroad depot at the west end of town. It also includes a small railroad museum.

**GUIDANCE—PARKS AND FORESTS** ✐ **Pisgah National Forest, Grandfather Ranger District** (828-652-2144; 109 East Lawing Dr., Nebo, NC 28761). Normal business hours. The Pisgah National Forest includes an arc of large mountainous tracts along the slopes and side ridges of the Blue Ridge, all along the northern edge of the Catawba Valley. The ranger station for these lands is a large, new building by exit 90 on I-40, at Nebo. It contains a staffed visitors center with a full range of maps and pamphlets, as well as a small book store and exhibits on forestry.

**GETTING THERE** *By Car* Interstate 40 runs up the center of the Catawba Valley for its entire length. With rugged mountains lining the valley's north and south edges, I-40 is the easiest approach no matter what direction you are coming from.

*By Bus* Greyhound Bus Lines schedules daily service through the Catawba Valley, with stops in both Marion and Morganton. Both of these towns have taxi services and car rentals; check with their visitors centers for details.

*By Air* Charlotte's major international airport is closest, at 75 miles from Morganton via four-lane highway.

**MEDICAL EMERGENCIES** **Grace Hospital** (www.blueridgehealth.org/grace -hospital.html; 828-580-5000; 2201 South Sterling St., Morganton, NC 28655). This major regional hospital, serving the eastern half of the Catawba Valley, is located at Morganton, by I-40 at the NC 18 exit.

**The McDowell Hospital** (www.mcdhospital.org; 828-659-5000; 430 Rankin Dr., Marion, NC 28752). This 65-bed local hospital with 24/7 emergency-room service sits by I-40 at exit 81 (Sugar Hill Road), 3 miles south of Marion, convenient to the western half of the Catawba Valley.

## ✶ Exploring the Area

**EXPLORING BY CAR** **The Swannanoa Grade** *Leg #1* (*9 miles*): From Old Fort, take US 70 west 0.2 mile to Old US 70 (SSR 1400); then go right 2.5 miles to Mill Creek Road (SSR 1407); then right 6.3 miles to Old US 70 (SSR 1400). Automobiles continue straight to Ridgecrest and I-40.

*Leg #2* (*3.4 miles*): For bicycles only. Turn left as you regain Old US 70, at the white gate. Follow the concrete road, former US 70, now abandoned, downhill for 3.4 miles.

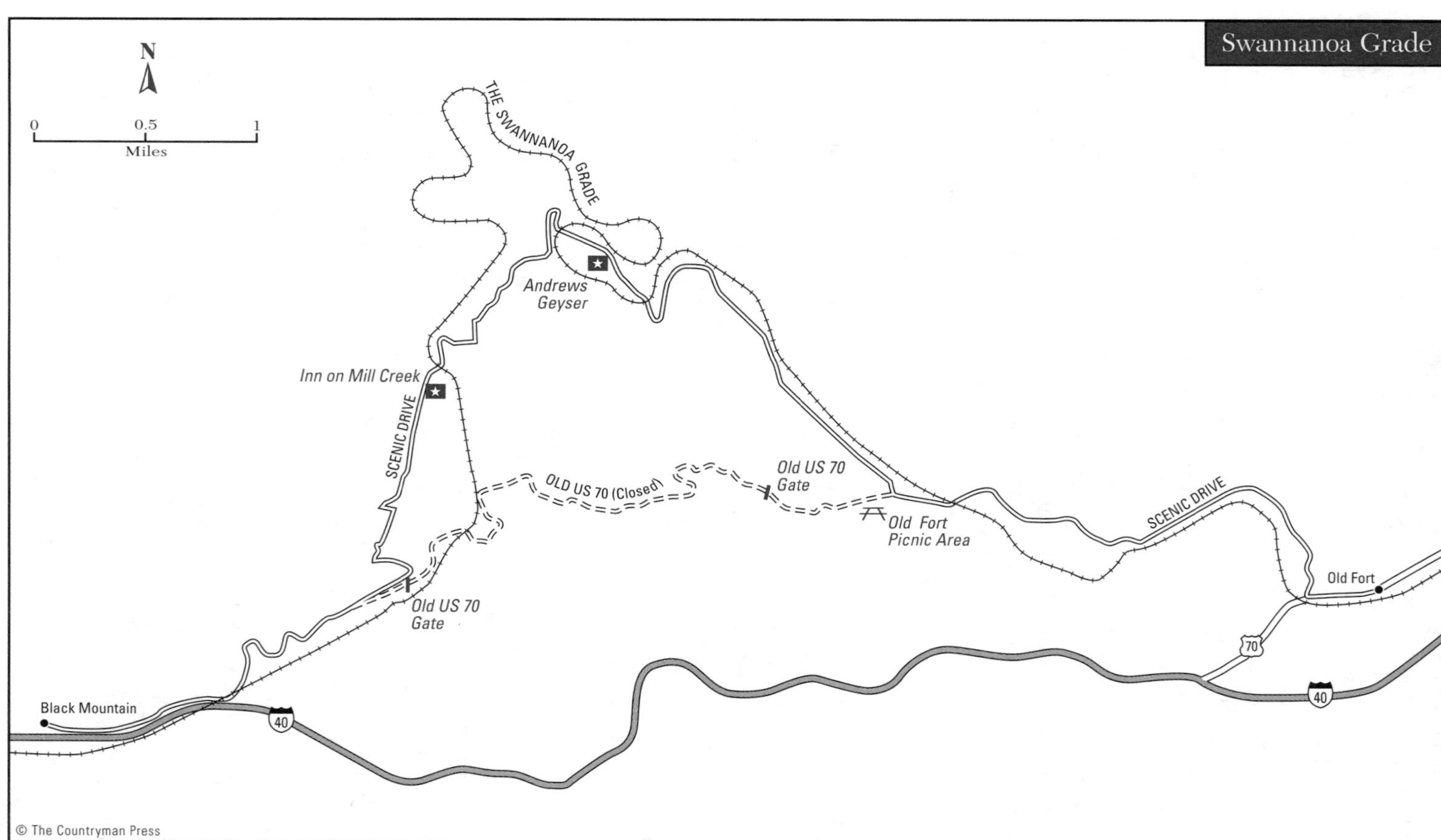
Swannanoa Grade
N
0
0.5
1
Miles
THE SWANNANOA GRADE
Andrews
Geyser
Inn on Mill Creek
SCENIC DRIVE
OLD US 70 (Closed)
Old US 70
Gate
Old Fort
Picnic Area
SCENIC DRIVE
Old Fort
Old US 70
Gate
70
Black Mountain
40
40
© The Countryman Press

Built in the 1870s with convict labor, the steep railroad known as the Swannanoa Grade takes 10 miles to cover a distance that a crow could fly in just over 4 miles. In doing so it climbs 1,000 feet in elevation, loops back on itself five times, and goes through seven tunnels with a total underground distance of 0.75 mile. More to the point, most of these engineering wonders (and the rugged scenery that brought them into existence) can be easily viewed by automobile-bound visitors—just as well, as there's been no passenger service on this line for a half-century.

Start this 12-mile drive at downtown **Old Fort**, where two small museums give historic perspective—on pioneer life at the **Mountain Gateway Museum**, and on 19th-century railroading at the **Old Fort Railroad Museum**. After that, follow the signs westward to Andrews Geyser. You'll be on the former main highway as far as the classic CCC-built **Old Fort Picnic Area**, then up the pastoral Mill Creek valley as far as **Andrews Geyser**. The railroad built the "geyser" (a 30-foot fountain) to impress passengers disembarking at a resort hotel; passengers and hotel are long gone, but the "geyser" remains, kept in operation by dedicated local residents. The geyser is placed in the center of three pigtail loops, and railroad enthusiasts will enjoy tracing the railroad on its mountain slope gyrations. This is a busy main line, so be patient. When a long freight train reaches Andrews Geyser it will pass below you, then curl above you, then curl once again on an even higher level; if you are lucky, the engines will enter the highest level while the last of the cars are still passing below you, filling the valley with a cacophony of raw power. From Andrews Geyser the road climbs the Blue Ridge as a good gravel lane through Pisgah National Forest lands. Attractive hardwood forests surround the road all the way up, except for a small orchard (privately owned) at the luxurious **Inn at Mill Creek**; the small pond behind the inn is the source of Andrews Geyser.

A bit farther you suddenly regain the old paved main highway, open to the right but gated to the left. The gated leftward road is **Old US 70**; a half-mile walk down its old concrete surface will lead to a series of four railroad tunnels, as well as a good view. From here, automobiles should complete the drive by following the old concrete road right to Black Mountain and I-40. However, bicyclists can follow the abandoned highway downhill for wonderful views and a close look at those railroad tunnels. The old highway circles back to the Old Fort Picnic Area. You can rent bicycles in Black Mountain.

♿ **Linville Gorge Rim Drive** *Leg #1* (*10.4 miles*): From Linville Falls on US 221, go east on NC 183 for 0.8 mile; then right on gravel Kistler Memorial Highway (SSR 1238) to Wiseman's View, 4.8 miles. Return to NC 183.

*Leg #2* (*21.5 miles*): Continue right on NC 183, 3.8 miles; then right on NC 181, 2.9 miles; then right at Table Rock Road (SSR 1265, becoming gravel FS 210), 6.1 miles; then right on steep, twisting, gravel FS 99 for 1.3 miles to Table Rock Picnic Area. Return to NC 181.

*Leg #3* (*23 miles*): Right on NC 181 for 23 miles to Morganton.

This 55-mile drive explores both rims of rugged **Linville Gorge**, the first eastern forest to be declared a wilderness area. For the most part it follows *gravel forest roads* to some spectacular viewpoints.

This drive starts at the intersection of US 221 and the **Blue Ridge Parkway**, at the rural community of **Linville Falls**. This settlement is noted for its handsome stone buildings constructed by the parkway stonemasons, and for its simple, turn-of-the-century farm-style houses built as summer homes by an early generation of tourists. From Linville Falls you take the oddly named "Kistler Memorial Highway," a poorly maintained gravel backroad. It's worth the trouble, though, as it follows the ridgeline that defines the edge of the wilderness, running through a dry oak forest for the most part. The first path on the left (parking) leads to the 90-foot-tall **Linville Falls** (see "The Blue Ridge Parkway: Blowing Rock & Grandfather Mountain," *To See*), where the Linville River drops dramatically into its gorge; all the later paths on the left descend steeply to the gorge bottom. After 4 miles, stop at disabled accessible **Wiseman's View** on the left, and take the short, easy path to impressive cliff-top views over the gorge. Beyond Wiseman's View, the Kistler Highway is very bad indeed; return the way you came.

The route continues through pretty rural countryside to the unremarkable mountaintop settlement of Jonas Ridge, where a brown recreation sign points down the road to Table Rock Picnic Area. This good-quality gravel forest road slowly winds its way through a large, handsome hardwood forest, with the edge of the wilderness following your right side most of the way. After you turn right at the T-intersection you'll get a great view straight up the gravel road toward the impressive **Table Rock**, then climb up seven switchbacks to reach the eastern edge of the Linville Gorge, almost opposite Wiseman's View, at a lovely, tree-shaded **picnic area**. Here footpaths stretch north and south along the gorge rim to spectacular clifftop views and strange geological formations at Table Rock and **The Chimneys**. Return the way you came.

The final leg follows a good quality state highway downhill to Morganton, a remarkably pleasant drive. In 2 miles, a trail to **Upper Creek Falls** is on the left, with **Bark House Picnic Area** just beyond. For the next 5 miles the highway follows the top of Ripshin Ridge, with excellent views back toward Table Rock and The Chimneys—here more impressive than ever. At the bottom of the mountain, commercial nurseries keep large fields of blooming trees, an amazing sight in the spring. NC 181 leads to the center of Morganton, with its early-19th-century courthouse once used by the North Carolina Supreme Court for its summer sessions.

**EXPLORING ON FOOT Waterfalls and Views in the South Mountains** The South Mountains offer a wide variety of first-rate walks and hikes; these two, each steep but short, lead to an 80-foot waterfall and a wide panorama. Both are reached from the **Jacobs Creek Picnic Area** within the South Mountains State Park, and are well signposted.

Start by following the signs to the *High Shoals Falls Trail,* a well-built waterfall walk that will take you on a 2-mile round trip with many, many steps. Go straight to the falls by taking the left fork of this loop trail—the one marked WARNING: STEEP AND RUGGED PATH. The path follows the violent little High Shoals Creek for a short distance, then turns suddenly and crosses an astonishing field of truck-sized boulders on a long, stepped boardwalk. Here the stream breaks up around the boulders, forming many small waterfalls. From this point up it's all steps, flight after flight, until you reach a large viewing platform at the base of 80-foot High Shoals Falls—where the powerful stream plunges straight down over a vertical gray cliff to a large, deep pool. The steps continue upward, hugging the cliffs near the falls, to reach the top, with a narrow view over the falls into the gorge. The loop trail continues on through second-growth forest; it's more fun to return the way you came, appreciating the fine cliff scenery from a leisured descent.

If you still have the energy, take *Chestnut Knob Overlook Trail* on the way back for great views across a deep gorge to High Shoals Falls and beyond; you'll pass the trailhead on your return to the picnic area. This trail ascends the dry hemlock and pine forests of the steep south-facing slopes, climbing 1,000 feet in 2 miles, to reach the wide clifftop views at Chestnut Knob. You'll reach the first view after 1 mile of uphill trudging—a fine view over the deep gorge of Jacobs Creek with High Shoals Falls clearly visible on the opposite side. From here the trail continues to ascend gently to the cliffs of Chestnut Knob. Here, more than anywhere else in North Carolina, you can see the end of the mountains, the sudden plunge to the Piedmont and the endless plains of the Deep South. Return the way you came.

**Table Rock Walks on the Linville Gorge Rim Table Rock Picnic Area** gives access to one of the most interesting and spectacular day hikes in the area, following the rim of the Linville Gorge. (For driving instructions, see the **Linville Gorge Rim Drive**.) To the north, *Table Rock Trail* climbs steeply (500 feet in a half-mile) up to the cliff-lined, flat-topped **Table Rock**, a remarkable mesa-like formation protruding 600 feet above the trees of the surrounding ridge. The cliff tops give a sweeping view over the entire gorge and the Blue Ridge beyond, as well as out over the Catawba Valley to the south.

WATERFALL IN SOUTH MOUNTAINS STATE PARK

The *Chimneys Trail* heads south along the rim to the rocky hoodoos known as The Chimneys. Much easier and only slightly longer (100 feet up in 0.7 mile), the path starts as a gentle ridgetop climb to an exposed rocky cliff with wide views, including one back toward Table Rock. From there the trail descends gently to a gap as the ridge becomes increasingly knife-like. More rocky cliffs give views over the gorge, with tall spires eroded along its edge. The trail continues along the knife ridge to the top of The Chimney, a phallic spire towering above the rest. Return the way you came.

Both trails are now part of the **Mountains-to-Sea Trail**, and carry its distinctive round white blaze.

**LONG-DISTANCE PATHS The Mountains-to-Sea Trail** At NC 80, the Mountains-to-Sea Trail drops down from the Blue Ridge Parkway to spend the next 71 miles exploring the rugged lands beneath it. This may be the most beautiful section of the trail in the mountains, and the most difficult. This chapter holds the first 46 miles of this section, from NC 80 to NC 181.

From NC 80 the trail descends gradually southeastwards away from the parkway on remote Woods Mountain, yielding good views within 1 mile of the trailhead. This continues as a ridgetop hike with more views from outcrops and ledges, reaching the base of the mountains in 9 miles, and US 221 at a local park in 4 more miles.

From here it's 33 miles to the next paved trailhead—the scenic and difficult part. It starts by jumping a low ridge (with some good views and a streamside meadow along the way) to a 200-foot bridge over the North Fork Catawba River, specially constructed for the trail. From there the trail takes 4 miles of uphill walking to cover 2 miles of linear distance, climbing nearly 2,200 feet using 30 switchbacks to reach the very beautiful top of Bald Knob. Here panoramic views stretch from the North Fork Catawba immediately below to Linville Gorge, Lake James, and Morganton. Now the trail is an easy downhill ridge hike along a gated forest road, then a path over to the Kistler Memorial Highway, here a very bad gravel road that may not be passable to passenger cars.

SUNRISE ON LAKE JAMES

From this ostensible trailhead the trail enters the **Linville Gorge Wilderness**. First it passes close to The Pinnacle, where a short side trail leads to wide clifftop views over the mouth of the gorge. Next it drops 1,300 feet down to the mouth of the gorge and fords the Linville River, only to climb very steeply 1,500 feet up to the opposite side. From here it's a cliff walk, mile after mile along the gorge's eastern cliff side with view after view, passing the great spires of **The Chimneys** to **Table Rock Picnic Area**, the only reasonable trailhead within this 33-mile length. The trail continues along the cliffs, passing the short side trail to the mesa-top of **Table Rock** then finally bending away, into the forests to the east. The trail now drops yet another 1,600 feet. There the scenery once again kicks into high gear as the path turns to follow the creek uphill, past waterfalls and a chasm, through mature forests and a tiny hidden pocket valley, then up through old growth to a forest road and a trailhead on NC 181.

## ✷ Villages

**Morganton** Founded in the late 1700s as the pioneer settlement of Morganborough, Morganton gained its prosperity as a furniture mill town in the 19th century. The mountain hardwood forests furnished the raw material, and the railroad shipped out the final product. This is still the arrangement—Morganton retains the division headquarters of major furniture manufacturer Henredon. Late-19th-century Morganton also gained major medical centers, and for similar reasons—good rail access, and closeness to the healthy air of the mountains. Today the late-19th-century campuses of the Broughton Hospital (a state psychiatric hospital) and the North Carolina School for the Deaf make up a large National Register Historic District, occupying the same hill on the south end of town. It's a gentle place of stately old buildings, wooded glades, and wide mountain views over grassy meadows.

Settled since the middle of the 18th century, Morganton has several worthwhile historic sites. However, its main attraction is its downtown—a classic small town Main Street, anchored by a lovely Courthouse Square, dominated by its old square courthouse (now an historic museum). A good quality shopping district, full of active, interesting stores and cafés, runs along the north side of the Courthouse Square, while two complexes of historic buildings are being renovated into more shops nearby. Parking is plentiful and free, with lots of street parking as well as large municipal lots behind the storefronts.

**Marion** This thriving county seat sits on an important railroad junction, where two major freight lines fight their separate ways up the face of the Blue Ridge. It centers on a four-block-long downtown of two-story brick storefronts from the late 19th century, and a golden brick 1920s courthouse faced with 12-foot windows. Downtown shops still center mainly on the old small-town standbys, well kept but lacking restoration. However, the little downtown has character, and improves a bit every year, as projects such as the Shamrock Inn and Eagle Hotel restore the buildings one by one, filling them with interesting and worthwhile things.

**Old Fort** Nestled at the base of the Blue Ridge, Old Fort has been a working railroad town since the 1870s. Its large siding, where steam engines used to get a second "pusher" engine to help them up the mountain, has long attracted mills, and modern Old Fort has a half-dozen or so clean factories. For a visitor, Old Fort is worthwhile for its two museums (one to pioneer life, another to the railroad) and its attractive little downtown. Downtown Old Fort sports a single block of 19th-century brick storefronts, a bright yellow depot containing the railroad museum, a tiny park with a gazebo, and a 25-foot-tall granite arrowhead set on a 15-foot stone plinth, erected in the 1920s as a memorial to frontier peace.

THE CHIMNEYS OF LINVILLE GORGE

# ✷ Wild Places



**THE GREAT FORESTS** **Linville Gorge Wilderness** One of the earliest wilderness areas created by Congress, this 11,000-acre tract preserves a deep, 13-mile-long gorge cut into the face of the Blue Ridge. The gorge starts with the massive 90-foot plunge of the Linville River over **Linville Falls**, then quickly drops away in near-vertical slopes to a river bottom that's a third of a mile below the gorge edge. The fierce river and steep slopes have prevented logging, leaving the gorge in pristine shape—a rich, riverside old-growth forest. Access to the gorge bottom is by foot paths that go straight down the gorge sides, making for an extremely difficult return. Even the riverside trail can be difficult, finding its way along the rough, rocky gorge bottom. Nevertheless, the gorge bottom is reasonably popular with day hikers, backpackers, and fishermen. Fortunately for the less athletic, the gorge rims are easier to reach (see *Exploring by Car*), and the finest viewpoint, **Wiseman's View**, is disabled accessible.

✐ 🐾 ♿ **South Mountains State Park** (www.ncparks.gov/Visit/parks/somo/main.php; e-mail: south.mountains@ncdenr.gov; 828-433-4772; fax: 828-433-4778; 3001 South Mountain Park Ave., Connelly Springs, NC 28612). Open all year during daylight hours. The 16,664-acre South Mountains State Park occupies the rugged central heart of the South Mountains, an outlier of the Blue Ridge. With about 1,000 feet of valley-to-peak relief, the South Mountains are smaller than much of the Blue Ridge—but they more than make up for it with rugged scenery. Streams twist and dash through deep gorges; the sharp points of gray cliffs emerge from deep forests; truck-sized boulders litter the bottoms of steep gulches; great waterfalls plunge over cliff edges. The mixed forests are dominated by hemlocks, a conifer with pine-like bark and fir-like needles that grows rapidly to great sizes. On exposed cliffs, pines and hemlocks twist into bonsai shapes.

Heavily logged in the 20th century, South Mountains State Park is laced by a network of slide roads (used to skid timber downhill), jeep trails, and even former automobile roads—nearly all now closed to vehicles. The best of these are marked as bicycle and/or horse trails, while other paths are strictly for foot travel only. The rugged topography makes nearly all paths difficult, but the short local relief limits the pain. The **two most popular paths** give breathtaking (figuratively and literally) climbs to a high cliff view and an 80-foot waterfall. Many other worthwhile paths exist, some requiring backpacking. The park has a new visitors center, **two picnic areas**, and an equestrian camping area.

OLD FORT DEPOT, NOW A HISTORY MUSEUM

The park's trail system is vast and complex, yet it occupies less than half of the park's total acreage; the western half, only recently purchased, is still in its planning stages. (A recently published master plan decided to leave this area to its remoteness, and called for the ever-popular "further study" on hiking, horses, and backcountry camping.) Nor is this all. On the immediate south of the park are the South Mountain Game Lands, with 19,781 acres and no official paths. The game lands are state owned and open to hikers during the off-season and on Sundays. Together, these two giant tracts encompass 57 square miles.

South Mountains State Park is 20 miles south of I-40, exit 104 (Enola Road). Take Enola Road south for 9 miles to its end at Old NC 18, then go right 5 miles. From here, large brown state park signs will guide you in for the remaining 6 miles.

**RIVERS The Catawba River** (www.ncwaterfalls.com/catawba1.htm). The 220-mile Catawba River rises from the Blue Ridge above Old Fort to flow eastward through this chapter's area. Its uppermost section has long been known for its incredible series of waterfalls, but access was closed by its landowner shortly before the first edition of this book went to press. Great news! In 2010 the Forest Service acquired the waterfalls (a gift from The Nature Conservancy) and negotiated an access agreement. This is one of the great waterfall walks of the area (including a ruinous 1923 concrete dam) that is fully described in the website, above.

River access starts as the river emerges from the mountains at Old Fort. For the next 18 miles the river meanders through a half-mile-wide floodplain as the mountains gradually recede on both sides, a nice canoe stream with Class I–II water. For the most part it's an attractive small river, with generally healthy environments and attractive riverside scenery, although passing several factories and gravel pits along the way. This flows into **Lake James**; after that it flows another 18 miles, passing Morganton, to leave this chapter's area as it enters another hydropower lake, Lake Rhodhiss. Surprisingly, this section is more wild in character than the upstream one, and, except for Morganton itself, is mainly riverside forests and an occasional farm. Inside Morganton, a 3.8-mile **greenway** parallels the river, giving continuous bank access and some canoe launches.

**RECREATION AREAS Lake James State Park** At one time little more than a lake access area, this state park, located 18 miles west of Morganton via NC 126, has been steadily expanding and upgrading. Its main area flanks the Catawba River Dam with two large boat ramps, then extends into the lake on two fingers. A tree-shaded picnic area sits near a sandy swimming beach; hiking paths loop through the woods to lakeside overlooks. New land purchases on the other side of the lake bring the park up to 3,000 acres, and master planning has just been completed for a large area of hiking, boating, swimming, and camping.

♿ **The Catawba River Greenway in Morganton** (e-mail: tsuther@ci.morganton.nc.us; 828-438-5350; Morganton, NC 28680). This city of Morganton Park stretches along the south bank of the Catawba River for 3.8 miles, starting at Judges Barbeque off US 70 and extending downstream (north) to US 64. It's an easy, paved walk with plenty of views over the wide Catawba as it enters the Piedmont, as well as a dramatic 226-foot steel truss pedestrian bridge over the river. The upstream terminus at Judges has ample parking and picnicking facilities, as well as a canoe launch and fishing docks.

**PICNIC AREAS Table Rock Picnic Area** This small primitive picnic area sits in a handsome hardwood forest on the rim of the **Linville Gorge Wilderness**, between the rock pinnacles of **Table Rock** and **The Chimneys**. The drive into the picnic area is worthwhile in itself, and short hiking trails lead to stunning views.

**Bark House Picnic Area** This small, attractive picnic area sits in a shady hardwood glade atop a small knob, an easy 6 miles south of the Blue Ridge Parkway on NC 181 in the Linville area. It's a lovely little place, with a low fee (free) that reflects its single pit toilet and water from a hand pump. Nearby, two short but steep hiking trails lead down into the gorge-like Upper Creek Valley to reach the large and beautiful **Upper Creek Falls**.

✐ ♿ **South Mountains Picnic Areas** South Mountains State Park has two fine streamside picnic areas. **Jacobs Fork Picnic Area** sits beside the main parking lot, its dozen tables spread widely underneath tall hemlocks and rhododendrons. The first-rate **Hemlocks Nature Trail**, disabled accessible, starts in the picnic area and follows the banks of Jacobs Creek for 0.38 of a mile. Just beyond the end of the nature trail is the primitive **Shimmy Creek Picnic Area**, with no automobile access, toilets, or water.

**Old Fort Picnic Area** This lovely national forest picnic area on the back road to **Andrews Geyser**, offers streamside picnicking in an old CCC-style site. Tables sit under tall old trees, spaced well apart, with small stone walls and steps forming scenic accents. The entrance road furnishes a wonderful view up Mill Creek Valley, past a quiet farming community, to the forested wall of the Blue Ridge.

## ✷ To See

**BIG DAMMED LAKES** ✐ **Lake James** (828-652-5047; P.O. Box 340, Nebo, NC 28761). Giant electric utility Duke Power created this huge reservoir at the foot of the Blue Ridge between Marion and Morganton by damming two separate watersheds—the Catawba River and the Linville River—and linking them with a canal. They actually needed three dams to do this, with the third preventing the combined impoundments from slipping into a side stream. Like all such lakes, Lake James provides lots of room for motorboat-based sports, and lots of public and private boat launches. One of these is at **Lake James State Park**, along with a number of short walking trails, a sandy beach, and a very good picnic area.

Sitting at the foot of the Blue Ridge, Lake James gives exceptional mountain views—particularly toward the cliff-lined mouth of the **Linville Gorge Wilderness**. The easternmost dam, known as Bridgewater Dam, gives the best shore views; from the top of this tall earthen dam, traversed by a paved state road, you can see the sweep of the Blue Ridge curving in front of you, from the Linville Gorge cliffs on your right to the mile-high peaks of the Black Mountains on your left. This is a first-rate sunset spot, especially when the air is still and the water glassy. To reach this spot, take NC 126 west out of Morganton for 9 miles, then left at a fork onto North Powerhouse Road; Bridgewater Dam is 3 miles farther on.

**HISTORIC SITES** ✐ **The Old Burke County Courthouse** (www.historicburke.org; 828-437-4104; P.O. Box 915, Morganton, NC 28680). Open all year, 10 AM–4 PM, Tues.–Fri. The tiny old Burke County Courthouse sits at the center of downtown Morganton, on its nicely kept square, with its Civil War statue out front. It's a square structure whose outside stairs lead to grandly columned second-story porches, topped by an elaborate Victorian cupola. However, it's much older than its Victorian trim; it was built in 1837 as a simple, elegant Federal-style structure, and served as the summer seat of the North Carolina Supreme Court until the Civil War. Inside, the Historic Burke Foundation maintains a small historic museum with exhibits that change annually; the second floor is taken up by a single 150-seat auditorium, where you can view a good slide presentation on Burke County history. Also in the building are the offices of the Historic Burke Foundation and the Travel and Tourism Commission, either of which will welcome your visit and your questions.

**Quaker Meadows Plantation (The McDowell House)** (www.historicburke.org; e-mail: historicburke@compascable.net; 828-437-4104; P.O. Box 915, Morganton, NC 28655). Open April–November, 2 PM–5 PM, Sun.; other times by appointment. The 1812 McDowell House sits on the 6 remaining acres of the vast Quaker Meadows Plantation. In Colonial times the McDowells were leaders of the western settlers, and their plantation hosted the gathering of the Overmountain Men as they marched to meet the British forces at Kings Mountain. The restored McDowell House shows the post-revolutionary success of this early family. A high-ceilinged two-story structure made of on-site red-brick, the two front doors show a Pennsylvania Dutch influence (even though the McDowells were Scots-Irish). Despite encroaching urbanization, the house remains beautifully situated amid rolling lawns. The Historic Burke Foundation has carefully restored it to its 1812 appearance and rebuilt the detached kitchen, and is in the process of locating authentic period furnishings. To reach the McDowell House, take NC 181 4 miles northwest from Morganton's town center to the end of the four-lane; then turn right on St. Mary's Church Road.

OLD COUNTY COURTHOUSE IN MORGANTON

**Morganton's National Historic Districts** Morganton has nine National Historic Districts listed on the National Register of Historic Places. This adds up to a lot of old buildings. However, it means more than this; a historic district preserves the look and feel of the past, and is an experience in itself. The Historic Burke Foundation has an excellent color brochure listing all nine districts and giving details of the major buildings in each one. It's a good way to get a deep insight into the way an American small town used to be.

**Andrews Geyser** (www.oldfort.org/andrews_geyser.htm). Built as part of the Swannanoa Grade railroad in the

1870s, Andrews Geyser shoots 30 feet up in the air continuously—that is, as long as it's turned on. The geyser, named after a railroad pioneer, sits in a small park surrounded by railroad; it's in the crook of a hairpin turn that the railroad makes as it climbs the face of the Blue Ridge. In the early days, the geyser served as a scenic focal point for railroad passengers entering (or leaving) this spectacular mountain climb, impressing the passengers as their train circled around it. Today it's an historic artifact from a bygone era, kept in loving repair by locals such as the innkeeper of the **Inn on Mill Creek**; the lovely little lake that feeds the geyser is on the inn's property, and the innkeeper is the one who turns the valve on and off daily. The geyser, shooting straight up in the middle of a pentagonal reflecting pond, is surrounded by shaded picnic tables. If you are lucky, a train will pass while you visit it, looping around you with half its cars going toward you and the other half away. To find Andrews Geyser take US 70 west from Old Fort and follow the signs, first onto Old US 70, then up Mill Creek Road.

**Carson House** (historiccarsonhouse.com; e-mail: info@historiccarsonhouse.com; 828-724-4948; 1805 Highway 70 West, Marion, NC 28752). Open May–October: 10 AM–5 PM, Tues.–Sat.; 2 PM–5 PM, Sun.; closed Mon. November–April: by appointment. Revolutionary war soldier and prominent North Carolina politician Col. John Carson built this large family home at the center of his plantation in 1790, an elaborate two-story farmhouse built of 12-inch walnut logs. Fifty years later his son modernized this sophisticated log home by covering it in clapboard and adding the wide first- and second-story porches with their Greek Revival trim. McDowell County was organized in the Carson House; it served as the new county's first courthouse; and the Carsons donated the site of the permanent county seat, Marion, 3 miles to the east (but still on the family plantation). Today, the Carson House is an independent not-for-profit museum displaying pioneer objects and furnishings. It's on US 70 west of Marion, near the intersection with NC 80.

**CULTURAL SITES** **Senator Sam J. Ervin, Jr. Library** (www.samervinlibrary.org; 828-448-6195; fax: 828-448-6173; 1001 Burkemont Ave., Morganton, NC 28655). Open 8 AM–5 PM, Mon.–Fri. Those of us old enough to remember Watergate will no doubt remember the late Senator Sam Ervin, chairman of the Nixon impeachment hearings, for his fairness, shrewdness, sharp intelligence, deep knowledge of the Constitution—and frequent protestations that he was "a simple country lawyer." Senator Sam was a Morganton man, born and bred, and Western Piedmont Community College has commemorated their local-boy-made-good in a most appropriate way: by preserving his large personal library. Western Piedmont Community College has gone well beyond saving the senator's personal papers and 7,500 books. It has faithfully recreated his large, wood-paneled library, every piece of furniture the way the senator left it, every book it its original place on the shelf. Located in its own room within the college's library, the Ervin Library offers a window into a great mind.

Apart from the Ervin Library, Western Piedmont Community College is worth a visit for its wide views and handsome campus. Crowning a hillock on the southwestern edge of town, its modern buildings form a tight group surrounded by wide meadows. To the north and east are views toward the 19th-century historic districts of Broughton Hospital and the North Carolina School for the Deaf, each facing the college with its own farm land and crowning its own hill with cupola-topped buildings. On the horizons are the silhouettes of the Blue Ridge and the South Mountains.

To reach the Ervin Library, follow the signs from exit 103 on I-40; once on campus, you'll find the library on the second floor of the Phifer Learning Resource Center. Then explore the views by strolling this compact campus. Parking is ample and no permit is needed.

**Jailhouse Gallery (Burke Arts Council)** (www.burkearts.org; e-mail: assistant@burkearts.org; 828-433-7282; 115 Meeting St., Morganton, NC 28655). Open 10 AM–4 PM, Mon.–Fri. No old courthouse square would be complete without an old jail. Morganton's 1950s-era Andy-of-Mayberry-style sheriff's office and jail now houses an art museum dedicated to local and regional artists. Expect more than the traditional displays of small-town art students; with national headquarters of major furniture manufacturers, Morganton is a serious venue, where artists can get their work seen and appreciated by art-buying professionals. The thorough-going displays, professionally presented, wander through two good-sized galleries, while a third room houses a small gift shop. Displays change every two months, so it's always worthwhile to stop in for another look.

**The Mountain Gateway Museum** (828-668-9259; Old Fort, NC 28762). Located at the center of Old Fort, this small state museum features exhibits on pioneer life and folk culture in a 1936 WPA building made of native stone. Permanent exhibits include mountain folk arts, a log cabin reconstructed from a pioneer church, and a reconstructed still; temporary exhibits, on a variety of topics, change every couple of months. Next door are two beautiful old log cabins, authentically furnished with period antiques.

**The Old Fort Railroad Museum** (828-668-4244; corner of Catawba Avenue and Main Street, Old Fort, NC 28762). Old Fort's canary yellow depot sits at the center of its single-block downtown, the site of the town's 25-foot-tall granite arrowhead, a monument to frontier peace. Today the depot houses a small but charming railroad museum, with rooms furnished as a late-19th-century depot, and exhibits on the dramatic **Swannanoa Grade**, 10 miles of railroad that loop up the face of the Blue Ridge just outside of town.

**MYSTERIOUS PHENOMENA** **The Brown Mountain Lights** Since 1900 (and perhaps earlier, according to local tales), mysterious lights have danced and flickered over the 2,725-foot peak of Brown Mountain, a side ridge off the Blue Ridge 13 miles north of Morganton. Attempts to explain them have all failed, including train lights (they appear when trains don't run), auto headlights (no autos), and swamp gas (no swamps). Most of the remaining explanations involve ghosts in some way. So find a good viewpoint on a clear night, bring to mind your favorite campfire tale, and wait for the lights to come out. With luck, you can view the Brown Mountain Lights from Wiseman's View on the rim of Linville Gorge, and from overlooks along NC 181.

## * To Do

**GOLF** **Silver Creek Plantation Golf Club** (www.silvercreekplantation.com; 828-584-6911; 4241 Plantation Dr., Morganton, NC 28655). Open all year. This

18-hole Tom Jackson–designed, semi-private course wanders along hilltops west of Morganton, with sweeping views toward the South Mountains and the Blue Ridge. **Fairway Oaks Bed & Breakfast** is located on this beautiful course, overlooking the fifth green.

**Pine Mountain Golf Course** (828-433-4950; Hwy. 18, Connelley Springs, NC 28612). This 18-hole Paul Mallard–designed course rests high in the South Mountains, adjacent to South Mountain State Park. Originally created as part of South Mountains Resort, this golf course with its wide and lovely views continues to thrive even as the resort business is being reorganized (and largely phased out).

**Old Fort Golf Course** (828-668-4256; Rte. 2, Old Fort, NC 28762). This semi-private nine-hole par-36 course, built in 1962, sits south of Old Fort in the rolling hills of the Catawba River Valley, with views toward the Hickorynut Mountains to the south. To find it, take exit 73 (Old Fort) from I-40, then follow the signs south for 3 miles.

**Marion Lake Golf Club** (828-652-6232; Hwy. 126, Nebo, NC 28761). This par-70 course, first opened in 1933, wanders along hill tops on the south side of Lake James, with stunning views over the water toward the cliffs of the Blue Ridge.

**GOLD MINING** ✐ **Thermal City Gold Mine** (www.HuntForGold.com; e-mail: info@thermalcitygoldmine.com; 828-286-3016; 5240 US 221 N. Hwy., Union Mills, NC 28167). Open all year during daylight hours. The South Mountains, and the hills to their east, formed the site of America's first gold rush, when a 12-year-old boy picked up a 12-pound (yup, that's pounds, not ounces) gold nugget from a Piedmont creek. Within the South Mountains, gold was quickly found along the Second Broad River, 13 miles south of modern-day Marion (and 9 miles south of I-40) just off US 276. One of the first gold mines in 1830 was the Thermal City Mine. Today visitors can pan for gold along a half-mile of the Second Broad River. (In a placer mine, gold dust and nuggets are washed from streamside sediments, not dug out of hard rock.) Panning is done with unsalted on-site deposits in an attractive riverside setting, for an authentic experience. There's an on-site camp store, and campsites and cabins are also available for overnight stays. Serious gold bugs can enjoy one of the three weekend-long common digs held each year.

## ✷ Lodging

**BED & BREAKFAST INNS Fairway Oaks Bed & Breakfast** (fairwayoaksbandb.com; e-mail: fairwayoaks@charter.net; 828-584-7677; 4640 Plantation Dr., Morganton, NC 28655). It only looks like a traditional southern farmhouse, with its wide wood porches and tall windows; Fairway Oaks was built as a four-room bed & breakfast in 1997. Set inside the gated golf community of Silver Creek Plantation 10 miles west of Morganton, this course-side inn has sweeping views over the links toward the majestic South Mountains. The guest lounge is warm and inviting, with hardwood accents, plush new furniture, and a gas log fireplace. Upstairs, each of the four sizeable guest rooms is furnished around its own theme with antiques and reproductions, and has its own phone, data port, and desk. Guests receive a discount on the semi-private **Silver Creek Plantation Golf Club**.

✐ 🐾 **College Street Inn** (828-430-8911; 204 S. College St., Morganton, NC 28655). Located near downtown Morganton in the prestigious West Union Historic District, the four-room

College Street Inn occupies a simple, well-kept cottage. While the exterior may be simple, the inside is nothing less than a road warrior's Valhalla. Handsomely furnished with blond hardwood accents, the rooms are large, comfortable, and business ready, with desks, phones, and data ports. The smallest room matches that of a good hotel; the largest room has a king bed, a full-sized executive desk, and a separate sitting area with two sofas and full-size windows. Guests with business meetings can use the cottage's conference room, with its own private entrance, fax, computer, and large screen TV/video player. Guests receive a hot breakfast in the large and comfortable common room, or can make up their own meals in the fully furnished guests' kitchen. The College Inn welcomes pleasure travelers as well as business travelers, and is a good choice for touring Morganton's handsome downtown and nine historic districts.

**The Inn on Mill Creek** (www.inn-on-mill-creek.com; e-mail: info@innonmillcreek.com; 877-735-2964, 828-668-1115; P.O. Box 185, Ridgecrest, NC 28770). Open all year. To reach the Mill on Old Creek, leave I-40 at Ridgecrest (exit 66) and follow the bed & breakfast signs east 3 miles. This peaceful, beautiful haven lies deep within the Pisgah National Forest, the only home on a country lane that winds up the Blue Ridge through 9 miles of forestland. Beside the inn, a 1916 dam forms a small lake stocked with rainbow and brown trout; its outfall, through a pipe regulated by the innkeepers, feeds **Andrews Geyser**. Uphill, carefully trimmed fruit trees march in neat rows; the fresh fruit finds its way into the gourmet breakfasts. Old tracks radiate through the miles of public forest that cover the Blue Ridge slope in all directions, all carefully mapped and perfect for exploring on foot or mountain bike. The home itself is a large modernist structure from the early 1980s, whose large common areas include fireplaces and a library balcony. The four en suite rooms are furnished with reproduction antiques in a country style; and are moderate to large in size.

**CABIN RENTALS** ✐ **Robardajen Woods Bed & Breakfast** (www.robardajenwoods.com; 828-584-3191; 5640 Robardajen Woods, Nebo, NC 28761).When Bill Reep retired he took up a hobby: he moves historic log cabins onto his large forested property near Lake James, rebuilds them, and renovates them to a high degree of comfort. The result is sort of a log cabin bed & breakfast; you stay in an historic pioneer log cabin with a porch overlooking deep woods, then join the Reeps and the other guests for a fine country breakfast. Or make breakfast in your own cabin—they all have full, well-equipped kitchens. In addition, the Reeps occasionally take guests into the Main Lodge, their personal home—a 1790 two-story log farmhouse from South Carolina with a stunning interior that meanders through five different levels. All cabins have a full quota of old country antiques, as well as access to some more modern comforts such as a swimming pool and an exercise room. (Yes, it's a log exercise room.) Robardajen Woods is a five-minute drive from I-40, halfway between Morganton and Marion, three minutes from Lake James, and equal distance between the Blue Ridge and the South Mountains.

**The Cottages at Spring House Farm** (www.springhousefarm.com; e-mail: thecottages@springhousefarm.com; 877-738-9798, 828-738-9798; 219 Haynes Rd., Marion, NC 28752). Open all year. This ecology-minded retreat has six widely spaced cabins on a wooded 92-acre farm in the Hickorynut Mountains (part of the South Mountains), 15 miles south of Marion. It prides itself of its sense of remoteness and solitude, yet is by no means hard to reach, 12 miles south of I-40's exit 81 via Sugar Hill Road (SSR 1001). All cabins have private porches or decks with full-size outdoor hot tubs, and all cabins have either a wood-burning stone fireplace or stove. Each cabin has its own unique elements: a view over a trout pond; through the woods to mountains beyond; a tree growing through a deck; a bedroom opening onto a large, airy porch; or an interior barn door that slides aside to unite the great king bed with the living room's wood fire. Decor is based around craftsman-style furniture, each piece handmade locally from salvaged historic lumber left over from the Ledbetter House restoration; the massive king-size beds are particularly impressive. Kitchens are not only fully furnished with everything you need to cook well and serve well, they are also stocked with milk, sausage, fresh-made bread, real butter, local jams, and brown eggs from a neighbor's farm. The owners live on-site, in the 1836 Ledbetter House that retains its original interior paint.

## ✱ Where to Eat

**EATING OUT** ✐ **Yiannis Restaurant** (828-430-8700; 112 West Union, Morganton, NC 28655). Open for lunch and dinner, every day. Behind the narrow storefront of this downtown Morganton restaurant is a bright, sparkling space with hand-painted murals on white walls, hardwood floors and tables, and an original high ceiling. The menu is large and eclectic, with traditional Greek recipes mixing with Southern and American favorites. Not surprisingly, this bright and airy restaurant has gained a broad audience in this sophisticated little mill town, with its appealing mix of simplicity and sophistication, quality and price.

✐ **Judges Riverside Barbeque** (www.judgesriverside.com; e-mail: judgesriverside@fulenwider.net; 828-433-5798; fax: 828-433-9842; 128 Greenlee Ford Rd., Morganton, NC 28680). Open daily, all year, 11 AM–9 PM. This large new restaurant sits on a remote, shaded spot on the south bank of the Catawba River, at the end of Greenlee Ford Road, hard by the upstream terminus of the **Catawba River Greenway**. Inside it's an open, wood-paneled layout with hardwood tables and an exposed ceiling; its floor-to-ceiling windows give wide views over the Catawba River, as does its multi-level deck. It features a varied menu and imaginative daily specials, but here's all you really need to know: the barbeque is great. It's freshly made, slow cooked, mild, smoky, tender, and moist, with just the right amount of crust—chopped pork, beef brisket, chicken, or ribs. They serve sauce on the side, not on the meat, and they make it themselves—a wonderfully spiced hot sauce and a sweeter mild sauce. The home-made sides include a wonderful cayenne-hot coleslaw made, not with mayonnaise, but with the vinegar sauce they use to baste the meat (a North Carolina tradition, worthy of imitation elsewhere). The onion rings are also worthy of note—made fresh daily, thick cut, and sweet. If you order a sandwich they'll use a sourdough bun "made special for us by a lady in town," as a waitress put it. "She makes the pound cake too. You should try it." Good advice.

**The Crooked Door Coffee House** (www.uniquegalleriesnc.com/CrookedDoorCoffeeHouse/Webpages/CrookedDoorCoffeecoverpage.html; 828-652-

6216; 11 N. Main St., Marion, NC 28752). Open 8 AM–10 PM, Wed.–Sat. This attractive second-story coffee shop sits behind the arched windows of Marion's beautiful old Eagle Hotel, an 1895 three-story brick building on the north end of downtown. It features Italian and American coffees and homemade pastries, along with lots of old Victorian wood trim, a sofa sitting area by a fire, and good views over downtown.

## ✷ Entertainment

**City of Moganton Municipal Auditorium (CoMMA)** (www.commaonline.org; 800-939-7469, 828-433-7469; South College St., Morganton, NC 28655). This handsome auditorium, larger and nicer than you might expect for a small town, sits on a hill above downtown, surrounded by the well-kept Victorian mansions of the South King Street Historic District. Their summertime Back Porch series features outdoor evening concerts with a picnic dinner. To find it, follow the signs for "CoMMA," which stands for "City of Morganton Municipal Auditorium."

**Old Fort Mountain Music** Every Friday, from 7 PM until late at night. Free. Old Fort Mountain Music shares space with Old Fort EMS in an old brick building at the center of town. On the one hand, it doesn't provide any on-site parking, as the EMS vehicles can't be blocked. (However, there's plenty of free parking within a half-block walk.) On the other hand, the wide, empty EMS driveways provide a place for the musicians to tune up, practice, and talk. Inside, a long, narrow hall with folding chairs forms the venue for this free weekly mountain concert and jam session. Bands range from first-rate to enthusiastic, playing a variety of mountain music, bluegrass, and country—but the emphasis is on mountain music.

## ✷ Selective Shopping

### *Morganton*

**Downtown Morganton** Morganton's Old Courthouse Square, well-kept and handsomely landscaped in a traditional style, sits at the center of a four-block downtown of turn-of-the-century two-story storefronts. Downtown Morganton still preserves the charm of a small town center, its old buildings immaculately kept and filled with clothing stores, restaurants, and boutiques. Shopping is concentrated along Union Street (Business US 70) on the north side of the Old Courthouse Square. Traditional old storefronts stretch westward from the square; to the east sits the newly restored Morganton Trading Company, offering more specialty shops in a restored 19th-century mill complex that includes the city hall.

**Apple Hill Orchard & Cider Mill** (applehillorchard.com; e-mail: hprewitt@applehillorchard.com; 828-437-1224; 2075 Pleasant Hill Ave., Morganton, NC 28655). Open August–December. This working apple orchard, located on the lower slopes of the South Mountains south of Morganton, has been producing apples since the 1930s. During the harvest season they open their orchard to the public and sell a variety of fresh-made apple products—including cider pressed on the site. While the well-kept buildings are modern, the site and the orchard are very scenic. To find it, take the Enola Road exit (exit 104) from I-40 south for 4 miles, turning right onto Pleasant Hill Road at the large brick church.

**South Mountain Crafts Village** (828-433-2607; 409 Enola Rd., Morganton, NC 28655). Open 9 AM–4 PM, Mon.–Fri. This unique craft shop features handmade crafts and furniture produced by the residents of Western Carolina Center, a large regional facility for the mentally handicapped.

Founded in 1980, the crafts village occupies seven of a mile-long line of small, square wooden houses that face Enola Road, built half a century ago as employee housing for the center. The crafts village exists to give training and work opportunities, and the skilled and original products found in its shop testify to its success. In it you'll find wooden craft items, pottery weaving, candles, soaps, potpourri, quilts, early American pine furniture, and fine finished oak tables and chairs—all handmade on the premises. In season, you may find fruits, vegetables, and flowers grown in the village's gardens and greenhouses—although the center's kitchens get first crack at the edibles. To reach the crafts village from I-40, take the Enola Road exit 104, then go south a quarter-mile.

### *Marion*

**Downtown Marion** Marion's downtown spreads along four blocks, centered on a 1903 bank with a fake dome and a wonderful 1922 golden brick courthouse with 12-foot art deco windows. Downtown is busy and improving steadily but is still recovering its shopping and architecture. Shops tend to be functional rather than funky, and all too many historic storefronts remain barnacled by "modernizing" facades from the 1950s and '60s.

### *Old Fort*

**Downtown Old Fort** Old Fort may well have the nicest one-block downtown in the mountains. A single row of one- and two-story turn-of-the-century stores lines one block of US 70, anchored by the old railroad depot and the giant arrowhead statue at its west end. Half of one side is taken up by a nice little park with a gazebo, while half of the other side is occupied by Old Fort EMS and Mountain Music (mixed together in the same old brick building). There is just enough room remaining for three nice, largish shops of antiques, collectables, memorabilia, and stuff. It's definitely worth poking around, particularly as it's next door to the Old Fort Railroad Museum and only two blocks from the Mountain Gateway Museum.

## ✷ Special Events

**SPRING** **Assault on Mount Mitchell** Second weekend in May. Sponsored by Freewheelers of Spartanburg, a South Carolina bicycle club, this bicycle race goes from Spartanburg, South Carolina, to the top of Mount Mitchell, North Carolina. The thousand or so racers cover 100 miles of road and bicycle 11,000 feet uphill; the final stretch, from Marion to Mount Mitchell, climbs 6,700 feet in 27 miles.

**SUMMER** **Freedom Celebration and Rodeo** Fourth of July weekend. Old Fort Ruritans sponsor an old-fashioned cowboy rodeo as the main event in the town's celebration; there's also a parade and fireworks.

**Historic Morganton Festival** Weekend after Labor Day. This large downtown street fair features arts and crafts booths, food vendors, and live music.

**AUTUMN** **Mountain Glory Festival, Marion** Second Saturday in October. This two-block-long street fair in downtown Marion features a hundred booths with crafters, artists, and food vendors, plus live entertainment in front of the county courthouse. It is held in association with a month-long quilter's show.

**WINTER** **Appalachian Potters Market**, Marion First Saturday in December. Held annually at McDowell High School in Marion, this major regional market, open to the general public, is a serious meet between regional potters and their buyers. It draws 60–80 potters each year.

# Asheville's Mountains

2

THE BLUE RIDGE PARKWAY CIRCLES ASHEVILLE

THE CITY OF ASHEVILLE

THE BLUE RIDGE PARKWAY APPROACHES THE SMOKIES

THE BLUE RIDGE: CHIMNEY ROCK & SALUDA

THE BLUE RIDGE: HENDERSONVILLE & BREVARD

NORTH OF ASHEVILLE: THE BALD MOUNTAINS

# ASHEVILLE'S MOUNTAINS

The highest mountains in the East mark the point where the Blue Ridge enters the Asheville region. Here the Black Mountains extend a solid wall of 6,000-foot peaks northward, including Mount Mitchell, the highest mountain in the eastern United States. The Craggy Mountains, famous for their natural rhododendron gardens, merge with the Blacks just north of Asheville. The Blue Ridge Parkway hugs these high ridgelines, furnishing easy access to spectacular tracts of Pisgah National Forest land.

THE PARKWAY IN THE CRAGGY MOUNTAINS

Despite this rugged beginning, one of the largest and gentlest valleys in the Smokies/Blue Ridge region forms behind the Blue Ridge—the valley of the French Broad River. A major tributary of the Tennessee, the French Broad River (like the geologically similar New River farther north), is one of the most ancient in North America, and perhaps the world. It twists sluggishly through a wide area, cutting through hard Blue Ridge rock like so much butter. It forms a natural path for trans-mountain roads and railroads, and the convergence of these roads forms the mountains' only city, Asheville.

The mountain's first stagecoach road, known as the Buncombe Turnpike, was constructed in the 1820s from Charleston, South Carolina, to Asheville and down the French Broad into Tennessee. For decades it made much of its money from drovers, men who would drive hundreds of cattle, pigs, and even turkeys from mountain farms to markets in South Carolina. However, it quickly generated a new an

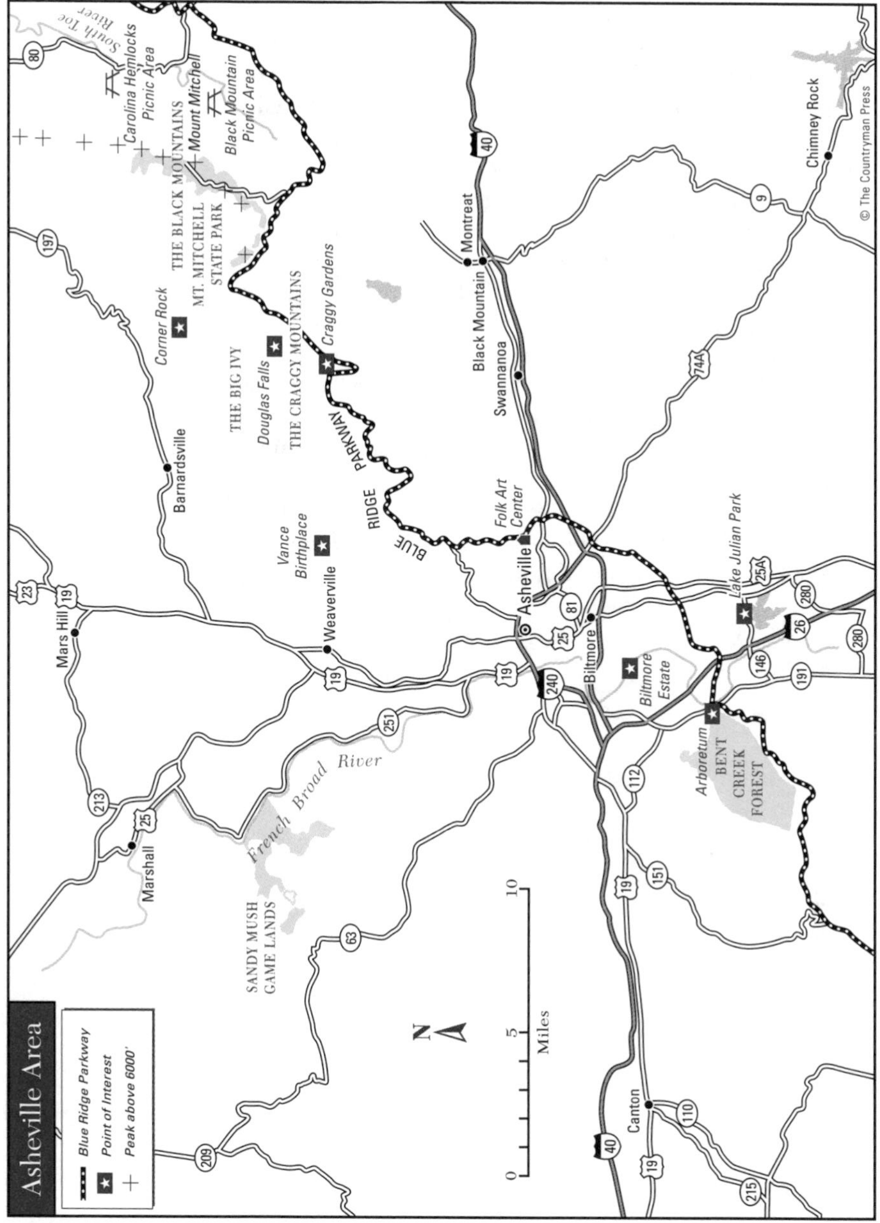


unexpected industry: tourism. Rich South Carolina plantation owners would take their coaches up the turnpike to large summer estates in the cool mountains. The greatest of such early resorts settlements was at Flat Rock, well established by the 1840s, but other great summer estates of the wealthy stretched along the Blue Ridge as far as Cashiers.

Asheville is surprisingly sophisticated for its size (83,400 residents in 2010), with a large downtown that's both lively and historically fascinating. While its early tourism industry helped, much of its big city air comes from its richest homeboy, George Vanderbilt, whose 1890 Biltmore Estate is now the region's premiere tourist attraction outside the Great Smoky Mountains National Park. In the decades before World War I, society families flocked to Asheville to be near Vanderbilt, and society architects followed. A century later, Asheville remains a striking early-20th-century city, resplendent in Craftsman and art deco architecture.

The Blue Ridge itself, now divorced from its parkway, swings due south from Asheville, once again reverting to type with a rugged, steep eastern face and a gentle, hilly western face. In this area the gentle, western slopes are heavily planted in apple orchards, the subject of apple festivals, roadside stands, and u-pick-ems. The east face is particularly rugged, a gapless cliff that runs due south to South Carolina, then turns westward in a line so dramatic it's known as the Blue Wall.

Meanwhile, the mountains to the west of Asheville and the French Broad Valley rise in a confusing mass of mile-high peaks, carrying names like the Bald Mountains, the Newfound Mountains, the Pisgah Mountains, and the Great Balsam Mountains. The Blue Ridge Parkway leaves the actual Blue Ridge to climb into these high peaks, reaching 1 mile in elevation in the Pisgahs then climbing above 6,000 feet in the rugged wilderness of the Great Balsam Mountains. From there, the Smokies are only a short distance away.

# THE BLUE RIDGE PARKWAY CIRCLES ASHEVILLE

Northeast of Asheville, the Great Craggy Mountains and the Black Mountains come together to form the highest mountain complex in the eastern United States. This amazing knot of mountains includes Mount Mitchell; at 6,684 feet, it is the highest peak in the East. It also has the second highest peak in the East (Mount Craig), as well as the 5th, 7th, 8th, 13th, 14th, 15th . . . well, honestly, it's hard to come up with an accurate count when 13 miles of near-continuous ridgeline tops 6,000 feet. Easily reached from the Blue Ridge Parkway, this high ridge provides stunning panoramas, deep forests, rough crags, and fields of wildflowers. The section of the Craggy-Black complex known as Craggy Gardens provides a large natural rhododendron garden with wide views; blooms peak in mid-June with some color lingering into mid-July.

This chapter covers the Blue Ridge Parkway as it traverses the Craggy-Black complex, then circles the wonderful little city of Asheville. It also includes two villages within the Craggy-Black complex, Weaverville (to the north of Asheville) and Black Mountain (to the east of Asheville). Asheville itself is so full of interest that it gets its own chapter.

**GUIDANCE—TOWNS AND COUNTRYSIDE** **Black Mountain/Swannanoa Chamber of Commerce** (www.blackmountain.org; 800-669-2301; 201 East State Street, Black Mountain, NC 28711). This chamber runs a visitors center out of a small storefront in the town of Black Mountain, a short distance east of downtown on US 70. It covers the four towns on the uphill side of the Blue Ridge's Swannanoa Gap—Black Mountain, Swannanoa, Ridgecrest, and Montreat.

**Weaverville Business Association** (www.visitweaverville.com). Weaverville's new website covers the basics, including detailed listings on the businesses within this quaint town of 2,500 to the north of Asheville. It's a good place to check up on bed & breakfasts and restaurants.

**GUIDANCE—PARKS AND FORESTS** **The Blue Ridge Parkway** (www.nps.gov/blri; 828-271-4779; 99 Hemphill Knob Rd., Asheville, NC 28754). Its street address notwithstanding, park headquarters for the Blue Ridge Parkway faces the

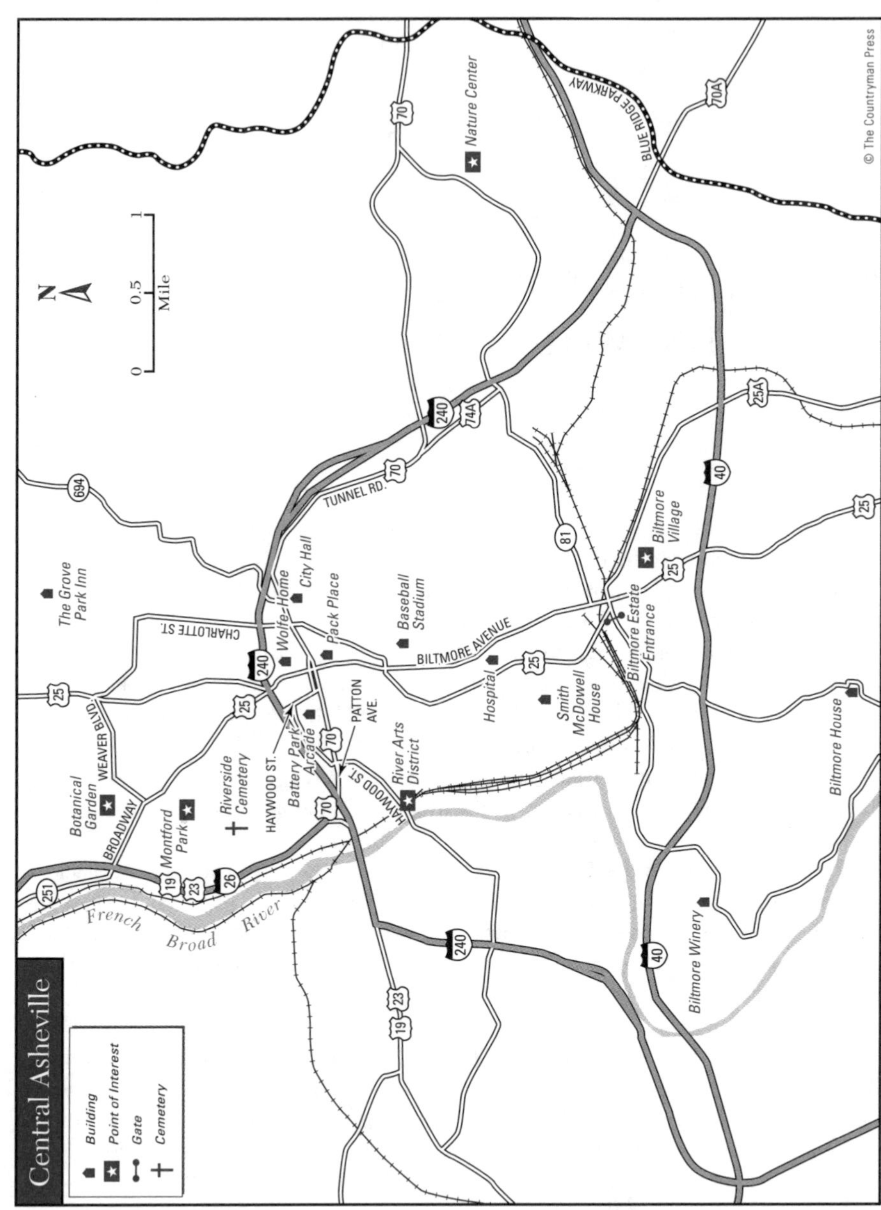


parkway at milepost 382. Directly adjacent to the large administrative center is a new visitors center, and a small garden behind the administrative center is open to the public.

**GETTING THERE Getting to the Black and Craggy Mountains** The Craggy-Black complex of mountains is immediately adjacent to Asheville, and you get to it just like getting to Asheville (see "The City of Asheville").

**MEDICAL EMERGENCIES** **Mission Memorial Hospital** (www.msj.org; 828-213-1111; 509 Biltmore Ave., Asheville, NC 28754). Asheville is very close to this entire area, and its major hospital is your best bet in an emergency.

## ✷ Exploring the Area

**EXPLORING BY CAR** **The Blue Ridge Parkway** *Leg #1* (*37.8 miles*): Start at NC 80. Follow Blue Ridge Parkway to US 70.

*Leg #2* (*11 miles*): From US 70 outside Asheville, follow Blue Ridge Parkway to NC 191.

*Leg #3* (*11.7 miles*): From NC 191 follow the Blue Ridge Parkway to NC 151.

As with all other sections of the parkway, this 60-mile segment is described as for a through-traveler heading south. If you are staying in Asheville, however, this segment is best done as a there-and-back-again, first up Leg #1, then down the other legs.

The first leg follows the Blue Ridge Crest, climbing uphill through increasingly rugged country. The road breaks out of the forest on both sides for frequent views; Mount Mitchell, the highest point in the East, can be clearly seen on the right, distinguishable by its tower. In 9.25 miles the parkway leaves the Blue Ridge forever; at Pinnacle Bald the Blue Ridge heads south into South Carolina and Georgia, and the Parkway climbs northward into the **Black Mountains**. A mile later, the Mount Mitchell Spur Road heads 4.5 miles right to **Mount Mitchell State Park**, a remarkable drive that leads to wonderful views from the highest point anywhere east of the Rockies. Along the spur road you will pass a trailhead for the **Mountains-to-Sea Trail** that explores the 6,000-foot peaks to your left; then, once inside the state park, the restaurant (run by a local family) offers good food with wide views.

CRAGGY GARDENS TUNNEL ON THE BLUE RIDGE PARKWAY

Back at the parkway, the road continues through high spruce-fir forests and frequent views. Along this stretch, any land that slopes downward to the left is part of the Asheville watershed, where gray cliffs surround a pretty little lake; this area is so off-limits to the public that you are not even allowed to stop your car on the verge, for fear that a tiny droplet of oil will leak into the ground. You can, however, park at Black Balsam Gap (it's on the other side of the ridge), and incidentally pick up the Mountains-to-Sea Trail as it descends from that 6,000-foot ridge. Ahead, an overlook on your left gives you a view to Glassmine Falls far on the other side of the watershed. After that, you've entered the **Craggy Gardens** area, noted for its views and its June rhododendron display. Three overlooks in this area (all on the right) take you first to a trail that climbs Craggy Pinnacle for one of the parkway's best views, then to a small visitors center and a trail to the famous rhododendron meadow, and finally to a nice picnic area. The visual climax of the Craggy area comes between the second and third overlooks, as the roadway becomes a ledge blasted into the cliff for a mile, then dives into a long curving tunnel.

From here the parkway drops two-thirds of a mile vertically, from the 5,520-foot Craggy Gardens Visitors Center to Asheville's Swannanoah River at 2,080 feet. There's a number of good overlooks along the way, but much of the interest is observing the forests (and, most days, the temperature) change—this descent is long enough to pass through a couple of climate zones. Near the bottom of this stretch is the **Folk Art Center**, built to promote native mountain crafts but now largely devoted to university-trained artists.

The second leg bypasses Asheville on a series of low mountains (or high hills), a pretty, forested section with few views. On a weekday, you might notice traffic pick up a bit, as some commuters use it as a shortcut. There are no intersections with any of the interstates, however, so you need to plan your exits. The first intersection, US 70 (Tunnel Road) marks the start of this leg, and leads into eastern Asheville's mall district. After that you'll pass over the Swannanoa River (nice view to your right), then the **Park Headquarters Building**. In 2 miles, there's an exit onto US 74A, with access to I-40 and downtown Asheville, followed by a 4-mile forest drive to the US 25 exit, the best approach to the **Biltmore Estate**. For the next (nearly) 5 miles the parkway is actually inside the Biltmore Estate, but you won't see anything except forest until you cross the dramatic high bridge over the **French Broad River**. Just after that is the last Asheville exit, NC 191, which leads to the **North Carolina Arboretum**, I-26 north and south, I-40 westbound, and (in the other direction) **Hendersonville**.

VIEW FROM CRAGGY GARDENS

STONE STEPS IN LAKE POWHATAN RECREATION AREA

From here, the third leg climbs steadily away from Asheville and into the wilderness. The views start immediately, over the gorge of the French Broad River; look carefully for the Biltmore House. In 6.5 miles, gravel Bent Creek Road gives access to **Lake Powhatan Recreation Area**. A series of tunnels brings you above 4,000 feet as you approach the NC 151 exit. Ahead are the **Pisgah Mountains and the Great Balsam Mountains**, the grand finale of the parkway, and the subject of another chapter. NC 151 provides a beautiful drive back to Asheville.

**LONG-DISTANCE PATHS** **The Mountains-to-Sea Trail** This 75-mile section, between NC 151 and NC 80, for the most part follows the Blue Ridge Parkway fairly closely without, however, any significant amount of road walking, part of the 300 miles of continuous path that starts at US 19's Soco Gap and ends at Stone Mountain State Park, in the far north of the state. Starting at NC 151, the path follows Shut-In Trail, created by George Vanderbilt in the 1890s and restored by volunteers in the 1980s, switching between parkway lands (where camping is prohibited) and the Pisgah National Forest (where camping is allowed), and exploring the upper slopes of the **Bent Creek Forest**. At the French Broad River, both the parkway and the trail enter Asheville's urban area, even if it doesn't look like it, as they cross the private property of the **Biltmore Estate**; during this segment, the trail never wanders far from the parkway. After 29 miles the trail passes in front of the **Folk Art Center** and once again gains some elbow room, courtesy of the adjoining national forest. From here the parkway climbs 3,500 feet—and the trail climbs a lot more, climbing knobs and plunging back into gaps. Despite the difficulty, there are notable features here: the ruins of Rattlesnake Lodge, the 1900 home of beloved local conservationist Dr. Chase Ambler, destroyed by fire in 1925; wildflower meadows; long walks on rock ledges with wide views; and, at the top, a traverse of **Craggy Gardens** with stunning views framed (in June) by masses of rhododendron blooms. From here the trail once again stays close to the parkway (and even follows it for a quarter-mile), reaching Balsam Gap in 23 miles from the Folk Art Center.

In the final 23 miles of this section the Mountains-to-Sea Trail leaves the parkway to explore the 6,000-foot peaks of the **Black Mountains**, traversing the highest mountains in the East. The trail immediately switchbacks up to 6,000 feet, then stays there for more than 3 miles, with many views along the way. This is not destined to be a peak-baggers path, however, and it drops down the south side of the Black Mountains to finally level out at 5,600 feet. Here it follows a logging railroad through high alpine forests and wildflower meadows, then climbs up to the ruins of Camp Alice, a logging camp that for a while served as a tourist resort. From here it's a short, steep walk up to **Mount Mitchell**; at 6,684 feet it's the highest point east of the Rockies. From here there's a scenic but ludicrously steep drop—3,700 feet in 5 miles—made worthwhile by waterfalls, views, and large tracts of virgin forest, along with a climate change equivalent to walking northward a thousand miles. This bottoms out at the **Black Mountain Recreation Area**. From there a ridge climb leads back to the parkway, with a view backward toward Mount Mitchell.

## ✷ Villages

**Black Mountain** The village of Black Mountain sits in a high mountain valley 15 miles east of Asheville, just off I-40. Located just below Swannanoa Gap on the Blue Ridge, it has historically been a major entry point to the western mountains—first by wagon road, then by the **Swannanoa Grade railroad**. Today you will find it a handsome small town. Its lively downtown fills two blocks with old brick-front stores, now filled with antique shops, gift shops, and restaurants. Its **historic depot** on the edge of downtown, handsomely restored, holds an important regional crafts gallery.

**Weaverville** Located on the north edge of Asheville's urban area, Weaverville has managed to retain its small-town look and feel. Its two-block downtown lines the former US 19 with nice old brick-front stores and three good restaurants, with a fourth nearby. Its handsome residential districts, with houses dating to the 1840s,

MOUNT MITCHELL, THE TALLEST MOUNTAIN IN THE EAST

host several nice bed & breakfasts that offer a small-town ambiance within an easy drive of downtown Asheville.

**Barnardsville** This remote village, pronounced BAR-nurds-vill, sits along NC 197 well north of Asheville, under the shadow of the Craggy Mountains. It has a recognizable center, but is mainly noted as a gateway to the Pisgah National Forest's extensive and spectacular holdings in the Craggies, the **Big Ivy Tract**. You will find the turnoff to Barnardsville well signposted on Future I-26 (US 19/23) 14 miles north of Asheville, then 6 miles east on NC 197.

## ✷ Wild Places

**THE GREAT FORESTS** **Mount Mitchell and the Black Mountains** Quite simply, this is the highest mountain range in the East. In the mid-19th century, New Englanders were astonished to learn that **Mount Mitchell**, the tallest of the Blacks at 6,682 feet, was taller than New Hampshire's impressive Mount Washington (6,288 feet). By the end of that century, people knew that *eight* Black Mountain peaks topped Mount Washington, and that more than 11 miles of the 16-mile ridgeline had elevations above 6,000 feet.

There's something else remarkable about the Blacks—paved, mile-high highways run along the top of this rugged and remote mountain for 6 of its 16 miles. From the Black Mountains' traditional terminus at Balsam Gap, the **Blue Ridge Parkway** parallels the crest for 4.6 miles to the Mount Mitchell Spur Road; this spur road then turns left to parallel the Black Mountain Crest for another 4.8 miles, finally reaching 6,500 feet (take that, Mount Washington!) at a parking lot a quarter-mile below Mount Mitchell. (Because of curves, the 9.4 miles of road occupy only 6 miles of ridgeline.) These roadways form a continuous corridor of views and trailheads, including the short, easy path to the Top of the East itself. There's even a **good restaurant**.

There's no reason, however, to confine yourself to a car, or limit yourself to short, easy walks. From the start of the spur road, the crest and the entire eastern slope of the Black Mountains is owned by either Mount Mitchell State Park or Pisgah National Forest, and the trails are endless, beautiful, and famously difficult. The most famous is the Black Mountain Crest Trail, which should be the easiest and isn't. Starting at the Mount Mitchell parking lot, it ascends and descends 12 peaks over 6,000 feet along its 11.3-mile length, before dropping to a remote trailhead on a country lane south of **Burnsville**, with a final descent of 3,200 feet in 4.4 miles; the National Forest Service calls it "the most scenic and difficult trail in the area." Four other trails descend the east slope at various points, with nonstop drops (or climbs, if you are so inclined) ranging from 3,000 feet to 3,700 feet. The longest and most popular of these carries the **Mountains-to-Sea Trail** from the top of Mount Mitchell to the **South Toe River**; another, also starting in the state park, has been specifically graded for horses. The remaining two, just as difficult, lead to remote gaps along the unroaded crest, and allow more chance for solitude. All four feature waterfalls, views, and virgin forests.

**The Craggy Mountains** Rising from the northeast edge of the City of Asheville, the aptly named Great Craggy Mountains quickly reach above a mile in elevation and beyond, with the tallest peak topping 6,000 feet. The highest peaks are characterized by sharp crags and thick heath balds—a beautiful but impenetrable combination of rhododendron, mountain laurel, azalea, and blueberry. Its most beautiful peak is **Craggy Gardens**, where the thick heath is broken by wide areas of grassy meadows and wildflowers, for wide views framed by deep purple rhododendrons. The Blue Ridge Parkway traverses the high gaps of the Craggies, passing above a mile in elevation in 17 miles from Asheville's US 70—on a hot summer day, an easy and most pleasant drive. It gives access to the **Mountains-to-Sea Trail**, running along ridgetops previously too thickly grown with heath to be accessible, now giving wide views from rock ledges. The western slopes of the Craggies are mainly owned by the Pisgah National Forest; known as the **Big Ivy**, it's an important recreation and conservation area in its own right. The east slope, wild and stunningly beautiful, is the Asheville watershed and closed to the public.

**Big Ivy** This large tract of the Pisgah National Forest occupies the western slope of the **Craggy Mountains**. It's named for its previous owner, the Big Ivy Timber Company, who sold it to the National Forest Service in 1914. With such long government ownership, the Big Ivy forests are rich and tall, and some are old growth. Rough terrain gives the Big Ivy more than its share of cliffs, waterfalls, and geologic oddities. And just for good measure, most of its 30 miles of trail are open to trail bikes and horses.

To reach the Big Ivy, go to **Barnardsville** on NC 197, then go right on Dillingham Road (SSR 2173), which becomes a good gravelroad, FS 74, at the forest boundary in 5.1 miles. From here, FS 74 delves deep into the Big Ivy, to dead-end in 8.3 miles and 1,800 feet of elevation gain. Apart from leading to eight trailheads, the road is remarkable in its own right:

- At 0.2 mile from the start of FS 74 is the pretty **Corner Rock Picnic Area**, set in a wildflower meadow.
- At 1.9 miles is Corner Rock itself; it's not altogether remarkable, but 200 yards upstream is a *rock house,* a room-sized shelter formed by a heavily overhanging rock.
- At 2.6 miles look carefully to your left as you cross a stream (Little Andy Creek) for a tiny but exceptionally pretty waterfall.
- At 3.4 miles a tall gray cliff looms over the road for 200 yards.
- At 3.8 miles, **Walker Falls** is hard by the road on your left.
- At 8.3 miles, the end of the road, an easy half-mile path leads to 70-foot-tall **Douglas Falls**.

**RIVERS The South Toe River's Headwaters** The 6,000-foot ridgeline of the Black Mountains creates unusually high rainfalls, upward of a hundred inches a year. These rains feed the South Toe River, a remarkably active and interesting stream on the east slope of Mount Mitchell. Wholly within the Pisgah National Forest, much of the upper South Toe is paralleled by gravel FS 472, with many opportunities for fishermen, as well as families looking for a good swimming hole. It enters private lands as it reaches NC 80, except for the popular swimming hole at **Carolina Hemlocks**.

**WATERFALLS Roaring Fork Falls** This particularly beautiful triple cascade is easily reached from NC 80, 2.2 miles north of the Blue Ridge Parkway, then left

ROARING FORK FALLS

onto South Toe River Road (FS 472), then immediately left onto FS 472A, to the trailhead. The trail itself is a pleasant 0.7 mile stroll along a level loggers' roadbed, passing a few interesting artifacts along the way. When it reaches Roaring Fork, the waterfall is directly above you.

**Walker Falls and Douglas Falls** These two **Big Ivy** waterfalls are easily reached from FS 74. The first, **Walker Falls**, is a 30-foot-tall double cascade only 20 feet from the road, and on the way to impressive **Douglas Falls**. Douglas Falls, named for Supreme Court Justice William O. Douglas (who is said to have hiked the Craggies as a young man), is a 70-foot-tall plunge over an overhanging cliff. The path into Douglas Falls is a half-mile railroad-grade walk.

**SWIMMING HOLE Carolina Hemlocks Recreation Area** Open April–November. This picnic and camping area on NC 80, maintained by the Pisgah National Forest, has as its main attraction a long and lovely stretch of the South Toe River, with wonderful views toward Mount Mitchell (the tallest peak in the East). The CCC developed its popular swimming hole, where sand and boulders line a deep hole in the South Toe; there's also a riverside path and a nature trail.

## ✷ Recreation Areas

**PICNIC AREAS Corner Rock** This exceptionally pretty picnic area is at the entrance to the Pisgah National Forest's **Big Ivy** tract, just south of Barnardsville. Tables are spread in a forest glade that lines a wide wildflower meadow. The access road, gravel FS 74, passes the picnic area to lead to the Corner Rock itself, a remarkable roadside cliff, many trailheads, and **Walker Falls and Douglas Falls**.

**Lake Tomahawk Park, Black Mountain** This town park, located in a Black Mountain neighborhood, centers on a lovely little lake surrounded by a walking path. As well as picnicking, you will find tennis, golf, a swimming pool, and croquet. Lake Tomahawk is the venue for Black Mountain's "Park Rhythms" summer music series.

## ✷ To See

*Along the Blue Ridge Parkway*

**Mount Mitchell State Park** (www.ncparks.gov/Visit/parks/momi/main.php; e-mail: mount.mitchell@ncdenr.gov; 828-675-4611; 2388 State Hwy. 128, Burnsville, NC

28714). Open summer: 8 AM–9 PM. Closes earlier at other times of the year, and closes completely when the Blue Ridge Parkway is closed. This 1,700-acre state park centers on the highest peak in the East—6,684-foot Mount Mitchell, more than 1.25 miles above sea level. The park stretches along the high ridgeline of the Black Mountains, with three other 6,000-footfoot peaks in its 2.5-mile length. The remainder of the Blacks are largely owned by the Pisgah National Forest, with a large chunk of the western slopes in private hands. A spur road runs from the Blue Ridge Parkway to the park, a 2.5-mile drive through Pisgah Forest lands, just below the crest of the Black Mountain (and beneath two more 6,000-foot peaks). At the park entrance the road passes above 6,000 feet with wide meadow views, and stays above 6,000 feet to its end on Mount Mitchell. The road continues to climb along the Black Mountain Crest, through subarctic spruce-fir forests, reaching 6,200 feet at the **park restaurant** in 1.25 miles; this full-service restaurant serves up good country food and wonderful views. Beyond the restaurant, the road slabs up Mount Mitchell to gain the ridge again at 6,400 feet, with some good roadside views. From there it passes just beneath the peak of Mount Mitchell to end on the ridgeline a bit downhill from the summit. Here you will find plenty of parking, a firs-rate picnic area, a snack bar, and a small visitors center. Expect it to be cold and windy, even in the summer. The wide, easy path to the summit passes through forests and wildflower meadows to reach the peak in a quarter-mile. A newly constructed tower allows you to climb above the trees for a 360-degree view, with the entire eastern United States beneath your feet.

Mount Mitchell is the high point on the dramatic and rugged Black Mountain, 15 miles of high crest named for the dark spruce-fir forest that covers its highest slopes. Eighty percent of the Black Mountain Crest exceeds 6,000 feet in elevation, with 10 peaks officially listed as 6'ers. Six of these mountains string out northward from Mount Mitchell, along the rough and difficult ridgeline trail that starts at the picnic area. Within the park, however, are a number of fine hiking paths, all of them considerably easier. Of special note is the nearly flat path that follows the old toll road from **Montreat**, itself built on a logging railroad bed. After 1.2 miles of profuse wildflowers and dense fir forests it reaches Camp Alice, an early-20th-century lumber camp that became, for a while around World War I, a backcountry tourist attraction. Here you will find some scant ruins and a lovely waterfall.

**Craggy Gardens** (www.visitblueridgeparkway.com/craggygardens.php). This recreation area on the Blue Ridge Parkway takes in the three highest peaks of the Craggy Mountains: Craggy Dome (6,080 feet, ranked 30th in the East), Craggy Pinnacle, and Craggy Gardens. Views are great—but there is more here than views from high mountains. Each June, the Craggies have one of the finest rhododendron displays in the mountains.

Driving up the parkway from Asheville, you enter the Craggies at Potato Field Gap, MP 368, with views left over the town of Woodfin's watershed. In a half-mile, a paved spur road leads left 1 mile to Craggy Gardens Picnic Area, a lovely tree-shaded meadow. This is the lower end of the Craggy Gardens Trail, climbing 400 feet in 0.4 mile to Craggy Gardens, a stunning natural rhododendron garden. Craggy Gardens mixes clumps of June-flowering heath shrubs with expanses of grassy meadows. The grassy meadows give wide views over lush displays of perennial flowers, framed in June and July by the wild displays—huge mounds of purple

Catawba rhododendrons, mixed with rosebay rhododendrons, flame azaleas, blueberries, and mountain laurels.

Back at the parkway, the road curves wide past Craggy Gardens, out of its view on a breathtaking ledge. In 3 miles the road reaches Pinnacle Gap, with wide views in both directions. Here a tiny visitors center has several exhibits about the Craggy Mountains and a gift shop. Here too is the uphill end of the Craggy Gardens Trail. From here Catawba rhododendrons line the parkway and frame changing views over the Asheville watershed. The Craggy Pinnacle Overlook is a half-mile from the visitors center, with wide views that improve dramatically as you walk up the easy path to the rhododendron-covered summit. Here a clifftop overlook gives views back toward Craggy Gardens, with the parkway dramatically cut into the side of the mountain.

♿ **The Folk Art Center & Allanstand Craft Shop** (www.southernhighlandguild.org/folkart.html; 828-298-7928; milepost 382, Blue Ridge Pkwy., Asheville, NC 28805). Open daily, 9 AM–6 PM (January–March, 9 AM–5 PM). Free. Founded in 1930 to help poor mountain folk refine their skills and find markets for their crafts, the Southern Highland Craft Guild has evolved into a juried membership organization of fine craft artists from a large area centered on the southern Appalachian Mountains. In the 1970s the National Park Service collaborated with the SHCG to provide a facility to interpret southern Appalachian mountain culture on the Blue Ridge Parkway. To achieve this, the Park Service built the present Folk Art Center, a large building on the Blue Ridge Parkway just north of US 70, and turned it over the the SHCG. The Craft Guild has utilized this building by moving their Allanstand Craft Shop into it from downtown Asheville, and by installing a medium-sized gallery in an upstairs mezzanine. Although the gallery features items from the Guild's collection of 3,500 mountain craft pieces, for the most part it displays contemporary art by its current members, with university trained fine artists far outnumbering native mountain folk crafters.

**HISTORIC SITES** ♿ **Vance Birthplace State Historic Site** (www.nchistoricsites.org/vance; e-mail: vance@ncdcr.gov; 828-645-6706; 911 Reems Creek Rd., Weaverville, NC 28787). Open Mon.–Fri., 9 AM–5 PM; closed Sat.–Sun. This log farmstead east of Weaverville on Reems Creek Road accurately reconstructs the early-19th-century birthplace of Zebulon B. Vance, one of North Carolina's most beloved politicians. In the mid-19th century, Vance led the movement to democratize North Carolina's patrician planter-controlled government; during the Civil War, Governor Vance (an anti-Confederate and anti-successionist, but not a Unionist) protected North Carolina from

ZEBULON VANCE BIRTHPLACE, WEAVERVILLE

lawlessness, preserved civil liberties, and sheltered his state from the Confederate government's worst excesses. This state historic site memorializes his life, and presents an accurate picture of the frontier mountain life that shaped his boyhood.

The farmstead is a well-crafted two-story log home, set on a grassy hill, shaded by large old trees, and surrounded by mountains. It has been carefully furnished to reflect the frontier period of Vance's boyhood. A vegetable garden separates the farmhouse from several log outbuildings—a weaving house with a period loom, a toolhouse, a smokehouse, a corncrib, a springhouse, and a slave house. Beautiful views stretch from the split-rail worm fence, past the log buildings, and to the mountains beyond.

Throughout the season, this is a venue for various programs interpreting early life on the mountain frontier. There's a visitors center with a small museum on Vance's life. Only the visitors center, the restrooms, and the picnic area are fully disabled accessible.

**CULTURAL SITES** **The Old Depot Gallery & Museum** (olddepot.org; e-mail: webmaster@olddepot.org; 828-669-6583; 207 Sutton Ave., Black Mountain, NC 28711). Black Mountain's old-fashioned passenger depot anchors the southern end of this small-town downtown. Painted bright yellow, it sits hard against Sutton Avenue with a row of old brick storefronts across the street. The Old Depot Association, which took it over and renovated it in 1976, runs a good-sized crafts gallery there, dedicated to high quality hand crafts in traditional mountain styles. The works of over 75 local and regional mountain craft artists can be seen at any one time, and artists frequently volunteer to run the gallery. Behind the gallery, a restored caboose houses a local history museum.

MILEPOST ON THE BLUE RIDGE PARKWAY

**Montreat** (www.montreat.org; e-mail: central@montreat.org; 800-572-2257, 828-669-2911; fax: 828-669-5054; 401 Assembly Dr./P.O. Box 969, Montreat, NC 28757). Of the 20 or so religious retreats and conference centers, Montreat is one of the two most worthwhile for a casual visit, as well as friendly toward a casual visitor (the other being **Lake Junaluska**). Founded in 1897 and now run by the Presbyterian Church USA, Montreat is really a town in itself, combining its major retreat center with a liberal arts college and a collection of summer homes, all grouped around a lovely recreation center on Lake Susan. Located at the end of NC 9, 2 miles north of **Black Mountain**, Montreat features a major concentration of early-20th-century resort architecture, from its impressive front gate (now permanently open) to the large and beautiful Assembly Inn, built of local stone. Historic stone and wood buildings face Lake Susan on one side; a garden-like park lines the other. Uphill, winding gravel roads lead past early 20th century cottages to reach various hiking trails. The best-known and most popular trail follows the old Mount Mitchell Road, abandoned in 1940 in favor of the Blue Ridge Parkway.

**ORCHARDS AND VINEYARDS** **Dogwood Hills Farms** (dogwoodhillsfarm .com; e-mail: bfridlin@verizon.net; 828-645-6286; 369 Ox Creek Rd., Weaverville, NC 28787). Please call in advance, before 9 AM of the day you plan to arrive. *From I-26 north of Asheville, take exit 21 onto New Stock Road, then go east 1 block to Bus US 19; turn right and go 0.8 mile to a right fork onto Reems Creek Road (SSR 1003); then go 4.5 miles to a right fork onto Ox Creek Road (SSR 2109), and go about 2 miles to the farm on the right. From the Blue Ridge Parkway, turn west at milepost 375.3 onto paved Ox Creek Road, then go about 2 miles to the farm on the left.* This attractive u-pick fruit orchard offers cherries, blueberries, blackberries, raspberries, and apples in a season that lasts from mid-June through October.

## ✱ To Do

**BICYCLING** **Epic Cycles** (828-669-5969; epiccyclesonline.com; 102 Sutton Ave., Black Mountain, NC 28711). This full-service bike shop in Black Mountain rents bikes, and offers detailed information on area trails.

**GOLF** **Reems Creek Golf Course** (www.reemscreekgolf.com; e-mail: info@ reemscreekgolfcourse.com; 828-645-4393; 36 Pink Fox Cove Rd., Weaverville, NC 28787). This 1984 course, designed by English firm Hawtree & Son, sits among the Blue Ridge Mountains east of Weaverville. Rated four-star by *Golf Digest,* its scenery is particularly beautiful.

**Black Mountain Municipal Golf Course** (blackmountaingolf.org/index.php; 828-669-2710; fax: 828-669-2842; 17 Ross Dr., Black Mountain, NC 28711). This 1929 18-hole public course has hilly terrain, water on most holes, and spectacular mountain scenery. While most greens are short, hole 17 is 747 yards, par 6.

## ✱ Lodging

**BED & BREAKFAST INNS** **Dry Ridge Inn** (www.dryridgeinn.com; e-mail: dryridgeinn@aol.com; 800-839-3899, 828-658-3899; 26 Brown St., Weaverville, NC 28787). This 1849 farmhouse, rebuilt into a stylish Victorian mansion in 1888, sits in a quiet residential neighborhood blocks from Weaverville's quaint little downtown. Surrounded by a white picket fence, the house's wide front porch looks out on well-kept gardens, with a water garden in the rear. The eight rooms are individually decorated in country-themed antiques, and range in size from cozy to large. Full breakfast is included in the brightly lit breakfast room or on the brick patio by the water garden.

**The Inn on Main Street** (www.inn onmain.com; e-mail: relax@innonmain .com; 877-873-6074, 828-645-4935; 88 S. Main St., Weaverville, NC 28787). Built by a local doctor in 1900, this country house in Weaverville, two blocks south of downtown, represented high living in a small town. Today this late Victorian house, with its two-story projecting bay windows and wide porches, continues to give high comfort in a small town. This seven-room bed & breakfast is furnished throughout with antiques. Rooms tend to be normal to large in size, each theme furnished in antiques and reproductions that feel comfortable in a turn-of-the-century home. A full breakfast is included.

**Ox-Ford Farm Bed & Breakfast Inn** (www.bedandbreakfast.com/north-carolina-weaverville-oxfordfarm.html; 828-658-2500; 75 Ox Creek Rd., Weaverville, NC 28787). Open April–December. *From I-26 north of Asheville, take exit 21 onto New Stock Road, then go east 1 block to Bus US 19; turn right and go 0.8 mile to a right fork onto Reems Creek Road (SSR 1003); then go 4.5 miles to a right fork onto Ox Creek Road (SSR 2109), and go about 2 miles. From the Blue Ridge Parkway, turn west at milepost 375.3 onto paved Ox Creek Road, then go about 2 miles.* Ox-Ford Farm Bed & Breakfast Inn is part of an authentic working farm, who's history dates back to 1876, when it was given as a wedding gift to the area's only country doctor. The farmhouse is now a bed & breakfast inn, with comfortable, homey bedrooms. A farmyard rooster or resident peacock may wake you up in the morning to get down to an exceptional country breakfast of all naturally grown products, including fresh eggs and home-baked bread.

**The Red Rocker Inn** (redrockerinn.com; e-mail: info@redrockerinn.com; 888-669-5991; 136 N. Dougherty St., Black Mountain, NC 28711). This large old inn sits on an acre of landscaped grounds in a residential neighborhood just three blocks from Black Mountain's quaint downtown. It's most notable feature is its huge wraparound porch and plentiful, bright red rocking chairs. It has garnered numerous kudos, both for its food and its 17 individually decorated en suite rooms. A full breakfast is included in the price.

**The Black Mountain Inn** (www.blackmountaininn.com; e-mail: jbergeron@mindspring.com; 800-735-6128, 828-669-6528; 1186 West Old Hwy. 70, Black Mountain, NC 28711). This historic inn sits on 3 wooded acres just west of Black Mountain, off Old Highway 70. Old Highway 70 is now a back lane, but it was once the main coach road over the Blue Ridge—and the Black Mountain Inn was built as a coaching inn in the 1830s. Today it has seven beautiful en suite rooms, all individually furnished in antiques. Unusually for bed & breakfasts, the Black Mountain welcomes well-behaved children and small pets, but you must make arrangements in advance. A full breakfast is included.

**Arbor House Inn** (www.arborhousenc.com; e-mail: info@arborhousenc.com; 866-669-9303, 828-669-9302; 207 Rhododendron Ave., Black Mountain, NC 28711). Open June–October. Located in a Black Mountain residential neighborhood, this is a modern, purpose-built inn facing Lake Tomahawk. Designed in the style of the Arts and Crafts Movement, the Arbor House has four good-sized rooms, the largest and most expensive having a private balcony overlooking the lake. A full breakfast is included.

**RENTAL CABINS** **Oxglen Vacation Rentals** (www.oxglen.com; e-mail: jim@oxglen.com; 800-326-2373, 828-645-2974; 376 Ox Creek Rd., Weaverville, NC 28787). *From I-26 north of Asheville, take exit 21 onto New Stock Road, then go east 1 block to Bus US 19; turn right and go 0.8 miles to a right fork onto Reems Creek Road (SSR 1003); then go 4.5 miles to a right fork onto Ox Creek Road (SSR 2109), and go 2.1 miles to the cabins on the left. From the Blue Ridge Parkway, turn west at milepost 375.3 onto paved Ox Creek Road, then go 2.2* *miles.* This 13-acre forested tract sits just 2 miles off the Blue Ridge Parkway's Craggy Mountain section via paved road. Five chalet-style cottages, varying in size from one to four bedrooms, are handsomely and comfortably furnished; each has a satellite TV, gas fireplace, private phone line, porch or balcony, washers and dryers, as well as a full kitchen.

## ✱ Where to Eat

**EATING OUT Blue Mountain Pizza** (www.bluemountainpizza.com; 828-658-8777; 55 N. Main St., Weaverville, NC 28787). Open Tues.–Sun., 11 AM–9 PM. This friendly neighborhood eatery, located in downtown Weaverville's oldest building, happens to make some of the best pizza in the Blue Ridge. They also have good salads and sandwiches, and the best cheesecake in the region (made by a local woman in her home). They have outdoor seating, and music nightly. Local favorite **Highlands Gaelic Ale** is on tap. Of all the outstanding restaurants listed in this book, this joyful little pub remains your author's favorite. I guess you just can't beat a good pizza.

**Well-Bred Bakery and Cafe** (www.well-bredbakery.com; 828-645-9300; 26 N. Main St., Weaverville, NC 28787). Open all day, Tues.–Sun. This sparkling clean deli in a downtown Weaverville brick storefront started as a bread-making bakery (a rarity in these mountains), and has since expanded into a coffee shop and deli, with live music on weekends. Their deli counter is spectacular, with regularly changing gourmet dishes, and their dessert display will keep you in happy indecision.

**Mount Mitchell State Park Restaurant** (828-675-9545; fax: 828-682-6510; NC 128 [Mount Mitchell Spur Rd.], Burnsville, NC 28714). Open May–October, daily at 10 AM. Closes: 7 PM in May; 8 PM in June–August; 7 PM in September; 6 PM in October. Closed November–April. *In Mount Mitchell State Park. Access from the Blue Ridge Parkway, milepost 355, Mount Mitchell Spur Road.* This pleasant lodge-style restaurant sits on the crest of the Black Mountains inside **Mount Mitchell State Park**, with stunning vistas from its large windows. Inside, it's all native stone and polished wood, kept immaculately clean. The restaurant is uncrowded, and table service is friendly and helpful. The food is best described as Southern Roadhouse, but better than ususal. You choose a main dish, then sides from a list—two sides with a dinner, one with a sandwich. This lets you pick fried okra with your hamburger, a surprisingly good combination. Desserts are particularly worthwhile. Prices are higher than most roadhouses, but more than justified by the food's quality and the wonderful views. This is a worthy stop for anyone doing the parkway.

**DINING OUT The Weaverville Milling Company** (www.weavervillemilling.com; e-mail: Wmilling@aol.com; 828-645-4700; 1 Old Mill Ln., Weaverville, NC 28787). Open for dinner, daily except Wed. This early-20th-century watermill, just off Reems Creek Road, continued in operation into the 1960s. Today it houses a fine restaurant, specializing in Southern foods, imaginatively yet traditionally prepared. The exterior looks just the way it did a century ago; inside it's beautifully converted, with polished bare wood and open rafters, decorated with authentic country objects from the area. Some of the original machinery is still in place, and a loft houses a collection of quilts and other mountain antiques. To find it, go north on Alt US 19/23 at Future I-26's exit 21 for 1.4

miles, to a right on Reems Creek Road (SSR 1003), then 0.6 mile farther on the right.

## ✷ Entertainment

**BLACK MOUNTAIN Park Rhythms** (828-669-2052). July and August, Thursdays, 7 PM. Free. These free concerts at Black Mountain's Lake Tomahawk Park feature a variety of bluegrass and alternative music.

**Swannanoa Chamber Music Festival** (swannanoachambermusic.com; e-mail: chamber@warren-wilson.edu; 828-771-3050). June and July. This annual series consists of five weekly concerts, each one performed first at Warren Wilson College (between Asheville and Black Mountain), then repeated at Waynesville and Hendersonville.

## ✷ Special Events

**SPRING** ✐ **Lake Eden Arts Festival** (www.theleaf.com; e-mail: info@theLEAF.com; 828-686-8742; 377 Lake Eden Rd., Black Mountain, NC 28711). Last weekend in May; repeated in mid-October. This twice-annual festival is an eclectic mix of New Age and traditional mountain elements, heavy on music and crafts, families and good times. Limited to 5,000 attendees at any one time, it's held at Camp Rockmont, a large and beautiful facility in the mountains west of the town of Black Mountain. People camp out by the lakes, go swimming and kayaking. The three-day schedule mixes traditional and New Age arts, with music, dancing, concerts, handcrafting, healing arts, special children's programs, and workshops.

**Black Mountain Arts & Crafts Show** (olddepot.org/craftshow; e-mail: craftshow@olddepot.org; 828-669-6583; 207 Sutton Ave., Black Mountain, NC 28711). First weekend in June. Art show is free. This juried sidewalk art show, limited to the best 70 exhibitors, occupies downtown Black Mountain's Sutton Avenue by its historic old depot. On Saturday night, "A Taste of Black Mountain" offers a sampling of foods from a dozen or more Black Mountain restaurants for one ticket price.

**SUMMER Mount Mitchell State Park Heritage Day (NC).** Last Saturday in August. Traditional mountain music and dancing on the highest peak in the east, along with a variety of traditional foods and crafts, a raptor demonstration, an annual tree-planting event, hikes, and workshops.

**Sourwood Festival at Black Mountain** (blackmountain.org/festivals; e-mail: info@blackmountain.org; 800-669-2301, 828-669-2300; fax: 828-669-1407; 201 E. State Street, Black Mountain, NC 28711). Free last weekend in August. This annual street fair, held in downtown Black Mountain, features craft and art exhibits and food vendors.

**AUTUMN** ✐ **Fall Pioneer Days at Vance Birthplace State Historic Site** (www.ah.dcr.state.nc.us/sections/hs/vance/vance.htm; 828-645-6706; 911 Reems Creek Rd., Weaverville, NC 28787). Free third weekend in September. This annual event has craft and pioneer skill demonstrations, along with a frontier militia encampment, at this fully preserved early-19th-century log farmstead.

**Fall! By the Tracks** (Black Mountain, NC). Second Saturday in October. Black Mountain's local art and history association, the Old Depot Association, sponsors this annual fall fest, featuring crafters demonstration, making your own mountain toys, cake-walks, local honey, mountain barbeque, and made-while-you-watch apple cider.

# THE CITY OF ASHEVILLE

The previous chapter zipped around Asheville on the Blue Ridge Parkway, while the next chapter will follow the Blue Ridge Parkway into the mountains west of Asheville. Now it's time to visit Asheville itself, the chief city of the Smoky Mountains.

Asheville may be a mountain city, but don't expect to find bearded hillbillies holding jugs. Asheville is an amazingly sophisticated place, a city of 83,400 (with an urban area of perhaps 200,000) that has the arts, shopping, music, and night life you'd expect in a giant metropolis—as well as the intellectual atmosphere and alternative lifestyles. Of course, being physically smaller than a huge metropolis, everything in it is jammed together in the most delightful mélange imaginable; there's really nothing else like it north of Key West. It has a wonderfully retro downtown, a 60-block area with exuberant little buildings from the 1890s to the 1930s. During the day, shoppers fill a dozen or more shopping blocks lined with small, independent shops; at night, streets bustle as people explore the restaurant and music scene. Some of this sophistication is the natural result of being the only city for miles around. However, much of it springs from the influence of George Vanderbilt, who made Asheville his home in 1889 and constructed the spectacular Biltmore Estate, reputedly the largest private home in America.

Physically, Asheville sits behind the Blue Ridge in a huge oval bowl, the Asheville Basin, a figure-eight that is 45 miles long and ranges from 3–18 miles wide—a total of 430 square miles in size. Asheville formed early in the 19th century in the narrowest part of the figure-eight, a squeeze point for turnpikes, then railroads, and now interstates. The French Broad River drains through the middle of the basin from south to north, cutting downward as it goes, so that the streams that drain into it cut downward as well; this gives the basin's bottom sort of a lumpy texture, resembling tiny mountains. The Asheville urban area and the Asheville Basin are one and the same thing; even at the farthest, most rural corners, the homes of commuters mix with those of the farmers.

**GUIDANCE—TOWN AND COUNTRYSIDE** **Asheville** Visitors Center (www.ashevillechamber.org; e-mail: member@ashevillechamber.org; 800-257-1300, 828-258-6101; fax: 828-254-6054; 36 Montford Ave., Asheville, NC 28802). This chamber covers Asheville and the surrounding area. It runs a large and sophisticated visitors center (with a nice gift shop) just north of downtown Asheville, off I-240's Montford Avenue exit.

**www.ExploreAsheville.com** This excellent website is aimed specifically at tourists, and is run by the Buncombe County Tourism Development Authority, a county government agency.

**Asheville Bed & Breakfast Association (ABBA)** (www.ashevillebba.com; 877-262-6867). This association is made up of 17 small bed & breakfasts, all of them in private homes located in quiet neighborhoods in and around Asheville. You can use either their website or their toll-free number to find and reserve the room that's right for you.

**GUIDANCE—PARKS AND FORESTS North Carolina's National Forests** (www.cs.unca.edu/nfsnc; 828-257-4200; 160A Zillicoa St., Ste. A, Asheville, NC 28802). The headquarters for all the national forests in North Carolina are located in Asheville, off the US 19/23 Freeway (Future I-26), NC 251 exit, and follow the signs. They maintain an information desk and bookstore, and—like all national forest stations—are more than happy to help you. Hikers take note: this office sells USGS topographic maps overprinted with current trail data.

**GETTING THERE** *By Car* Asheville is located at the intersection of I-26 (which runs north and south) and I-40 (which runs east and west). Downtown Asheville is several miles north of I-40 via a spur, I-240. At this writing, points north are reached via a new freeway, now marked as Future I-26 but officially designated US 19/23.

VIEW OF DOWNTOWN ASHEVILLE

Internally, Asheville has 700 feet of vertical relief in a 2-mile distance—and 83,000 people live on this broken and contorted slope. Streets run every which way, and getting lost is a lot easier than getting where you want to go. So here's the layout:

- *The shape of the city* is a long oval, oriented north and south.
- *Downtown Asheville* sits on a shelf in the middle of the city, immediately south of I-240.
- *I-40* is 2.7 miles south of downtown.
- *US 25* is the main road going north from downtown, and is named *Merrimon Avenue.*
- *US 25 south of downtown* is also the main artery. It has three names.

In the center of downtown, its name changes to *Biltmore Avenue.*

- As it leaves downtown it slants two blocks west to follow *McDowell Street.*

Lastly, when it intersects with I-40 on the south edge of town, its name changes to *Hendersonville Road.*

- *Biltmore Avenue* continues to parallel McDowell Street; this is where the main **hospital** is located. Biltmore and McDowell converge again in **Biltmore Village**.
- *US 19* leads west of downtown, first as *Patton Avenue,* then as *Smokey Park Highway.*
- *US 70* leads east of downtown; it's called *Tunnel Road* and has the mall commercial district.
- *In the suburbs,* NC 191 (Brevard Road) heads south, and NC 63 (New Leicester Highway) heads north. Both are west of downtown, as are nearly all the suburbs.

And that's it! Nearly every place you'll want to visit is off one of these roads. Asheville isn't big—just confusing.

*By Air* **Asheville Regional Airport** (www.flyavl.com; e-mail: pr@flyavl.com; 828-684-2226; 61 Terminal Dr., Ste. 1, Fletcher, NC 28732). Asheville's small regional airport is located 15 miles south of downtown off I-26, exit 9 (NC 280). It's an old-fashioned terminal from the 1950s, with a central one-story terminal and radiating gates, but has been remodeled and modernized in recent years—less quaint but more comfortable. It is served by four airlines, with daily service to Atlanta, Charlotte, Detroit, Minneapolis, Orlando, Cincinnati, Houston, and Newark. Several car-rental agencies are located within or near the airport.

*By Bus* (www.greyhound.com; 828-253-8451; 2 Tunnel Rd., Asheville, NC. Asheville is served by Greyhound Bus Lines, with several arrivals each day. The terminal is located a mile east of downtown on US 70 (Tunnel Road), in the Asheville Mall commercial area. Car rentals are nearby, including an Avis at the Sears in the mall.

**MEDICAL EMERGENCIES** **Mission Memorial Hospital** (www.msj.org; 828-213-1111; 509 Biltmore Ave., Asheville, NC 28801). This major hospital complex has a huge campus south of downtown Asheville, straddling Biltmore Avenue. Its Class II trauma center (the only one in western North Carolina) is a left turn as you go south on Biltmore, into the St. Joseph's Hospital area of the campus. You might want to call for directions.

## ✷ Exploring the Area

**EXPLORING BY CAR** **The Buncombe Turnpike** This 30-mile drive traces the route of the most important road ever to be built in the Smoky Mountains—the 1827 Buncombe Turnpike.

*Leg #1* (*5 miles, urban*): From the Smith McDowell House, take Victoria Street south for 0.7 mile to a right onto Meadow Street, then go 2.9 miles (Meadow Street becomes Lyman Street) to the US 19/23 (Future I-26) entrance ramp. Enter, merge left, and exit on Patton Avenue (0.7 mile). Take Patton Avenue to Pack Square, 0.7 mile.

*Leg #2* (*2 miles, urban*): From Pack Square in downtown Asheville, take Merrimon Avenue (US 25) north one block to a left onto Lexington Avenue, which becomes Broadway Street as it leaves downtown. When Broadway Street crosses under Future I-26 (US 19/23) in 1.9 miles it becomes NC 215.

*Leg #3* (*16.7 miles*): Continue on NC 215, following the French Broad River, for 16.7 miles to its intersection with US Bus 23.

*Leg # 4* (*6.3 miles*): Continue straight on US Bus 23 into Marshall, following the railroad, to the far side of downtown in 2.8 miles. Just as US Bus 23 turns sharply right and uphill, go straight on Redmon Road (SSR 1136) for 2.1 miles to a right fork uphill onto Sweetwater Road (still SSR 1136), then go 0.4 mile to a right onto Little Pine Road (SSR 1135), then 1 mile to a right onto US 25; Asheville and Pack Square are 22 miles ahead.

John Smith built the **Smith-McDowell House** in 1840 out of profits from the Buncombe Turnpike. Completed in 1827, the turnpike made a beeline from Charleston, South Carolina (the South's biggest city at the time), through the heart of the Blue Ridge mountains, to the rich farmlands of Virginia, Tennessee, and Kentucky. The South Carolina slave plantations concentrated on cash crops, such as cotton, rice, indigo, and (most important to the economy) more slaves. In fact, many played-out plantations made all their money as human stock-breeders—and all this stock took a lot of food. The food came on the hoof, driven down from beyond the mountains: hogs above all, but also cattle, sheep, and turkeys. (And a turkey drive was truly a sight to behold.)

Hundreds of thousands, even millions, of animals walked and fluttered down the turnpike every fall of every year, from 1827 to 1860. And every last one of them had to pass in front of the Asheville County Courthouse, then cross the French Broad River at Smith's Ferry. In 1834, John Smith replaced his ferry with a bridge, and his wealth billowed. He grew corn all along the French Broad flood plain, and in the process prevented any competitors from building another bridge. He died, rich as Croesus, in 1858.

This route starts at John Smith's house, restored to its original splendor, and then drops quickly to the giant railroad yard that lines the French Broad River; look for the round house on your right, designed to service steam engines; just beyond, the bridge to your right leads to parks and **greenways** along the river. Now the road is passing through Asheville's newest arts district, the **River Arts District**, where artists take advantage of the empty, but beautifully built red-brick warehouses to create wonderful new studio and gallery spaces. At 2.4 miles you reach Smiths Bridge on your left, the third-generation successor to John Smith's money machine, today a modern concrete structure leading to (fittingly) livestock auctions on the other shore. You can follow the actual turnpike roadbed right, very steeply uphill, but this route takes an easier detour into downtown, to the site of the old Courthouse on Pack Square.

Leg #2 starts on **Pack Square**, with its monument to local boy Governor Zebulon Vance, who also made pots of money selling corn to drovers. Stop to note the **Urban Trail** bronze sculpture of pigs and chickens walking along the turnpike, marking the location of the roadbed. Modern interstates obscure the route out of downtown; but you regain the roadbed on Broadway, with a greenway along the left side probably closer to its actual location. A mile north of the interstate, the beautiful **Asheville Botanical Gardens** is on your right; apart from the obvious reasons to visit this lovely place, it has a preserved length of the turnpike roadbed, exactly where a group of old men and boys fought off marauding Yankees in the "Battle of Asheville."

Leg #3 regains the roadbed and the riverside, meandering first through an industrial district; look for the state prison and the restored-brick warehouses. This ends as you pass the sewage works (the geodesic domes over the settlement ponds making it look oddly New Age) and the solid waste compound—the old South never did value its rivers. Now the highway gives broad views over the **French Broad River**, with a couple of parks and kayak launch sites. This stretch of highway was evidently restored sometime around World War I (replacing **Old NC 20** in the Sandymush Drive), becoming first the Dixie Highway, then (in 1927) US 25. Now that it's been demoted to backroad status, you can enjoy it without worrying about traffic. You'll pass Alexander Bridge, the start of the **Sandymush Drive**, at 8.8 miles; another 8 miles later, you rejoin US 25.

Leg #4 is a bonus leg, for those left wanting more. It goes through the center of the quaint little county seat of **Marshall**; be sure to stop at **Zumas** if you are ready for a cup of coffee. As US Bus 25 is about to lift itself out of the riverside gorge that holds Marshall, look for a small lane straight ahead. This is the turnpike's original roadbed, and it's a hoot, twisting safely above the French Broad's floods, passing through meadows with wide views over the gorge. This (minus the pavement) is what the turnpike was really like 180 years ago.

ASHEVILLE'S URBAN TRAIL

**A Sandy Mush Drive** This 19-mile drive explores the most rural and beautiful section of the Asheville Basin, following Sandy Mush Creek from its mouth to its source. On the way, it leads to the **major trailheads of the Sandy Mush Game Lands**, and explores some historic early highways.

*Start* on NC 215 at the Alexander Bridge, 8.8 miles north of its intersection with Future I-26 (US 19/23) in Asheville.

*Leg #1 (6.4 miles)*: Turn left onto Fletcher Martin Road (SSR 1620), crossing the bridge, and go 1.3 miles to a right onto SSR 1634, still Fletcher Martin Road. At the fork, in 1.5 miles, go straight on Cedar Hill Road (SSR 1632) to its end in 1.8 miles. Return to the fork.

*Leg #2* (*12.5 miles*): Back at the fork take a very sharp left onto Old NC 20 (SSR 1629) for 2.9 miles; then continue straight on paved Piney Knob Extension (SSR 1846) for 0.3 mile; then continue straight on Bear Creek Road (SSR 1607, becoming SSR 1114) for 3.1 miles; then turn left onto Meadows Town Road (SSR 1001) for 3.6 miles; then turn left onto Sandy Mush Road and reach NC 63 (New Leicester Highway) in 2.6 miles.

This drive starts off dramatically, with a long bridge high over the **French Broad River**. From there, the road meanders through a pleasant sort of scenery common enough in the Asheville Basin, as meadows and farmlands mix with commuters' homes. Soon the road passes an old, abandoned country store and an impressive farmhouse, relics (as we will see below) of a first-generation highway. Now the route passes a fork and follows a ridgetop meadow with wide views, much of it over the open public lands of the **Sandy Mush Game Lands**. On your left, you'll pass gravel Martin Chandler Road (SSR 1633), which leads to more hilltop views and a trailhead for the game lands. Continuing ahead, you'll pass a country church on your left, with more trailhead parking just beside it; from it, you can wander through hilltop meadows, kept in hay for the benefit of wildlife. The road and Leg #1 both end at yet another trailhead into the game lands; here the former road continues into the game lands, closed to vehicles but open to walkers. To start Leg #2, return to the fork.

In *Leg* #2, Sandy Mush Creek breaks into the steep northern side of the Asheville Basin and hacks it into a rough, broken land—the heart of the Sandy Mush Game Lands. (Yes, they're spelled differently.) It's a hard place to build a road, and successive waves of road improvements (starting before World War I) have added a confusing layer of conflicting names. It can be interesting as well as frustrating—the frequent name changes document this little area's history.

From the fork your road is **Old NC 20**—a name that dates before World War I, when the State of North Carolina was establishing its first highway network. The even number indicates that this was meant to be an important north-south highway between Asheville and Marshall. It's strange that they should choose this route, which crosses the French Broad River twice, instead of the nearby **Buncombe Turnpike**; it probably indicates that, at that time, the turnpike was in too bad repair to be rehabilitated, and a detour was necessary.

Old NC 20 quickly proves itself to be a highway designed when cars sped along at 15 mph—and 10 mph was seen as not unreasonable in a mountain area. Narrow and twisting, it plunges quickly into a pretty little gorge carved by a rushing stream, and almost immediately enters game lands. There is yet another trailhead parking area where the road crosses the stream, and game lands extend along this stream for miles in both directions. Indeed, the road stays within or along the game lands for most of the next 1.6 miles, and much of what looks like farmland on your right is actually open to casual exploration (check for game land signs to be sure). Leaving the game lands behind, Old NC 20 climbs a hill—then wanders away to the right at the next intersection, to an eventual dead end; this highway ended its life around 1927, when the U.S. Primary Highway Network came into existence, and US 25 took its place. You will continue straight on the modern main road that replaced the curvy and erosion-prone old one—the result of a third generation of road building, a burst of rural road upgrading in the mid-1980s to mid-1990s. It follows a hill line with more views, then passes attractive Redmon

Church with the last of the hilltop panoramas. Just beyond on the left is the last game land trailhead, this one on a track that leads down a forested ridge to Sandy Mush Creek. The road crosses the creek just beyond; look for a handsome old farmhouse on the left.

In a mile your road connects with the generation of road-building that came between it and NC 20. Today it's SSR 1001, but in the years after 1927, when the Works Project Administration was paving America, it proudly sported the number NC 213, and connected Marshall with Luck. By the time of the third generation, NC 213 was too out of date for a modern highway, and the state demoted it to a secondary road. Its western reaches live on, upgraded and improved, as NC 63, the New Leicester Highway. SSR 1001 is a pleasant country drive today, ending at NC 63. To return to Asheville, follow NC 63 right.

**EXPLORING ON FOOT** **Downtown Asheville Urban Trail** (828-259-5855; fax: 828-259-5832; P.O. Box 7148, Asheville, NC 28802). This 1.6-mile loop is not your ordinary downtown historic walk. A City of Asheville public art project, the Urban Trail marks each of its 30 interpretive stations with a unique work of art. Some are solemn historic statuary with explanatory plaques, such as the monument to Elizabeth Blackwell, M.D., the Ashevillian who became the first American woman to get a medical degree. However, the most notable pieces are whimsical tributes to Asheville's past. A little girl drinks from a fountain in City Hall Plaza; author Thomas Wolfe's size 13 shoes sit outside his mother's boardinghouse; a giant flat iron, accurately reproducing one used in downtown's Asheville Laundry, stands in front of the Flat Iron Building. You might sit down on a bench to rest a spell, only to find yourself beside a bronze fiddle, a bag of apples, or a little boy; or facing dancers swirling to mountain music. Historic buildings, never completed due to timidity, rise in the glorious form imagined by their architects.

The **Asheville Visitors Center** is your headquarters for taped interpretive guides, guided walks, and even Segway tours. Amazingly, this treasure has no dedicated website.

## ✷ Villages

**Asheville** Until 1889 Asheville was just another mountain town, a bit larger and more prosperous than most. By then, several rail lines had converged upon Asheville, guaranteeing its future success (at least in comparison to its neighbors). Convenient rail connections gave Asheville more than its share of the emerging mountain tourism market; from this, Asheville gained a couple of truly spectacular hotels (now, alas, gone), which in their turn attracted a more highfalutin clientele. One of these society high rollers was George Vanderbilt, grandson of the railroad magnate, who visited an Asheville hotel in 1888. A year later he returned, buying up over 100,000 acres and creating a grand baronial estate for himself, the **Biltmore Estate**.

What followed Vanderbilt and his Biltmore Estate wasn't just more tourism—it was a cultural upheaval. Vanderbilt caused part of this directly and intentionally. Unhappy with the way American loggers destroyed their forests, Vanderbilt brought Gifford Pinchot (a German-trained forester, born in America) to his estate to develop European-style forestry, and teach forest conservation to the locals. He founded a model village, **Biltmore Village**, to provide humane and comfortable housing and stores for his workers. He started **craft schools**, and built a cultural center for his African American workers, the **YMI Cultural Center**. All of these efforts may have fallen short of turning a raw Southern town into a sophisticated and diverse European settlement, but they certainly had their effect. Vanderbilt's indirect impact was even more important. He brought America's greatest society architect, Richard Morris Hunt, to Asheville, and America's greatest landscape planner, Frederick Law Olmsted. Hunt and Olmsted received local commissions, many from socialites attracted to Asheville by the presence of the Vanderbilts. Hunt's assistant, William Sharp Smith, set up his practice in Asheville and developed a distinctive type of Queen Anne style with wood, stone, and pebbledash that has become an Asheville signature; other, later, architects erected gloriously eccentric art deco structures, including the **Grove Arcade** and the **City Hall Plaza**. Asheville was raw no more.

ASHEVILLE CITY HALL

In the 1920s, Asheville's blossoming attracted investors—including land speculators looking for the next Florida. After 1925 Asheville land prices soared and building boomed, and the 1926 collapse of the Florida Land Boom only seemed to bring more land speculators to Asheville. Author Thomas Wolfe publicly ridiculed the speculators—and privately advised his mother (who ran an Asheville boardinghouse) to buy more land on credit. Asheville's bubble burst in November 1930, leaving a 60-block downtown so vastly overbuilt that its gorgeous Land Boom architecture remained largely unviolated 70 years later. Careful land-use planning, instituted in the 1990s, has kept it that way, allowing the beautiful old buildings to slowly fill with wonderful small shops.

## ✶ Wild Places

**THE GREAT FORESTS The Bent Creek Forests** (www.srs.fs.fed.us/bentcreek/index.html; e-mail: juliamurphy@fs.fed.us; 828-667-5261; fax: 828-667-9097; 1577 Brevard Rd., Asheville, NC 28806). This tract of the Pisgah National Forest, on the southwest edge of Asheville, centers on the watershed of Bent Creek, a 6,000-acre bowl surrounded by 3,500-foot ridgelines. George Vanderbilt consolidated this tract in 1909 from 70-odd small farms and homes, because it linked his estate with his huge **Pisgah Forest** holdings, and because it was in the middle of the view from his terrace. Seven years later, his widow sold it to the U.S. Forest Service for $5 an acre. Since 1925, the bulk of this land, including all of the Bent

Creek watershed, has been managed as the Bent Creek Experimental Forest. At first the forest was dedicated to experiments in regrowing healthy hardwood forests on devastated lands, but since World War II the experiments have concentrated on managing mountain hardwood forests for their logging resources. For the last 75 years, most of these experiments have included systematically altering small forest areas and measuring the difference, creating a patchwork of forest scenery. Two large tracts have been carved out of the experimental forest for recreational users: the **North Carolina State Arboretum** and the **Lake Powhatan Recreation Area**. A network of trails wander through all parts of the forest, most of them open to mountain bikes and horses as well as walkers. Its ready accessibility (and relatively easy gradients) make this a popular area. To reach it, take NC 191 south from I-26 for 2 miles to a left onto Bent Creek Ranch Road (SSR 3484); this enters Bent Creek Forest in 1 mile, becoming FS 806.

**Sandy Mush Game Lands** One of the most exciting public land acquisitions by the State of North Carolina sits at the far northern edge of the Asheville Basin, at a place where Sandy Mush Creek is cutting a canyon into its mountainous northern edge. The 2,600 acres of the Sandy Mush Game Lands sprawl over farming and forestlands, in a district where suburban homes are only now beginning to appear.

As a public land, Sandy Mush is virtually unique; instead of deep, wild forest, it is a collection of farmland and woodlots on the edge of a rapidly expanding urban area. Its hills (you might call them mountainettes) are frequently covered in grasslands, with wide views of the mountains jumping out of the ground at the edge of the basin. There are many relics of abandoned farms throughout the area. The forests are worthwhile as well. Mostly farm woodlots, the trees are healthy and young, and quite varied—an interesting environment that's very different from the national forest and park forests based on abandoned logging lands. The tiny gorge of Sandy Mush Creek is particularly beautiful and interesting—and very hard to reach, as this area is completely pathless. While it may have no trails, it has six trailheads, located at farm tracks that wander unpredictably into this giant tract. It is open for hunting in season, but only on Monday, Wednesday, and Saturday, making it an exceptionally good place to explore for fall color on the other four days (wearing hunter orange, just in case). Just be sure to bring a map.

QUILT GARDEN AT THE NORTH CAROLINA STATE ARBORETUM

**RIVERS The French Broad River** The French Broad River spends 34 miles in this chapter's area as it flows northward through the Asheville Basin. As you might expect for a mountain river in a basin, it is overwhelmingly Class I–II. Along this stretch its uppermost section is the most interesting; here the river spends several miles within the bounds of the **Biltmore Estate**, with long reaches of Class II to add a bit of excitement on top of the uniquely beautiful scenery. The Biltmore Estate lands end as the river passes under an interstate, and the Asheville urban area begins, with a long-decaying industrial district. This district, however, is rapidly improving as a city masterplan finally starts to take hold, and a greenway has already spread for several miles along its left bank. As the river passes the central city (marked by a prison and a closed landfill) it enters an attractive rural zone, with good access opportunities on its right bank from NC 215, **The Buncombe Turnpike**.

**RECREATION AREAS Lake Powhatan Recreation Area** This Pisgah National Forest recreation area sits just outside Asheville off NC 191, in the **Bent Creek Experimental Forest**. It has a large lake with a swimming beach, picnicking, and camping. A large network of hiking trails, very popular with Ashevillians, spreads throughout the surrounding hills, and an easy gravel road leads uphill to the Blue Ridge Parkway.

**Lake Julian County Park** (buncombecounty.org/governing/depts/Parks; e-mail: parks@buncombecounty.org; 828-250-4260; 75 Long Shoals Rd., Asheville, NC, 28704). This county park centers on a large cooling pond used for a major regional power plant, "Lake Julian," covering some 300 acres. Wilderness it ain't, but the fishing is excellent, with an abundance of bass, catfish, brim, crappie, and talapia. It has a pretty picnic area as well. Johnboat rentals are available. You will find it on Long Shoals Road (Asheville's south side), off I-26, exit 6, then east a half-mile on NC 146.

**PICNIC AREAS Montford City Park** This attractive city park has a garden-like appearance—well-kept, deeply shaded, and climbing a steep hill in stone terraces. A full-service recreational park, it's located on Montford Avenue about a mile north of downtown Asheville.

## ✷ To See

**The Biltmore Estate** (800-411-3812; 828-225-1333; biltmore.com; 1 Lodge St., Asheville, NC, 28803). Open all week, January–March, 9 AM–4 PM; April–December, 8:30 AM–5:00 PM; locations within the estate have different hours. Adults: $47–$59; youth (10–17): $23.50–$29.50. Varies by season and day of week; some days have timed entries. In 1889, 28-year-old George Vanderbilt decided to become a medieval nobleman. The grandson of railroad tycoon Cornelius Vanderbilt, George was a sensitive and intellectual young man who left the coarse work of running the family enterprises to his older brothers. Like many of the Victorian aristocracy, he looked back on medieval Europe as a happy, stable society where the laboring classes found satisfaction through fine craftsmanship while the nobility watched over all with fatherly concern. Vanderbilt wanted to create such a society with himself as the nobleman, and chose Asheville as his new demesne.

George Vanderbilt had discovered Asheville on his many travels. He loved the mild climate and the scenic beauty, and appreciated the advantages of forming a great estate from cheap Appalachian land. And Vanderbilt had a very large estate in mind. Before he was done he had purchased 125,000 acres—nearly 200 square miles stretching from the southern edge of Asheville to the Pisgah Mountains on the far horizon. He then assembled a remarkable team of experts to convert this tired-out land into a noble domain: leading architect Richard Morris Hunt to design the house; Frederick Law Olmsted, the designer of Central Park and the U.S. Capitol grounds, to design the gardens and develop a management plan; and America's first forester, Gifford Pinchot, to restore and manage 100,000 acres of logged-out forest. He had Hunt build the largest house in America, a 250-room French château, and emparked this house with several hundred acres of Olmsted's gardens. Beyond the gardens he laid out a thousand acres of farmland and dairy to establish the self-sufficiency of a great medieval estate. He built a medieval village at the estate gates, today's **Biltmore Village**, to provide his workers with housing and shops.

After George Vanderbilt's death in 1914, his wife continued to live on the estate and manage its farms and forests, becoming the first woman president of North Carolina's agricultural society. Being more of a practical manager than a medieval baroness, she sold 87,000 acres of forest to the U.S. Department of Agriculture (run by her husband's old employee Gifford Pinchot), to form the nucleus of the **Pisgah National Forest**. She sold off Biltmore Village and other holdings as well, shrinking the estate to a mere 11,000 acres. When she remarried and moved north, her daughter and son-in-law, Cornelia and John Cecil, continued to live in Biltmore, opening it to the public in 1930.

The Vanderbilt heirs ceased living at Biltmore in 1958, but have continued to run it as a self-sufficient estate; it is now owned by John and Cornelia's son and grandson, who run it as a profit-making, tax-paying enterprise. Currently possessing 8,000 acres, the estate continues its extensive farming and forestry operations as well as a distinguished winery and vineyard. But the core of the estate remains the house and gardens, carefully preserved and restored to reflect the way it looked to George and Edith Vanderbilt, an Appalachian lord and lady at the height of the Gilded Age.

The Biltmore Estate is located on Lodge Street, 0.6 mile north of I-40, exit 50.

**The Biltmore House** All week; 9:00 AM–5:30 PM. On busy days, visitors are given a pass which specifies their visit time. Included in admission; special tours available at an additional cost. Famed architect Richard Morris Hunt personally supervised the construction of this 250-room French château from 1889 to 1895, and helped its owner, George Vanderbilt, pick out the furniture in a series of European buying sprees. Today, still fully furnished as in Vanderbilt's day and immaculately preserved by his heirs, the Biltmore House is completely overwhelming.

The front entrance is a delightful surprise—a bright, open place, where white marble floors surround a glass-roofed atrium, opening into arches that lead into great spaces. This is the Winter Garden, with its great palms overhanging rattan and bamboo garden furniture. To one side of the entrance is the grandest room in the house, the baronial Banquet Hall—a huge space with a barrel-vaulted wooden ceiling 70 feet high, five gigantic 16th-century Flemish tapestries, and a leaf table, which expands to hold 64 guests. Opposite the hall, the Library has balconied two-story-tall walls, completely covered with 10,000 books—less than half of Vanderbilt's personal collection.

Walk onto any one of a series of terraces that line the rear of the house, and one of the grandest views in the region opens up. Meadows and glades drop away from the steep stone sides of the terraces to the farmland lining the French Broad River far below. Then, after miles of steeply rolling forestlands, the grand cliff-like sides of the Pisgah Range form a tall, unbroken wall along the horizon. Vanderbilt owned this view; every bit of land in this wide panorama was his.

Upstairs, on the second and third floor, are the family's private quarters and a very large number of guest rooms. Vanderbilt disliked formal entertainment but he enjoyed having houseguests, informal house parties of the sort popular in the great houses of Europe. There were so many guests, and so many guest rooms, that Vanderbilt had the halls color-coded so that guests would know where they were. Downstairs, the basement housed servants quarters, kitchen and laundry facilities, and indoor recreation rooms including a swimming pool, bowling alley, and gymnasium.

In all, the self-guided house tour leads through 23 rooms upstairs and 11 rooms downstairs, and has disabled access. Two other tours, each requiring an additional payment and at least six flights of steps, take visitors through closed portions of the house, from the fourth-floor servants' quarters to the Victorian boilers and electric panels in the sub-basement; and up onto the roof for sweeping views.

**Biltmore Gardens** All week; 9 AM–dusk. Included in the admission ticket. Designed by Frederick Law Olmsted after he had already completed New York's Central Park, the Biltmore Gardens flow downhill from the house, covering several hundred acres. Formal gardens, patterned after Italian Renaissance styles, frame the house and offer striking views both of the house and the mountains beyond. Then, downhill from the house's Italianate gardens, an informal Ramble allows visitors to explore an intimate mountain draw covered with flowering shrubs. Beneath the Ramble is a large, formal Walled Garden, patterned after the gardens found in English country houses, and ending in a large and impressive series of glasshouses called the Conservatory, with displays of delicate tropical vegetation. Beneath the Walled Garden stretch a series of intriguing informal gardens spread about the mountain slopes and reached down a long series of paths. Most notable here is the stunning Azalea Garden, with an extensive collection of local and exotic azaleas, and the beautiful Bass Pond and Waterfall, restored to its original appearance.

The exit road takes visitors through parts of the garden, including the Walled Garden, the Conservatory (with a parking lot), and the Bass Pond. The estate's brochure, included with the admission ticket, has an excellent and detailed map of the garden's many twisting paths.

**The Biltmore Winery** Open January–March, Mon.–Sat., 11 AM–6 PM, and Sun., noon–6 PM; April–December, Mon.–Sat., 11 AM–7 PM, and Sun., noon–7 PM. Included in admissions ticket. Biltmore opened its ambitious winery in 1985, in a dairy barn designed by Hunt and built as part of the original estate construction. The short winery tour includes a seven-minute video and a self-guided walk through the winemaking areas and the basement. The tour ends with a delightful tasting in the old calf barn, where you can interact with wine-serving bartenders at U-shaped bars. The wines include one of Biltmore's top-end estate-grown wines, plus several white and red blends of North Carolina and California grapes. Those interested in tasting more of Biltmore's estate wines and champagnes can pay $5 for an additional tasting.

**Biltmore Shops & Restaurants** (Asheville, NC). There is quite a variety of shops and eateries within the estate that are available only to ticket holders. The largest concentration of these is by the house, in the old stables. Here are shops that specialize in Victorian-style gifts, Biltmore wines, Christmas items, old-fashioned toys, old-fashioned candies, and books related to local sites, Victorian arts and crafts, and the Vanderbilts. Food service includes the Stable Cafe (11 AM–5 PM), an ice-cream parlor, and a bakery. In the winery is another gift shop with Biltmore wines and other food and gift items, as well as The Bistro (9 AM–9 PM), serving lunch and dinner. Finally, a garden shop located at the Conservatory offers plants from the Biltmore nurseries and a variety of garden items. The Deerpark Restaurant, also on the estate, is open to the public for buffet lunches.

The estate's eateries are not cheap. Visitors who wish to spend less on lunch can find a large variety of good local cafés in **Biltmore Village** immediately outside the main gate. Your ticket allows you to leave the estate and reenter on the same day.

♿ **Pack Place** (packplace.org; e-mail: info@packplace.org; 828-257-4500; fax: 828-251-5652; 2 South Pack Sq., Asheville, NC 28801). Open Tues.–Sat., 10 am–5 pm; Sunday (June–October only), 1 pm–5 pm; closed Monday. Located on downtown Asheville's Pack Square, this arts and sciences center's small entrance is deceiving. Behind the entrance, a large complex of museums, public spaces, and the Diana Wortham Theatre stretches back through several buildings, including the marble-clad 1920s neo-Classical Public Library Building. The not-for-profit Pack Place Foundation runs the multilevel public area at the center of the complex, including the fascinating free exhibition on the history of the square. Off the public area are three independent museums—the art museum, the gem and mineral museum, and the hand-on health museum—and the Diana Wortham Theatre. Behind this main structure in its own historic building is the YMI Cultural Center, a major part of Asheville's African American community. Pack Place will sell you combined tickets at various complex prices (every tenant sets its own price rules), or you can buy tickets at each venue separately. Combined tickets are cheaper.

SIDEWALK CAFÉS ON PACK SQUARE

♿ **The Asheville Art Museum** (ashevilleart.org; e-mail: mailbox@ashevilleart.org; 828-253-3227; fax: 828-257-4503; 2 South Pack Sq.).

Founded in 1948 by a group of Asheville area artists, the Asheville Art Museum has a permanent collection of over 1,500 pieces of 20th-century art. Part of the Pack Place Center, it occupies much of the old Italian Renaissance public library adjacent to Pack Square. Wandering through three stories of display space, the museum will have two or three exhibitions going at any one time, making the overall experience quite diverse. As you might expect, the permanent exhibitions emphasize western North Carolina, with one gallery displaying art inspired by the Blue Ridge Mountains from the 19th century to the present, and another displaying pieces by the contemporary craft masters of the western mountains. However, the displays are by no means limited to area artists, and pieces by nationally known figures are splashed throughout the museum.

✐ ♿ **Colburn Gem & Mineral Museum** (828-254-7162; Pack Place). Founded in 1960, this first-rate mineral museum combines an extensive collection of North Carolina gems and minerals with educational and interpretive exhibits aimed at families with children. Exhibits include locally mined precious stones, mountain-building, and mountain minerals. Summer field trips lead to some of the most fascinating and little-known corners of the Asheville area.

✐ ♿ **The Health Adventure** (828-254-6373; Pack Place). Founded in 1968, the Health Adventure is a hands-on health and science museum. Originally a museum for school children, they have been expanding their exhibits to appeal to adults and older children, and to include biology and physics as well as health.

✐ ♿ **The YMI Cultural Center** (828-252-4614; Pack Place). George Vanderbilt constructed this National Register Tudor-style brick building as a cultural center for his African American workmen. Originally known as the Young Mens Institute, it continues to this day as the YMI Cultural Center. Exhibitions on African American arts and history, particularly in the Asheville area, are always featured, as are plays, storytelling, and hands-on craft classes. Considered part of Pack Place, it's building is across the street to the south.

**CULTURAL PLACES** **The River Arts District** (riverartsdistrict.com). In the early 20th century Asheville's industrial district trailed along the railroad tracks that hugged the banks of the French Broad River, swinging around town center in a broad semicircle. This was a common pattern in the industrializing South, as was its modern sequel of slow abandonment, leaving behind dozens of tall brick factories, semiruinous. Asheville, however, has an advantage over other small cities—a huge population of artists, artists who need large amounts of very cheap square footage for studio and gallery space, and who easily fall in love with the bricks and timbers of the old factories. And so the old industrial district has been reborn as The River Arts District.

The River Arts District has reached critical mass, and is growing fast. Its website, maintained by one of the artists, lists ten buildings, each with a variety of studios, galleries, and businesses. Some studios are open daily, others on Friday or Saturday, and some by appointment. Check the website before you visit, where you can download a map of this confusing area.

**Grovewood Galleries** (www.grovewood.com; e-mail: grovewood@grovewood.com; 877-622-7238, 828-253-7651; fax: 828-254-2489; 111 Grovewood Rd., Asheville, NC, 28804). Open Mon.–Sat., 10 AM–6 PM; Sun., 1 PM–5 PM. This collection of two museums, a gallery, and a lovely little café occupy a group of historic buildings in their own little garden by the Grove Park Inn. This complex was erected by the Vanderbilts in 1901, as a training school for traditional mountain weavers and woodworkers. After George Vanderbilt's death, his widow sold the school to the adjacent Grove Park Inn, which added three English cottage–style buildings to the complex in 1917. From then until the 1980s, the small complex produced fine homespun cloth for the craft market. Independent of the Grove Park Inn since 1942, Grovewood became a crafters' center again in the 1990s. Its large fine crafts gallery represents regional craft artists in a wide variety of media, including a large furniture gallery. It rotates solo exhibits every two months or so, and has actively supported artists groups in areas such as woodworking and jewelry. Adjacent are two museums, one dedicated to the Vanderbilt's school and the homespun industry of the early 20th century, and the other with a collection of 30 antique cars. All of these buildings front on a lovely tree-shaded garden, with sculptures scattered about, and a wide view over the Grove Park Inn and its golf course toward downtown Asheville. To find the Grovewood Galleries, go to the Grove Park Inn, enter its parking lot, and follow the signs.

**New Morning Gallery** (newmorninggallerync.com; e-mail: newmorning@bellsouth.net; 828-274-2831; 7 Boston Way, Asheville, NC 28803). New Morning Gallery looks like a tiny storefront, sitting a half-block from the center of Biltmore Village. Looks can deceive; the gallery stretches back deep into the building, then climbs up the stairs to sprawl through nearly a block of elegant second-floor space. New Morning specializes in "functional art," handcrafted stuff you can use (if only as a paperweight). It features artists from all over America, but with a special emphasis on regional artists. The New Morning Gallery sponsors the annual **Village Arts and Crafts Festival**. An affiliated gallery in the village, Bellagio, offers handcrafted clothing and accessories.

**HISTORIC PLACES** **Smith-McDowell House Museum** (www.wnchistory.org; 828-253-9231; 283 Victoria Rd., Asheville, NC 28801). Open Thurs.–Sat., 10 AM–4 PM; Sun., noon–4 PM. One of the oldest brick houses in the area, the 1840 Smith-McDowell House sits on a hilltop south of downtown Asheville, on what is now the campus of Asheville-Buncombe Technical Community College. The post-frontier farmhouse of a prominent family, this handsome, symmetric structure sports first- and second-story full-front porches, and double fireplaces on each gable end. Now a historical museum, different rooms are furnished for different periods of the house's 19th-century heyday. The kitchen shows the earliest period, the 1840s; a bedroom reflects more prosperous antebellum tastes; and the parlor and dining room show the style of the succeeding generation. The garden behind the house preserves a design of Frederick Law Olmsted, executed during his days at the nearby Biltmore Estate.

**Thomas Wolfe Memorial State Historic Site** (www.wolfememorial.com; e-mail: contactus@wolfememorial.com; 828-253-8304; fax: 828-252-8171; 52 North Market St., Asheville, NC 28801). Open April–October, Mon.–Sat., 9 AM–5 PM, and Sun., 1 PM–5 PM. November–March, Tues.–Sat., 10 AM–4 PM, and Sun., 1 PM–4 PM. Free. Author Thomas Wolfe, acclaimed for his autobiographical novels during the 1930s, spent his childhood in his mother's boardinghouse, My Old Kentucky Home, on the eastern edge of the Lexington Hill section of downtown Asheville.

That boardinghouse, and the town of Asheville, became the thinly veiled subject of his most famous novel, *Look Homeward Angel: A Story of the Buried Life,* published in 1929 to high acclaim (and great embarrassment among Asheville's worthies). Today, the boardinghouse and a modern visitors center make up the Thomas Wolfe Memorial. For many years the boardinghouse has fronted a pedestrianized street opposite a downtown hotel tower, furnished as it was when Wolfe lived there in the 1910s, and housing a considerable collection of Wolfe memorabilia and artifacts. An arsonist brought this to a halt in 1998, causing massive destruction to the house and collection. Fortunately, most of the collection has been salvaged and restored; and the house's reconstruction is complete and the house is now open. The visitors center houses a display of Wolfe artifacts and an audiovisual show on Wolfe's life and works.

**The Grove Arcade** (www.grovearcade.com; e-mail: info@grovearcade.com; 828-252-7799; 1 Page Ave., Asheville, NC 28801). This astonishing 1920s downtown mall reopened for shopping in 2002, for the first time in 60 years. It's a five-story elaborately decorated structure, covering two entire city blocks in downtown Asheville's **Battery Hill shopping district**. Outer walls are covered with terra cotta tiles and limestone; stone-carved lions and gryphons guard the entrance. Built by the developer of the **Grove Park Inn** in 1929, it functioned successfully as an "indoor market" throughout the Depression, only to be taken over by the Federal government in 1942 as part of the war effort. (Curiously, it was the home of the federal research effort into global warming until that government agency moved to new digs two blocks away.) In 1995 the City of Asheville bought it from the Feds with the intent of restoring it to its original glory. They've succeeded. There are about 70 stores, many specializing in unique local products.

**PARKS AND GARDENS** **The Botanical Gardens at Asheville** (ashevillebotanicalgardens.org; e-mail: bgardens@bellsouth.net; 828-252-5190; fax: 828-252-1211; 151 W. T. Weaver Blvd., Asheville, NC 28804). Free. This 10-acre garden in central Asheville is dedicated to preserving and exhibiting the native plants of the western North Carolina Mountains in their natural surroundings. Designed in 1960 by Doan Ogden, the gardens follow a narrow draw formed by Reed Creek.

ASHEVILLE BOTANICAL GARDENS

Four bridges cross the creek, each with its own view. Special environments include a Sunshine Garden, a Woods Garden, a Rock Garden, a Heath and Azalea Garden, and a Garden for the Blind, emphasizing textures and smells. Also on the property are an historic log cabin, earthworks from a Civil War skirmish, and a length of the original Buncombe Turnpike, the historic 1820 road that opened up the mountains. This volunteer-run garden sponsors regular walks and talks. The gift shop sells a detailed guide to the garden, and sells native landscaping plants; their website is a good resource for native Blue Ridge gardening.

**Asheville City Hall Plaza** (packsquarepark.org; e-mail: info@packsquarepark.org; 828-252-2300; 1 West Pack Sq., Ste. 513, Asheville, NC, 28801). This urban park covers four blocks of downtown Asheville, between Pack Square and the seats of local government—the Asheville City Hall and the Buncombe County Courthouse. It's a lovely place to stop and rest, with ample tree-shaded benches and well-kept flower beds. Its courthouse is an attractive 1927 Neoclassical "skyscraper" of 17 stories, with an elaborately decorated interior. However, the real star of the square is the Asheville City Hall, a 1927 nine-story art deco masterpiece in rich gold brick, white limestone, and rose terra cotta trim. Its octagonal stepped roof is topped by a tall torch-shaped carillon belfry, all covered in pink terra cotta tile with green accents. It's architect, Ashevillian Douglas D. Ellington, designed several other stunners within an easy walking distance—the adjacent Fire Department, the octagonal First Baptist Church two blocks north, and the S&W Cafeteria Building two blocks south. The entire park complex was redesigned and expanded in 2007, eliminating a major highway in the process. The new version extends, unbroken, all the way to the center of downtown at **Pack Place**, and is officially known as "Pack Square Park." The old version was great, and the new version is very special indeed.

**Riverside Cemetery** (828-258-8480; 53 Birch St., Asheville, NC 28801). Open Mon.–Fri., 8 AM–4:30 PM. This 87-acre historic cemetery, owned by the City of Asheville and operated by Parks and Recreation, features park-like grounds with winding hillside paths, large shade trees, many dogwoods and azaleas—and over 9,000 unusual headstones, monuments, and mausoleums. In use since the Civil War, it holds the graves of such notable Ashevillians as O. Henry, Thomas Wolfe, and Gov. Zeb Vance. It's a popular place to stroll on a warm spring day.

♿ **The North Carolina State Arboretum** (www.ncarboretum.org; 828-665-2492; fax: 828-665-2371; 100 Frederick Law Olmsted Way, Asheville, NC 28806). Gardens open daily, 8 AM–9 PM. Buildings keep shorter hours. Founded in 1992, this 426-acre arboretum has 36 acres of formal and informal gardens, greenhouses, educational programs, and miles of walking paths. As an arboretum (and part of the University of North Carolina) it is dedicated to conserving native plant resources and educating the public. The entrance drive, off the Blue Ridge Parkway at the NC 191 exit, is spectacular—beautifully landscaped in an unobtrusive style that blends in with the native habitats, including a viaduct over a delicate stream environment. The handsome main building of stone and gray wood combines contemporary architecture with such homey touches as a large porch with rocking chairs; it has an information desk, a café, and a gift shop, with the rest of the building given over to classrooms and offices. Outside stretch a series of contemporary formal gardens, designed by the original architect and rather severe and intellectual. More successful is the informal garden beneath the porch and stretching down the mountainside. Known as "Plants of Promise" (or POP), it contains a riot of native garden plants, both showy and practical, in a setting designed by the arboretum staff and maintained with home garden equipment and methods. Behind the main building are the greenhouses, now the source of nearly all the seasonal and potted plants in the arboretum, and an active participant in the campaign to conserve rare and endangered native species. Paths stretch downhill through forests to reach **Bent Creek**, where an old road has been converted to a walking and biking path. Along the creek are more gardens, both existing and planned. The most interesting site for a May visit is the National Azalea Repository, containing all but two of the native American azalea species. Picnicking is allowed, as are dogs on leashes. Segway tours are available.

**Western North Carolina Nature Center** (www.wildwnc.org; 828-298-5600; fax: 828-298-2644; 75 Gashes Creek Rd., Asheville, NC 28805). Open daily, 10 AM–5 PM. Run by Buncombe County Parks and Recreation, this large and sophisticated nature study museum concentrates on the animals and plants of the western North Carolina Mountains, occupying 42 acres on the east side of Asheville, off NC 81. Much of the museum is taken up with live animal and plant displays that put their subjects in their environmental context. Habitat displays include predators (red wolf, black wolf, cougars, and bobcats), river otters, turkeys, deer, and bears. A Nocturnal Hall displays animals found only at night—bats, owls, rabbits, flying squirrels. The Educational Farm has farm animals (including a petting area) and exhibits. The Main Hall has 75 live animal exhibits and encourages touching (except for the poisonous snakes and spiders). There are also raccoons, foxes, turtles, hawks, and eagles, as well as a log cabin, herb garden, and nature trail. Their excellent web page has a huge compendium of nature information, a calendar of local nature-oriented events, and a whole lot of links.

**MICROBREWERIES** With 11 microbreweries in or near town, Asheville must set some sort of brewery per capita record. All sponsor their own pubs; otherwise, they range all over the map in character as well as location. Here's a complete list.

**Highlands Brewing Company** (highlandbrewing.com; e-mail: info@highlandbrewing.com; 828-299-3370; fax: 828-299-7223; 12 Old Charlotte Hwy., Ste. H, Asheville, NC 28803). Founded in 1994, Highlands is Asheville's oldest and most popular microbrew. Their English-style Highland Gaelic Ale is ubiquitous in Asheville bars, restaurants, and supermarkets. For eight years they were located in a downtown basement; now they have their own factory in East Asheville, with a tasting room attached.

**Green Man Brewing and Tasting Room** (jackofthewood.com; 828-252-5502; 23 Buxton Ave., Asheville, NC 28801). Open weekdays, 5 PM–10 PM. This is the brewery for the popular brewpub, **Jack of the Wood**—Green Man's only outlet. Brews are heavy and distinctive, and one of them is nearly always available as a cask ale.

**Asheville Brewing Company** (ashevillepizza.com/beer; 828-255-4077; 77 Coxe Ave., Asheville, NC 28801). Lunch and dinner. This small downtown brewery supplies a theater-pizza pub in northern Asheville. But it has its own down-to-earth pub in front, with ample seating and full kitchen to accommodate their menu selections. A weekday, all-you-can-eat pizza buffet at lunchtime is a local favorite. It has outdoor seating as well, where your leashed dog is welcome.

**French Broad Brewing Company** (frenchbroadbrewery.com; 828-277-0222; 101 Fairview Rd., Asheville, NC 28803). Open weekday evenings. This brewery, located just east of **Biltmore Village**, produces a range of Belgian and German inspired beers that are distributed at 75 Asheville area restaurants, pubs, and stores. They have a tasting room on-site, with live music in the evenings.

**Wedge Brewing Company** (wedgebrewing.com; e-mail: info@wedgebrewing.com; 828-505-2792; 125 B Roberts St., Asheville, NC 28801). Open daily, in the afternoons and evenings. This small brewery and its tasting room are part of a gallery complex in the **River Arts District**, in a fine old warehouse. Brews are as sophisticated and varied as the art district that serves as their host.

**Craggie Brewing Company** (craggiebrewingco.com; e-mail: contact@craggiebrewingco.com; 828-254-0360; 197 Hilliard Ave., Asheville, NC 28801). Open Tues.—Sat. evenings. Located in an old warehouse space on the southernmost edge of downtown, this small brewery offers exceptionally good brews with some adventuresome recipes from its attached pub.

**Lexington Avenue Brewery** (lexavebrew.com; e-mail: bookings@LexAveBrew.com; 828-252-0212; 39 N. Lexington Ave., Asheville, NC 28801). Open daily, lunch and dinner. Recently created in an old downtown storefront in the **Lexington Avenue Shopping District**, this brew pub functions as a nightspot for the sophisticated young, with modernist designs set in the old wood and brick, an up-to-date gastropub menu, and live music.

**Oysterhouse Brewing** (oysterhousebeers.com; 828-350-0505; 35 Patton Ave., Asheville, NC 28801). Asheville's smallest brewery is located inside downtown's best seafood restaurant, The Lobster Trap, and produces beers only for that restaurant and its bar. It's specialty is a wonderful oyster stout, made in the authentic Irish manner, with oysters. Not just the meaty parts, mind you, but the whole things, shells and all. It's delicious, and a wonderful complement to seafood. They have other brews as well for the less adventurous in your party, including a blonde ale.

**Pisgah Brewing Company** (pisgahbrewing.com; e-mail: info@pisgahbrewing.com; 828-669-0190; 150 Eastside Dr., Black Mountain, NC 28711). Open Thurs., 4 PM–7 PM.

**Heinzelmännchen Brewery** (yourgnometownbrewery.com; e-mail:

LEXINGTON AVENUE SHOPPING DISTRICT, DOWNTOWN ASHEVILLE

gnome@yourgnometownbrewery.com; 828-631-4466; 545 Mill St., Sylva, NC 28779). Much farther afield, this unique Sylva brewery is in a downtown Sylva storefront, 47 miles west of Asheville (see "Near the Park: Sylva & Dillsboro," *To See*). About a dozen restaurants serve their beer on tap, including a couple in the Asheville area; check their website for a list.

**Catawba Brewing Company** (828-430-6883; Fax: 828-430-6867; catawbavalley brewingcompany.com) 212 South Green Street, Morganton, NC, 28655. E-mail: wscottpyatt@gmail.com. The furthest of the Asheville vicinity microbreweries, Catawba is 57 miles east of Asheville, in downtown **Morganton**. In operation since 1999, Catawba has been developing a regional style based on mountain ingredients and flavors. Its storefront brewery offers tastings on Friday evenings.

**The Asheville Brews Cruise** (brewscruise.com; e-mail: info@brewscruise.com; 828-545-5181). And just to top it all off, you can take a guided tour of three of Asheville's in-city breweries. The brews cruise stops for tastings and plant tours at Highands Brewing Company, Asheville Brewing Company, and French Broad Brewing Company.

## ✷ To Do

**WHITEWATER ADVENTURES** **Southern Waterways** (www.paddlewithus .com; 800-849-1970; 828-232-1970; 521 Amboy Rd., Asheville, NC 28806). Southern Waterways offers gentle, self-guided trips on the French Broad River as it cuts through the Biltmore Estate—several miles of private wilderness, little changed since Frederick Law Olmsted designed its landscape in the 1880s. You have your choice of raft, canoe or kayak, or they will shuttle your private boat for a modest fee. A guided sunset paddle goes down the same stretch in the twilight hours.

**Nantahala Outdoor Center in Asheville** (888-622-1662; 828-232-0110; 52 Westgate Pkwy., Asheville, NC 28806). This large Bryson City outfitter maintains a base and outdoor shop in Asheville, at the Westgate Shopping Plaza off I-240 just across the river from downtown.

**HORSEBACK RIDING** **Biltmore Estate Equestrian Center** (828-277-4485; 1 Biltmore Estate Dr., Asheville, NC 28803). The Biltmore Estate's stables offer riding on the hundred miles of estate trails that George Vanderbilt constructed in the 1890s.

**FISHING** **Hunter Banks Co.** (www.hunterbanks.com; 800-227-6732, 828-252-3005; 29 Montford Ave., Asheville, NC 28801). This large fly shop, occupying a fine old brick store in Asheville's historic Montford section, offers guide services to local trout streams. Their web page is worth a peek for its detailed stream reports and fly recommendations. You'll find the store located just north of downtown Asheville off I-240's Montford Street exit.

**BICYCLING** **Bio-Wheels** (www.biowheels.com; e-mail: asheville@biowheels.net; 828-236-2453; 81 Coxe Ave., Asheville, NC 28801). This large bicycle shop on the south edge of downtown Asheville (on US 25) offers rentals and tours, with your choice of off-road mountain biking, road touring, or leisure biking.

**Liberty Bicycles** (www.libertybikes.com; e-mail: Ride@libertybikes.com; 800-962-4537; 828-684-1085; 1378 Hendersonville Rd., Asheville, NC 28803). This full-service bike shop on US 25 south of Asheville, popular with the area's serious bicyclists, rents mountain bikes.

**ROCK CLIMBING** **ClimbMax** (www.climbmax.com; e-mail: stuart@climbmax nc.com; 828-252-9996; 43 Wall St., Asheville, NC 28801). Located in the Wall Street shopping district, this complete climbing shop has equipment and a large indoor climbing wall in addition to guide services for day trips and overnighters.

**Mountain Adventure Guides, Inc** (www.mtnadventureguides.com; e-mail: guide@mtnadventureguides.com; 866-872-7238, 423-743-7111; 2 Jones Branch Rd., Erwin, TN 37650). This adventure guiding service does all levels of rock climbing that includes equipment, with beginner instructions for children as young as eight. They also offer guided day hiking and backpacking.

**Black Dome Mountain Sports** (www.blackdome.com; 800-678-2367, 828-251-2001; 140 Tunnel Rd., Asheville, NC 28805).This large outdoor supplier offers guide services for rock climbing, fly-fishing, and backpacking. Their store is located in its own building on US 70 (Tunnel Road) just east of downtown Asheville, and is worth a visit.

**GOLF** **Grove Park Inn Resort Golf Course** (groveparkinn.com/Leisure/Golf; 828-252-2711; 290 Macon Ave., Asheville, NC 28804). This scenic course sits in an historic neighborhood a short distance north of downtown Asheville, overlooked by the mammoth stone-built Grove Park Hotel and Beaucatcher Mountain. Built in 1899, it was substantially redesigned by Donald Ross in 1923; a major renovation was completed in 2001.

**Crowne Plaza Hotel and Resort** (ashevillecp.com/home; 800-733-3211, 828-254-3211; fax: 828-285-2688; 1 Resort Dr., Asheville, NC 28806). This 18-hole 1976 course sits on a hilltop overlooking the French Broad River and downtown Asheville. In the center of Asheville, it's right off I-240.

**Buncombe County Golf Course** (golfholes.com/nc/buncombe-golf; 828-298-1867; 226 Fairway Dr., Asheville, NC 28805). Designed in 1927 by Donald Ross, this 18-hole par-72 course is located on the east side of Asheville, just off US 70. The front nine parallel the Swannanoa River, while the back nine climb a fairly substantial hill with narrow, short fairways. Built as part of a 1920s subdivision, it's now surrounded by a pleasant urban neighborhood and run by the Buncombe County Department of Recreation as a fully public course.

**BALLOONING** **Asheville Hot Air Balloons** (ashevillehotairballoonrides.com; e-mail: info@ashevillehotairballoonrides.com; 828-242-5275; 1 Page Ave., Ste. 316, Asheville, NC 28801). The R. O. Franks Aviation Company offers hour-long, private hot-air balloon rides over downtown Asheville and its surrounding areas. Headquartered in the historic Grove Arcade in the center of the city. Balloons accommodate a maximum of four passengers and they fly year-round, weather permitting.

## ✱ Lodging

**Blue Ridge Mountain Host of North Carolina** (www.ncblueridge.com; e-mail: info@ncblueridge.com; 828-285-9907; fax: 828-285-9908; P.O. Box 1806, Asheville, NC 28802). This organization of independent hotels and bed & breakfasts covers the area around Asheville and Boone.

### COUNTRY HOTELS AND LODGES

♿ **The Haywood Park Hotel** (www.haywoodpark.com; e-mail: info@haywoodpark.com; 800-228-2522, 828-252-2522; fax: 828-253-0481; 1 Battery Park Ave., Asheville, NC 28801). This small luxury hotel sits at the center of downtown Asheville's Battery Hill shopping district, in a recently renovated historic four-story brick building. The lobby centers on a four-story glass-roofed atrium; inside the atrium are exotic shops and restaurants. The hotel has room service, an exercise room, and a sauna, and covered valet parking. The 33 rooms are stylishly and elegantly decorated with custom-designed contemporary furniture, and all rooms have sitting areas, wet bars, and Spanish marble baths with garden tubs. A continental breakfast is delivered to each room, included in the room rate. Child-care facilities are available.

♿ **The Grove Park Inn Resort & Spa** (www.groveparkinn.com; e-mail: bookit@groveparkinn.com; 800-438-5800, 828-252-2711; fax: 828-253-7053; 290 Macon Ave., Asheville, NC 28804). Open all year. This impressive stone inn occupies a hillside above Asheville, just north of downtown. Built in 1913, it was a focal point for Asheville's early development; now it's at the center of an upscale historic neighborhood. The large old inn is built of huge granite stones and topped with a bright red roof—a grand sight viewed across its 1899 golf course (redesigned by Donald Ross in 1923). This old inn is flanked by two modern wings, built in the 1980s; together, they offer 510 rooms. These rooms are all furnished in Arts and Crafts–style furniture—reproductions in the new wings, the hotel's custom-built original furniture in the old inn. Resort activities include the 18-hole golf course with its wide mountain views, three indoor and three outdoor tennis courts, a sports complex with exercise equipment, aerobics class, and racquetball, a swimming pool, and a new40,000-square-foot spa. The hotel also has seven restaurants, cafés, and bars, as well as a number of shops (including a golf pro shop and a tennis pro shop). This child-friendly inn offers fully supervised children's programs (age 3 to 12) in a summer camp format for half days, full days, and (some) evenings. Child-averse adults can stay in the child-free Club Floor, which has oversized rooms, its own private lounge, free evening cocktails, and free continental breakfast. Apart from the Club Floor, breakfast is not included in the tariff.

**Inn on Biltmore Estate** (www.biltmore.com/plan/stay/stay.shtml; e-mail: innsales@biltmore.com; 800-624-1575, 828-225-1600; 1 Antler Approach Rd., Asheville, NC 28803). This 213-room hotel stands six stories tall on a hillock within the Biltmore Estate, about 2 miles from the house and garden. A monolithic modern structure built in 2001, it has been given exterior decorative flourishes reminiscent of the Biltmore House's French château architecture. The same sort of decorated modern architecture carries on in the interior, where distinctly contemporary lines and room designs serve as backdrops for English and French country house furniture. Please note: the room rate does NOT include a ticket to the Biltmore House and Gardens, even though the hotel is on the estate grounds.

**BED & BREAKFAST INNS The Albemarle Inn** (www.albemarleinn.com; e-mail: info@albemarleinn.com; 800-621-7435, 828-255-0027; fax: 828-236-3397; 86 Edgemont Rd., Asheville, NC 28801). Occupying a large Greek Revival mansion in Asheville's elegant Grove Park district, the Albemarle Inn is spacious, elegant and quiet. Greek columns support its great front porch nearly two stories high; inside, a grand oak staircase winds up past a semicircular sitting area before reaching the second story. Guests are served wine and cheese in the early evening; a sunroom, roomy and bright, is the site for breakfast. The 11 guest rooms are large, with high ceilings, period furnishings, and claw-footed baths. A full breakfast is included.

**Abingdon Green Bed & Breakfast Inn** (www.abbingtongreen.com; e-mail: info@abbingtongreen.com; 800-251-2454; 828-251-2454; fax: 828-251-2872; 46 & 48 Cumberland Circle, Asheville, NC 28801). This 1908 Colonial Revival mansion, listed in the National Register, sits on a large tree-shaded lot in Asheville's Montford Historic District, not far from downtown. Carefully tended English gardens surround the house and fill the back of the property. Inside, antique furnishings grace the common rooms. The eight guest rooms (including three suites in the separate Carriage House) are theme-furnished with antiques, and range in size from cozy to large. Full breakfasts are served in the elegant dining room.

**Chestnut Street Inn** (www.chestnutstreetinn.com/index.html; e-mail: innkeeper@chestnutstreetinn.com; 800-894-2955; 828-285-0705; 176 E. Chestnut St., Asheville, NC 28801). This large brick Victorian home is located three blocks north of downtown Asheville, in the Chestnut Hill National Historic District. Its wide porch looks out on a large lot landscaped as an English garden. Common areas have their original heavy woodworking and period antiques, and each of the six rooms is theme decorated in Victorian antiques. The tariff includes a full breakfast and afternoon tea.

🐾 **WhiteGate Inn & Cottage** (www.whitegate.net; e-mail: innkeeper@whitegate.net; 800-485-3045, 828-253-2553; fax: 828-281-1883; 173 E. Chestnut St., Asheville, NC 28801). Located in Asheville's Chestnut Hill National Historic District, just three blocks north of downtown, the hilltop WhiteGate is surrounded by gardens, with the tops of downtown Asheville's tallest buildings visible over the white picket fence. Gravel paths loop through its English-style gardens, with a 1,200-square-foot greenhouse and conservatory holding an orchid garden. Inside, the common rooms are wood paneled and decorated with Edwardian antiques. The four rooms in the main house are large, each theme decorated with period antiques; two have separate sitting rooms. A small garden cottage, original to the house, makes up the fifth room in the inn. A full breakfast is included. Dog friendly. Check policies for information.

**The Wright Inn & Carriage House** (www.wrightinn.com; e-mail: info@wrightinn.com; 800-552-5724, 828-251-0789; fax: 828-251-0929; 235 Pearson Dr., Asheville, NC 28801). Located in Asheville's Montford National Historic District just north of downtown, the National Register–listed Wright Inn occupies an elaborate Queen Anne mansion. The thickly gingerbreaded verandah curves around the front in a witch's hat turret; on the side, elaborate steps lead down the rock wall foundation to the Victorian garden. The seven rooms and three suites are all elegantly decorated in period, and range in size from cozy bedrooms to multi-room apartments. A full breakfast is included, along with afternoon tea and cookies in the gazebo.

**1900 Inn on Montford** (www.innonmontford.com; e-mail: Info@innonmontford.com; 800-254-9569, 828-254-9569; 296 Montford Ave., Asheville, NC 28801). Tree lovers take note: the 1900 Inn on Montford has the North Carolina State Record Norway Maple in its front yard. Business travelers take note: this century-old historic house a couple of blocks north of downtown Asheville has high-speed Internet in every room. This fine old Victorian house in Asheville's Montford National Historic District is painted brick red, has flanking front gables, and a huge wraparound porch overlooking its English garden landscaping. Common areas as well as the five rooms are elegantly furnished in a turn-of-the-century style, allowing you to plug in your laptop with some homey comfort. A full breakfast is included.

**North Lodge Bed & Breakfast** (www.northlodge.com; e-mail: stay@northlodge.com; 800-282-3602; 828-252-6433; 84 Oakland Rd., Asheville, NC 28801). This 1904 house sits on a large lot in Asheville's hospital and medical district. It was built in the fashionable cottage style, heavily influenced by the Arts and Crafts Movement, with stonewalls on the first floor and cedar shakes covering the second floor. Beautifully restored, the house is isolated from the surrounding neighborhood by its landscaped lot and long drive. There are six theme-furnished rooms, one of them with one single bed at a lower price. A full breakfast is included in the tariff. Located halfway between downtown Asheville and the Biltmore Estate, this bed & breakfast inn is only a few blocks from both of Asheville's major hospitals.

**Cedar Crest, a Victorian Inn** (cedarcrestvictorianinn.com; e-mail: stay@cedarcrestinn.com; 877-251-1389, 828-252-1389; 674 Biltmore Ave., Asheville, NC 28803). This 1890s Victorian mansion graces its upscale Asheville neighborhood with a full panoply of gables, gingerbread, turrets, balconies, and verandahs. The influence of the nearby Biltmore Estate is clearly visible in the elaborate woodwork in the common areas and on the grand staircase. Gardens surround the property, making for a pleasant view from the rocking chairs on the porch. The nine guest rooms in this huge house are all individually decorated in period antiques. Full breakfasts are served in the formal dining room or on the verandah, and fresh cookies and lemonade are served each afternoon.

**The Blake House** (www.blakehouse.com; e-mail: blakehouseinn@gmail.com; 888-353-5227, 828-681-5227; fax: 828-681-0420; 150 Royal Pines Dr., Asheville, NC 28704). Built as a summer home in 1847, the Blake House is now in a quiet southern suburb of Asheville, convenient to the airport. Built entirely of granite, it sports 22-inch thick granite walls and 14-foot high ornamental plaster ceilings, as well as a wide front porch with rocking chairs. Common rooms are beautifully decorated and quite roomy. The spacious five rooms are individually and elegantly decorated with antiques. A full breakfast is served in the dining room.

**Honey Hill Inn and Cabins** (honeyhillasheville.com; e-mail: sweetdreams

@honeyhillasheville.com; 877-338-1004, 828-633-1110; 2630 Smokey Park Hwy., Candler, NC 28715). This elaborately Victorian 1885 farmhouse sits on the western edge of the Asheville area, on 12 acres of meadowland with beautiful views. Even for a Victorian house the porches are a wonder, wrapping around a corner turret on two floors, with plenty of gingerbread and fine wood trim. The five guest rooms are decorated with Victorian antiques, and range in size from roomy to large. A full breakfast is included. Honey Hill also offers six clean and comfortable self-contained cabins situated on a hilltop with porches with a panoramic view of the Blue Ridge Mountains.

## ✷ Where to Eat

**EATING OUT** ✐ **Barley's Taproom and Pizzaria** (barleystaproom.com; 828-255-0504; 42 Biltmore Ave., Asheville, NC 28801). This favorite downtown watering hole has long been noted for its huge selection of microbrews on tap—45 of them, with both regional and European breweries well represented, and no taps wasted on the mass-market stuff. Barley's has the singular distinction of being the pub that introduced microbrews to Asheville audiences, who promptly went nuts; the Asheville urban area now has 11 **craft breweries**. Barley's downstairs is family friendly, and nearly always has a lot of kids scarfing down pizza. Its upstairs (no elevator) is strictly grownups only, and has pool tables. The food is good, basic bar fare, and very reliable.

✐ **The Laughing Seed Cafe** (laughingseed.jackofthewood.com; e-mail: owner@laughingseed.com; 828-252-3445; 40 Wall St., Asheville, NC 28801). Open Mon., Wed., Thurs., 11:30 AM–9:00 PM; Fri.–Sat., 11:30 AM–10:00 PM; Sun., 10 AM–9 PM; closed Tues. Any vegetable lover will enjoy this downtown Asheville vegetarian café for its wide choice of fresh, exotic produce, and its imaginative preparation that fuses a variety of ethnic themes and ideas. It occupies its own little building on Wall Street, reminiscent of a 1940s snack bar; inside, it's bright and sparkling, with a big mural and lots of blond wood. The menu is huge, with plenty of cheese dishes, and vegan (no dairy or egg) choices clearly labeled. All food is prepared from scratch with fresh ingredients (including the bread), and they strive to find local organic suppliers for their huge selection of exotic produce. They offer a superb choice in organic wines, and their own brand of home-brewed beer, the England-inspired Green Man (brewed downstairs).

✐ **The Early Girl Eatery** (earlygirleatery.com; e-mail: mail@earlygirleatery.com; 828-259-9292; 8 Wall St., Asheville, NC 28801). Open for breakfast 7:30 AM–11:30 AM, weekdays; lunch 11:45 AM–3:00 PM, weekdays; dinner 5:30 PM–10:00 PM, Thurs.–Sat.; brunch 9 AM–3 PM, weekends. This small storefront in the Battery Hill shopping district specializes in original food with a Southern twang, made fresh from locally grown ingredients. The café is bright and airy, with windows overlooking a downtown park two floors below; service is fast and attentive. Breakfasts have traditional egg and pancake dishes, complemented with less usual courses such as shrimp in brown gravy over grits. Lunches have fresh soups and sandwiches, plus a large blackboard of specials such as shrimp and andouille sausage in a rich brown sauce full of fresh spring onions, served over stone-ground yellow grits. Dinners feature duck, chicken, salmon, and pork in a variety of blackboard specials. There are always vegetarian and vegan choices, and the extensive vegetable list will show you just what the mountain farms are harvesting right now. Beer and wine are available, with a good choice of microbrews and quality wines by the glass.

**Jack of the Wood** (www.jackofthewood.com; e-mail: pubmanager@jackofthewood.com; 828-252-5445; 95 Patton Ave., Asheville, NC 28801). Open daily, 4 PM–2 AM. Free parking adjacent after 6 PM. Unlike many "Irish pubs," this downtown Asheville brewpub has a distinctly Celtic slant. Located in a storefront on Patton Avenue, Jack of the Wood makes its own beer and its own food fresh daily. Simple bar meals of sandwiches, stew, curry, fish cakes, or chili complement the British-style ales brewed in the basement. An interesting and original lineup of bands entertain on Friday and Saturday nights, while jam sessions are a regular feature on Sundays (Celtic, 5 PM), Wednesdays (mountain music, 9:30 PM), and Thursdays (bluegrass, 9:30 PM).

**DINING OUT** **The Market Place Restaurant and Wine Bar** (www.marketplace-restaurant.com; e-mail: contact@marketplace-restaurant.com; 828-252-4162; fax: 828-253-3120; 20 Wall St., Asheville, NC 28801). Open for dinner, Mon.–Sat. One of the attractive storefronts on Wall Street in downtown Asheville, the Market Place offers a fusion of continental and global cuisine with fresh mountain ingredients. Outside, wrought-iron gates welcome Wall Street strollers into a courtyard and dining patio; inside, diners are greeted by cool, contemporary lines in tall spaces, with elegant, muted colors. The dinner menu changes daily, depending on the fresh, seasonal fruits, vegetables, and seafood available. It may feature meats from local farms, perhaps smoked with apple wood, or berries from the Biltmore Estate. The wine list includes hundreds of different bottles, with many rare vintages priced over $100, and a limited choice of wines under $30.

**Rezaz Mediterranean Cuisine** (www.rezaz.com; e-mail: info@rezaz.com; 828-277-1510; 28 Hendersonville Rd., Asheville, NC 28803). Mon.–Sat. Restaurant: lunch and dinner. Enoteca: 9am to late. Located in a large brick storefront on the northern edge of **Biltmore Village**, Rezaz has long been noted for its elegant and original cuisine from North Africa, the Middle East, Spain, and Italy. Its wine list is excellent, with a good choice below $30 (but nothing below $20). Now they've turned an adjacent building, *Rezaz Enoteca,* into an Italian wine bar (*enoteca* translates as "wine library"), a very informal hangout that offers finger food and sandwiches along with dozens of Italian wines by the glass.

## ✷ Entertainment

### *Asheville*

**The Asheville Symphony Orchestra** (ashevillesymphony.org; e-mail: info@ashevillesymphony.org; 828-254-7046; fax: 828-254-1761; 87 Haywood St., Asheville, NC 28801). Since 1960, the Asheville Symphony Orchestra has been bringing professional symphony to the mountains. Seasons typically include six masterworks concerts, two pops concerts, and a fully staged opera in conjunction with the Asheville Lyric Opera Company.

**Asheville Community Theatre (ACT)** (www.ashevilletheatre.org; 828-254-1320; fax: 828-252-4723; 35 E. Walnut St., Asheville, NC 28801). Asheville's amateur theater maintains an ambitious program of eight or more sophisticated plays from their permanent downtown theater near the Thomas Wolfe Home.

**The Diana Wortham Theatre** (www.dwtheatre.com; e-mail: tom@packplace.org; 828-257-4530; fax: 828-251-5652; 2 S. Pack Sq., Asheville, NC 28801). This 500-seat theater, part of the Pack Place complex, hosts around 150 performances a year, of every conceivable type.

**Shindig on the Green** (folkheritage.org/shindigonthegreen; e-mail: info@folkheritage.org; 828-258-6101; P.O. Box 1010, Asheville, NC 22802. July–August, 7 PM–10 PM, Sat. Free. Asheville sponsors this weekly outdoor musical get-together on the large green in front of the downtown City Hall, featuring old-time mountain music, bluegrass, and dancing.

**The Asheville Tourists** (asheville.tourists.milb.com; e-mail: pspence@theashevilletourists.com; 828-258-0428; fax: 828-258-0320; McCormick Field, 30 Buchanan Pl., Asheville, NC 28802). Asheville's minor league baseball team has its headquarters in a handsome new red-brick stadium, McCormick Field, just south of downtown off US 25. Founded in 1909 as the Asheville Red Birds, the team's been known as the Tourists since 1915 and have been playing at their current site since 1924. Members of the A-rated South Atlantic League, the Tourists have been affiliated with the Colorado Rockies since 1994.

## ✷ Selective Shopping

### *Downtown Asheville*

Asheville's 1920s-era downtown spreads over a 60-block area, just south of I-240 at US 25 (exit 5A). Frozen in time by the Great Depression, it somehow survived the late 20th century with most of its charm intact. Nearly all of the large downtown area is dominated by two-story and three-story buildings, dating from the early 20th century. "Newer" buildings show art deco's industry-inspired design features, while many of the older structures sport the elaborate frills of the 19th-century Art Nouveau Movement. Indeed, you will find only four modernist buildings in the entire district (one of them by I. M. Pei), and few buildings higher than 10 stories. Without glass towers to sterilize the streets below, Asheville retains a downtown district of charm and grace. Shoppers stroll past buildings crusted with fancy brickwork, colored tile, stone trim, and sculptures small and large. Sidewalks are filled with people, and storefronts filled with shops.

Asheville's downtown is large enough to split into four districts, each with its own distinct personality. To the west, **Battery Hill** has the largest concentrations of vintage 1920s architecture and small boutiques. **Pack Square** marks the busy heart of downtown, its banking and office district, and its arts district. To the north of Pack Square, **Lexington Park** houses businesses and people pursuing alternate or New Age lifestyles. And to the east, the **Courthouse Plaza** area (heavily urban-renewed in the 1960s) holds the institutions of urban life—the City Hall, the courthouse, the glass-tower hotel, the YMCA, and lots of parking lots.

Below are descriptions of the main shopping streets of the three shopping districts. Some of the shops are mentioned by name; others are left for you to discover. When visiting downtown Asheville, be sure to park in one of the city-owned garages, for 50 cents an hour with the first hour free.

**The Pack Square Downtown Shopping District** Pack Square sits at

Asheville's center, a classic urban square with benches, trees, sculptures, and storefronts—four-story old brick buildings from the late 19th century. On its north side, two of Asheville's modernist glass towers choke off interest; paradoxically, the squat anonymous one on the right now houses the corporate offices of the Biltmore Estate, having been designed by I. M. Pei for a chemical company in 1979. On its south side, the city's **Pack Place** museum and theatre complex sits beside the marble-clad public library. Restaurants crowd around its edge, including Cafe on the Square and Bistro 1896 on the gourmet side, and (much less expensive) the Noodle Shop, the Sisters McMullen coffee shop, and (around the corner) Salsas for Mexican-Caribbean.

Asheville's arts district extends south of the square along Biltmore Avenue (US 25). Its centerpiece is the large commercial gallery, Blue Spiral I, representing major regional artists in a 14,000-square-foot display area that wanders through a three-story brick building. Next door, the Fine Arts Theatre plays a full schedule of independent films. Storefronts up and down the street house smaller galleries, but not all is art; a **Mast General Store** inhabits a 1940s-era department store building. **Barley's Taproom** is one of several good restaurants on the south edge of the district; other good choices include Ed Boudreaux's Bayou Barbeque and the City Bakery. The district ends at the French Broad Food Co-op, with a large line of natural and organic products, and the Asheville Wine Market, a large wine shop with a full selection of beers and cheeses as well.

**Battery Hill Downtown Shopping District** The Battery Hill shopping district wanders through back streets lined with fine old 1920s-era buildings in the western part of downtown Asheville, the largest and most varied of the four shopping districts. Start your excursion at the little triangular-shaped park on Patton Avenue at Haywood Street. Although most of the action is to your north and west, you definitely want to explore a block east on Patton to the Kress Emporium, where the individual booths of handcrafters fill the delicious old Kress Department Store building. Back at the park, Ten Thousand Villages carries gifts and art objects from third world countries. Just ahead on the right, the old Woolworth's building houses another craft cooperative.

Go north, then left onto Battery Park. There's an amazing number of good, up-scalish restaurants within a block of this corner: **The Flying Frog** (noted for its appetizers), the **Early Girl Eatery**, the **Laughing Seed Cafe**, **The Market Place**. Straight ahead is the amazing **Grove Arcade**, a 250,000-square-foot 1920s-era mall, encrusted with elaborate statuary, now fully restored and filled with small, independent merchants. These include (on the outside west) Natural Selections, a nature store with regional art, books, telescopes, and optics—everything that has to do with appreciating nature. When you finish with the arcade, go down the alley-width Wall Street, pedestrianized and lined with shops. Rock-climbing store **Climbmax** has gear and an indoor climbing center. At the end of Wall Street, the monolithic glass-walled Federal Building houses the World Data Center for Meteorology, our nation's major repository for global warming data.

Return along Battery Park, then go left up Haywood Street. There are several interesting shops and restaurants here. Be sure not to miss Malaprop's Bookstore, winner of *Publishers Weekly* Bookseller of the Year 2000 Award, with a wide selection of hard-to-find titles. At the end of the long block, the Asheville Public Library is a friendly refuge, and library patrons who park in the garage behind it can get their parking receipts validated. Beside that is the Asheville Civic Center and Thomas Wolfe Auditorium, a popular venue for all sorts of stuff, from symphony orchestra concerts to minor league ice hockey.

**Lexington Park Downtown Shopping** At one time, Lexington Park would have been known as the Bohemian Quarter, or perhaps the hippie district. In the New Millennium, it's the place where the New Age hangs out its shingle. The smallest of the districts, it includes Broadway (US 25) north of the plain modernist glass towers that flank Pack Square, and Lexington Avenue, one block to the west. This is the least boutiquey of the three districts, and the most likely spot to find stores that decorate with spray paint. It's also the best place to find that odd-little something that would never appear inside of a mall shop. The best shopping is on Lexington Avenue. A row of shops (Native Expressions, Cosmic Vision, and The Natural Home) feature gifts, clothing, jewelry, and home accessories from third world countries. TS Morrison & Company, a downtown department store in continuous operation since 1891, now specializes in a broad selection of nostalgia items. An equally venerable institution, The Downtown Bookstore, anchors the upper end of Lexington with a huge set of magazine racks. At the far northern end, **Rosettas** offers up superb vegetarian fare from local ingredients.

**BILTMORE VILLAGE** In the 1890s, George Vanderbilt constructed Biltmore Village (biltmorevillage.com; e-mail: stanbooks@aol.com) outside the gates of his Biltmore Estate as the home for his hundreds of workers. Frederick Law Olmsted planned the village, and Richard Morris Hunt designed its buildings, giving it a unique appearance that survives to this day. Sold off after Vanderbilt's death in 1914, Hunt's handsome buildings and Olmsted's landscaping remain—now holding an upscale shopping district.

To understand the village, picture the idyllic rural world that Vanderbilt tried to create. Vanderbilt placed his village across from the main gate of his estate, separated from it by an old narrow coach road and an expanse of green lawn. On one side of the village he placed an elegant little train station to serve the needs of the estate. In the ensuing decades, a large industrial rail yard grew up beside the little depot. The narrow coach road became US 25 and slowly expanded to 10 lanes. The grassy lawn, sold off and divided into pieces, came to hold a 1950s motel, three gas stations, and two fast-food franchises. Fortunately, the noise and ugliness stop as if cut off by a curtain as soon as you enter the tiny back streets of the village. The center of the village remains pretty much as Vanderbilt left it.

The large selection of independently owned shops include a half-dozen antique stores, several galleries, five clothiers, and a dozen or so gift shops. If you get a might peckish, there are a number of small independent restaurants inside the village, including **Rezaz** for dinners both fancy and casual. The village features free street parking, usually (but not always) with enough spaces to handle all the shoppers.

## ✷ Special Events

**SPRING** **Spring Herb Festival** (828-689-5974; WNC Farmer's Market, NC 109 at I-26). Early May. Free. This annual gathering brings together all of the region's many herb farmers, selling seedlings and meeting new customers.

**Asheville Gem & Mineral Show** (828-254-7162). Mid-June. Free. This weekend show at Pack Place's Colbern Gem & Mineral Museum has booths displaying crystals, gemstones, meteorites, handcrafted jewelry, from collectors and rock shops all over the East.

**SUMMER** **Fourth of July Celebrations** Asheville has a large downtown party with live entertainment, food, children's activities, and evening fireworks.

**Belle Chere** (belechere.com; e-mail: belechere@ashevillenc.gov; 828-259-5800; fax: 828-259-5606; P.O. Box 7148, Asheville, NC 28802. Free. Last weekend in July. This annual street festival boasts of being the largest free outdoor festival in the South. Taking over most of downtown Asheville for three days, Belle Chere is best known for its multiple, on-going music venues (featuring bluegrass, jazz, rock, pop, and whatever), its street food, its copious beer sales, and its hundreds of arts and crafts vendors.

**Village Art & Craft Fair** (newmorninggallerync.com; e-mail: newmorning@bellsouth.net; 800-933-4438, 828-274-2831; 7 Boston Way, Asheville, NC 28803). First weekend in August. This large fine crafts and arts show, held on the shaded grounds of the Cathedral of All Souls in **Biltmore Village**, attracts 140 or more artists from all over America. Held annually since 1972, its posters are notable for their original art featuring cats. It's sponsored by the **New Morning Gallery**.

**The Mountain Dance & Folk Festival** (828-257-4530; Asheville, NC). First weekend in August. Founded by Bascom Lamar Lunsford in 1927, this annual festival is dedicated to mountain folk music and dancing. It's held in the Diana Wortham Theatre in Pack Place.

**AUTUMN** **Craft Fair of the Southern Highlands** (828-298-7928; Thomas Wolfe Auditorium, Asheville, NC). Mid-October. Founded in 1930 to promote crafters of the southern mountains, the nonprofit Southern Appalachian Craft Guild has been holding these craft fairs since 1948. Held in downtown Asheville's Civic Center, it has a large juried show of member artists, craft demonstrations, and live music. They hold a show in mid-July as well.

# THE BLUE RIDGE PARKWAY APPROACHES THE SMOKIES

The penultimate section of the Blue Ridge Parkway forms a high altitude half-circle that arcs around Waynesville for nearly 50 miles. It's the parkway's highest section, passing close to 12 peaks above 6,000 feet and reaching its high point at 6,158 feet, 1.16 miles above sea level. Indeed, 19 miles of this drive are 1 mile or more above sea level, and virtually all of it is above 4,000 feet. As the parkway gets higher, its views get better—broad, panoramic views that cover ridge upon ridge, not only from the overlooks, but also from long roadside stretches as the roadway becomes a ledge perched high in the sky. This is the most remote section of the Blue Ridge Parkway, almost continuously bordered by giant tracts of national forest lands, including two large wilderness areas; little wonder that only three roads intersect it between its start and end points.

At the foot of these mountains, Waynesville is a classic red-brick small town with a bustling three-block Main Street filled with interesting stores; its historic neighborhoods have an astonishing selection of high-quality bed & breakfast inns. Nearby is the lovely little Methodist retreat village of Lake Junaluska, with its historic center and landscaped lakeside walks.

**GUIDANCE—TOWNS AND COUNTRYSIDE** **Haywood County Tourism Development Authority** (www.visitncsmokies.com; e-mail: hctda@visitncsmokies.com; 800-334-9036, 828-452-0152; 1233 North Main St., Ste. 1-40, Waynesville, NC 28786). This quasigovernmental agency uses the room tax to promote tourism. They are the people to call to get a packet of brochures and information.

**Haywood County Tourism Development Authority** (www.visitncsmokies.com; e-mail: info@visitncsmokies.com; 800-334-9036, 828-452-0152; fax: 828-452-0153; 44 North Main St., Waynesville, NC 28786). This private not-for-profit promotes business members. It maintains a staffed visitors center where you can get maps, brochures, postcards, etc.

**GUIDANCE—PARKS AND FORESTS** **Pisgah National Forest** The large tracts of national forest lands between the Blue Ridge Parkway and Waynesville are part of the Pisgah National Forest's Pisgah Ranger District. Their office is 35 miles south of Waynesville via US 276.

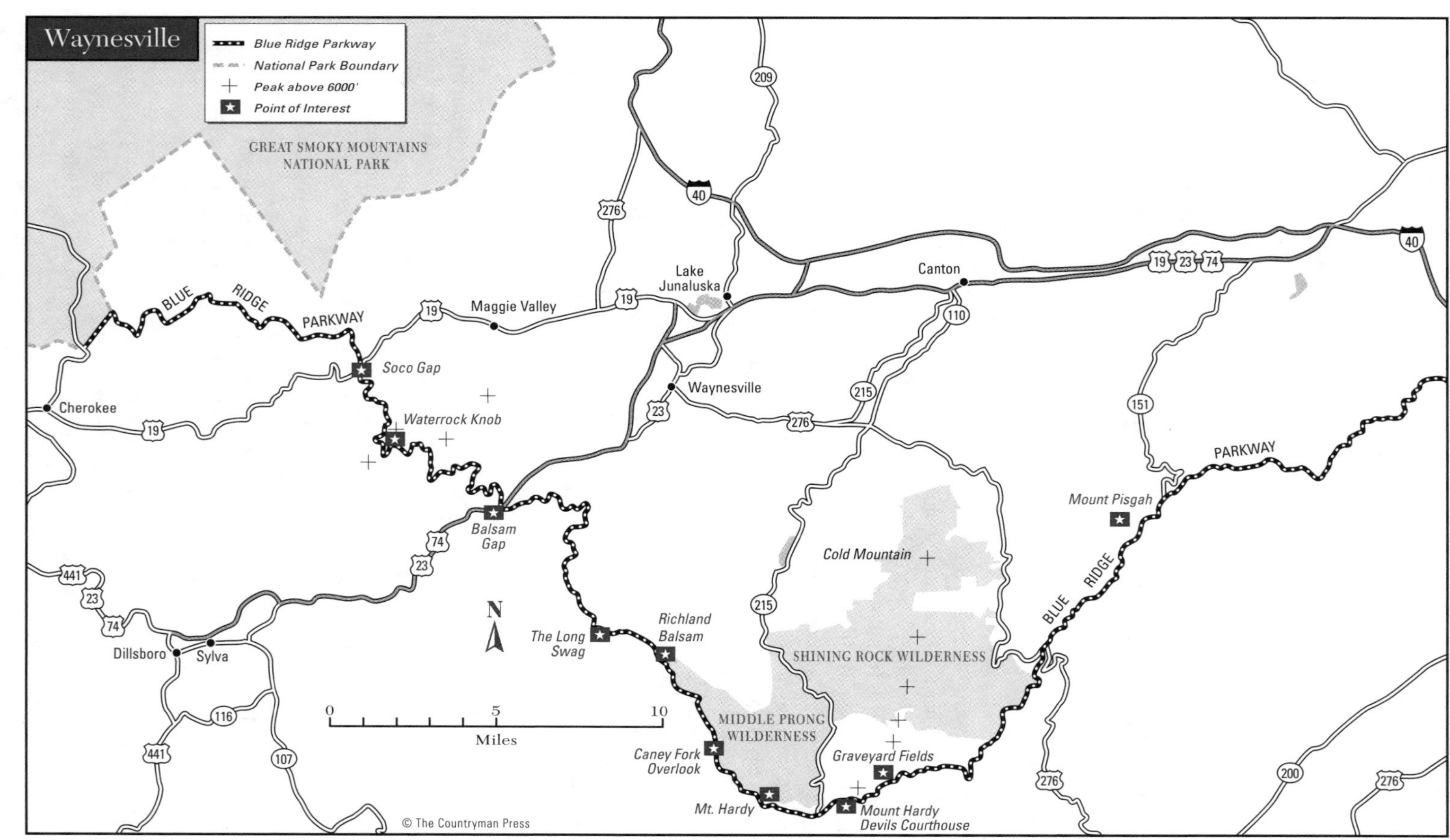
Waynesville
Blue Ridge Parkway
National Park Boundary
Peak above 6000'
Point of Interest
GREAT SMOKY MOUNTAINS NATIONAL PARK
BLUE RIDGE PARKWAY
Cherokee
Soco Gap
Waterrock Knob
Maggie Valley
Lake Junaluska
Waynesville
Canton
Balsam Gap
The Long Swag
Richland Balsam
Cold Mountain
SHINING ROCK WILDERNESS
MIDDLE PRONG WILDERNESS
Caney Fork Overlook
Mt. Hardy
Graveyard Fields
Mount Hardy Devils Courthouse
Mount Pisgah
Dillsboro
Sylva
N
0
5
10
Miles
40
209
276
19
23
74
110
215
151
441
116
107
200
© The Countryman Press

**GETTING THERE** *By Car* I-40 provides the main access from all directions. US 276, which runs north-south through this area, should be treated as a back road.

*By Air:* **Asheville Regional Airport** (see "The City of Asheville") is 35 miles southeast via I-26 and I-40.

*By Bus or Train* Greyhound (www.greyhound.com) Lines's east–west route through North Carolina and Tennessee stops twice a day in the Waynesville area. The city of Waynesville has a weekday bus service that connects the town's residential areas with its shopping districts. There is no train service.

**MEDICAL EMERGENCIES** **Haywood Regional Medical Center** (www.haymed.org; e-mail: publicrelations@haymed.org; 800-834-1729, 828-456-7311; 262 Leroy George Dr., Clyde, NC 28721). This major regional hospital has a walk-in clinic on its campus, as well as a full-service emergency room. It's 5 miles east of downtown Waynesville via US 23; take the NC 209 exit, then parallel the freeway to Jones Cove Road.

## ✷ Exploring the Area

**EXPLORING BY CAR** **The Blue Ridge Parkway** *Start:* Take I-40 east to exit 37 (Chandler), then right one block to a left onto US 19/23/74, then go 3.9 miles to a right onto NC 151, which ends at the parkway in 11.9 miles. Expect this 49-mile drive to take a half-day at least.

*Leg #1 (17.3 miles)*: From the parkway's intersection with NC 151, go right to the intersection with NC 215.

*Leg #2 (31.8 miles)*: From NC 215, continue along the parkway to US 19.

LOOKING GLASS ROCK, FROM THE BLUE RIDGE PARKWAY

This starting point, already 4,200 feet above sea level (and 2,200 feet above Asheville), is on the crest of the Pisgah Ridge—a crest you'll be following for the next 17 miles. Your first landmark will be the short dead-end Mount Pisgah Spur Road, on the left. Go down it a few hundred yards for a good view southward over the forests of the Mills River, then continue to the end if you want to pick up the popular (but steep and rocky) 2.5-mile round trip hike to the 5,720-foot cone of **Mount Pisgah**, where an observation deck offers 360-degree views only partially spoiled by a TV tower. Back at the parkway, the **Mount Pisgah Picnic Area** is a short distance away, with the **Mount Pisgah Inn** (with a good restaurant and views from every room) a bit farther on. From here the views open up to the south over the rhododendron-covered cove known as **The Pink Beds**, with the enormous rock dome of **Looking Glass Rock** behind it; then scenic US 276 furnishes an excellent side trip south to **The Cradle of Forestry in America**, an outstanding historic site. Now the parkway climbs to 5,000 feet through increasingly rugged and dramatic scenery, to **Graveyard Fields**, a meadow-covered cove perched high among mile-high peaks. In another mile, Black Balsam Spur Road leads left to the trailhead for the **Shining Rock Wilderness**, and access to six peaks topping 6,000 feet. Back at the parkway, look for the great stone outcrop known as **The Devils Courthouse**, and don't miss the short, easy path to its top, with panoramic views. At the end of this leg you are 24 miles from Waynesville via NC 215 north to a right on US 276; there are no services for the first 6.5 miles.

The second leg follows the crest of the **Great Balsam Mountains**, with seven more 6'ers along its 32 miles of ridgetop wilderness. Built in the 1960s, this modern highway slashes through the wilderness landscape in huge cuts, with long sweeping views from its wide, clear shoulders. The views start suddenly as the parkway turns upward along the cliff-like flanks of 6,110-foot **Mount Hardy**, with continuous and wide panoramas southward. More views open up as the parkway sweeps toward 6,000 feet in elevation, with exceptional panoramas near **Caney Fork Overlook** and at **Cowee Mountain Overlook**. After that, the parkway reaches its highest elevation as it crests out at 6,190 feet at the **Richland Balsams Overlook**. From there it follows the mile-high meadows of **The Long Swag** before it starts its long drop to Balsam Gap. On this downward leg the parkway gives impressive views of itself as approaches the long, curving Pinnacle Ridge Tunnel; beyond, look for sunrise views at **Waynesville Overlook**.

The parkway dips into **Balsam Gap**, where it intersects with the four-lane US 23/74 and the first services since Mount Pisgah (go right 1 mile; Waynesville is 7 miles east). After Balsam Gap the parkway climbs steadily for the next 8 miles, as

THE BLUE RIDGE PARKWAY IN THE GREAT BALSAM MOUNTAINS

good views open up. The parkway crests out as it crosses the massive side ridge known as **Plott Balsams**, at 5,710 feet (see "Near the Park: Sylva & Dillsboro," *Wild Places*). Here a spur road leads to the impressive **Waterrock Knob Overlook**, with a new visitors center, water, toilets, and picnic tables. To the left, a side trail follows a high, narrow ridgeline to form the **Plott Balsams Walk**, with excellent views back toward Balsam Gap. As the parkway descends from Waterrock Knob it passes a series of good views west over the Cherokee lands, before dropping into the forests of **Soco Gap**. Waynesville is 13 miles east on US 19 to US 276.

**EXPLORING ON FOOT** **A Walk in the Middle Prong Wilderness** The **Mountains-to-Sea Trail** makes for an easy 3.5 mile round-trip to the lush, spreading meadows on the 5,800-foot-tall crest of this otherwise remote wilderness area. Park your car on the Blue Ridge Parkway as it traverses the Great Balsam Mountains, at Rough Butt Bald Overlook (milepost 425.3) about 2 miles from Beech Gap (NC 215). A path directly opposite the overlook links you to the Mountains-to-Sea Trail with its white circular blazes. Follow the blazes to your right. The trail quickly passes into the **Middle Prong Wilderness** and follows an old logging tramway, level, wide, and easy. This balsam forest, like other high altitude forests on Balsam Mountain, had survived heavy logging and acidic paper mill emissions throughout most of the 20th century, only to fall to a natural enemy—the fir-killing wooly adelgid, accidentally introduced to North America around 1900. At 1.2 miles, the Mountains-to-Sea blazes turn uphill to the right, climbing a half-mile to the crest of Fork Ridge, remarkable for its mountaintop meadows. Formed by logging fires in the early 20th century and still occupying most of the Fork Mountain Crest, the grassy meadows extend along the top of this high ridge for 2.3 miles, with a maze of paths leading through wildflowers and berries. Views are frequent and stunning, with the best views from rocky outcrops on the east side, looking over the gorge of the West Fork Pigeon River toward the sweeping meadows of the **Shining Rock Wilderness**.

**Richland Balsams Nature Trail** This 1.2-mile nature trail climbs 350 feet to the 6,410-foot peak of Richland Balsams (10th highest in the East), the highest point on the lands of the Blue Ridge Parkway. Once a forest walk where giant firs and spruces shaded an open floor of needles and moss, it now crosses an ecology undergoing rapid and radical transition. Around 1980 a parasitic insect known as the wooly adelgid (an exotic introduced into Canada around 1900) reached the Balsam Mountains in its slow southward migration through the Appalachians. Within a few years all the fir trees (more than half the forest) had died, leaving the remaining spruces exposed to harsh weather and high wind, and the forest floor exposed to a whole host of sun-loving competitors. The trail now travels through wildflower meadows, thick patches of blackberries, stands of mountain ash saplings, occasional groves of old spruces, and thick masses of fir seedlings and saplings competing with each other as well as the wooly adelgids. Once viewless because of the dense forest, the path now offers several views over newly formed meadows and briar patches; one such view lets you look down on the sign claiming to mark the highest point on the parkway. A guide to this nature loop, available at its beginning, gives full information on the forest succession going on around you.

**A Walk Around Lake Junaluska** After you've explored the high, windy ridges and mountaintop meadows in the rugged wilderness surrounding the Blue Ridge

Parkway, you may find yourself ready for a level walk, on a paved path, through landscaped parklands along a lakeshore. If so, you're in luck. The historic **Lake Junaluska Retreat**, run by the United Methodist Church, maintains a parkland walk along their centerpiece lake, open to public use. You'll find Lake Junaluska just off US 19, 4 miles north of Waynesville; turn right on Lakeshore Drive and proceed to the large public lot by the administration center. Admire the stunning mountain view from the lot, and the handsome buildings at the center of this retreat; then follow the paved path left. You will quickly reach the monumental cross that serves as the centerpiece for the retreat, on a hill above you. Then, at a quarter-mile, you will walk across the handsome old dam that impounds the lake. For the next mile the level, paved path goes through landscaped parklands along the lakeshore, with stunning views west toward the 6,000-foot peaks of the Plott Balsams. Then the path crosses the lake on a long footbridge and reenters the main retreat area, passing historic and modern buildings still used as a center for refreshing the spirit. When you regain your car, you'll have walked 2.25 miles.

**LONG-DISTANCE PATHS** **The Mountains-to-Sea Trail** As the Mountains-to-Sea Trail enters this area it leaves its only remaining mountain road walk behind. It does not, however, leave the Blue Ridge Parkway by any real distance. Rather, it zigs and zags over the parkway, exploring the peaks and slopes missed by the automobile-bound. Some of its sections are remarkable. In the **Middle Fork Wilderness** it explores the wildflower meadows of Fork Ridge. In the **Graveyard Fields** it ignores the meadows below to follow the grassy, wind-blown ridges above, then dives into the sharp canyon of the Yellowstone River, only a short distance below the huge Yellowstone Falls. Immediately beyond Pisgah Inn it leads to the site of George Vanderbilt's log hunting lodge (whose ruins were removed in 1990 for safety reasons), with a view to Mount Pisgah. From there it follows The Shut-In

WAYNESVILLE AND THE GREAT BALSAM MOUNTAINS

Trail, carefully engineered by Vanderbilt, abandoned upon his death in 1914, and then restored by volunteers in 1978.





## ✱ Villages

**Waynesville** In the early days of the Republic, Waynesville sat at the border of the Cherokee Nation, literally the end of the road for European settlers. As the Cherokees were pushed back into Tennessee, and then exiled to Oklahoma, Waynesville gained in importance as the gateway to the tangled valleys of the Smokies and the Blue Ridge. Today it remains the main gateway and the largest of the western mountain towns. At first glance it's more sprawling and industrial than the other Smoky/Blue Ridge towns; however, attractive and genteel neighborhoods, rich in historic architecture, sit only a scant half-block off the main drag. These historic neighborhoods have become a prime destination for knowledgeable visitors, as a dozen or so bed & breakfast inns have moved in. Waynesville has a charming downtown, three blocks of historic red-brick structures with a good choice of interesting shops. Downtown parking is free, but limited; however, there is plenty of parking on the back blocks. Every July this wonderful town center becomes the main venue for **Folkmoot**, a large-scale gathering of 10 or more national dance troupes with performances throughout the Smoky Mountains region.

**The Town of Lake Junaluska** This small lakeside town 4 miles north of Waynesville off US 19 is dominated by its large and historic retreat, the headquarters for the United Methodist Church in the Southeast. The town centers on its 180-acre lake, created in the 1920s as part of a retreat for missionaries; now open to the public, the retreat remains the main focus of the village. The Methodist Church headquarters and retreat sits on the north side of the lake, an impressive grouping of buildings both historic and modern, dominated by the 1922 **Lambuth Inn** with its giant memorial cross. The south side, a quiet residential area, is lined by landscaped parklands with a 2-mile paved path—a wonderful **lakeview walk**.

**Canton** Founded as the home of Champion Paper in 1906, Canton remains dominated by its giant mill, still one of the largest in America despite being over a century old. Champion located here because the high altitude boreal forest furnished large numbers of spruce trees, valued for producing a high-quality pulp. Parts of these Champion forests have since become the **Shining Rock and Middle Prong Wildernesses**, and the **Smokemont** area of the Great Smoky Mountains National Park—all with large areas significantly altered to this day by huge clear-cut fires. Champion Paper finally left this area in the late 1990s, selling its plant to its employees and divesting itself of its last forest lands in 2001. Still a working mill town, Canton has few tourist facilities, but its small museum is worth a visit.

## ✱ Wild Places

**THE GREAT FORESTS The Shining Rock Wilderness** The 18,400 acres of the Shining Rock Wilderness center on the high Shining Rock Ledge, a north-trending side ridge of the Pisgah Range with three 6,000-foot peaks (and four more in the protected recreation lands on its immediate south). Champion Paper purchased all of these lands in 1906, building the huge paper mill at **Canton** to exploit the spruces found in these high-altitude forests. This was not a success, and Champion turned to the Smokies for spruce pulp, selling Shining Rock to a succession of lumber companies. The loggers used tramways and locomotives to clear-cut the area; in 1926 sparks from a locomotive touched off a 25,000-acre wildfire that denuded the Shining Rock Crest, creating the broad grassy meadows that remain the wilderness' most distinctive feature. Logging ceased after the fire, and the tract passed into the hands of the Pisgah National Forest in 1935. Congress created the Shining Rock Wilderness in 1964.

Shining Rock's mile-high crest is completely covered by huge meadows, the results of that 1925 fire. The mountaintop meadows are rich in wildflowers and punctuated by unusual rock outcrops—including the large Shining Rock, a great mass of quartz that shines in the sun. The meadows extend southward all the way to the crest of the Pisgah Range and the **Blue Ridge Parkway**, and northward to **Cold Mountain** (6,030 feet, the 40th highest in the East), the same mountain used as the title for the best-selling novel. Because this 12-mile ledge is both stunningly beautiful and easily reached from the Blue Ridge Parkway, it tends to be popular. A good trail follows the crest from **Black Balsam Knob** all the way to Cold Mountain; it's easy going in its early sections but gets gradually more difficult as it proceeds, with the final ascent of Cold Mountain being notoriously difficult. A number of side trails, very rough and difficult, lead down the ridge to the forested valleys in the wilderness' lower slopes.

**The Middle Prong Wilderness** (828-877-3265; P.O. Box 8, Pisgah Forest, NC 28768). Created by Congress in 1984, the 7,900-acre Middle Prong Wilderness occupies some of the highest, roughest, and most difficult land in the eastern wilderness system—the southern terminus of the Great Balsam Mountains. Within this wilderness the mountains rise from 3,200 feet to 6,400 feet—over 3,000 feet of local relief—in only 2 linear miles. The Middle Prong runs through the center of this wilderness, a mountain river in a deep, gash-like valley; Fork Mountain rises from it to the east, wholly within the wilderness, while the Great Balsam Mountains (with the Blue Ridge Parkway on its crest) rings the wilderness to the south and west.

RHODODENDRONS IN THE GREAT BALSAM MOUNTAINS

Like the neighboring Shining Rock Wilderness, the Middle Prong was clear-cut in the 1920s, then devastated by fire. The forests have rested since then, becoming very mature and attractive. Upper slopes are covered by balsam forests, while lower slopes are covered in maturing mixed hardwoods. The high crest of Fork Ridge, contained within the wilderness, is covered by a series of grassy wildflower meadows stretching for 2 miles along its ridgeline, affording spectacular views; at the south end of Fork Mountain stands 6,010-foot Mount Hardy, the 30th tallest mountain in the East. The

**Mountains-to-Sea Trail** gives safe and easy access to these mountaintop meadows; otherwise, the Middle Prong Wilderness trail system, although extensive, consists mainly of unblazed, unmaintained logging tramways, making for difficult and even dangerous hiking.

**PICNIC AREAS** **Mount Pisgah Picnic Area** This large picnic area on the **Blue Ridge Parkway** is part of the Mount Pisgah area, the last full-service recreation area on the parkway. It sits in a ridgeline forest just shy of 5,000 feet high—very breezy and cool on a hot summer day.

## ✷ To See

### *Along the Blue Ridge Parkway*

**Mount Pisgah** This large recreation area has picnicking, camping, a camp store, a good restaurant, and a nice lodge, all at an elevation around 5,000 feet. Its centerpiece is 5,721-foot-tall Mount Pisgah, whose summit is reachable by a 2.6-mile (round trip) trail that gains 700 feet in elevation. The path is a pleasant forest walk, fairly steep and generally busy; at its end is a large observation platform near an even larger TV tower, with a 360-degree view. Of special interest is the cable-driven rail car used by the television technicians to service the tower.

**Looking Glass Rock** This giant granite dome, a classic monadnock, sits off the main ridgeline, 2 miles south of the parkway. It's huge, rising 1,000 feet above the forests that completely surround it, and well over 1 mile long. Although located in another chapter's area (see "The Blue Ridge: Hendersonville & Brevard," *Wild Places*), it is best seen from the parkway. Indeed, you can hardly miss it. As you drive west from the **Mount Pisgah** area it dominates the wide views to your left, and remains a prominent landmark as far west as **Devils Courthouse**. It's the ultimate Blue Ridge cliff, formed like most Blue Ridge cliffs, through exfoliation rather than erosion; with miles of overburden eroded off it, it's actually expanding, causing the rock to flake off in little chips. Its slopes are popular with rock climbers, and a hiking trail sneaks up its southern slope for fine views and a close-up look at a large rocky bald.

**Graveyard Fields and Black Balsam Knob** This high-perched valley sits nearly 1 mile above sea level, flanked by seven 6,000-foot peaks, just off the Blue Ridge Parkway 3 miles east of NC 215. Once covered by huge old-growth forests—the "graveyard" refers to the grave-like mounds left by fallen giant trees as they return to the soil—it was devastated by clear-cut fires in the early 20th century and remains meadow-covered to this day. A lovely system of hiking trails, most starting at the Graveyard Fields Overlook on the Blue Ridge Parkway, loops around the wildflower-carpeted meadows, along the clear mountain river that cuts through its center, down to the roaring waterfall that marks its foot, and up to the tall, graceful waterfall that sits at its head.

Above the fields, the 6,214-foot Black Balsam Knob (23rd highest peak in the East) and the adjacent 6,040-foot Tennant Mountain (34th highest) can be easily reached via the Black Balsam Trail, starting on the Black Balsam Spur Road off the parkway just west of the fields. This 1.8-mile round-trip (with 1,200 feet of total climbing) follows the high ridgeline through mountaintop meadows and past large rock outcrops, with nearly continuous views over waving wildflowers. Turn around when you reach the deep gap with the old abandoned road—or continue forward into the stunning high ridge meadows of the Shining Rock Wilderness with three more 6,000-foot peaks.

GRAVEYARD FIELDS

**The Devils Courthouse** This classic Blue Ridge cliff projects out a bit from the main ridgeline, giving it an appearance a bit like a large, grotesquely proportioned building. A short, easy hiking trail leads to its top for spectacular views.

**Beech Gap and Mount Hardy** NC 215 intersects the parkway at Beech Gap, running south to **Lake Toxaway** and north to **Waynesville**. The drive north is especially pretty, and leads past a waterfall to several trailheads, finally leaving the Pisgah National Forest at a nice picnic and camping area named Sunburst. Beyond Beech Gap the parkway slabs around the south-facing slope of 6,110-foot Mount Hardy, whose peak marks the southern tip of the **Middle Fork Wilderness**. Old maps show a hiking trail climbing around the east slope of Mount Hardy to curve around to its peak; it long ago disappeared from government maps but nevertheless remains on the ground, very faint, for those who dare.

**Caney Fork and Cowee Mountain Overlooks** Although Caney Fork Overlook itself is mildly disappointing, the mile-long stretch of parkway on either side gives dramatic roadside views (with easy verge parking) down a 3,000-foot drop into a mountain valley, and beyond to the Tuckaseegee River, the Cowee Mountains, and the Nantahala Mountains. Sunset lovers will appreciate the way the sun dips down into the lowest part of the deep valley, dropping below the horizon to throw orange sidelights on the tall ridges to its right and left, then falls behind layered mountains that recede endlessly into the background. Two miles later, Cowee Mountain Overlook gives a 270-degree view from a promontory, nearly 6,000 feet in elevation, that thrusts westward from the parkway over the deep valleys of the Balsams. A quarter-mile north, the Haywood-Jackson Overlook supplies the missing 90-degree view, eastward over the deep gorge of the West Fork to the mountaintop meadows of the **Middle Prong and Shining Rock Wilderness**; fans of the best-selling novel *Cold Mountain* should look for this 6,030-foot peak in the far background.

**Richland Balsams** A large sign prominently declares the Richland Balsams Overlook as the highest point on the parkway, at 6,190 feet. By this it means the roadway itself; the peak named Richland Balsams is within the parkway's boundaries, and, at 6,410 feet, is 220 feet above the overlook. A **nature trail** allows you to ascend to the true high point and look down on the sign; it starts at the previous overlook. The views from the Richland Balsams Overlook are good, but anticlimatic after the Caney Fork/Cowee Mountain section.

**The Long Swag** Two miles beyond the Richland Balsams Overlook, the parkway slabs along the west side of a long, narrow, meadow-covered ridge. This is The Long Swag, and, although there are no overlooks, there is nothing whatever to stop you from pulling safely onto the verge and walking through the meadow on your own, looking for wildflowers and views. On the Long Swag's far end, the meadows climb up almost to the 5,780-foot summit of Old Bald, and gives very good views back over the roadway. Notice that the parkway circles the shoulder of Old Bald in a deep cut; at the top of this cut, on the downhill side, the **Mountains-to-Sea Trail** follows a 5,500-foot ridgeline for 0.7 mile to give access to a large, little-visited area of the Nantahala National Forest, with no formal trails but lots of informal ones and four more mile-high peaks ahead.

**Waynesville Overlook** At this point the north-to-south traveler is quickly descending from the rarified hieghts of the Great Balsams along one of the parkway's most notorious grades, a steady drop of nearly 2,000 feet in 6 miles. The parkway has curved its closest to Waynesville, a crows flight of 4.9 miles. This overlook gives a particularly good view eastward over the entire town—and incidentally, toward the rising sun on a summer's morning. The best part is, it's only 2 miles from the main expressway, US 23/74, and easily reached while zipping toward the Great Smoky Mountains from a Waynesville inn. The best place for a sunrise is the grassy verge immediately beyond the overlook.

**Balsam Gap** The parkway crosses this deep gap at right-angles as it follows the crest of the Balsams, making long ascents on both sides. Balsam Gap was (and is) the gateway to the western mountains of North Carolina, the only good eastern approach to the deep valleys of the Tuckaseegee, the Nantahala, and the Little Tennessee Rivers. Nowadays it's traversed by a railroad and a four-lane highway, US 23/74. The historic community of **Balsam** occupies the western side of the gap, where the old railroad hotel **The Balsam Mountain Inn** still thrives. However the closest facilities are on the eastern side of the gap, where a wayside park furnishes picnic tables, toilets, and phones, with gas stations only a little bit farther on.

**Waterrock Knob** In its climb northward out of Balsam Gap, the parkway passes a number of good overlooks with views west and south. However, you might want to save your film for the top; as the parkway finally reaches the crest, it sends a 0.33-mile spur to a series of three overlooks with stunning 270-degree views. These overlooks

THE BLUE RIDGE PARKWAY ON THE CREST OF THE BALSAMS

(with views west, south, and north over the Balsams) occupy the high, grassy crest of a great wall-like side ridge known as Plott Balsams, after the local frontiersman who bred the Plott bearhound for hunting these slopes. The collection of overlooks makes up a small recreation area, with a modest visitors center, water, toilets, several tables, many wildflowers, and large grassy verges perfect for picnic blankets or tossing a Frisbee. Beyond the overlooks a wide, heavily used trail climbs very steeply to the peak of Waterrock Knob, for some good views.

TRAIL TO WATERROCK KNOB

**MUSEUMS The Museum of North Carolina Handicrafts** (blueridge-heritage.com/useum-of-north-carolina-handicrafts; 828-452-1551; Shelton House, 49 Shelton St., Waynesville, NC 28786). Open May–October, Tues.–Sat., 10 AM–5 PM. Call for winter hours. Located on the south edge of Waynesville on US 276, the 1875 Shelton House is home to this extensive display of both home crafts and fine art crafts from the Smokies, other parts of North Carolina, and the Navajo Nation. This beautifully restored mountain farmhouse, surrounded by meadows, has two-story verandahs along its front and walnut trim throughout its interior. Inside are traditional 19th-century farm furnishings and a wide array of mountain crafts—pottery, baskets, quilts, toys, and dulcimers. It has a large collection of Seagrove pottery, and items from fine craft artists throughout the state. A gift shop offers handmade craft items for sale.

**Canton Historic Museum** (828-646-3412; 58 Park St., Canton, NC 28716). Open Mon.–Fri., 10 AM–noon, 1 PM –4 PM; Sun., 2 PM–4 PM. Free. This small local museum occupies the former public library in downtown Canton, next to the City Hall. It has some items from the pioneer era, but most of its exhibits are about its controversial paper mill, often cited as the largest in the South, in operation next door since 1906.

## ✷ To Do

**GOLF Waynesville Country Club Inn** (e-mail: info@wccinn.com; 800-627-6250, 828-452-4617; fax: 828-456-3555; P.O. Box 390, Waynesville, NC 28786). This golf resort built its first nine-hole course on a dairy farm in 1926; the barn served as the clubhouse. It now has three nine-hole courses, which are played in three 18-hole combinations; views from the links extend to the surrounding mountains. The large resort has buildings from nearly every decade from the 1930s to the 1990s. It's located on the edge of Waynesville, 1 mile west of downtown on Business US 23.

**Iron Tree Golf Course** (828-627-1933; Iron Tree Dr., Hwy. 209, Waynesville, NC 28786). Open daily, 7 AM–7 PM. Located 5 miles north of Waynesville off NC 209 (exit 24 off I-40), this 1991 course recently expanded to 18 holes. The course is hilly, with excellent mountain scenery.

**Lake Junaluska Golf Course** (828-456-5777; 19 Golf Course Rd., Waynesville, NC 28786). This 18-hole public course, built in 1919, is located 2 miles north of Waynesville on US 19, on the south edge of the Methodist retreat community.

**Springdale Resort & Country Club** (www.springdalegolf.com; e-mail: info@springdalegolf.com; 800-553-3027, 828-235-8451; fax: 828-648-5502; 200 Golfwatch Rd., Canton, NC 28716). Open all year at 7 AM. Despite its Canton mailing address, this golf resort is deep in the Pisgah Mountains, in a scenic valley 11 miles south of Waynesville on US 276. The 18-hole par-72 course offers stunning scenery, with views toward Cold Mountain and the Shining Rock Ledge, with play accentuated by hilly terrain and mountain streams.

**GEM MINING** **Old Pressley Sapphire Mine** (www.oldpressleymine.com; 828-648-6320; 240 Pressley Mine Rd., P.O. Box 263, Canton, NC 28716). Open daily, 9 AM–6 PM. This remote mine has produced record-setting sapphires in years past. It remains one of the few recreational gem mines in these mountains to be located at an authentic mine, using unsalted ore from onsite (which you can dig yourself). To find it, take exit 33 from I-40, then go north 1 mile on Newfound Road; from there, follow the signs for another 1.5 miles down back roads.

## ✷ Lodging

**COUNTRY HOTELS AND LODGES**

**The Old Stone Inn** (www.oldstoneinn.com; e-mail: reservations@oldstoneinn.com; 800-432-8499, 828-456-3333; fax: 828-452-1567; 109 Dolan Rd., Waynesville, NC 28786). Open April–December. In operation since 1946, this rustic lodge in a Waynesville residential neighborhood has 23 rooms and a well-respected gourmet restaurant in its seven buildings scattered over 6 acres. The Main Lodge, with stone walls and tuliptree logs, houses the restaurant, wine bar, and two rooms; its long front porch overlooks the well-kept garden. Seventeen other rooms and four cottages (no kitchens) are found elsewhere on the property. Breakfast, included in the tariff and available only to guests, starts with coffee, muffin, and newspaper left outside the room, and continues with a full, gourmet buffet in the lodge (table service on weekends).

**RESORTS** ✐ ♿ **The Pisgah Inn** (www.pisgahinn.com; 828-235-8228; P.O. Box 749, Waynesville, NC 28786). Open April–October. This modern motel-style inn fronts on the Blue Ridge Parkway in the 4,900-foot-high MountMount Pisgah area—a National Park concessionaire, and a good one. Two long, low buildings face over a sharp drop, giving incredible views from every room. Standard rooms are normal hotel size, with two double beds and a private balcony with rocking chairs overlooking that fabulous view. The deluxe rooms have the same great views from the balcony, but are larger, more recently renovated, and have larger windows for an unobstructed inside view. The one suite is a two-roomer with a wood-burning fireplace. The attached restaurant is consistently good, specializing in fresh, simply prepared mountain dishes.

✐ ♿ **The Lambuth Inn at the Lake Junaluska Assembly** (www.lakejunaluska.com; e-mail: Information@lakejunaluska.com; 800-222-4930, 828-452-2881; fax: 828-456-404; 91 N. Lakeshore Drive, Lake Junaluska, NC 28745). Open all year. This Methodist retreat complex, owned and operated by the Southeastern Conference of the United Methodist Church (whose headquarters are on the premises), is open to individual vacationers and families, whether or not they wish to participate in any of the religious programs. The retreat includes modern motels, apartments, and private cottage rentals—but its most striking property is the 1922 Lambuth Inn, with 130 en suite hotel rooms. This large hilltop hotel dominates the Lake Junaluska skyline with its bright yellow walls, white trim, and Neo-Federalist Classical styling. Needless to say, views from the Lambuth are first-rate.

**BED & BREAKFAST INNS The Yellow House** (www.theyellowhouse.com; e-mail: info@theyellowhouse.com; 800-563-1236, 828-452-0991; fax: 828-452-1140; 89 Oakview Dr., Waynesville, NC 28786). Open all year. This outstanding luxury bed & breakfast occupies a century-old house on a pond, surrounded by beautiful gardens, in the pastoral Plott Creek Valley, 3 miles from downtown Waynesville. Built by the prominent Lykes family of Tampa in the late 19th century, the Yellow House is a simple, elegant late Victorian structure with wraparound porches and a second-story balcony. Common rooms are rich in polished hardwood and Victorian antiques; guests enjoy a wine and cheese reception in the afternoon, and refrigerator full of beverages in the kitchen. The full gourmet breakfast is served on china and crystal in the elegant dining room. All of the six large guest rooms are individually theme-decorated, each reminiscent of a favorite place.

**Andon-Reid Inn** (www.andonreidinn.com; e-mail: info@andonreidinn.com; 800-293-6190, 828-452-3089; 92 Daisey Ave., Waynesville, NC 28786). This large 1902 Victorian-style farmhouse sits in a quiet residential neighborhood three blocks uphill from downtown Waynesville. It features wide porches, tall ceilings, high windows, and lots of wood trim and Victorian furniture in the ample common rooms downstairs. The four rooms range from cozy to large; all are individually decorated and sound insulated, and two have private sun decks. The full breakfast, served in the dining room, features four courses.

♿ **Herren House** (www.herrenhouse.com; e-mail: BedandBreakfast@HerrenHouse.com; 800-284-1932, 828-452-7837; 94 E St., Waynesville, NC 28786). Originally built as a boarding house in 1897, the completely renovated Herren House sits a short block off the center of Downtown Waynesville, on a quiet residential side street. Its large wraparound porch looks out over a garden, with a roomy gazebo. Decor, both in the ample common areas and in the six guest rooms, is elegantly Victorian, with antiques and reproductions. Afternoon tea consists of homemade goodies, and a full breakfast is served in the dining room.

**CABINS Rivermont Cabins** (www.rivermont.com; e-mail: vacation@rivermont.com; 888-648-6373, 828-648-3066; 126 Deer Run Dr., Canton, NC 28716). This 70-acre wooded property has a half-mile frontage on the West Fork Pigeon River in the Sunburst area, 9 miles south of Waynesville. The nine cabins are all individual structures with their own histories, ranging from modest cabins to full-size houses, and from contemporary log structures to the local 1855 schoolhouse.

## ✱ Where to Eat

**EATING OUT** ♿ **The Pisgah Inn** (www.pisgahinn.com; 828-235-8228; fax: 828-648-9719; P.O. Box 749, Waynesville, NC 28786). Open April–October. Breakfast: 7:30 AM–10:30 AM, lunch: 11:30 AM–4 PM, and dinner: 5 PM–9 PM. This National Park concessionaire sits by the side of the Blue Ridge Parkway, high and remote on the flanks of Mount Pisgah. The casual, simply furnished restaurant has dramatic views from huge windows that cover its entire southern side, flanked by large timber beams. The menu emphasizes fresh ingredients and mountain recipes, although there are plenty of old favorites available too. Full breakfasts can be ordered with fresh mountain trout, and local hickory-smoked trout can be ordered from the appetizer menu. Burgers and sandwiches can be ordered for lunch or dinner, but a more formal dinner is also available, with specials that are prepared from scratch and change daily. Wine and beer are available.

**Maggie's Galley** (www.dininginthe smokies.com/_waynesv/wdmgobar.htm; 828-456-8945, 49 Howell Mill Rd., Waynesville, NC 28786). Open for lunch and dinner, Tues.–Sun. Despite its name, Maggie's Galley is not located in Maggie Valley; this seafood restaurant occupies a log building just off US 276, a mile north of downtown Waynesville. Built in 1975 from logs salvaged from historic log cabins, this cozy and comfortable eatery features casual dining from a menu heavy with seafood favorites. Don't expect any masterful gourmet specialties here—just good food, prepared in the traditional way.

**DINING OUT The Old Stone Inn** (oldstoneinn.com; e-mail: reservations @oldstoneinn.com; 800-432-8499, 828-456-3333; fax: 828-452-1567; 109 Dolan Rd., Waynesville, NC 28786). Open April–December, 6 PM–8 PM, by reservation only. Part of a rustic lodge, this Golden Fork–winning restaurant sits in a quiet residential neighborhood 0.75 mile north of downtown Waynesville. Owner Cindy Zinser serves as the chef, designing a short but selective menu that imaginatively exploits seasonally fresh ingredients. The wine list is excellent, and the Wine Bar offers wine by the glass with hors d'oeuvres from 5 pm. The stone and log lodge, with a large porch overlooking 6 landscaped acres, has a rustic look and feel.

**The Sourwood Grille** (www.spring dalegolf.com; e-mail: info@springdale golf.com; 800-553-3027; fax: 828-648-5502; 200 Golfwatch Rd., Canton, NC 28716). Open April–November for lunch and dinner. Located on the grounds of the Springdale Country Club 11 miles south of Waynesville on US 276, this scenic and popular spot offers fine dining for lunch and dinner. Lunch menus include a range of interesting and unusual hot and cold sandwiches, burgers, fish cakes, salads, and pasta dishes, none of it particularly expensive. Dinners are fancier, with fresh and highly original fare.

## ✱ Entertainment

**Haywood Arts Repertory Theatre (HART)** (828-456-6322; 114 Church St., Waynesville, NC 28786). This local theater group performs seven shows each summer season (including two musicals) in their purpose-built 250-seat theater behind the Museum of North Carolina Handicrafts.

**Pickin' in the Park** (828-646-3411). May–August. Free. Every Friday night at 7 PM, the city of Canton presents local blue grass, mountain, and country groups, free of charge, by the Pigeon River at the Canton Recreation Park. Bring your own lawn chair.

**Mountain Street Dances** (828-456-3517). July–August, every other Saturday, 6:30 PM–9 PM. Free. Clogging and square dancing to live bluegrass music on the front lawn of the county courthouse in downtown Waynesville.

## ✷ Selective Shopping

### *Waynesville*

(www.downtownwaynesville.com; e-mail: downtownwaynesville@charter.net; 828-456-3517; 19 S. Main St., Waynesville, NC 28786). Downtown Waynesville furnishes one of the more interesting and varied shopping districts in the Smokies. A classic small-town district, it stretches for three blocks along the former main highway, from the county courthouse to the city hall. Its 86 retailers and restaurants are dominated by small craft galleries and boutiques, but you'll also find antique stores, kitchen supplies, books, cafés, wine sellers . . . almost anything except the franchised or the dull.

**Craft Galleries & Studios in Downtown Waynesville** Twelve craft galleries and studios group together in the three blocks of downtown Wayneville—a bonanza for the fine crafts shopper. There are galleries displaying local professional artists' clay sculpture, stoneware, jewelry, textiles, photographs, woodcarving, watercolors, pencil sketches, and numbered prints. Four of these shops incorporate the working studios of their artist/owners.

## ✷ Special Events

**SPRING The Garden Party** (828-642-7925) Second Saturday in May. This Canton street fair celebrates the coming of Spring with plant sales, craft displays, live music, and a Mad Hatter contest.

**SUMMER Art in the Mountains** (828-456-3517; 19 South Main St., Waynesville, NC 28786). Third Saturday in June. The downtown Waynesville artists open up their galleries and studios for this annual open house and walking tour.

**Fourth of July Celebrations** Waynesville celebrates Independence Day with a downtown street fair, with sidewalk sales, entertainment, and refreshments. Nearby Lake Junaluska has an 11 AM parade, followed by live mountain music, clogging, and craft displays until 3 PM. Waynesville's fortnightly evening of Mountain Street Dancing starts the following Saturday.

**Folkmoot USA** (www.folkmoot.com; 877-365-5872, 828-452-2997; 112 Virginia Ave., P.O. Box 658, Waynesville, NC 28786). Last two weeks in July. This major folk dance event brings 10 to 12 international dance troupes to the Smoky Mountains region, with Waynesville at the center of the action. As many as 350 dancers and musicians perform folk music and dance in native costume, at venues scattered throughout the mountains. The festivities start with a day-long street fair in downtown Waynesville, with dancers and musicians giving impromptu performances and mixing with visitors and locals. After that, the festival concentrates on indoor performances, with admission charges partially defraying costs.

**The Canton Labor Day Celebration** (828-648-7925). Canton, with its giant paper mill, makes quite a celebration out of Labor Day. Starting the Thursday before, five days of music and special events at Canton Recreation Park climax with a parade down Main Street on Labor Day.

**AUTUMN** **The Haywood County Fair** (828-456-3575). Last week in September. Held at the Haywood County Fairgrounds in Waynesville, this classic county fair has carnival rides, live entertainment, and plenty of food along with the livestock shows, home extension exhibits, and agriculture competitions.

**Church Street Arts and Crafts Show** Second Sunday in October. This downtown Waynesville street fair features regional crafters along with mountain music and dance, entertainment, and food.

**WINTER** **Christmas Celebrations** Waynesville has its Christmas Parade during the last week in November; Canton follows with its Festival of Lights Night Parade a week later. Canton continues its celebration throughout December with home tours, lighting displays, and a "drive through Nativity" organized by Canton churches.

# THE BLUE RIDGE: CHIMNEY ROCK & SALUDA

East of Asheville, the Blue Ridge (the mountain, not the parkway) extends due south in a straight line, reaching South Carolina after 50 miles of rugged valleys and gray cliffs. It is quite a barrier, and towns have formed where gorges break through it. On its north end, the Hickory Nut Gorge carried a 19th-century coach road up the Blue Ridge, now US 74A; along this old road sits the village of Lake Lure and the settlements of Chimney Rock and Bat Cave. On the south end of the Blue Ridge, the Pacolet River Gorge allowed the railroad to break through from the south, bringing the handsome little depot towns of Tryon and Saluda, one at each end of the notorious "Saluda Grade."

Between these two settled areas stretches 40 miles of empty, rugged mountains. The southern half of this remote stretch is forest-covered wilderness, broken by the deep wilderness gorge of the Green River; much of this wild land is open to the public as part of the 18,000-acre Green River Game Lands, owned by the State of North Carolina. North of these wild lands stretch Apple Country, rolling orchard lands with wonderful views from a confusing network of back roads.

**GUIDANCE** **Hickory Nut Gorge Chamber of Commerce** (www.thehickorynutgorge.com; 877-625-2725, 828-625-2725; 2926 Memorial Hwy., Lake Lure, NC 28746). This association of merchants from Lake Lure, Chimney Rock, Bat Cave, and Gerton runs a visitors center and information desk on US 64/74A, at the center of Lake Lure on the west end of the lake.

**Polk County Travel & Tourism** (www.nc-mountains.org; 800-440-7848, 828-894-2324; fax: 828-894-6142; 20 E. Mills St., Columbus, NC 28722). This agency, covering the Saluda, Tryon, and Columbus area, has a visitors center and information desk at the Tryon City Hall, on US 176 at the north end of downtown Tryon.

**Rutherford County Tourism Development Authority** (rutherfordtourism.com; 800-849-5998, 828-287-6113; 117 W. Court St., Rutherfordton, NC 28139). This agency provides tourist information for Lake Lure and Hickory Nut Gorge, as well as for parts of Rutherford County east of the mountains. It's located in Forest City, a Piedmont town some distance from Lake Lure.

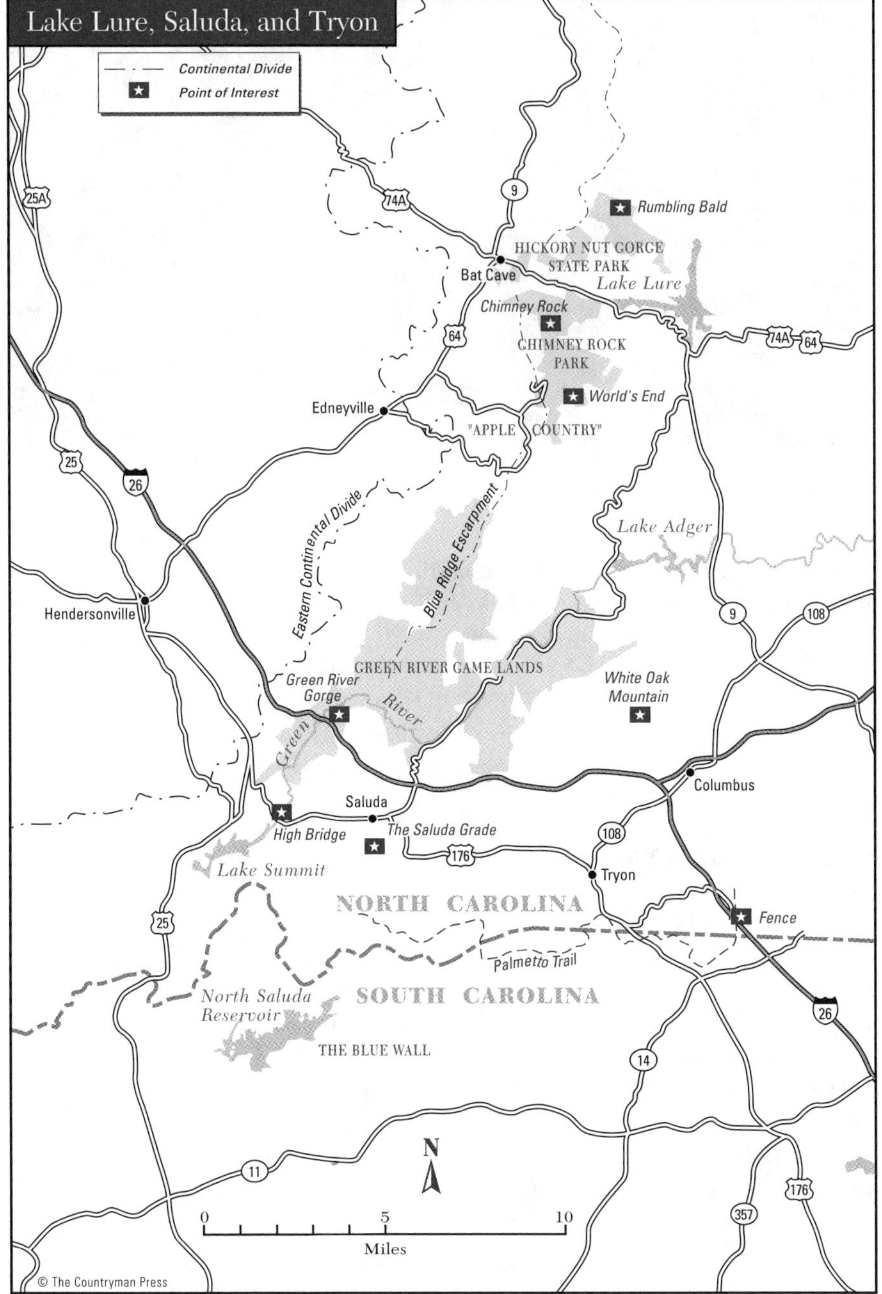
Lake Lure, Saluda, and Tryon
Continental Divide
Point of Interest
Rumbling Bald
HICKORY NUT GORGE STATE PARK
Lake Lure
Bat Cave
Chimney Rock
CHIMNEY ROCK PARK
World's End
Edneyville
"APPLE COUNTRY"
Eastern Continental Divide
Blue Ridge Escarpment
Lake Adger
Hendersonville
GREEN RIVER GAME LANDS
Green River Gorge
Green River
White Oak Mountain
Columbus
Saluda
High Bridge
The Saluda Grade
Tryon
Lake Summit
NORTH CAROLINA
Fence
Palmetto Trail
North Saluda Reservoir
SOUTH CAROLINA
THE BLUE WALL
N
0 5 10
Miles
© The Countryman Press

CHIMNEY ROCK STATE PARK

**GETTING THERE** *By Car* I-26 runs north and south up the middle of the region. The interstate-quality US 74 freeway links this region to Charlotte and points east, meeting I-26 outside Tryon. Everything else is a back road—including the US primary highways (US 176 from South Carolina to Tryon and Saluda; US 64 from Hendersonville to Lake Lure; and US 74A from Asheville to Lake Lure).

*By Air* Greenville-Spartanburg Airport (GVL) is probably your best bet for an air connection, located only a short distance south of this region. Asheville is also very convenient, but frequently costs more.

**MEDICAL EMERGENCIES** **Mission Memorial Hospital, Asheville** (828-231-1111) This huge regional hospital is just north of this region in the center of Asheville, via I-26 or US 74A (see "The City of Asheville").

**Pardee Hospital, Hendersonville** (www.pardeehospital.org; e-mail: info@pardeehospital.org; 828-696-1000; 800 N. Justice St., Hendersonville, NC 28791). Located in downtown Hendersonville, this hospital is closer to most parts of this region, via US 176 from Saluda, I-26 from Tryon or Columbus, or US 64 from Lake Lure. They maintain a walk-in clinic near I-26 off US 64.

## ✷ Exploring the Area

**EXPLORING BY CAR** **The Blue Ridge without the Parkway** *Leg #1 (11.9 miles)*: From Asheville, follow US 74A to NC 9, east of Lake Lure.

*Leg #2 (20.6 miles)*: Turn right onto NC 9, for 1.2 miles; then right on Owl Hollow Road (SSR 1164) for 2 miles; then ahead on Silver Camp Road (SSR 1138) for 6.5 miles; then right on partially gravel Green River Cove Road (SSR 1151) for 10.9 miles to a T-intersection with Holbert Cove Road (SSR 1142), with I-26 visible to your right.

*Leg #3 (15.6 miles)*: Turn right on Holbert Cove Road, then go 1.3 miles to a right onto US 176 in Saluda, then 0.3 mile to town center. From there, turn left onto narrow gravel Pearson Falls Road (SSR 1102), and take it to its end at US 176 in

3.7 miles. Turn right for 6.3 miles (passing through Tryon in 5 miles) to a left onto Ridge Road on the South Carolina state line, then go 0.6 mile (reentering North Carolina) to a left onto Hunt Country Road (SSR 1501); then right 3.4 miles to FENCE.

This 48-mile drive follows the Blue Ridge after the Blue Ridge Parkway has deserted it, using U.S. highways and gravel back roads to stay as close to it as possible. You'll be surprised how different the Blue Ridge looks away from the care of the National Park Service. The first leg follows the **Broad River** along the base of the **Hickory Nut Gorge**. As you pass the village of Bat Cave you'll get good views of the rough little Broad River; look to your right for views of the 400-foot **Hickory Nut Falls**. Gift shops and motels increasingly block the views as you approach the 1920 stone gates of **Chimney Rock State Park**, and the western edge of **Lake Lure** a mile later. US 74A follows the lake shore through the 1927 town center, with views backward over the lake to the **cliffs of the Blue Ridge**, now behind you.

As you enter *the second leg* you will be on the flatland side of the Blue Ridge, the western edge of the Piedmont, with the Blue Ridge sometimes visible as a faraway wall that rises out of rolling meadows. This route curves through some lovely farmland then quickly passes **Lake Adger**, a largish 1920s hydro lake. A mile later the route turns to reenter the mountains, following the **Green River** upstream in a deep gorge, surrounded by the magnificent **Green River Game Lands**, with a few scatterings of vacation cottages. The road gives many wide views over this lovely river, as well as several parking areas. At 4.4 miles from the turn, look for lovely Laurel Branch Falls on your right. At 7 miles from the turn is the trailhead for the extensive system of **hiking trails**, following the gorge bottom and climbing

LAKE LURE FROM CHIMNEY ROCK

HICKORY NUT GORGE

up its sides for clifftop views. At the end of the gorge, the road climbs steeply up the face of the Blue Ridge, with 17 switchbacks in less than 2 miles—a shocking stretch of road. By rights you should have a grand view from the top of this, but you won't.

*The third leg* continues on to lovely little **Saluda**, an important craft center despite its tiny size. Its downtown, facing US 176 and the railroad, gets nicer every year; the **High Bridge** over the Green River Gorge is 3 miles beyond town on US 176. This route leaves downtown Saluda by turning left onto Pearson Falls Road, the historic road down the mountain to Tryon. Look for waterfalls and precariously perched cabins as it follows a deep defile downhill; then it tunnels under the **Saluda Grade**, the steepest mainline railroad in the East and becomes a more reasonable road. Look for the turnoff to **Pearsons Falls** on the right. Once back on US 176 the railroad wanders in and out of view; look for a waterfall in a rocky gorge on your left, after which the road opens up, with broad views over the gorge to the right. **Tryon** sits at the bottom of the gorge; this route continues straight through downtown, past Morris the giant toy horse and the old depot. This route continues into **"hunt country,"** using back roads to drive past horse farms and the trails used in the hunt. The drive ends at the unique **Foothills**

FOOTHILLS EQUESTRIAN NATURE CENTER, NEAR TRYON

**Equestrian Nature Center**, with its combination of nature exploration and horse competitions.

**Apple Country** Here's a backroad orchards tour, a loop just 19 miles long but with lots of scenery—and plenty of places to get lost, as the complexity of these directions imply. As a bonus, it takes you to Worlds End, the stunning new unit of **Hickory Nut Gorge State Park**. Along the way, you will cross and recross both the geological **Blue Ridge** and the Eastern Continental Divide (see sidebar).

*Start:* From Bat Cave and the intersection with US 64 and US 74A, take US 64 south to a left onto Hog Rock Road (SSR 1703).

*Leg #1 (3.6 miles)*: Continue on Hog Rock Road for 1.6 miles, then continue straight on Bald Ridge Road (SSR 1710) for 0.6 mile to a fork; take the left fork, still Bald Ridge Road for 0.5 mile; continue straight on Sugarloaf Mountain Road (SSR 1602) for 0.9 mile to a fork.

*Leg #2—**Worlds End** (7.6 miles)*: Note that this is a three-way fork, with the middle fork starting 400 feet down the left fork. First, take the *left fork,* still Sugarloaf Mountain Road (but now SSR 1708), becoming gravel and ending at a summit in 2.7 miles; return. Now take the *middle fork,* Worlds End Road (SSR 1602) to its end at 1.1 miles; return.

*Leg #3—Orchards on the Blue Ridge (7.8 miles)*: Now take the *right fork,* Spicer Cove Road (SSR 1708, becoming gravel SSR 1196, then paved SSR 1715) for 2.5 miles to a right onto Summer Road (SSR 1713) for 2.6 miles, then bear left onto Sugarloaf Mountain Road (SSR 1602, and well might you wonder how you got here). Continue on SSR 1602 (becoming Gilliam Mountain Road in 0.5 mile) to US 64 in 2.7 miles; the start of this loop is 1.9 miles left.

Along the Blue Ridge Crest south of Hickory Nut Gorge, a maze of small, deep-sided valleys form a protected environment for apples, and have been covered with orchards since the late 19th century. The orchards bloom in late April, and come into full fruit from mid-August to mid-October. During the harvest, the growers put up stands along US 64 to allow passersby to buy bushels of fresh-picked mountain Rome apples. Behind the main highway, country lanes reach deep into the orchards and along the ridges for some beautiful scenery and stunning views—including views from the cliffs at Worlds End.

*Leg #1* takes you slowly into Apple Country along narrow, twisting Hog Rock Road, which among other eccentricities takes you up a triple switchback for no apparent reason; you can see the actual Hog Rock on your right at 1.25 miles. As you enter a better road you start across a series of small high valleys lined with orchards. This ends as you get within a mile of the edge of the Blue Ridge, at a triple fork.

*Leg #2* uses the left and middle forks to explore the Blue Ridge Crest, an area known as Worlds End. The left fork, still Sugarloaf Mountain Road, looks like a farm lane as it climbs through orchards; then it suddenly crosses a ridge and slabs out onto the **steep eastern face of the Blue Ridge**, with a near-vertical 3,000-foot plummet on the right. This remarkable view is now part of the **Hickory Nut Gorge State Park**, as is everything downhill to your right as far as the first switchback. The road, now gravel and rather scary, uses four switchbacks to reach the 3,900-foot meadow summit of Sugarloaf Mountain, with four or five houses and wide views. Back at the triple fork, a *very* sharp backtrack takes you onto the middle fork, for a pretty orchard drive to the border of the state park's Worlds End tract, again on the crest of the Blue Ridge; from here, the access road (closed to traffic) leads a mile along the crest to more clifftop views over the Piedmont.

*Leg #3* explores deep into Apple Country, crossing the Blue Ridge Crest two more times and the Eastern Continental Divide three times. Despite all this mountain crest crossing, the scenery is dominated by farmland and orchards; it is precisely these high, perched valleys that are perfect for apples. The first stretch of road crosses the Blue Ridge twice, giving it three different state road numbers, as it passes through orchards and along ridges with frequent views. Then this route turns away from the Blue Ridge to the protected valleys behind it, first diving into a small canyon carved by the Big Hungry River. From here it twists through two rural valleys with many orchards, then reaches an intersection with yet another section of Sugarloaf Mountain Road (SSR 1602). As this road crosses another orchard-clad valley it will also cross the Eastern Continental Divide twice, briefly entering, then leaving, the Mississippi Valley. A steep, switchbacked drop brings you down from the highest of the perched valleys. Here the Eastern Continental Divide, labeled "The Blue Ridge" on federal government maps, is barely visible as a slight hillock a hundred feet to your right, and you actually cross it (back into the Mississippi Valley) when you drive in front of the small church. You regain US 64 at the apple-packing town of Edneyville, only 2 miles from where you started. If you are completely turned around at this point, Bat Cave is to your right, and Hendersonville is to your left.

**EXPLORING ON FOOT Walking the Green River Gorge** (eco-wnc.org; 828-692-0385; fax: 828-693-0942; 121 Third Ave. West, Ste. 4, Hendersonville, NC 28792). Fifteen miles of hiking trails loop along the cliff tops over the Green River Gorge, climb down to the river's edge, and reach into the chasm known as The Narrows. Three paths start from Big Hungry Road (SSR 1802), a country lane running from US 64 east of Hendersonville to a dead end in the game lands. The three Big Hungry trails run through rolling terrain covered in rich old forests, typically reaching the cliff edge in 2 miles for some spectacular views over the gorge. Other paths run parallel to the cliffs, linking the main paths into loops, while two

APPLE COUNTRY

CURVES ON THE GREEN RIVER COVE ROAD

more paths make their way down the gorge side to the river's edge. The final trail, reached from the road that follow's the gorge bottom, hugs the river's edge for 3 miles to reach The Narrows.

All of these remarkable paths explore but 1,500 acres of the huge Green Mountain Game Lands—only about 10 percent of the total public lands. Perhaps we'll be seeing more of this beautiful tract in years to come. To find the Big Hungry trailheads, leave I-26 at exit 22, Upward Road, and go east 1 mile to a right turn onto Big Hungry Road (SSR 1802). The three trailheads are on the right, the first one at 4 miles. The riverside trail starts at the new bridge on Green River Cove Road, 1 mile downstream from the Fishtop Access Area.

**LONG-DISTANCE PATHS** **The Palmetto Trail** South Carolina's ambitious path from the Blue Ridge to the Atlantic Coast is about half completed—but has large blank areas in the mountains. In this chapter's area, there are two sections, called "passages," totaling about 20 miles. The eastern trailhead is at **FENCE** in North Carolina's Piedmont; from there it dives into South Carolina and heads westward to the Saluda Mountains. At its far western end it dips into North Carolina once more, to end at a trailhead at South Fork Creek Road (SSR 1840); from downtown Saluda, take Greenville Street (becoming Mountain Page Road, SSR 1846) south for 3 miles to a left onto SSR 1840, marked with a brown sign, then 1.8 miles farther. Much of the trail has the character of a road hike—on actual roads from leaving FENCE to entering preservation lands 9 miles later, then on closed roadbeds for much of the next 5 miles. The final 5 miles follow the crest of Seneca Mountain along the state line, until now an inaccessible area.

## ✷ Villages

**Saluda** Saluda's short downtown lines one side of US 176 with turn-of-the-century brick buildings, facing the railroad that marks the uphill end of the **Saluda Grade**. The buildings are immaculately kept, and filled with fascinating places to poke into: an old-style country store with a soda fountain; a wood-floored hardware shop; a fine craft gallery featuring the works of the nationally known artists who live nearby; the forge of a blacksmith who incorporates his wife's hand-painted tiles in his creations; an elegant little storefront café with live music. The railroad itself is well known as the steepest grade now existing in the East, and Saluda is the siding created to furnish the special services needed for such a steep grade. Across from the railroad, a nice little town park climbs up the hillside with views of downtown, good picnicking, and lots of happy children.

**Tryon** Located at the base of the Blue Ridge, Tryon has been a summer retreat for the South Carolina aristocracy since the turn of the last century. The rolling hills that extend from the end of the mountains had immediate appeal to the horse-and-hounds set, and Tryon has long been a center for hunt-oriented equestrian activities. Its short, railroad-facing downtown has art galleries and restaurants, watched over by Morris, a giant toy horse and the town's mascot since 1928. Across the tracks, the **old depot** holds an excellent history museum and the hunt club; just uphill is the **Tryon Fine Arts Center**, whose galleries and gardens cover half a block.

**Columbus** Located at the foot of **White Oak Mountain**, Columbus is an attractive, old-fashioned county seat. It has a sleepy, Piedmont flavor, very much a flatland Southern town—even though the mountains are in sight from its streets. It centers on its handsome old courthouse, sitting on a square with a Confederate soldier statue, and surrounded by a downtown that's only a scattering of old brick buildings. Travel services are limited; tourists are Tryon's job, 8 miles to the west.

## ✷ Wild Places

**THE GREAT FORESTS** **Hickory Nut Gorge** It's best to say it right up front: Hickory Nut Gorge doesn't look the slightest bit like a wild place when you drive through it on US 64/74A. This winding two-lane road that runs down the gorge's bottom has become lined—very close to continuously—by an assortment of businesses clamoring for tourists' attention. What many tourists never realize is that all this development is just one building lot thick. The rest of Hickory Nut Gorge is just plain beautiful.

Hickory Nut Gorge is an 8-mile slash through the heart of the Blue Ridge, a U-shaped valley 1.25 miles wide and 1,900 feet deep. Much of the gorge's upper slope is near-vertical, and its lowermost 2 miles are framed by sheer gray cliffs. Its stream, the **Broad River**, is even stranger. Upstream from its short and narrow gorge, the Broad fans out in a series of parallel and perpendicular tributaries that collect a tremendous volume of water from all over Buncombe and Henderson Counties. You can see the result clearly in the gorge—rocks the size of pickup trucks have been tossed about the streambed all the way down. As active as this river looks on a hot summer's day, it seems unbelievable that it could roll these rocks down from Asheville. Believe it; the Broad is noted for its devastating floods. It's quite an experience to camp by it, watch your kids splash around in the water, and listen to an old-timer talk about the flood of 1998.

Until 2005 the Hickory Nut Gorge was privately held in its entirety. In that year the State of North Carolina announced that it would create **Hickory Nut Gorge State Park**, has since purchased 3,260 acres, and expects to purchase 800 acres more. This includes the spectacular **Chimney Rock Park**, a thousand acre attraction and nature preserve that has stunning clifftop views, amazing geological formations (including the Chimney Rock, a huge freestanding spire reachable via a long bridge over a chasm), and a 400-foot waterfall. Other major areas are owned by resorts and are open to their guests. **The Chalet Club** gives its guests access to miles of trails on the north rim opposite the Chimney Rock, while the **Hickory Nut Gap Inn** lets its guests explore the mountains along the upper parts of the gorge.

**Green River Game Lands** (919-733-7291). Like the **Broad River** 13 miles to its north, the **Green River** drains a wide area above the Blue Ridge, then uses its heavy water flow to cut a long, deep gorge through the hard center of the mountain. However, the gorge of the Green River remains in a nearly wild state, with more than 18,000 acres protected by the State of North Carolina as the Green River Game Lands. Like other Blue Ridge water gaps, the Green River Gorge is U-shaped with sheer gray cliffs visible along its upper slope, its lower slopes clad in botanically rich mature cove hardwoods. Camping is prohibited, but 15 miles of blazed and maintained **hiking trails** explore one of its most scenic corners. The bulk of the forest, however, has no formal paths—only old roads and hunters tracks.

**South Carolina's Blue Wall** South Carolina's impressive mountain escarpment, the **Blue Wall** extends into this area as the Saluda Mountains. Lower and less rugged than the mountains near Brevard, they are nevertheless beautiful and full of variety. Most of this section of the Blue Wall is taken up by the city of

**WHERE'S THE BLUE RIDGE?**

If you stand on the shores of **Lake Lure**, the answer seems obvious: that great line of gray cliffs surrounding the upper end of the lake couldn't be anything else. But if you look at the **USGS topographic map** of the area you'll see that the Federal mapmakers disagree. They put the Blue Ridge some miles to the west, following little orchard-covered hills while the great gray cliffs march on elsewhere.

It depends on what you mean by the "Blue Ridge." Here in southwestern North Carolina, the official federal definition was set by the big dam-building agency, the Tennessee Valley Authority (TVA). Created in the 1930s, the TVA was interested only in the waters that flowed into the Tennessee River, and so formed the Tennessee Valley. In this chapter's area they defined the Blue Ridge so as to divide the waters of the Tennessee Valley from the waters of the Atlantic Ocean.

It's a counter-intuitive definition. Here, as everywhere from Maryland to Georgia, a wall of super-hardened granite forms a line of cliffs that face the Atlantic and loom high above the flatlands—the wall that pioneers named the Blue Ridge. In this chapter, however, two rivers have actually breached that wall, the **Green River** to the south and the **Broad River** to the north. Both have carved deep "water gaps" through the granite cliffs, and drain several valleys behind it into the Atlantic. The official government definition puts the line that marks the "Blue Ridge" behind these headwaters, to divide them from adjacent streams that flow toward Tennessee.

So who's right? Actually, geologists class the entire area between the cliff wall and the Tennessee state line as the "Blue Ridge Region." This entire region—the subject of this book—exhibits Blue Ridge geology nearly everywhere: twisted ridgelines controlled by erosion instead of the underlying rock, V-shaped valleys, contorted Precambrian bedrock, waterfalls, and those strange gray cliffs.

Greenville watershed and closed to the public as tightly as Area 51, and much of the remainder is in private hands. A hiking trail known as the Blue Wall Passage traverses Nature Conservancy lands and is worth the walk, passing ponds and climbing through old-growth forests to reach stunning mountain views. (Directions: take US 176 south of Tryon to a right at the Lake Lanier entrance just before the state line; follow the West Lakeshore Road around the lake for 2 miles to a right on Dug Hill Road; follow Dug Hill Road to the entrance of The Nature Conservancy's Blue Wall Preserve.)

**RIVERS** **The Green River** The Green River is noted for the deep gorge it cuts as it passes through the Blue Ridge, flowing eastward toward the Atlantic. The gorge's upstream terminus is marked by tiny old Summit Lake Dam, 3 miles north of Saluda. Public access starts at the **High Bridge**, a 1920s structure preserved by its modern replacement, US 176. From there it digs deeply into the mountain wilderness. The Green River becomes increasingly wild, with Class III and IV rapids, as it reaches its deepest and most rugged point—"The Narrows," where the river rushes between cliffs. After The Narrows, the gorge widens out to form a flat valley floor beneath tall cliffs, the river becoming wider and much less wild. This section, called Green River Cove, is traversed by a back road and contains scattered houses between blocks of state game lands. The gorge ends suddenly as the Green River drains into the Piedmont and enters Lake Adger.

Kayakers enjoy both the rowdy upper section of the Green River Gorge and its somewhat less technical lower section, and the NC Wildlife Resources Commission maintains a launching point just downstream from The Narrows, as well as a nice riverside picnic area. Five miles of hiking paths allow easy exploration of the deepest and most rugged section of the gorge, including The Narrows and the cliffs to its north.

**RECREATION AREAS** **Hickory Nut Gorge State Park** In 2005 the State of North Carolina announced that it was assembling Hickory Nut State Park by purchasing lands on both sides of Hickory Nut Gorge. The resulting 4,000-acre park opens up one of the South's most beautiful and unique places. The state will not

MORNING FOG ON SUMMIT LAKE

release any details until planning is completed and the park declared open, once set for 2008 but now stretching indefinitely into the future. In broad terms, this is what you can expect:

- *Chimney Rock Park.* This 130-year-old environmental park, described below, has passed into state ownership.
- *Worlds End.* This 1,500-acre tract, adjacent and to the south of Chimney Rock Park, protects the cliffs that face eastward toward the Atlantic. As its name implies, the views are incredible. Trailhead access is described in the **Apple Country Drive**.
- *Bat Cave.* This 100-acre tract, long protected by The Nature Conservancy, might become part of the state park. The actual Bat Cave is the largest granite fissure cave in North America, with a gigantic central chamber that's home to four endangered species, three of them unknown elsewhere. Don't expect any public access to this highly sensitive site.
- *Roundtop Mountain.* This Nature Conservancy tract will likely become part of the park. It protects a mile of cliffs on the northwestern side of the gorge. Trailheads, if any, are uncertain; no public roads come within a mile of this remote and difficult tract.
- *Rumbling Bald Mountain.* This large and impressive rocky bald projects for two miles eastward toward Lake Lure, and nearly all of it will be within the state park. A state road approaches the top of this tract and may provide a future trailhead, but there was no public access when this book went to press.

The state wants to create a giant horseshoe of protected and recreation lands around the gorge, but expects that this could take as long as 20 years to accomplish, as it relies on willing buyers.

🖍 🐾 ♿ **Foothills Equestrian Nature Center** (www.fence.org; e-mail: info@fence.org; 828-859-9021; 3381 Hunting Country Rd., Tryon, NC 28782). Free. This beautiful and unusual center (known as FENCE) is in the foothills of the Blue Ridge near Tryon. It combines an educational nature center with a large, national quality horse show and steeplechase venue. Best known as the host of Tryon's famous equestrian events, it also has 320 acres of picnic areas, walking paths, forests, and wildflower meadows. Its rolling foothills location provides an astonishing variety of environments for its 5 miles of paths—hardwood forests, pine forests, hilltops, open meadows (with lovely views), marshlands, and ponds. A historic building at the center, shaped like a stable, holds the offices and a shop; next door, an herb garden surrounds a log cabin. One of the trails is disabled accessible.

On the other side of I-26 sits the equestrian center, with an 8-furlong track and stalls for 200 horses. Some sort of equestrian event is scheduled for almost every weekend, and is worth looking into.

**PICNIC AREAS** **McCreery Park, Saluda** This small park at the center of Saluda climbs a hill opposite downtown, with good views from the picnic tables toward the Main Street shops. It's a popular playground for local kids.

**Fishtop Access Area, Green River Cove** Part of the **Green River Game Lands**, Fishtop Access Area offers limited riverside picnicking at the deepest and most rugged part of the Green River Gorge, the mouth of The Narrows.

## ✱ To See

**BIG DAMMED LAKES Lake Lure** The village of Lake Lure includes the large hydropower lake of that name and all of the land surrounding it. The Morse family, former owners of **Chimney Rock Park**, built the lake and founded the town in 1926. They wanted to expand Chimney Rock's appeal by adding a scenic lake, recreational opportunities, and upscale vacation development; it was the Morses who created the vintage 1928 town center and the 1926 Donald Ross golf course. However, the Depression intervened, and Lake Lure was sold off in bankruptcy. That's too bad; the Morses have shown themselves to be masters of tasteful and environmentally friendly development at Chimney Rock Park.

Lake Lure remains an attractive little resort settlement, despite its haphazard development. The towering cliffs of the Blue Ridge form a crescent around the lake's western end, and **Hickory Nut Gorge** cuts deeply into this gray-green escarpment. This great wilderness escarpment frames a lakeshore largely encrusted by vacation homes of all types and sizes, extending two to five lots uphill on twisting gravel roads. Access to the town is by US 64/74A, a narrow prewar relic that hugs the lake's southern coastline; traveler services stretch out along this highway, but become thicker toward the village center at the lake's western end. A city-owned park at the western end gives great views over the lake toward the cliffs, and is a pleasant place to picnic.

**HISTORIC SITES Polk County Historical Association** (828-894-3351; 60 Walker St., Columbus, NC 28722). Open Tues. and Thurs., 10 AM–1 PM; Sat., 10 AM–4 PM. This office, located at the intersection of Highway 108 and Walker Street, offers a walking tour of Columbus, and their gift shop has a nice variety of local interest items, books, and maps.

**High Bridge over the Green River Gorge** Built in 1927, High Bridge spans the Green River Gorge in one large concrete arch. It carried US 176 between Hendersonville and Saluda for over 70 years; now it carries only pedestrians, with the highway running beside it on a new, nondescript structure. From the center of High Bridge you get good views down to the rocky Green River. There is no access to the river itself.

**CULTURAL SITES Upstairs Artspace** (www.upstairsartspace.org; e-mail: frontdesk@uptairsartspace.org; 828-859-2828; 49 S. Trade St., P.O. Box 553, Tryon, NC 28782). Open Tues.–Sat., 11 AM–5 PM. This well-respected contemporary arts gallery displays the works of professional regional artists and fine crafters from their digs in downtown Tryon. A not-for-profit art organization, the Upstairs Artspace occupies a 3,000-square-foot historic red-brick storefront, divided into three galleries. Exhibits, which change every two months, are typically themed collections that feature the works of established artists, with a leaning toward the experimental and avant-garde.

**Tryon Fine Arts Center** (tryonarts.org/index; 828-859-8322; fax: 828-859-0271; 34 Melrose Ave., Tryon, NC 28782). Founded in the mid-1960s, the Tryon Fine

Arts Center (TFAC) is an umbrella organization made up of nine local arts groups, including the Little Theatre. TFAC occupies a half-block campus a block away from downtown across the tracks, with several public gardens and art galleries. On-site is Tryon Crafts, a craft school and one of the founding members. Also on site is the gallery for the Tryon Painters and Sculptors, a co-op made up of local professional artists.

**GARDENS AND PARKS** **Chimney Rock Park** (chimneyrockpark.com; 800-277-9611, 828-625-9611; fax: 828-625-9610; Hwy. 64/74A/P.O. Box 39, Chimney Rock, NC 28720). Open daily. Ticket plaza opens 8:30 AM; closes 5:30 PM, May–October and 4:30 PM, November–April. Owned by the same family from 1902 until purchased by the state in 2007, Chimney Rock is a very old, very traditional, and very beautiful scenic attraction off US 74A in Hickory Nut Gorge. The park centers on a series of stunning cliffs along the south edge of the gorge, where unusual geological formations frame overwhelming panoramas over Lake Lure, Hickory Nut Gorge, and the Blue Ridge. Entering the park in the middle of Chimney Rock Village, you'll travel a mile through park lands before reaching the 1920 stone-built ticket booth. Two more miles brings you to the base of the cliffs, with views up to the Chimney Rock—a 300-foot rock tower with a flat top, crowned by a giant American flag. From here you walk through a 200-foot tunnel and zoom up a 25-story elevator to a cliff ledge large enough to hold a gift shop and snack bar. Outside are wide views from large rock-floored balconies placed in the ledge—views over to the Chimney Rock, now only a little ways up, along the cliffs, and over Lake Lure. This is the end of the disabled accessible area. Now a cliff-side path and steps climb up to a bridge across the chasm that separates the Chimney Rock from the cliff face; the wide top of the Chimney furnishes more views. From there the trail continues, climbing the cliffs in stairs, looking down on the Chimney Rock, getting even better views from the cliff top, cutting through the cliff face on a narrow ledge, and viewing the unique cliff-side forest, stunted into bonsai shapes by harsh winds. The climax of the cliff walk: a huge, violent waterfall that plunges straight down for 400 feet without so much as a bounce off a ledge until it crashes to the bottom. (This is the same waterfall featured in the 1992 movie *The Last of the Mohicans.*) A separate (much easier) path leads to the bottom of the falls, with astonishing views upward. The pre-elevator steps to the Chimney, built in 1920, are still there, and are a fun trip down. If you bring your dog, you are required to use the steps instead of the elevator.

Below the cliffs, an area called the Meadows provides a large picnic area and a museum that explains the natural history of the cliffs above.

In 2007 the State of North Carolina purchased Chimney Rock Park as part of their planned Hickory Nut Gorge State Park. Since then the park has operated as before, including the admission, under its original management. The state has, however, been upgrading the infrastructure, replacing the elevator and rebuilding the trails. A new 15-mile backpacking trail will explore the backcountry above the cliffs, linking with **Worlds End**.

**Pearson's Falls** Open March–October: Tues.–Sun., 10 AM–6 PM; November–February: Wed.–Sun., 10 AM–5 PM. Since 1931 the Tryon Garden Club has preserved this extraordinarily beautiful and botanically rich gorge, located off US 176 (on Pearsons Falls Road, SSR 1102) between Tryon and Saluda. From a small picnic area, a mile trail climbs gently up a limestone ravine, alive with every sort of wildflower and fern imaginable, to the lovely 20-foot Pearson's Falls.

**White Oak Mountain** Long a popular beauty spot outside Columbus, this tall outlier of the Blue Ridge is being loved to death, its summit taken over by condominiums and vacation houses. To find it, take Houston Road (SSR 1137) north from Columbus for 1.1 miles, to a left on White Oak Mountain Road (SSR 1136)—and a 1,500-foot climb to the summit. As you reach the top of the mountain the road will cross the beautiful and tall Shunkawaken Falls. Then, as you top out on the summit, what's left of a mountaintop meadow sits in front of a condo development, with some truly remarkable views south over the Piedmont.

**RAILROADS The Saluda Grade** As the Norfolk Southern Railroad runs south from Asheville to Spartanburg, South Carolina, it meets the steep escarpment of the Blue Ridge at Saluda. Here's how it gets down: it turns 90 degrees to plunge into the steep defile formed by Joels Creek, and then makes a second right-angle turn to enter the Pacolet River Gorge. At the point where the railroad makes this second turn, it has dropped 400 feet vertically in just 1.45 miles—at a 5.22-percent grade, the steepest drop of any mainline railroad in America, and known as the notorious Saluda Grade.

Captain Charles Pearson chose this route for the Spartanburg and Asheville Railroad in the 1870s as the best of a bad lot. The route started servicing traffic in 1878, and by 1903 had racked up an unenviable death toll of 29 lives lost, all of them crews of runaway freight trains. In that year a runaway survivor, engineer W. P. Ballew, suggested safety tracks at the two most dangerous points, the right-angle turn (Sand Cut) and the bottom of the 3-mile grade (Slaughter Pen Cut)—sort of runaway train ramps. Just one year later, the Sand Cut safety track saved a passenger train from destruction. While the deaths stopped, the derailments continued, the last one being in 1971. Downhill trains were restricted to 8 miles per hour.

Passenger service ended in 1968, and freight service ended in 2001. Coal no longer shipped north up the grade, and the slow speeds and troublesome grade made it unprofitable for what commodities remained. Norfolk Southern has not abandoned the line, however, and is ready to reopen it should circumstances warrant.

The scenic drive, **The Blue Ridge without the Parkway,** closely parallels the Saluda Grade as it leaves downtown Saluda on Pearson's Fall Road; look for the grade above the cottages that line Joels Creek. When you cross underneath the railroad in a long tunnel you are at Sand Cut, the right-angle turn at the bottom of the steepest grade in America. When the railroad again comes into sight it will be above you, across the Pacolet River on your left. You go under the railroad once more near the base of the grade; to your left, the railroad has just crossed the Pacolet River as well as your road using the same trestle, and the Saluda Grade ends 0.3 mile to your right.

One rail fan has written, "Following [a train] down on Pearson's Falls Road is an experience every rail fan should have! . . . The screeching sound of the brakes as they fight to hold back the awesome weight of the train against the grade is a sound that will stay with you always." Maybe someday.

## ✷ To Do

**STILL-WATER SPORTS** **Lake Lure Marina** (lakelure.com/tours; e-mail: bo@lakelure.com; 877-386-4255, 828-625-1373; 2930 Memorial Hwy., Lake Lure, NC 28746). This marina on Lake Lure rents a variety of human- and machine-powered boats, including canoes and kayaks.

**HORSEBACK RIDING** **Cedar Creek Riding Stables** (cedarcreekstables.com; e-mail: hakbarnman@aol.com; 877-625-6773, 828-625-2811; 542 Cedar Creek Rd., Lake Lure, NC 28746). Open 7 days a week, 8 AM–5 PM. Located deep in the mountains north of Lake Lure, Cedar Creek offers scenic one- and two-hour trail rides on their own 360-acre ranch. Two-night pack trips in the Pisgah National Forest include all equipment and meals.

**GOLF** **Lake Lure Municipal Golf Course** (828-625-4472; Hwy. 64/74, Lake Lure, NC 28746). This nine-hole course, designed by Donald Ross in 1929, follows rolling terrain between Lake Lure and US 74A.

**Colony Lake Lure Golf Resort** (828-625-2626; 201 Blvd. of the Mountains, Lake Lure, NC 28746). This golf resort is located north of Lake Lure at the development complex known as Fairfield Mountains. It has two 18-hole courses with notable views of the rock cliffs of the Blue Ridge.

**Pine Links Golf Club** (828-693-0907; S. Orchard Rd., Flat Rock, NC 28731). This nine-hole Apple Country course, designed in 1997 by Sidney Blythe, features short greens and a number of water hazards.

**Red Fox Country Club** (redfoxcc.com; 828-894-8251; 106 Club Rd., Tryon, NC 28782). This 18-hole course, designed by Ellis Maples in 1966, sits in the Piedmont underneath Tryon, with views toward the Blue Ridge some distance away. Described as "scenic and serene," it has a number of streams and a 30-acre lake in play.

## ✷ Lodging

**COUNTRY INNS AND HOTELS**
**The Orchard Inn** (www.orchardinn.com; e-mail: innkeeper@orchardinn.com; 800-581-3800, 828-749-5471; 100 Orchard Inn Ln. [Hwy. 176], P.O. Box 128, Saluda, NC 28773). Sitting on its own little mountaintop, at the end of a winding private drive, surrounded by 12 acres of gardens and woods, this 1910 National Register country hotel offers mountain views from its wide, wraparound veranda. Located near Saluda, the Orchard Inn has nine rooms furnished with antiques, along with four small kitchen-free cottages, each with fireplace, whirlpool bath, and private deck. Well-known for its fine dining, the Orchard serves a full breakfast, included in the tariff.

**The Pine Crest Inn** (www.pinecrestinn.com; 800-633-3001, 828-859-9135; 85 Pine Crest Ln., Tryon, NC 28782). This National Register 1917 hotel sits on three hilltop acres above downtown Tryon. Built as a meeting place for Tryon's horses and hounds set, today it's run as an elegant English-style country inn with a full gourmet restaurant. The main lodge holds four of the 35 rooms as well as the restaurant. Long and deep, its side-on front entrance looks a bit like a farm house, but its long side is set upon a stone terrace and covered with a verandah overlooking gardens. Most of the rooms are in cottages (no kitchens)—five multiroom cottages and five individual cottages. The cottages range widely in style, from historic log cabins to contemporary, with most in a 1930s style. The rooms range in size from comfortable to very large, and continue the decorating theme of an English country house. The full breakfast, included in the tariff, is in the restaurant and from the same menu offered to the public.

**The Melrose Inn** (828-859-0234; tryon-melrose-inn.com; 55 Melrose Ave., Tryon, NC 28782). This 1889 hotel sits on a hill above downtown Tryon, in a quiet residential neighborhood. It has wide verandahs with mountain views as well as a full-service restaurant that serves lunch and dinner. Its guest rooms are individually decorated with antiques and reproductions in a late Victorian theme. Special guest rooms are dedicated to families traveling with children or pets. The room rate includes a full breakfast.

**The Mimosa Inn** (carolina-foothills.com; e-mail: MimosaInn@charter.net; 828-859-7688; Mimosa Inn Ln., Tryon, NC, 28782). This 1903 mansion, built in the style of an antebellum Classical plantation, sits on the north end of Tryon on 4 acres of landscaped grounds. An impressive sight when viewed from busy NC 108, it is dominated by a 50-foot-tall verandah framed by classical columns—a popular site for breakfast on pleasant summer mornings. The 10 upstairs guestrooms are antique furnished and individually themed. A guest house with kitchen and private entrance is also available on the property. A full breakfast is included in the room rate.

**RESORTS** **The Chalet Club** (www.chaletclub.com; e-mail: reservations@chaletclub.com; 800-336-3309; fax: 828-625-9373; 532 Washburn Rd., Lake Lure, NC 28746). Open all year. The Washburn family has run this intimate resort above Lake Lure on the rim of Hickory Nut Gorge since they founded it in 1934. Even though classed as a private club, they welcome all visitors with no restrictions; the modest annual fee is used to maintain the surrounding wild lands. With five guest rooms and six cottages, it is nevertheless a traditional full-service resort, including all meals and all activities in the price; guests can also get a "bed & breakfast" limited to breakfast and only a few of the activities. The main lodge, built in 1927 as the family vacation retreat, is in a chalet-style with plenty of period charm and panoramic views. It contains the five comfortable guest rooms and the large common areas. The cottages were all built as private houses, and range from a quaint 1927 caretaker'slog cabin to a comfortable 1962 home. Meals are prepared from fresh ingredients, with breakfasts served from a menu, a simple lunch served buffet style or taken as a picnic. Dinners are more formal, with gentlemen expected to wear a coat. Outdoor activities, for which there is no extra charge, include two tennis courts, a platform tennis court, 7 miles of hiking and biking trails, basketball, shuffleboard, and horseshoe courts, two swimming pools, lake swimming, water skiing, canoeing, kayaking, electric boating (for lake fishing), and power boating. Discounts or special packages are available for golf, horseback riding, rock climbing, and several nearby attractions.

**Hickory Nut Gap Inn** (www.hickorynutgapinn.com; 828-625-9108; P.O. Box 246, Bat Cave, NC 28710). This mountaintop lodge with six guest rooms is notable for its remarkable building and guest facilities. It sits above Hickory Nut Gorge near Bat Cave, at the end of a mile-long private drive, with wide views from its 40 acres, and extensive recreation on the site and in its elaborate game room. The founder of the Trailways Bus line built the lodge in the 1940s out of wood and stone taken from his surrounding 5,000-acre estate. With a modest exterior, the lodge is sited to gain a stunning view over the cliffs of Hickory Nut Gorge. Its interior is completely paneled with fine hardwoods—including floors and ceilings. The game room downstairs, paneled in gleaming hardwoods, has a full-size bowling alley as well as pool and ping-pong tables. All six guest rooms are fully paneled as well, and furnished in simple comfortable period furniture reminiscent of the 1940s. The tariff includes a continental breakfast on the large covered porch. The 40-acre site offers excellent walking opportunities, and horseback riding can be arranged.

**BED & BREAKFAST INNS The Oaks Bed & Breakfast** (www.theoaksbedandbreakfast.com; e-mail: theoaksbedandbreakfast@gmail.com; 800-893-6091, 828-749-2000; 339 Greenville St., Saluda, NC 28773). Built in 1895 for a local banker, this fine old Victorian house in a Saluda neighborhood has a witch's hat turret, a wraparound porch with turned woodwork, and gables in all directions. Four rooms in the main house are furnished with antiques; three of these rooms are en suite, while the turret room has a private bath down the hall. Two suites in a separate guest house have sitting rooms and a deck or balcony. The price includes a full breakfast.

✐ **Gaestehaus Salzburg** (www.gaestehaussalzburg.com; e-mail: gaestenhaus@bellsouth.net; 828-625-0093; 1491 Memorial Hwy., P.O. 228, Lake Lure, NC 28746). Located on a woodland plot on the east side of Lake Lure just off US 74A, the Salzburg has been built in the folk style of the Alpine borders by its Austrian founder, its three guest rooms, all furnished in a traditional Alpine style with natural wood accents. There's a pool and hot tub by the gaestehaus, as well as the German-Austrian restaurant Das Kaffeehaus. The included traditional German breakfast consists of fresh baked breads and fresh fruits, the Kaffehaus' Austrian pastries, soft-boiled egg (in a cup), and a selection of cold cuts, cheeses, and sausages. In addition to the bed & breakfast, there's a cottage on the property, and a set of eight modern condo-style efficiencies.

**CABIN RENTALS Sandy Cut Cabins** (sandycutcabins.com; e-mail: sandycutcabins@peoplepc.com; 828-749-4689; Pearson's Falls Road/P.O. Box 386, Saluda, NC 28773). Open all year. These three modern cabins are located on 15 acres near Saluda, set between the North Pacolet River and the inactive Saluda Grade railroad. The cabins are clad in stained clapboards, one built in a simple mountain style with a full porch, the other more contemporary with a deck. All have full kitchens with dishwashers, and either a hot tub or a whirlpool bath.

## ✷ Where to Eat

**EATING OUT The Purple Onion Cafe and Coffee House** (www.purpleonionsaluda.com; e-mail: scasey@tds.net; 828-749-1179; 16 Main St., Saluda, NC 28773). Open for lunch, 11 AM–3 PM; dinner, 5 PM–8 PM; closed Wed. and Sun. This small upscale eatery occupies a well-kept storefront in downtown Saluda. Its menu offers California-style cuisine, with lots of fresh and exotic ingredients. It has a good wine list and a selection of microbrews.

**Wildflour Bakery** (www.saluda.com/wildflour/bakery.htm; 828-749-9224; 173 E. Main St., Saluda, NC 28773). Open Mon., Wed.–Sat., 8 AM–4 PM; Sun., 11 AM–3 PM; closed Tues. Located at the east end of downtown Saluda on US 176, this small local bakery is well known for its scratch-made breads and pastries, fresh each morning. Breakfast pastries are featured in the morning, while lunches have soups, salads, and sandwiches.

**Tosh's Whistle Stop Cafe** (www.saluda.com/icecream; e-mail: tosh91@tds.net; 828-749-3310; 101 E. Main St., Saluda, NC 28773). Open for lunch. Located in a handsomely redone 1940s-style gas station on the south end of Saluda's Main Street, this fine little sandwich shop offers indoor and outdoor seating for their first-rate sandwiches, wraps, salads, and burgers. They have locally made ice cream as well as wine and beer.

**Old Rock Cafe** (www.chimneyrockpark.com/park/facilities/oldrock.php; 800-277-9611, 828-625-2329; Hwy. 64/74A, Chimney Rock, NC 28720). Located in Hickory Nut Gorge right outside Chimney Rock Park, the Old Rock Cafe offers salads, burgers, trout, and seasonal specials. In addition to indoor dining, they offer tables on a large deck overlooking the Rocky Broad River.

**Das Kaffeehaus Austrian Pastry Shoppe** (www.gaestehaussalzburg.com/shoppe.html; e-mail: gaestehaus@bellsouth.net; 828-625-0093; 1491 Memorial Hwy., P.O. Box 22, Lake Lure, NC 28746). Open Wed.–Sat., serving lunch 11 AM–2:30 PM; dinner by reservation only: 6 PM–8 PM. Part of the Gaestehaus Salzburg Bed & Breakfast on the east end of Lake Lure, Das Kaffeehaus offers freshly made Austrian pastries and authentic German entrées. You'll find it off US 74A down its own private drive, deep in the woods, built in the folk style found in the Alpine borders where restaurateur and innkeeper Werner Maringer was born. They have a full selection of German wines and beers.

**DINING OUT The Orchard Inn** (www.orchardinn.com; e-mail: innkeeper@orchardinn.com; 800-581-3800, 828-749-5471; fax: 828-749-9805; 100 Orchard Inn Ln. [Hwy. 176], P.O. Box 128, Saluda, NC 28773). By reservation only, Wed.–Sat., 7 PM. Well known for its fine dining, the Orchard Inn is a 1910 National Register country hotel south of Saluda off US 176 in the scenic Pacolet River Valley. It's a fine old building, sitting on a grassy hilltop, with wide verandahs wrapping around its front and sides, elegantly furnished with antiques. The dining area occupies a glassed-in porch overlooking the gardens and vineyard. Gentlemen should wear coats and ties. The Orchard has an excellent wine list; however, the choices below $25 a bottle are extremely limited.

**The Pine Crest Inn** (www.pinecrestinn.com; 800-633-3001, 828-859-9135; 85 Pine Crest Ln., Tryon, NC 28782). Open for breakfast and dinner. Reservations requested. Located in the hotel's historic main lodge, its two dining rooms are decorated as an English tavern. The menu features new American cuisine and favors original taste combinations with distinctive flavors. An extensive wine list is available.

## * Entertainment

### *Tryon*

**The Tryon Little Theatre** (www.tryonarts.org; 828-859-8322; fax: 828-859-0271; Fine Arts Center, 34 Melrose Ave., Tryon, NC 28782). This local amateur theater performs four plays a year at the Tryon Fine Arts Center.

**The Pickin' Parlor** (828-894-8091). First Friday each month, 7 PM–9 PM. Donations at the door. This monthly jam brings local musicians together for folk and bluegrass music. It's held in the Trade Street Cafe and Gallery, in Tryon's old-fashioned downtown.

### *Saluda*

**The Purple Onion Cafe** (www.purpleonionsaluda.com; e-mail: scasey@tds.net; 828-749-1179; P.O. Box 778, Saluda, NC 28773). On Saturday nights, downtown Saluda's Purple Onion Cafe features live acoustic performances in a coffeehouse atmosphere, tending toward folk and alternative music. Performances start at 8 PM; dinner service ends at 9 PM (but you can order desserts and coffees until closing); and performances typically end at 10 PM.

## ✷ Selective Shopping

**LAKE LURE AND HICKORY NUT GORGE A Touch in Time** (828-625-1902; P.O. Box 101, Bat Cave, North Carolina 28710). Open daily, 10:00 AM to 5:30 PM. A wide-porched 1902 Victorian farmhouse overlooking US 74 in Bat Cave (at the high end of Hickory Nut Gorge) carries a wide variety of crafts.

### *Tryon*

**Silver Fox Gallery** (silverfoxonline.com; e-mail: silverfoxart@bellsouth.net; 828-698-0601; fax: 828-698-0604; 508 N. Main Street, Hendersonville, NC 28792). This downtown Hendersonville gallery presents "art for living" as they put it—art for the home, practical and otherwise. Their selection can have a whimsical touch, and they have a special selection of "horses & hounds."

### *Saluda*

**Heartwood Contemporary Crafts Gallery** (heartwoodsaluda.com; 828-749-9365; 21 E. Main St., Saluda, NC 28773). Open Mon.—Sat., 10 AM–5 PM; Sun., noon–5 PM. This downtown Saluda gallery features American fine crafts with a strong contemporary flair. Handsome, roomy, and brightly lighted, this historic storefront offers a wide range of items—handmade wearables, jewelry, paper, paintings, fine porcelain, stoneware, glass, metal, and wood.

**Saluda Mountain Crafts Gallery** (828-749-4341; 1487 Ozone Dr., Saluda, NC 28773). Don't let the interstate-side location fool you; this is no chintzy gift shop. Located in a rusticized modern building by I-26's exit 28, Saluda Mountain Craft Gallery stocks original craft art with a traditional tone, featuring the works of local and regional artists. They have a wide front porch with rocking chairs and a quilter upstairs every Saturday.

## ✷ Special Events

**SPRING St. Patrick's Day Parade & Celebration** A parade through downtown Tryon is followed by live music, an antique car show, and plenty of food.

**The Blockhouse Steeplechase** (blockhouseraces.com; e-mail: office@trhcevents.org; 828-859-6109; 289 S. Trade St., Tryon, NC 28782). Late April. Ticket sales to the public begin on February 15. Gates open at 10 AM. Races start at 2 PM. The Tryon Riding and Hunt Club has been holding this sanctioned steeplechase annually since 1947. Race day activities include a parade of hounds, antique carriages, the Parade of the Old Tryon Foot Beagles, and awards for Best Tailgate Picnic and Most Creative Hat. The 1-mile kidney-shaped track, located at the Foothills Equestrian Nature Center (FENCE), sits in a hollow surrounded by low hills. Spectators' tickets gain them a parking space within view of the track, and they watch the races from their car (or mingle about and admire each others tailgate picnics and hats). The cheapest seats are in the infield, while the most expensive seats are hillside and RV parking.

**SUMMER Tryon Riding and Hunt Club Horse Show** (blockhouseraces .com; e-mail: office@trhcevents.org; 828-859-6109; 289 S. Trade St., Tryon, NC 28782). Mid-June. This hunter-jumper show has been held in Tryon since 1928. It's a four-day event at the FENCE equestrian center—one of a number of such events held throughout the spring and summer months.

**Annual Coon Dog Day** (saluda .com/events_coondog; e-mail: admin @cityofsaludanc.com; 828-749-2581). Early July. Free. This annual coon dog show has been held in Saluda since 1964. Along with the coon dog judging is a coon dog race, a craft fair, a parade, live music, and a street dance.

**AUTUMN Any & All Dog Show** (blockhouseraces.com; e-mail: office @trhcevents.org; 828-859-6109; 289 S. Trade St., Tryon, NC 28782). Early October. A Tryon tradition since 1933, this show has categories such as Most Interesting Tail, Looks Most Like Master, Best Costume, Most Doubtful Ancestry, Best Trick, Happiest, and (of course) Best Horse-Show Dog.

**Foothills Highland Games** (828-859-2050). First weekend in November. This two-day event, held at Harmon Fields on the north side of the town of Tryon, features Scottish athletic competition, the calling of the Clans, bagpipe bands, Scottish dance, border collie demonstrations, live (nonbagpipe) music, and Scottish food.

**WINTER Tryon Christmas Stroll** First weekend in December. Downtown Tryon celebrates Christmas with carriage rides, refreshments, an open house, carol singing, and a crafts sale. The celebration extends to nearby towns; in the evening, Saluda has its Home Town Christmas open house and celebration, while Columbus has a Christmas parade the next day.

# THE BLUE RIDGE: HENDERSONVILLE & BREVARD

At the far northern border of South Carolina, the hot, humid southlands end abruptly at the foot of a remarkable cliff. Two thousand feet high and 35 miles long, South Carolinians call it the **Blue Wall**. Part of the Blue Ridge, its crest forms the boundary between South and North Carolina. In back of this crest, in North Carolina, sits a high-perched valley, bowl-shaped, with small mountains at its center. This valley is large enough to contain two counties, high enough to be cool and pleasant in the summer, and mountainous enough to be exceptionally beautiful. This chapter describes the Blue Wall, the valley behind it, its two county seats (Hendersonville and Brevard), and the mountains that surround it.

Since the construction of the Buncombe Turnpike in the 1820s, rich South Carolinians have fled here in the summer, escaping the sticky heat of Charleston and Columbia. Antebellum second homes are still scattered throughout this valley, as are vacation homes from every historic period thereafter. Today, these historic homes play host to elegant inns and sophisticated restaurants. Art galleries dot brick-front main streets. Two symphony orchestras and the State Theater of North Carolina headquarter in these tiny rural towns, and a major classical music festival stages full-scale operas from its own lakeside campus. Tourism here is refined, cultured, and understated.

Hendersonville and Brevard offer excellent shopping and restaurants in their revived and restored downtowns, and both have a good choice in bed & breakfast inns. Hendersonville, the larger and more industrial of the two, plays urban host to the 19th-century tourist settlement of Flat Rock, only a few miles south. Brevard, much deeper in the mountains, is quieter, with more of a small-town atmosphere; its summer music festival, held on its own lakeside campus, is one of the cultural highlights of the mountains. The valley itself is largely flat, so much so that the French Broad River wanders through it in a long series of tightly twisted meander loops. However, a series of small mountains runs up the middle of the valley; near Brevard, the westernmost of these low mountains make up the waterfall-rich DuPont State Forest.

**GUIDANCE—TOWNS AND COUNTRYSIDE** **Henderson County Travel & Tourism** (historichendersonville.org; 800-828-4244; 201 S. Main St., Hendersonville, NC 28792). Open daily. Weekdays, 9 AM–5 PM; weekends, 10 AM–5 PM. The

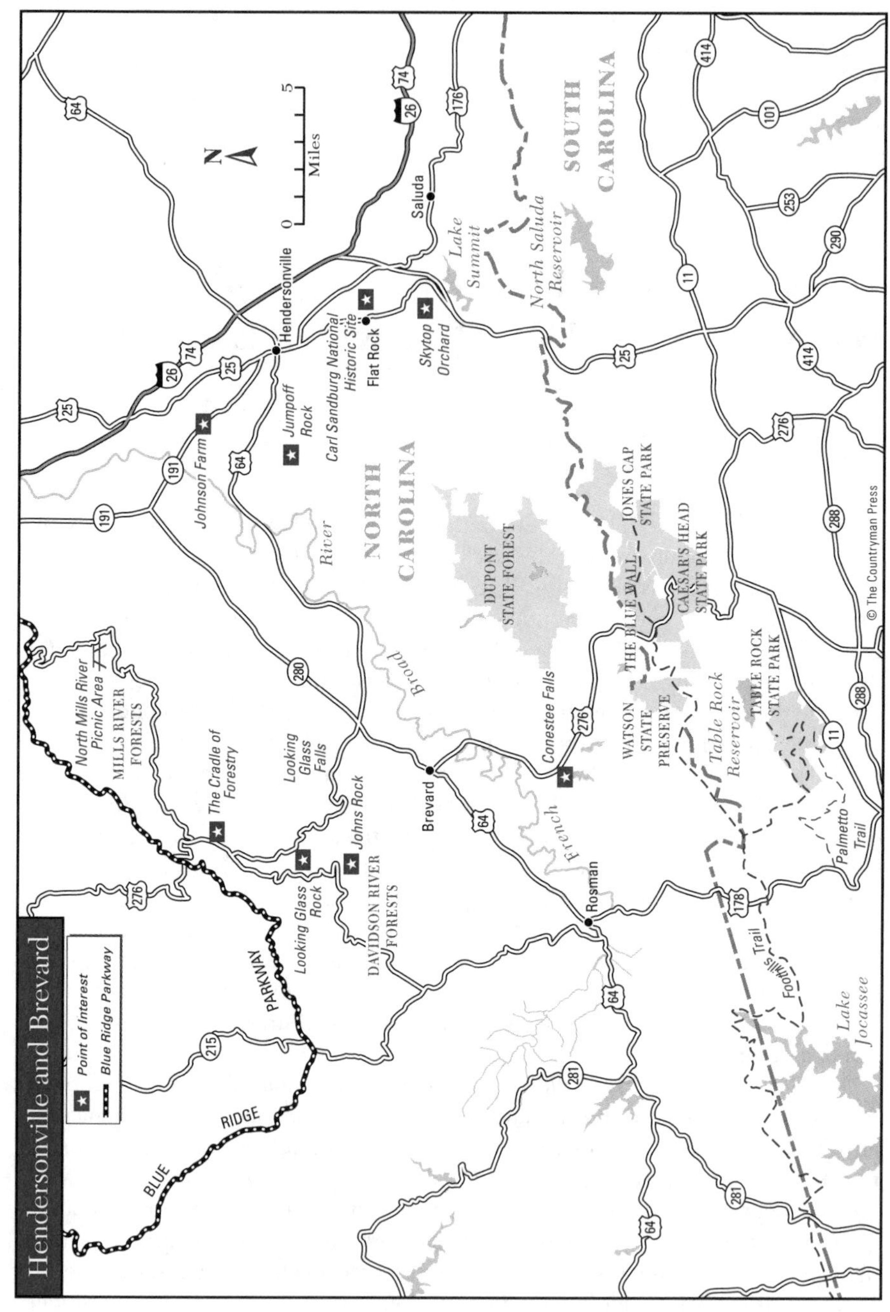


visitors center occupies its own building on the south edge of downtown Hendersonville, just beyond the old county courthouse.

**Transylvania County Tourism Development Authority** (visitwaterfalls.com; 828-883-3700; fax: 828-883-8550; 175 E. Main St., Brevard, NC 28712). The visitors center for the combined Chamber of Commerce and Tourism Development

Authority is in a small storefront in the center of downtown Brevard. They have a specialized tourism site, visitwaterfalls.com, as well as a traditional chamber site with complete business listings.

**GUIDANCE—PARKS AND FORESTS** **The Pisgah National Forest, Pisgah Ranger District** (828-877-3265; 1001 Pisgah Hwy., Pisgah Forest, NC 28768). Located on US 276, 4 miles north of Brevard, this National Forest Service visitors center has interpretive displays, a bookstore, and an information desk as well as the administrative offices of the Pisgah District.

**GETTING THERE** *By Car* From I-26, 24 miles south of Asheville, take US 64 (exit 18) west. You'll hit the north edge of downtown Hendersonville in 2 miles, and the north edge of downtown Brevard in another 20 miles. If you are approaching from Greenville, South Carolina, US 25 makes for a scenic four-lane shortcut to Flat Rock and Hendersonville. Other routes, including those with U.S. highway numbers, are not recommended for any purpose other than sightseeing down steep and winding mountain roads.

*By Air* Asheville Regional Airport is actually closer to Hendersonville than it is to downtown Asheville—9 miles compared to 13. It's 20 miles away from Brevard.

*By Train* (amtrak.com; 877-276-2767;) This is the only location in this book to have a reasonably convenient train connection. Hendersonville is 35 miles from the Amtrak depot in Greenville, South Carolina, served twice daily (once in each direction) by the Crescent from New York to Atlanta and New Orleans.

*By Bus* There is no longer any bus service to this region.

**MEDICAL EMERGENCIES** ♿ **Pardee Hospital, Hendersonville** (pardee hospital.org; e-mail: info@pardeehospital.org; 828-696-1000; 800 N. Justice St., Hendersonville, NC 28791). This full-service major regional hospital offers 24/7 emergency-room service from its campus on the northwest edge of downtown Hendersonville.

♿ **Pardee Urgent Care at Four Seasons** (pardeehospital.org/urgent_care; 828-697-3232; 212A Thompson St., Hendersonville, NC 28791). Open Mon.–Sat., 9 AM–9 PM; Sun., noon–6 PM. This walk-in clinic, run by the area's regional hospital, is located just off Four Seasons Boulevard beside Epic Theaters.

♿ **Transylvania Regional Hospital** (trhospital.org; 828-884-9111; 260 Hospital Dr., Brevard, NC 28712). This small but full-service local hospital is located just east of Brevard off US 64, between downtown Brevard and Pisgah Forest.

**Park Ridge Hospital, Hendersonville, NC** (parkridgehospital.org; e-mail: info@parkridgehealth.org; 828-684-8501; 100 Hospital Dr., Hendersonville, NC 28792). *The Park Ridge Hospital is located between Hendersonville and Asheville, off I-26 at exit 13.* This 103-bed hospital, founded in 1910, is part of the Adventist Health System, operated by the Seventh-day Adventist church. Its large 24/7 emergency room promises a wait time of 20 minutes or less.

## ✷ Exploring the Area

**EXPLORING BY CAR** **US 276** The 42-mile scenic drive down US 276 is a perfect way to get acquainted with this part of the mountains. For its first 15 miles this route passes through the Pisgah National Forest, descending steeply off the Pisgah Ridge. In less than 4 miles the highway passes a Forest Service picnic area at **The Pink Bed**, named for its rhododendrons, and **The Cradle of Forestry in America**. In the next 5 miles the highway drops into a gorge-like valley, passing **Slide Rock**, a popular swimming hole, and **Looking Glass Falls**, a classic river-over-a-cliff waterfall. A quarter-mile later, a paved side road leads right to the **Pisgah Center for Wildlife Education**.

Leaving the national forest, US 276 immediately turns and follows four-lane US 64 to **Brevard**, temporarily losing its charm but picking up a wide array of roadside services as partial compensation. After 3.4 miles of this the highway reaches the middle of Brevard, turns, and becomes Main Street through Brevard's handsome old downtown. It quickly leaves Brevard to follow the old, slow, meandering **French Broad River** for 2 miles, then enters a long series of straight stretches through pastoral scenery; look for craft artists' studios and galleries scattered about. Five miles south of Brevard, the twin waterfalls of **Conestee Falls** cascade beside the highway. At 11 miles south of Brevard, a side road to the left (paved Cascade Lake Road) leads to the **DuPont State Forest**, with its first-rate waterfall walks.

Soon the highway crosses the **Blue Ridge** and suddenly tips over the edge of the world. No other road gets so up close and personal with **South Carolina's Blue Wall**. The highway follows the flat top of a side ridge for 3 miles out into the cliff lands, reaching **Caesars Head State Park** with its stunning panoramic views and **walks** to gorges and waterfalls. Then the highway drops down off the ridge top and switchbacks wildly down the steep slopes of the Blue Wall. In 7 miles of continuous twists the highway drops 2,200 feet to the floor of the South Carolina Piedmont. Five miles into this (it will feel longer) you will reach a graffiti-covered roadside rocky bald called **Bald Rock**, with wide views over this sudden end of

THE CRADLE OF FORESTRY IN AMERICA

the mountains to the endless flatness of the Deep South. Four miles later, at the base of the mountain, look for **Wildcat Falls** on your left, with a nature trail following the stream. In 4 more miles the highway reaches the flatlands, with views over fields toward The Blue Wall.

**Driving Through the Pisgah National Forest** This 40-mile drive winds its way on gravel roads through the heart of the Pisgah Forest, the forests that George Vanderbilt brought into his **Biltmore Estate** in 1889. In the early decades of the 20th century, when giant logging companies were devastating much of the Smoky Mountain forest, Vanderbilt's foresters tended these forests with thought and care. Today they are very beautiful.

Start at **Lake Powhatan Recreation Area** (see "The City of Asheville," *Wild Places*), turning onto the gravel FS 479. Your road follows Bent Creek gently uphill through increasingly handsome mixed forests, then climbs steeply to the Blue Ridge Parkway on the crest of the Pisgah Ridge. Cross the parkway and continue downhill on the gravel Forest Service road (FS 5000), winding downhill for nearly 6 miles to **North Mills River Recreation Area**. Turn right onto the gravel Yellow Gap Road (FS 1206). For the next 12 miles, Yellow Gap Road climbs two ridges, follows three streams, and enters four high mountain coves. Watch how the mature forests change from the rich diversity of the coves to the dry oak and pine forests on the ridgelines. The last of the coves is known as **The Pink Beds**, named for its rhododendron displays in June, and the center of Vanderbilt's early forestry operations.

Yellow Gap Road ends at **US 276**; turn left and follow the highway for 1.5 miles, passing The Pink Beds Picnic Area and the Biltmore's historic forestry school, **The Cradle of Forestry in America**. Then turn right onto FS 475B, another gravel forest road. This road takes you around the west side of the gigantic schist monolith **Looking Glass Rock**, best viewed from the Blue Ridge Parkway. In 3.5 miles the road passes through Gumdrop Gap, the trailhead for rock climbers attacking the north face of Looking Glass Rock, and drops down into the lush valley of Rockhouse Creek. Look for the attractive Slick Rock Falls on your left about 1.5 miles into the valley. In 2.75 miles you reach the Davidson River at **John Rock**; turn right onto FS 475, passing the **Pisgah Center for Wildlife Education**, a first-rate museum on wildlife management and conservation. This gravel road follows the Davidson River for nearly 5 miles upstream through a popular hiking area with many trailheads, topping out at Gloucester Gap to descend 3 miles to NC 215. Turn left on NC 215 to reach US 64 at Rosman in 7.6 miles; Brevard and Hendersonville are east (left) on US 64.

**EXPLORING ON FOOT** **A Pisgah Forest Hike** Looming a thousand feet over the **Pisgah Center for Wildlife Education**, the long expanse of gray cliff known as John Rock is hard to resist. This 6-mile loop climbs from the Pisgah Center to the top of John Rock, with good Pisgah Forest scenery along the way and a stunning panoramic view at the top. The path, named Cat Gap Loop Trail, starts at the far end of the Pisgah Center's parking lot. It follows a lovely little mountain stream, staying level for a half-mile, then turning south and starting its steady climb up a side valley known as Horse Cove. In 1.5 miles from the parking lot (and a climb of 500 feet), a side path peels off right across the stream and up to John Rock, reaching the summit in another mile (and another 500 feet up). The views north take in the gorge-like valleys of the Davidson and Looking Glass Rivers, the gray cliff-sided dome of **Looking Glass Rock**, and the mile-high crest of the Pisgah Ridge. From the summit, the trail heads south along the rock's narrow ridgeline, reaching a trail intersection in 0.60 mile. While all three choices will take you back to your car, this walk follows the rightmost trail, Cat Gap Bypass. This path circles around the high forests above a little side valley, then merges with the Cat Gap Loop Trail (which has strayed uphill away from John Rock since we last met it). Follow the Cat Gap Loop Trail downhill along a dry ridgeline, then past the Picklesimer Fields, and down Cedar Rock Creek to the Pisgah Center.

**A DuPont Forest Waterfall Walk** Four lovely waterfalls, each with its own unique personality, group tightly together at the center of the DuPont Forest. A single walk to all four waterfalls, following a roaring mountain river most of the way, takes a total of 5 miles with 750 feet of total climbing. To reach the trailhead parking, take US 276 11 miles south of Brevard to Cascade Lake Road; then take Cascade Lake Road north 2.4 miles to its fork with Staton Road; then take Staton Road 2.3 miles (passing the abandoned Agfa plant, now being environmentally restored) to a parking lot on the left just after a bridge.

Your first destination is **Hooker Falls**—through the gate at the end of the parking lot, then 0.35 mile along the river on a level old road. Here the Little River, 130 feet wide, pours straight down over a 13-foot ledge. Retrace your steps to the parking lot, then cross the river on the paved road bridge to continue upstream on the opposite bank. As the scenery becomes more mountainous the trail ascends to a view of **Triple Falls** on the Little River—three separate cascades that together drop 120 feet. From here a path leads to the base of the fall, and a roadbed leads to a picnic shelter. Continue on the main trail, first uphill, then along the riverbank. As your trail goes uphill again, a side trail along the river leads to the base of **High Falls**, where the Little River slides straight down a 150-foot cliff. The main trail continues uphill to views from the top of High Falls, then more views from a picnic shelter.

At this point you have walked 1.75 miles and climbed 250 feet, and you are 1.4 miles from your car (downhill all the way). If you want to continue, there is one more waterfall nearby, a tall slide rock on Grassy Creek that will add 2 miles and 500 feet of climbing to your walk. Cross the Little River on the bridge upstream from High Falls, then continue left on Buck Forest Road (at one time the main road through these parts). After about a mile, you will cross Grassy Creek on a bridge, then turn left on Imaging Lake Trail (another old roadbed, leading a couple of miles to a pretty little lake built by the film factory in years past). The newly built path to the base of **Grassy Creek Falls** is just beyond, to your left.

**Raven Cliff Falls on the Blue Wall** South Carolina's Blue Wall is a rugged and difficult area; with few exceptions, its rewards must be earned by hard effort. This walk is comparatively easy—by Blue Wall standards. By any reasonable standard, it's a tough day hike. However, with a 400-foot waterfall at the end, it's well worth it.

The 4- to 8-mile round-trip walk to Raven Cliff Falls, one of the tallest in the East, follows a well-built footpath in **Caesars Head State Park**, 13 miles south of Brevard on US 276. Trailhead parking is a mile north of the park's headquarters. For the first mile the path follows the gently rolling ridgeline along the top of the cliff wall, passing through handsome forests with occasional views over the Blue Ridge, with about 300 feet of climbing and dropping. At the intersection with Gum Gap

Trail, continue left on Raven Cliff Falls Trail, dropping into the rugged terrain around the waterfall. The trail will drop 700 feet in the next 0.9 mile, and you will have to reclimb every step on your way back. At the bottom of the trail is an observation deck giving a wide view across this narrow, forested gorge to the waterfall, a strong cataract that hurls down the cliff in three large jumps. When its time to go back, you have a thousand feet of climbing to reach your car, for a round-trip of 4 miles. If you are feeling energetic, you may double this length and add 300 feet of climb by taking the right-hand fork at Gum Gap Trail, leading around to Naturaland Trust Trail and a suspension bridge over the waterfall—another first-rate view from a completely different angle.

**LONG-DISTANCE PATHS** **The Foothills Trail** In this chapter the Foothills Trail reaches its eastern terminus—two of them, actually. Just 3 miles after crossing US 178 (9 miles south of Rosman, North Carolina), the trail reaches the crest of the Blue Ridge at the North Carolina–South Carolina state line. Here it forks. The right fork, staying in South Carolina, leads 7.8 miles to **Table Rock State Park** and enters the park very near the top of the rock itself, with its spectacular views from vertical cliffs. From here there is a choice of descents to the trail's end at the park's Nature Center—either straight down, past a viewpoint and a waterfall, or along Table Rock's ridgeline, passing the side path to the top of Table Rock (another 1 mile and 300 feet of climb). The left fork (15.5 miles long) crosses the Blue Ridge into North Carolina for 5.5 miles, bypassing Greenville's watershed, before reentering South Carolina at **The Mountain Bridge Wilderness**. Here it passes some of the Blue Ridge's most dramatic scenery, including **Raven Cliffs Falls** and the view from **Caesars Head**, before descending the beautiful Middle Saluda River into **Jones Gap State Park** and its alternate end.

**The Palmetto Trail** Someday this long path will link the Blue Ridge Mountains with the Atlantic Coast of South Carolina, spending many miles within this chapter's area. At press time, however, the trail had only one section completed in this area, the 9.5-mile Jocassee Gorges Passage. This section runs westward from **Table Rock State Park**, with a trailhead a half-mile from the park's Nature Center (where the Foothills Trail starts), crossing the foothills of the ridge traversed by the **Foothills Trail**. It ends at US 178, 3.5 miles south of the Foothills Trail, allowing for a loop of 24.6 miles, including 4 miles of road walk.

## ✷ Villages

**Hendersonville** This busy little city of 12,000 sits in a wide valley 20 miles south of Asheville via I-26. A successful small center of commerce, it's surrounded by a ring of modern, sprawling development, its highways busy and noisy. However, its quiet little downtown is a wonderful place. Almost completely preserved from the early 20th century, it has five blocks of Italianate red-brick storefronts, with wide, landscaped sidewalks and free street parking; downtown shopping is varied and sophisticated, and the choice of restaurants is excellent. The town's most historic (and ritzy) neighborhoods stretch westward from downtown along Fifth Avenue, then up a little mountain on the 1920s-era Laurel Park Highway—ending at **Jump off Rock**, a lovely city park with a high view rock.

**Flat Rock** This attractive village of 2,500 residents stretches along US 25, 3 miles south of Hendersonville. Like many Southern settlements, it lacks a well-defined center; shops and inns are spread out along the highway, widely separated by tree-lined fields. Flat Rock has been a tourist destination since the late 1820s, when the stagecoach road known as the Buncombe Turnpike (following the route of modern US 25), made it accessible to wealthy South Carolinians. By the 1850s, Flat Rock was a fashionable summer destination for heat-struck Southerners who could afford it, and not even the Civil War could alter this. Today it remains genteel and beautiful, a village of elegant country inns and fine restaurants hidden down remote lanes. Flat Rock was the home of **Carl Sandburg** and his wife for 22 years (1945 to 1967); their ante-bellum home and modern goat farm are a National Historic Site, a wonderful example of an early Flat Rock plantation.

JUMP OFF ROCK IN HENDERSONVILLE

**Brevard** This small mountain town of 6,800 people, the seat of Transylvania County, sits on a hillside by the French Broad River, 20 miles west of Hendersonville via US 64. The main approach to town on US 64 doesn't do it justice, passing through several miles of sprawling industry and commercial development before briefly diving in and out of the town's center. However, leave the main highway to explore the traditional center of town, and you will find a perfectly preserved red-brick downtown filled with interesting shops, galleries, and cafés, surrounded by well-kept old neighborhoods with lovely little parks and plenty of trees. Brevard gains a surprising level of cultural sophistication from its small Methodist liberal arts college (Brevard College), and its first-rate summer program for aspiring young professional musicians, the **Brevard Music Center**.

## ✷ Wild Places

**THE GREAT FORESTS The Pisgah Forest** The Pisgah National Forest wanders through much of western North Carolina, with important tracts stretching from the eastern edge of the Great Smoky Mountains National Park to Roan Mountain and on to the slopes of Grandfather Mountain. However, to most people in North Carolina, the Pisgah Forest is the great stretch of wild lands on the south slopes of the Pisgah Ridge, north of Brevard and Hendersonville.

Originally part of George Vanderbilt's **Biltmore Estate**, Vanderbilt had carefully tended and restored its forests over a 30-year period. Vanderbilt's foresters had set up America's first forestry college in log cabins on this 100,000-acre tract to train the assistants they needed; its buildings, still preserved, make up the core of the forestry museum, **The Cradle of Forestry in America**. More than a century later, Vanderbilt's Pisgah Forests are remarkably diverse and beautiful, with a network of gravel roads and hiking trails leading to its scenic wonders.

The Pisgah Forest splits naturally into two halves. To the east, the Mills River and its tributaries drain a series of watersheds. To the west, the Davidson River drains southward toward the headwaters of the French Broad River. In the center, roughly straddling these two areas, runs **US 276**, a winding and scenic drive that links many of the finest sites of the forest. Gravel forest roads run cross-grain through the area, giving ready access to most corners of the forest. The Blue Ridge Parkway, running along the mile-high crest of the Pisgah Ridge just outside the northern border of this chapter, lets you drive up to the high points of many of these trails and enjoy their best views without raising a sweat. These tracts are multiple-use national forest lands, not wilderness; yet they are largely given over to outdoor recreation, with little or no logging. Trails are extensive and well developed, with the majority open to bicycles and horses as well as hikers.

**DuPont State Forest** (828-251-6509; 14 Gaston Mountain Rd., Asheville, NC 28806). This 10,300-acre North Carolina state forest, purchased from the DuPont Corporation in 1997, lies in a high plateau 13 miles south of Brevard via US 276 and Cascade Road (SSR 1536). It's noted for its many waterfalls, and its excellent views from a number of exceptionally large rocky balds. Its forests are young and varied, and its slopes are much gentler and shorter than other mountain tracts. It has four lakes, one of them quite large—remnants of old real estate schemes and summer camps. It has nearly a hundred named trails, most of them old roadbeds, and nearly all of these gentle, old paths are open to bicyclers and horses as well as walkers. In the middle of this large, popular recreation site once sat a large film factory, like a hole in a doughnut. Although it was razed in 2003, it remains an environmental remediation site and access is strictly prohibited. Access to everything else is free and open.

CARL SANDBURG HOME NATIONAL HISTORIC SITE

About a quarter of this forest, including nearly all of the prime recreation sites, was seized by the State of North Carolina in 2000 from a developer who had started to construct an exclusive gated community on the site; the gate is still there, now part of the state forest.

For the traveler, the DuPont Forest is worthwhile for its seven major waterfalls and rock slides, the views from its large rocky balds, and its refreshingly easy walking. The largest and most remarkable waterfalls are on the Little River, easily reached from paved roads. The **DuPont Forest Walk** describes a stroll to three of these, from a roadside parking area at the center of the forest. A second scenic area can be reached from a trailhead parking lot on Cascades Road, about 2 miles north of US 276 (10 miles south of Brevard). From here, easy trails lead to Bridal Veil Falls, a wide, tall waterfall with a high water volume that you can walk behind, featured in the movie *The Last of the Mohicans;* to Cedar Rock, claimed as the longest rocky bald in the Blue Ridge with panoramic views; and to Corn Shoals, a slide rock and popular swimming hole. A loop walk to all three points is 4.4 miles long with 950 feet of total climbing (hint: do Cedar Rock first, and the Corn Shoals swimming hole last).**The Mountain Bridge Wilderness of South Carolina** Rising 2,000 feet nearly straight up from the South Carolina Piedmont, this cliff-like 35-miles of the Blue Ridge is known as the Blue Wall. The terrain is extraordinarily beautiful, with lush forests, deep gorges, huge waterfalls, and high cliffs. It's also extremely difficult—a rough and broken land with extreme elevation changes in short distances. Much of this wild territory is protected by the government of South Carolina in a series of state parks, game lands, and heritage preserves, while other large tracts are protected by private conservation foundations and city watersheds. All together, these state, local, and private conservation tracts make up more than 40,000 acres of coterminous wild lands, termed "The Mountain Bridge Wilderness and Recreation Area" by the state of South Carolina.

SOUTH CAROLINA'S BLUE WALL AT CEASAR'S HEAD STATE PARK

Three state parks make up the bulk of the recreational opportunities in this area. **Table Rock State Park**, on the western edge of this chapter's region off SC 11, centers around an outlying dome of hard, gray rock that looms 2,000 feet above the park's lakeside picnic area; history buffs will want to check out its extensive **CCC architecture**, listed on the National Register. **Caesars Head State Park**, bisected by US 276 in the center of the region, protects a long series of cliffs and waterfalls—the only place on the Blue Wall with cliff-top views you can drive to. **Jones Gap State Park** protects the upper reaches of the Middle Saluda River, with some spectacular cliff scenery.

**RIVERS The French Broad River** The French Broad River begins at the far western edge of this chapter's area, as three fast mountain streams drain off the slopes of the Blue Ridge and merge near the small village of Rosman, on US 64. At this point the river is deep in the mountains at 2,200 feet above sea level—yet it will spend the next 52 miles meandering gently across a flood plain. In this length it manages to travel only 26 linear miles, describing a gentle crescent that passes through Brevard before passing out of this chapter's area north of Hendersonville. Its constant meandering, doubling the length the water must travel, cuts its gradient in half and makes it a slack-water Class I canoe trip. Riverside scenery is pastoral, with nearly continuous farmland and all in private ownership.

**RECREATION AREAS Table Rock State Park** (864-878-9813; fax: 864-878-9077; 158 E. Ellison Ln., Pickens, SC 29671). Open every day, 7 AM–9 PM. Built in 1936, this 3,000-acre park preserves a 3,100-foot mountain dome, plus enough historic **CCC architecture** to place the entire park on the National Register of Historic Places. The central attraction is, of course, Table Rock, a cliff-sided outlier of the Blue Ridge that towers 2,000 feet above the picnic area—a horizontal distance of only 1.4 miles. Most visitors enjoy the view from the lovely little lake or the wildflower meadows at its base; but more than a few climb the very steep 3.5-mile trail to its peak, for wide views over the Blue Ridge and out over the level plains of the Deep South. The park has a CCC picnic area on a small lake, CCC-built log rental cabins, a lakeside restaurant with dining room views toward Table Rock, and a nature center.

**Caesars Head State Park** (864-836-6115; 8155 Greer Hwy., Cleveland, SC 29635). Open April–September, 9 AM–9 PM; October–March, 9 AM–6 PM. Bisected by **US 276**, Caesars Head State Park occupies a 3,200-foot cliff-faced ridge projecting out into South Carolina's Blue Wall country. A roadside overlook offers stunning views over the rugged Blue Ridge, toward **Table Rock** and the plains of the Piedmont. Nearby, a visitors center has an information desk, gift shop, and exhibits on area history. **Raven Cliff Falls**, at over 400 feet (one of the tallest in the East), is in this park.

**Jones Gap State Park** (864-836-3647; 303 Jones Gap Rd., Marietta, SC 29661). Open April–October, 9 AM–9 PM; November–March, 9 AM–6 PM. This 3,300-acre park protects the rare forests and unique rock formations at the foot of the Cleveland Cliffs, along South Carolina's Blue Wall. Rugged (but well-maintained) paths climb the high cliffs, follow side ridges, or explore the Middle Saluda State Scenic River. At the park's headquarters up a quiet rural lane off SC 11, the park's Environmental Education Center has nature exhibits, and the CCC-era Cleveland Fish Hatchery has been restored and stocked as a demonstration.

**PICNIC AREAS Silvermont Park** This odd Brevard city park offers good picnicking three blocks south of downtown on US 276. It takes up the house and grounds of an historic neoclassical brick mansion—but with no attempt at restoration. Quite the contrary; the house itself, used for meetings, is in bad shape, and much of its extensive formal gardens have been paved over with tennis and basketball courts. However, it has a nicely kept, shady picnic area with a good playground, as well as a lovely little herb garden and a gravel exercise path through a forest garden.

**North Mills River Recreation Area** At the end of the paved North Mills River Road, and the start of two scenic gravel Forest Service roads, this Forest Service site offers picnicking in a great hemlock grove by a mountain river.

**The Pink Beds Picnic Area** This National Forest Service picnic area sits just off the Blue Ridge Parkway on US 276. Apart from the famous rhododendrons from which it is named (and that display in June), it's notable for its attractive and level loop trail, which leads to beaver dams (and may be flooded by beaver ponds).

## ✱ To See

**HISTORIC SITES** ✐ ♿ **The Cradle of Forestry in America** (www.cradleofforestry.com; e-mail: ccarpenter02@fs.fed.us; 828-877-3130; fax: 828-884-5823). Open May–October; 9 AM–5 PM. When George W. Vanderbilt founded Asheville's **Biltmore Estate** as his private residence in the 1880s he surrounded it with vast tracts of forest lands, including much of the Pisgah Ranger District of the Pisgah National Forest. With no scientific forestry in existence in America at the time, Vanderbilt imported professional foresters from Germany to manage his forests—first the German-trained American Gifford Pinchot, then the German scientist Carl A. Schenck. With no trained assistants or staff available in the United States, these scientists were forced to start a training school on Biltmore property. This training school is now preserved as The Cradle of Forestry in America, a beautiful and fascinating collection of historic log structures. The tour starts at the large modern museum, where historic and modern forestry practices are explained. Then a loop trail leads to the historic site, with a log school room, store, and cabins (including some built in a proper German style by Dr. Schenck), where craft demonstrations are held. A second loop trail leads through a demonstration of historic forestry practices. Run by the National Forest Service, the Cradle of Forestry is on US 276, 14 miles north of Brevard and 3.5 miles south of the Blue Ridge Parkway.

✐ ♿ **Carl Sandburg Home National Historic Site** (www.nps.gov/carl; 828-693-4178; fax: 828-693-4179; 81 Carl Sandburg Ln., Flat Rock, NC 28731). Open all year, 9 AM–5 PM. Free admission to grounds and goat barn. House additional charge for adults; children under 17 free. In 1945, poet and scholar Carl Sandburg and his wife, Paula, moved from Michigan to Flat Rock, North Carolina. Mrs. Sandburg was a dedicated goat farmer and serious goat breeder, and the mild climate of Flat Rock was a superior place to raise goats. They purchased Connemara, a large farm with a beautiful antebellum house and a large pond, at the center of Flat Rock. Carl Sandburg remained at Connemara until his death in 1967; a year later, Connemara became Carl Sandburg National Historic Site, part of America's national park system.

BARBARA MILLER SPINS YARN AT THE CRADLE OF FORESTRY IN AMERICA

GOAT FARM AT CARL SANDBURG HOME

Connemara would have been worthy of preservation under any circumstance. One of the oldest farmsteads in this region, it was built in 1838 as a vacation home for a rich South Carolinian, Christopher Memminger, later treasury secretary for the Confederate States of America. His heirs sold it to a Captain Smyth (it was known locally as The Smyth House when the Sandburgs bought it), and Smyth's heirs sold it to the Sandburgs with 240 acres of farmland and forest. Despite this history, the National Park Service realizes that nothing more distinguished has happened to this fine old house than the Sandburgs. They keep the house, the grounds, and the goat farm the way Carl and Paula left them.

Connemara is an extraordinarily beautiful place, easily worth a full day's exploration. From the roadside parking lot, you walk along a lovely pond with views toward a meadow-covered hill and the columned old house. The path crosses a wooden bridge, then climbs along wood fences and through meadows for 0.3 mile to the surprisingly modest house, with its columned porch and lush azaleas. The basement visitors center has a small bookstore and information desk. From there you can tour the house, carefully preserved the way the Sandburgs left it, a slice from a warm and comfortable life in the 1940s. From the house, you continue up into the farm area with 21 buildings preserved from the Sandburg era. It's still a functioning goat farm, and kids wander out from the giant red barn to great visitors. Beyond the goat dairy, walking paths lead through woods to mountaintop viewpoints.

**Historic Johnson Farm** (828-891-6585; 3346 Haywood Rd., Hendersonville, NC 28791). Open all year, 9:00 AM–2:30 pm, with guided tours at 10:30 AM and 1:30 PM; in May–October, closed Sun. and Mon.; in November–April, closed Sun.–Tues. Run by a not-for-profit on behalf of the Henderson County school system, this 15-acre museum complex preserves a late-19th-century tobacco farm. It centers on a restored-brick 1870s farmhouse listed on the National Register andis furnished as a late-19th-century farm residence. There are nine other historic structures, all original to the farm, including a boarding house and a barn museum.

**CULTURAL SITES** **Brevard Music Center** (brevardmusic.org; 888-384-8682, 828-862-2100; fax: 828-884-2036; 349 Andante Ln./P.O. Box 312, Brevard, NC 28712). From its beautiful lakeside campus on the north edge of Brevard, the Brevard Music Center furnishes summer instruction in professional music practice and theory for talented, serious musicians from age 14 to post-college. Its 50 faculty members teach 400 students each summer. Brevard's unique program emphasizes performance experience with professional musicians under real-world conditions—the sorts of rehearsals and audiences that students will encounter in their first professional jobs. For this reason the Music Center sponsors the annual **Brevard Music Festival**—two months of performances (50 in all), in which the Music Center's students perform with top-ranked professionals. Founded in 1936 as a band camp, the campus consists of 145 rolling, wooded acres with around a hundred separate buildings and two lakes. Its main venue, the Whittington-Pfohl Auditorium, is open sided, with seating both under cover and on the open lawn by Milner Lake.

**MUSEUMS** ✐ ♿ **Pisgah Center for Wildlife Education** (828-877-4423; fax: 828-877-4792; P.O. Box 1600, Pisgah Forest, NC 28768). Open every day, 8 AM–5 PM. Located 10 miles north of Brevard, this wildlife museum "sponsored by the sportsmen of North Carolina" (actually, the North Carolina Game & Fish Commission) is 1.5 miles off US 276, down a signposted paved forest road. Deep in the Pisgah National Forest, this small museum occupies a beautiful site at a working fish hatchery, bordered by the rocky Davidson River and with views up toward the gray cliffs of **John Rock**. Inside the small, gray government-style museum building, exhibits follow a stream from the mountains to the sea, including aquaria of mountain, Piedmont, and coastal species. Then the museum path leads outside for an easy streamside walk, with first-rate exhibits on Appalachian forest ecology, wildlife, and management. The museum tour ends with a walk through the working fish hatchery, its long concrete troughs filled with trout. Given the ownership of this museum, as well as its being funded by hunting and fishing licenses, expect a subtle prohunting (and an unsubtle profishing) slant to the displays. There is a good picnic area at the far end of the parking lot, as well as trails to the top of John Rock with stunning views.

W.N.C. AIR MUSEUM

**Western North Carolina Air Museum** (wncairmuseum.com; e-mail: inf02009@WNCAirMuseum.com; 828-698-2482; P.O. Box 2343, Hendersonville, NC 28793). Open Wed., Sat., and Sun. in the afternoon. This small air museum, run by local enthusiasts, has beautifully restored and fully operational small historic aircraft, including World War I fighters and small private aviation craft. It occupies a modern metal hanger on the grounds of Hendersonville's small airport, south of town off US 25 on Brooklyn Ave.

**GARDENS AND PARKS Skytop Orchard** (www.skytoporchard.com; 828-692-7930; P.O. Box 302, Flat Rock, NC 28731). Open daily. August–October, 9 AM–6 PM. Located on a side road off US 25 near the center of Flat Rock, this u-pick apple orchard has stunning views from 50 acres of handsome orchards straddling the Blue

Ridge. Pickers have 20 varieties of apples to choose from; there are also hayrides, farm animals to pet, picnicking, and a farmstand during the picking season. From US 25, turn west on Pinnacle Mountain Road and follow the signs.

**Conestee Falls** Although signs along US 276 south of Brevard advertise a residential subdivision named Conestee Falls, there is an actual waterfall and it is definitely worth a stop if you are in the area. You'll find it behind the development's realtor office along side the main highway, 6 miles south of town. A well-built path leads perhaps a hundred feet to a railed overlook with an excellent view over a double waterfall.

**South Brevard Park** This local park, two blocks west of downtown Brevard on US 64, offers a small but worthwhile native plant garden. Covering perhaps half a block, it has a wide range of flowers blooming April to October, displayed from a system of wide rectangular paths with plenty of benches.

**Jump off Rock Park** This local park outside Hendersonville offers panoramic 270-views over the valley of the French Broad River, toward the mile-high crest of the Pisgah Ridge, from a large projecting rock. To find it, take 5th Avenue west from downtown Hendersonville; then continue on Laurel Park Highway until you reach its end, 4.4 miles from downtown. Actually, Laurel Park Highway is a hoot—a genuine 1920s-era main road, complete with its original concrete surface, that curves uphill through an old, wealthy, mountainside subdivision with 80-year-old mansions spread through the trees. Jump off Rock Park, at its end, is a landscaped picnic and walking area, where the cliff-like sides of this small mountain become undeniable cliffs. Apart from the views, this is a pleasant, cool, and attractive spot.

## ✷ To Do

**WHITEWATER ADVENTURES** **Headwaters Outfitters** (headwatersoutfitters.com; 828-877-3106; P.O. Box 1057, Rosman, NC 28772). Open daily. April–October, 9 AM–5 PM.Headwaters Outfitters is located approximately 9 miles west of Brevard on the right at the intersection of US 64 and NC 215. Comprised of 50 miles of serpentine still water on the French Broad River, Headwaters Outfitters offers canoe and kayak sales, rentals, and shuttled trips.

**FISHING** **Davidson River Outfitters** (davidsonflyfishing.com; e-mail: info@davidsonflyfishing.com; 888-861-0111, 828-877-4181; 95 Pisgah Hwy., Pisgah Forest, NC 28768). This full-service fly-fishing shop, located north of Brevard near the intersection of US 64 and US 276 (in the same building as Hawg Wild BBQ), dispenses good advice as well as arranging guide service to the rich streams of the Pisgah National Forest. Their web page is worth checking for information on local streams.

**BICYCLING** **Backcountry Outdoors** (www.backcountryoutdoors.com; e-mail: info@backcountryoutdoors.com; 828-884-8670; 49 Pisgah Hwy., Ste. 6, Pisgah Forest, NC 28768). This outdoor supply store, located north of Brevard on US 276, specializes in outdoor activities in the Pisgah National Forest; they have trail bike rentals, trail maps, and guided trail bike trips.

**GOLF** **Etowah Valley Country Club and Golf Lodge** (etowahvalley.com; e-mail: info@etowahvalley.com; 800-451-8174, 828-891-7022; 470 Brickyard Rd.,

Etowah, NC 28729). Open all year. Three nine-hole courses give a choice of play in this championship course, noted for its mountain views and beautifully landscaped floral edges.

**Crooked Creek Golf Club** (828-692-2011; 764 Crooked Creek Rd., Hendersonville, NC 28739). Located just south of Hendersonville, this mainly rustic course follows a stream along a valley bottom, with water in play in 12 of its 18 holes. The clubhouse occupies an old Warner Bros. retreat.

**Orchard Trace Golf Club** (828-685-1006; 942 Sugarloaf Rd., Hendersonville, NC 28792). This 1993 18-hole course is located in Apple Country, just north of Hendersonville a mile or so off US 64. It features large greens and sloping terrain.

**Highland Lake Golf Course** (828-692-0143; 111 Highland Lake Rd., Flat Rock, NC 28731). Open all year. This nine-hole course near the center of Flat Rock (not part of the Highland Lake Inn resort) is fairly level, with four water hazards.

## ✷ Lodging

### COUNTRY INNS AND HOTELS

**The Claddagh Inn** (www.claddaghinn.com; e-mail: innkeepers@claddaghinn.com; 866-770-2999, 828-693-6737; 755 N. Main St., Hendersonville, NC 28792). Open all year. This lovely old inn sits on downtown Hendersonville's Main Street, a large late-Victorian mansion surrounded by its own lawn and shaded by giant oak trees. It's an oasis of calm charm within an easy stroll of downtown's first-rate restaurants and shopping. The three-story Classical-Revival house, listed on the National Register, features an extra-wide wraparound front porch and a cute second-story balcony. The 14 en suite guest rooms, all comfortable to large in size with telephone, television, and air conditioning, are individually furnished in Victorian antiques and reproductions. Guests are treated to a hearty country breakfast and an evening glass of sherry.

**The Woodfield Inn** (www.woodfieldinn.com; e-mail: info@woodfieldinn.com; 800-533-6016, 828-693-6016; 2905 Greenville Hwy., P.O. Box 98, Flat Rock, NC 28731). Open all year. In operation since its founding in 1852, this National Register ante-bellum stagecoach inn sits on 28 acres at the center of Flat Rock. Surrounded by landscaped parkland, the 18-room Italianate structure has wide verandahs on its first and second floor. The en suite rooms are individually themed with Victorian decor, including antiques; guests can choose rooms with private verandahs, whirlpool tubs, and views. The hearty breakfast is served in the inn's restaurant, which serves lunch and dinner to the public.

### RESORTS

**The Highland Lake Inn** (www.hlinn.com; e-mail: ksmith@hlinn.com; 800-635-5101, 828-693-6812; 86 Lilly Pad Ln., Flat Rock, NC 28731). Situated amongst 26 gently wooded acres on a serene lake, this full-service resort in the center of Flat Rock has a modern inn and a historic lodge. Resort amenities include fishing, lake swimming, pool swimming, canoeing, paddle boating, volley ball, horse shoes, and on-site walking trails. The site also boasts an extensive organic farm operation that supplies its first-rate restaurant. The contemporary inn has 16 large and airy rooms; the historic lodge, recently renovated, has 20 more rooms. Modest cabin duplexes, simple structures with board-and-batten walls and covered porches, make up the economy end of the lodgings, while quaint cottages with full kitchens make up the high end.

## BED & BREAKFAST INNS

**The Flat Rock Inn** (flatrockbb.com; e-mail: fribb@bellsouth.net; 800-266-3996, 828-696-3273; fax: 828-692-7755; 2810 Greenville Hwy./P.O. Box 308, Flat Rock, NC 28731). Open all year. A classic four-room bed & breakfast, this 1888 National Register mansion sits comfortably off US 25 on its own tree-shaded property at the center of the village of Flat Rock. Originally built as a summer residence for a wealthy Charlestonian, its wraparound porches and second-story balconies peek out from between the trees. Homemade afternoon sweets are served from the wide porch, or in the parlor, while a traditional formal dining room furnishes the venue for the gourmet country breakfasts. A butler's pantry has tea and custom blended coffee for guests, as well as a guest refrigerator well-stocked with wine and ice cream as well as the usual soft drinks. Each of the large air-conditioned guest rooms is individually furnished in Victorian antiques and has a private bath; two have private porches.

**Mélange Bed & Breakfast** (www.melangebb.com; e-mail: mail@melangebb.com; 800-303-5253, 828-697-5253; 1230 Fifth Ave. W, Hendersonville, NC 28739). This five-room bed & breakfast occupies a 1920 Colonial-Revival mansion in an upscale residential section of Hendersonville. The interior of this simple Colonial design is an elaborate French Empire concoction, first installed by a 1960s francophile owner and lovingly restored by the current owners. All five en suite rooms are large, with decor both luxurious and comfortable; features (varying by room) may include wood-burning fireplaces, whirlpool baths, sitting areas, wet bars, and a private deck. Full gourmet breakfasts are served on a flagstone patio in the rose garden, weather permitting.

**The Red House** (www.brevardbedandbreakfast.com; e-mail: info@brevardbedandbreakfast.com; 828-884-9349; 412 West Probart St., Brevard, NC 28712). Open all year. Established as a trading post before Brevard existed, the Red House served as the town's first train station and as the founding location for Brevard College, a local four-year liberal arts school. The inn sits on a hill just north of downtown, surrounded by lawns. Painted brick red, it has first- and second-story wraparound porches and third-story dormers. Inside, its furnished with Victorian antiques in rather a country style, including the four guest rooms. The rate includes a full country breakfast.

**Key Falls Bed & Breakfast** (keyfallsinn.com; e-mail: keyfallsinn@citcom.net; 828-884-7559; 151 Everett Rd., Pisgah Forest, NC 28768). This large two-story farmhouse from the 1860s sits on 35 acres by the French Broad River, 3 miles east of Brevard. Its well-kept gardens and meadows give views toward the river and the mountains beyond, while the large property contains a pond, tennis courts, and hiking trails (including one to the lovely Key Falls, on site). Comfortable common areas and five guest rooms are furnished with Victorian decor, including antiques. The room rate includes a full breakfast.

## CABIN RENTALS

**Lakemont Cottages** (www.lakemontcottages.com; e-mail: reservations@lakemontcottages.com; 800-597-0692, 828-693-5174; fax: 828-693-5174; 101 Lakemont Dr., Flat Rock, NC 28731). Open all year.

Lakemont features 14 pleasant modern cottages spread around a rolling, wooded tract south of Hendersonville, not far off US 176. A small lake (or large pond) makes up the centerpiece of this little village. Cottages have separate bedrooms and full kitchens, as well as enclosed porches.

## ✷ Where to Eat

**EATING OUT Cypress Cellar** (828-698-1005; 321-C N. Main St., Hendersonville, NC 28792). Located in a roomy, airy space below sidewalk level in downtown Hendersonville, the Cypress Cellar features authentic dishes from southern Louisiana, for lunch and dinner. The lunch menu features hot Cajun dishes as well as sandwiches and burgers, including muffulettas and po-boys on bread from Gambino's of New Orleans, fried green tomatoes on jalapeño cheddar grits, gumbo, red beans and rice, jambalaya, and crawfish cakes. The dinner menu drops the sandwiches, and adds a variety of steak, pasta, and seafood entrées. On weekend evenings, it's a popular venue for live music.

**Rocky's Soda Shop & Grill** (ddbullwinkels.com/Rockys; 828-877-5375; 46 South Broad St., Brevard, NC, 28766). Open Mon.–Sat., 11:00 AM–5:30 PM; Sun., noon–5 PM; extended hours in summer. *In downtown Brevard, on US 64.* This nostalgic store front in the center of downtown Brevard has burgers, hot dogs, and sandwiches, but the emphasis is on its old-fashioned soda fountain. Counter service with round stools and round tables with red-backed wire chairs, it's decor steps back in time a half century—as does its ice creams, floats, sundaes, and banana splits.

**DINING OUT The Highlands Lake Inn** (www.hlinn.com; e-mail: ksmith@hlinn.com; 800-635-5101, 828-693-6812; 86 Lily Pad Ln., Flat Rock, NC 28731). Open for breakfast, 7:30 AM–10:00 AM; lunch, 11:30 AM–2:00 PM; dinner, 5 PM–9 PM; closed Sun.; closed January–April. The dining room of the Highlands Lake Inn describes its fare as "fine country garden cuisine." The description is literal; much of the Highlands Lake's vegetables, salads, and even their herbs and seasonings come from the inn's organic gardens. Sitting on 180 lakefront acres in Flat Rock, just off US 25, this attractive restaurant offers all three meals to nonguests. Lunches offer salads made from their own garden vegetables, and sandwich favorites with an original twist. The extensive dinner menu marries fish, fowl, or meat with exciting combinations of vegetables and cheeses, and includes some impressive vegetarian dishes.

## ✷ Entertainment

**HENDERSONVILLE AND FLAT ROCK Flat Rock Playhouse** (flatrockplayhouse.org; e-mail: boxoffice@flatrockplayhouse.org; 828-693-0403; fax: 828-693-6795; 2661 Greenville Hwy./P.O. Box 310, Flat Rock, NC 28731). The State Theater of North Carolina, this professional Actor's Equity Company performs nine or so productions at its barnlike theater on US 25 in Flat Rock. The town's namesake rock is on its property.

**Hendersonville Symphony Orchestra** (www.hendersonvillesymphony.org; 828-697-5884; 228 Sixth Ave. East, Ste. A/P.O. Box 1811, Hendersonville, NC 28793). Hendersonville is probably the only small-town rural county seat with its own full-size symphony orchestra. Made up of talented local musicians, it's led by Music Director and Conductor Thomas Joiner, Professor of Violin and Orchestra Activities at Furman University and Concertmaster of the

Brevard Music Festival. Performing at various local venues (including the high school auditorium), its typical concert season includes a pops concert, a Christmas concert, and a couple of traditional classical concerts with guest soloists.

**BREVARD** ♿ **Brevard Music Festival** (brevardmusic.org; 828-862-2100; fax: 828-884-2036; 349 Andante Ln./P.O. Box 312, Brevard, NC 28712). June—August (box office opens in April). Students at the Brevard Music Center combine with top-notch professional musicians to put on a summer-long series of performances—typically 50 or so. Events include symphony orchestras, chamber music, popular music, musicals, and fully staged operas.

## ✱ Selective Shopping

**DOWNTOWN HENDERSONVILLE**

Hendersonville's five-block downtown remains utterly dominated by turn-of-the-century two- and three-story buildings, facing a landscaped Main Street. The main highway, US 25, splits down one-way streets that flank the back sides of these downtown blocks, leaving Main to shoppers and people looking for parking places. Now one of the classier shopping districts in the mountains, downtown's old storefronts are dominated by art and fine crafts galleries, antique shops, gift shops, specialty shops, and restaurants—90 retailers and eateries in all. The Main Street shopping district is bordered on the north by US 64, and on the south by the old and distinguished Henderson County Courthouse. Parking is free along Main Street, and 25 cents for two hours on four metered lots along US 25.

**Dad's Cats** (dadscats.com; e-mail: dadscats2@aol.com; 828-698-7525; 221 N. Main St., Hendersonville, NC 28792). Dad's Cats one-ups your normal model railroad shop with a large selection of model industrial cranes and construction equipment. Owned by a retired design engineer who specialized in earthmoving equipment, Dad's Cats likes to stock limited, serial-numbered diecast scale models. They also have model cars, trucks, fire equipment, and—yes—train layout items, as well as educational toys and collectable model horses.

**Wickwire Fine Art/Folk Art** (wickwireartgallery.com; e-mail: info@wickwireartgallery.com; 888-692-6220, 828-692-6222; fax: 828-692-6870; 330 N. Main St., Hendersonville, NC 28792). This commercial fine arts gallery features a wide variety of arts and fine crafts from local and regional artists. It's artists include three Smithsonian artisans and two artists who have been declared "North Carolina Living Treasures."

**Henderson County Farmer's Curb Market** (828-692-8012; 221 N. Church St., Hendersonville, NC 28792). Open May–December: Tues., Thurs., and Sat., 8 AM–2 PM; January—April: Tues. and Sat., 9 AM–1 PM. Located just outside downtown behind the Old County Courthouse (facing southbound US 25), this nonprofit organization has 137 vendors, all of whom are from Henderson County and all of whom offer only locally made or grown items. In continuous operation since 1924, some of its vendors are now in their third or fourth generation.

**FLAT ROCK Hand in Hand** (www.handinhandgallery.com; e-mail: info@handinhandgallery.com; 828-697-7719; fax: 828 697-7702; 2720 Greenville Hwy./P.O. Box 735, Flat Rock, NC 28731). Open Tues.–Sat., 10 AM–5 PM.

This fine crafts gallery, specializing in professional local artists, offers a wide variety of fine crafts, both traditional and contemporary. Look for the bright blue roadside building toward the center of Flat Rock.

**Forge Mountain Foods** (forgemountain.com; 800-823-6743, 838-692-9470; fax: 828-692-9917; 1215 Greenville Hwy., Flat Rock, NC 28731). This small specialty food company maintains its outlet store in an attractive modern building along US 25 in Flat Rock. Forge Mountain makes a wide variety of traditional southern-style gift foods—jellies, jams, fruit butters, honey, molasses, sorghum, syrups, relishes, ciders, candies, shortbreads, cakes, hams, and that sort of thing—and sells them all from this roadside company store.

TRANSYLVANIA COUNTY COURTHOUSE, DOWNTOWN BREVARD

**DOWNTOWN BREVARD Heart of Brevard** (brevardnc.org; e-mail: heartofbrvd@comporium.net; 828-884-3278; fax: 828-884-4209; 175 East Main St., Ste. 200, Brevard, NC 28712). This four-block classic small-town Main Street centers on its beautiful and well-kept Transylvania County Courthouse. For the past decade it's been evolving from rural downtown to an upscale shopping district; you can still get your hair cut and shoes repaired, but you can browse for art and antiques as well.

**Number 7 Arts** (number7arts.com; e-mail: info@number7arts.com; 828-883-2294; 7 East Main St., Brevard, NC 28712). This fine arts and crafts cooperative, sponsored by the Transylvania County Arts Council, is made up of local artists selected by an impartial jurying process. It displays a wide range of media and styles, and always has a local artist/member on hand.

**Red Wolf Gallery** (redwolfgallerync.com; e-mail: redwolfgallery@comporium.net; 828-862-8620; 8 East Main St., Brevard, NC 28712). This fine arts gallery represents well-known professional artists, mainly from the Appalachian region, with a decidedly contemporary slant.

**The Forest Place** (theforestplace.com; 800-660-0671; 66 Broad St., Brevard, NC 28712). This ecology-oriented gift and book shop is owned and operated by The Cradle of Forestry Interpretive Association, a nonprofit organization that supports The Cradle of Forestry in America and other educational efforts of the Pisgah National Forest. You'll find a wide range of books, gifts, art, toys, and educational material—all dealing with forest ecology in the Smokies and the Blue Ridge.

**CEDAR MOUNTAIN COMMUNITY** This rural community, stretched along US 276, 10 miles south of Brevard, is home to several highly respected craft artists who maintain galleries and open studios.

**Mountain Forest Studio** (828-885-2149; Greenville Hwy.). Open Mon.–Sat., 10 AM–5 PM. This white stucco farmhouse on US 276, 3 miles south of Brevard holds the studios of potter Mary Murray. It features the work of several other local artists as well.

## ✷ Special Events

**SPRING Poetry Celebration at the Carl Sandburg Home** (828-693-4178). Last weekend in April. This two-day festival, sponsored by the National Park Service on the grounds of the Carl Sandburg Home National Historic Site, features poetry readings by school children, college students, and well-known guest poets, in addition to poetry workshops.

**Johnson Farm Festival** (828-891-6585). Last Saturday in April. This fundraiser for the nonprofit organization that runs the Johnson Farm museum features mountain crafters and musicians (including fiddles and dulcimers), old-time mountain food, craft exhibits, and farm demonstrations—as well as the full range of museum features.

**SUMMER The North Carolina Apple Festival** (ncapplefestival.org; e-mail: apple@ncapplefestival.org; 828-697-4557; fax: 828-698-1629; P.O. Box 886, Hendersonville, NC 28793). Labor Day weekend. This four-day festival in downtown Hendersonville celebrates the local apple industry. Six blocks of Main Street are filled with 150 vendors and two music stages, while apple-related activities and demonstrations go on throughout the county. The festival ends with a downtown Labor Day parade.

**AUTUMN** ✐ **Brevard Halloween Festival** (828-883-3700). Last Saturday in October. This annual festival features a costume parade, crafts, food vendors, and music.

# NORTH OF ASHEVILLE: THE BALD MOUNTAINS

North of Asheville, the mountains extend in a grand tumble for mile after mile. This is an area of tangled ridgelines where craggy tops can suddenly change to wide, broad meadows, a place where streams drop over waterfalls into sharp-sided valleys. It's also a region of broad rivers that flow through deep gorges to empty into broad, rich valleys, where isolation keeps towns tiny and unspoiled. Opportunities for outdoor enjoyment are remarkable and widespread: the French Broad River, a first-rate kayaking and rafting river with spectacular gorge scenery; the Bald Mountains, straddling the state line with 50,000 rugged acres open to the public; Max Patch, one of the most beautiful sunset peaks anywhere. Most tourism focuses on the tiny, remote town of Hot Springs, where there is a good choice of quality bed-and-breakfasts and restaurants.

**GUIDANCE—TOWNS AND COUNTRYSIDE** **Madison County Tourism Development Authority** (www.visitmadisoncounty.com; 877-262-3476, 828-680-9031; fax: 828-689-2217; P.O. Box 1527, Mars Hill, NC 28754). This agency maintains a visitors center in a restored historic house near the center of Mars Hill.

**Madison County Chamber of Commerce** (www.madisoncounty-nc.com). This chamber maintains a thorough-going website, worth consulting.

**Greene County Partnership** (www.greenecountypartnership.com; e-mail: vandrew@greenecop.com; 423-638-4111; fax: 423-638-5345; 115 Academy St., Greeneville, TN 37743). This consolidated agency promotes tourism and economic development for Greene County, Tennessee, in the northeastern part of this chapter's area. Their website, heavy on multimedia, has a lot of information; but understand that this county stretches a very long distance away from the mountains, and you need to check distances before you commit.

**Newport/Cocke County Tourism Council** (cockecounty.com; e-mail: Tourism@CockeCounty.com; 423-625-9675; fax: 423-623-7216; 433 B Prospect Ave., Newport, TN 37821). Again, heavy on the multimedia, this website nevertheless has lots of good information about the northwestern part of this chapter's area. As with adjacent Greene County, Cocke County extends for some distance outside the mountains, so check locations first.

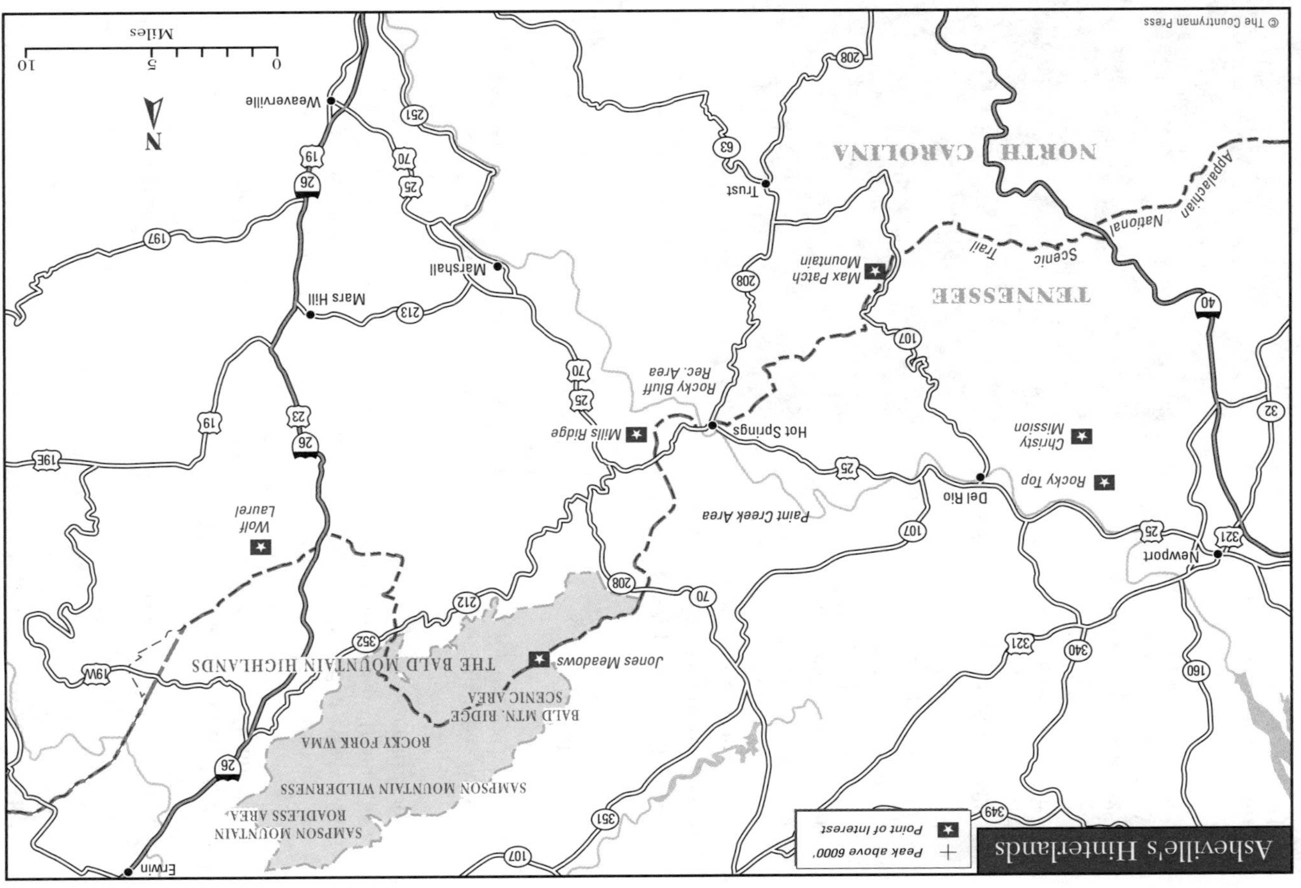
Asheville's Hinterlands
Peak above 6000'
Point of Interest
SAMPSON MOUNTAIN ROADLESS AREA
SAMPSON MOUNTAIN WILDERNESS
ROCKY FORK WMA
BALD MTN. RIDGE SCENIC AREA
THE BALD MOUNTAIN HIGHLANDS
Erwin
Wolf Laurel
Jones Meadows
Mars Hill
Marshall
Weaverville
Mills Ridge
Rocky Bluff Rec. Area
Hot Springs
Paint Creek Area
Trust
Max Patch Mountain
Del Rio
Rocky Top
Christy Mission
Newport
TENNESSEE
NORTH CAROLINA
Appalachian National Scenic Trail
N
0 5 10
Miles
26
19W
19E
19
23
197
352
212
107
351
208
70
25
213
251
63
349
321
340
160
32
40
© The Countryman Press

**GUIDANCE—PARKS AND FORESTS** **Pisgah National Forest, North Carolina** (828-622-3202; P.O. Box 128, Hot Springs, NC 28743). The French Broad Ranger District is responsible for all of the Pisgah National Forest lands in this region. It maintains an information desk at its office on US 25 in Hot Springs.

**Cherokee National Forest, Tennessee** (www.fs.fed.us/r8/Cherokee; 423-638-4109; fax: 423-638-6599; 4900 Asheville Hwy. [TN 70], Greeneville, TN 37743). The ranger station for the Tennessee half of this chapter's area is located just north of the national forest lands on TN 70, 5 miles south of Greeneville, Tennessee.

**GETTING THERE** *By Car* This area is bisected by US 25/70, a two-lane U.S. highway running between I-40 at Newport, Tennessee, and I-26 at Weaverville, North Carolina; all four of the region's villages are on this highway. Tennessee's Bald Mountains, in the northeast quadrant of this area, are best reached from Greeneville, via TN 107 or TN 351.

*By Air* **Asheville Regional Airport** is the closest to most of this area. **Tri-Cities Regional Airport**, near Johnson City, Tennessee, is closer for those who are mainly interested in the Tennessee Bald Mountains.

*By Bus or Train* This region has no scheduled passenger service by either train or bus.

HOT SPRINGS VIEWED FROM THE APPALACHIAN TRAIL

**MEDICAL EMERGENCIES** **Hot Springs Health Program** (hotspringshealth-nc.org/centers; e-mail: info@hotspringshealth-nc.org). The Hot Springs Health Program is not a hospital, and does not maintain an emergency room. Rather, it is a rural primary care program with four clinics. For routine medical problems in this area, these are good people to contact.

**Mars Hill Medical Center** (828-689-3507; 119 Mountain View Rd., Mars Hill, NC 28754). Open Mon.–Sat., 9 AM–9 PM; Sun., 1 PM–9 PM.

**Mashburn Medical Center** (828-649-3500; 590 Medical Park Dr., Marshall, NC 28753). Open Mon.–Fri., 9 AM –5 PM; Sat., 2 PM–5 PM.

**Hot Springs Medical and Dental Center** (828-622-3245; 66 N.W. Hwy. 25/70, Hot Springs, NC 28743). Open Mon.–Fri., 9 AM–5 PM; Sat., 8 AM–noon.

**MEDICAL EMERGENCIES: NEARBY HOSPITALS** **Mission Memorial Hospital, Asheville,**

**North Carolina** (www.missionhospitals.org; 828-231-1111; 509 Biltmore Ave., Asheville, NC 28801). With western North Carolina's only Level II trauma facility, this huge hospital is located just south of downtown Asheville on Biltmore Avenue. This is the closest hospital for Mars Hill and Marshall; for Hot Springs, it's a toss-up between Asheville and the smaller hospital in Newport, Tennessee.

**Newport Medical Center** (laughlinmemorial.org; 865-625-2200; 435 Second St., Newport, TN 37821). Located near the center of Newport, Tennessee, this 103-bed hospital has the closest emergency room to the Del Rio area.

**Laughlin Memorial Hospital, Greeneville, Tennessee** (423-787-5000; 1420 Tusculum Blvd., Greeneville, TN 37745). This 230-bed hospital within Greenville, Tennessee, just east of the town center on US 11E, is the closest hospital to Tennessee's Bald Mountains.

## ✷ Exploring the Area

**EXPLORING BY CAR A Hot Springs Drive** *Leg #1* (*29.9 miles*): From Hot Springs, follow US 25 north 13 miles to Del Rio, Tennessee; then right on TN 107 13 miles to the state line; then continue straight ahead 3.3 miles on gravel SSR 1182, Max Patch Road, to Max Patch Parking Area.

*Leg #2* (*19.7 miles*): Continue on Max Patch Road 4.5 miles to Meadow Fork Road (SSR 1175); then left 3.6 miles to Caldwell Corner Road (SSR 1165); then right 2 miles to NC 209; then left 11.6 miles to Hot Springs.

This chapter's featured scenic drive links Hot Springs with Max Patch, visiting the western part of the district on the way there and back. Its first leg starts along the recently rebuilt US 25, switchbacking out of Hot Springs past a monument, then leaving town to make broad sweeps high above the **French Broad River**. As the river drops into a gorge far away on the right, the highway sweeps upward and away from it toward the Tennessee border, marked by a classic state line bar (once a common sight when much of the rural South was dry). From there the highway curves back to the French Broad River, crossing it on a long, old bridge with good views. The highway now follows the river closely, with broad views over it toward the fields and mountains beyond, reaching **Del Rio** in 4.5 miles. Despite its tiny size and obscurity, Del Rio featured prominently in two pop culture icons from the late 1960s—Catherine Marshall's best-selling religious novel ***Christy***, and the ribald bluegrass standard **"Rocky Top."** From there, the route runs through beautiful, hilly farming valleys, then climbs very steeply uphill to the crest of the Bald Mountains. Finally the road crosses the mountains into North Carolina, and immediately turns into the gravel Max Patch Road (SSR 1182). **Max Patch** itself, with its wide wildflower meadows and stunning 360-degree views over the Smokies and the Balds, is just beyond.

Past Max Patch, Max Patch Road becomes a beautiful ridgetop drive that alternates between deep forests and wide views over mountaintop pastureland. From there, our route turns east off the mountaintop, dropping through lovely valleys and over a side ridge to reach NC 209. Here a right turn will take you 2 miles to the tiny village of **Trust**, with a beautiful roadside chapel. However, the route goes left instead, heading back toward Hot Springs. On this stretch NC 209 passes through well-tended farm valleys with some fine old buildings, then curves steeply uphill to run along the top of the dramatic Spring Creek Gorge. There are three good views over the gorge, plus more views from the paths in **Rocky Bluffs Recreation Area**. From there, Hot Springs is only 3 miles away, for a total loop of 50 miles.

RAILROAD CROSSES THE FRENCH BROAD RIVER NEAR HOT SPRINGS

**EXPLORING ON FOOT** **Sampson Mountain Wilderness Walks** Sampson Mountain Wilderness trails are known for their waterfalls, their handsome forests, their good views—and their steep uphill pulls from the ends of valley roads. The trails that lead into the wilderness from **Horse Creek Picnic Area** possess all these virtues. The easier of the two follows Squibb Creek uphill, climbing 600 feet in 2.2 miles, through beautiful cove forests to a small, but particularly lovely waterfall. The second path, a mountain-climbing loop, leaves Squibb Creek after 0.4 miles, marked as TURKEYPEN CREEK TRAIL. This path climbs a steady 18-percent gradient through rich and varied forests, following a small, steep creek to finally gain a ridgeline. Then there's more steep climbing up along the ridge, whose xeric forests give way to large rock outcrops with spectacular views over the Sampson Wilderness. The trail reaches a ridgetop trail intersection at 2.5 miles, having gained 1,600 feet in that short distance. Turn right for a ridgeline walk back down to Squibb Creek.

**Max Patch Walks** A 4,630-foot peak marking the western end of the Bald Mountains, the Pisgah National Forest's Max Patch offers easy and dramatic walking across miles of mountaintop meadows. This walk starts at the trailhead parking lot. Go uphill through meadows, climbing 200 feet in a scant half-mile, gaining increasingly spectacular views on the way up. You'll probably pass hay bales; the Forest Service keeps these old cattle pastures from returning to scrubby forests by regular mowing and burning. At the top you will find a surveyor's monument marking the summit, and posts with white blazes marking the route of the Appalachian Trail through the grasses and flowers. Here the view is a complete circle of endlessly receding mountains. The mountains on the west are the Great Smokies; the ridges passing on to the northeast are the Bald Mountains. The Max Patch summit is a wonderful place for a sunset, and it's not uncommon to see people all over the ridge, picnicking and camping in an impromptu sunset party.

To extend the walk, follow the Appalachian Trail downhill to the left, dropping 400 feet. As the trail reaches a lower set of meadows it briefly merges with an old farm track running along the ridge. Follow this track along the ridge for another mile of stunning meadow views. When you reach the end, return by following the farm track all the way back to Max Patch Road. When you reach the road, your car is parked a thousand feet to the right.

**LONG-DISTANCE PATHS** **The Appalachian Trail** The Appalachian Trails spends 58 miles within this chapter's area, the first section northward from the Great Smoky Mountains National Park. It starts at the Pigeon River, 1,400 feet above sea level, and follows a ridgeline for 13 miles to the 4,629-foot peak of **Max Patch**, with its meadows and panoramic views. Here the trail finally leaves the state line and dives into North Carolina, this time skirting within view of farmland for its first time. This stretch is 17 miles of up-and-down—but mainly down, as the trail drops all the way back to 1,400 feet to go right through the middle of **Hot Springs**, the first of only two towns it enters. From there the trail crosses the **French Broad River** on US 23/70, then spends 5 miles exploring the 2,500-foot ridgeline along the river's right bank, a particularly pleasant walk with great views and large meadows. This is a good time for northerly through-hikers, who are welcomed into Hot Springs with the annual **TrailFest**, just in time for spring color to break out all through these lower elevation areas.

Then it's back to work as the trail once again enters deep forests and high elevations within endless national forestlands, in this case a climb back up to the crest of the Bald Mountains, a 19-mile section that finally regains the state line, then stays above 4,000 feet for 10 miles and a number of fine views, reaching 4,800 feet or more within the **Bald Mountain Scenic Area**. After that it drops precipitously for its last 5 miles to a good trailhead on NC 212, 23 miles east of Hot Springs via US 23/70.

## ✷ Villages

**Mars Hill** Mars Hill is a handsome hilltop college town, with a one-block downtown adjacent to the tree-shaded, red-brick campus of **Mars Hill College**. Both the college and the village are compact, more like a New England college town than a Southern one, and people tend to get around on foot—along the downtown sidewalk with its old red-brick storefronts, through the campus on tree-shaded walks, and into the neighborhoods with their historic old houses. Mars Hill is located a mile off the main freeway, US 19/23 (Future I-26), on NC 209. Its single traffic light marks the center of town, with the campus straight ahead, the visitors center to the left, and downtown to the right.

THE APPALACHIAN TRAIL CROSSES MAX PATCH

**Marshall** Madison County's seat sits deep in a gorge, stretching for six blocks along the French Broad River. The river here is broad enough to have an island that once held the local elementary school, and is now a park—a popular venue for festivals. A major railroad line stretches along the river's east bank; then the town's center stretches along the railroad; then the town's residential area terraces up the side of the gorge behind downtown. The handsome old courthouse sits in the middle of downtown, its dome set against the green forests of the gorge wall behind it. A long, long time ago the main road from Asheville passed through the center of town; however, Marshall was bypassed in the 1950s, then the bypass was bypassed in the 1960s, then (in 2004) the bypassed bypass's bypass was bypassed by the new I-26. Nowadays, Marshall is very much off the beaten track, north of Asheville and a bit west of US 25.

**Hot Springs** Hot Spring's old downtown tries to stretch itself to three blocks. On those blocks are a little bit of everything—restaurants, a neat hardware store, a 1950s-style motel, a Forest Service ranger station, some houses, and several shops. However, this central business district gets an unusual boost from its sidewalk; this particular stretch of concrete is known to the world as **the Appalachian Trail**. The famous Georgia-to-Maine path descends into town from the mountains on the west, follows the sidewalk through town and across the French Broad River, then dives into the woods again. You'll see hikers with backpacks walking the sidewalk, sitting and resting on a bench, or inside one of the stores with their gear stored neatly in a corner.

COUNTRY ROAD NEAR MARSHALL

The other notable thing about Hot Springs is its remoteness. It's 30 minutes to the nearest town in either direction, down a twisting, two-lane highway (US 25). After a 1998 ice storm it took 10 days to restore power to parts of the area. Hot Springs tends to attract people who like it quiet and isolated, making for a tightly knit community of mountain people, free spirits, and folk dedicated to some serious relaxing. Most services are available at Hot Springs, including beer and wine service in the restaurants. US 25 runs through town from Asheville to Newport, Tennessee, and NC 209 forks away at the center of town to wander southward toward Waynesville.

**Del Rio** Del Rio is an old depot town in the Bald Mountains of Tennessee. Sitting by a siding near the banks of the French Broad River, it consists of a straggle of old buildings along TN 107 just off US 25. While Del Rio itself offers little reason to slow down (aside from an occasional dog sleeping on the road), the surrounding mountains are remarkably scenic. Del Rio was the model for "El Plano" in Catherine Marshall's 1968 novel ***Christy*** and the actual mission portrayed in that novel makes for an interesting visit.

## ✱ Wild Places

### *The Bald Mountain Highlands*

For the most part, the steep-sided Bald Mountains are known for two things: dividing North Carolina from Tennessee, and carrying 20 miles of the **Appalachian Trail**. Less well known are its nearly **50,000 contiguous acres** of recreational wild lands—about 75 square miles. To the hikers, fishers, hunters, and campers who use this area, it's one giant tract of remote mountain land, a land filled with craggy ridgelines, mountaintop meadows, hidden coves, waterfalls, and a single, continuous hardwood forest that has not been disturbed for more than 60 years. However, to the powers-that-be it's five separate tracts: one (Shelton Laurel Backcountry Area) owned by the Pisgah National Forest in North Carolina, three (Sampson Mountain Wilderness Area, Sampson Mountain Roadless Area, and Bald Mountain Ridge Scenic Area) owned by the Cherokee National Forest in Tennessee, and one (Rocky Fork/Cherokee WMA) leased by the State of Tennessee from a lumber company.

**Shelton Laurel Backcountry Area** This remote tract of North Carolina's Pisgah National Forest was the site of one of the most notorious of the Civil War's killings: the Shelton Laurel Massacre, where Confederate regulars, acting under orders, murdered 13 local Unionist farmers and hid the bodies in a mass grave. The victims were traditionalist mountain folk who believed that God had established the Union and that the flatlander Confederates were rebels against God's will. In turn, the most radical Confederates considered these Unionist mountain folk to be traitors who deserved death. Such killings occurred throughout the mountains, but were usually done by marauding gangs of irregulars. The Shelton Laurel Massacre was exceptional for its brutality—13 males killed, some of them children—and for being an official act of the Confederate Army.

Today, Shelton Laurel is a backcountry forest, managed by the Pisgah National Forest for rugged outdoor recreation. Here, mixed hardwood forests cover the steep southern slopes of the Bald Mountains, crossed by hiking trails that not uncommonly climb 2,000 feet or more. Two popular (and very difficult) loops climb from Big Creek to the Appalachian Trail, with stunning views back over the Laurel; to find the trailhead, take NC 212 to Big Creek Road (SSR 1312, opposite Carmen Church), then north to the trailhead. A second trailhead (NC 212, then north on Hickey Fork Road, SSR 1310) leads to an easy forest walk up and old road to remote, meadow-covered Whiteoak Flats, where a half-mile trail goes right to a waterfall.

**The Sampson Mountain Wilderness Area and Roadless Area** Part of Tennessee's Cherokee National Forest, these two areas protect nearly 15,000 acres of the north slope of the Balds, near Erwin, Tennessee. They cover an area of quickly maturing second-growth forest, last logged in the 1920s. These two areas are noted for their **waterfalls**, as well as their attractive forests and good views. In fact, a waterfall deep in the unpathed backcountry is claimed by some to be the tallest in the East rather than **Whitewater Falls** (see "The Blue Ridge: Cashiers & Highlands," *Wild Places*)—but lack of access, poor views, and no official measurements leave the matter in doubt. The Sampson Mountains are also noted for trails with long, steep uphill pulls, starting at the ends of the valley roads and going straight up the steep flanks of the Balds. The most popular trailhead, at **Horse Creek Picnic Area**, gives a good sampling of all of these qualities.

**Bald Mountain Ridge Scenic Area** West of the Sampson Mountain Wilderness, the Tennessee Bald Mountains are protected for recreationists as the Bald Mountain Ridge Scenic Area. Unlike a wilderness area, this scenic area allows a broad range of recreation (while prohibiting logging). ORVs are allowed on some trails, and three remote sites can be reached by passenger cars. One, Forge Creek Campground (a side road from Horse Creek Picnic Area), is a seasonal campground and trailhead for the notably beautiful Jennings Creek Trail. The second, **Round Knob Picnic Area**, features a hair-raising mountain drive to a lovely little CCC picnic spot. The third leads to the remarkable **Jones Meadows**, high on the crest of the Balds.

**The Rocky Fork Unit of the Cherokee Wildlife Management Area** This 10,000-acre tract of private land has been leased by the state of Tennessee as a hunting area for the last 60 years. At this writing the state still leases it, and it remains open to hikers when hunting isn't going on. It's an important tract, separating the Sampson Mountain Wilderness from the Appalachian Trail, and abutting the Shelton Laurel Backcountry. It shares the virtues of these publicly owned tracts—spectacular views, waterfalls, rugged & rocky scenery, and deep gorges. Trails are not developed, but hunters' trails exist, and access tracks lead deep into its center. Approach it from I-26 south of Erwin, Tennessee, by taking TN 352 4.4 miles to a right on Rocky Fork Road, then another 0.9 mile to the trailhead.

**THE FORESTS OF HOT SPRINGS** **The Paint Rock Area** Just east of Hot Springs a large tract of national forest land extends upward from the French Broad River, with high peaks, wildflower meadows, impressive waterfalls, and a long section of the **Appalachian Trail**. Historically, its most famous landmark has been Paint Rock, a tall red cliff that loomed above the Buncombe Turnpike, an 1820s road that opened up the mountains—a section now preserved as gravel Paint Rock Road, on the east bank of the French Broad River. The road follows the river until it passes under Paint Rock, then crosses into Tennessee and turns abruptly inland to follow Paint Creek. This is an impressive drive, hugging close to Paint Creek to pass a whole series of waterfalls, some quite large. There are several good picnic areas as well.

Over the river from Hot Springs and south of US 25, the Appalachian Trail climbs the bluffs above the French Broad River for wide, clifftop views. From there it wanders into a series of meadows on the rolling 2,500-foot top of Mill Ridge. Passenger cars can make it to the near edge of the Mill Ridge meadows by taking US 25 about 4 miles west of town, to make a left onto a side road and cross over the highway on a viaduct; from there it's only a mile up a gravel Forest Service road. There's a loop bicycle path and lots of good exploring. Nearby (at the intersection of US 25 and NC 208), another hiking/biking path leads gently downhill to the French Broad River at the remote, abandoned siding town of Runion. The trail follows an old lumber railroad grade along the remarkably beautiful Laurel Creek, gently falling ever deeper into the gorge.

**Max Patch** Known as the "Jewel of the Appalachians," remote 4,600-foot Max Patch is crowned with wide wildflower meadows. The best known and best loved part of a large tract of Pisgah and Cherokee National Forest lands, Max Patch is an easy introduction to this little-visited corner of the country, with a trailhead on **Max Patch Road** scarcely a half-mile from the summit. Grasslands cover its wide, rolling summit, and grasslands continue to flow down to the ridgelines 400 feet below. A 360-degree panorama surrounds a summit nearly always buffeted by high winds; the Great Smoky Mountains National Park is clearly visible to the west. Westward from Max Patch, the Harmon's Den Area of the Pisgah National Forest is crossed with hiking and horse trails. To the north, Tennessee's Cherokee National Forest conceals the lost mountain community of Wasp, its ruins hidden deep in the forest that has taken over its high, perched cove. Farther east, the Appalachian Trail pokes its way through a number of interesting little corners before making its final drop into Hot Springs.

**RIVERS The French Broad River** For most of its 218-mile length, the French Broad River meanders lazily through a wide flood plain, the haunt of canoeists rather than kayakers or rafters. For its uppermost 60 miles it remains steadily Class I, then breaks into Class II as it passes through the Asheville area and reaches Marshall, within this chapter's area. Then it gets lively. For 8 miles, between the settlement of Barnard just north of Marshall, to the US 25/70 bridge at Hot Springs, the French Broad bounces through a deep gorge, surrounded by national forest lands, with Class III–IV+ rapids. Then, as it reaches Hot Springs, the river reverts to its old self, becoming once again a fine Class I–II canoe stream through the mountains with lots of fishing access. Altogether, the French Broad River spends 48 miles in this chapter's area.

**RECREATION AREAS Jones Meadows on the Bald Mountains** Wide grassy meadows top the crest of the Balds at Jones Meadows, a remarkable site within the Bald Mountain Ridge Scenic Area of the Cherokee National Forest. The 8-mile gravel approach road, Bald Mountain Road (CR 58), can be charitably described as thrilling, with rough bumps up 4 miles of hairpin switchbacks. Nevertheless, it's worth the thrill, as wide wildflower meadows spread along the 4,500-foot crest. An attempted vacation subdivision went bankrupt here in 1989, to be snapped up by the Forest Service at auction; you'll see abandoned and decaying vacation cottages in the woods on all sides. The **Appalachian Trail** enters the meadows on your right, crosses them, and exits on your left. Park and follow it left (east). You'll quickly come to a side trail that leads 15 yards right to Whiterock Cliffs, with wide views south over North Carolina's **Shelton Laurel Backcountry**. Continue on, for another short trail left to the Blackstack Cliffs, with panoramic views north over the face of the Balds to Tennessee's Great Valley. There are no formal facilities up here, but plenty of places to spread a picnic blanket.

**Rocky Bluffs Recreation Area** NC 209 twists and turns its way south of Hot Springs to hack its way along the cliffs of the Spring Creek Gorge, with a couple of impressive views along the way. Three miles south of town along this scenic stretch of highway, the Rocky Bluffs Recreation Area furnishes picnicking and camping on the edge of the gorge. A short loop trail goes to a viewpoint before descending into the gorge, while a longer loop trail explores the steep slopes above the road.

**PICNIC AREAS** **Horse Creek Recreation Area** The Cherokee National Forest's Horse Creek Recreation Area centers on a deep, clear pool in a mountain creek, a popular swimming hole. The picnic area is up the road a short distance, with several tables under tall old trees. A popular **Sampson Mountain Wilderness** trailhead is here, with some fine walking. To reach it, take TN 107 to Horse Creek Road, CR 94, and follow the Forest Service signs.

**Round Knob Picnic Area** This tiny **CCC**-era picnic area snuggles deep under tall trees, halfway up Bald Mountains steep slopes. While this heavily forested site has no views, it is so high and steep that it gives the impression of an aerie. It has a shelter built of great logs, and a hand pump, along with a few tables. The 4.5-drive up the mountain is on Round Knob Road (FS 88), a one-lane gravel road, very steep and narrow, with some stunning views off the side. Directions: Find the intersection of TN 350 and TN 351 (it will be southeast of Greeneville on your map). From there, go toward the mountains (southeast) on Jones Bridge Road; and stay on it 1.25 miles as it curves left and becomes McCoy Road. In another mile, go right on Greystone Road, and stay on it 2.5 miles to a right on Round Knob Road.

## ✷ To See

### HISTORIC SITES

**The Christy Mission** (423-487-2648; 1425 Chapel Hollow Rd., Del Rio, TN 37727). Novelist Catherine Marshall based her best-seller *Christy* on her mother's life and work as a young teacher in a remote Appalachian mission above Del Rio, Tennessee (called El Plano in the novel). That original Presbyterian mission site, and all that remains of its buildings, are signposted, interpreted, and preserved by local resident Larry Meyers—whom fans of the novel will be delighted to learn is the grandson of "Fairlight Spencer" (Flora Corn). Such remote missions, bringing education, medicine, and religion to the inaccessible coves, were an important feature of the turn-of-the-century mountains. Times have changed, and formerly well-known missions have been lost; the Salvation Army's Max Patch Mission has long disappeared into the Pisgah National Forest, and the Methodist Church's Pittman Center Mission is now a country club and golf resort. The Christy mission is now the best place to get a feel for those difficult times. To find the mission at Chapel Hollow ("Cutter Gap" in the novel), take TN 107 south from Del Rio for 1 mile, then go right on Old 15th for 4.4 miles to Chapel Hollow Road.

A final note for fans of the 1996 CBS TV series: the location shots were done at **Townsend,** Tennessee, 60 miles west of Chapel Hollow (see "Townsend, Cades Cove, and the Northwest Quadrant," *Villages*). The actual Chapel Hollow sites lack the breathtaking mountain backdrops of the set created for television in Townsend. If you want to see the Townsend location sites, ask for directions at the visitors center.

**Rocky Top, Tennessee** Oddly enough, Felice and Boudleaux Bryant wrote the racy bluegrass standard "Rocky Top" at about the same time Catherine Marshall was writing *Christy*. You might not recognize these two pop icons of the 1960s as being about the same place—but they are. Rocky Top is a 2,400-foot peak separating Chapel Hollow (Christy's "Cutter Gap") from the town of Newport. The real life Christy, Leonora Whitaker, ran her small mountain school and mission immediately beneath Rocky Top, on its eastern slope, presumably not far from where the song's good old boys were making moonshine and whooping it up with the girls. Of course, this proximity is a complete coincidence; the Bryants picked "Rocky Top" merely because it sounded good in the song, and had no knowledge of the actual locale. Catherine Marshall's version is the one based in fact—not the Bryants.

So, can you visit Rocky Top? Well, yes. It's owned by the Cherokee National Forest, who maintains the bad narrow gravel Rocky Top Road (FS 402) to a high gap a few hundred yards from its summit. When field inspected in 2006, the road was passible, with some difficulty, by a passenger car in good weather. A large clear-cut made the peak itself unrewarding, but there was a nice view from a rocky outcrop near the gap. To get there from Newport, Tennessee, take US 25/70 east for 3.3 miles from its intersection with TN 73 to a right onto Pig Trot Road, then go 1 mile to a left onto Rocky Top Road, which becomes bad gravel FS 402 in 1.6 miles and reaches its effective end at Rocky Top Gap a mile later.

**CULTURAL SITES** **Country Workshops** (www.countryworkshops.org; e-mail: langsner@countryworkshops.org; 828-656-2280; 990 Black Pine Ridge Rd., Marshall, NC 28753). This craft school for serious hand-tooled woodworking occupies a remote farmstead high in the Shelton Laurels area. Founded by Drew Langner in 1978, it offers two- to six-day residency seminars and workshops that cover a wide variety of woodworking with hand tools; while most courses deal with furniture making, others deal with folk vernacular styles, woodcarving, green woodworking, making hand tools on a forge, and making a timber-frame building. Students stay in a dorm on the property, and eat hearty homemade meals together. Anyone serious about woodworking will want to visit the school's store, with a thorough line of high-end woodworking equipment and books. The school welcomes visitors, who should call ahead for directions (and to ensure that someone is there).

**Trust Chapel** (chapelofhopestories.com). Beverly Barutio built this 12 x 14-foot log chapel, dedicated to St. Jude, in 1990 in thanks for the curing of her cancer. It's a beautiful structure, built of logs and outfitted with a variety of handcrafted art objects. It's open during daylight hours, on NC 63 just south of its intersection with NC 209 in the community of Trust.

♿ **Mars Hill College** (www.mhc.edu; 866-642-4968; 100 Athletic St./P.O. Box 370, Mars Hill, NC 28754). The town of Mars Hill remains firmly centered on its 150-year-old Baptist liberal arts school, Mars Hill College, a four-year college with 1,500 students. Founded in 1856, it was one of a number of church-run boarding high schools, called "academies," in these mountains; such academies were the only real way that a mountain child could obtain any education beyond the local one-room schoolhouse. Mars Hill College entered its modern phase in 1896, when it began the long journey to becoming a fully accredited four-year college (in 1962). The modern campus evolved over this century. It's dominated by handsome red-brick buildings from every period, from elegant and beautiful late Victorian structures to recent modernist structures, looking slightly racy on this rural Baptist campus. The grounds are shaded and parklike, beautifully landscaped with native vegetation.

**Rural Life Museum** (www.mhc.edu/ramsey-center/rural-life-museum; 828-689-1262). Mars Hill College's History Department maintains the on-campus Rural Life Museum (the Montague Building), dedicated to the history and culture of the southern Appalachian Mountains. It includes a fascinating section on the hand-hooked rug industry, which was a Depression-era, three-million-dollar-a-year cottage industry in the Mars Hill area. **NOTE:** *At press time, this museum was CLOSED, undergoing extensive renavations, with no estimated reopen date. If you want to visit this facility, CALL FIRST to see if it has opened.*

**Weizenblatt Gallery** (www.mhc.edu/art/weizenblatt-gallery; e-mail: pmurray@mhc.edu; 828-689-1396). Mars Hill College Campus, Mars Hill, NC, 28754. Free. Part of the Art Department at Mars Hill College, the on-campus Weizenblatt Gallery features the works of students, faculty, and regional artists, and has regular exhibits highlighting the works of Southern artists.

## ✷ To Do

**WHITEWATER ADVENTURES** **Huck Finn River Adventures** (huckfinnrafting.com; 800-303-7238; 158 Bridge St./P.O. Box 366, Hot Springs, NC, 28743. Headquartered in Hot Springs, North Carolina, this outfitter leads whitewater rafting trips on the remote and beautiful French Broad River upstream from Hot Springs, and float trips on the calm waters downstream from Hot Springs. Special trips include an evening float trip with a sunset steak dinner, and an overnight river camping trip with a steak dinner and pancake breakfast.

**French Broad Rafting Company** (frenchbroadrafting.com; e-mail: raft@frenchbroadrafting.com; 800-570-7238; fax: 828-649-0516; 9800 US Hwy. 25/70, Marshall, NC 28753). Located north of Marshall, North Carolina, off US 25 near the French Broad River, this outfitter offers both whitewater and calm-water trips on different sections of the French Broad.

**Nantahala Outdoor Center (NOC)** (800-232-7238) This large outfitter, headquartered in Bryson City, North Carolina, has an outpost north of Marshall, North Carolina, on US 25 for whitewater trips on the French Broad River.

**USA Raft** (800-872-7238) This large rafting chain headquartered in Rowlesburg, West Virginia, maintains an outpost north of Marshall, North Carolina, on US 25, for excursions on the French Broad River.

**HORSEBACK RIDING AND LLAMA TREKKING** On a horseback ride, the horse carries you around. On the whole, llamas are too small to carry people. On a llama trek, llamas will carry all your food, water, and equipment, while you walk. The picnic lunch is the main point of most llama treks, and the main reason you take those llamas along. Another reason is that llamas are really, really cute, with an appealing, if unsettling, habit of coming up silently behind you to nuzzle your ear from above.

**English Mountain Llama Trekking** (www.hikinginthesmokies.com; e-mail: info@hikinginthesmokies.com; 828-622-9686; 767 Little Creek Rd., Hot Springs, NC 28743).Varies. Call or e-mail for rates. Owner Lucy Lowe leads llama treks in the Pisgah National Forest. Day treks include lunch; overnight treks include all gear and meals.

**Sandy Bottom Trail Rides** (www.sandybottomtrailrides.com; e-mail: info@sandybottomtrailrides.net; 800-959-3513, 828-649-3464; 155 Caney Fork Rd., Marshall, NC 28753). April–October. This stable offers half- and full-day trail rides, as well as overnighters, from their location in a beautiful rural valley west of Marshall.

**SKIING** **Wolf Laurel** (www.skiwolflaurel.com; e-mail: marketing@skiwolfridgenc.com; 800-817-4111, 828-689-4111; 578 Valley View Circle, Mars Hill, NC 28754). This ski slope is located on the leeward side of snow-magnet Bald Mountain, just below its crest. Maximum vertical drop is 700 feet from a high elevation of 4,650 feet, with 14 runs and four chairlifts. All runs have artificial snow and night lights.

## ✷ Lodging

**RESORTS** **Gannon's French Broad Outpost Ranch** (www.frenchbroadriver.com; 800-995-7678, 423-487-3147; 461 Old River Rd., Del Rio, TN 37727). Open all year. This ranch sits on the French Broad River near Del Rio, Tennessee, extending from the riverside meadows to the ridges above. A classic dude ranch, one price covers accommodations, all meals, and all activities. The ranch has a central lodge and related facilities built to look like an Old West town, which they dub "Rough Cut." Along with the four-room lodge, it contains the dining room, a dance hall, and a saloon. Accommodations consist of four good-size lodge rooms, four ridgetop cabins, and four tiny log "pioneer cabins" rather like old-fashioned tourist camp units. While all activities are optional, they include five days of horseback trail riding, three rafting trips (including one with some Class IV rapids), a 1-mile cattle drive ("it may not be a long drive, but it's the only one east of the Mississippi"), a fishing trip with a chuck wagon lunch, and a guided Appalachian Trail hike on Max Patch. There's also nightly entertainment, which may include live bluegrass, square dancing, campfires, naturalist talks, and wagon rides. Children of all age are welcome, and there are special activities just for kids under 12.

**BED & BREAKFAST INNS**

**The Magnolia Mountain Inn** (www.mountainmagnoliainn.com; e-mail: innkeepers@magnoliamountaninn.com; 800-914-9306, 828-622-3543; 204 Lawson St., Hot Springs, NC 28743). This elaborate 130-year-old Victorian house in Hot Springs, North Carolina, has been beautifully restored to a five-room bed & breakfast. It was built in 1868 by the only member of the South Carolina legislature to vote against succession at the outbreak of the Civil War; and it is no coincidence that it is located in the most Unionist corner of the South. It has 3 acres of gardens with a 100-year-old boxwood maze, vegetable and herb gardens (used in the food prepared for guests), and rhododendrons, all framed by spectacular mountain views. The five rooms (some with balconies) range from cozy to large, each with its own personality. There's also a 20th-century Garden Cottage, overlooking the vegetable gardens, with a beautifully decorated open plan very suitable for retreats or family gatherings. A full breakfast is included in the price (except for the Garden Cottage). Dinner is available to guests and nonguests on Fridays and Saturdays, for an extra charge.

**Duckett House Inn & Farm** (duckethouseinn.com; e-mail: duckett houseinn@frontier.com; 828-622-7621;

433 Lance Ave., P.O. Box 441, Hot Springs, NC 28743). Open all year. This 1900 Victorian-style house sits by NC 209 a half-mile outside of Hot Springs. It's the sort of fancy farmhouse that a wealthy man might have built, three stories with a wraparound front porch and lots of dormers. Today it is beautifully kept, with an eye-catching red tin roof. Inside, six tastefully decorated rooms are furnished with period antiques; all share baths. Breakfasts feature homemade breads and free-range eggs. In addition, there is a two-bedroom cottage on the property. Children of all ages are welcome in the cottage, while the main house is restricted to children over 12.

**Marshall House Bed & Breakfast Inn** (marshallhousebandb.com; e-mail: ruth@marshallhouse.org; 828-649-9205; fax: 828-649-2784; 100 Hill St., Marshall, NC 28753). Located in the center of the quaint and quiet town of Marshall, North Carolina, the Marshall House rises in stone terraces above the handsome old county courthouse. Designed by the same architect who built Biltmore Village, this 1903 National Register mansion is covered with pebbledash, with a 50-foot-long verandah rising from a tall stone wall and turreted on one end. The views from the verandah extend over the courthouse and town below, framed by the French Broad River and the mountains behind. Inside, the home is decorated with period antiques. One of the eight rooms has a queen bed, the remainder having twins or doubles; some of the rooms share baths. A full breakfast is included, and pets, children, and smokers are welcome.

**Bed and Breakfast at Ponder Cove** (pondercove.com; 828-689-7304; 1067 Ponder Creek Rd., Mars Hill, NC 28754). This bed & breakfast welcomes dogs and their people to its 90-acre tract in Ponder Cove, a particularly beautiful valley 6 miles from I-26 and 9 miles east of Mars Hill. The modern rural-style house has a large deck with views over the nicely landscaped property; the three en suite rooms range from large to very large, and have wood paneling and fireplaces.

**CABINS** **Mountain Valley View Cabins** (www.ncmountainview.com; e-mail: cabins@ncmountainview.com; 828-622-9587; 225 Mountain Valley Dr., Hot Springs, NC 28743). Open all year. Two log-clad traditional cabins sit on a grassy and shaded ridgetop 9 miles south of Hot Springs off NC 209. These bright, one-bedroom cabins are nicely decorated in a country style, and have picnic areas with barbeque pits, full front porches with rocking chairs, living rooms with wood stoves (plus gas heat), and full kitchens, along with such amenities as phones, washers and dryers, and satellite TV with HBO.

## ✱ Where to Eat

**EATING OUT** **Zuma Coffee** (828-649-1617; 7 North Main St., Marshall, NC 28753). Open for lunch. Located in an historic downtown building, across the street from Marshall's handsome old courthouse, this café serves truly excellent coffee, fresh baked goods, and sandwiches. Despite its trendy coffee shop persona this is a classic courthouse hangout, and sure to be full of suited lawyers and uniformed sheriff's deputies sipping espressos and lattes.

## ✱ Entertainment

### *Mars Hill*

**Southern Appalachian Repertory Theater (SART)** (sartplays.org; e-mail: sart@mhc.edu; 828-689-1384; fax: 828-689-1272; 44 College St., Mars Hill, NC 28754). Located in the 175-seat Owen Theater on the campus of Mars Hill College, SART is a nonprofit professional theater company whose performance schedule of plays and musicals always includes original plays from Appalachian authors.

*Del Rio*

**Hillbilly's Music Barn** (423-487-2655; Newport, TN 37727). Open Sat., 7 PM–10 PM. Free. Located deep in the mountains, Hillbilly's offers weekly live bluegrass music. It has a large dance floor and is family oriented. There's plenty of munchies and soft drinks, but no alcohol permitted. Near downtown Newport.

## * Special Events

**SPRING TrailFest at Hot Springs** Last weekend in April. This celebration of the **Appalachian Trail** brings the entire town out to commemorate the first great long-distance path in the world, and to welcome the throughhikers just beginning to walk along the downtown sidewalk that the trail follows.

**SUMMER Fourth of July Celebrations** All three Madison County, North Carolina, towns—Mars Hill, Marshall, and Hot Springs—have special Independence Day celebrations that climax with fireworks. Mars Hill and Hot Springs have live music and food (Mars Hill has a fish fry), with special attractions for the kids. Marshall's Volunteer Fire Department sponsors a rodeo on the island in the French Broad River opposite the courthouse.

**AUTUMN Madison County Heritage Festival** (828-689-9351). First Saturday in October. This Mars Hill street festival, just outside the 150-year-old Baptist college, celebrates its mountain heritage and traditions with booths and craft demonstrations from a variety of local mountain people.

# The Great Smoky Mountains National Park

3

GATLINBURG &
THE NORTHEAST QUADRANT

TOWNSEND, CADES COVE, &
THE NORTHWEST QUADRANT

BRYSON CITY &
THE SOUTHWEST QUADRANT

CHEROKEE &
THE SOUTHEAST QUADRANT

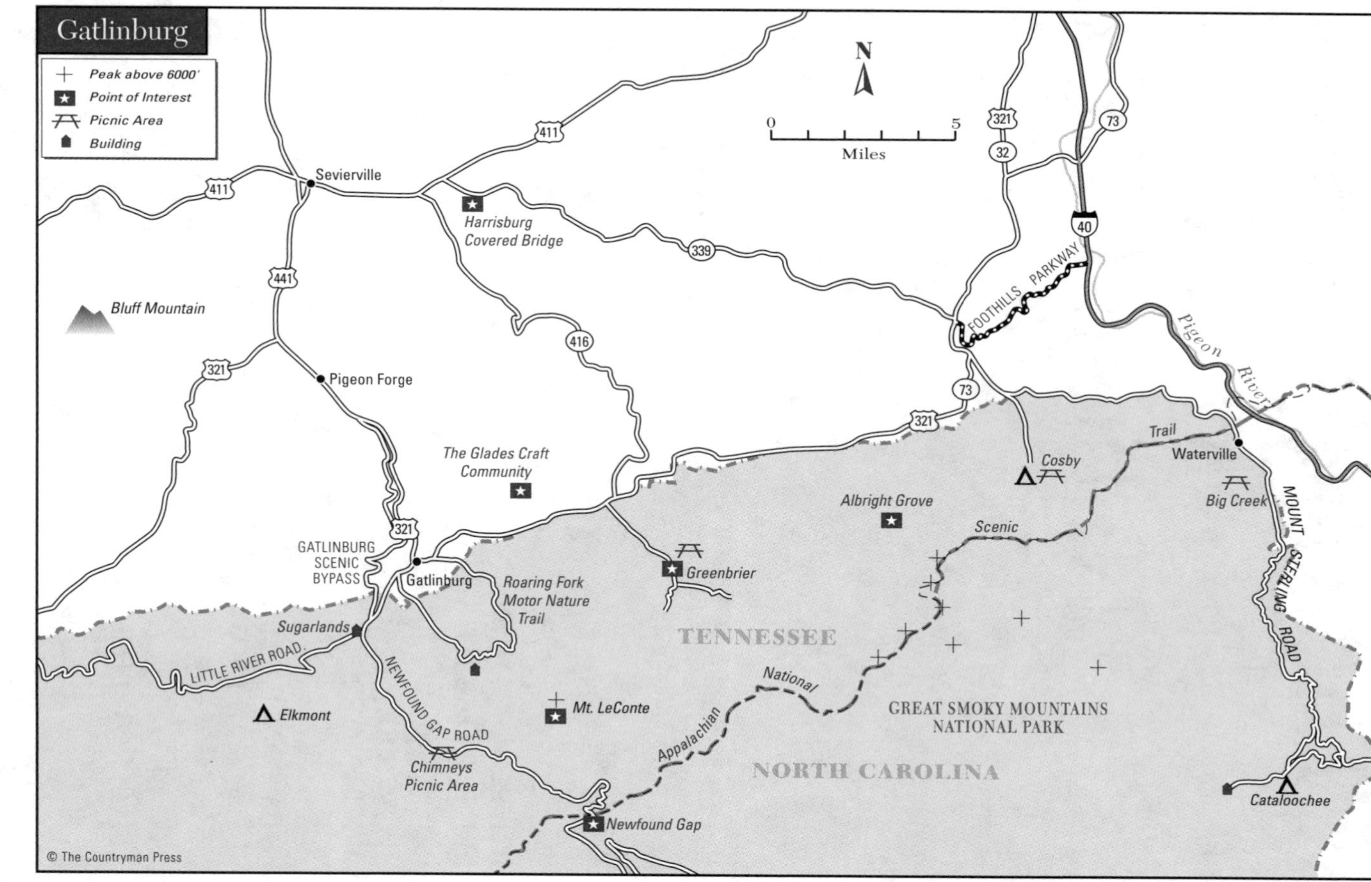
Gatlinburg
Peak above 6000'
Point of Interest
Picnic Area
Building
N
0
5
Miles
Sevierville
411
441
321
Bluff Mountain
Pigeon Forge
Harrisburg Covered Bridge
339
416
32
73
40
FOOTHILLS PARKWAY
Pigeon River
The Glades Craft Community
GATLINBURG SCENIC BYPASS
Gatlinburg
Roaring Fork Motor Nature Trail
Sugarlands
LITTLE RIVER ROAD
Elkmont
NEWFOUND GAP ROAD
Chimneys Picnic Area
Mt. LeConte
Newfound Gap
Greenbrier
TENNESSEE
Albright Grove
Cosby
Scenic
Trail
Waterville
Big Creek
MOUNT STERLING ROAD
National
Appalachian
GREAT SMOKY MOUNTAINS NATIONAL PARK
NORTH CAROLINA
Cataloochee

# THE GREAT SMOKY MOUNTAINS NATIONAL PARK

The Great Smoky Mountains make up the craggy climax to the southern Appalachians. While the nearby Black Mountains may be taller by a few dozens of feet, no other eastern range is more steep, more twisted and knotted, or more rugged. The Smokies run as an unbroken wall for 60 miles along the state line, blocking North Carolina from Tennessee with a cliff-sided razor's edge that has mile-high gaps and 6,000-foot peaks. Then, at Tricorner Knob, the Smokies suddenly twist south, change their name to the Great Balsam Mountains, and run as a mile-high wall for another 45 miles. Behind this great L-shaped range (to its south and west) lie a tangle of tall knotted mountains with deep gaps and slashing narrow valleys.

While the Smokies may have missed the honor of having the highest peak in the East, they are without doubt the most difficult, rugged, and impenetrable range in the Southern Appalachians. Where most eastern mountains struggle to push their peaks more than a half-mile above sea level, the Smokies and the Balsams quickly reach an elevation of three-quarters of a mile above sea level—then stay there or higher for a hundred miles. Indeed, the ridge stays a mile above sea level for fifty miles (in four stretches), with 107 mile-high peaks and gaps. Mile-high peaks and gaps are so common in these ranges that folks haven't bothered naming 35 of them, a nonchalance unheard-of in other eastern ranges. Slopes plunge 4,000 to 5,000 feet nearly straight down from these high ridges to narrow valley floors, then jump straight up to the next ridge. This tangle of valleys and ridges forms a chaotic nonpattern in which all ridge names are arbitrary. Other mountains may be as tall, but the Smokies and the Balsams are the worst barrier.

Mountains this tall make their own climate. Valley floors as low as 800 feet above sea level have a hot Southern climate with oak and pine forests. Looming above these valleys, the mile-high ridgelines extend into a subarctic climate zone typical of Canada, dominated by spruces and firs (known locally as a balsam forest). Between these two forest types are every type of hardwood forest imaginable, changing by slope, elevation, local rainfall, exposure to the sun, history, and pure luck. The trees cover nearly every slope, no matter how steep, with the most rugged slopes covered in "laurel hells," dense tangles of rhododendron and mountain laurel. High rainfall, on some ridges more than a hundred inches a year, can bring about a lush temperate rainforest of wondrous variety and beauty, where springs ooze out of the rocks to become raging rivers within 3 miles. With all this variety, it comes as no surprise that the Great Smoky Mountains National Park is an International Biosphere Reserve, said to contain more tree species than Europe.

In these tangled ridges, stage roads and railroads followed the few river valleys with any width, while towns and farms followed the roads. Away from the railroads and turnpikes, settlement fanned out among the steep draws and coves as a thin cover of small subsistence farms. A high mountain family would live in a one-crib log cabin and grow the food they planned to eat—mainly corn—in a small steep plot cleared by girdling trees. They would probably have a log barn with a horse or mule and a few cattle, as well as a corncrib, a chicken coop, and (perhaps) a spring house. Uphill, where it was too steep to farm, the ancient forest spread to the ridgeline; the men hunted the forest, but did not log it. These small plots spread up streams wherever there was enough land to grow a little corn. The Great Smoky Mountains National Park preserves quite a number of these high mountain farmsteads, some as major open-air museums, others as cabins sitting by a path.

The Great Smoky Mountains National Park combines all of these areas of interest—scenic grandeur, ecological diversity, and pioneer history. It forms a half-million-acre oval with the highest and most difficult ridges running lengthways along its center, and roads penetrating in from its periphery. Only one road, the popular Newfound Gap Road, penetrates deep into the park's interior to emerge on the other side. All other roads skitter along its edge, or run up valleys to dead-end at the mountain wall. Those roads lead to all sorts of places: wide views, deep forests, noisy rivers, beautiful waterfalls, and quaint log farmsteads. And footpaths—over 800 miles of foot and bridal paths wander through the national park's backcountry. If you stay in your car, you will miss most of the park.

The Great Smoky Mountains National Park is run as a wilderness experience. Apart from campgrounds and camp stores, there are no restaurants or lodgings inside the park. The largest concentration of rooms and restaurants is at Gatlinburg, Tennessee, a congested tourist town at the park's main entrance. To the west of Gatlinburg, the settlement of Townsend, Tennessee, offers a quieter alternative. On the North Carolina side, much of the land bordering the park is within the Qualla Boundary, the reservation of the 10,000-member Eastern Band of the Cherokee Nation; its tribal town of Cherokee straddles the park's main entrance in North Carolina. Not too far away are the unspoiled county seats of Bryson City and Sylva, each with an excellent choice of bed-and-breakfasts and restaurants.

**GETTING ALONG IN THE NATIONAL PARK** **Fishing** Inside the national park, fishing for rainbow and brown trout is allowed year-round; you must have a state license, use a single hook on an artificial lure, and not take brook trout (a native species the National Park Service is trying to restore). Despite the fact that the park service stopped stocking streams over 35 years ago, the fishing is excellent and most streams are at their trout population maximums. Fishing within the Qualla Boundary requires a tribal license, but no state license; fishing on some streams is limited to tribal members.

**Bicycling** For the most part, the National Park Service treats bicycles as vehicles, on par with automobiles, and requires them to follow the same rules. As a practical matter, this means that bicycling opportunities are limited, as the automobile roads are narrow, shoulderless, and crowded. There are some exceptions. The scenic drive from Cades Cove up Parsons Branch Road and back on the **Foothills Parkway** is well suited for bicycles (see "Townsend, Cades Cove, & the Northwest Quadrant," *Exploring the Area*), as is the loop around **Heintooga** (see "Cherokee & the Southeast Quadrant," *Exploring the Area*). The park service allows bicycles up the **Deep Creek and Indian Creek Trails** near Bryson City, even though it's closed to vehicles (see "Bryson City & the Southwest Quadrant," *Exploring the Area*). Last and best, the wonderful **Cades Cove Loop Road** is closed to automobiles Wednesday and Saturday mornings until 10 AM, to allow bicyclists and walkers to enjoy it without noise and fumes (see "Townsend, Cades Cove, & the Northwest Quadrant," *Exploring the Area*).

**Day Hiking** (800-436-1200) Day hiking is unrestricted in the national park, and this guide includes many suggested paths. Paths are normally high in quality, wide and properly graded (although maintenance may vary in quality). Nearly all paths are forest walks, including those along ridgetops—forests cover even the steepest slopes in the Smokies.

Two dangers confront even the casual walker. The first is bears, discussed below. The second, and by far the more deadly, is hypothermia, dehydration, and exhaustion. Hypothermia—sudden body cooling leading to disorientation—can occur in the hottest weather when altitudes exceed 5,000 feet and rain storms blow up suddenly. Exhaustion and dehydration can occur whether or not a person is overcooled, particularly when pulling up a 25 percent gradient that stretches for miles without a break. In either case, a disoriented person can wander off the trail—a very dangerous place to be in this twisted, craggy land. The Park Service posts a daily web report on trail conditions, weather, trail closures, and bear problem locations.

**Backpacking** (423-436-9564) Weekdays, business hours. Couch potatoes may be surprised to learn that backpacking in the Great Smoky Mountains National Park is so popular that it has had to be rationed for the last 35 years. The rationing system takes the shape of backcountry camping permits, required for all overnight trail use. The most popular backcountry areas require reservations and assigned camping spots, while the less visited areas have fewer restrictions. This system has succeeded in its goal of spreading backpackers throughout the park, instead of concentrating in the hundreds along the Appalachian Trail. You can get a permit from any of the ranger stations, or by calling in advance of your trip.

Many people are interested in hiking the **Appalachian Trail**, as a special and famous place. Day hiking the trail is unrestricted, and this book includes suggestions. However, the Appalachian Trail remains badly overcrowded by backpackers at all times of the year except the dead of winter, and is strictly regulated by the permit system. Here as elsewhere, the trail has three-sided shelters with shelf bunks every 5 miles or so, but these are completely full nearly all the time. Overuse can make these camping spots unpleasant. In addition, there are bear problems, as bears sometimes raid the Appalachian Trail camping areas for food. It's a good idea to backpack down other park trails, or on sections of the Appalachian Trail outside the park. Near the park, the **Cheoah Mountains** section of the Appalachian Trail is a good alternative (see "The Northern Unicois: Robbinsville & Tellico Plains," *Exploring the Area*), as are **Max Patch** (see "North of Asheville: The Bald Mountains," *Exploring the Area*) and **Standing Indian** (see "Franklin & the Nantahala Mountains," *Exploring the Area*).

**Automobile Camping** (great.smoky.mountains.national-park.com/camping; 800-365-2267). Most campgrounds close seasonally; ask in advance. Auto-based camping is allowed at 10 campgrounds, all of them scenic but primitive, with unheated toilet rooms, no hookups, no electricity, and no showers. Despite these conditions the national park campgrounds are extremely popular and fill up fast. You can get advanced reservations at the most popular campgrounds—Cades Cove, Elkmont, and Smokemont. Of the remaining first-come first-serve campgrounds, **Deep Creek** is an excellent alternative to the Big Three, with a convenient location right outside of Bryson City, a fair amount of room at 92 spaces, and some neat waterfalls (see "Bryson City & the Southwest Quadrant," *Exploring the Area*). But on a really hot summer's day, try to get into Balsam Mountain Campground on the **Heintooga Spur Road**—at 5,300 feet, one of the coolest places in the park (see "Cherokee & the Southeast Quadrant," *Exploring the Area*). If you want remoteness the 12-site **Abrams Creek** is hard to beat; you may be two hours from Gatlinburg or Cherokee, but the campground is lovely, the foot paths are some of the park's easiest and most beautiful, and the fishing is great (see "Townsend, Cades Cove, & the Northwest Quadrant," *Wild Places*).

**Pets** The Great Smoky Mountains National Park is definitely not a pet-friendly place; the National Park Service sees them as an environmental risk, period. Pets are prohibited on all trails, to the extent that through hikers on the Appalachian Trail are required to kennel their dogs until they clear the park. Dogs are allowed only in the overlooks and picnic areas, and they must be on leashes at all times.

**Bears** The park's first ever black bear fatality happened in March 2000, on the Little River Trail about 4 miles from Elkmont. In this incident, two bears attacked two adult hikers without apparent provocation, killing one and guarding the body as bears do to a carcass they intend to eat, until rangers could arrive and kill the bears. Bears are extremely dangerous. They should never be approached or fed.

**GUIDANCE** **Smoky Mountain Host of North Carolina** (visitsmokies.org; 800-432-4678, 828-369-9606; 4437 Georgia Rd., Franklin, NC 28734). This innkeepers organization will help you find a room throughout the North Carolina side of the Smoky Mountains. They run a large, friendly visitors center on US 441 south of Franklin, near the Georgia state line.

# GATLINBURG & THE NORTHEAST QUADRANT

The great majority of the 10 million people who visit the Great Smokies every year get their first sight of the national park from the tourist town of Gatlinburg, Tennessee. With 3,800 full-time residents, this intensely busy collection of motels, restaurants, and shops straddles US 441 as it passes up a narrow valley and into the park. Brought into existence by the millions of visitors who have visited the park every year since the end of World War II, Gatlinburg tempts would-be nature lovers away from the park with a carnival-like atmosphere. It also plays host to an exceptionally large and rewarding crafts community, with 80 or more craft artists perpetuating mountain craft traditions.

Whatever the attractions of Gatlinburg, the Great Smoky Mountains National Park remains the main event, with its entrance abutting the southern edge of town. The park preserves a solid wall of mountains whose highest peaks loom a mile over Gatlinburg's main street, and whose crest extends 30 miles in both directions without a break. Despite its cliff-like slopes, this mountain front is covered with the richest and most varied forest in North America, a forest where 130 tree species form nine distinct ecologies (including successional fields and heath balds). In the areas of the park nearest Gatlinburg, visitors are faced with a wide range of exceptional sites. Views encompass the great crest of the Smokies, so high that the hills around Gatlinburg appear flat next to them. Old-growth forests form groves of giants, trees that tower 150 feet in the air on trunks 15 feet across. Waterfalls range from graceful, lacy curtains to raging torrents that plunge over 90-foot cliffs. Historic log homesteads, barns, and mills remain scattered about the hills above Gatlinburg. While some of these sites can be reached by automobiles, this is very much a walker's park, and most of the best sites are well-removed from the noise and fumes of the park's busy main roads.

**GUIDANCE—TOWNS AND COUNTRYSIDE Gatlinburg Department of Tourism** (gatlinburg-tennessee.com; 800-343-1475; 303 Reagan Dr., Gatlinburg, TN 37738). This city of Gatlinburg agency runs the convention center, and works with the chamber to promote the area. It runs a small visitors center in the center of town, on the corner of US 441 and US 321, at traffic light #3.

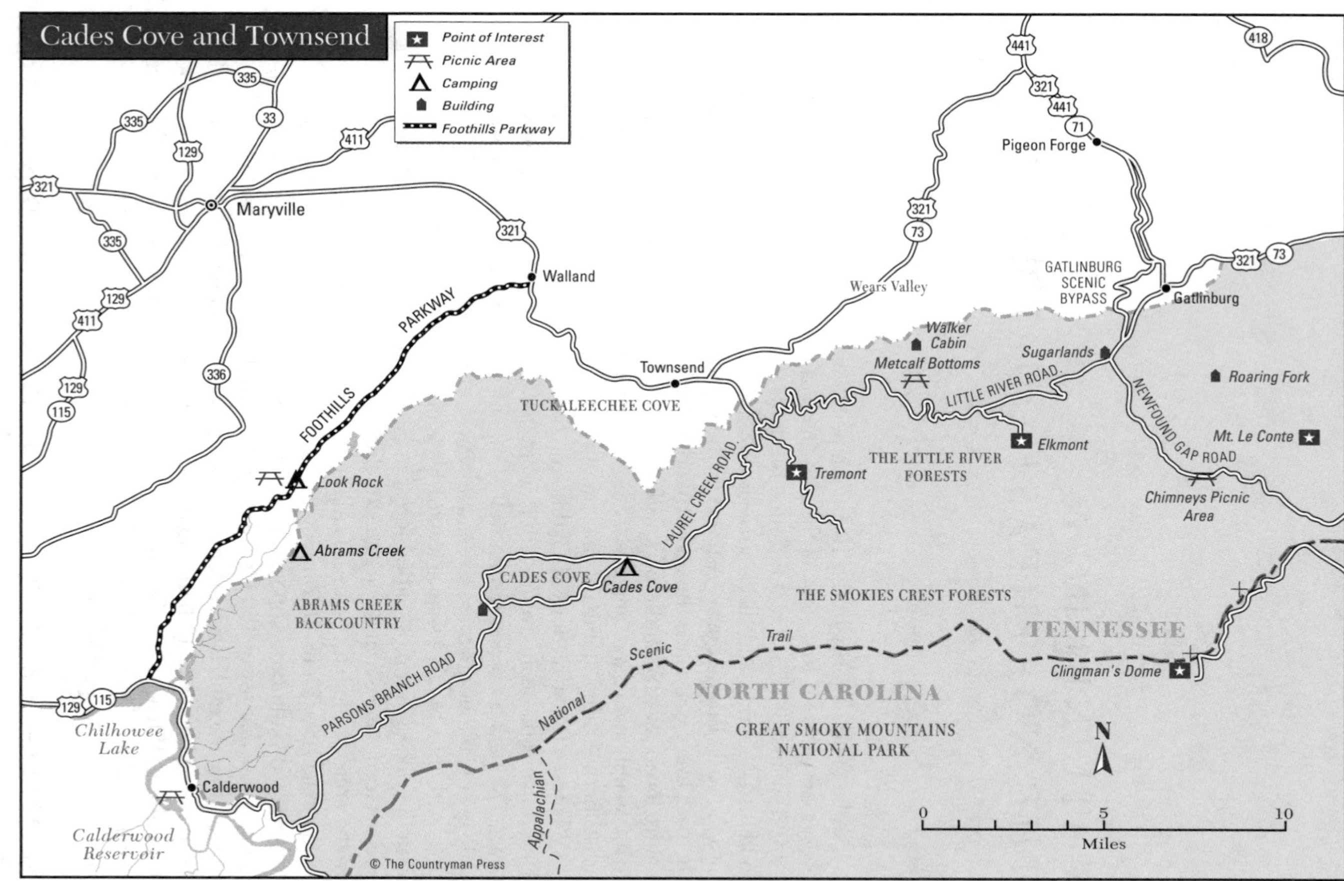
Cades Cove and Townsend
Point of Interest
Picnic Area
Camping
Building
Foothills Parkway
Maryville
Walland
Townsend
Pigeon Forge
Gatlinburg
GATLINBURG SCENIC BYPASS
Wears Valley
Walker Cabin
Metcalf Bottoms
Sugarlands
Roaring Fork
LITTLE RIVER ROAD
NEWFOUND GAP ROAD
Mt. Le Conte
Elkmont
Tremont
THE LITTLE RIVER FORESTS
Chimneys Picnic Area
TUCKALEECHEE COVE
FOOTHILLS PARKWAY
Look Rock
Abrams Creek
LAUREL CREEK ROAD
CADES COVE
Cades Cove
ABRAMS CREEK BACKCOUNTRY
THE SMOKIES CREST FORESTS
TENNESSEE
PARSONS BRANCH ROAD
National Scenic Trail
Appalachian
Clingman's Dome
NORTH CAROLINA
GREAT SMOKY MOUNTAINS NATIONAL PARK
Chilhowee Lake
Calderwood
Calderwood Reservoir
N
0 5 10
Miles
© The Countryman Press
321
335
33
411
129
336
115
441
71
73
418

**Gatlinburg Visitors Center (Chamber of Commerce)** (www.gatlinburg.com; e-mail: info@gatlinburg.com; 800-588-1817; 811 E. Pkwy., P.O. Box 527, Gatlinburg, TN 37738). The Gatlinburg Chamber of Commerce cooperates with the National Park Service to run this large welcome center on US 441 at the eastern entrance to the town. It's also a major terminus (with free parking) on Gatlinburg's elaborate trolley network, making it a good place to park while visiting the rest of the town.

**Sugarlands Ranger Station** (www.nps.gov/grsm; 865-436-1200; 107 Park Headquarters Rd., Gatlinburg, TN 37738). This large 1950s-style complex offers an information desk, museum, and some really worthwhile interpretive trails. The administrative headquarters for the national park is located just behind.

**Mount LeConte Geology Web Page** (geology.er.usgs.gov/eespteam/Mtleconte; 703-648-6501; e-mail: aschultz@usgs.gov). This web page, sponsored by the U.S. Geological Survey at the request of the National Park Service, gives detailed information on the geology of the Smoky Mountain Front, accompanied by a large number of color photos to aid in rock identification. Rock hounds and geology enthusiasts will want to look up the detailed descriptions (with photos) of the geology along each of the trails up Mount LeConte. The USGS team responsible for this page has compiled a similar page for **Cades Cove**.

**GETTING THERE** *By Car* To reach Gatlinburg from any direction (including south), take Interstate 40 to TN 66 (exit 407), then go south on TN 66 to pick up US 441 in Sevierville. Gatlinburg is 13 miles south of Sevierville on US 441. Don't worry about getting lost; Gatlinburg is well signposted the entire distance.

*By Air* If you are staying on the Gatlinburg side of the Smokies, you will want to fly into Knoxville, a full-service regional airport with on-site car rentals. The Knoxville airport is a 44-mile drive from Gatlinburg, more than half of it on two-lane roads; expect it to take at least an hour and a quarter. If your primary destination is the **Cades Cove** area of the park, you should note that the Cades Cove entrance at Townsend, with a full range of tourist facilities, is only a 20-mile drive from the airport via multi-laned highways.

*By Bus* There is no regularly scheduled bus service into Gatlinburg. Many tour operators offer bus tours to Gatlinburg; check with your travel agent.

**MEDICAL EMERGENCIES** **Fort Sanders Sevier Medical Center** (www.fssevier.com; 865-453-9355; 709 Middle Creek Rd., Sevierville, TN 37864). Despite its Sevierville address, Sevier (pronounced Se-VERE) Medical Center is located in Pigeon Forge, 1.2 miles east of US 441 on Middle Creek Road; if you are coming from Gatlinburg, you will find this to be a right turn, 7 miles north of downtown. A branch of Knoxville's massive regional hospital company, Covenant Health, Sevier is a small, full-service local hospital with surgery facilities and a 24/7 emergency room.

## ✱ Exploring the Area

It's not my habit to start by talking about how plain a place is. But honestly, if you drive into this area from the north (as most folk do), it's going to get ugly. You will pass through miles of suburban-style sprawl, then find yourself in stand-still traffic in the carnival-like town of Gatlinburg. (Gatlinburg is actually a lot of fun—but only on foot.) So be warned: the main approach from the north is downright unpleasant. To avoid it altogether, move your base of operation westward to Townsend, Tennessee, or southward to the Bryson City, North Carolina, area.

There is some good news, however. Although this dreary river of traffic is nearly 14 miles long, it is seldom more than a few hundred yards wide. Once you leave this thoroughly beaten track, the scenery is worth every effort you've spent getting here.

At Gatlinburg, the Smoky Mountains form what may be the tallest mountain front in the East, a vertical rise of 1 mile between downtown Gatlinburg and **Mount Le Conte**, just 7 miles away. This wall-like mountain traps rain systems, and the heavy rains form raging rivers, large waterfalls, and deep gorges. Forests range from subarctic at the top to subtropical at the bottom. You can find more tree species in a few acres of gorge-bottom than exist in most European nations.

Most remarkable is the suddenness of this great wall of mountains. Geologically, the Smoky Mountain Front marks the western edge of the Blue Ridge, a fault line that separates the hard ancient rock of the Smokies from the softer, newer rock of the Great Valley. As soon as you leave the Blue Ridge region, the mountains form into linear ridges that seldom reach the height of the Smokies, and quickly dwindle to mere hills. Farmlands alternate with forests, with farms gaining the upper hand the farther you go.

To drive straight up and over the Smoky Mountain Front, take the **Newfound Gap Road**. The easiest crest-top view over the Great Valley is at **Clingmans Dome Overlook**. For the best view of the Smoky Mountain Front from the valley, take the **Foothills Parkway** at Cosby, I-40's exit 443.

**EXPLORING BY CAR** **The Newfound Gap Road in Tennessee** Built in 1932 as a scenic tourist highway, the **Newfound Gap Road** climbs up the steep Ten-

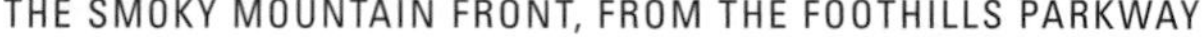

THE SMOKY MOUNTAIN FRONT, FROM THE FOOTHILLS PARKWAY

FARM IN THE NEWFOUND MOUNTAINS

nessee face of the Great Smoky Mountains National Park to top out in the 5048-foot-high **Newfound Gap**. From there the highway enters North Carolina to descend to **Cherokee**, a beautiful stretch with spectacular views. This two-lane highway is a fairly easy drive as mountain roads go, but heavy traffic and inconsiderate drivers can make it slow going. You'll enjoy it more if you approach it as a recreational drive, taking plenty of time to pull over and enjoy the scenery.

Most people start this drive at the national park entrance at the south edge of Gatlinburg. A better plan is to start at the north end of Gatlinburg, entering the **Gatlinburg Bypass** from the southbound lanes of US 441 a mile south of the Smoky Mountains/Gatlinburg Visitors Center. This 5.-mile scenic parkway, part of the Great Smoky Mountains National Park, winds along the mountain slopes west of Gatlinburg with two stunning 180-degree **views over the town** and toward the high slopes of **Mount LeConte**. This little used road will zip you around Gatlinburg and into the park just south of the **Sugarlands Visitor's Center**, to join the Newfound Gap Road proper. For the next 2. miles the highway curves gently uphill through a young hardwood forest growing on the site of the former Sugarlands community. A nature trail and two "quiet walkways" give you an opportunity to explore the forests for **signs of its former inhabitants**—old foundations, chimneys, and tulip trees growing on abandoned fields, even a motel and some paved roads and concrete bridges. After that the highway climbs above Sugarlands for sweeping views over the valley and toward the face of Mount LeConte. At 5 miles you will reach the streamside **Chimneys Picnic Area**, where a nature trail explores a **virgin cove hardwood forest**. Now the highway becomes more rugged as it climbs away from the valley, with good views to the **Chimney Tops**, two gigantic rock spires protruding from the ridgeline above. Beyond that, the highway goes through a 360-degree **pigtail curve**, circling over itself to gain a high, gentle-floored stream valley. When the highway finally runs out of valley its switchbacks turn steeply up to become **a ledge cut into cliffs**, a low stone wall guarding its downhill edge. Finally it reaches **Morton Overlook**, with striking views into the deep valley below and receding ridges beyond. Newfound Gap, with its large parking lot, views, and **Appalachian Trail** access, is just beyond.

**Roaring Fork Motor Nature Trail** This nature trail for the auto-bound leads down old farm roads that once wandered through the settlements south of Gatlinburg, before this area was included in the Great Smoky Mountains National Park and allowed to go back to forests. This scenic drive starts in downtown Gatlinburg, turning onto Historic Nature Trail (that's the name of the street) from US 441 at light 8. Continue past the lovely little **Mynatt Park** to enter the national park just beyond. The road goes through gentle curves to climb through hardwood forests to the Bud Ogle Place, a log cabin with running water piped in using hollow logs. Just beyond, the road breaks into a mile-long one-way loop through Cherokee Orchards, an apple orchard and commercial nursery until 1940. As the road loops uphill and around (to return to the Bud Ogle Place), turn onto the one-lane, one-way Roaring Fork Motor Nature Trail to the right. Passing the **Baskins Creek Trail** in a quarter-mile, the road twists up to a ridge with a good view, then twists around to a second ridgeline with a great view—westward, toward Sugarlands, with receding ridges fading into the background. Passing the **Grotto Falls** trailhead, the road twists through a hemlock forest, then follows a boisterous creek; look for the stone wall on its opposite side. After a half-mile a parking lot will mark the far end of the Baskins Creek Trail and the second historic site, the Jim Bales Place, a log cabin and outbuildings overlooking a small waterfall. Then the road reaches the **Ephraim** Bales Place, a modest dogtrot log cabin and barn, with an impressive stone wall marking the location of the old farm road. A half-mile farther the road passes the last and most colorful of the four sites, the brightly painted Alfred Reagan Place, with a restored horizontal wheel "tub mill" by the stream. A double stream crossing marks the point when the stream drops suddenly down into a small gorge, the road following it on a ledge hewn into the rocky slopes above. Here are dramatic views down the stream, and two wonderful waterfalls dripping down the rocks above the road. The road finally leaves the park to reenter Gatlinburg; return to downtown by taking the turn to the left.

**EXPLORING ON FOOT** **Five Popular Hikes Near Gatlinburg** These five hikes, all within 10 miles of Gatlinburg, are overwhelmingly popular. Each is extraordinary, even by Smoky Mountain standards, with a magnificent view, remarkable feature, or beautiful waterfall. Each is well-maintained (one is paved) and capable of handling its visitors, although parking can be a problem. In fact, the only thing wrong with any of these hikes is their lack of solitude. On a sunny weekend, expect these hikes to be more like a carnival than a wilderness experience.

1. *Laurel Falls Trail,* 4 miles west of Sugarlands Visitor's Center on Little River Road. This 1.3-mile paved trail, partially blasted through solid rock by the CCC in 1935, leads past a view to a strong 75-foot waterfall.
2. *Chimneytops Trail,* 6.7 miles south of Sugarlands Visitors Center on Newfound Gap Road. This 2-mile uphill slog leads through old-growth forest to a popular, but dangerous, clifftop viewpoint. This is a really bad place to take children.
3. *Alum Cave Trail,* 8.6 miles south of Sugarlands Visitors Center on Newfound Gap Road. The lowermost 2 miles of this Mount LeConte access trail features huge boulders, an interesting geological formation known as Arch Rock, old-growth forests, and spectacular views from exposed bluffs.

GROTTO FALLS, NEAR ROARING FORK MOTOR NATURE TRAIL

4. *Grotto Falls* (on Trillium Gap Trail), 3.5 miles from Gatlinburg on the **Roaring Fork Motor Nature Trail**. This easy 1-mile walk leads through mature forests to a large waterfall.
5. *Ramsey Cascades Trail,* at the end of the left fork within the **Greenbrier area**. This difficult hike (an 8.-mile round-trip distance with 2,000 feet of climbing) runs through old-growth forest with giant hemlocks and tulip trees, to end at an exceptionally beautiful 90-foot waterfall.

**Old Settlement Walks Near Gatlinburg** One of the best ways to escape the crowds near Gatlinburg is to take a walk through the old mountain settlements of Sugarlands and Baskins Creek, abandoned in the 1930s to make way for the national park. These interconnecting paths are so close to Gatlinburg that you can start from the center of downtown, do them all in a day, and return to where you started—a total distance of 11 miles with an elevation gain of 1,600 feet. If you want to try this loop hike, follow the downtown sidewalk toward the park, then continue along the pretty riverside *Gatlinburg Trail* to the national park headquarters at Sugarlands, a level 2-mile stroll past old home sites and a lovely cascade.

*Old Sugarlands Trail* starts near the park headquarters (where you can park)—across the Newfound Gap Road, over the bridge, and on your right. This little-used path follows old abandoned roads, some once paved, through the heart of the Sugarlands community. You will walk past foundations, stone walls, stretches of abandoned macadam, old automobile bridges, and a **CCC camp** beneath the trees. The walk is 4 miles to the start of the **Roaring Fork Nature Trail** on Cherokee Orchards Road; the first 2 miles are particularly interesting, and nearly level.

To continue the loop walk, pick up *Trillium Gap Trail* at the end of Old Sugarlands Trail. This trail goes through an old commercial apple orchard absorbed into the park in 1942 and still shows signs of its former use. This trail connects with the next walk.

*Baskins Falls Walk* follows a little-used path 1.75 miles through an old settlement to a lovely waterfall. Its trailhead, marked BASKINS CREEK TRAIL, is just beyond the start of the Roaring Fork Motor Nature Trail. This trail climbs up a piney ridge, then descends into a small canyon with some impressive bluffs. As the main trail turns away, a side path continues downhill along the stream to Baskins Falls, a 30-foot plunge that settlers used as a shower in the summer. This is the end of the official path, and most folk return to the main trail. From there you can retrace your steps to your car, or continue left along the trail, through overgrown farms and woodlots, to an old cemetery and log cabin farther along on the Roaring Fork Road. If you take the latter you will have walked 2.7 miles, and will be about 2.5 miles from your car (to the left along Roaring Fork Road).

However, you may want to continue ahead, along Baskins Creek to Gatlinburg, to complete the loop. This little-used informal path (a "manway" in park parlance) follows the banks of the creek through the heart of another old community. This rough, overgrown walk passes many signs of the old settlement, as well as wildflowers and beautiful stream views. The path leaves the national park and enters Gatlinburg at the end of the town's Baskins Creek Road; follow the paved roads downhill to return to downtown.

**Albright Grove** Named after a National Park Service administrator who did much to ensure the park's integrity from developers, Albright Grove is a remarkable stand of virgin old-growth forest. It's a moderate hike, 6.7 miles round trip with 1,600 feet of uphill climb, all through forests. The trailhead is hard to find. Go 15.5 miles east of downtown Gatlinburg on US 321, then turn right onto Baxter Road, by Smoky Mountain Creekside Rentals; from there, turn right at the T-intersection with Laurel Springs Road, going a short distance until you reach the park service sign for the *Maddron Bald Trail.* You will hike uphill on the Maddron Bald Trail for 3 miles to reach Albright Grove, walking along an old settlement road through forests that have grown over former farms. After a half-mile you will pass one of the old farm houses, a chestnut log cabin with a shake roof, built by Willis Baxter in 1889. The old settlement road ends after 2 miles, and the forest becomes deeper, dominated by large hemlocks; you are now entering a classic Appalachian cove hardwood forest, with a rich variety of old, large trees. At 2.8 miles, the *Albright Grove Loop Trail* forks right to enter a segment of the forest that has never been logged. Giant tulip trees (yellow poplars) exceed 25 feet in diameter; similar gargantuan hemlocks and beeches are scattered about, as are huge silverbells, the signature tree of the cove forest. In all, the loop trail leads through this cathedral-like forest for 0.7 mile before returning to the Maddron Bald Trail. To go straight back to your car, turn right; it's downhill all the way. Strong hikers may be interested in taking a left here, going deeper into the wilderness and higher up the mountain. This path reaches a large, wild bald on remote Maddron Bald, with 360-degree views over the Smokies Crest and down into Tennessee—an addition of 6.5 miles and 1,800 feet of climb added to an already long walk.

**LONG-DISTANCE PATHS** The **Appalachian Trail** follows the high crest of the Smokies along the southern edge of this chapter's area, to meet up with the **Benton MacKaye Trail** at the far eastern edge of the Great Smoky Mountains National Park; both are described in the Cherokee chapter.

## ✷ Villages

**Gatlinburg** In the late 1920s Gatlinburg was just another poor mountain crossroads. It was where the road up from the flatlands reached the foot of the Smokies—a fork with a general store and a gas pump. The left fork (now US 321) went to the Methodist mission at Pitman Center, which furnished limited, but lifesaving, medical services to the isolated mountain folk. The right fork (now the **Newfound Gap Road)** went deep into the Smokies to dead-end at the poverty-stricken community of Sugarlands, also known as "Blockader's Heaven" according to local moonshine expert Horace Kephart. Then came the park. Gatlinburg found itself the main entrance to a park that attracted a million automobile-driving visitors in 1941. A short time later, all those tourists had turned the mountains crossroads into a small city.

Gatlinburg is a city built for tourists. It's still centered on that old fork in the road, but now the fork is a busy multilaned intersection in the middle of a crowded downtown. Here two-story buildings, jammed against the sidewalk and each other, are filled with every sort of tourist enticement imaginable—gift shops, restaurants, candy shops, old-timey photo places, sideshows (labeled "museums" and "attractions"), amusement rides . . . you name it. It has more than a passing resemblance to a really large county fair, complete with bad parking, high prices, and a stiff dose of hucksterism. It's easy to complain about it, but it's a lot more fun to grab a corn dog and enjoy it.

Unlike **Cherokee**, Gatlinburg is continuously tearing itself down and rebuilding itself. Its downtown is crammed into a narrow river gorge, a single block wide and a mile long, so that real estate is at a premium. The entire length is built with commercial structures two to three stories high, attached to each other and the sidewalk. The latest commercial craze has been to take what had been normal-size stores and turn them into "malls" with tiny shops opening onto a central corridor. This has allowed the number of downtown shops to multiply like rabbits, with small merchants scrambling to offer something new and different to browsing tourists—and, more often than not, succeeding. Behind this long, thin downtown strip, scores of motels with thousands of rooms climb down to the river and up the mountain sides.

Apart from this full-time street fair, Gatlinburg has a serious, mountain-oriented side. On the rural east side of town, **the Glades area** hosts a community of 80 craft artists—some newcomers, others from old mountain craft families. A series of crafter-owned shops string out along this scenic mountain cove, with members of the community proudly displaying a logo certifying that they make what they sell. Indeed, most have their studios in their shops, and will welcome you in as they work.

Gatlinburg traffic is always slow, and can grind to a stop during the season. If you wish simply to get beyond Gatlinburg to the other side, take the **Gatlinburg Bypass**, a scenic road maintained by the National Park Service. Outside of the winter season, there is no street parking in downtown Gatlinburg. Instead, downtown parking is in a couple of city garages, plus an outdoor lot near the auditorium at a somewhat lower price. As an alternative, you can park for free at the **visitors center** at the north end of town or the city hall at the east end of town on US 321, and take a trolley (cost from $0.50 to $2.00).

**Pigeon Forge** This sprawling suburb of Gatlinburg, 6 miles north of downtown, consists of a 2-mile string of chain restaurants and franchise motels stretching along a six-lane segment of US 441. Pigeon Forge's landscape is that of a recently built up area on the edge of a large city, with no real mountain views or traditional mountain culture. If you long for the certainty of familiar surroundings and brand names you recognize, you will certainly find them at Pigeon Forge. However, if you want to immerse yourself in mountain scenery and culture, you might want to look elsewhere.

**Sevierville** Sevierville (Se-VERE-vull) is the seat of Sevier County, Tennessee—the county that contains Gatlinburg. Travelers along US 441 will see little of it beyond a continuous suburban-style sprawl that merges seamlessly with Pigeon Forge. However, two blocks off the highway is a quaint old downtown centering on an old brick courthouse with a statue of Dolly Parton in front. Many businesses in the foothills of the Smokies sport Sevierville addresses, even though they are not particularly near town.

**Cosby** Cosby is a dispersed rural settlement with no defined village center, stretching along US 321 about 16 miles east of Gatlinburg. It offers access to the little-visited northeastern fringe of the Great Smoky Mountains National Park. However, services are slight and choices are limited.

## ✷ Wild Places

**THE GREAT FORESTS** **The Smoky Mountains Front** A drop of rain, falling on the highest point of Mount LeConte, travels through 7 miles of wilderness before it reaches the river in downtown Gatlinburg. It also drops 1 mile vertically—in all likelihood the longest slope in the eastern United States. This slope is wet as well as steep, with 7 *feet* of rainfall in a typical year. This combination of high rainfall and high, steep slopes does more than create big rivers and impressive waterfalls; it creates one of the richest temperate forests in the world.

Start at the top, with that drop of water on the 6,593-foot peak of Mount LeConte. You'll be in a boreal forest, an extension of the great subarctic forest that covers much of Canada, whose Christmas tree species of spruce and fir form a forest canopy over thin, rocky soils. Below that will be a mosaic of forest types: New England–style hardwood forest, oak-hickory forests, beech-maple forests, pine-oak forests on warm, dry ridgelines, northern riverine forests along many streambanks. Unique to the Smokies and other nearby mountains is the cove hardwood forest, with the highest species richness in temperate North America. A cove forest can mix and match as many as 25 tree species in an acre of old-growth forest, covering a thick, shrubby understory that bursts into colorful blooms every spring—rhododendron, mountain laurel, flame azalea, dogwood, redbud, and silverbell. These thick forests cover even the steepest slopes with trees that grow 6 to 10 stories high.

And there's a lot of slope that has to be covered. The front of the Smoky Mountains at Gatlinburg forms an unbroken wall 65 miles long. The central 56 miles of that wall, immediately behind Gatlinburg, stays continuously above 4,000 feet, with half of that length above a mile high. On the western (Tennessee) side of the crest, the Smokies drop to a valley that appears flat-bottomed from a crest-top viewpoint, and stretches off to the horizon as far as the eye can see. On the eastern

(North Carolina) side, other mountains, nearly as tall, fill the view in a confused jumble.

Access to this great forest is either from the **Newfound Gap Road**, or from a series of four trailheads along its perimeter: **Roaring Fork Motor Nature Trail**, **Greenbrier Picnic Area**, **Cosby Picnic Area**, and **Big Creek Picnic Area**. All four of these trailheads are gateways into rich and varied forests, with stunning wildflowers, roaring rivers, large waterfalls, and magnificent views. Almost without exception, the hiking and horse trails that lead from these trailheads are well built, well kept, and incredibly beautiful; it should go without saying that nearly all of them are very steep as well.

**RIVERS The Pigeon River** The Pigeon River rises in North Carolina's **Shining Rock Wilderness** to drain northward, cutting a deep water gap through the Great Smoky Mountains to join the Tennessee River, 72 miles from its origin. An 8.9-mile stretch within this chapter's area has become particularly popular with kayakers and commercial rafters. The uppermost half, starting at the Waterville powerplant downhill from **Big Creek**, is the livelier of the two, with plentiful Class II–III+ water. A midway takeout is the segue to a somewhat milder lower section, Class II–II+, ending in a Class III drop. The entire length is paralleled by I-40, so that all access points are easily reached.

**RECREATION AREAS Greenbrier Picnic Area** Six miles east of Gatlinburg on US 321, a right turn on a narrow paved lane leads 4 miles up a broad valley named Greenbrier Cove. Inhabited by scattered farms in the 1920s, Greenbrier Cove is now grown over by a young riverside forest along the noisy, boulder-strewn Middle Prong of the Little Pigeon River. The modest, pleasant picnic area is 2.5 miles up the lane. In another half-mile, a side road crosses the Middle Prong at a particularly scenic spot, then winds through forests to the start of the **Ramsey Cascades Trail**, one of the park's most popular hikes. Straight ahead, the road follows Porters Creek to end at a gate in 1 mile. You can park here and continue up the road on foot. This was once the road to a farming community; you will pass old stone walls, steps leading up hills, boxwoods and roses growing rank where houses once stood. At the end of the road, in a mile, a short path leads right to an old cantilevered barn in the woods, and a log cabin nearby.

ABANDONED STEPS IN GREENBRIER COVE

**Cosby Picnic Area** Cosby Picnic Area is at the far northeast corner of the Tennessee Smokies; go 18 miles east of downtown Gatlinburg on US 321 to TN 73 at Cosby community, then right 0.4 mile to TN 32, then right 1.3 miles to a park service lane on the right. This lane leads 2 miles into the national park, through a rich forest growing on a fan of river deposits at the foot of the Smokies. This forest is particularly beautiful in spring, when it gets its color early, and in fall, when its color lingers a few extra days. The picnic area at the upper end of the road (there is also a campground here) is small and forest covered, along the lovely Cosby Creek. Here you will find a trailhead to the Lower Mount Cammerer Trail—a lengthy trail along the middle slopes of the Smokies, here lower than at Gatlinburg. The first 1.5 miles of this well-built path, climbing only 260 feet, are definitely worth your while. At first it leads along old roadbeds, with stonewalls indicating a formerly settled area. Then, after a half-mile, the old roads end and the trail (built by the CCC in 1935) rises gently for a mile to Sutton Ridge. Here a side trail uphill to the right leads to a wonderful view out over the foothills and the Great Valley. Beyond, the trail descends slightly to Riding Fork. Here you'll find a lovely little cascade upstream to your right, a place where the water trickles and dashes over the rocks in a hundred little steps—a good place to turn around.

COSBY PICNIC AREA

**Big Creek Picnic Area** This remote valley hides just over the state line in North Carolina, at the extreme northeast tip of the park. The drive there is part of its charm. Take US 321 east to Cosby, then turn right onto TN 32. This narrow road must set a state record for twists, as it slowly feels its way through a lovely young hardwood forest on the park's northeast flank. There's a really nice view or two at first; then the forest closes in, and the road becomes a serpentine tunnel through the trees for mile after mile after mile . . . You cross the state line and the **Appalachian Trail** at the same time, then descend quickly on the now-gravel road to an intersection. The right turn takes you into the Big Creek area; straight ahead leads to **Cataloochee Cove** (see "Cherokee and the Southeast Quadrant," *Exploring the Area*); and the left turn takes you through the attractive settlement of Waterville to I-40, for a much faster return to Gatlinburg.

LITTLE PIGEON RIVER AT CHIMNEYTOPS PICNIC AREA

Once at Big Creek you will be on a narrow gravel road that leads 1 mile into the park, to end at a creekside camping and picnic area. The picnic tables sit near the lovely Big Creek, noisy and full of rapids, sheltered by tall, young hardwoods. Beyond the picnic area, the road continues on up the stream as a foot and horse path. Logged in the 1920s, this valley is now covered by a healthy young forest of tall tulip trees and maples; the stream, glanced frequently to the left of the road, is exceptionally beautiful. At 1.4 miles up this gentle roadway is *Midnight Hole,* a 6-foot cascade between two large boulders into a deep pool. At 2.1 miles is *Mouse Falls,* where the creek pours 20 feet over gray stone.

**PICNIC AREAS** **Chimneys Picnic Area** This large picnic area offers forest-shaded tables strung along the Little Pigeon River, 7 miles from Gatlinburg on the **Newfound Gap Road**. It's attractive, cool, and quiet, even on a busy summer day. A nature trail explores the Smoky's unique hardwood cove forest, leading 0.75 mile to a virgin old-growth stand. Picnickers should note that Chimneys is the last picnic area on the Newfound Gap Road for 22 miles—the next place to picnic is **Collins Creek** (see "Cherokee & the Southeast Quadrant," *Wild Places*), way on the other side of the mountain.

**Mynatt Park** This attractive city park inside Gatlinburg offers a number of forested, streamside picnic tables in a quiet residential neighborhood, as well as a full range of recreational facilities (including tennis, if you remembered your racket). Parking is adequate. You'll find it a mile from downtown on Historic Nature Trail.

## ✷ To See

**HISTORIC SITES** **Harrisburg Covered Bridge** Built in 1875 by a local mill owner, this simple wood truss bridge spans a gap between two high bluffs above the East Fork, in this scenic rural location 5 miles east of Sevierville. Like all true covered bridges, the cover protected the heavy wood trusses from rotting; the wood trusses, in turn, allowed the bridge to span the long distance between the bluffs. (Doubting Thomases in the Tennessee DOT have stuck a big concrete pier in the middle, just in case.) The covered truss bridge still carries local traffic on this pastoral back road, thanks to a 1972 restoration funded by the local DAR chapter. To find it, go east from Sevierville on US 411 for 4 miles; then right onto TN 339, continuing onto TN 35, for a total of 1 mile; then right onto Harrisburg Road for 0.2 mile, to the bridge.

**MUSEUMS** **Sugarlands Visitors Center** (865-436-1200; 107 Park Headquarters Rd., Gatlinburg, TN 37738). Located outside Gatlinburg, Tennessee, at the start of the Newfound Gap Road, the Sugarlands Visitors Center has an information desk, gift shop, exhibits, a multimedia show, and a native plant garden. Its exhibit area, recently revamped, explores the Smoky Mountains' unique environment in detail. However, its most rewarding feature is its least visited. Fighting Creek Nature Trail leads you on a 1-mile ramble through forest growing on old farmland; it will take you along an old wagon track, along a stream, past stonewalls and springs, to a restored log cabin deep in the woods.

**FINE CRAFTS** **The Glades** (gatlinburgcrafts.com; 800-565-7330; Gatlinburg, TN 37738). This scenic rural cove on the east side of Gatlinburg has been known as a center for mountain crafts for over half a century. An 8-mile loop road, well signposted off US 321 3 miles east of town, runs through the center of this crafters' community, becoming increasingly beautiful as it draws away from Gatlinburg's center; along it, small craft shops sit in meadows with views over the low mountains of the foothills. In 1937 the craft artists of the Glades have formed their own association, the Great Smoky Arts and Crafts Community, limited to crafters who feature their own work in their own studios. There are now more than 80 such studio/galleries displaying the "Arts & Crafts Community" logo. According to member and porcelain artist Judy Baily, "People feel free to take their time in our shops. Many times they ask us a lot of questions about what we do, and we are glad to spend time with them." These fine crafters, rather than the downtown souvenir shops, are Gatlinburg's main attraction for serious shoppers.

**Galleries and Gardens of the Arrowmont School** (www.arrowmont.org; e-mail: info@arrowmont.org; 865-436-5860; 556 Pkwy., Gatlinburg, TN 37738). Weekdays, normal business hours. The prestigious **Arrowmont School**, founded by the Pi Beta Phi women's fraternity, has occupied its campus in the middle of downtown Gatlinburg since the 1920s—long before downtown Gatlinburg existed. You'll find it to be a string of handsome buildings ranging from old log cabins to contemporary structures, climbing up from busy downtown in beautiful park-like gardens. Five galleries in the main educational facility, a 1970 prairie-style homage that echoes the mountain peaks behind it, display works of faculty and students, as does a sculpture garden farther up the site. The campus starts behind the venerable Arrowcraft Shop, on US 441, in the center of downtown just south of River Road.

**DRAMATIC VIEWS** **Foothills Parkway East** This short length of the long-delayed **Foothills Parkway** (see "Exploration Themes," *Parkways*) links I-40 with US 321—sort of a short cut for people heading from Asheville to Gatlinburg. It's worth a visit, even if it's out of your way. This 6-mile section of parkway climbs to the 2,200-foot top of Green Mountain, the first foothill beyond the northeast end of the Smokies. Overlooks give panoramic views of the Great Smoky Mountains as they rise almost a mile above the foothills and valleys in front of you; other viewpoints look westward, over the foothills as they descend in waves into the Great Valley.

**WHITEWATER ADVENTURES** ✐ **Rafting in the Smokies (Pigeon River Outdoors, Inc.)** (www.raftinginthesmokies.com; e-mail: rafting@raftinginthe smokies.com; 800-776-7238, 865-436-5008; fax: 865-436-6360; P.O. Box 592, Gatlinburg, TN 37738). March–October. From their downtown Gatlinburg location, this company runs whitewater rafting trips and float trips on two different sections of the Pigeon River, a half-hour shuttle from town. The intermediate-level rapids of the Pigeon are restricted to children over eight who weigh more than 60 pounds, but the float trip is open to anyone over the age of three.

✐ **Smoky Mountain Outdoors** (www.smokymountainrafting.com; 800-771-7238, 865-430-3838; 453 Brookside Village Way, Gatlinburg, TN 37738). This outfitter offers Pigeon River whitewater rafting adventures and leisurely floats from their headquarters deep in the country, on the banks of the Pigeon River a mile down Hartford Road from I-40's exit 447, on the Tennessee side of the state line. They maintain a location in Gatlinburg as well, on the east side of town on US 321.

✐ **USA Raft** (usaraftpigeonriver.com; e-mail: info@usaraftpigeonriver.com; 800-872-7238, 423-487-4303; 3630 Hartford Rd., Hartford, TN 37753). This West Virginia rafting company maintains an outpost on the Pigeon River in the Hartford community, just off I-40's exit 447, just beyond the Tennessee/North Carolina state line.

**STABLES** **Smoky Mountain Riding Stables** (smokymountainridingstables.com; 865-436-5634; Hwy. 321-East Pkwy., Gatlinburg, TN 37738). The second of two national park concessionaires in the Gatlinburg area, Smoky Mountain Stables offers trail rides up the little-visited Dudley Creek area of the national park from a stable on US 321, 4 miles east of downtown.

**HIKING AND CAMPING** **A Walk in the Woods** (awalkinthewoods.com; e-mail: Erik@awalkinthewoods.com; 865-436-8283; 4413 Scenic Dr. East, Gatlinburg, TN 37738). Erik and Vesna Plakanis offer half- and whole-day guided nature walks within the Great Smoky Mountains National Park, as well as custom trips and backpacking trips. All walks include a guide, car shuttles, and a picnic lunch. They also rent camping equipment. Appalachian Trail hikers should note that the Plakanis offer through-hiker support.

**GOLF** **Bent Creek Golf Resort** (bentcreekgolfcourse.com; e-mail: bentcreekgc@ yahoo.com; 800-251-9336, 865-436-3947; 3919 East Pkwy., Gatlinburg, TN 37738). This par-72 golf course, designed in 1972 by Gary Player, is located at Pittman Center, 10 miles east of Gatlinburg on US 321. Owned by Sunterra, there are a large number of time-share condos available for rent along the course, as well as some very nice cottages.

**Gatlinburg Muncipal Golf Course** (800-231-4128, 865-453-3912; 520 Dollywood Ln., Pigeon Forge, TN 37863). Open all year. Owned by the city of Gatlinburg, this 1955 Bob Cupp–designed course is noted for its dramatic 12th hole—teeing over a 200-foot drop down a near-cliff-like slope to reach the green 194 feet away. This handsome course offers beautiful views along its length, plus a lake on the 18th.

**SKIING** **Ober Gatlinburg** (obergatlinburg.com; e-mail: fun@obergatlinburg.com; 800-682-4386, 865-436-5423; 1001 Pkwy., Gatlinburg, TN 37738). Open all year, except for the first two weeks in March (dates vary). Ski season runs December to February; summer amusement park from April to November. You can drive to the ski slopes of Ober Gatlinburg, but it's a lot more fun to take the **Swiss-made cable car** from downtown Gatlinburg. The enclosed cars sweep over the Gatlinburg rooftops, up a hollow, and over a ridge to a wide panorama—Mount LeConte towering on the right, the much lower hills of eastern Tennessee on the left, and Gatlinburg deep in the valley directly below. The clean and orderly ski hall, which doubles as a fun center in the summer, is a wide-spanning metal building with exposed girders and a sloping floor of exposed concrete. Inside, county fair–style concessions surround a skating rink, with the floor spiraling down. The eight ski trails have a longest run of 5,000 feet and a maximum drop of 600 feet, with a maximum elevation of 3,300 feet. A snow report can be obtained by dialing 800-251-9202.

**CRAFT AND ENVIRONMENTAL SCHOOLS** ♿ **Arrowmont School of Arts & Crafts** (arrowmont.org; e-mail: info@arrowmont.org; 865-436-5860; 556 Pkwy., P.O. Box 567, Gatlinburg, TN 37738). In the early 20th century, the Pi Beta Phi women's fraternity founded the Settlement School just south of the mountain crossroads known as Gatlinburg, a charitable effort to bring schooling into the remote coves and hollows of the Smoky Mountains. Today known as the Arrowmont School, it has evolved over the years into one of the mountain's premiere craft schools. Still occupying its original 70-acre campus at the center of Gatlinburg, it offers one- and two-week intensive residency courses in a wide variety of craft arts.

🖍 **The Smoky Mountains Field School** (www.ce.utk.edu/Smoky; e-mail: utnoncredit@utk.edu; 865-974-0150; University of Tennessee; 313 Conference Center Bldg., Knoxville, TN 37996). Courses run spring through late fall. This cooperative program between the National Park Service and the University of Tennessee offers outdoor walking-based courses, taught by experts. The range of courses is truly incredible, from the expected offerings on Smoky Mountain plants, animals, and history, to special programs in the arts and nature writing, to wonderfully specialized programs on such topics as land snails and slime molds. A typical course will meet in a picnic area inside the park, then travel (most likely, walk) to the course's various locations over a period of four to eight hours. Many of the courses are specifically structured for parents to share with their children, with separate courses aimed at parents with teens and parents with youngsters. The Field School's headquarters is far outside the park, at the University of Tennessee's Knoxville Campus.

## ✷ Lodging

**BACKPACKERS' CABINS**

**LeConte Lodge** (www.leconte-lodge.com./home.html; e-mail: reservations@lecontelodge.com; 865-429-5704; fax: 865-774-0045; 250 Apple Valley Rd., Sevierville, TN 37862). Open mid-March–mid-November. Deep within the national park's backcountry and accessible only by hikers, LeConte Lodge sits just shy of the 6,593-foot peak of Mount LeConte. This collection of log buildings and primitive cabins is surrounded by old balsam forests, with only a short walk to wide sunset and sunrise views off clifftops. Hikers stay in bunk beds (linens and blankets supplied) in tiny board and batten cabins, heated by kerosene and lighted by oil lamps; there's no electricity or running water at LeConte Lodge. Meals, served in the rustic lodge and included in the price, are plain and hearty, not surprising as the food has to be packed in by llama. On any given day it's the coolest place to stay in the South—it's typically 20 degrees cooler than nearby Knoxville. It's also one of the rainiest and foggiest (and no, they won't give you a rain check on your reservation). However, if the weather cooperates you will experience the finest sunrises and sunsets anywhere in the South, from clifftops 1.25 miles above sea level. Reservations are required, and very hard to get. Try calling the first week in October for the following year.

**COUNTRY INNS** **Eight Gables Inn** (www.eightgables.com; 800-279-5716, 865-430-3344; 219 North Mountain Trail, Gatlinburg, TN 37738). Open all year. The Eight Gables Inn sits in forests on the northern edge of Gatlinburg, 2 miles from downtown and a short distance off a section of US 441 maintained as a scenic corridor. Built in the 1990s, the handsome, stylized exterior reminds one of a prosperous Victorian farmhouse, with wide porches (complete with rocking chairs, swings, and checkers), high windows, powder-blue clapboarding, and two gables on each side. Inside, a large common area occupies half or more of the first floor, with sofas and two wood-burning fireplaces. There are 16 rooms in all—eight upstairs, four downstairs, and four in an adjacent "cottage," a home-like annex that blends quietly into the woods. All rooms are comfortable and full-sized, theme-furnished with reproduction antiques. A full breakfast is served promptly at 9 AM, and guests typically gather before breakfast for coffee and a chat by the fire, or to read a morning paper on the wide verandah. In the evening, a homemade sweet and coffee offers another chance to socialize.

**Hippensteal's Mountain View Inn** (www.Hippensteal.com; e-mail: VernHippen@aol.com; 800-527-8110, 865-436-5761; fax: 865-436-8917; P.O. Box 707, Gatlinburg, TN 37738). Open all year. Prominent Gatlinburg watercolorist Vern Hippensteal and his wife, Lisa, own and operate this modern luxury inn on a hilltop deep in the countryside east of town. Set on 25 acres, the three-story inn has one of the finest views in the area, a sweeping 180-degree panorama over dense forest toward the high wall of the Great Smoky Mountains. Even better, every single one of the 12 rooms has its own share of this view from a wide covered porch furnished with rockers. Purpose-built during the 1990s, the three-story inn and its two-story annex have an old country look about them, with covered porches on every floor, French doors, and floor-to-ceiling sash windows. A hearty full breakfast is served between 8 am and 10 am.

**Blue Mountain Mist Country Inn** (www.bluemountainmist.com; e-mail: relaxed@bluemountainmist.com; 800-497-2335, 865-428-2335; 1811 Pullen Rd., Sevierville, TN 37862). Open all year. Built as a country inn in 1987, this bed & breakfast looks like a turreted Victorian farmhouse, powder-blue and surrounded by wide porches. Located in the hills above Pigeon Forge on the innkeeper's 60-acre family farm, its hilltop vantage point offers wide views toward the Great Smoky Mountains 7 miles away. The 12 rooms are ample in size and elegantly furnished with antiques and heirloom quilts. Five simple clapboard cabins are luxuriously furnished, and include Jacuzzis and kitchenettes. All rooms and cabins include a full breakfast and evening dessert.

**Hilton's Bluff Inn** (bnblist.com/tn/hiltons_bluff_inn; e-mail: info@hiltonsbluff.com; 800-441-4188, 865-428-8765; fax: 865-428-8997; 2654 Valley Heights Dr., Pigeon Forge, TN 37863). Open all year. A modern cedar-sided building conveniently located just outside Pigeon Forge (on a dead-end residential road just off US 321), Hilton's Bluff has 10 nicely decorated, country-themed rooms, each with its own door to a balcony or deck The cedar-clapboard building, in a plain modern style, is amply supplied with decks, porches, and balconies; it sits on a well-landscaped property surrounded by forests on all sides.

**COUNTRY RESORTS** **The Buckhorn Inn** (www.buckhorninn.com; e-mail: buckhorninn@msn.com; 866-941-0460, 865-436-4668; 2140 Tudor Mountain Rd., Gatlinburg, TN 37738). Open all year. Located in the beautiful, rural Glades area east of Gatlinburg, this historic 1930s resort is set in the midst of its own 25 private acres, surrounded by meadows and woodlands carefully set out by its original founder. From the approaching road the inn appears as a simple, modest white-painted wood structure; the inn turns its more elegant side to the Smokies, with a lovely view over wildflower meadows and hemlock forests to the peak of Mount LeConte. The six inn rooms are each theme-decorated with English country antiques and reproductions, and range in size from comfortable to large; one is a charming two-level retrofit on the inn's old central tower (which held a water tank during the 1930s). Attached to the old inn is a new annex with three new luxury suites, each with its own sitting area, gas log fireplace, and Jacuzzi. Down from the main inn are seven kitchenette cottages in a 1930s style (two are originals), with porches, decks, and wide picture windows overlooking the meadows. Breakfasts are hearty and fresh, with a choice of four items from a menu that changes daily.

**Christopher Place, An Intimate Resort** (www.christopherplace.com; e-mail: stay@christopherplace.com; 800-595-9441, 423-623-6555; 1500 Pinnacles Way, Newport, TN 37821). This luxury retreat sits on a remote site, north of Cosby on English Mountain. A modern structure purpose-built as a deluxe country inn, the Christopher Place looks for all the world like a Colonial mansion, perched high above the valley and surrounded by meadows with wide views. It has more amenities than other country inns, with a pool table, heated outdoor pool, tennis, fitness room, sauna, on-site trails, and llama trekking. Most rooms are large, with private sitting areas; all are elegantly furnished, and all have some special feature. The restaurant serves a hearty breakfast, and offers an elegant table d'hôte evening meal, available to the public with a 24-hour reservation.

**BED & BREAKFAST INNS** **Berry Springs Lodge** (www.berrysprings.com; e-mail: stay@berrysprings.com; 888-760-8297, 865-908-7935; 2149 Seaton Springs Rd., Sevierville, TN 37862). Open all year. A farmhouse-style lodge built in 2000, this nine-room bed & breakfast is located deep in the hills above Pigeon Forge. Quiet and remote, its hilltop location offers spectacular views over the foothills toward the Great Smoky Mountains, 7 miles to the south. The rooms are handsomely theme-furnished with reproduction antiques; each room has a fireplace and a private door that opens to either a deck, porch, or balcony with a view. A full breakfast is included.

**Bluff Mountain Inn** (bluffmountain inn.com; 865-908-0321; 1887 Bluff Mountain Rd., Sevierville, TN 37876). This modern four-room bed & breakfast sits in the fascinating Bluff Mountain area above Pigeon Forge, a steep, rock-bound mountain on the outward edge of the Smokies, 7 miles from the national park. All of the four rooms are beautifully decorated with country-style antique reproductions, and three of them are extra large—sitting areas with plush furniture around a fireplace, two-person whirlpool tubs—the works. Breakfasts are large and luxurious.

**MOTELS** Gatlinburg has several thousand motel rooms, and nearby Pigeon Forge has several thousand more. Gatlinburg tends more toward independent motels, set tightly on small pieces of property, frequently with unusual architectural flourishes. Pigeon Forge units are more interstate-style—chain motels, of standard construction, surrounded by large parking lots and fronting on a six-lane highway. Some of the more interesting-looking Gatlinburg motels sit along the river, a block below downtown. Contact the chamber of commerce for more information.

## ✷ Where to Eat

**EATING OUT** **Smoky Mountain Brewery and Restaurant** (865-436-4200; 1004 Pkwy., Gatlinburg, TN 37738). Open for lunch and dinner. This tavern and pizzeria has its own on-premise microbrewery, the only one in Gatlinburg. A two-story eatery toward the back of the Calhoun Village retail area, it is decorated in rough wood and 1950s-style furniture and flooring. It's immaculately clean, the atmosphere is neat, and the food is great—but the real story is the beer. If you have any taste for beer at all, you will want to try their fresh-brewed product, with a selection of five regular beers that the brewmaster continues to refine and adjust. The food is made with the same attention to detail, with original twists on old favorites. The pizza is excellent, and the sandwiches are made with bread baked fresh on the premises. Next door, Calhouns is run by the same people and presumably has the same high-quality food; it is more of a sit-down restaurant with ribs and steaks dominating the menu.

**The Fox and Parrot Tavern** (fox-and-parrot.com; e-mail: brian@foxandparrot.com; 865-436-0677; 1065 Glades Rd., Gatlinburg, TN 37738). Gatlinburg's best place for a friendly meal won't be found among the tourist-crowded downtown shops; instead, it sits above photographer Brian Papsworth's first-rate gallery in the Glades Arts and Crafts Community. Brian's Fox and Parrot Tavern recreates the atmosphere and spirit of a great village local in the heart of England. It's a place where locals and visitors meet and talk over a game of darts while enjoying a locally brewed ale and a freshly prepared bar meal. Every item on the menu is made from scratch ingredients on the premises, with a mix of American and British pub fare, including a really good chili. Desserts are first-rate, including an amazing Eccles cake, a Scots pastry filled with rum-soaked raisins. Ale lovers should note that Brian tries to stock a cask-conditioned ale on a hand pump during the season.

**DINING OUT** **The Buckhorn Inn** (www.buckhorninn.com; e-mail: info@buckhorninn.com; 866-941-0460,

865-436-4668; 2140 Tudor Mountain Rd., Gatlinburg, TN 37738). Open all year. Gatlinburg's historic resort inn offers an elegant, yet friendly dining experience. The Buckhorn offers only one seating for the small number of tables in its 1938 main lodge, so that service is attentive and food is prepared specifically for each table. The lodge furnishes an intimate atmosphere, with sofas grouped around a large hearth, encouraging conversation. All diners are seated at one time and presented with five courses of a fixed menu; reservations are required, as preparation starts long before the seating time. The imaginative and exquisitely prepared food varies daily, but tends to combine familiar favorites in new and exciting ways. Located in a dry area of the county, the Buckhorn has no wine list, but welcomes you to bring your own and charges nothing for corkage.

## ✷ Selective Shopping

**DOWNTOWN GATLINBURG** "We don't want to be noticed as T-shirt City, USA," the mayor of Gatlinburg once told a newspaper reporter, but "evidently it's easier to make a dollar selling T-shirts than anything else." Yes, downtown Gatlinburg has a lot of T-shirt shops. However, there are a lot of other downtown shops as well: old-timey photographs, tattoo parlors, NASCAR memorabilia, wedding chapels, souvenir stores, fudge shops, funnel cakes, gaudy jewelry, four different Thomas Kincade stores (the California-based "painter of light"), museums of the curious and weird (filling the role of side shows), amusement arcades, even carnival rides. It's easy enough to sneer at this "rundown, haphazard collection of buildings ranging from the good to the bad to the ugly," as did the **Sonoran Institute** in a report funded by the Gatlinburg Chamber of Commerce, no less; "Gatlinburg is widely viewed as one of the most unattractive and inappropriate gateways to a national park in the United States," the Institute sniffed. But it's also easy to relax and have fun, at Tennessee's **giant unofficial permanent state fair**. Message to the Sonoran Institute: grab a funnel cake, guys, and chill.

**Arrowcraft** (southernhighlandguild.org/pages/guild-shops/arrowcraft; 865-436-4604; 576 Pkwy., Gatlinburg, TN 37738). Open daily, off-season, 10 AM–6 PM; summer and fall, Mon.–Sat., 10 AM–8 PM; Sun., 10 AM–6 PM. The Arrowcraft crafters gallery predates the downtown area that crowds around it on all sides; this wandering log building has been selling fine crafts by local artists since 1926. Originally part of the adjacent Arrowmont School of Arts and Crafts, it is now run by the not-for-profit Southern Highland Craft Guild, and features only items handmade by Craft Guild artists.

**Beneath the Smoke** (kenjenkins.com; e-mail: ken@kenjenkins.com; 888-818-2262; 446 East Pkwy., Ste. 12, Gatlinburg, TN 37738). Beneath the Smoke is Gatlinburg nature photographer Ken Jenkin's homage to the Great Smoky Mountains, an 8,000-square-foot nature store, outfitter, bookshop, and gallery of Ken's stunning wildlife and scenic photography.

**THE GLADES ARTS AND CRAFTS COMMUNITY** Out of the 70 or more craft artists who are members of the Arts and Crafts Community in Gatlinburg's scenic, rural Glades neighborhood, it's impossible to select only three or four "best" or "most worthy." The listings that follow are more in the line of appetite-whetters than anything else. Poke around and choose your own favorites.

**The Historic Cliff Dwellers** (cliffdwellersgallery.com; e-mail: info@cliffdwellersgallery.com; 865-436-6921; 668 Glades Rd., Gatlinburg, TN 37738). Constructed in 1933 as an art gallery and studio, for decades this distinctive, multigabled wood structure served as a prominent landmark in downtown Gatlinburg. When threatened with demolition in 1995, it was moved to its present site at the heart of the Glades Community. The Gallery is now owned and operated as a cooperative by five local artists and carries the work of approximately 60 other area artists. These include weaving, pottery, decorative paper, watercolor, and doll and basket making.

**Church Mouse Gallery** (jimgraygallery.com; e-mail: office@jimgraygallery.com; 865-573-0579; c/o Greenbriar Inc., P.O. Box 735, Gatlinburg, TN 37738). Open daily, 10 AM–5 PM. Watercolorist and sculptor Jim Gray creates a wide range of landscapes, portraits, and florals—by no means all of the Smokies, although Smoky Mountain scenes predominate. The detail and colors of his watercolors are remarkable, as are the liveliness and sympathy of his sculpture—which include the statue of Dolly Parton in front of the Sevier County Courthouse. His Church Mouse Gallery offers reproductions from a lovely restored country church in the Glades Community, next door to the Cliffdwellers historic structure.

**Gatlinburg Ceramics** (e-mail: jbailey40@msn.com; 865-436-4315; 805 Glades Rd., Gatlinburg, TN 37738). Judy Baily has been handcrafting fine porcelains in her Glades studio-gallery for over 35 years, taking each piece painstakingly from raw kaolin to finished ceramic. The bulk of her work is in a traditional, even Victorian style, but her range is wide. She is frequently in her studio, visible from the showroom, and welcomes visitors.

**Ogle's Broom Shop** (oglesbroomshop.com; e-mail: toglebs@aol.com; 865-430-4402; 670 Glades Rd., Gatlinburg, TN 37738. One of the original craft studio/galleries in the Glades, David Ogle is a third-generation mountain crafter, native to Gatlinburg. He produces a variety of traditional mountain brooms, walking sticks with carved handles.

**G. Webb Gallery** (gwebbgallery.com; 865-436-3639; 795 Buckhorn Rd., Gatlinburg, TN 37738). Watercolorist G. Webb specializes in highly detailed studies of local landscapes; recent

DOLLY PARTON STATUE AT THE SEVIER COUNTY COURTHOUSE, SEVIERVILLE

works include the Temple Feed Store in Sevierville and the Emerts Cove Bridge near his home. His Glades Community gallery occupies a restored 1910 board and batten farmhouse surrounded by wildflower gardens and giant hemlocks.

## ✷ Special Events

**SPRING Annual Spring Smoky Mountain Wildflower Pilgrimage** (www.springwildflowerpilgrimage.org; 865-436-7318; 115 Park Headquarters Rd., Gatlinburg, TN 37738). Last week in April. For over half a century, a group of East Tennessee organizations has sponsored this weeklong exploration of the national park's spring wildflowers. There are exhibits and vendors at the Gatlinburg Convention Center, but the real action takes place in a long series of field trips into the park—by foot, bicycle, and automobile. Wildflower walks predominate, but there are daily field trips for birders, and specialized trips for geology, plant identification, medicinal plants, moss, algae, fungi, insects, spiders, salamanders, bats, bears, old-growth forests, second-growth forests, logging, history, folk art, plant sketching, photography, and environmental issues.

**The Cosby Ramp Festival** Since 1954, Cosby has celebrated that pungent herald of spring, the ramp. A ramp is a type of wild onion also known as a wild leek. It has a sweet, mild taste with a hint of garlic, but is notorious for the strong odor it leaves behind. One of the first plants to emerge in the spring, the ramp has traditionally been a center of community celebration in the mountains—typically a ramp supper given by the volunteer fire department. The Cosby Festival is unusual in being a big shindig thrown

DOWNTOWN GATLINBURG

for tourists as much as locals, with a full slate of mountain and bluegrass music.

**Gatlinburg Scottish Festival and Games** (800-568-4748; P.O. Box 1487, Gatlinburg, TN 37738). Third weekend in May. This traditional Scottish festival includes bagpipes, drums, Highlands dancers, sheepdog demonstrations, entertainment, clan tents, and Scottish food (yum!), in addition to Scottish games. It's held in Mills Park, a largish city park near the Glades Crafts Community.

**SUMMER Fourth of July Celebrations** Gatlinburg's July Fourth celebrations start promptly at midnight, with a night parade through downtown that includes marching bands, lighted floats, and helium balloons. During the day there's a "River Raft Regatta" in which unmanned craft race down the river in the middle of town.

**WINTER Winterfest Kickoff** November 14. Gatlinburg starts its season of winter illumination—light displays that continue through Christmas to Valentine's—with a festival at the new Ripley's Aquarium featuring a chili cook-off, live music, clowns, and magicians, as well as trolley tours of the lights. Christmas hayrides start two weeks later and continue through most of December.

**New Year's Eve Space Needle Spectacular** A New Year's street party centers on downtown Gatlinburg's Space Needle attraction, with a ball drop and a stunning display of fireworks launched from the 340-foot observation tower.

# TOWNSEND, CADES COVE, & THE NORTHWEST QUADRANT

This quadrant of the Great Smoky Mountains National Park contains one of the most beautiful and rewarding sites in the eastern United States—the remarkable Cades Cove, a large flat-bottomed valley covered in pastureland, dotted with log cabins, and surrounded on all sides by great mountain walls. The Park Service maintains this huge valley, 5 miles long and nearly 2 miles wide, as a 3,000-acre outdoor museum of pioneer life, with 12 major structures and many more outbuildings. An 11-mile-long, one-way loop road skirts the cove's edge, giving wide views and easy access to all of its sites.

The drive to the cove tells another story. The twisting paved road follows the bed of an historic logging tramway along a roaring mountain stream—as do most of the roads in this part of the park, the former lands of the Little River Lumber Company. The handsome young hardwood forests you see in these parts have grown since the Park Service gained control of the stripped-out land in 1940. Two old lumber camps, at Elkmont and Tremont, offer recreation opportunities, while the scattered remnants of the Little Greenbrier farming community survive in a little-visited corner of the woods.

Outside the park, another large cove straddles the main highway (US 321). Tuckaleechee Cove furnishes a scenic mountain setting for a variety of bed & breakfast inns, resorts, cabin rentals, cafés, and restaurants. It also contains the main settlement of Townsend, a former logging town where restaurants, shops, and motels spread along the four-lane highway. It has a visitors center in a new log building in the center of town—a good place to get oriented. Townsend is a lot less trafficked and more mountainy than the Gatlinburg/Pigeon Forge area, for those who prefer a more personal, homelike experience and are willing to do without chain restaurants.

**GUIDANCE—TOWNS AND COUNTRYSIDE** ♿ **Smoky Mountain Convention & Visitor's Bureau** (www.smokymountains.org; 800-525-6834; 7906 E. Lamar Alexander Pkwy., Townsend, TN 37882). Open every day, normal business hours. This nonprofit organization, dedicated to promoting economic growth and tourism in the Blount County area of the Smokies, maintains a visitors center in a

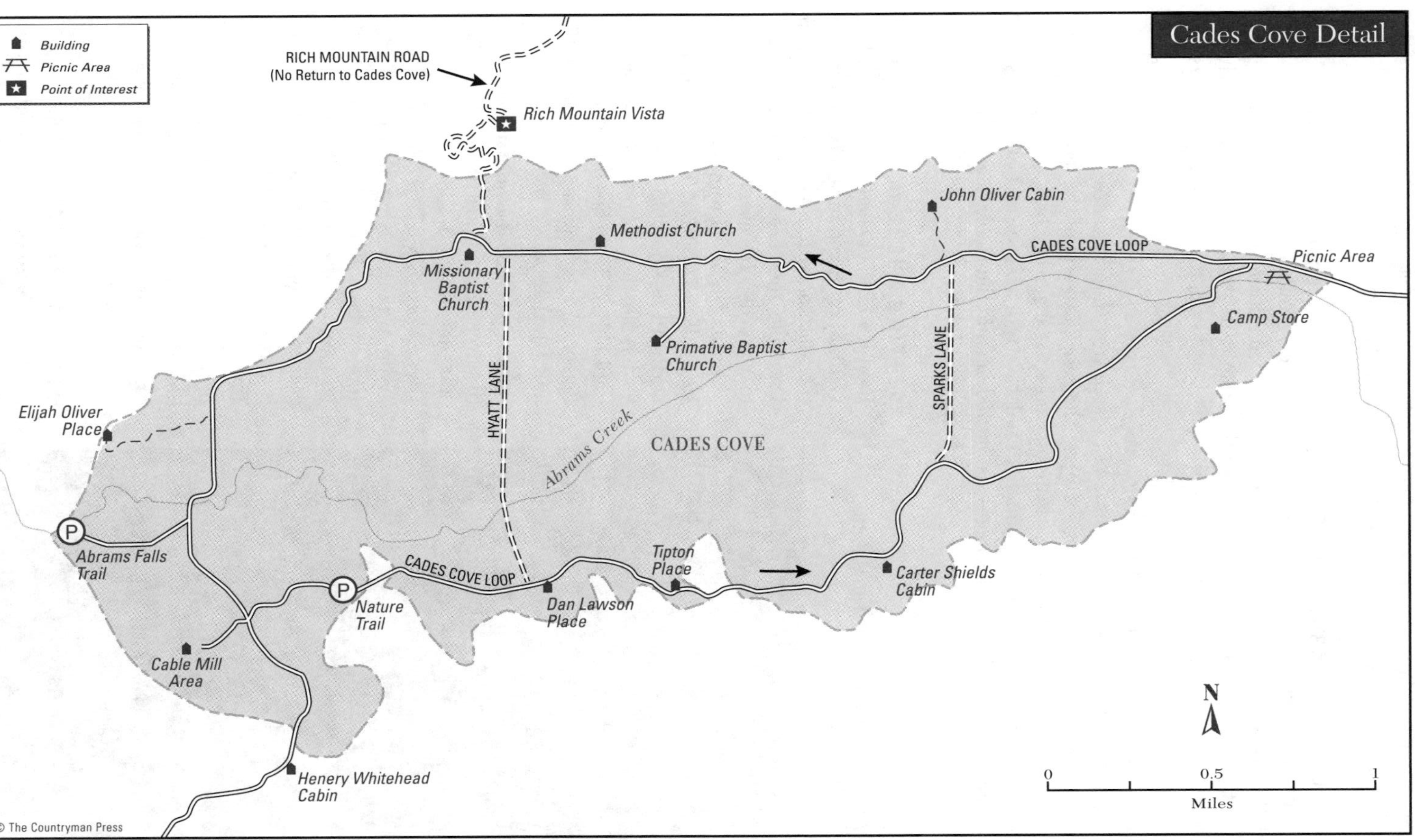
Cades Cove Detail
Building
Picnic Area
Point of Interest
RICH MOUNTAIN ROAD
(No Return to Cades Cove)
Rich Mountain Vista
John Oliver Cabin
Methodist Church
CADES COVE LOOP
Picnic Area
Missionary Baptist Church
Primative Baptist Church
Camp Store
HYATT LANE
SPARKS LANE
Elijah Oliver Place
Abrams Creek
CADES COVE
P
Abrams Falls Trail
CADES COVE LOOP
Tipton Place
Carter Shields Cabin
P
Nature Trail
Dan Lawson Place
Cable Mill Area
Henery Whitehead Cabin
N
0
0.5
1
Miles

modern log building in Townsend. This visitors center has a good gift shop and displays of local artists, as well as a staffed information desk.

**GUIDANCE—PARKS AND FORESTS** **The Great Smoky Mountains National Park—Ranger Stations** (www.nps.gov/grsm). The Park Service maintains a ranger station at Cades Cove with a staffed information desk. You'll find it off to the left as you enter the cove, in the main recreation area across from the camp store. For general phone inquiries, it's best to call the Sugarlands visitors center.

**Digital Geologic Map of Cades Cove** (geology.er.usgs.gov/eespteam/smoky/ResearchAreas/smokys/cadesCove/Cades Home2.htm). The U.S. Geologic Survey, the geological arm of the federal government, maintains an extensive website on Cades Cove geology based on their own, recent, research. They also maintain a similar website for **Mount LeConte**. Sorry about the long URL—these pages are buried deep in the Geological Survey's master site.

VIEW OVER CADES COVE FROM RICH MOUNTAIN ROAD

**GETTING THERE** *By Car* Townsend is on US 321 between Maryville and Gatlinburg. If you're approaching from the south or west, take the interstate to Knoxville, then take I-140 and US 129 to Maryville; Townsend is another 20 miles via US 321. From the north or east, follow I-40/81 to TN 66 (exit 406), northeast of Knoxville. Take TN 66 to Sevierville, then follow US 441 south until US 321 branches off right at Pigeon Forge; Townsend is another 15 miles farther on.

*By Air* **McGhee Tyson Airport** (tys.org; e-mail: info@tys.org; 865-342-3000; fax: 865-970-4113; 2055 Alcoa Hwy., Alcoa, TN 37701). McGhee Tyson Airport, serving the Knoxville area, is about 20 miles from Townsend. It's large enough to have all the major car rental agencies on-site, which is just as well; there is no bus service into Townsend.

*By Bus, Train, or Public Transportation* The Townsend area has no railroad, no bus service, and no public transportation.

**MEDICAL EMERGENCIES**

♿ **Blount Memorial Hospital** (www.blountmemorial.org; 865-983-7211;

907 East Lamar Alexander Pkwy., Maryville, TN 37804). Located 20 miles west of Townsend on US 321, this 250-bed regional hospital serves all of Blount County from the county seat of Maryville. It has 24-hour emergency facilities.

## ✷ Exploring the Area

The northwest quadrant of the Great Smoky Mountains National Park has, as its southern border, the western half of the Smoky Mountains, descending from its high point at Clingman's Dome (at 6,643 feet, or 1.26 miles above sea level) to its end at the Little Tennessee River's water gap (at 1,086 feet, or 0.21 mile above sea level). That's right—within this quadrant, elevations drop more by more than a mile. And they do it pretty much all at once; the wall of the Great Smoky Mountains looming above Cades Cove makes for one of the greatest sights of the Appalachian Mountains.

Down from this massive barrier ridge, you'll find a series of much lower ridges that parallel it. The largest and closest of these ridges forms the park's northern border. This chapter continues beyond that, taking in a broad area of privately owned land, and ends at the last parallel ridge, Chilhowee Mountain, with its impressive views over Tennessee's Great Valley.

These ridges frame three of the largest examples of a most peculiar geological feature, which geologists call a *limestone* (or *karst*) *window,* known to the locals as *coves.* These are places where a river has eroded down through ultrahard mountain rock onto a flat bed of limestone. As water can dissolve limestone, the river makes short work of it, forming it into a completely flat bottomed valley with incredibly rich soil. Where the limestone ends, the mountains rise suddenly, forming a box valley; the river must then exit through a gorge.

The three limestone windows in this area are **Cades Cove** within the park, along with **Tuckaleechee Cove** and **Wear Cove** outside the Park. The park's original plan was to purchase and preserve all three coves, but the money ran out before that happened. Now Cades Cove has been returned to its pioneer area appearance, and is one of the East's premiere beauty spots. Tuckaleechee Cove (which contains Townsend) and Wear Cove serve the needs of the 2 million people who make the annual trek to admire that beauty.

**EXPLORING BY CAR Cades Cove Loop Road** To reach the start of the 10.3-mile, one-way Cades Cove Loop Road, enter the park at Townsend and follow the signs 7.3 miles to Cades Cove. This one-lane loop furnishes a scenic ramble through the national park's most historic and beautiful corner. Meandering through forests and fields, with sweeping views toward the Smoky Mountains, this lane passes 10 **separate historic sites**, each one preserving one or more pioneer-era structures from the cove's past; you'll find full descriptions under *To See: Cades Cove Historic Sites.*

The loop road begins at a large meadow where the **Cades Cove Stables** pastures its horses; in the morning, the grazing horses provide foreground for the wide view over the fields toward the Great Smoky Mountains. There is parking here, and an information kiosk. From there, the road wanders through forests and meadows for 1.1 miles, where gravel, two-way **Sparks Lane** on the left cuts straight across the width of the cove floor to meet the loop 1.7 miles from its end. Just beyond on the

BEAUTY SPOT, IN TENNESSEE'S UNAKA MOUNTAINS

right is the parking lot and path for the **John Oliver Place**, the cove's oldest and most photogenic log cabin, set back a quarter-mile from the road. At 2.4 miles, the narrow, winding lane takes you to a short, gravel side lane to the **Primitive Baptist Church**, during the Civil War a hotbed of Unionism and a stop on the Underground Railway. At 2.7 miles you reach the loveliest of the three surviving cove churches, the white clapboard **Methodist Church**. You'll find wide views from the wildflower meadows above the church.

At 3.1 miles, **Hyatt Lane** leads off to your left across the cove floor, a two-lane, two-way gravel road that regains the loop road at the far side of the cove, a 1.3-mile drive. This tree-lined lane is your best place to admire the view from the middle of the cove, a substantially different perspective from the loop road. It is lined with wide meadows that invite wandering, and is full of wildlife, including deer and bear. If traffic has snarled beyond endurance (as sometimes happens on a fine fall weekend), this is your best escape route.

DEER IN CADES COVE

Next comes the **Missionary Baptist Church** at 3.2 miles, across the lane from the one-lane, one-way gravel Rich Mountain Road, leading 10.9 miles out of the park to the village of Townsend. If you venture 1.1 miles up this road you will find the single **best road view in the entire park**, a spectacular 180-degree panorama over the whole cove, with the wall of the Great Smoky Mountains revealed in all its glory, and the tiny, white Methodist Church on a hill below. And from there, you have an achingly slow 9.8-mile drive through heavy forest, passing over two gaps with many switchbacks, all the way to Townsend; there is no return to the cove.

Now that you've reached the western end of the cove, the views reach their finest. At 4.6 miles there's parking for the 0.6-mile easy walk to the **Elijah Oliver Cabin**, a full-sized farmstead set in remote meadows. You are now driving along the "Hayfields" stretch of the loop road, 1 full mile of continuous views in all directions, the longest and widest view from a paved road within the park. In the middle of this stretch a 0.5-mile lane on your right goes to the Abrams Creek Trailhead, the start of the popular hike to **Abrams Falls**. Toward the end of the Hayfields, a split-rail fence on the right frames views over wildflower meadows toward a large farmstead—**the Cable Mill Area** (entrance at 5.6 miles), for many the high point of the loop with its visitors center, working water mill, restored farmhouse, cantilevered barn, collection of pioneer farm tools, and craft demonstrations. Another good reason to stop: Cable Mill has the only toilets on the loop road.

From Cable Mill, the loop road turns sharply left as the paved two way Forge Creek Road goes 0.7 mile to the **Henry Whitehead Cabin**, an unusual merging of two cabins. Another half-mile leads to the end of the two-way road and the start of **Parsons Branch Road**, a one-way, one-lane gravel road that preserves (all too well) an antebellum mountain road.

Back at the loop, a long, twisty forest section passes the Cades Cove Nature Trail on the right at 6 miles, and (at 6.8 miles) reaches the **Dan Lawson Place**, a log cabin behind split-rail fences. Hyatt Lane enters at this point, and a short jaunt up the lane will give you a good view over meadows to the Lawson Place nestled in the forests. At 7.4 miles on the rightsits the elaborate **Tipton Place**; its impressive cantilevered barn, a unique folk feature, is the first building you'll see of this complex. The final cabin on the loop, the modest **Carter Shields Cabin** at 8.6 miles, sits in an open glade rich in spring dogwoods. From here you have 1.5 miles of pleasant, if anticlimatic, scenery before reaching the Cades Cove Recreation Area and two-way traffic; the ranger station is a short distance to your right. The loop's start and the road out of the cove is 0.2 mile ahead on your left.

A final word of warning: loop road traffic can be very bad. It's one lane wide with no passing, so you'll go no faster than the slowest car on the loop. On a weekend the loop road can become a parking lot, with traffic inching forward slower than a walking pace. There's a great alternative, though; on Wednesday and Saturday mornings (until 10:30 am) the loop road is open to bicyclists and walkers only.

HYATT LANE IN THE CENTER OF CADES COVE

**Driving the Little River Railroad**

East of Cades Cove, 23 miles of park roads follow the railroad beds of the **Little River Lumber Company**. By the time the Little River Lumber Company finished logging in 1940 they had laid over 400 miles of railbed, mostly to dead ends in the valleys they were logging. These abandoned railbeds form many of the hiking trails and nearly all of the roads in this part of the park.

### THE AMAZING SHAY LOCOMOTIVE

There's a Shay Engine on display at **Townsend's Little River Railroad and Lumber Company Museum**, and it is definitely worth a gander. From the museum side, its stubby chassis gives no hint of its immense power; but walk around it and you'll see that each wheel has gear teeth on its rim that connects directly to the engine. This little beast doesn't go very fast, but boy, can she pull!

In 1876, Michigan logger Ephraim Shay invented this locomotive specifically for pulling heavy loads on steep, curvy, badly laid tracks—an engine for the timber industry. It was short, massively geared, with an engine designed to create even power and a chassis designed to hug the worst track imaginable. His engine cut the cost of logging Michigan's primeval forests by 60 percent or more—money in his pocket, as neither he nor any other lumberman was about to pass on the savings. Shay-based logging devastated Michigan, and when that state was denuded moved into the more challenging southern Appalachians. By the 1890s the Shay tracks had reached the Smokies.

Until the 1890s there was little logging on the upper slopes anywhere in the Smokies or Blue Ridge Mountains. It was just too hard; a lumberman could lose his investment just trying to move the logs over the rough terrain to a railhead. The Shay engine, however, allowed the loggers to extend standard gauge track along steep, twisty, poorly laid track into the most remote defiles, and slide the logs down the stripped clay slopes to the train. The Shays were powerful enough to keep long trains from jumping the

Starting at the **Cades Cove Picnic Area**, this drive follows Laurel Creek Road out of the cove toward Townsend. Just beyond the Schoolhouse Gap Trailhead the highway takes to the old logging railbed, acquiring its even gradients and sharp curves. Frequently the road becomes a narrow shelf cut into the mountain slope, with the stream racing along on one side and a vertical rock face on the other. You'll pass a tunnel and a waterfall, then the side road to **Tremont**, before you reach the fork to Townsend (1 mile on the left) at a great **swimming hole** with a sandy beach. From there, the old railbed goes right, following the Little River upstream. Now the road/railbed winds sharply while hugging this full-volume, cascading river. Views over the river are continuous for miles, with many opportunities to fish, wade, or admire the scenery. At **The Sinks** (parking at right, over the bridge) there's a clifftop view of a stone bridge framed by two large waterfalls. A few miles farther down the road you'll reach the **Metcalf Bottoms Picnic Grounds** and a side road leading to the historic **Little Greenbrier community** with its log schoolhouse and a remote log cabin that was inhabited as late as the 1960s. When you reach the side road to **Elkmont**, take it; you will still be follow-

tracks or sliding out of control as they descended 6-percent slopes and steep curves; in one spot near Elkmont, the tracks crossed a cliff-sided gorge on a sagging suspension bridge. None of these dead-end logging lines was meant to last more than a dozen years; when a watershed was stripped bare, the steel tracks would be lifted up and moved to the next stream. When the National Park Service took over these lands, it found the slopes denuded, the trees all carried away by the Shay engines.

To a large extent, the Shay engine formed this area. Townsend was founded as the place where the logging cars were transferred from slow-moving Shays to normal locomotives. Names such as Tremont and Elkmont remember the temporary logging towns that serviced each watershed-based operation. And there is a reason why the modern roads that link Townsend with Cades Cove, Tremont, and Elkmont are all so narrow and twisty, yet so gentle in their grades; they are all built on railroad beds constructed specifically for the Shay engine.

While time and good management by the National Park Service have healed the damage caused by Shay-based logging in the Townsend area, other places were worse hit. **Charlies Bunion** (see "Cherokee & the Southeast Quadrant," *Exploring the Area*) formed where fires and floods on denuded slopes caused all the soil to slip down into the valley, leaving the bedrock exposed as a sheer cliff. Further south, the Pisgah National Forest's **Shining Rock and East Fork Wildernesses** (see "The Blue Ridge Parkway Approaches the Smokies," *Wild Places*) preserve thousands of acres of mountaintop meadows, formed when clear cut fires burnt so fiercely that they consumed the soil itself.

ing the old railbed. Abandoned buildings and a security fence mark the start of the old lumber camp, then a long straight stretch of road follows Elkmont's railroad siding. The paved road ends at the parking area for the Little River Trail, which continues to follow the railbed upstream. A gravel road, right, leads to the **Elkmont National Historic District**, an early-20th-century vacation settlement.

**The Foothills of Cades Cove** The Foothills Parkway, part of the National Park Service's scenic highway system since 1944, has only two short completed segments. This scenic drive

SCHOOLTEACHER ELSIE BURRELL AT GREENBRIER SCHOOL

follows the longer of the two segments, Chilhowee (kill-HOW-ee) Mountain, for 17 miles, using historic old roads to make a loop trip.

To start this scenic drive, go through Cades Cove to the Cable Mill **site** then take Forge Creek Road through young forests growing up on abandoned fields. In 2 miles, Parsons Branch Road forks right. This is one of the earlier pioneer roads out of the cove, and the only motorable road that **preserves the look and feel of a** 19th-century turnpike—9 miles of twisting, steep, one-lane, one-way gravel road, with fords instead of bridges. It climbs in and out of small mountainside defiles as it rises; forests near the streams have giant hardwoods and hemlocks, while forests on the dry ridgelines have small pines and oaks. You'll reach the first of many fords at 2.7 miles; these fords consist of a concrete ramp into, then out of, a small stream. The road tops at **Sam's Gap** (2,780 feet), then drops into a steep defile so narrow that it's forced into a dozen fords before it ends at an historic 20th-century road—US 129.

US 129 is a relic of the 1930s **Works Projects Administration**; built for a Depression era when cars were few and slow, it is so curvy that motorcyclist use it for rallies. Turn right. US 129 spends the next 5 miles twisting under giant power lines that lead from the ALCOA-owned hydropower dams upstream. Views climax as the highway occupies an entire ridgetop, and the Little Tennessee River twists through a deep canyon below. Just beyond is the turnoff to the **Calderwood Power Station**, and the site of a very nice lakeshore recreation area. The highway finally descends to the banks of **Chilhowee Reservoir**, with 3 miles of wide and continuous views across the lakes. Turn right onto the **Foothills Parkway**.

Wide-shouldered, straight, and easy, the parkway curves gently up **Chilhowee Mountain** to its dry, sandstone ridgeline. Once there, you'll get the first of many sweeping views east toward the high crest of the Great Smoky Mountains National Park. Along this stretch, the **Look Rock Recreation Area** offers picnicking and 360-degree views from an observation tower. From there the Foothills Parkway goes more than 3 miles without a view, then makes up for it with a westward view over the flat Tennessee Valley—a great sunset location. The parkway ends a few miles later, 7 miles from Townsend on US 321.

**EXPLORING ON FOOT** **Tremont Logging Camp Walk** The Little River Lumber Company did its best to jam a full-gauge railroad into every stream valley between Elkmont and Cades Cove. Eighty years later, these **old lumber railroads** can make for some great walking, combining wide, even paths and easy gradients with stunning streamside views. This quiet stroll follows one such path, starting from the old logging settlement of Tremont and going up the railroad grade used to log out Lynn Camp Prong.

You'll find the trailhead, with ample parking, at the end of the Tremont Road, at the **old town site**. Constructed in 1925, Tremont operated for 8 years as the company stripped the upstream valleys bare. Tremont had a hotel, general store, electrical generator, machine shop, doctor's office, and combination church/school/movie theater (known as the House of Salvation, Education, and Damnation)—now all gone. A brochure, available from a roadside kiosk at the end of the Tremont Road's pavement, gives details of family life in the Tremont Camp as well as a map of the town.

A footbridge perches on old railroad piers in the center of the former town; a flat place beyond marks a siding and a fork in the railroad. Take the left grade up Lynn Camp Prong, a strong mountain torrent full of water in the driest weather, with many cascades in its narrow, steep valley. You'll immediately notice the coolness of this valley, and the fine smell of mountain water that hangs in its moist air. Straight young hardwoods and hemlocks shade the path and fill the valley on both sides. In a quarter-mile, the grade gives a clear view straight toward a 30-foot-**waterfall**, where the stream slides down a great exposed dome of a rock. From here the grade gives lovely views of rapids, then another set of waterfalls, before reaching a set of still pools. For the next half-mile the stream continues to furnish good views of small cascades, still pools, moss-covered boulders, and trees clinging to high bluffs. Then the valley becomes more U-shaped, allowing the railroad to straighten and retreat from the more dramatic and difficult terrain to a flat valley floor. This is a good place to turn around.

**Chestnut Top Trail** Cades Cove Ranger Steven McCoy calls Chestnut Top Trail "**the best wildflower walk in the Smokies**, both for variety and sheer numbers." Located right outside Townsend, this well-maintained footpath follows the ridgeline of Chestnut Top Lead just inside the national park boundary. You'll find the trailhead a half-mile inside the park on the Townsend entrance road, at the large riverside parking lot. The trail starts by climbing up the slope above the road, shaded by straight young hardwoods. Frequent limestone outcrops indicate the source of the lush wildflowers—rich limestone soil, similar to that of Cades Cove, supports a diverse ecosystem here. As the path climbs away from the road, the trees become large and the forest more open. Hemlocks reach 2 feet in diameter and rhododendrons arch over the path, as the trail reaches a narrow but beautiful view over Townsend and the mountains beyond the park. Then the trail gains the ridgeline and leaves the tiny limestone cove, to enter a dry pine forest with a rocky outcrop floor and a rich pine smell. Continuing gently uphill the path reaches a second gap, where trees cover a cliff-like plummet on the left; listen for the river noise from this direction, as you have spent nearly 1 mile doubling back to a point 400 feet above the trail's beginning. As the trail continues up the ridgeline, the forest gradually yields to a dry ridgetop pine/oak forest, very sunny and dusty with a faint smell of dry rot on a hot day. When the trail levels and enters the fourth gap, you've gone 2 miles and climbed 800 feet; it's a good place to turn back. If you continue, the path will climb another 300 feet and lose it again, before reaching the Schoolhouse Gap Trail in 2 more miles.

**LONG-DISTANCE PATHS** **The Appalachian Trail** The Appalachian Trail follows the Smoky Mountain Crest along the southern edge of this chapter's area; it is described in the Bryson City chapter.

**EXPLORING BY BICYCLE** **Bicycling in Cades Cove** Faced with jammed auto traffic on Cades Cove Loop Road, a large number of people prefer to bicycle around the 11-mile valley-bottom loop. In order to accommodate all these cyclists, the Park Service closes the loop road to automobiles on Wednesday and Saturday mornings until 10 am during the summer season. This is by far the best way to enjoy the continuous beauty of this 10-mile loop road, at just the right speed, with a breeze in your face. You can rent bicycles from a concessionaire in the cove or from a shop in Townsend (see *To Do*).

## ✷ Villages

**Townsend** Founded as a lumber mill town in 1901, Townsend sits on the first piece of flat land outside the national park boundaries, straddling the main road into this area of the park. This makes it **the closest town to Cades Cove**, and the closest collection of travel facilities (including food and gasoline) for the cove's 2 million annual visitors. Nevertheless, Townsend has always been dwarfed in popularity by Gatlinburg (23 miles east on US 321), and this has allowed it to retain some of the character of a quiet mountain cove. Today it consists of a scattered (but increasing) number of modest commercial buildings widely spread along a 2-mile stretch of four-lane US 321. It retains little of its past as a mill town apart from a worthwhile (and free) **historical museum** at the mill site, and it lacks any real town center or historic structures. However, views are good, and the town parallels the lovely Little River as it exits the Smokies. Townsend has only a scant few franchise motels and eateries, but it does have a decent selection of independent motels and restaurants as well as craft shops, antique shops, and gift shops. Compared to the mess at Gatlinburg, traffic and parking pose few problems.

**Wears Valley (Wear Cove)** Wears Valley (traditionally known as Wear Cove) is a wide rural valley just outside the national park between Townsend and Gatlinburg. Although isolated by bad roads for many years, Wears Valley started getting tourists when US 321 entered it in 1980. Since then it has become a popular spot for second-home **subdivisions**; its open views over rolling meadows are increasingly apt to include a large number of modern houses. A side road, Little Greenbrier Road, leads 2 miles into the park, ending at the **Metcalf Bottoms Picnic Area** on Little River.

## ✷ Wild Places

**THE GREAT FORESTS The Forests of the Smoky Mountain Crest** The Smokies Crest forms a giant half circle around the southern edge of Cades Cove. Lower here than at Gatlinburg, the crest rises abruptly from under 2,000 feet at the park's boundary at Deals Gap to reach 4,700 feet at Parsons Bald, there beginning its gradual rise to over 6,000 feet without any significant gaps. Although the Smokies formed a barrier here as well as elsewhere, it was a porous barrier, broken by a network of footpaths that allowed a low but steady commerce between the cove people and North Carolina. The cove folk would use these paths to bring their cattle up to graze in the **great grassy balds** that straddle the ridgeline. These balds, probably formed by the Cherokees and enlarged by the cove settlers, are some of the most varied and beautiful places in the park, with stunning views over the Smokies Crest and the infinitely receding ridges of North Carolina. Today's park trails retrace the old pioneer paths, ascending steadily through handsome young forests to the great mountaintop meadows above the cove at Gregory Bald, Russell Bald, and Spence Bald. Several of these paths make a challenging but doable all-day hike, with elevation gains between 2,000 and 3,000 feet and 6 to 12 miles of hiking one-way.

LOG CABIN IN CADES COVE

**The Forests of the Little River** When the Tennessee National Park Commission started buying land for the Great Smoky Mountains National Park in 1925, the Little River Lumber Company owned the entire Little River Drainage, some 77,000 acres. The company agreed to sell the land for a national park, but only if it could retain logging rights for 15 years. The Park Commission agreed; after all, how many trees could they harvest in 15 years? The answer turned out to be, "All of them." The company attacked the slopes, stripping them of every tree it could sell before the deadline came and logging ended forever. They beat the deadline by a year, denuding the virgin forests of the Little River by 1939. Then they took up the last of the rails from the railbeds, disassembled the Townsend mill, and turned control of the wrecked Little River Basin over to the National Park Service. The logging company had purchased a huge tract of old-growth forest, removed every tree, left a destroyed land bereft of economic value—and sold it to the government for a 50- percent profit.

The forests you see today are a product of this clearcut logging—a forest of young, straight hardwoods, mostly less than 70 years old. Hiking trails are more plentiful than you might expect, and many of these trails are remarkably easy and well built. Little wonder—they follow the gentle, even grades of logging rail beds, up the streams to end at the great mountainous wall of the Smokies Crest.

**Lower Abrams Creek Backcountry** The national park extends westward of Cades Cove to take in 60 square miles of rugged, little-visited backcountry centered on the lower reaches of Abrams Creek. This is a jumbled region of low ridges, with elevations seldom reaching 3,000 feet—short, stubby, linear ridges, placed close together between parallel creeks. The entire backcountry is thickly forested, with dry pinelands on the ridges and rich mixed hardwoods and hemlocks along the creeks. Access is by foot and horse only, with three trails running across the lay of the land and many more occupying the linear stream beds. Abrams Creek Trail, the only well-used trail in the area, follows the gorge of Abrams Creek as it cuts through the middle of these ridges, while the beautiful old cove roads, Cooper Road and Rabbit Creek Road, allow easy and lonely walking through the backcountry's northern and southern marches. All three of these access trails start in Cades Cove and converge at the Abrams Creek Ranger Station at the western edge of the park in Happy Valley (best reached from Happy Valley Road at US 129 just east of the Foothills Parkway, then follow the signs). This ranger station has a fine little campground, a couple of picnic tables, and good fly-fishing access.

**RIVERS** **The Little River** This important tributary of the Tennessee River rises from the 6,000-foot slopes under **Clingmans Dome** to flow for 34 miles before leaving the mountains, with 21 of these miles within the Great Smoky Mountains National Park. Back in the early 20th century it was the main corridor for the lumber railroad used to clearcut these slopes, and a railroad bed carries automobile traffic along its banks within the national park for 16 miles. Above this, the railroad bed continues as a hiking path, easy and level, giving good access for fishing.

Kayakers can join in the fun as far upstream as **Elkmont**, but the next 9 miles, rated Class II–III, are not favored. Instead, boaters flock to the 5.8 miles that start at **The Sinks** for a Class II–IV+ thrill ride through some very beautiful scenery. The dramatic 10-foot waterfall at The Sinks always has plenty of sightseers on hand, for those who like a little theater. As the river approaches the park border it becomes slack, so that its final 11 miles before leaving the mountains has only occasional Class II rapids; there is a dam portage on this section, and a second, demolished dam provides some artificial Class III action. Handsome limestone bluffs add to the pastoral scenery.

**RECREATION AREAS** **Cades Cove Recreation Area** This large, tree-shaded recreation area sits at the beginning of the Cades Cove Loop Road, a short distance down the paved road on your left. Its lovely streamside picnic area follows Abrams Creek as it flows into the cove from the mountains on its east. Just beyond is the large, wooded camp ground, the most popular in the park. Between the two is a recreation hall and camp store in a 1950s-style building, and a ranger station with an information desk. You can rent bicycles at the camp store, and a concessionaire-run stable offers trail rides across the road (see *To Do*).

Although the official picnic area is very nice indeed, serious picnickers will want to bring a blanket and enjoy the fine meadows on the cove floor. Hyatt Lane is a particularly good place to look for picnic spots, as is the stretch of loop road between the Primitive Baptist Church and the Elijah Oliver Cabin.

**PICNIC AREAS** **Metcalf Bottoms Picnic Area** This large picnic area, 10 miles west of Townsend on the Little River Road, occupies a long, flat-bottomed wide space on the otherwise twisty and cliff-sided Little River Gorge. Now covered in tall forest, this used to be a small, isolated farm and a whistlestop on the Little River Railroad. Metcalf Bottoms nearly always has a large choice of tables along its **long riverfront**—a particularly calm and wadeable stretch of the Little River. Little Greenbrier Road sneaks out behind this picnic area to the **Little Greenbrier historic area**, then out of the park to Wears Valley.

**Look Rock Picnic Area** This striking picnic area, about halfway along the Chilhowee (Chill-HOW-ee) Mountain section of the Foothills Parkway, features a row of picnic tables along **a rock precipice**, the view only partially blocked by tree stubbornly growing in the rock cracks. This is a dramatic, breezy place for a warm summer's lunch. The nearby observation tower, built in the 1960s and given to casual vandalism, offers fine views west over the flat lands of Tennessee's Great Valley.

## ✱ To See

**CADES COVE HISTORIC SITES** Cades Cove's stunning scenery is not merely a matter of a mountain wall rising from a flat valley. In truth, if the National Park Service had let the valley go to nature (which it seriously contemplated back in the 1930s), there would be no views at all, as the forest would block them. Instead, the Park Service manages the entire cove as a museum of pioneer life, not only preserving 10 separate historic building sites, but also keeping the valley floor under agriculture (primarily hayfields) to preserve the giant views of the prepark era. Here are the 10 historic sites, with mileages given along the one-lane, one-way 10.3-mile park loop road.

**The John Oliver Place** *Mile 1.2.* The first log cabin on the Cades Cove Loop Road, the John Oliver Place may well be the **most visually impressive**. It sits a quarter mile off the paved road, clearly visible across a meadow, framed by a split-rail "worm" fence, set against a backdrop of hardwood forest and steep slopes. Like all cove log cabins, its logs are "planked," hewn with flat fronts and backs, to prevent rot from entering along the rounded undersides of the logs. It works; the John Oliver Cabin has been standing for over 180 years. The cabin is built as a single log cube (called a "crib"), one log in length, with logs that interlock with dovetail joints—the same type of joint still used in making good quality cabinet drawers. The dovetail joints left large gaps between the logs, which the farmer chinked with mud mortar. Inside, the cabin is a single large room heated by a fireplace, with a second-story loft. The chimney is set outside the cabin against the gable end, and is made of local stone held with mud mortar. Southerners will see nothing unusual in this, but Northerners might wonder about the heat loss from an outside chimney. The mountain people preferred it cool, particularly after a long day cooking in the middle of the summer. At night, the sparse furniture would be moved out of the way; parents and girls would sleep downstairs, while the boys would sleep in the loft.

**Primitive Baptist Church** Mile 2.4. Cades Cove's Primitive Baptist Church was organized in 1826; the surviving church building is an 1887 white frame structure 0.33 mile down a gravel road. The Missionary Baptist Church is a short distance away, down the loop road.

Why two Baptist churches in such a small community? The Primitive Baptists were (and are) a deeply conservative and traditionalist group. They believed that every person should remain in the place given to them by God, and that missionary work was interfering with God's will for the heathen and a first step toward establishing a permanent, paid priesthood. In contrast, the upwardly mobile Missionary Baptists encouraged people to improve their position through business activity, had little fear of creating a priestly class, and funded missionaries. During the Civil War the Primitive Baptists were strongly pro-Union; God had created the Union, and to rebel against it was to rebel against God's will. Although the Primitive Baptist Church stopped meeting during the Civil War, its members resisted the Confederacy and formed **a way station of the Underground Railroad** that smuggled escaped Union prisoners to safety. For this they were targeted for assassination by rebel marauders who would cross the border from North Carolina, receiving information from Rebel sympathizers in the cove. This viciously murderous pattern repeated itself in isolated coves on both sides of the Tennessee–North

Carolina border, most famously at North Carolina's **Shelton Laurels** (see "North of Asheville: The Bald Mountains").

**Methodist Church** 2.7 miles. The current building is the prettiest of the cove's three churches, a beautifully proportioned 1902 white frame structure with a bell set in a small tin-roofed steeple. Built by a cove carpenter and blacksmith who later served as its minister, it replaced an old log church that the congregation had used since the 1820s. Like the other two surviving cove churches, it has a pioneer cemetery. Large meadows stretch uphill from it, a good place to ramble for views and wildflowers.

**Missionary Baptist Church** 3.2 miles. The cove's Missionary Baptist Church was formed in 1839 by dissidents from the Primitive Baptist Church. It, too, went inactive during the Civil War, its congregation split between Unionists and Rebels; it reorganized after the war without its Rebel families. The current white frame building dates from 1915, and served the congregation until it closed in 1944. Springtime visitors should look for the daffodils in the back of the church, planted by the cove's CCC troop in the 1930s to form the phrase "Co. 5427."

Across the lane, Rich Mountain Road—steep, gravel, and one-way—heads 10.9 miles north, out of the park, to US 321 west of Townsend.

**Elijah Oliver Place** 4.6 miles. The Elijah Oliver Place is a pleasant half-mile walk from the loop road. Elijah Oliver, a son of John Oliver, built this cabin after the Civil War. It is larger and more elaborate than his father's cabin, with an attached wing and a board-and-batten enclosure on the porch. It's interesting to note that Elijah used smaller logs than his pa had 40 years earlier; great trees had become harder to find in the cove. You'll find a number of interesting log outbuildings near the cabin, including a spring house used to protect the cabin's water supply.

♿ **Cable Mill Historic Area & Visitor's Center** Halfway: 5.6 miles. This complex of seven historic buildings occupies the site of the cove's mill, store, and most prosperous farm. When founded by John P. Cable in 1870 it had a gristmill and sawmill, both powered by a large overshot wheel that got its water down a long millrace from Mill Creek. The water mill is still in business, its overshot wheel turning its huge grist stones every weekend in season. The short walk along the mill race to the modest mill dam is interesting and peaceful. The adjacent frame house, built from lumber sawed at the Cable Mill, was a store and boardinghouse run by "Aunt Becky" Cable from 1887 until her death in 1944, 10 years after becoming part of the national park. It's now furnished like a late-19th-century cove boardinghouse. Nearby are all the outbuildings of a prosperous cove farm: a smokehouse, corncrib, barn, and sorghum mill. Nearby, a large cantilevered barn houses a collection of farm wagons and implements. The cantilevered barn, a folk form unique to these mountains, uses two log cribs as a foundation for a large loft, which is cantilevered out on all sides. Hay was stored in the large loft, stables created in the cribs, equipment kept dry under the overhang, and wagons pulled through the space between the cribs.

When you're scheduling your cove loop tour, be sure to check for craft demonstrations. These can include sorghum milling, blacksmithing, dying and flint knapping as well as milling corn. Every October the hayfields beside the Cable Farm are mowed with authentic 19th-century horse-drawn equipment.

**Henry Whitehead Place** 5.7 miles. This cabin is 0.7 mile down a two-way side lane, Forge Creek Road. In the 1880s, Matilda Gregory's husband deserted her and their son; in this emergency, her brothers quickly erected a crude log cabin for them. Then, a few years later, Matilda married Henry Whitehead, a widower with three daughters. Whitehead built them a fancy new cabin, attached to Matilda's tiny, crude one. The Whitehead Cabin is made of logs milled to 4-inches thick at the Cable sawmill, fitted snugly together, and covered with milled clapboards. It's the most sophisticated log cabin in the cove, and it's attached to the crudest.

**Dan Lawson Place** 6.8 miles. This well-built 1856 cabin is made of large hand-hewn logs fitted tightly together, with a frame extension added some years later. It has two log outbuildings, a granary and a smokehouse. Located at the intersection with Hyatt Lane, it is the most visible log cabin from the floor of the cove. Its split-rail fences provide space for wildflowers and a favored subject for photographs.

**The Tipton Place** 7.4 miles. Col. "Hamp" Tipton, a Mexican War veteran who lived in nearby Tuckaleechee Cove, built this frame house in the early 1870s for his daughters who taught school in Cades Cove. In the 1880s, the Tiptons sold the house to a blacksmith, James McCaulley, who built a smithy that still stands behind the house. Quite a farmstead survives from McCaulley's era. In addition to the smithy, there's a smokehouse and woodshed in the front yard, and a corncrib and cantilevered barn across the road.

**The Carter Shields Cabin** 8.5 miles. Little is known of the history of this modest log cabin, set in a lovely glade 2 miles from the end of the loop road. It's named after George Washington "Carter" Shields, a wounded Civil War veteran, who lived in it with his wife from 1911 to 1922.

TUCKALEECHEE COVE

**OTHER HISTORIC SITES** **Little Greenbrier Community** Little Greenbrier Community is one of the least known and least visited historic sites in the national park. It is also the place where the mountain folk lingered longest after the coming of the park. To find it, take Wear Gap Road from the middle of the Metcalf Bottoms Picnic Area, a half-mile to a gravel road on the right, then another half-mile up this narrow gravel road to its end.

You'll be parked by a **one-room log school house** that started life as a church—hence the incongruous presence of a pioneer cemetery on the hill above it. The Greenbrier school house is still in use, being the site of special classes for the schoolchildren of

Blount and Sevier Counties. With a bit of luck you'll find it open and class in session, with a full set of turn-of-the-century texts and teaching aids. The teacher uses an old map of Greenbrier Community that shows how these woods used to be filled with a network of cabins linked by paths and tracks. As late as 1999, you might have even caught Miss Elsie Burrell, the school's last full-time teacher back in 1942, in front of the blackboard; few of the students realized that this kindly old mountain woman was one of Tennessee's most distinguished educators. Since then, "Miss Elsie" has passed on, the last living link to the pre-park days; Tremont's Elsie Burrell Activity Center is named in her honor.

One of the Greenbrier cabins still survives, a remote 1.2-mile (one-way) walk from the school, along the gated jeep track across from the cemetery. A lovely and nearly level walk, the track follows Little Brier Creek upstream for a mile, then goes right at a fork to cross the stream and continue 0.2 mile to **the Walker Cabin**. This fine log cabin, set in a clearing with a springhouse and barn, was the home of the Walker sisters, who refused to move out of the park and continued to live in their family cabin until the 1960s. No other site in the park gives quite the feeling of remoteness, of quiet, and of simplicity as the Walker Place.

**Elkmont National Historic District** In 1908, the first logging train climbed up the Little River Gorge to the new lumber camp, Elkmont—then a typical company town, temporary but with a full range of services for the lumbermen and their families. However, the 18-mile rail journey up the Little River Gorge was so scenic, and Elkmont so cool and pleasant during the summer's heat, that tourists started coming up the rail line to stay at the modest little company hotel. By 1912 there were so many tourists coming to Elkmont that the company built a luxury hotel, the Wonderland, and subdivided a lovely nearby valley for vacation homes. These early-20th-century vacation developments, popular with Knoxville's power-

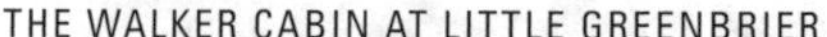
THE WALKER CABIN AT LITTLE GREENBRIER

ful elite, easily survived the lumber camp's closure in 1926. In fact, they survived until 1992, as an enclave of privilege inside the national park.

Why did the National Park Service allow the vacation homes of Knoxville's socialites to survive while they systematically demolished 6,600 farms, homes, and businesses? Many have jumped to the obvious conclusion—but the Park Service maintains that no one received any special treatment. When the National Park Service condemned the privately held lands, they gave every landowner the option of retaining a lifetime lease in exchange for giving up much of the purchase money. Mountain folk, who had to earn a living, took the money and left, while the Elkmont vacation-home owners accepted the lease option. Then, in 1972, the Elkmont elite used their clout to gain a 20-year extension from Congress. Enraged, the National Park Service formally stated their intention of tearing down every structure in Elkmont as soon as they got control. However, by then the vacation home subdivision had become **Elkmont National Historic District** with 69 of its structures on the National Register of Historic Places. This made the park's wholesale demolition plan illegal, and required independent review and approval for any substitute plan.

When the first edition of this guide came out, the National Park Service was still refusing to back off its wholesale demolition of an entire National Historic District, and was still refusing to maintain the rapidly deteriorating historic structures, despite the passage of nearly 10 years. Since then, the situation has advanced, albeit glacially. The National Park Service has approved an Environmental Impact Statement that acknowledges they are legally required to preserve the Elkmont Historic District, and that it is illegal for them to neglect maintenance. They have abandoned their former plan of demolishing the historic district and abandoning the property to nature (which would have added 60 acres of second growth to the 77,000 acres they already have). In 2010 the Park Service started implementing a plan that will demolish 57 historic structures, leave 12 as a museum area, and actively restore the environment to a cove hardwood forest. The first step, the restoration of the old Appalachian Clubhouse at the center of the new museum district, may well be completed by the time you visit.

**RAILROADS** ✐ **The Little River Railroad and Lumber Company Museum** (www.littleriverrailroad.org; e-mail: president@littleriverrailroad.org; 865-448-2211; P.O. Box 211 [Town Center on Old Highway 73], Townsend, TN 37882). Open Mon.–Sat., 10 AM–2 PM; Sun., 2 PM–6 PM. Between 1902 and 1938, the Little River Lumber Company stripped over a half billion board-feet of lumber from the Great Smoky Mountains and milled it in Townsend. This small local museum seeks to preserve the memory of the days when logging, not tourism, dominated the mountains of Tennessee. Headquartered in an historic railroad depot moved in from nearby Walland, this volunteer-run museum contains a first-rate collection of local logging artifacts. The artifacts are interesting in themselves and are arranged intelligently to give a thorough and coherent picture of Smoky Mountain logging and the way of life that logging briefly created. If you're lucky, you'll be shown around by a volunteer such as Georgia Bradshaw, who can expand on the exhibits with tales from her own childhood in the lumber camps high in the mountains. Outside the museum sits one of the Little River Lumber Company's original Shay engines—an amazing piece of machinery with its huge geared wheels.

**SPECIAL PLACES** ✐ **Tuckaleechee Caverns** (tuckaleecheecaverns.com; e-mail: info@tuckaleecheecaverns.com. 865-448-2274; 825 Cavern Rd., Townsend, TN 37882. Open April–October, 9 AM–6 PM; late March and early November, 10 AM–5 PM; closed mid-November–mid-March. The limestone-floored Dry Valley, just 1 mile east of Townsend, is home to one of the most dramatic show caves in the southern Appalachians, Tuckaleechee Caverns. The 170-step descent (no disabled access) leads to a deep underground river, then follows it for a half-mile. The 75-minute tour passes underground waterfalls, rapids, and sandy beaches on a gently curving stretch of stream. Long stretches of the path appear to travel through a western-style canyon, with steep rock walls rising on all sides. Stalactites, stalagmites, and flowstone of all sorts decorate the cave walls. The path ends in one of the South's largest underground rooms open to the public, big enough to hold three football fields and containing a stalactite column five stories tall. Tuckaleechee Caverns is lighted with uncolored incandescent lamps—this cave doesn't need to be frilled up with colors. It's particularly dramatic in rainy weather, when its underground river rises and the waterfalls become lively. As the path is not a loop, the total tour requires a mile's walk and 340 steps, so be prepared. To find Tuckaleechee Caverns, follow the signs south from US 321, just east of Townsend.

## ✷ To Do

**WHITEWATER ADVENTURES** ✐ **Smoky Mountain River Rat Tube Rentals** (smokymtnriverrat.com; 888-390-1190, 865-448-8888; 205 Wears Valley Rd., Townsend, TN 37882). The River Rat offers tube floats (with shuttle service) and kayak rentals with a choice of routes.

**BICYCLING** ✐ **Cades Cove Bike Shop** (www.cadescove.net/bicycling_cades_cove.html; 865-448-9034; P.O. Box 4923, Maryville, TN 37802). Open daily, April–October. This national park concessionaire offers reasonable day-long rentals on sturdy, well-kept machines. They are located at the Cades Cove Camp Store at the start of the Cades Cove Loop Road.

**FISHING Little River Outfitters** (www.littleriveroutfitters.com; e-mail: Info@LittleRiverOutfitters.com; 877-448-3474, 865-448-9459; fax: 865-448-3407;106 Town Square Dr., P.O. Box 505, Townsend, TN 37882). This large outdoor specialist offers fishing guides and a fly-fishing school in addition to their large line of fly-fishing gear and clothing. Owner Byron Begley is a fly-fishing expert.

**GOLF** ✐ ♿ **Laurel Valley Country Club** (e-mail: info@laurelvalleygolftn.com; 865-448-6690; 702 Country Club Dr., Townsend, TN 37882). Open daily. The Laurel Valley Country Club is a modest but comfortable facility at the center of a large gated community a scant 3 miles east of Townsend. Fully open to the public, its 18-hole par-70 golf course offers sweeping views toward nearby Rich Mountain (the northern border of the Great Smoky Mountains National Park), only a half-mile away.

**HORSEBACK RIDING** ✐ **Davy Crockett Riding Stables** (davycrockettridingstables.com; e-mail: Davy@DavyCrockettRidingStables.com; 865-448-6411; 505

Old Cades Cove Rd., Townsend, TN 37882). Located in scenic, rural Dry Valley east of Townsend, the Crockett Stables specializes in groups, but welcomes walk-ins for half-hour to two-hour guided rides; longer rides, including overnighters, are available by appointment. You can find the Crockett Stables by following the signs for Tuckaleechee Caverns, which is nearby.

**Next To Heaven Stables** (thesmokiemountains.com/customer_next_to_heaven_riding_stabels; 800-407-2231, 865-448-9150; 1239 Wears Valley Rd., Townsend, TN 37882). Open Mon.–Sat., 10:00 AM–5:30 PM; closed Sun. This stable, located 3 miles east of Townsend on US 321, offers guided and unguided rides.

**Cades Cove Riding Stables** (cadescovestables.com; 865-448-9009; 10018 Campground Dr., Townsend, TN 37882). Open daily, April–October, 9 AM–5 PM; closed November–March. This national park concessionaire operates guided trail rides within Cades Cove. If you visit the cove early in the morning, you'll see their horses grazing the wide fields at the start of the loop road. They also offer carriage rides and hay rides inside Cades Cove.

**OF SPECIAL INTEREST** **The Great Smoky Mountains Institute at Tremont** (www.gsmit.org; e-mail: mail@gsmit.org; 865-448-6709; 9275 Tremont Rd., Townsend, TN 37882). Multi-day programs run all year; reservations are required. For more than 30 years the Great Smoky Mountains Institute at Tremont has been giving youth and adult programs in environmental topics from their headquarters in the old YCC camp near Tremont. The Tremont Institute offers an immersive, intense experience with a great deal of group interaction, in the setting of a rustic camp surrounded by deep forest. While many of the activities are for school groups or professional educators, the institute also offers regular programs for the general public, typically three- to five-day residency programs with extensive outdoor time; meals are taken in a large mess hall. Youth and teen camps are scheduled throughout the summer, while adult multi-day programs include nature observation, wildflowers, geology, fall colors, photography, backpacking, and elder hostels.

## ✷ Lodging

**COUNTRY INNS** **Dancing Bear Lodge** (www.dancingbearlodge.com; e-mail: info@dancingbearlodge.com; 800-369-0111, 865-488-6000; fax: 865-448-3075; 137 Apple Valley Way, Townsend, TN 37882). Formerly known as the Maple Leaf Inn, this is a modern log-built lodge in the grand style, sitting on a large tract of woods and meadows adjacent to the center of Townsend. Each of its 12 lodge rooms and 16 cabins are individually decorated, and the cabins have kitchens, wood-burning fireplaces, indoor whirlpool tubs, and porch hot tubs. A continental breakfast is served in the lodge restaurant, which offers a full menu and bar in the evenings. The property has 3 miles of nature trails and paved bicycle paths, with views over meadows toward the Smokies.

**COUNTRY RESORTS** **Blackberry Farm** (blackberryfarm.com; 800-557-8864; 1471 West Millers Cove Rd., Walland, TN 37886). Open all year. Formerly a 1920s-era summer estate on 1,100 acres adjacent to the national park, Blackberry Farm has evolved into a luxurious 44-room mountain resort.

United by an architecture that combines the American Shingle Style of the original Main House with motifs from England's Cotswold District, the resort's facilities spread across 100 landscaped acres in groupings of large houses and small cottages. The landscaped grounds give the appearance of a thoroughbred horse farm through which guests can hike, bicycle, or jog on 7 miles of hiking paths and 3 miles of paved jogging trails; there are tennis, basketball, and shuffleboard courts, a swimming pool, and bicycles available to guests. All rooms are individual and unique, decorated in a simple, elegant English Country style. The elegant candlelight dinners are available to guests only, and are fully included in the room rates (excluding wine and beer), along with breakfast, a picnic lunch, a light tea, and ample day-long snacks (including Dove Bars).

## BED & BREAKFAST INNS

**The Richmont Inn** (www.richmontinn.com; e-mail: info@richmontinn.com; 866-267-7086, 865-448-6751; fax: 865-448-6480; 220 Winterberry Ln., Townsend, TN 37882). Open all year. Inspired by the unique local cantilevered barns found in nearby Cades Cove, this modern purpose-built small hotel has a log-built ground floor and a much larger second and third floor cantilevered out a good 10 feet in all directions. Located on 11 wooded ridgeline acres, the Richmont's site combines spectacular views with lovely woodland walks. Its 12 rooms, ranging in size from cozy to full-size luxury suites, are each individually decorated around a theme from Smoky Mountain history, and each has either a fireplace, a private balcony, or both. Room rates include a full gourmet breakfast and a candlelight dessert. Separate antique log buildings house the Cove Cafe, an intimate dinner place specializing in fondue, and a gift shop. Golfers receive a discount on the Laurel Valley golf course only a short walk away.

**Gracehill** (www.gracehillbandb.com; e-mail: info@gracehillbandb.com; 866-448-3070, 865-448-3070; 1169 Little Round Top Way, Townsend, TN 37882). This large, new bed & breakfast sits on the top of a small knob on the western edge of Wear Valley; it's encircling decks and porches furnish 360-degree views. The inn, purpose built as a bed & breakfast, is modern rural in design, with gray cedar shakes, local stone, and high ceilings. The four rooms are all large and luxuriously furnished.

**CABIN RENTALS** Although the Townsend area has only a few bed & breakfast inns, it has an enormous number of high-quality cabin rentals at very reasonable prices. The listings below are just a sampling of the units available to you, chosen to give the flavor of this area. With nightly rental rates competitive with bed & breakfasts and Gatlinburg motels, these cabins—all with full kitchens and separate living, dining, and bedroom areas—are the bargains of the Smokies. And, while the fellowship of a bed & breakfast is nice, there is something to be said for enjoying a mountain view from your own porch.

🖉 🐾 ♿ **Mountain Mist Cabins** (www.mtnmistcabins.com; e-mail: mistcabins@aol.com; 800-686-9288, 865-448-6650; 345 Boat Gunnel Rd./PO Box 162, Townsend, TN 37882). Open all year. Formerly a family farm, this is now a small community of country-style cabins, each set in its own woods separate from the others. Distinctive red tin roofs sit above full-size wraparound porches; walls are sided with rough-cut 12-inch planks. Each porch has rockers and a hot tub.

Inside, doors are handmade, and on-site wood is used for decorative accents with the log country furnishings. Fireplaces are finished in local stone, with gas log insets. All cabins are pet friendly.

**Blue Smoke Cabins** (www.bluesmokecabins.com; e-mail: bradycabin@aol.com; 865-448-3068; 1233 Carrs Creek Rd., Townsend, TN 37882). Open all year. Retired fireman Ron Brady and his wife, Linda, run this collection of handsome log cabins high on top a pine ridge 3 miles north of town. These well-furnished and roomy cabins have fine views from the rocking chairs and hot tubs on their wide porches, yet each cabin is completely isolated from its neighbors. You'll find the site's gravel roads to be mountainy verging on breathtaking, but within the abilities of the family sedan.

**Bradley Mountain Retreat** (www.smokycabins.com/bradley_mtn_retreat.htm; e-mail: reservations@smokycabins.com; 877-766-5915; 339 Bradley Retreat Rd., Townsend, TN 37882). All year. This ridgetop site southwest of Townsend offers stunning views over the town toward Rich Mountain. These roomy log cabins, set far enough apart on this wooded site to offer good privacy, are furnished comfortably and with a lot of personality; all have porches and hot tubs. Also on-site is a two-story log building with three motel-style kitchenettes, at a reduced price.

**Carnes' Log Cabins** (www.carneslogcabins.com; e-mail: info@carneslogcabins.com; 865-448-1021; P.O. Box 153, Townsend, TN 37882). Open all year. Small pets are allowed, with restrictions; please call ahead well in advance. This lovely little community of four hand-hewn log cabins is conveniently located in a hollow above Townsend. The cabins form a rough circle around the end of the approach drive, scattered in a wooded, grass-floored glade that gives privacy without impeding the views. The roomy cabins, which range from one to three bedrooms, are modern-built, with porches with rocking chairs, fireplaces, and whirlpool baths. Guests have free access to the Olympic-sized swimming pool at Tremont Outdoor Resort, a nearby private campground.

**Gilbertson's Lazy Horse Retreat** (www.lazyhorseretreat.com; e-mail: lazyhrse@comcast.net; 865-448-6810; 938 Schoolhouse Gap Rd., Townsend, TN 37882). Open all year. Melody Gilbertson boards horses and their people from her spread in scenic Dry Valley, 4 miles southwest of Townsend. Horses board in 10 indoor box stalls in a handsome and well-kept modern barn, with a half-acre of paddock surrounded by wooden fences. Their people get stabled in four cabins: two modern log cabins, a small house, and a farm hand's cabin right by the barn. This is a great location for trail riders, with 12 horse trails within 14 miles.

**Old Smoky Mountain Cabins** (oldsmokymountaincabins.com; e-mail: olsmokymtn@aol.com; 800-739-4820, 865-448-2388; fax: 865-448-9917; 238 Webb Rd., Townsend, TN 37882). Open all year. Possibly the oldest cabin rental in Townsend, Old Smoky has a wide range of properties scattered about, including a number of roomy, well-appointed log cabins. Their centerpiece property is a small modern hotel in a quiet rural location just north of town, with three suites overlooking a pool. All their cabin rentals have free access to the pool as well.

**Whisperwind Cabin Rentals** (www.whispercabins.com; 800-993-9928, 865-448-1979; 1177 Shuler Rd., Townsend, TN 37882). Open all year. The Hobbes family offers seven cabins in Dry Valley, each on a separate property but none far from their house and office. These excellently kept rentals cover quite a range, from a modest little cabin to a large luxury house; all properties offer privacy, and some are very secluded. Various cabins offer log construction, mountain views, whirlpool baths, hot tubs, wide porches, and great rooms with cathedral ceilings.

**CABIN RESERVATION SERVICES** **"Bear"ly Rustic Cabin Rentals** (bearlyrustic.com; e-mail: info@bearlyrustic.com; 888-448-6036, 865-448-6036; P.O. Box 283, Townsend, TN 37882). Open all year. A reservation service for renting second homes, they offer their selection of more than two dozen homes through a color brochure and web page.

**Dogwood Cabins** (dogwoodcabins.com; 888-448-9054, 865-448-1720; fax: 865-448-1721; 101 Painted Trillium Way/P.O. Box 485, Townsend, TN 37882). A reservations service managing and renting second homes. Some accommodations, such as the River Loaf Farm, offer horse stalls and fenced grazing on-site.

## ✱ Where to Eat

**EATING OUT** **Trailhead Steak House** (865-448-0166; 7839 E. Lamar Alexander Pkwy. [US 321], Townsend, TN 37882). Open for dinner all year. Grill your own steaks on the Trailhead's large, open outdoor grill! Actually, owner Tim Byrd is a masterful griller with an obsession for quality. Most people prefer to let Tim do the work while they relax in this western-themed restaurant, enjoying the large, flavorful salad, homemade bread, and a cold beer. Apart from four types of steak, Tim will grill up Alaskan halibut or salmon, caught wild and flown in, local trout, chicken breasts, kabobs, or shrimp; all get a treatment of his lightly seasoned olive oil.

## ✱ Entertainment

*Townsend*

**The Pickin' Porch at Nawgers Nob** Twice a week, on Tuesdays and Saturdays, local musicians and performers show up in front of Mike Clemmerer's dulcimer shop in the Nawgers Nob craft community. Mike will play a bit, and introduce the other acts. It's free, but don't forget your lawn chairs.

*Walland*

**Appalachian Music at the Community Center, Walland, TN**. Every Friday night, year-round, local musicians come to the Walland Community Center to jam. What happens next depends on who shows up; bluegrass musicians might be playing in one

GOSPEL MUSIC AT TOWNSEND

room, while old-time fiddlers hold court in another.

*Cades Cove*

**Mountain Music Program** The Great Smoky Mountains National Park sponsors a monthly program of authentic Appalachian mountain music at the Cades Cove Amphitheater, next to the camp store. In these programs, skilled musicians perform the historic music and ballads of the Smokies, and talk about this heritage music. Traditional dance may also be performed. This event occurs on the third Saturday of every month, from June through October; for details, call the park office (see "Gatlinburg & the Northeast Quadrant," Guidance).

## ✷ Selective Shopping

*Townsend*

**Wood-N-Strings**
(clemmerdulcimer.com; 865-448-6647; 7645 E. Lamar Alexander Pkwy./P.O. Box 383, Townsend, TN 37882). Mike Clemmer handcrafts fine Appalachian stringed instruments, from fiddles to the strange and beautiful stringed psaltery. But his favorites are dulcimers, lovingly crafted from walnut, cherry, or butternut. Mike is a soft-spoken man, as gentle and as sweet as the mountain instruments he loves, and he never seems to tire of showing off his sweet-toned dulcimers.

## ✷ Special Events

**SPRING** ✐ **Townsend in the Smokies Spring Festival and Old Timers Day** (www.smokymountains.org; 800-525-6834; 7906 E. Lamar Alexander Pkwy., Townsend, TN 37882). Last week of April, and last week in September, 9 AM–6 PM. Most events are free. This free weeklong festival, held in a large grassy field behind the Townsend Visitors Center, features daily live bluegrass music, craft demonstrations, and wildflower walks, with occasional special features such as mountain storytelling, antique tractors, and a barbeque competition.

**AUTUMN Cades Cove Fall Harvest Hayride** Each evening, last full week in October. The National Park Service collaborates with the Cades Cove Stables concessionaire to offer this evening hay ride around the Cades Cove Loop Road. As you progress around the cove you meet people from the cove's history: a cove farmer, a Cherokee, perhaps an escaping Union soldier or a Confederate raider.

# BRYSON CITY & THE SOUTHWEST QUADRANT

Bryson City sits at the southern edge of the Great Smoky Mountains National Park, within a deep, narrow bowl surrounded by mile-high peaks. To the north looms the third tallest peak in the eastern United States, Clingmans Dome, 6,643 feet above sea level, and almost a mile above Bryson City's small-town main street. To the south lie the knotted peaks of the Cowee Mountains, within the Nantahala National Forest. Between these two mountain systems, the Tuckaseegee River drains a deep, narrow valley, where fertile bottomland supplies a half-dozen produce stands. The town itself straddles the river, a fine old-fashioned county seat.

The Great Smoky Mountains National Park takes up a massive amount of remote, broken backcountry north of Bryson City, much of it little visited and hard to reach. South of Bryson City is the Nantahala Gorge, a whitewater venue that has produced a number of Olympians, including medalists. Fontana Lake stretches far to the west, where its monumental 1942 dam can be explored and crossed; its original workers settlement remains to this day as the Fontana Village resort.

**GUIDANCE** **Swain County Chamber of Commerce** (www.greatsmokies.com; e-mail: chamber@greatsmokies.com; 800-867-9246, 828-488-3681; fax: 828-488-6858; 210 Main St., Bryson City, NC 28713). The chamber of commerce is located at the center of downtown Bryson City, immediately adjacent to the old courthouse. You'll find it well staffed and extremely helpful. When the train is in town, they open a substation in an old red caboose within easy walking distance of the depot.

**The Great Smoky Mountains National Park Ranger Stations** For backcountry permits and other related questions, visit the ranger station at Deep Creek, in the campground. The nearest visitors center, with a staffed desk seven days a week, is at Oconaluftee, 2 miles north of Cherokee on US 441.

**Wayah Ranger District, Nantahala National Forest** (828-524-6441; 90 Sloan Rd., Franklin, NC 28734). The 15,000 acres of Nantahala National Forest in the Bryson City area are run from the Nantahala Ranger Station in Franklin (see

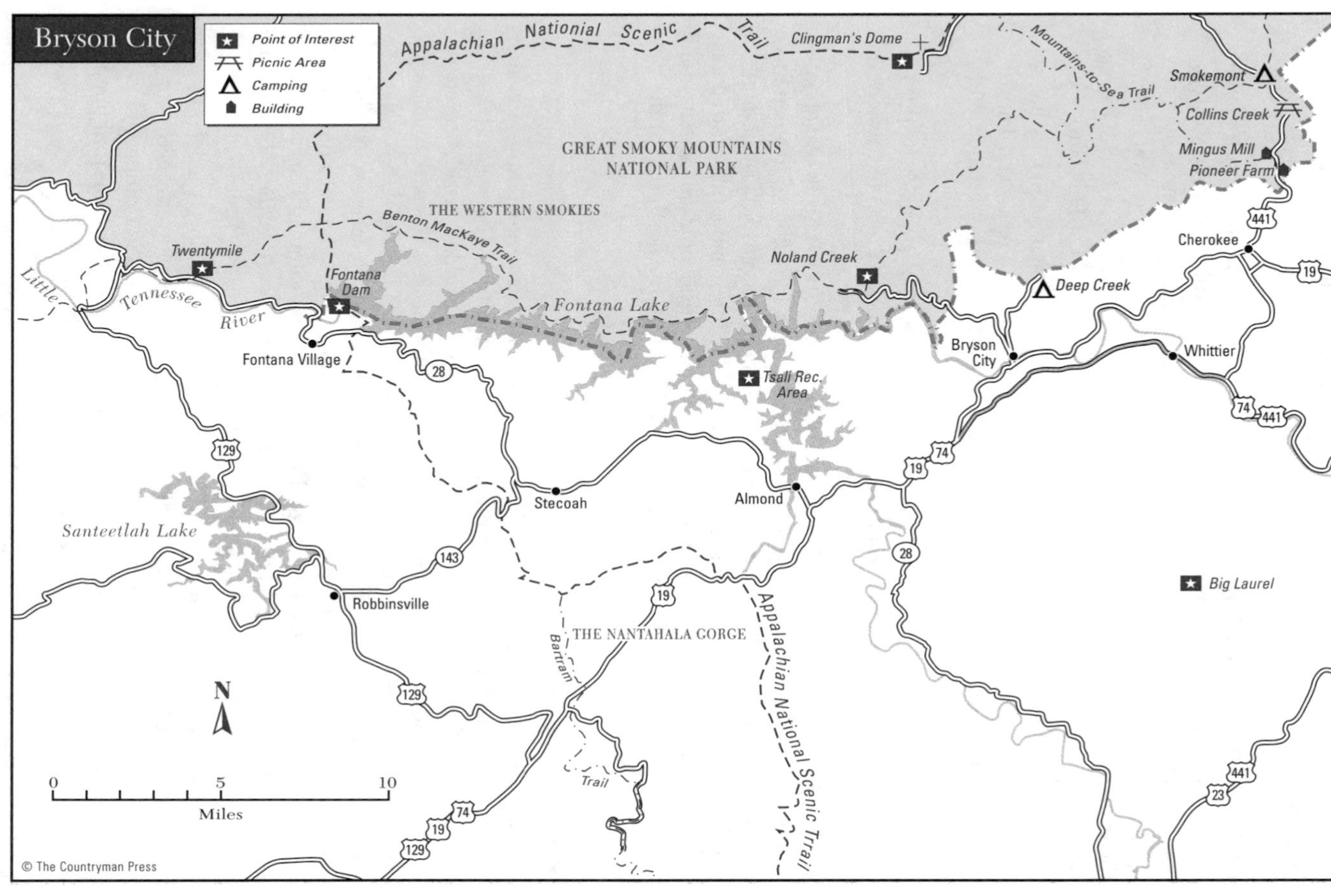
Bryson City
Point of Interest
Picnic Area
Camping
Building
Appalachian National Scenic Trail
Clingman's Dome
Mountains-to-Sea Trail
Smokemont
Collins Creek
Mingus Mill
Pioneer Farm
GREAT SMOKY MOUNTAINS NATIONAL PARK
THE WESTERN SMOKIES
Benton MacKaye Trail
Twentymile
Fontana Dam
Fontana Lake
Noland Creek
Deep Creek
Cherokee
Whittier
Bryson City
Tsali Rec. Area
Little Tennessee River
Fontana Village
Santeetlah Lake
Robbinsville
Stecoah
Almond
THE NANTAHALA GORGE
Bartram Trail
Appalachian National Scenic Trrail
Big Laurel
441
19
74
28
129
143
23
N
0
5
10
Miles
© The Countryman Press

"Franklin and the Nantahala Mountains,"), 33 miles south via the four-lane US 74 and US 441.

**GETTING THERE By Car** Bryson City sits at the far western end of the four-laned Smoky Mountain Expressway that links North Carolina's rugged western counties with the rest of the state. For this reason, it's almost always easiest to approach it from the east, even if it means driving out of your way. You can pick up the expressway from Asheville by following I-40 west to US 64, or from Georgia by following US 441 north into North Carolina, reaching US 74 at Dillsboro.

**By Air** Asheville, North Carolina, has the closest airport. As Bryson City has no bus service from Asheville (or anywhere else), you'll have to rent a car. The 70-mile driving distance is stop-free expressway virtually the entire distance, and should take about an hour and a quarter.

**By Bus or Train** Bryson City has no bus or train links to the outside world. Like most of these poor mountain counties, Swain County has no rural bus system.

**MEDICAL EMERGENCIES** ♿ **Swain Medical Center** (64.85.191.80/about-westcare/westcare-affiliates/swain-medical-center; 828-488-4205; 45 Plateau St., Bryson City, NC 28713). A rare survival from earlier days, this fully accredited small-town hospital has 25 beds, general surgical facilities, and a fully staffed Class II 24/7 emergency room. You'll find it on an obscure residential side street, uphill from the train depot; look for the blue hospital signs on the north side of the depot.

## ✷ Exploring the Area

Although (or perhaps because) the national park's tallest and steepest region abuts Bryson City, only limited areas of the nearby backcountry can be reached easily by automobiles. The Deep Creek area, reached down a paved local road, centers on a lovely stream noted for its waterfalls, and is the only place in the park to allow off-road bicycling. The seldom visited Lakeshore Drive (aka the Road to Nowhere) offers a short, scenic drive down a dead-end park road, with access to Noland Creek, a former mountain settlement cut off by the rising waters of Fontana Lake, as well as the Benton MacKaye Trail. Further west, the waters of Fontana Lake block the park's backwater all the way to Fontana Dam; even farther, the remote Twentymile Ranger District has worthwhile (and little-visited) walks.

Thirteen miles southwest of Bryson City lies the Nantahala Gorge, a deep tree-lined canyon. US 19 runs along the floor of the gorge, allowing easy access to numerous whitewater outfitters—a popular destination on a hot summer day. There's a scenic drive for this area as well, extending well upstream from the popular areas to explore some deep gorge scenery and waterfalls.

**EXPLORING BY CAR Driving the Nantahala Gorge** This scenic drive follows the Nantahala Gorge, a 1,600-foot deep, heavily forested gorge carved by the Nantahala River. It starts 13 miles west of Bryson City on US 19, as that highway drops into the gorge to follow the gorge floor. The highway hugs the river closely, with many places to pull over and admire the scenery. You will only have to wait a few minutes to see kayakers paddling furiously through the rapids and rafters carried happily with the current. After 8 miles US 19 continues straight ahead, but the gorge swings left in an almost perfect right-angle; follow the gorge left onto Wayah Road. Now the gorge turns rugged, its river violent and boulder-strewn beneath black rock walls—the scenery of a western gorge moved into the lush East and covered with trees. The highlight is Camp Creek Falls, a 200-foot jet of water pouring over the sheer rock wall of the gorge, 2.6 miles up Wayah Road. In another mile Wayah Road climbs out of the gorge without making any noticeable curve; once again, the gorge has swerved 90 degrees. Here you turn right onto Old River Road, a good gravel road maintained by the Nantahala National Forest. You'll immediately cross Whiteoak Creek, with an impressive 20-foot waterfall visible on your left from the concrete bridge. Beyond, the gorge is less rugged and the river smaller. The Nantahala River passes over a beautiful small waterfall, then becomes starved for water by the TVA's Nantahala Dam, only a few miles upstream. In another mile the road catches up with some of that missing water—a giant penstock crosses the road then follows it for 0.5 mile. Old River Road ends at a T-intersection with paved state secondary road SR 1401 (Junaluska Road). A left turn will take you 2.5 miles back to Wayah Road; follow it left to US 19 in a bit less than 10 miles.

**The Remote Western Smokies** The waters of giant Fontana Lake isolate much of the western Smokies from casual visitors. As a result, it has little by the way of development to intrude upon its stunning scenery. To explore this area by car, pick up NC 28 westbound, 9 miles west of Bryson City on US 74. You'll find this section partly four-laned, the result of a regional development project surviving from Lyndon Johnson's War on Poverty in Appalachia. In ten miles you'll pass the sleepy village of Stecoah, off on sideroads to your left. Shortly beyond, NC 143 peels off to the left, a shortcut to Robbinsville (see "The Northern Unicois: Robbinsville & Tellico Plains," Villages) and the corridor for future four-lane highways, assuming Johnson's road project ever gets finished. From here, NC 28 becomes a lot more steep and curvy. Views will open up on your right, including a wonderful 180-degree sweep over Fontana Lake toward the crest of the Smokies, from a wayside picnic area.

RAFTS IN THE NANTAHALA GORGE

You'll reach the turnoff to **Fontana Dam** after 22 miles. It's worth a visit for the good views and generator tours at its visitors center—but the biggest thrill is driving over the narrow dam top, high above the gorge below. Turn left at the far end (inside the national park) for a great view of the dam. Continue on NC 28 to the **Little Tennessee River**; now NC 28 hugs the river, impounded as **Cheoah Lake**, with several beautiful views. In 8 miles you will reach the national park's remote **Twentymile** section, then reach US 129 in another 3 miles. Go left on US 129 for 2 miles to an old bridge over the Little Tennessee River. Here you will get a good view of **Cheoah Dam**, a 265-foot structure built in 1919 by ALCOA. This was the site of Harrison Ford's dramatic dam jump in the 1992 movie, *The Fugitive.*

**EXPLORING ON FOOT** **Noland Creek Trail** Up until 1942 Noland Creek was the site of a streamside settlement, 50 or so families in scattered farmhouses that ranged from log cabins to modern bungalows. Then the Tennessee Valley Authority built Fontana Dam and flooded their road access. Rather than rebuild the road, the TVA condemned the Noland Creek community, evicted its residents, and donated their land to the Great Smoky Mountains National Park. To visit their old community, take Lakeshore Drive to the trailhead at Noland Creek Overlook. You can go either up or down the valley—but the more interesting parts of the trail are up the valley, a 4-mile walk along an old road at a steady upward gradient of 6 percent. Although the National Park Service demolished nearly all of the structures in Noland Creek for safety reasons, signs of the settlement still remain. Boxwoods and roses grow rank around old homesites, where a set of steps or an old chimney might poke up through the trees. Because the valley was never logged, the forests are extraordinarily beautiful, a combination of old woods and young trees growing in former farmland.

At 3.70 miles, the track enters a flat-floored stretch known as Solola Valley, a heavily settled area named for the Cherokee word for squirrel. The remains of this settlement include the ruins of a large mill, its wheelhouse foundations emerging from the streambed. At 4 miles a side trail, the Springhouse Branch Trail, leads uphill to the left, passing house and field ruins to reach a large old-growth forest in 0.75 mile. At 4.2 miles an unmarked side trail leads uphill a short distance to a cemetery, still used by the families evicted from Noland Creek. Another quarter-mile leads to a nice waterfall—a good place to turn around.

**A Twentymile Walk** The western backcountry of the Great Smoky Mountains National Park has numerous choices for good walks, all the more enticing for being remote and little used. Most are cut off from roads by the waters of Fontana Dam, and require boat access. However, a collection of little-used trails radiate out from the Twentymile Ranger Station, on NC 28 nine miles west of Fontana Dam (and 37 miles west of Bryson City).

Like many of the trails in these parts, the Twentymile Creek Trail follows a prepark road—in this case, an old narrow-gauge lumber railroad built in the 1920s and converted to a jeep track by the CCC. Closed to autos and bicycles, it makes for gentle and pleasant walking through attractive young forests, grown up since this area was logged 80 years ago. After 1 mile it reaches **Twentymile Cascades**, where the little Twentymile Creek jumps down a steep sloping rock about 40 feet high. At 3 miles the track reaches a trail intersection at Proctor Field Gap, where remnants of stonewalls and old foundations poke up through the level forest floor.

At this point, you have climbed 1,000 feet above the Twentymile Ranger Station. Should you continue on the old track (to the right), you will gain another 1,500

TWENTYMILE CREEK FALLS

feet in only 1.5 miles—a steep pull. When you finally reach the ridgeline you will be on the **Appalachian Trail**. A third of a mile to the right (and uphill, alas) is the Shuckstack Fire Tower, with one of the finest panoramic views anywhere in the Smokies. To your north the entire Smoky Mountain Crest marches along the horizon, while the deep gorge of the Little Tennessee River cuts across the ridges that recede forever into the south.

**LONG-DISTANCE PATHS** Two long-distance paths run through the southwest quadrant of the Great Smoky Mountains National Park: the Appalachian Trail and the Benton MacKaye Trail. When linked via the Mountains-to-Sea Trail, the two paths form a 73-mile loop that explores both the long crest of the Smokies and the valleys, lakeshore, and abandoned villages of the backcountry that extends for miles along its south.

**The Appalachian Trail** The 2,160-mile Appalachian Trail spends 30 miles in this chapter's area, including its first 4 miles as it descends from Cheoah Mountain and crosses Fontana Dam to enter the national park. Your first climb is a lollapalooza, 2,000 feet in 2.5 miles to the top of Shuckstack Mountain; a 0.5-mile walk to your right leads to a famous view, if you are up for it. The trail then follows a side ridge northward at a more reasonable upward pitch, and reaches the Smoky Mountain Crest 6.2 miles (and 3,700 feet of climbing) from the dam. From here on the path closely follows the crest, frequently splitting its treadway between Tennessee and North Carolina. This leads through stunning scenery, passing through high-altitude forests and mountaintop meadows. It also leads to a great deal of knob-hopping, so much so that it adds 6,000 feet of climb and descent to the 1,000 feet of actual elevation gain experienced in the next 19 miles. Eight miles into this stretch, one of your climbs will briefly bring you up above the mile-high mark, onto the 5,527-foot summit of Thunderhead Mountain, but you'll lose 1,000 feet of it over the next two up-and-downs. Do not be discouraged; it is the price you pay for some of the most breathtaking scenery in the East. At the end of this 19-mile stretch you reach the mile-high mark again, and will stay above it for the next 29 miles, a section described in the next chapter.

**The Benton MacKaye Trail** While the Appalachian Trail may take the high road, its grandson the Benton MacKaye Trail takes the low road, exploring the lower reaches of the huge wild area beneath the crest. It starts with a 3.4-mile road walk to get it from Deals Gap to the nearest trailhead at Twentymile Ranger Station, then uses Twentymile Creek to gently climb the 2,300 feet to Shuckstack and an intersection with the Appalachian Trail. Over the next 3 miles it loses all of its elevation gain while it drops to the shores of Fontana Lake at Eagle Creek, followed by a couple of ridge hops. The first hop brings you to the site of the former town of Proctor, where an old state road climbs out of the lake to lead past the scant ruins of this former settlement. The second hop, and the last big one on this section, brings you down close to the lakeshore and stays there for the next 14.5 miles, jumping a lot of minor ridges but no more big ones; one 2-mile stretch follows Old NC 288, the former main highway flooded by the lake in 1944. A final 1,000-foot climb takes you away from the lake for good, and then goes through a ridge in a tunnel—built in the late 1960s for a recreational road that was abandoned for environmental reasons after construction had started. At the other side of the tunnel you will reach a trailhead at the motorable section of this road, now officially known as Lakeshore Drive but better known as The Road **to Nowhere**.

**EXPLORING BY BICYCLE Deep Creek Trail** This easy path, following an old prepark road up Deep Creek, is well known for its three beautiful waterfalls, as well as its lovely streamside scenery. The gravel road portions are open to bicycles, and make a pleasant, beautiful morning's ride; bicycles are prohibited on the footpaths. You'll find the trailhead at the end of Deep Creek Road, just inside the national park.

Walkers should start with the 0.25-mile spur trail to **Junywhank Falls**, which leaves the northwest corner of the parking lot. Junywhank Falls is a thin trace of water that hurls itself over a 50-foot ledge, dashes under a wood log bridge, then bounces down another 30 feet of rock. Be sure to take the footpath to the log bridge for the best views, then return the way you came.

TOM BRANCH FALLS ON THE DEEP CREEK TRAIL

For Deep Creek Trail, walk or bike up the old roadbed 0.2 mile to view **Tom Branch Falls**, a side stream that enters Deep Creek by pouring over a 30-foot rock wall. Farther along, the track follows Deep Creek as it bounces over rapids and rock shelves then climbs above it to give views up the deep V-shaped cleft. At 0.7 mile the old road forks at a bridge where Indian Creek pours in from the side, through a chute into a still pool that throws rippling reflections onto the overhanging rocks. Both forks are open to bicyclists. Walkers will want to take the right fork—then listen for the roar of a waterfall. A short side trail leads to the base of the third and most impressive waterfall, **Indian Creek Falls**. Here a wide wall of water pours over a 50-foot ledge into a deep, still pool with a natural pebbly beach. A short distance beyond the side trail, the main path offers a good view over the top of the falls. Return the way you came.

## ✷ Villages

**Bryson City** Visitors to Bryson City will find it a handsome town of about 1,500 inhabitants, with an old-fashioned downtown stretched into a T-shape and possessing a full range of services. The Old Swain County Courthouse sits by the main downtown intersection and furnishes an unmissable landmark. It's guarded by a World War I doughboy instead of the traditional Confederate soldier, showing Swain County's post-Civil War origin. The town's Main Street follows US 19 east and west from the Old Courthouse, ending at the town's beautiful hilltop cemetery. Down from the courthouse, the downtown district crosses the Tuckaseegee River to reach the old railroad depot, now housing the Great Smoky Mountain Railroad with daily scenic excursions. Parking is ample and free. Apart from its quaint downtown with some interesting shops, Bryson City offers some of the better lodging and dining in the mountains, with several first-rate establishments in town or nearby.

**The Nantahala Gorge** Located 13 miles southwest of Bryson City along US 19, this 8-mile-long gorge has recently acquired its own community of tourist-oriented businesses, drawn by the increasing popularity of rafting and kayaking on the Nantahala River. Most of it consists of roadside businesses of recent architecture, separated by long stretches of beautiful national forest land. Apart from the outfitters, you'll find several places to eat and at least one good lodge. Traffic can be very slow on a warm summer weekend, with lots of pedestrians, cars entering from parking lots, and old repainted busses loaded high with inflated rafts.

PRODUCE STAND IN BRYSON CITY

**Almond** Formerly a riverside stopping place along US 19, 9 miles southwest of Bryson City, the settlement of Almond was flooded in 1942 by the rising waters of Fontana Reservoir. US 19 moved elsewhere, and the remnants of the village rose up the mountain slope until they were just above the high-water line. The NC 28 bridge over Fontana Reservoir, in the center of Almond (if Almond is big enough to have a center), gives good views over the giant lake. Some Nantahala Gorge businesses have Almond addresses.

**Stecoah** This tiny village off NC 28, 18 miles west of Bryson City, is the main center of population of this remote corner of the Smokies. It's old stone school, now a community center, marks the center of town. It has few services beyond gas, a café, and a couple of general stores.

**Fontana Village** Fontana Village was founded in 1942 as the construction camp for Fontana Dam. After the dam was completed in 1944 the construction camp became a resort. And so it remains—the main administrative building converted into a lodge, and the temporary workers' quarters becoming a small city of modest vacation cabins. A log cabin in the center has displays on pioneer life. The surrounding countryside is very remote, with few facilities. You'll find Fontana Village 31 miles west of Bryson City on NC 28.

## ✷ Wild Places

**THE GREAT FORESTS The Southwest Quadrant of the Great Smoky Mountains** The high crest of the Smokies sweeps southwest from Bryson City, starting some 10 miles north of town and 4,800 feet above it. For much of this area the crest comes to a sharp, rocky point and drops down almost cliff-like—but still covered by trees more typical of New England or Canada than the South. In other places, the crest becomes wide and rolling, the scene of great open meadows. Side ridges branch off to the south, separating valleys that drop straight down to a sharp point, with scarcely enough bottomland to contain a fierce little river. Before the park was created in the 1930s, these valleys frequently contained roads that would peter out at high dead ends—some made by farmers, others by loggers. In 1944 many of these roads were cut off from the rest of the world by the waters of the newly impounded Fontana Lake, running along the southern edge of the park for 24 miles. Today they are hiking trails.

Within the wild southwestern quadrant of the park, two areas are easily reached from Bryson City: **Deep Creek** and **Noland Creek**. These valleys were once heavily settled, their upper reaches valued for hunting—effectively protecting them from the destructive large-scale logging that decimated many of the more remote valleys. Instead, these valleys had either been selectively logged, leaving a continuous cover of old hardwoods, or cleared for pasture, leaving rich, well-conserved soil that supported fast-growing, healthy forests when abandoned. Both valleys are rich in traces of their former inhabitants (although all the structures have been removed for safety reasons), and the upper slopes of Noland Creek preserve some large stands of old-growth forest.

**Big Laurel** This tract of National Forest land centers on a high meadow-covered valley perched near the top of Cowee Mountain, a scenic 16-mile drive southwest of Bryson City. At this time the Forest Service is protecting the meadows and keeping up the roads—and little else, leaving this little-known cove in its natural state. At the far end of the cove a jeep track heads gently downhill to your right, leading in a half-mile to the lovely Alarka Creek Falls, a 30-foot set of waterfalls, framed by rhododendrons, with a Japanese garden type of beauty. (To find the waterfall, look for an unsigned side trail on your left.) To find Big Laurel, take US 23/74 east of Bryson City to the Whittier exit, then follow the signs for the Smoky Mountain Golf Course through Whittier and beyond; when you reach the golf course, just keep going on Conley Creek Road, which becomes a steep and narrow (but well-maintained) Forest Service road as it climbs up to Big Laurel. A word of caution: visitors during the October leaf season will find the whole area taken over by bear hunters.

**RIVERS The Nantahala River** One of the South's most popular rivers, the Nantahala has produced a number of Olympians and several medals, thanks to the excellent facilities provided by the Nantahala Outdoor Center at the river's outlet. On any given summer day, the lowermost 8 miles become a continuous parade of rafters and kayakers. There's more to the Nantahala, however, than its last few miles.

The Nantahala starts at the **Standing Indian Basin**, west of Franklin off US 64 (see "Franklin and the Nantahala Mountains," *Exploring the Area*). Its uppermost section is popular with fishermen, but by the time it gathers enough water for kayakers it has entered private lands. Within 17 miles, it sinks beneath the waters of **Nantahala Lake**, a large hydropower reservoir from the 1940s, now owned by Duke Energy. Because the lake's waters are routed through a penstock to a downstream power station, the next 9 miles can be kayaked only when recreational releases are scheduled. First comes a 5.8-mile section that has been substantially dewatered, and is closely followed by a good gravel forest service road; the last mile of this stretch has some handsome waterfalls and rapids. Then a substantial steam, Whiteoak Creek, drops into the Nantahala over a good-sized waterfall, just as the gravel road joins paved Wayah Road (SSR 1310). At this point the Nantahala enters a 0.8-mile section of waterfalls and boulders, Class IV–V when Whiteoak Creek furnishes enough water; then it cruises through another 3.3 miles of Class II–III to finally reach the power station and meet up with the rest of its water.

Now fully watered, the Nantahala River enters its most famous stretch, the Nantahala Gorge, 8 miles of Class II–III water paralleled by US 19. A host of outfitters run rafts down this section, while kayakers play in the eddys. With even water provided by the upstream generator, this river runs whenever Duke is making electricity, basically all year except for November dam maintenance. The gorge itself is beautiful, despite some slight tracts of private lands embedded in the large National Forest Service holdings. The Forest Service provides picnic areas, put-in and take-out points, and overlooks, as well as carefully keeping commercial and private boaters from tangling each other up.

**RECREATION AREAS Tsali Recreation Area** This large recreation area on the shores of Fontana Reservoir, devoted to off-road bicycling and horseback riding, occupies the site where the Cherokee Tsali hid with his family during the Trail of Tears—a turning point, as it happened, in the 1838 expulsion of the Cherokees from their homeland. Federal troops tracked Tsali and his people to these remote cliffs overlooking the Little Tennessee River, and took them peacefully; but younger men in the group hid weapons and killed most of their captors, allowing their clan to escape. The local Qualla Cherokees—legally inhabitants of North Carolina and not part of the Cherokee Nation being expelled—saw this as simple murder, and helped track down and execute the killers, taking and executing Tsali without help from federal troops. As a result of this chilling episode, the federal officer in charge of the district ruled that the Qualla could remain on their lands. Today the Qualla make up the Eastern Band of the Cherokee Nation, in Cherokee.

This is the story told by the federal troop's official records. More details are available from the stories told by the Qualla and recorded by Smithsonian anthropologist James Mooney in the 1890s. Tsali's womenfolk had been attacked by federal troops, and the clan had fled to protect them. The young men were determined that no such outrage would be repeated, and took murderous action to protect their family from the brutal troops. Tsali voluntarily gave himself up to his tribal leaders, knowing he would be executed, to save the remainder of the Cherokee in North Carolina.

This large recreation area features 39 miles of marked bicycle and horse paths, ranging from old roads to rough tracks. Paths lead to lake and mountain views, wildflower meadows, and old home sites, through a predominantly pine forest. But don't expect to see the rugged gorges that sheltered Tsali's family; they are all under the waters of Fontana Reservoir. There's also a boat ramp and a small picnic area.

**PICNIC AREAS** **Deep Creek Picnic Area** Small by Smoky Mountains National Park standards, this ample picnic area offers stream-cooled air under a hardwood forest. It's less than 3 miles from Bryson City by well-marked paved roads, but quiet and away from traffic. The Deep Creek walk starts from nearby, leading to three impressive waterfalls.

**Picnicking in the Nantahala Gorge** The Nantahala Gorge's major picnic area is the Ferebee Memorial, 1.30 miles south of the Nantahala Outdoor Center on US 19. It centers around a memorial, carved in local marble, to Percy B. Ferebee, who donated the Nantahala Gorge to the American people. It's a very pleasant area, with a few tables scattered over a grassy, tree-shaded field. In addition to this major site, the N.C. Department of Transportation operates four free roadside tables, each set a mile or so from the other, and each with a river view.

**Riverfront Park in Downtown Bryson City** This fine small riverside picnic area with a pavilion is located in the center of Bryson City at the new Swain County Courthouse. The picnic area is shaded by trees and rhododendrons, and has a short, lovely riverside walk that gives you views of the backs of the downtown buildings across the river. A flock of Muscovy ducks hang along the river and will be sure to pay you a visit as soon as you start eating. The courthouse is an attractive modern structure on Mitchell Street two blocks west of downtown's Everett Street, and its picnic area is on the river on its west side.

**TVA Park on Old NC 288** Old NC 288 is the gravel road along the north shore of the Little Tennessee River that was flooded by the rising waters of Fontana Reservoir in 1944. It leaves Bryson City as Bryson Walk, runs along the river past a large lumber drying kiln, changes its name to Old 288, then slowly drops toward the lake surface to disappear under the water. The TVA has converted the last half-mile of the old road into a linear picnic ground with a large boat ramp at the end. It has six tables, each set a tenth of a mile from the next. All tables are on grassy swaths with shade trees, and all have wide views over the lake toward the mountains beyond. To find it, take Bryson Walk west out of town—it's the first left beyond the railroad depot, by the collection of old brick shops.

## ✷ To See

**BIG DAMMED LAKES Fontana Lake** The Tennessee Valley Authority (TVA) built the giant reservoir to provide power during World War II for nearby ALCOA aluminum smelters. In doing so, they destroyed a dozen small mountain communities, cutting them off with rising flood waters. The TVA handled this by condemning the hundreds of small farms, removing all the structures, then donating the land to the Great Smoky Mountains National Park.

The lake they created stretches for 25 miles to Bryson City, with many long side arms. It has 238 miles of shoreline, half of which are inside the national park and much of the rest owned by the National Forest Service. Despite this, it has only 16 square miles of surface; this is one long, skinny lake. There are several marinas along it, and you can rent a boat at the marina run by **Fontana Village**.

**GARDENS AND PARKS Bryson City Cemetery** Bryson City's cemetery occupies a tree-shaded hilltop at the west end of downtown. It's worth a visit for its lovely views over the town's Main Street, as well as a nice view of the Smoky Mountains. Its graves include a Thomas Wolfe angel—one of the angel statues imported from Italy by Wolfe's father and described by Wolfe in a famous passage in his novel *Look Homeward, Angel*. Another, nearly identical, angel statue sits in a cemetery in East Flat Rock, North Carolina, but the Bryson City Wolfe angel has the distinction of gazing over the Great Smoky Mountains. Nearby is the grave of writer and historian Horace Kephart, a plaque set on a large boulder.

FONTANA VILLAGE MARINA

**RAILROADS** ✐ **The Great Smoky Mountain Railroad in Bryson City** (gsmr.com; 800-872-4681, 828-586-8811; 226 Everett St., Bryson City, NC 28713). All year; schedule varies. As a major visitor attraction, the Great Smoky Mountain Railroad takes second place only to the national park itself. Organized to save a dead-end freight spur line from closing, its imaginative management has revamped it into a touring excursion line by day, with 53 miles of spectacular mountain sightseeing, steam and diesel engines, and a wide variety of special events. By night, this Cinderella railroad becomes a freight line again. The railroad runs excursions from Bryson City's historic old depot, with occasional special trips from other depots.

The Bryson City depot hosts three basic excursions. The most common excursion crosses Fontana Lake on a high old iron trestle, then follows the lakeshore up into the flooded lower reaches of the Nantahala Gorge. It stops for lunch at **Nantahala Outdoor Center**, then travels up the gorge to its end, returning the way it came. An alternative trip travels the same route but omits the lunch stop at NOC; instead, it uses the extra time to continue past the end of the gorge through spectacular mountain scenery to the small mountain town of **Andrews**. A third variant follows the same route as the first Nantahala Gorge excursion—but its passengers disembark at the head of the gorge to raft their way back. You will have a choice of an open excursion car, an air-conditioned Crown Coach, or an adults-only Club Car, a beautifully restored historic lounge car with wine and beer service.

**SPECIAL PLACES** **Yellow Branch Cheese** (www.yellowbranch.com; e-mail: mail@yellowbranch.com; 828-479-6710; Yellow Branch Farm, 136 Yellow Branch Circle, Robbinsville, NC 28771). Open Saturdays, 2 PM–5 PM; or by appointment; or just drop by. Free. This family-owned organic dairy, near Fontana Dam off NC 28, produces farmstead cheese from their own cows. It's a pretty, little place, a ways up a valley and not far from Fontana Lake. The fat, sassy cows produce a high quality, all-organic milk which yields a mild, buttery, full-bodied cheese. They make a jalepeño cheese from organic peppers they grow themselves. Next door is Yellow Branch Pottery, the studio and gallery of potter Karen Mickler, open Tues.–Sat., 2 pm–5 pm. It's worth a visit too, and Karen sells the Yellow Branch cheese.

**Fontana Dam** (1804 Hwy. 321 North, Ste. 300, Lenoir City, TN 37771). Sitting at the base of the Smoky Mountains, 22 miles west of Bryson City, Fontana Dam is the tallest dam in the eastern United States, blocking the gorge of the Little Tennessee River with a concrete wall 480 feet high and over a half-mile wide at the top. Built in a great hurry between 1942 and 1944, Fontana was an emergency wartime project, intended to insure that the Knoxville, Tennessee, area had enough electrical power for the strategically important ALCOA aluminum plant and the top-secret Oak Ridge Research Laboratory. Its impoundment created the 29-mile long Fontana Lake, flooding the gorge of the Little Tennessee River and forcing the abandonment of a half-dozen mountain communities.

Fontana Dam is an impressive sight, and well worth a visit. A modernist visitors center sits at its southern end, with a large observation deck giving fine views of the mammoth structure. From the center, those wanting to tour the dam take an inclined tram down the gorge wall to the generators at the base. A public road crosses the 2,600-foot dam top to national park trailheads on the opposite side—a fascinating drive.

## ✷ To Do

**RAFTING AND KAYAKING** **Nantahala Outdoor Center (NOC)** (www.noc.com; 800-232-7238; 13077 Hwy. 19 West, Bryson City, NC 28713). This complex of a half-dozen handsome buildings straddles both the Nantahala River and the Appalachian Trail, and qualifies as a tourist attraction all by itself. The employee-owned NOC offers kayaking and rafting, mountain biking, instruction at a variety of levels, three restaurants, cabin rentals, and an outdoor store.

**Endless Rivers Adventures** (www.endlessriveradventures.com; e-mail: info@endlessriveradventures.com; 800-224-7238, 828-488-6199; fax: 828-488-2259; 14157 US Hwy. 19 West, P.O. Box 246, Bryson City, NC 28713). This outfitter offers whitewater rafting on the Nantahala and other rivers, as well as workshops for kayaking and rock climbing, and fly-fishing guide service.

**Rolling Thunder River Company** (www.rollingthunderriverco.com; 800-408-7238; 10160 Hwy. 19 West, Bryson City, NC 28713). Rolling Thunder offers a variety of inflatable rentals as well as guided raft trips on the Nantahala and other rivers. They have on-site camping and a bunkhouse.

**Wildwater, Ltd. Nantahala** (800-451-9972, 828-488-2384; wildwaterrafting.com; P.O. Box 190, Almond, NC 28702). This outfitter offers a variety of guided and unguided rafting trips, as well as the popular Raft & Rail trip in association with the Great Smoky Mountain Railroad.

**USA Raft** (www.usaraft.com; e-mail: raft@usaraft.com; 800-872-7238; 1104 Hwy. 19 West, Bryson City, NC 28713). This Rowlesburg, West Virginia, company has a presence in the Nantahala Gorge, offering raft trips and inflatable rentals.

**STABLES** **Nantahala Village Riding Stables** (nvnc.com/horseback; e-mail: nvinfo@nvnc.com; 828-488-9649; 9400 Hwy. 19 West, Bryson City, NC 28713). Open daily during the summer, 9:00 AM–6:30 PM; spring and fall, Fri.–Sun., 10 AM–5 PM; closed in winter. Guided trail rides in the Nantahala Gorge area, 9 miles west of Bryson City.

**BICYCLING** **Nantahala Outdoor Center** (www.noc.com; 888-662-1662; 13077 Hwy. 19 West, Bryson City, NC 28713). NOC offers a large range of mountain and road bicycling programs, from simple rentals to overnight trips.

**GOLF** **Great Smoky Mountains Golf Club** (www.smokymountaincc.com; 800-474-0070; 1112 Conley's Creek Rd., P.O. Box 937, Whittier, NC 28789). Located in Conley Creek Valley, this 18-hole par-71 course climbs up the mountainsides 500 feet above the clubhouse. Views are stunning, and the play is challenging, even though only four holes play uphill.

## ✷ Lodging

### COUNTRY INNS AND HOTELS

✐ **The Fryemont Inn** (www.fryemontinn.com; e-mail: fryemont@dnet.net; 800-845-4879, 828-488-2159; P.O. Box 459, Bryson City, NC 28713). The main lodge and restaurant are open mid-April through Thanksgiving; suites are open all year. Built by timber baron Amos Frye in 1923, this National Registry lodge sits on a hill above downtown Bryson City, with sweeping views from its wide front porch. The inn's large grounds are beautifully landscaped with native rhododendrons and hemlocks, isolated and very quiet. The bark-clad lodge has a large, comfortable lobby, filled with original craftsman-style furniture. The 37 en suite rooms in the main lodge all have wormy chestnut paneling and simple, comfortable furnishings in a country style. Room tariffs include a full breakfast and dinner, ordered from the menu, at the inn's excellent dining room. A separate building, constructed in 1940 as a recreation hall, has been redone into large and comfortable "fireplace suites," each with a living room with fireplace, a separate king bedroom, and a wet bar.

**Charleston Inn Bed & Breakfast** (www.charlestoninn.com; e-mail: info@charlestoninn.com; 888-285-1555, 828-488-4644; 208 Arlington Ave., Bryson City, NC 28713). Open all year. Built by a local attorney in 1927, the large and beautiful house sits on a wooded piece of property on a hillside within the town on Bryson City. Beautifully renovated in 1996, the Charleston Inn has 20 rooms—six in the main house, and 14 in an annex built in the 1940s and converted to excellent-quality rooms. In the main house, the common rooms are elegant and comfortable, with a game room, a glassed porch, a dining room, and an elaborate multi-layer deck with mountain views. All rooms are carefully decorated with new furniture in an elegant English Country style. The main house's six rooms are more like bedrooms in a wealthy home, while the annex's 14 rooms are larger, with separate sitting areas and semi-private porches.

✐ **Historic Calhoun Country Inn** (www.calhouncountryinn.com; e-mail: innkeepernc@gmail.com; 828-488-1234; fax: 828-488-0488; 135 Everett St., Bryson City, NC 28713). Open all year. Innkeeper Sue Hyde was raised on her mother's stories of Bryson City's Calhoun Hotel, where she worked as a cook—the good country food and a warm country welcome that the old owner, Granville Calhoun, had brought to it. Now Sue has restored this 1920s depot area hotel to its glory days as a country hotel. Its extra-wide front porch has rockers facing downtown's Everett Street, and its public rooms are large, bright, and airy. The rooms are reminiscent of a fine old country hotel—small to medium in size, bright, with antiques mix into the decor. Of the 23 rooms, eight have shared baths. The price includes a hearty country breakfast served in the sunny dining room.

**RESORTS** **Hemlock Inn** (www.hemlockinn.com; e-mail: hemlock@dnet.net; 828-488-2885; fax: 828-488-8985; Galbraith Creek Rd., P.O. Box 2350, Bryson City, NC 28713). Open May–October. Built as a country inn in 1952, the Hemlock Inn sits just 3 miles from the Great Smoky Mountains National Park's Deep Creek area, on its own 50 acres down a paved country lane. A low, modern structure of rustic gray wood, it has a large common area and two motel-style wings. Breakfast and dinner—both included in the tariff—are hearty country fare, authentically mountain and made fresh from scratch on the premises. Meals are served family style, with the food placed in great bowls on lazy Susans in the middle of round tables.

**BED & BREAKFAST INNS**

**Folkestone Inn Bed & Breakfast** (www.folkestone.com; e-mail: innkeeper@folkestone.com; 888-812-3385, 828-488-2730; fax: 828-488-0722; 101 Folkstone Rd., Bryson City, NC 28713). Open all year. This beautifully restored 1920s farmhouse, sits a quarter-mile from the Great Smoky Mountains National Park on Deep Creek Road. It's a bit of a cross between a Victorian farmhouse and a large bungalow, set in a grove of giant spruces by a tiny stream. A wide full-front porch faces Deep Creek with comfortable chairs, with another porch on top serving the second floor. The 10 comfortable rooms feature Victorian and country reproductions, including three ground-floor rooms with stone flag floors and low tin ceilings. This facility is also horse-friendly, so you can stable your horse at a barn one block from the inn, making it easy to enjoy Smoky Mountain trail riding in the area.

**CABIN RENTALS** **Falling Waters Adventure Resort** (www.fallingwatersresort.com; e-mail: wwltd@nuvox.net; 800-451-9972; fax: 864-647-5361; 10345 US Hwy. 74 West, Bryson City, NC 28713). Although well known in the Pacific Northwest, luxury yurts are a new concept in the South. These are tents, round in shape, pitched on a wood platform. However, these are not ordinary tents. These tents are 16 feet in diameter, with French doors opening up onto wood decks, skylights over the queen-size four-poster beds, and area rugs on the polished knotty pine floors. Not to mention ceiling fans, refrigerators, and coffee makers. This is definitely the luxury end of tent camping.

**Hidden Creek Cabin Rentals** (www.hiddencreekcabins.com; e-mail: hiddencreekcabins@yahoo.com; 888-333-5881; Bryson City, NC 28713). These four cabins overlook Hidden Creek on 23 private acres just outside the Lakeshore Drive entrance to the Great Smoky Mountains National Park. Two of the cabins are traditional second homes; one is a modern log cabin; and one is a 1930s farm house. All four are on a stocked trout stream, and each has its own 7-person hot tub on an outdoor deck.

**CABIN RESERVATION SERVICES** **Yellow Rose Realty** (yellowroserealty.com/vacation; e-mail: rentals@yellowroserealty.com; 800-528-0760, 828-488-2797; fax: 828-488-9855; 203 Slope St./P.O. Box 326, Bryson City, NC 28713. This local realtor manages 50 or so vacation properties throughout the Bryson City and Cherokee area.

## ✱ Where to Eat

**EATING OUT** **Everett Street Diner** (828-488-0123; 126 Everett St., Bryson City, NC 28713). Open Tues.–Sun., 7 AM–3 PM. This busy café may occupy a brick storefront in downtown Bryson City, but it's no grits-and-ham small-town eatery; the Everett Street Diner offers an upscale menu filled with fresh foods and intelligent recipes. Inside you'll find indirect lighting, bamboo chairs, dark green carpets, and light gray walls hung with original art. Despite this decidedly big-city sophistication, you'll find the prices remain comparable to downtown Bryson City venues, tightly grouped between $5 and $7.

**DINING OUT** ✐ ♿ **The Fryemont Inn** (www.fryemontinn.com/dining.htm; e-mail: fryemont@dnet.net; 800-845-4879, 828-488-2159; 245 Fryemont St., Bryson City, NC 28713). Open for breakfast: 8 AM–10 AM; dinner: Sun.–Thurs., 6 PM–8 PM, Fri.–Sat.; 6 PM–9 PM; bar opens at 5 PM; closed winter. The historic Fryemont Inn, on a hill overlooking Bryson City and the Great Smoky Mountains from its wide porch, opens its dining room to the public for breakfast and dinner from mid-April to late November. This large room is in keeping with a 1923 mountain lodge, with its wood rafters, polished hardwood floors, giant stone fireplace (with a wood fire cackling merrily away in chilly weather), and wormy chestnut paneling. Its full-service bar is comfortable and quiet, with lots of old wood and two pool tables. The dinner menu is noted for its local trout. Breakfasts emphasize simple country foods, well prepared: eggs, omelets, French toast, and pancakes.

**Relia's Garden Restaurant** (www.noc.com/relias-garden-restaurant; 828-488-7176; 13077 Hwy. 19 West, Bryson City, NC 28713). Open Sun.–Thurs., noon–9 PM; Fri.–Sat., noon–10 PM; closed winter. Terraced herb gardens, curved and stepped like an amphitheater, flank the entrance walk to the fanciest of the Nantahala Outdoor Center's three restaurants. The handsome modern building, clad in unpainted board and batten, also steps up in multiple levels, with wide porches and high-pitched roofs. Entrees emphasize fresh ingredients and careful use of herbs, frequently from the garden outside.

**Nantahala Village Mountain Resort & Meeting Center** (www.nvnc.com; e-mail: nvinfo@nvnc.com; 800-438-1507, 828-488-2628; fax: 828-488-4857; 9400 Hwy. 19 West, Bryson City, NC 28713). This 200-acre resort and conference center, a local tradition since 1948, sports an excellent restaurant in its new lodge. The large dining room features a cathedral ceiling and plenty of wood trim; large windows offer a wide sunset view deep into the Nantahala Gorge, then over the mountains. Dinner entrées run from the simple (fried chicken, ribeye steak) to the imaginative (spinach mushroom strudel). Expect the simplest entrées to be fresh and well prepared, such as a local trout, butterflied and sauteed in butter and herbs, served with capered butter.

## ✷ Selective Shopping

### *Bryson City*

**Downtown** You don't really expect a small-town main street to be a center for high-fashion shopping; yet it can have its charms. Bryson City furnishes some interesting storefronts in an L-shaped district radiating from the old courthouse. Foremost among these is Clampett's Hardware, which maintains a separate store for farm-related products that may well have the single most compelling collection of country items in the Smokies. Next door, watercolor artist Elizabeth Ellison maintains her studio and gallery from a small storefront. A bit farther down, The Charleston Station offers antiques and gifts from an attractive early-20th-century house. And don't forget to stop for lunch at the Everett Street Diner.

**The Depot Area** Bryson City's classic small-town depot, on the north edge of downtown, is once again lively with passenger traffic—this time on the Great Smoky Mountain Railroad. And just like in the old days, the depot area is coming alive with small shops. A quilt shop and discount bookshop occupy the old car dealership on one side, while the old brick buildings across the street hold a variety of shops, including one specializing in mountain fiddles. Sideways across the street are more old brick storefronts with antiques and collectibles.

## ✷ Special Events

**SPRING Dogwood Train Ride** (800-872-4681). Late April. The special train excursions are always extra fun, and this one has the added attraction of benefiting the local Rotarians' scholarship fund. The 4.5-hour train ride into the Nantahala Gorge includes a barbeque lunch and plenty of spring color.

**Heritage Day Festival** (800-867-9246, 828-488-3681). Memorial Day. This annual celebration of mountain heritage features traditional food, music, and crafts, as well as a toy duck race on the Tuckasegee River.

**SUMMER Singing in the Smokies** (828-497-2060; P.O. Drawer JJ, Bryson City, NC 28713). This gospel music festival, sponsored by the successful Bryson City male gospel group The Inspirations, features a large number of gospel groups over a week-long festival centered on the Fourth of July. The festival is held at Inspiration Park; follow the signs from the Ela exit off US 23/74 east of Bryson City.

**Freedom Fest on the River** (800-867-9246, 828-488-3681). July Fourth. Bryson City's town celebration takes place in its attractive Riverfront Park, with live entertainment, food, crafts, and fireworks.

VIEW OVER THE TUCKASEEGEE VALLEY TO THE GREAT SMOKY MOUNTAINS

**Folkmoot USA** (800-867-9246, 828-488-3681). Late July. Bryson City hosts three groups of international folk singers and dancers in their native costumes, as part of this major mountain-wide folk celebration.

**AUTUMN Fireman's Day Festival** (828-488-9410). Labor Day. Apart from the music, entertainment, crafts, and barbecue dinner, this fundraiser for the local volunteer fire department features a Parade of Fire Trucks and a Miss Flame competition.

**Nantahala Village Fall Dinner Concert Series** (800-438-1507, 828-488-2826). November and December. After the tourist season winds down and night starts falling early in the evening, the excellent restaurant at Nantahala Village schedules a series of dinner concerts, where musicians from the Asheville Symphony perform their choice of acoustic music. The full dinner, included in the charge, has a choice of three entrées (one of which will be a steak or prime rib, with the other two being more adventuresome chicken, fish, or vegetarian fare).

**WINTER Bryson City Merchants Christmas Parade and Festival** (800-867-9246, 828-488-3681). First Saturday in December. Sponsored by the merchants of Bryson City, this Christmas celebration features a parade with floats, bands, horses, and clowns; a breakfast with Santa; an auction; special discounts for shoppers; and a local theater presentation. A week later, the Rotarians sponsor "A Visit from Inn to Inn," visiting five historic old inns decorated for Christmas, with plenty of Christmas music and hors d'oeurves (tickets: $15 single/$25 couple).

# CHEROKEE & THE SOUTHEAST QUADRANT

This chapter covers the southeastern quadrant of the Great Smoky Mountains National Park and the adjacent lands of the Qualla Cherokees. It includes the rugged and remote ridges that run down from the Smokies Crest into the North Carolina half of the national park; the large Cherokee Reservation, properly known as the "Qualla Boundary," on the park's southern edge; the populous tourist area now called Maggie Valley; and the remote mountain coves of Cataloochee and Little Cataloochee, once heavily settled and now preserving mountain heritage deep within the national park.

This corner of the Smokies was settled by traditionalist Cherokees in 1819, led by the respected Chief Yonaguska. Known as the Qualla, they wished to avoid both the white settlers and the Europeanized leaders of the Cherokee Nation; they built their riverside villages along the Oconaluftee deep in the Smoky Mountains, on land uncoveted by whites and outside the Cherokee Nation. In 1838, President Andrew Jackson supported the State of Georgia in its efforts to expel the Cherokee Nation, seize its land for white people, and send the Cherokees west to the "Indian Territory" (now Oklahoma). The result was the genocidal Trail of Tears, where Federal soldiers forced Cherokee families from their houses at gunpoint, into holding compounds, then on a long and brutal trudge in the dead of winter. However, the Qualla were not part of the Cherokee Nation, and legally not subjected to the expulsion; after much debate, federal authorities allowed the Qualla to stay. Today, the Qualla are the Eastern Band of the Cherokee Nation, their tribal headquarters of Cherokee located on the border of the national park.

**GUIDANCE—TOWN AND COUNTRYSIDE Cherokee Visitor's Center (Cherokee Tribal Travel & Promotion)** (www.cherokee-nc.com; e-mail: travel@nc-cherokee.com; 800-438-1601, 828-497-9195; fax: 828-497-2505; P.O. Box 460, Cherokee, NC 28719). The visitors center offers information and brochures from a small stand-alone building in the center of Cherokee, by the Pizza Inn.

**Maggie Valley Area Visitors Bureau** (maggievalley.org). This website gives complete details on the Maggie Valley area, including food and lodging.

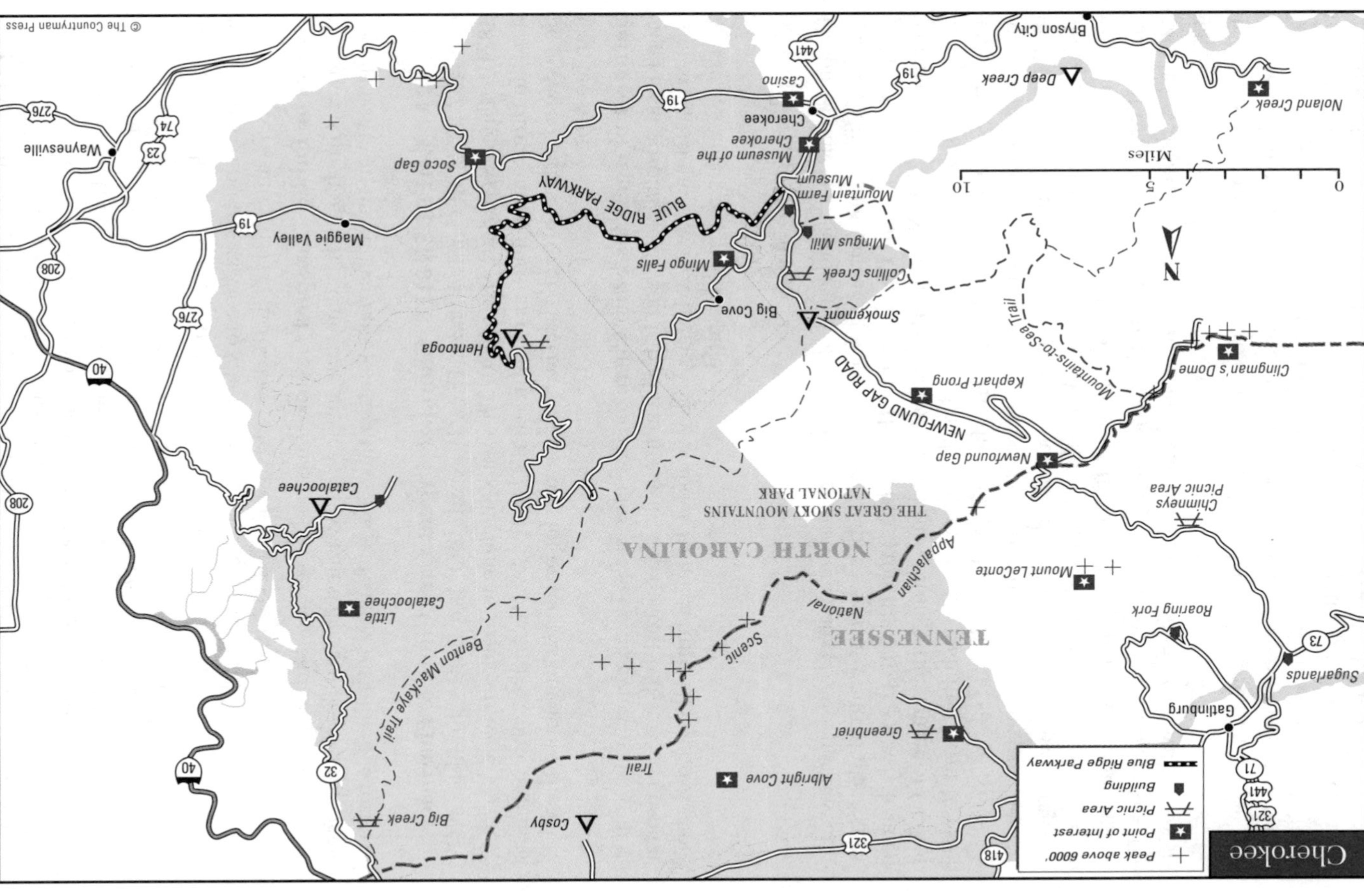
Cherokee
Peak above 6000'
Point of Interest
Picnic Area
Building
Blue Ridge Parkway
Gatlinburg
Sugarlands
Roaring Fork
Mount LeConte
Chimneys Picnic Area
Clingman's Dome
Newfound Gap
NEWFOUND GAP ROAD
Kephart Prong
Mountains-to-Sea Trail
Noland Creek
Deep Creek
Bryson City
Miles
0
5
10
N
TENNESSEE
NORTH CAROLINA
THE GREAT SMOKY MOUNTAINS NATIONAL PARK
Appalachian National Scenic Trail
Greenbrier
Albright Cove
Cosby
Big Creek
Benton Mackaye Trail
Little Cataloochee
Cataloochee
Hentooga
Big Cove
Mingo Falls
Smokemont
Collins Creek
Mingus Mill
Mountain Farm Museum
Museum of the Cherokee
Cherokee
Casino
BLUE RIDGE PARKWAY
Soco Gap
Maggie Valley
Waynesville
© The Countryman Press

**GETTING THERE** *By Car* Cherokee is located at the main south gate of the Great Smoky Mountains National Park, at the intersection of US 441 and US 19. As US 19 is a narrow, winding two-lane road between Maggie Valley and Cherokee, it's nearly always faster to use the nearby freeway, US 74 to US 441 a few miles south of town. If your destination is Maggie Valley rather than Cherokee, approach it via US 276, either from I-40 or from US 74 in Waynesville.

**By Air** The closest airport is in Asheville Regional Airport. You will need a rental car, as there is no bus service to Cherokee. Ignore your GPS and follow freeway quality US 74 and US 441, instead of twisty two-laned US 19.

**By Bus or Public Transport** Cherokee has no bus service, and no public transportation. Greyhound has daily bus service into Waynesville, 9 miles from Maggie Valley; however, no public transporation links Maggie Valley with the bus terminal.

**MEDICAL EMERGENCIES** **Cherokee Urgent Care Clinic & Pharmacy** (828-497-9036; El Camino Plaza, Hwy. 19 North, P.O. Box 2039, Cherokee, NC 28719). Open weekdays, 9:30–4:30. This walk-in clinic welcomes travelers with non-life-threatening illnesses or injuries. It's located by Harrah's Casino, and must be accessed either through the Harrah's parking lot or the parking lot of the El Camino Motel.

**Serious Emergencies** From Cherokee, the closest 24/7 emergency room is in the small local hospital at Bryson City, 11 miles away; the nearest full-service hospital is in Sylva, 18 miles away. Maggie Valley is about 10 miles from Haywood Regional Medical, a major regional hospital.

## ✷ Exploring the Area

Despite a mile-high landscape of knotted ridgelines separated by deep valleys, this quadrant offers some amazing opportunities to explore by car. Pride of place goes to The Newfound Gap Road, built in 1932 to bring tourists into the newly formed national park. This National Park Service Road runs through the center of Cherokee, past a pioneer log farmstead and mill, then up the Oconaluftee River to reach a high ridge, for some of the best views in the park. From the top of the Newfound Gap Road, Clingman's Dome Road leads along the crest of the Smokies to the highest point in the park. From the bottom, the Blue Ridge Parkway wraps along the park's southern border, for wonderful views of the Smokies Crest and the receding ridges of the North Carolina Blue Ridge—then generates a scenic spur road that dives deep into the park's back country. East of the Qualla Boundary, the national park preserves the remote and beautiful Cataloochee Cove, with its twisting gravel roads, wide meadows, and historic farm houses.

There is some prime hiking here as well. Day hikes highlighted in this section lead to mile-high meadows where azaleas and rhododendrons frame wide views, trace an active little mountain stream, and discover an 80-year-old environmental disaster that furnishes one of the most remarkable scenes in the Smokies. No fewer than three long distance paths cross and recross: the **Appalachian Trail**, the **Benton MacKay Trail**, and the **Mountains-to-Sea Trail**.

**EXPLORING BY CAR** **The Newfound Gap Road in North Carolina** It's good to get an early start to the national park's premiere scenic drive, both to avoid the crowds and to catch a sunrise. For a sunrise go straight up to the top, then go down to the first overlook on the North Carolina side, where the sun will rise over a deep mountain cleft. After the sun is up, you'll want to go on up to Newfound Gap to enjoy the way that the early morning sun lights up the road as it dives into the deep valleys of North Carolina. From there the spur road to Clingmans Dome has more sunrise views.

While the Newfound Gap Road continues northward to descend into Tennessee and **Gatlinburg**, this drive goes down the North Carolina side, south toward **Cherokee**. The road drops down from Newfound Gap onto the crest of Thomas Divide. For the next 3 miles the road twists along the narrow ridgeline, giving **panoramic views** over the deep valleys of the Smokies, toward the twisted high ridges of the Cowee and Nantahala Mountains. On many mornings, the early light will be reflecting off great sheets of fog that blanket the valleys thousands of feet below, with the ridgelines poking through like archipelagoes. The road finally plunges down the side of Thomas Divide to give one final view over a sharp-sided valley and back up toward Newfound Gap. A quiet walkway on the left follows the original 1932 roadbed, abandoned in the 1960s; it looks like a footpath along a grassy terrace, with bits of asphalt occasionally showing through. After that, the road loops down into the valley for a long, easy streamside drive, reaching the Oconaluftee River at the **Kephart Prong Trail**. From here the road hugs the river closely, sometimes looming over it from a high granite wall, sometimes swerving away from it through grassy meadows. Along this segment you'll pass **Collins Creek Picnic Area** at 10.6 miles and **Smokemont** at 12.5 miles. Beyond are two first-rate historical sites: **Mingus Mill**, a restored turbine water mill, and the **Oconaluftee Farm Museum**, a reconstructed mountain farm complete with crops, gardens, and farm animals. At the end of this drive, the Newfound Gap Road loops around broad meadows with wide views toward the log farm museum and the mountains beyond. On the far side of the meadow, the **Blue Ridge Parkway** makes its southern terminus. Just beyond is the park boundary and the town of Cherokee.

**Clingmans Dome Scenic Drive** This 7-mile spur road follows the crest of the Smokies westward from Newfound Gap to its dead-end at Clingmans Dome. It's the easiest way to enjoy the unusual Canadian-style spruce-fir forest found only at the highest elevations, as this high-altitude road stays inside the forest most of its length. This forest (known locally as "balsams") is an isolated remnant of a great subarctic forest that blanketed the Southeast at the peak of the last Ice Age—preserved here by the subarctic conditions at the top of the Smokies. It's also one of only four roads in the eastern United States that passes above 6,000 feet in elevation.

More than any other park road, The Clingmans Dome Spur Road has the look and feel of a 1930s Works Project Administration (WPA) scenic drive. It's narrow and twisting, shaded by the balsam forest crowding its edge, with trimmed rock walls on the downhill side. Its cuts are too modest to provide the wide views of a more modern highway, and its shoulders are frequently too narrow to pull off and park. The first view (0.4 mile from the beginning) is one of the best, a 5,200-foot high bird's-eye view straight down Beech Flats Prong to the Oconaluftee Valley, with the **Newfound Gap Road** curving away below. Your next landmarks are an **Appalachian Trail** access point (at 1.2 miles) and an interpretive nature trail about the spruce-fir forest (at 2.5 miles). However, you can combine both interests at the next trailhead (3.5 miles), where a short access trail leads to the Appalachian Trail, then half a mile left and uphill through a fir forest devastated by insects (the wooly aselgid, an illegal immigrant from Europe), to views and wild berries on the peak of **Mount Collins** (6,188 feet, the 25th tallest in the East). Then, at 5.3 miles, Webb Overlook gives another fine view eastward. However, save some film for the final overlook at the road's end, with wonderful panoramic views east, south and west over endless mountain ranges—another good place for a sunrise. At the end of the overlook is the paved path that leads to the summit of **Clingmans Dome** as well as a great Appalachian Trail walk to **Silers Bald**. The walk to the wildflower-framed views from **Andrews Bald** starts here as well.

**The Blue Ridge Parkway and the Heintooga Spur Road** The Blue Ridge Parkway's final 13-mile section runs from Soco Gap on US 19 to the Newfound Gap Road just inside the Great Smoky Mountains National Park. From Soco Gap, the parkway climbs uphill through forests for the next 3 miles—a particularly fine stretch for spring wildflowers, reaching the Heintooga Spur Road (described later) at Wolf Laurel Gap. From here the parkway picks its way down a side ridge, dropping 3,200 feet to reach the Oconaluftee River. Although heavily forested, the terrain is rough enough to require five tunnels, and the parkway gets its share of views. The best views are found on a 2-mile stretch between Big Witch Gap Overlook and Noland Divide Overlook, where the wall-like Great Smoky Mountains are framed in June by a stunning rhododendron display. There are more good views near the end, where the Oconaluftee River Overlook gives an aerial of the Mountain Farm Museum. The parkway ends at an intersection with US 441 just outside Cherokee and just inside the Great Smoky Mountains National Park.

Back on the parkway, the unusual and fascinating Heintooga Spur Road (mentioned above) loops 27 miles through the park's **Great Balsam Mountain** backcountry, a leisurely forest drive that ends deep in the Qualla Boundary. The first of the spur's three major views arrives quickly, at Mile High Overlook—as its name implies, a 5,280-foot overlook with a 180-degree view toward the Smoky Mountain Crest. At 3.6 miles the road reaches Black Camp Gap and enters the national park; a pyramidal Masonic Monument sits a short distance off the road. From here the road is a pretty forest drive that climbs gently to **Balsam Mountain Picnic Area** on a high ridge top. Shaded by a handsome old spruce forest, this high, windy spot is definitely the place to cool off on a summer day. It also has the second of the road's three views, known as **Heintooga Overlook**, at the far end of the picnic area—a broad view sideways over the high crest of the Smokies, renowned for its fine sunset.

OCONALUFTEE MOUNTAIN FARM MUSEUM

From the picnic area, the road becomes a one-lane, one-way gravel road, of dependably good quality. The road is so narrow as to be a car path

VIEW FROM MILE HIGH OVERLOOK TOWARD THE GREAT SMOKY MOUNTAINS

through the great overhanging trees; fortunately, you don't have to worry about oncoming traffic. The third and last view comes 2 miles into this segment, a 90-degree view southward over the deep canyon-like valleys of the Smokies toward the Qualla Boundary. Six miles later the road reaches Pin Oak Gap, an important backcountry trailhead, and finally drops away from the high ridgeline into the stream valleys below. At 22 miles the road bottoms out at Round Bottom Horse Camp and becomes two-way again as it follows a lovely little stream to enter the Qualla Boundary. In 3.5 more miles it reaches Big Cove Road, its first real intersection since it left the Blue Ridge Parkway. A left turn will bring you to Cherokee in 11 miles.

**Cataloochee Cove Drive** Once the most heavily settled corner of the Smokies, Cataloochee is now the most remote part of the Great Smoky National Park accessible by car. To reach it you must drive over miles of narrow, winding gravel road, through deep forest. Once there you will find yourself in a wide valley, floored with broad meadows, dotted by historic buildings, and surrounded by mountains.

Start your drive to Cataloochee at the intersection of US 276 and I-40 (exit 20), 6 miles north of US 19 near Maggie Valley. Near the intersection you'll find a side road, Sutton Town Road (SSR 1331) heading west. Take it; then take the right fork in 1.5 miles onto Cove Creek Road (SR 1305). This switchbacks steeply uphill, then over a mountain and into the national park (turning into a gravel road along the way). When you reach the bottom you will find an intersection with a paved road, part of a long-abandoned project to turn Cataloochee into a major tourist attraction; turn left. The paved road winds through young forests, past a small campground to an intersection with a gravel road in wide meadows. Here stands the 1905 **Will Messer Barn**, beside a small ranger station with an information desk. Continue along the paved road to the left, passing through meadows to the lovely little 1898 **Palmer Methodist Chapel**, still occasionally used. Nearby is the 1901 **Beech Grove School**, a one-room schoolhouse authentically furnished.

After that the road turns gravel, continuing through meadows with wide, pastoral views. The road passes between a large barn and a 1906 Victorian-style farmhouse, **the Caldwell House**. Beyond, the auto road ends at a gate, but the old farm road continues to **the Woody House**, an 1866 log cabin with a 1910 addition.

Return to the Will Messer Barn and ranger station, then turn left onto the gravel road. In a short distance (through more meadows) you will reach the attractive **Palmer House**; Uncle Fate Palmer built this dog-trot log cabin in 1860, and his descendants added the hand-planed interior paneling (1905), brightly painted weatherboarding (in 1910), and kitchen wing (in 1924). Just beyond, the gravel road enters the woods, then reaches a T-intersection. The right fork goes back to Cove Creek Road and Maggie Valley. The left fork leads a few miles to an old road (now a footpath) up to the **Little Cataloochee Community**. This 5-mile walk leads to three more historic sites: the 1864 log Hannah Cabin with its handmade brick chimney; the hilltop Little Cataloochee Baptist Church, topped by a handsome belfry and steeple; and the scant remains of the Cook Place and Messer Farm at the top of the road. Back at your car, continue on the gravel road, leaving the park in 3 miles to pass through 9 miles of meadows and farmlands. When you reach the road to the **Big Creek** area of the national park, turn right into Waterville, reaching I-40 in 2 miles.

**EXPLORING ON FOOT** **A High Ridge Walk on the Appalachian Trail** This 3-mile walk follows the Smoky Mountain Crest westward from Clingmans Dome, staying above 6,000 feet with stunning views into both Tennessee and North Carolina. Starting at the Clingmans Dome Overlook parking lot, go a short distance down the Forney Ridge Trail to the Clingmans Dome Bypass Trail. This little-used cutoff will save you some climbing, while leading past some good meadow views into North Carolina. After 0.3 mile you gain the Appalachian Trail on the high, sharp ridge of the Smokies Crest. From here are first-rate views into Tennessee, toward Elkmont and over the side ridges that fall steeply downward to the foothills. Turn left onto the Appalachian Trail. You will be hiking along a razorbacked spine of a ridge, with grass growing between exposed rocks and long views over both North Carolina and Tennessee. The trail will remain more or less level to Mount Buckley, then start a moderate but inexorable drop, losing 1,000 feet in the next 2.5 miles. The trail remains scenic, passing through grassy areas and forests—but don't forget that going up this slope is going to be a lot more difficult than going down. When you decide to turn around, stay on the Appalachian Trail until it reaches the Clingmans Dome Observation Tower, to pick up a few good views you missed on the way out.

**Andrews Bald Walk** The high grassy balds of the Smokies remain one of the most important features of the park, playing a major part in the park's environmental diversity. They are also one of the most beautiful features—wide, ridgetop meadows, scattered with brushy azaleas, rhododendrons and laurels, a riot of wildflowers all spring and early summer, with wide views the rest of the year. Ironically, these balds are disappearing as a result of the National Park Service's conservation efforts. It seems these balds were brought into their present form by settlers using them for summer cattle pastures—and they return to forest after grazing stops. Since the National Park Service eliminated grazing over seventy years ago, all the balds have shrunk and some have disappeared altogether. Today the rangers main-

FONTANA DAM

tain just two of the many balds, and those at a fraction of their former size: remote Gregory Bald, and Andrews Bald.

Although Andrews Bald is a short 3-mile hike, it's no level stroll. Starting from the high ridge at Clingmans Dome, it drops 600 feet in 0.9 mile then rises 150 feet before the final 175-foot drop to the large ridgeline meadow. It offers wide views over North Carolina and Fontana Lake, framed by rhododendrons and azaleas in June. Not surprisingly, it's a popular walk, so expect a fair amount of company along the way.

**Charlie's Bunion Hike on the Appalachian Trail** This challenging all-day hike along the Appalachian Trail is worthwhile for its overwhelming high-cliff views. Charlie's Bunion, a large chimney on top of a sheer 1,000-foot cliff, is a man-made feature—unbelievably, this cliff was covered by trees until clear-cutting and wildfires in 1925 allowed all the soil to wash away. Horace Kephart, the chronicler of Smoky Mountain life and genial local character, discovered the feature during a hunting trip and named it after a member of his party who had been complaining about his feet.

You reach it by hiking eastward from **Newfound Gap** along the Appalachian Trail for 4 miles, climbing 900 feet, a hard uphill slog made harder by a badly eroded trail surface; be sure to bring food and water with you. Once there, you'll find that the Appalachian Trail along the Bunion is little more than a narrow shelf blasted into the rock, with wide and continuous views over the Tennessee front. When you are done admiring the Bunion, continue to the end of the cliff and return along the alternate (i.e., safe) trail on the back side of the peak, as it wanders through a wildflower-carpeted meadow with sweeping views over the layered ridges of North Carolina. This, too, is a disaster feature, formed when the 1925 fire burnt the area so thoroughly that the forest has yet to grow back.

**Kephart Prong Trail** Kephart Prong is a lively mountain stream named after Horace Kephart from nearby Bryson City; the town's librarian, "Kep" was a prominent national park activist and an outdoor writer who authored *Our Southern Highlanders* in 1913. This easy walk on the North Carolina side of the Newfound Gap Road follows an old road for 2 miles along a lovely mountain stream to a small trail shelter. It is particularly interesting for the remains of a Civilian Conservation Corp camp hidden in the woods along the trail. The well-signposted trailhead parking lot is 3.7 miles north of Smokemont, on the right.

**LONG-DISTANCE PATHS** The Smoky Mountain's three longest long-distance paths meet and mix deep in the Great Smoky Mountains National Park, within this chapter's area. The 2,160-mile Appalachian Trail follows the Smokies Crest throughout this chapter, while the Mountains-to-Sea Trail branches off it at Mount Collins, 3.1 miles east of its official start at Clingmans Dome, to drop down to the Mountain Farm Museum on its long journey to the Outer Banks. Meanwhile, the 300-mile Benton MacKaye Trail has been ridge-hopping 5 or 10 miles south of the Appalachian Trail; it intersects the Mountains-to-Sea Trail 7.8 miles south of the Smokies Crest, follows it for 6.9 miles, then branches off to head toward Smokemont and some more ridge-hopping.

This layout creates **two loops** within the national park, each of them furnishing a week's backpacking that combines remote, little-visited backcountry with the popular and scenic ridgeline trek. Within this chapter's area, an 83-mile loop connects **Newfound Gap** with the park's far eastern trailhead at Davenport Gap, with additional trailheads at Smokemont and the **Heintooga Spur Road**. In an adjacent chapter, a second 73-mile loop runs west from Clingmans Dome to a high viewpoint above **Fontana Dam**, then explores the north shore of **Fontana Lake**; Clingmans Dome and nearby Mount Collins furnish the upper trailheads, while the Noland Creek Overlook on the **Road to Nowhere** is the lower trailhead.

**The Appalachian Trail** The Appalachian Trail in the Smoky Mountains National Park may well be the most popular backpacking path in America. In this chapter it travels for 39 miles, the highest section in its entire 2,160-mile length. This starts as the trail gains 1 mile in elevation near Jenkins Knob, then crosses 6,643-foot Clingmans Dome, passes through 5,046-foot Newfound Gap, to reach the park's eastern edge at 2,000-foot Davenport Gap, then drops through 1 mile of national forestlands to reach 1,371-foot Pigeon River. Along this entire route it only leaves the crest of the Smokies by a few hundred feet in either direction. For the most part it follows the crest exactly, sometimes on a knife-edge, and you walk with one foot in Tennessee, the other in North Carolina. Scenery alternates between handsome high-altitude forest and wildflower meadows called "grassy balds."

The first 29 miles stay consistently above a mile in elevation except for Newfound Gap itself, very likely the highest multinight hike in the East. It's not as easy as you would expect; the trail's fondness for the ridgeline causes it to climb every knob and drop into every shoulder, for 10,400 feet of climbing and 14,600 feet of descent. The Big Drop to the Pigeon River takes up the last 10 miles, starting at 5,918-foot Inadu Knob. From this point you will lose 4,400 feet in elevation, with knob-hopping adding another 2,000 feet up and down.

Trail shelters are found every half-dozen miles or so, all of them the three-sided lean-to type, and all of them with serious problems from bears and overcrowding.

HORSE EATING SNOW AT THE OCONALUFTEE MOUNTAIN FARM MUSEUM

Side trails intersect every 2 to 4 miles along the entire length, and this contributes to the overcrowding as people hike up for a single night on the trail. This is really not a good idea. The bear-fenced shelters are reserved for long-distance hikers, not day-trippers, and bears have learned about tents containing candy bars.

**The Mountains-to-Sea Trail** North Carolina's Mountains-to-Sea Trail officially starts at Clingmans Dome, but is coterminus with the Appalachian Trail for the first 3 miles, to Mount Collins. From that 6,188-foot point, the trail drops for 21 miles to 2,050-foot Oconaluftee Ranger Station, where it passes through the Mountain Farm Museum, following the Oconaluftee River to the Blue Ridge Parkway's southern terminus. This is essentially a forest walk, with the forest changing as you drop through two climate zones, following the headwaters of lovely Deep Creek. You are not done yet; from Deep Creek the trail climbs 2,400 feet to cross Thomas Ridge, with the Benton MacKaye Trail coterminous (and forming two 80-mile loops within the park). For this reason, this section of the trail, from the crest to the ranger station, has 6,400 feet of drop and 2,400 feet of climb—a good reason to take it from the top.

As the trail gains the Blue Ridge Parkway it follows the roadway to Soco Gap, a 14.4-mile roadwalk—the only uncompleted section until you reach the far northern end of the mountains, 322 miles of path later. This section is planned as a footpath that roughly parallels the parkway, but route approval has been delayed, and this will remain a road walk for the next few years.

**The Benton MacKaye Trail** The Benton MacKaye Trail spends 42 miles in this chapter's area, as it continues its ridge-hopping route parallel to the Smokies Crest and 5–10 miles to its south. The trail enters this chapter's area at an intersection with the Mountains-to-Sea Trail at Deep Creek, then runs coterminous with it as it climbs 2,400 feet to a ridgetop—the first of four major climbs in this section. From there the trails separate, with the Benton MacKaye dropping directly to the Newfound Gap Road and passing through Smokemont. The next 12 miles bring two more ridges, separated by the Raven Fork Gorge, noted for its extraordinary scenery and first-rate fly-fishing, with the Benton MacKaye Trail furnishing the only access. The next drop brings the trail to a trailhead at Round Bottoms Horse Camp on the Heintooga Spur Road, followed by its final climb of 2,500 feet to the Great Balsam Mountains, from there following the crest of a side ridge to stay above the mile-high point for 5 miles. At the end of this, the trail reaches 5,842-foot Mount Sterling for grand views. From there it drops pretty much straight down 4,000 feet in 5 miles to reach the picnic area at Big Creek. Although its official end is 2 miles farther at Davenport Gap, this is a road walk, and Big Creek is a better place to stop.



## ✷ Villages

**Cherokee** The main administrative center of the Qualla Boundary since the 19th century, Cherokee sits astride US 19 and US 441, hard against the southern boundary of the Great Smoky Mountains National Park. It's much smaller and more modest than Gatlinburg, and its parking and traffic isn't quite so bad. Much of its modest appearance is due to rules within the Qualla Boundary, which restrict land possession to tribal members; this has discouraged outside business investment and kept Cherokee in sort of a 1950s time warp.

Here's the layout. US 441 goes north and south, while US 19 goes east and west. Cherokee sits at their intersection, with modest businesses stringing outward along these highways. The most densely developed area, called "Downtown Cherokee" on road signs, straddles US 19 just east of US 441. Compared to the Tennessee tourist towns, "Downtown Cherokee" is startlingly retro, with a look and feel that's changed surprisingly little since the early days of park tourism. Old-fashioned open-front souvenir stands, bursting with an astonishing variety of trinkets, still dominate "Downtown." Shops trundle out stuffed bears on wheeled platforms. Giant sheet metal teepees sit on flat 1950s roofs (Cherokees never lived in tepees), and totem poles hold up porches (Cherokees never used totem poles). The real center of Cherokee gathers around its government complex on US 441 about a mile north of "Downtown." The buildings here show standard government styles from the 1930s through the 1990s, with two new **parks**, a first-rate **museum**, and the Eastern Band's **craft cooperative**, as well as the Cherokee Historical Association's outdoor drama ***Unto These Hills*** and 18th-century Cherokee village **Oconaluftee Village**.

MINGO FALLS

**Big Cove** One of the five original towns of the Qualla Boundary, today's Big Cove is a large, scenic mountain valley following the gorge-like Raven Fork. To a visitor, it is most significant as the site of most of the commercial campgrounds, some good cabin rentals, and the spectacular Mingo Falls.

**Maggie Valley** This tourist strip town formed in Jonathan Creek Valley in the 1950s, when a new highway was built eastward from the Qualla Boundary and designated US 19. Sprawling suburban-style development slowly grew up along the new highway; now, 60 years later, the development is nearly continuous. Maggie Valley is not a convenient place to stay when visiting the Great Smoky Mountains National Park, as it has no park entrance, and the Cherokee entrance is 20 miles away by a narrow, winding, steep two-lane road. However, the Blue Ridge Parkway is nearby, as is Cataloochee Cove.

## ✷ Wild Places

**THE GREAT FORESTS** **The Forests of the Oconaluftee Valley** The Newfound Gap Road from Cherokee to Gatlinburg gives access to the large drainage basin of the Oconaluftee River. While this was the home of the Qualla Cherokees since 1819, the Qualla preferred the better lands toward the bottom of the drainage, and left the upper slopes as hunting grounds. The tribe did not bother to purchase much of this land when they constructed the Qualla Boundary in the mid-19th century, allowing Champion Paper of Waynesville to acquire it in the 1890s.

As with their Waynesville tracts (see "The Blue Ridge Parkway Approaches the Smokies," *Wild Places*), Champion's doubtful stewardship led to large-scale ecological catastrophe. Fires and floods swept over their badly managed clear-cuts so viciously as to destroy large forests, creating meadows and even rocky cliffs that exist today. Paradoxically, the largest of these sites is now a renowned beauty spot, **Charlie's Bunion**. Champion prized these high upper slopes for their giant spruce and fir trees, which yielded superior paper pulp. However, they logged the lower slopes with similarly enthusiastic abandon, removing every tree they could sell. They abandoned logging the Oconaluftee Drainage in 1929 as a result of the Great Depression. The forests you see have been recovering since that date.

At the northeast edge of this forest, the Great Balsam Mountains split off from the Great Smoky Mountains to run south for another 45 miles. Nearly all of this length is above 4,000 feet (there is one deep gap), and a majority of it tops a mile in elevation. This section of the Great Balsams rises from the **Heintooga Spur Road** to a high group of 11 peaks over 6,000 feet in elevation—over a quarter of all the 6'ers in the East.

**RECREATION AREAS** **Smokemont** Smokemont was originally constructed as a timber camp, the general headquarters of Champion Paper's logging operations in the Oconaluftee drainage during the first three decades of the 20th century. Champion valued the high ridges above the Oconaluftee for its spruce trees, which produced high-quality pulp for paper, and their aggressive logging practices led to the disastrous fires that created the meadows and cliffs around Charlie's Bunion, similar to the huge fire-caused mountaintop meadows of the Shining Rock Wilderness south of Waynesville. However, the Great Depression caused Champion to simply walk away from Smokemont in 1929; when the National Park Service took it over in the late 1940s they removed nearly every trace of the polluted, deteriorating lumber camp and converted it to a recreation area. Today it holds a large campground, a livery stable, and a variety of trailheads.

**Newfound Gap** This high gap marks the point where the Newfound Gap Road crosses the crest of the Smokies. Not surprisingly, it's heavily visited, with a huge parking lot. A monumental stone platform at its eastern edge served as the site of the 1940 dedication ceremony, personally attended by President Franklin Roosevelt (who gave a speech fromthe platform); nearby is a narrow, but impressive view of the highway wandering down the Tennessee side. The Appalachian Trail runs by the dedication platform, and furnishes a steep but beautiful day hike (9 miles round-trip) to Charlie's Bunion, a massive cliff with sweeping panoramic views. An overlook south of the platform has interpretive plaques and a handsome 180-degree sweep over the upper Oconaluftee drainage basin on the North Carolina side.

**Clingmans Dome** At 6,643 feet, Clingmans Dome is the highest point in the national park and the second highest peak in the eastern United States. It offers some of the best views in the Smokies. Many of these views can be found at its large cresent-shaped parking lot, almost 0.2 mile long, with a continuous south-facing panorama so broad that you have to walk its entire length to take it all in. The rest of the views are from the Dome's large, modern observation deck, a concrete pillar surrounded by a huge spiral ramp, a steep quarter-mile up a paved trail from the parking lot. Clingmans Dome is a major trailhead, where the Appalachian Trail reaches its highest point and the Forney Ridge Trail descends to beautiful Andrews Bald before it plunges deep into the North Carolina backcountry. It has flush toilets and drinking water in season, but no picnic tables. Access is by the Clingmans Dome Spur Road, which is closed in winter.

AN EARLY SNOW IN THE SMOKY MOUNTAINS

**Balsam Mountan Picnic and Camping Area** Part of the Great Smoky Mountains National Park, Balsam Mountain (also known as Heintooga) is certainly the place to be on a hot summer day. At 5,300 feet above sea level, it's the highest, coolest, and windiest picnic area and campground in the park. It may also be the loveliest, set in a fine old balsam grove. A very short walk takes you to Heintooga Overlook, with a sweeping 180-degree view over the entire Smoky Mountain Crest—probably the best place in the park to enjoy a sunset. To reach Balsam Mountain from Cherokee, go 12 miles up the Blue Ridge Parkway then 7 miles up the Heintooga Spur Road.

**PICNIC AREAS** **Collins Creek Picnic Area** This large, lovely picnic area is scattered along three loops through a cool, streamside forest, 6.65 miles up Newfound Gap Road from the park's boundary in Cherokee. Despite the fact that it is the only picnic area on the North Carolina Newfound Gap Road, it is little used, possibly because it has no recreation opportunities besides eating outdoors. Even its one CCC hiking trail has been closed for 30 years—a pity, as it climbed through a virgin forest to a good view.

**Oconaluftee Islands Tribal Park and Veterans Tribal Park** Isolated from the center of Cherokee by the waters of the Oconaluftee, Islands Park is an oasis of cool, quiet loveliness. Its picnic tables are widely scattered through a forested glade, and linked by an interpretive nature/history trail. Unfortunately, there is only limited parking on the gravel road shoulder by the bridge. The nearby Veterans Park in the center of the town's government district also has picnic facilities as well as ample parking. Both parks have full facilities.

## ✷ To See

### *Along the Blue Ridge Parkway*

**Soco Gap** The parkway intersects with US 19 in this high (4,345-foot) gap. Soco Gap has had some sort of trail in it since the early 19th century, but its great elevation and cliff-like sides has always prevented it from being a major entry point to the Smokies; it received its current highway, US 19, only in the 1950s. Apart from its height and steepness it's had another barrier to travel: it may well be the snowiest U.S. highway in these mountains, frequently having deep snow when most other areas have had only a cold drizzle. This is not always a bad thing. Although this section of the Blue Ridge Parkway is invariably closed in winter, you can drive up to Soco Gap on the plowed and salted US 19, park on the intersection verge, and join in the other families sledding, cross-country skiing, throwing snowballs, and building snowmen along the closed parkway. For other times of the year, if you need facilities at this exit, drive 4 miles east on US 19 to Maggie Valley.

**HISTORIC SITES** **Mountain Farm Museum** Located in the Great Smoky Mountains National Park on the Newfound Gap Road 1.35 miles outside Cherokee, the Mountain Farm Museum is one of the most complete, and one of the most handsome, exhibits on mountain farm life anywhere in the southern Appalachians. Unlike sites in the more famous Cades Cove, the Mountain Farm Museum portrays a full-sized operating farm—flowers along the porch, furniture in the house, corn in the field, chickens in the coop, and a horse in the barn.

The farmstead consists of log structures, all built around 1900, moved in from remote areas of the park (where other such buildings were being destroyed as safety hazards). The log farmhouse is a solid two-story structure with a kitchen wing and two porches, built in 1902 by local farmer John Davis. Today the farmhouse is furnished in late-19th-century style, and docents in period costume explain the way of life. The Davis House is surrounded by hand-split pickets and planted with beds of native flowers. The barn anchors the other end of the site. Original to this location, it's a large cantilevered log barn with an oversized clapboarded hayloft overhanging log cribs. Inside are examples of late-19th-century farm equipment, a horse, several stray chickens from the nearby coop, and a cat. The horse is a friendly old creature, who loves to meet gentle and well-behaved children.

Between the two main structures lies a working late-19th-century farmstead. Corn grows behind high, strong split-rail fences; beans and squash grow among the corn, a standard mountain practice. A vegetable garden, protected by pickets, grows a riot of tomatoes, squash, beans, and peas, as well as flowers for the kitchen table. Gourd birdhouses provide natural insect control. Log outbuildings include a corncrib, a chicken house, a springhouse, a smokehouse, an apple house with a stone foundation, a gear shed, a blacksmith shop, a pigpen (with pig), hollow-log beehives (with bees), and a sorghum press.

Adjacent to the Farm Museum is the modest Oconaluftee Visitor's Center, with an information desk, bookshop, and interpretive exhibits housed in a classic Depression-era stone building.

**Mingus Mill** Mingus Mill is a late-19th-century gristmill restored to operation, located on the Newfound Gap Road a short distance beyond the Mountain Farm Museum. In its time it was a modern facility, with two grist stones powered by an efficient store-bought turbine instead of the old-fashioned hand-carpentered overshot wheel. You can scramble under this large clapboarded building to see the turbine in operation, then go inside to watch the miller operate the great grist stones and buy a pound of stone-ground cornmeal. However, its most impressive part is

MINGUS MILL

its elevated millrace, standing 20 feet off the ground as it passes into the building to fall into the turbine. There's a short, pleasant walk that follows the millrace to the mill's small log dam on Mingus Creek.





**MUSEUMS The Museum of the Cherokee Indian** (www.cherokeemuseum.org; e-mail: eswimmer@cherokeemuseum.org; 828-497-3481; fax: 828-497-4985; US Hwy. 441 & Drama Rd., P.O. Box 1599, Cherokee, NC 28719). The Museum of the Cherokee Indian is one of the most intriguing, involving, and moving museum experiences in the western mountains. Its displays mix carefully chosen artifacts with artworks and state-of-the-art museum technology to tell the story of the Cherokee clearly, simply, and beautifully. And story-telling is just what it does. Starting with the Cherokee creation myth, the museum leads visitors gently through the ages, from Archaic times, to the pre-Columbian Cherokee culture and way of life, through their contact with Europeans and the chaotic dislocations that ensued, and ending with an emotional account of the Trail of Tears, the violent relocation of most of the Cherokee to Oklahoma. The museum, which is a wholly independent not-for-profit, has a first-rate gift shop. You'll find the museum in a handsome 1970s wood building constructed to remind one of the surrounding mountain peaks, in town at the intersection of Drama Road and US 441, 1.25 miles north of US 19.

**Oconaluftee Indian Village** (http://www.cherokeehistorical.org/OconalufteeVillage.html; e-mail: info@cherokeehistorical.org; 866-554-4557, 828-497-2111; fax: 828-497-6987; P.O. Box 398, Cherokee, NC 28719). Open daily, May 15–October 25, 9 AM–5:30 PM. Built in 1952 by the Cherokee Historical Association, the Oconaluftee Indian Village authentically recreates an 18th-century Cherokee settlement. Thatched log cabins group around a seven-sided council house, where Cherokee crafters in period costume demonstrate traditional tribal arts.

**The Qualla Arts and Crafts Mutual** (828-497-3103; fax: 828-497-4841; P.O. Box 310, Cherokee, NC 28719). The Qualla Mutual is a craft cooperative and gallery for several hundred crafters who are enrolled members of the Eastern Band. A museum area has a series of glass-case wall displays which explain the varieties of contemporary Cherokee crafts, including their history, style, materials, and methods: stone carving, basket weaving (several kinds), pottery, masks, dolls, wood carving, and jewelry. The main area of the building contains a large shop that wanders through several rooms, offering every kind of Cherokee craft at a wide range of prices. All crafts for sale are hand made by members, and carry an authentication mark. The Qualla Mutual is in a low-slung 1960s-era building across the street from the Museum of the Cherokee.

**GARDENS AND PARKS Mingo Falls Tribal Park** One of the most beautiful waterfalls of the Smokies, Mingo Falls is the highlight of a modest tribally run park and campground in Big Cove. A short, steep track leads a quarter-mile uphill to the base of the falls—a lacy curtain of water hung over a hundred foot cliff. You'll find it 6 miles north of Cherokee on Big Cove Road; turn left at Saunooke Village, then just keep going.

**OTHER Unto These Hills** (cherokee-nc.com/index; 866-554-4557, 828-497-2111; 688 Drama Rd., Cherokee, NC 28719). Jun 14–August 26, except Sundays;

preshow entertainment starts around 7:45 pm. Founded in 1950 by the nonprofit Cherokee Historical Association, this large-scale outdoor pageant, performed by a hundred actors and dancers over three stages, presents the history of the Cherokee people, from their contact with Hernando de Soto to the Trail of Tears.

**Harrahs Cherokee Casino** (harrahscherokee.com/casinos/harrahs-cherokee; 828-497-7777; fax: 828-497-5076; 777 Casino Dr., Cherokee, NC 28719). Open 24 hours a day, 7 days a week. The Eastern band owns, and Harrahs operates, this large, luxurious video gaming emporium, a short distance east of Cherokee on US 19. This new facility includes three restaurants and a 1,500-seat theater. Added recently is a 252-room,, 15-story high-rise luxury hotel, conveniently connected to the casino, which houses an indoor swimming pool, fitness center and gift shop and displays local Cherokee crafts and artwork throughout.

## ✷ To Do

**STABLES** **Smokemont Riding Stables** (828-497-2373; smokemontridingstable.com; e-mail: SmokyMtn@Hughes.net; 135 Smokemont Riding Stable Rd., Cherokee, NC 28719). May–October. This national park concessionaire offers guided horseback rides in the Smokemont area.

**Cataloochee Ranch Stables** (cataloocheeranch.com; e-mail: info@cataloochee-ranch.com; 800-868-1401, 828-926-1401;119 Ranch Dr., Maggie Valley, NC 28751). April–November. Part of Cataloochee Ranch, this stable offers trail rides on the ranch's spectacular 1,000 acres of mile-high ridgetop meadows and forests and into the adjacent Great Smoky Mountains National Park.

**FISHING** **Fishing on the Qualla Boundary** (828-497-5201). North Carolina's record brown trout (15 lb., 2 oz.) was caught on the Qualla Boundary in 1990. The boundary has 30 miles of trout streams open to visitors, plus several trout ponds. The tribe stocks these streams twice a week in season, and has a creel limit of 10 fish per day. Unlike the national park, you need no state fishing license; however, you must have a Tribal Fishing Permit, which costs $7 per day (children under 11 free with permitted adult). Permits are sold in most campground stores, outfitters, tackle stores, and general stores in the boundary.

CABIN IN LITTLE CATALOOCHEE COVE

**GOLF** **Maggie Valley Resort** (www.maggievalleyclub.com; e-mail: info@maggievalleyclub.com; 800-438-3861, 828-926-6013; 1819 Country Club Rd., Maggie Valley, NC 28751). This 18-hole par-72 course, constructed in 1961, winds uphill from the center of Maggie Valley, with excellent views of the surrounding peaks.

## ✷ Lodging

If you are looking for a bed & breakfast in Maggie Valley you'll find quite a choice. However, Cherokee has only motel rooms (2,500 of them) and cabins—no bed-and-breakfasts, country lodges, or resorts. A sampling of Cherokee cabin rentals is given below. You can also rent a private vacation home in the Cherokee area from any of several realtors in Sylva and Bryson City. There are also a number of first-rate bed & breakfasts and small country hotels a short drive from Cherokee, listed in the Sylva and Bryson City chapters.

**COUNTRY RESORTS** **The Swag** (www.theswag.com; e-mail: stay@theswag.com; 800-789-7672; fax: 828-926-2036; 2300 Swag Rd., Waynesville, NC 28785). This large log inn sits in a grassy swale 5,000 feet high, at the end of a 2.5-mile driveway that climbs over 1,000 feet in elevation. Remote and quiet, the views from its wide porches and balconies are spectacular. Rooms range in size from cozy to huge, each distinctively decorated with antiques and heritage quilts. Three log cabins (one with its own billiard room) give additional choices. The tariff includes three gourmet meals each day: a full breakfast, a picnic lunch, and an elegant, relaxed dinner. The 250-acre site includes a pond, a waterfall, a 3-mile nature trail with fine views, and four sheltered hideaways for a little private relaxing in the woods.

**Cataloochee Ranch** (www.cataloochee-ranch.com; e-mail: info@cataloochee-ranch.com; 800-868-1401, 828-926-1401; fax: 828-926-9249; 119 Ranch Dr., Maggie Valley, NC 28751). The Cataloochee Ranch has been operating from its current 1,000-acre ridgetop spread since 1938, under the ownership of the same family. It sits in sweeping mountaintop meadows above 5,000 feet high, directly above central Maggie Valley at the end of Fie Top Road. Its main compound has a log lodge with six rooms, a modern conference building with four rooms and two suites, and nine log cabins. The tariff includes a buffet breakfast and a family-style dinner with traditional southern cooking; there are frequent barbeques as well. The ranch offers horseback rides at an extra fee, as well as hiking trips (both on its beautiful site and into the adjacent Great Smoky Mountains National Park), pond fishing, an outdoor swimming pool, and such activities as story telling, clogging, square dancing, wagon rides, bonfires, and marshmallow roasts.

**BED & BREAKFAST INNS** **Timberwolf Creek Bed & Breakfast** (www.timberwolfcreek.com; e-mail: staff@maggiecabin.com; 888-525-4218, 828-926-2608; 391 Johnson Branch Rd., Maggie Valley, NC 28751). This classic luxury three-room bed & breakfast is in a modern ranch-style house by a mountain stream, on a side road convenient to central Maggie Valley. The rooms are beautifully furnished with antiques, and have views (either mountain or stream) and two-person hot tubs. The common area has plush country furniture around a stone fireplace, with beverages and fresh-baked goods on the counter. Full gourmet breakfasts are included.

**CABIN RENTALS** **Grandview Cabins** (www.thegrandviewcabins.com; e-mail: bobens@verizon.net; 828-497-1356; Cherokee, NC 28719). Open all year. The Grandview Cabins are located in the center of Cherokee, with a wide and unobstructed view over the western parts of the town toward the mountains beyond. The four log cabins are roomy and well appointed, with covered porches that face the sunrise. There are also rocking chairs, fireplaces, and good kitchens. The Grandview Cabins have a very convenient location, a few hundred yards uphill from the intersection of US 19 and US 441 in the center of town.

**Sycamore Log Cabins** (828-497-9068; P.O. Box 563, Cherokee, NC 28719). These three log cabins form a quiet little group along side Big Cove Road adjacent to the boundary of the Great Smoky Mountains National Park. The well-kept, recently built log homes have a great room with kitchen, plus two bedrooms. Each has a porch with rocking chairs, and is furnished in a rustic style.

**Great Smoky Mountain Log Cabins** (www.gsmcabins.com; e-mail: info@gsmcabins.com; 828-497-6182; 1056 Adams Creek Rd., Cherokee, NC 28719). This is made up of two sets of cozy log cabins, one in the pastoral Olivet Church area south of Cherokee, and another up Owl Branch, a more heavily settled section of the Qualla Boundary. All but two of the cabins are modern milled log structures with a combined living area and kitchen, plus two bedrooms and either a hot tub or a whirlpool bath. All of the cabins have wide covered porches with rocking chairs, and gas fireplaces in the living areas.

**Boyd Mountain Log Cabins** (www.boydmountain.com; 828-926-1575; 445 Boyd Farm Rd., Waynesville, NC 28786). Set on a 150-acre private farm in Maggie Valley's scenic Hemphill Creek area, these six log cabins are all authentic, restored pioneer structures ranging from 150 to 200 years old. These cozy, comfortable historic cabins set in beautiful meadows, by or near a fishing pond; all have full porches and fireplaces, with upstairs bedroom(s).

## ✷ Where to Eat

**EATING OUT** Frankly, this is not a good area to search for a memorable meal. The three restaurants inside Harrah's Casino all serve reliably good food, and there are several decent buffets for the all-you-can-eat crowd. Motel restaurants at Cherokee's Holiday Inn and Best Western are also reliable. However, there are some first-rate restaurants in nearby towns; see the chapters on Sylva and Bryson City (both near Cherokee), as well as Waynesville (near Maggie Valley).

## ✷ Selective Shopping

### *Cherokee*

**The Drama Road Gift Shops** Not surprisingly, the first-rate Museum of the Cherokee has a first-rate gift shop. Spacious, handsome, and full of stuff, this museum gift shop has Cherokee art and crafts, books, children's toys and books related to the museum, as well as a fascinating selection of tasteful and relevant gewgaws and knickknacks. The Qualla Mutual, a Cherokee crafters' cooperative, is just across the street and simply bursting with even more good stuff—all of it handmade on the Qualla Boundary and carrying a certificate of authenticity from the U.S. Bureau of Indian Affairs. You'll find these two locations on US 441 and Drama Road, 1.25 miles north of US 19.

**Great Smokies Fine Art Gallery** (greatsmokiesart.com; e-mail: gsfinearts@frontier.com; 828-497-5444; 1655 Acquoni Rd., Ste. 3, Cherokee, NC 28719). This storefront in the Saunooke Village area of Cherokee combines limited-edition prints by Native American artists with Native American crafts and North Carolina handcrafted furniture. With this mix, the shop has the comfortable feel of a luxuriously furnished home. Western Native American artists as well as Eastern Band artists are among those represented.

**The Old Mill** (282-497-6536; 3082 Hwy. 441 North, Whittier, NC 28789). This large, old clapboard mill, painted white and with a huge steel overshot wheel, ground corn through most of the 20th century. Nowadays it sells a wide variety of items, including locally made jams and honeys and stone-ground cornmeal (ground at a nearby mill—the Old Mill's workings were destroyed in a 1980s' burglary). The Old Mill is located on US 441, south of Cherokee, outside the Qualla Boundary.

## ✷ Special Events

**SPRING Honor the Elders Day** Mid-March. Cherokee stickball, a ceremonial (and very exciting) sport, combines with traditional dances and food, at the Cherokee Ceremonial Grounds.

**Ramp and Rainbow Festival** First weekend in April. Ramps—the mountain wild leek, with a taste redolent of both onion and garlic—traditionally herald the coming of spring throughout the Smokies and the Blue Ridge. This festival at the Cherokee Ceremonial Grounds celebrates the coming of spring with ramp and rainbow trout dinners, along with craft and fishing vendors.

**SUMMER Fourth of July Powwow** Fourth of July weekend. The tribe celebrates the Fourth of July with a powwow dance competition, arts and crafts displays, Native American foods, and a fireworks display, at the Cherokee Ceremonial Grounds.

**Maggie Valley Arts & Crafts Festival** Second weekend in July. Sponsored by the Maggie Valley Civic Association, this festival at the Maggie Valley Civic Center features over 100 craft vendors, plus food and entertainment. It's repeated on the third weekend in October.

# South of the Smokies

4

NEAR THE PARK:
SYLVA & DILLSBORO

THE BLUE RIDGE:
CASHIERS & HIGHLANDS

FRANKLIN &
THE NANTAHALA MOUNTAINS

THE NORTHERN UNICOIS:
ROBBINSVILLE & TELLICO PLAINS

THE SOUTHERN UNICOIS:
MURPHY & THE COPPER BASIN

# SOUTH OF THE SMOKIES

Mountains extend southward from the Great Smokies through North Carolina, to meet the Blue Ridge near the Georgia state line. These ridges are high and steep-sided, with most peaks above 4,000 feet and many topping a mile high. They zig and zag around with no obvious reason, hemming in narrow-bottomed little valleys. The major rivers—the Tuckaseegee, the Nantahala, the Little Tennessee, the Valley River, the Hiwassee, the Tellico—can run obediently between two low ridges, then turn suddenly to cut a deep gorge straight through a high barrier.

Early roads and railroads tried to pick their ways through the least difficult gaps and gorges, with settlements following. The state legislatures broke the mountains into increasingly small counties in a vain attempt to create courthouses within horseback distance of most of the settlers. Today, these courthouses sit at the center of compact, old downtowns in small county seats—Sylva, Franklin, Robbinsville, Hayesville, Murphy.

These are the lands in which the Cherokees made their last stand in the East. The Cherokee Nation gave up their most rugged areas to the European invaders, hoping to satisfy the land hunger and live unmolested in the lower mountains of north Georgia and southeastern Tennessee. When the invasion failed to abate, the tribe fought its battles in the American courts—only to discover that the whites simply ignored their own courts when they did not like the results. In 1838 the Jackson administration, disobeying a U.S. Supreme Court order, forcibly removed the Cherokees from their lands, marching them to Oklahoma on the bitter Trail of Tears on which many hundreds died. The modern town of Murphy, seat of Cherokee County, occupies the site of one of the concentration camps used to gather the Cherokees for the forced march. Today, the Robbinsville grave of Chief Junaluska, who had saved Jackson's life during the battle of Horseshoe Bend, is the sole monument to the Cherokee Nation in these lands. (The Qualla Boundary, modern home of the Eastern Cherokees, is outside the final boundaries of the old Cherokee Nation.) Some 600 descendents of Cherokees who escaped the expulsion form a community at Snowbird, also near Robbinsville.

More than most other Eastern mountains, these southern ridges are dominated by public ownership, with settled areas sometimes little more than islands in a sea of forest. In North Carolina, the Nantahala National Forest owns the majority of the mountain slopes; in Tennessee, it's the Cherokee National Forest. Where the

Blue Ridge overlaps into South Carolina, the Sumter National Forest takes over, and in Georgia the Chattahoochee National Forest rules the roost. All four of these national forests maintain ranger stations in the major towns throughout this area, and these stations always have staffed information desks, books, and maps. As with all national forests, public recreation (including hunting) is permitted nearly everywhere; however, these are not national parks or conservation areas, and active logging continues on many government-owned tracts.

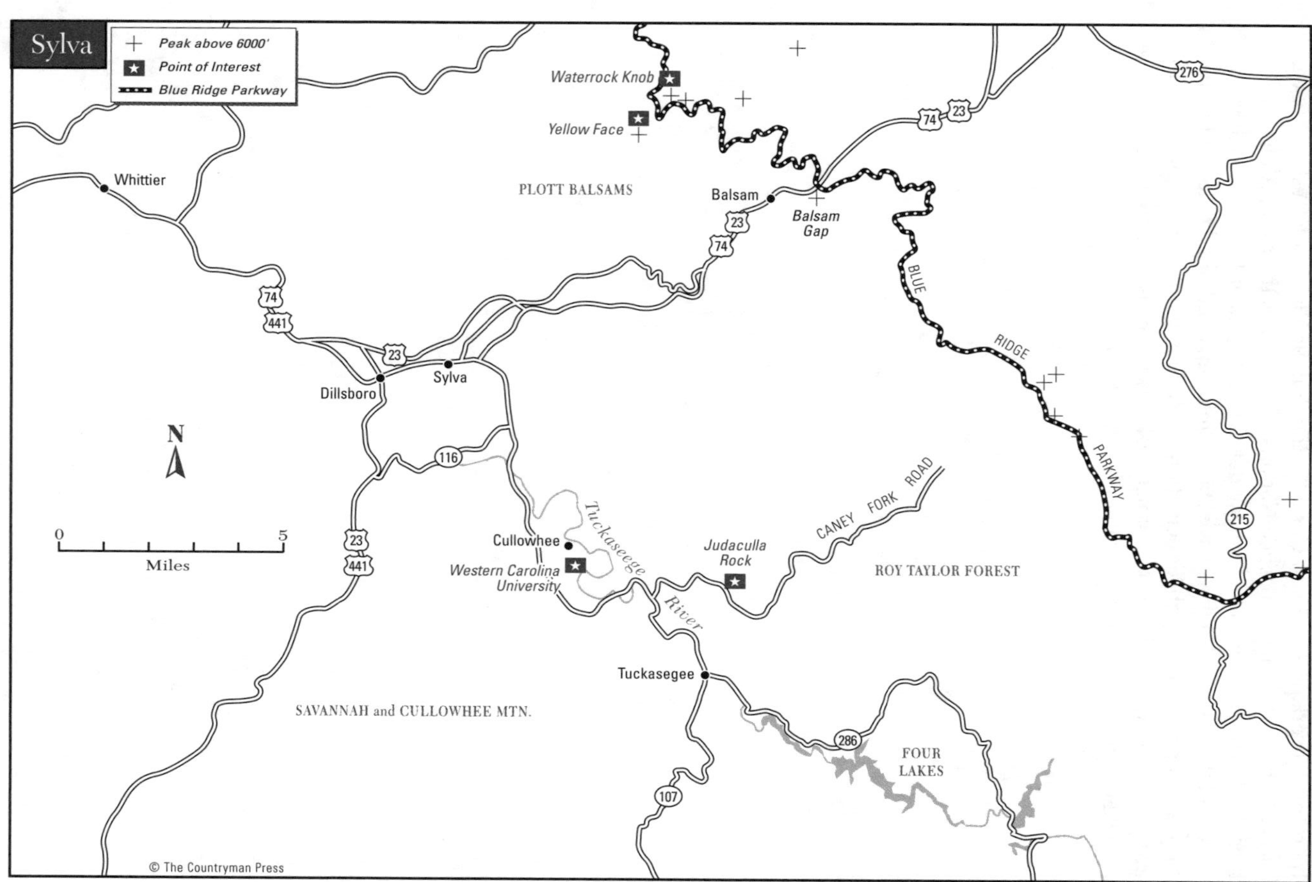
Sylva
Peak above 6000'
Point of Interest
Blue Ridge Parkway
Whittier
Waterrock Knob
Yellow Face
PLOTT BALSAMS
Balsam
Balsam Gap
BLUE RIDGE PARKWAY
276
74
23
441
Dillsboro
Sylva
116
N
0
5
Miles
Cullowhee
Western Carolina University
Tuckaseege River
Judaculla Rock
CANEY FORK ROAD
ROY TAYLOR FOREST
215
Tuckasegee
SAVANNAH and CULLOWHEE MTN.
286
FOUR LAKES
107
© The Countryman Press

# NEAR THE PARK: SYLVA & DILLSBORO

The tall, jumbled ridges of the Smokies don't end at the national park boundaries. The high peaks and deep valleys continue south of the Great Smoky Mountains National Park to encircle the beautiful little county seat of Sylva and its sister burg, Dillsboro. Nestled deep in a valley formed by the Tuckaseegee River, Sylva and Dillsboro remain red-brick and white-clapboard Victorian villages, surrounded by deep forests and mile-high summits. Other places have more chain restaurants and franchised motels; Sylva and Dillsboro are rich in authentic, old-fashioned comfort.

Sylva and Dillsboro command a deep mountain valley that has long served as the gateway to North Carolina's western mountains, including the Smokies. Ten miles to the east, the unusually deep and gentle Balsam Gap furnishes the only real break in the solid wall of the Smokies and their southward extension, the Great Balsam Mountains. In pioneer days the Rutherford Trace, a glorified footpath, ran through Balsam Gap to serve as the main route westward as late as 1850—an astonishing level of isolation, considering that railroads were entering much of the South by that time. In 1855 the Smokies first wagon road, the Nantahala Turnpike, opened through Balsam Gap to Dillsboro and Bryson City, then on through the Nantahala Gorge to Tennessee. It took the railroad almost 30 more years to reach this isolated backwater, paralleling the Nantahala Turnpike the entire way. US 74 roughly parallels the turnpike, while the Great Smoky Mountains Railroad still carries passengers on the old railroad.

Dillsboro was the original pioneer settlement; nearby Sylva, founded as a railroad siding, slowly acquired most of the businesses and jobs. Today, Sylva is the main town, little changed from the 1940s with brick storefronts marching up to a grand old county courthouse crowning a green hill. Adjacent Dillsboro is a village of nicely kept white-clapboard Victorian buildings, with one of the Smoky Mountain's finest concentration of craft and gift shops. To the south, the settlement of Cullowhee marks the center of a twisted knot of tall mountains and deep valleys. Throughout this area, the choice of restaurants and bed & breakfasts is unusually good (just as the usual array of chains and franchises are largely missing), the towns are small and unspoiled, and the scenery is spectacular. Access is good, with expressways leading to the Great Smoky Mountains in 15 miles and the Blue Ridge Parkway in 10 miles.

DOWNTOWN SYLVA

**GUIDANCE—TOWN AND COUNTRY Jackson County Chamber of Commerce** (www.mountainlovers.com; e-mail: info@mountainlovers.com; 800-962-1911, 828-586-2155; fax: 828-586-4887; 773 West Main St., Sylva, NC 28779). This countywide chamber handles both Sylva and Dillsboro tourist information. Its new walk-in visitors center occupies part of the beautifully renovated Hooper House, right by the old courthouse on Main Street. If you have any questions about the towns and valleys west of the Balsams, their website is the best place to start looking for answers.

**The Jackson County Home Page** (www.main.nc.us/Jackson; e-mail: bouchard@main.nc.us). Sponsored by the mountains' not-for-profit Internet cooperative, MAIN (Mountain Area Information Network), the Jackson County Home Page is a thorough and well-designed repository of community information and links about the western slopes and valleys of the Great Balsam Mountains.

**GUIDANCE—PARKS AND FORESTS The Nantahala National Forest** While this region has significant tracts of national forest land, none of them has any real recreation development beyond a footpath or two. It's all administered by the Nantahala Ranger Station in Franklin, North Carolina, 22 miles south via US 441.

**The Blue Ridge Parkway** The Blue Ridge Parkway's highest and most breathtaking section hugs the eastern border of this chapter's area, and is easily reached from Sylva by taking four-lane US 74 east for 12 miles. It is described in other chapters.

**GETTING THERE By Car** Sylva and Dillsboro sit near the intersection of US 441 and US 23/74, both excellent four-lane highways—scenic and lightly traveled access for visitors from the south, east, and west. Visitors from points north will find the Great Smoky Mountains National Park firmly in the way; while sightseers will enjoy crossing the park on the scenic Newfound Gap Road (formerly US 441) from Gatlinburg, Tennessee, anyone wishing to make time should take Interstate 40 around the east side of the Smokies, picking up US 23/74 at Canton, North Carolina, about 30 miles east of Sylva.

**By Air** (www.flyavl.com; 828-684-2226; 61 Terminal Dr.,(828-684-2226; flyavl.com) 61 Terminal Drive, Ste. 1, Fletcher, NC, 28732. The nearest airport is the

Asheville Regional Airport, 45 miles east of Balsam Gap. You'll need to rent a car, as the Sylva area has no bus service. It's a 45-minute drive, four-lane all the way, via I-26, I-40, and US 74.

**By Bus, Train, or Public Transportation** There is no bus or rail service to this area, and there is no local bus service.

**MEDICAL EMERGENCIES** **Harris Regional Hospital** (www.westcare.org; 828-586-7000; 68 Hospital Rd., Sylva, NC 28779). Sylva's 200-bed regional hospital has 24/7 emergency room service. If you want to see what it looks like, rent the movie The Fugitive, in which it had a starring role. It is a mile east of town on Business US 74, just off the easternmost of the three Sylva exits on US 23/74.

## ✷ Exploring the Area

**EXPLORING BY CAR** **The Nantahala Turnpike** In 1855, when most of America was being linked together by iron rails, the Smokies finally got their first wagon road—the Nantahala Turnpike. This 14-mile scenic drive gives the look and feel of traveling down the old turnpike. On the way it gives good views of the 1882 railroad, including two fine old trestles and the second steepest railroad grade in the East. Total length: 13.8.

*Leg #1—Balsam Gap (4.8 miles)*: From US 23/74 at Balsam Gap, go west 0.20 mile to a left onto Cabin Flats Road (SSR 1701), then go 0.5 mile to a right onto Old Balsam Depot Road (SSR 1700), then go 0.4 mile to left onto Dark Ridge Road; continue 3.7 miles to a T-intersection with Old Highway 19-23 (SSR 1432). US 23/74 is 0.2 mile right.

*Leg #2—Old US 19/23 (6.9 miles)*: Turn left onto Old Highway 19-23 for 6.6 miles to a right fork onto Chipper Curve Road in Sylva, then go 0.3 mile to a sharp uphill right onto Allen Street.

*Leg #3—The Nantahala Turnpike (2.1 miles)*: Follow Allen Street for 0.80 mile to a right onto Municipal Drive, then go two blocks to a right onto Grindstaff Cove Road, then take an immediate left onto Old Dillsboro Road, becoming SSR 1380.

VIEW FROM NEWFOUND GAP

Continue for 1.6 miles to a right onto Hometown Place Road (SSR 1381), then go one block to a right onto US Bus 23, then go one block to a left fork onto Front Street, which ends in three blocks. US 23/441 is one block right, then one block left.

Once you leave US 23/74, your road quickly reaches the railroad and runs parallel to it, past the abandoned Knights General Store, then crosses the railroad to pass the grand old **Balsam Mountain Inn**, a 1905 railroad hotel still in operation and restored to elegance. As you leave the inn behind, you'll follow an isolated mountain valley downhill through lovely remote scenery. Soon both the road and the stream cross under a fine old steel truss railroad bridge, a working piece of history from the late 19th century.

After another mile of this remote mountain valley, Leg #2 of this route turns left onto the former WPA-era main highway, Old US 19/23, at a T-intersection. This particularly scenic section snakes through the gorge carved by Scott Creek, zigging and zagging past the railroad. At one point the road passes over the railroad just as the railroad passes over the creek—a double bridge. A half-mile later, the railroad flies over both the road and the creek. From here, the road (and the railroad) passes into wide valleys.

As you enter the town of **Sylva** some miles later, Old 19/23 bends left to return to the main highway. Leg 3 stays on the old turnpike by following the alley-like Allen Street, with a dramatic uphill at its start. At first it seems odd that the turnpike avoids entering Sylva—but, of course, Sylva didn't exist when the turnpike was built. The turnpike was actually trying to miss valley mud and floods, pretty typical behavior for an early-19th-century coach road. As Allen Street enters Sylva, it passes City Hall, then zig-zags onto Old Dillsboro Road—the actual turnpike roadbed. This is a lovely drive that climbs and twists along hillsides to a **panoramic view** of the town of Sylva, which now fills the valley bottom that the turnpike was so careful to avoid. At the bottom of the hill, the Old Dillsboro Road returns you to Business US 23, the early-20th-century automobile road that replaced the turnpike. A block later, on the left, the turnpike forks off to run through the three-block center of **Dillsboro**, now an important craft center with many gift shops and a passenger station for the excursion **Smoky Mountain Railroad**. Here it ends, blocked by the tall banks of its successor, US 23/441.

**EXPLORING ON FOOT** **Plott Balsams Walk** Close to the popular Waterrock Knob, this little-used 1.3-mile round-trip follows the spectacular 5,800-foot ridgeline of Plott Balsams to the 6,032-foot peak of Yellow Face. It's part of the town of Sylva's effort to open up Plott Balsams for outdoor recreation, making paths through its watershed available to day hikers. You will find the trail along the side of the parkway opposite the intersection with the Waterrock Knob Spur; the closest parking is 0.12 mile up the spur road at the Cut-off Ridge Overlook.

The trail immediately dives into a high-altitude "balsam" forest. Like all such forests in the Balsam Mountains, it's undergoing a drastic ecological transition, as the deaths of most of the firs (due to wooly aselgid infections) clears out the forest canopy and allows a host of other species to gain a foothold. Look for berries and wildflowers where forest giants once shaded a floor of needles, moss, and rocks. In a quarter-mile the path reaches an open meadow with sweeping views east and south along the plunging slopes of the Balsams. Beyond, the trail climbs up a narrow, rocky ridgeline through tall spruces, gaining 300 feet in elevation; occasionally, it clambers up a rocky outcrop, with mosses and dwarf trees to give the look of a Japanese garden. Near the top of the peak, the trail scrambles left around a large outcrop to follow a rocky ledge to another stunning view. From here you can see the little settlement of Balsam hugging the slopes of the mountain, with Balsam Gap slashing through the mountain so deeply that it appears only as a gash; on a roiling summer day, rain clouds will sail through the gap a half mile below you. The viewless peak of Yellow Face (39th highest in the East), covered in blueberry and blackberry meadows, is a short distance beyond. This is a good place to turn back. If you decide to go on, the trail continues through high mountain meadows, knife-edged outcrops, and balsam forests to reach The Pinnacle, with panoramic views, adding 6 miles and 2,100 feet of rugged backcountry climbing to your journey.

## ✷ Villages

**Sylva** The county seat of Sylva snuggles in a narrow side valley of the Tuckaseegee River, under the mile-high peaks of Plott Balsams. Its four-block downtown hugs the hillside above Scotts Creek, so that each old brick storefront has a basement on Main Street that comes out at street level on Mill Street. Its Main Street is not so much restored as unchanged, frozen in a time where people went downtown to shop in tiny old brick buildings. Main Street ends at a flight of steps climbing a tall green hill—past a fountain, then past a Confederate soldier statue, and on up to the column-and-dome Old Courthouse. With its exterior recently restored, the Old Courthouse makes a stunning landmark visible as far away as the Blue Ridge Parkway (from Grassy Mine Ridge Overlook, milepost 437). The Old Courthouse is especially beautiful in the spring when framed by dogwoods, but is worth a visit at any time for its views over Main Street toward the Blue Ridge Parkway and the 6,000-foot peaks of the Great Balsam Mountains. Downtown street parking is free and plentiful.

**Dillsboro** During the 19th century, Dillsboro was the main town of the Tuckaseegee Valley, thriving decades before a nearby railroad siding was named "Sylva." However, a series of floods repeatedly inundated Dillsboro's low-lying downtown, driving its businesses uphill to find drier land along the Sylva siding. By 1970, upstream dams had solved the flood problem, but it seemed too late—Dillsboro was little more than a ghost town, with most of its old buildings abandoned. Then things started to change. Craft artists discovered that its roomy old buildings could be rented cheaply and started moving in. The Hartbarger family acquired the town's railroad hotel, the Jarrett House, and returned it to its former glory as a fine old bed & breakfast and country-style restaurant. Then a set of investors

BRANT BARNES, A DILLSBORO CRAFT ARTIST

bought out the recently abandoned freight railroad and turned it into a successful excursion line, the Great Smoky Mountain Railroad. Now Dillsboro is a beautiful old-fashioned village, reminiscent more of Old New England than the New South. Its three-block historic district, made up largely of original buildings tastefully restored, is crammed with more than 40 shops and craft studios.

**Whittier** In the early 20th century Whittier was the roughest town in the district. The favored siding of the large logging companies, Whittier was well known for its brawls along its saloon-lined main street. A hundred years of time and a modern freeway have both taken their toll, and Whittier is now a sleepy collection of a few scattered buildings 7 miles south of Cherokee. Two of the oldest surviving structures now house Stuff & Such, a local crafts cooperative run as a labor of love by a townswoman. Three miles east of town on US 74 you'll find the Smoky Mountain's largest collection of flea markets, open weekends from May through October. Whittier is off US 74 at a marked exit, 12 miles west of Sylva; you'll pass the flea markets on the way there, about 9 miles west of Sylva.

**Balsam** When the railroad finally crossed the 3,550-foot Balsam Gap in the 1880s, it became the highest point in the East to receive regular passenger service, and a resort village grew up around its small depot. By 1908 it had acquired a large wooden hotel, the Balsam Mountain Inn—now beautifully restored to a luxury full-service country inn, with gourmet food. The village is a quarter-mile south of the four-lane US 23/74, signposted down local roads. It remains the highest and coolest place to stay in this area, as well as the closest to this section of the Blue Ridge Parkway.

**Cullowhee** Settled in the 1850s, this rural community is located at the place where the Upper Tuckaseegee Valley narrows from a broad plain to a narrow gorge. Since 1889 it has been home to Western Carolina University—founded as a high school for training teachers, now a state university with 8,000 students and graduate programs in the liberal arts, sciences, business and education. Cullowhee remains unincorporated, and has only a scattering of businesses on the northern edge of the university.

WHITTIER COUNTRYSIDE

## ✷ Wild Places

**THE GREAT FORESTS** **Plott Balsams** Plott Balsams is a high side ridge running at right-angles to the main crest of the Great Balsam Mountains from Sylva to Waynesville. Stretching for 23 miles, it has four peaks over 6,000 feet tall in a central section that maintains continuous mile-high elevations for 7.5 miles. The eastern two peaks, Plott Balsam (6,088 feet, 31st in East) and Mount Lyn Lowry (6,240 feet, 19th in East), are on private lands; Mount Lyn Lowry is topped by a giant electrified cross, the site of an annual Easter Morning prayer service. The western half of the range, with 6'ers Waterrock Knob (6,292 feet, 16th in East) and Yellow Face (6,032 feet, 39th in East) is largely public, split between the Blue Ridge Parkway, the Nantahala National Forest, and the town of Sylva watershed—now open to the public as Pinnacle Park. Much logged in the early 20th century to support Sylva's paper mill, Plott Balsams is covered in a variety of mature second-growth hardwood. The high crest is mainly covered in the subarctic spruce-fir "balsam" forest, with isolated meadows and rocky outcrops offering impressive views. Waterrock Knob has a popular (and very steep) 1-mile trail to its summit, while Yellow Face can be easily reached in a pleasant 2.6-mile forest walk.

**National Forest Lands near Sylva** In addition to Plott Balsams, this area has two substantial National Forest tracts, both very beautiful and worthwhile, and neither with any meaningful recreation development. To the south of Sylva the large Roy Taylor Forest, named after a former congressman for this area, lies on the west slope of the Balsam Mountains below the Blue Ridge Parkway; it's mainly a logging area for the Nantahala National Forest. Across the Tuckaseegee River, the Savannah Mountain/Cullowhee Mountain tracts occupy the broken peaks to the south and west of Cullowhee—a large and beautiful tract of mature second-growth hardwood forest which the National Forest Service has not developed for public use in any way. In both cases, recreational use is possible (including camping, fishing, hiking, and hunting), but limited by a lack of trails, out-of-date maps, and possible logging operations.

**RIVERS** **The Tuckasegee River** People who know "the Tuck" can instantly recognize its appearance in the movie The Fugitive, where we see an obviously freezing Harrison Ford pulling himself out of the roiling brown water. Rising along the north slopes of the Blue Ridge around Glenville and Lake Toxaway, the Tuckaseegee (also spelled Tuckaseigee) flows for 40 miles northward through this chapter's area. In its headwaters, its East Fork and West Fork still offer some stunning gorge and waterfall scenery, but are mostly either flooded or dewatered by hydropower projects (including Glenville Lake). Then comes a 20-mile stretch of wide, clear, mainly calm water with stunning scenery, paralleled by NC 107 and several smaller lanes. As it passes Dillsboro, the Tuckaseegee picks up its characteristically brown color, along with several rafting outfitters. This final 10-mile section has numerous Class II and III rapids, a perfect venue for a family rafting trip. Minimum body weight for rafting on the Tuckaseegee is 40 pounds (compared to 60 pounds on the Nantahala), so all but the smallest children are allowed.

**PICNIC AREAS** **East Laporte River Access Area** Daily, 8 AM–dusk. This shady riverside picnic area, run by Jackson County Parks & Recreation, sits on the Tuckaseegee River 4 miles south of Cullowhee on NC 107. It offers several simple

THE TUCKASEEGEE RIVER NEAR CULLOWHEE

recreational facilities, the best of which is a little pebble beach where kids can splash in this calm mountain river.

**Mark Watson Park** Daylight and early evening hours This Jackson County park sits on the west side of Sylva, on Bus. US 23, just behind the Old Courthouse. Although mainly a neighborhood recreation park, it has a number of tables under a pavilion, well away from highway noise. Its main points of interest are a number of WPA-style stone structures, including a long set of steps going up to Sylva's beautiful Old Courthouse with its sweeping views.

**Dillsboro River Access Area** Daylight hours. This pretty little city of Dillsboro park sits on the Tuckaseegee River across the street from the Riverwood Crafters on River Road, a short distance east of US 441; its entrance might be hard to spot. It has a handful of tables and barbecue pits on a very scenic riverside location.

## ✷ To See

**BIG DAMMED LAKES The Four Lakes of the Tuckasegee River** These four lakes, none particularly big by Smoky Mountain standards, provide flood control as well as hydropower on the East Fork of the Tuckaseegee River. On the one hand it's a pity that this stunningly beautiful gorge should be almost completely drowned; on the other, no one misses the devastating floods that repeatedly wrecked riverside communities, including Dillsboro. All are owned by Duke Energy, the successor to their original builder, Nantahala Power and Light. All are easily reached from NC 281, 6.7 miles south of Cullowhee via NC 107. As you travel away from Cullowhee you will see them in this order: Cedar Cliff Lake, Bear Creek Lake (the largest), Wolf Creek Lake, and tiny Tanassee Creek Lake. Wolf Creek Lake is upstream on a side creek; the other three flood the Tuckaseegee such that only a dewatered 1.5-mile section remains. That section, however, is worth a visit, as a Forest Service path leads to it, then up it along a cliff-sided boulder-strewn gorge known for its most prominent landmark, **Bona's Defeat**, named for an over-enthusiastic hunting dog who chased a deer right over the 250-foot drop.

**HISTORIC SITES** **Judaculla Rock** A state historic site in scenic Caney Fork Valley south of Cullowhee, Judaculla Rock is a large boulder completely covered by pictograms, sitting in on the edge of a lovely mountain meadow. The Cherokees credited the rock to their god of the hunt, Judaculla, a terrifying giant who lived in Judaculla Old Fields on the high Balsams Crest. Examine the rock closely, and you can see the imprint of Judaculla's seven-fingered hand. Scholars cannot agree on the age or meaning of these carvings, or even if they were carved by the Cherokee. This mysterious site is located in a beautiful mountain valley with lovely views over its meadow. There is no office, visitors center, or even toilets onsite—just a few parking spaces in a field, and the strange stone. It's signposted off NC 107, 3 miles south of Cullowhee.

SUNRISE AND VALLEY FOG NEAR SYLVA

**CULTURAL SITES** **Mountain Heritage Center** (www.wcu.edu/2389.asp; 828-227-7129; Western Carolina University, 150 H. F. Robinson Bldg., Cullowhee, NC 28723). Open weekdays 8 AM–5 PM, all year; Sundays, 2 PM–5 PM, April–October. Closed on university holidays. Free. Run by Western Carolina University and located in its administrative building, this small museum tells the story of the pioneers who settled the deep coves and high hollows of the Smokies, and their descendants who followed the pioneer way of life. In addition to this permanent display it has changing displays on such diverse topics as blacksmithing, mountain trout, and handcrafting. In addition to running the small museum and maintaining its 10,000-item of mountain artifacts, the Center publishes scholarly and educational material, puts on educational programs, and cosponsors the highly popular Mountain Heritage Day in Cullowhee on the last Saturday in September.

**Western Carolina University** (www.wcu.edu; 828-227-7122; Western Carolina University, Cullowhee, NC 28723). The campus, Hunter Library, and A. K. Hinds University Center are open at all reasonable hours. The Belk Building Art Gallery is open 8 AM–noon, 1 PM–5 PM, weekdays. The most beautiful of the mountain colleges and universities, "Western" (as it is known) is a collection of red-brick buildings crowded into the narrow head of the Tuckaseegee Valley. Founded as a high school for teachers in the 1880s, materials for its earliest buildings had to be carried in by pack mules. Although it now sits at the end of a modern four-lane highway, NC 107, it still retains its sense of remoteness. One of the 16 campuses of the University of North Carolina, this 8,000-student university offers bachelor and graduate degrees in the liberal arts, sciences, business and education.

Visitors can gain year-round enjoyment from Western's superb native mountain landscaping, particularly lovely in the late spring when the rhododendrons and flame azaleas bloom. Western also sponsors the **Highlands Botanical Station**, the premiere botanical collection in the Smoky Mountains. Western's large Hunter Library houses a first-rate collection of mountain historic material, including the Kephart diaries. Casual visitors should enjoy the scenery and the views, visit the on-campus **Mountain Heritage Museum**, then check out the two permanent art galleries, one in the Belk Building and the other in the A. K. Hinds University Center.

**Heinzelmännchen Brewery** (yourgnometownbrewery.com; e-mail: gnome@yourgnometownbrewery.com; 828-631-4466; 545 Mill St., Sylva, NC 28779). Open Tues.–Sat., 11 AM–5 PM. A Heinzelmännchen (pronounced HIENZ-le-mention) is a Black Forest gnome; master brewer Dieter Kuhn brings Black Forest brews to the mountains in his Mill Street storefront behind downtown Sylva. This microbrew offers tastings and growlers, and their wide variety of unfiltered, cask-conditioned pilsners and ales are available in a number of restaurants in Sylva, Waynesville, and Asheville. They also brew traditional, nonalcoholic root beer and birch beer, the latter a bright orange in color.

## ✷ To Do

**WHITEWATER ADVENTURE** ✐ **Tuckaseegee Outfitters** (www.tuckfloat.com; 888-593-5050, 828-586-5050; 4909 Hwy. 74, Whittier, NC 28789). Open May–October, daylight hours. Tuckaseegee Outfitters offers nonguided rentals of inflatables for downstream floats and paddles on the Tuckaseegee. You'll find Tuckaseegee Outfitters on the river, 5 miles west of Sylva on US 74/441.

✐ **Carolina Mountains Outdoor Center** (www.cmoc-rafting.com; 888-785-2662, 828-586-5285; 5303 Highway US 74, Whittier, NC 28789). Open May–October, daylight hours. Located on the Tuckaseegee River in Dillsboro, Carolina Mountains Outdoor Center offers immediate starts with a shuttle at the end of the 4.5-mile downstream float. All trips are unguided on inflatables.

**FISHING Smoky Mountain on the Fly** (e-mail: smonthefly@aol.com; 828-586-4787; 100 Round Top Trail, Sylva, NC 28779). Open all year. William R. Cope specializes in fly-fishing for trout in mountain streams. A full-time guide, Willie is licensed by the state of North Carolina and permitted for guide service within the Great Smoky Mountains National Park and the Nantahala National Forest. He offers half-day, full-day, or backcountry trips, and will provide equipment if needed.

DAWN OVER WHITTIER

**HORSEBACK RIDING Arrowmont Stables and Cabins** (arrowmont.com; 800-682-1092, 828-743-2762; 276 Arrowmont Trail, Cullowhee, NC 28723). This stable offers fully guided trail rides, ranging from 45 minutes to 2 hours on the trail, on its 200-acre property deep in the mountains south of Cullowhee.

**WILDERNESS EXCURSIONS Slickrock Expeditions** (www.slickrockexpeditions.com/index.htm; e-mail: slickrock@slickrockexpeditions.com; 828-293-3999; P.O. Box 1214, Cullowhee, NC 28723). Burt Kornegay has been a professional guide since 1971, as well as being a free-lance writer and past president of the North Carolina Bartram Trail Society. His Slickrock Expeditions offers several unusual and interesting wilderness excursions in the western mountains of North Carolina.

## ✷ Lodging

### COUNTRY INNS AND HOTELS

♿ **The Balsam Mountain Inn** (balsaminn.com; e-mail: relax@balsaminn.com; 800-224-9498; 68 Seven Springs Dr., Balsam, NC 28707). Open all year. This beautifully restored Victorian railroad hotel is located well off the main road in Balsam Gap, 0.7 mile from the Blue Ridge Parkway's intersection with US 23/74. The 50 rooms all have original beadboard walls and ceilings. The comfortable furniture is rustic in style, covered in bright fabrics, with original prints on the walls, and either two double beds or a king bed; 16 of the rooms are expanded to include a large sitting area, and eight rooms are two-room suites. The breakfast (included in the tariff) is cooked to order and extremely good, while dinners (extra, by reservation) are of truly exceptional quality.

**The Jarrett House** (www.jarretthouse.com; e-mail: info@jarretthouse.com; 800-972-5623, 828-586-0265; fax: 828-586-6251; P.O. Box 219, Dillsboro, NC 28725). Open May–December. This three-story wood hotel in central Dillsboro has been in continuous operation since 1884, when it was built to serve the railroad depot. The hotel's most dramatic feature is its triple-level porches, allowing plenty of cool rocking on every floor. All rooms are en suite, and nearly all rooms have from one to three double beds. Tariffs include a full breakfast served country style in the restaurant.

### BED & BREAKFAST INNS

**The Chalet Inn** (www.chaletinn.com; e-mail: paradisefound@chaletinn.com; 800-789-8024, 828-586-0251; 285 Lone Oak Dr., Whittier, NC 28789). Open all year. This is a large, luxurious chalet, with an ample great room, seven guest rooms ranging in size from comfortable to huge, and a private balcony or porch for every room. The inn's 22-acre grounds are beautifully landscaped around a spring-fed mountain stream, and woven with graded footpaths. Rooms are simply but beautifully decorated, combining European flair with American amenities. Breakfast at the Chalet Inn is served in the style of a German gasthaus, a buffet including an exceptional variety of traditional German fare. Located in the Barkers Creek section of Jackson County down a tangle of paved country lanes, the Chalet Inn is only 2.4 miles from the four-laned US 23/74/441.

**The Freeze House** (www.freezehousebnb.com; e-mail: freezh@dnet.net; 828-586-8161; 71 Sylvan Heights, Sylva, NC 28779). This large, red-brick bungalow sits in a quiet Sylva neighborhood, on a shadedhilltop property large enough to be registered as a Backyard Nature Preserve by the National Wildlife Federation. Its L-shaped porch, wrapping around two sides of the house, furnishes a cool, shaded location for full-sized country breakfasts as well as a good place to rock and enjoy the view. The Freeze House offers three large and comfortable upstairs rooms, flooded with light from banks of gable-end windows. There are also two guest houses adjacent to the property, available for weekly and monthly rental.

**The Dillsboro Inn** (www.dillsboroinn.com; e-mail: info@dillsboroinn.com; 866-586-3898, 828-586-3898; 146 North River Rd., P.O. Box 270, Dillsboro, NC 28725). Open all year. This small bed & breakfast lodge overlooks a dam waterfall on the Tuckaseegee River, a short distance outside Dillsboro. It has 300 feet of landscaped riverfront, including a small fishing pier and a sitting area. Guests can enjoy wide views over the river and the falls from a large deck, or from a wood-burning hot tub. The Dillsboro Inn has two rooms and three suites (without kitchen facilities).

**The Olde Towne Inn** (www.dillsboro-oldetowne.com; e-mail: oldetown@mchsi.com; 888-528-8840, 828-586-3461; 364 Haywood Rd., P.O. Box 485, Dillsboro, NC 28725). Open February–December. This large 1878 wood farmhouse in the center of Dillsboro has a wide, full-length front porch where you can sit in a rocking chair and watch the town's historic center immediately below. While this inn has many steps, both down from the covered parking and up from the street, it gives ready access to the heart of Dillsboro.

**The River Lodge** (riverlodge-bb.com; e-mail: rvrldg94@frontier.com; 877-384-4400, 828-293-5431; 619 Roy Tritt Rd., Cullowhee, NC 28723). Open all year.

### CABIN RENTALS

**Mountain Creek Cottages** (www.mountaincreekcottages.com; e-mail: stay@

cherokeelogcabins.com; 828-508-6484; P.O. Box 2008, Sylva, NC 28779). Open all year. Located 2.5 miles up a paved mountain from the four-lane US 23/74/441, these four cabins share a beautiful streamside grove of giant hemlocks, laced with paths and centered on a log gazebo. These older cabins are bright, clean, roomy, and comfortably furnished with full kitchens and queen or king beds.

**Arrowmont Stables and Cottages** (www.arrowmont.com; 800-682-1092, 828-743-2762; 276 Arrowmont Trail, Cullowhee, NC 28723). This 200-acre stable offers a variety of rides on their own trails in the mountains high above Cullowhee. On the property are two cottages, modest on the outside but nicely furnished and well kept. One of the two has stunning views; the other fronts on the horse trails.

**Fox Den Cottages** (800-721-9847, 828-293-9847; foxdencottages.com; e-mail: info@foxdencottages.com; Cullowhee, NC, 28723). Open all year. Located deep in the mountains, 3.4 miles south of Cullowhee, Fox Den Cottages are completely modern, roomy, well furnished, and immaculately kept. They are set together on their own high slope tract, with enough land to give privacy and a feeling of remoteness. Some cabins have mountain views, and all have large porches and rockers, wood-burning fireplaces, and oak floors.

## ✷ Where to Eat

**EATING OUT** **Soul Infusion Teahouse and Bistro** (soulinfusion.com; 828-586-1717; 628 E. Main St. [NC 107], Sylva, NC 28779). Open Tues.–Sat., lunch and dinner. This lively local pub occupies a 1930s farmhouse on Sylva's Main Street. It features such fare as sandwiches and pizzas, but also has an ever-changing menu of specials. It has a good selection of microbrews on tap and in the bottle, wine, and of course 60 varieties of tea. There's live music most nights.

**The Jarrett House** (www.jarretthouse.com; 800-972-5623, 828-586-0265; P.O. Box 219, Dillsboro, NC 28725). Open May–December. Lunch: daily, 11:30 AM–2 PM; dinner: Fri.–Sat., 4 PM–8 PM. This historic inn in central Dillsboro, in continuous use for 120 years, serves good, plain food and plenty of it. Lunch is served as a plate, while dinner is served family-style, out of big bowls. Desserts consist of vinegar pie, cobblers, and French silk pie. No beer or wine service.

**Dillsboro Smokehouse** (dillsborobarbeque.com; e-mail: eat@dillsborobarbeque.com; 828-586-9556; 403 Haywood Rd./P.O. Box 269, Dillsboro, NC 28725). Open Mon.–Sat., 11 AM–8 PM; Sun., 11 AM–3 PM. This friendly spot in central Dillsboro is definitely where the locals go. It features hearty, fresh food, including old-fashioned mountain barbeque.

**The Well House** (828-586-8588; Hwy. 441, Dillsboro, NC 28725). Open Sat.–Wed., 11 AM–5 PM; Thurs.–Fri., 11 AM–8 PM. This Dillsboro café, in the basement of the Riverwood Crafters across the river from the main town, specializes in deli sandwiches, fresh salads, homemade soups, and made-from-scratch desserts. Inside it's roomy, if a bit dark, with many booths and an actual 19th-century well in one corner (still used for irrigation water). They'll pack you a picnic box if you ask them.

**DINING OUT** **The Balsam Mountain Inn** (www.balsaminn.com; e-mail: relax@balsammountaininn.com; 800-224-9498, 828-456-9498; P.O. Box 40, Balsam, NC 28707). Open 6 PM–10 PM, by reservation. This 1908 railroad hotel, a half-mile off US 74/23 near its intersection with the Blue Ridge Parkway, offers fine dining in a remote, rural setting. The hotel itself is worth a visit just to admire its authentically restored late Victorian architecture, and its 100-foot-long porches on two floors. The hotel's old dining hall has now become an exquisite restaurant without losing any of its early, earthy flavor, a place where classical columns contrast with beadboard paneling. The menu typically combines several traditional items, such as fresh-baked mountain trout or filet mignon, with two or three surprises. A sophisticated wine list completes the experience.

**Lulu's Cafe** (luluscafe.com; 828-586-8989; 612 Main St., Sylva, NC 28779). Open Mon.–Sat., 11:30 AM–9 PM. This handsome restaurant, occupying three red-brick storefronts in downtown Sylva, has gained a wide reputation for its sophistication and intelligence. The lunch menu offers original salads and sandwiches, with specials such as black bean and sweet potato enchiladas and seafood gumbo. At dinner the sandwiches disappear, replaced by a selection of entrées and specials, typically nontraditional and frequently adventurous. Lulu's wine list is as sophisticated as the rest of the menu; the beer list includes a choice of several microbrews and imported ales.

## ✷ Selective Shopping

### *Sylva and Dillsboro*

Dillsboro. These adjacent towns are a study in contrast. Sylva has an old-style downtown that has changed remarkably little from the 1940s. Dillsboro, on the other hand, is a lively crafters town, whose 40-odd stores include quite a variety of studios and galleries.

**Dogwood Crafters** (828-586-2248; P.O. Box 604, 90 Webster St., Dillsboro, NC 28725). Open all week, 9:30 AM–5:30 PM. This modest log building at the western edge of Front Street hides a half-dozen rooms jammed floor to ceiling with every kind of country craft and fine art imaginable. As the outlet store for Jackson County's Dogwood Crafters Cooperative, this volunteer-staffed shop offers the work—hand-made and deeply original—of the cooperative's 100 local members. You'll find quilts, wall hangings, stained glass, watercolors, fancy birdfeeders, Christmas decorations, pottery, baskets, calligraphy, lace, knickknacks, bric-a-brac, and souvenirs of all sorts.

**Riverwood Pottery** (riverwoodpottery.com; e-mail: riverwoodpottery@frontier.com; 828-586-3601; P.O. Box 801, Dillsboro, NC 28725). Open normal retail hours, Mon.–Sun., all year; individual shops may vary. Located across the river from the main part of town, this fine old Victorian structure now houses pottery and jewelry makers. All of the crafters welcome visitors into their studios, adjacent of each of their shops.

### *Dillsboro*

**The Dillsboro Chocolate Factory** (dillsborochocolate.com; 877-687-9731, 828-631-0156; fax: 828-631-0156; 28 Church St./P.O. Box 1126, Dillsboro, NC 28725). Open 10 AM–5 PM, Mon.–Sat. The aroma of melting chocolate mixes heavily with that of hot espresso as you walk in the door of this tiny candy and coffee factory. Owners Randy and Susan Lyons make their own fine chocolate candies and scratch fudges, while stocking several varieties of gourmet chocolates. There's only one table inside, but outside are café tables under some fine old birches—and coffee and chocolate can be a perfect pick-me-up in the middle of an afternoon.

*Whittier*

**Stuff & Such** (828-497-2393; 29 Main St., Whittier, NC 28789). Open Fri.–Sat., 10 AM–5 PM and 7 PM–8:30 PM; Sun., noon–3 PM; closed Mon.–Thurs. (but check, as Gloria opens when she is working in her museum). This artists' co-op features a large selection of homey, locally made crafts in one of the few old wooden storefronts surviving in Whittier. It's worth a visit for its giant scale model of Whittier at the turn of the century.

## ✷ Special Events

SPRING **Dillsboro Easter Hat Parade** Easter Sunday, Dillsboro. Months before tourist season begins, Dillsboro residents celebrate the coming of the first flowers of spring by dressing up in creative hats and parading through the center of town, escorted by antique cars. Totally uncommercialized and completely local, this is great fun.

DILLSBORO'S EASTER HAT PARADE

**Greening Up the Mountains Festival** Late April, Sylva. A combination of three smaller festivals, this downtown street party combines Appalachian heritage with environmental themes.

SUMMER **Dillsboro Heritage Festival** Mid-June. Dillsboro kicks off the tourist season with this large and popular street fair, featuring crafters who demonstrate their talents at their booths, along with performances by regional musicians.

**Sylva Independence Day Celebration** July Fourth. Sylva celebrates Independence Day with bluegrass street dances and fireworks over its beautiful hilltop courthouse.

AUTUMN **Mountain Heritage Day** Last Saturday in September, Cullowhee. The largest and most distinguished heritage festival in the North Carolina Smokies, Western Carolina University's Mountain Heritage Day features live performances, craft demonstrations, and a midway with over 200 mountain crafters and artists. Now in its third decade, this annual event draws tens of thousands of people to Western's beautiful rural campus.

WINTER **Dillsboro Lights and Luminaire** First two weekends in December. Dillsboro merchants close out the season with a nighttime program of Christmas lights, candle-lined streets, regional music, home-made treats and hot beverages served in the shops. A special train, sponsored by the Smoky Mountains Railroad, brings families in from Sylva.

# THE BLUE RIDGE: CASHIERS & HIGHLANDS

In this area the Blue Ridge has one of its more creative moments. Just to the east, it has just come off its long run as the Blue Wall (see "The Blue Ridge: Chimney Rock and Saluda," Wild Places), a solid granitic mass rising straight up from the plains of South Carolina. Now it retreats suddenly to the north, its crest lined up with the North Carolina towns of Lake Toxaway, Cashiers, and Highlands. Extending south of this crestline, well into South Carolina and Georgia, it twists into a mass of hard rock ridges, many separated by deep gorges in which rivers rage over high waterfalls—most notably, the Chattooga National Wild and Scenic River, of Deliverance infamy. Here the scenery mixes charming valleys with great gray cliffs; lovely little streams drain these valleys, only to fall off their edges in a fierce plunge over a waterfall. Much of this scenery is highly accessible from US 64, which runs east-west near the crest of the Blue Ridge, or from NC/SC 107 and NC/GA 28, which run north-south.

**GUIDANCE—TOWNS AND COUNTRYSIDE** **Cashiers Chamber of Commerce** (www.cashiers-nc.com; e-mail: sue@cashiers.org; 828-743-5941; fax: 828-743-9446; P.O. Box 238, Cashiers, NC 28717). The chamber has its offices in a log building in the center of town, on US 64 just west of NC 107.

**Highlands Area Chamber of Commerce** (www.highlandschamber.org; e-mail: visitor@highlandschamber.org; 282-526-2112; fax: 828-526-5803; P.O. Box 404, Highlands, NC 28741). This chamber maintains a visitors center in the middle of downtown, just off Main Street on US 64.

**GUIDANCE—PARKS AND FORESTS** **Nantahala National Forest, Highlands Visitors Center** (Highlands, NC 28741). Open June–October, Mon.–Sat.; April–May and November, Sat. only. Highlands' ranger station closed in 2007, a victim of budget cuts. The Forest Service funds a small downtown visitors center, staffed by volunteers and managed by the not-for-profit Cradle of Forestry Interpretive Association. If you need a permit, or a talk with a ranger, you will need to go to the Franklin station.

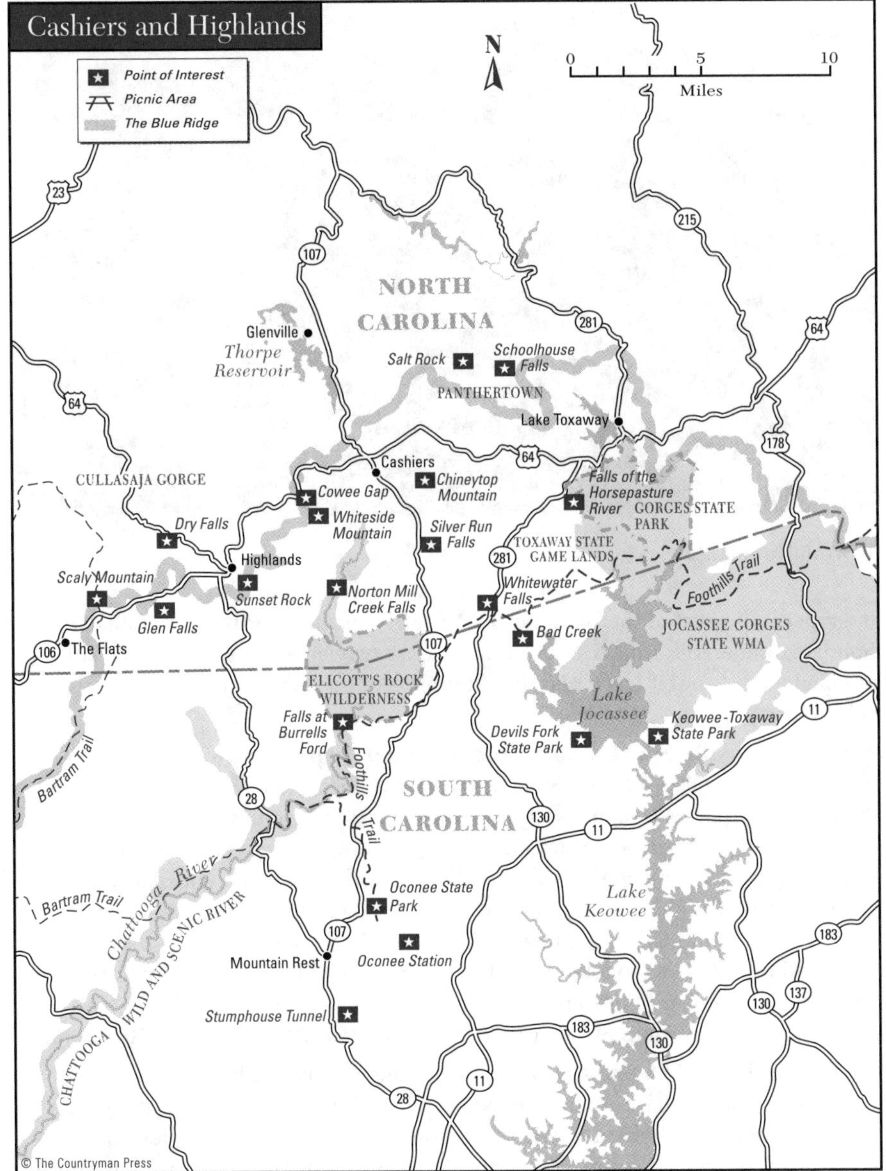


**Sumter National Forest, Andrew Pickens Ranger District** (864-638-9568; fax: 864-638-2659; 112 Andrew Pickens Circle, Mountain Rest, SC 29664). In South Carolina, most of the public forests are within Sumter National Forest. Their ranger station is located at the southern end of this chapter's area, on SC 28 just north of its intersection with SC 107.

**GETTING THERE By Car** This isolated area straddles the Blue Ridge Crest between the towns of Franklin and Brevard. No modern, high quality road enters this area. Even its one U.S. highway, US 64, was engineered in 1923 and never

TOWN OF HIGHLANDS

upgraded. The best of the bunch is SC/NC 107, heading north from Walhalla, South Carolina, to Cashiers,North Carolina; it's two lanes are full sized, its curves are engineered, and it has a real shoulder most of the way. All the other roads are substandard.

*By Air* **Greenville-Spartanburg International Airport** (www.gspairport.com; 864-877-7426; 2000 GSP Dr., Suite 1, Greer, SC 29651).te. The closest and most convenient airport is Greenville-Spartanburg, located 78 miles away in Greer, South Carolina. Greenville-Spartanburg is served by seven passenger airlines with direct flights to 16 cities. Asheville is only a bit farther, but the roads are worse. Atlanta's airport is about four hours away. Here's the directions from Greenville-Spartanburg, South Carolina:: take I-85 west for 12.5 miles to US 25; then north on US 25 for 3.5 miles to a left onto US 125; then go 34.5 miles to a right onto SC 28. Highlands is 36.8 miles on SC/GA/NC 28; for Cashiers, follow SC 28 for 15.2 miles to a right fork onto SC 107, then 23.2 more miles on SC/NC 107 to Cashiers.

**By Bus or Train** (828-526-4113). Highlands and Cashiers, like the rest of the western mountains, have no bus or train service. However, Highlands does have a shuttle service, the Highlands Transportation Company, which will pick you up from any of the regional airports (Asheville, Atlanta, Greenville), as well as take you to a restaurant once you're in Highlands.

**MEDICAL EMERGENCIES** **Highlands-Cashiers Hospital** (www.hchospital.org; e-mail: info@hchospital.org; 828-526-1200; 190 Hospital Dr., Highlands, NC 28741). This 104-bed independent not-for-profit hospital has full emergency services at its campus 4 miles east of Highlands on US 64.

## ✷ Exploring the Area

**EXPLORING BY CAR** **The Cullasaja Gorge** West of Highlands, US 64 follows the bottom of a rough little gorge carved into the backside of the Blue Ridge by the Cullasaja River—the 8-mile-long Cullasaja (Cul-la-SAY-jah) Gorge. The current roadway is utterly unchanged since being built in the 1920s; it's modernization ceased in the 1930s, when the CCC developed its scenic features for tourism. That is how it stands today, a highway built for farm wagons and Model Ts, running through a rugged mountain gorge, and lined with national forest sites with lovely CCC architecture. Leaving Highlands, it passes by Lake Sequoyah, one of the long lakes that meander through the town's neighborhoods; look for the dam on your left. A half-mile farther, lacy Bridal Veil Falls drops 30 feet from an overhanging cliff. Modern US 64 passes in front of the falls (a concession to safety made in 1954), while the original highway's roadbed still goes underneath the falls, maintained and drivable—very possibly the only such highway in existence. In 0.75 mile on the left, the Cullasaja River plunges 50 feet over a large overhang to form Dry Falls, so named because the footpath passes underneath the overhang, allowing walkers to pass dry (mostly) behind it. A mile farther, Cliffside Lake Recreation Area, with lakeside and clifftop walks, and a CCC picnic area, turns off right. Shortly after that the gorge road becomes rough and woolly, with plenty of twists and turns. Four miles from Cliffside the road becomes a narrow ledge carved into a perpendicular granite cliff, with barely enough room for two cars to pass each other. Views over the gorge are spectacular. However there is only one place to park, on the left, with room for only about four cars. Don't miss it—it's your only chance to view 200-foot Cullasaja Falls, a stunning double cataract. The gorge drive ends suddenly, dropping out onto flat farmlands in a suddenly widened valley.

**EXPLORING ON FOOT** **Walking the Blue Ridge** The Blue Ridge in this area is best explored on foot. Panthertown Valley is certainly one of the best walking and biking areas, although you will need to buy a map (available from the Forest Service Visitors Center in downtown Highlands) if you intend to stray off the gravel roads. High Hampton's Chimneytop and Rocky Mountains are probably the most exciting hikes in the area. Of course, the view off the highest cliff in the East, at Whiteside Mountain, is pretty hard to beat. The rivers that drain the Blue Ridge are pretty impressive, too. The Horsepasture River has a whole series of waterfalls in a deep gorge—remarkable, but just a taste of the 60,000-acre Jocassee Gorges now under development. And for a quiet riverside walk, the Upper Chattooga River from Bull Pen Bridge is exceptional.

**LONG-DISTANCE PATHS** **The Bartram Trail** This southernmost section of the Bartram Trail spends about 50 miles in this chapter's area, crossing from Georgia into North Carolina and climbing from 1,500 feet along the banks of the Chattooga River to the rocky cliffs of 4,800-foot Scaly Mountain. You'll find the Bartram Trail's southern terminus on the near side of the GA 28 bridge over the Chattooga River as you approach it from Highlands, North Carolina, a drive of 13.5 miles. The trail's first 8 miles parallel the **Chattooga** Wild and Scenic River, sometimes close to the bank and with good views, but other times some distance away. As it turns away from the river the trail begins a long and slow climb through the North Georgia mountains, following the 2,000-foot side ridges for 12 miles until finally reaching the Blue Ridge and the 3,000-foot contours at the same time. Seven miles later comes Rabun Bald, with grand views from its 4,700-foot peak, then another 7 miles of forest walking that slabs along one side of the Blue Ridge, crosses the state line into North Carolina, and finally reaches NC 106, 6 miles west of Highlands, North Carolina. At this point the trail leaves the Blue Ridge to climb 4,800-foot Scaly Mountain, with fine views from a large rocky bald, then continues north along this 4,000-foot ridgeline, bagging more clifftop views at 4,600-foot Jones Knob and 4,700-foot Whiterock Mountain. At the end of this section, the trail drops down to the valley of the Little Tennessee River to continue northward along roads to Franklin.

The Bartram Trail may end at the GA 28 bridge, but the long-distance hiking goes on. A 3.6-mile section of the Chattooga River Trail links it with the **Foothills Trail**, which in turn connects with the trails of South Carolina's **Mountain Bridge Wilderness** (see "The Blue Ridge: Hendersonville & Brevard," *Wild Places*). Together they stretch for 164 miles, from **Jones Gap State Park** in South Carolina to **Cheoah Bald** in North Carolina—and from there to Maine, via the Appalachian Trail.

**The Foothills Trail** (www.foothillstrail.org). The 76-mile-long Foothills Trail crosses the deeply incised side ridges of the Blue Ridge, roughly following the North Carolina—South Carolina border. For years it was almost completely within the gigantic Duke Power tract that surrounded Lake Jocassee, and built with their help and support by the independent Foothills Trail Conference; now, with Duke's donation of this land to the public, the trail is within South Carolina's Sumter National Forest and Jocassee Gorges Wildlife Management Area, and North Carolina's Nantahala National Forest, Toxaway Game Lands, and Gorges State Park. The trail stretches for 50 miles within this chapter's area, before climbing into the Mountain Bridge Wilderness.

The trail starts in South Carolina's **Oconee State Park**, where it links with the **Palmetto Trail** for hiking (eventually) to the Atlantic Ocean. From there it saunters northward for 7 miles along a ridge with some nice views, to the **Chattooga Wild and Scenic River**. Here it links up with the **Bartram Trail**, and from that, the **Appalachian Trail** for some truly long-distance hiking possibilities. It follows the Chattooga upstream (north) for another 7 miles; this entire 14-mile stretch varies between 1,600 and 2,300 feet. In the next 9 miles the trail starts its characteristic up-and-down as it explores a little-visited area of the Sumter (South Carolina) and Nantahala (North Carolina) National Forests, reaching its high point for this chapter (although not for its length) of 3,200 feet.

Now the trail reaches **Whitewater Falls**, reputedly the tallest in the East, plunges into its gorge, and follows the Whitewater River downstream to the **Bad Creek Project** and the spectacular **Lower Whitewater Falls**. This and the next section are noted for their superb construction and excellent trail structures, courtesy of Duke Power. From here the trail parallels the north shore of **Jocassee Lake**, going up and down a series of ridges. During this 20-mile stretch it reaches the lakeshore (at 1,200 feet) three times, and crosses the same number of 1,700-foot ridges, passing through two states and four agencies (including remarkable **Gorges State Park**). This section gives access to rough bushwacks up gorges where rare plants thrive and waterfalls have yet to be named.

This ends finally as the trail enters its last 7 miles with a long, leisurely climb up Laurel Fork Creek, with a truly fine waterfall along the way, to South Carolina's 1,000-acre **Laurel Fork Creek Heritage Area**, which preserves a half-dozen rare species in its cove and uplands forests. The trail reaches US 178 in 3 miles from the heritage area; the trailhead is 7 miles east of Lake Toxaway on US 64 to a right onto US 178, then 9 more miles.

**The Palmetto Trail** (palmettoconservation.org; e-mail: info@palmettoconservation.org). This 425-mile trail will, when completed, link the coast of South Carolina with the mountains, and ultimately the Appalachian Trail (via the Foothills and Bartram Trails). It is a project of the State of South Carolina, managed by the Palmetto Conservancy, an independent conservation organization. It's about 50 percent completed, with its first 100 coastal miles in place. Unfortunately, only four sections (called "passages") have been completed within the mountains, and there are three big gaps in the Piedmont as well. Within this chapter's area, 3.2 miles have been completed, from Oconee State Park down the mountain to Oconee Station Historic Site, with a nice waterfall along the way.

## ✷ Villages

**Highlands** The town of Highlands sits in a large bowl at the crest of the Blue Ridge, at an elevation above 4,000 feet. It was founded as a resort town in the 1870s, and numerous buildings date from the 19th century. It remains a high-end resort town, with a large summer population of Atlanta and Florida socialites. Strict zoning has left it looking more like a New England village than a southern town, nearly devoid of chain stores. It is a desert for those reliant on McDonalds and their ilk, and heaven for travelers who appreciate local, independent shops and cafés. It has a four-block downtown lining its Main Street with a wide variety of shops in an eclectic mix of buildings from every era. Parking is free and plentiful. Still true to its 19th-century origins, Highlands has quite a variety of small independent hotels, and almost no motels.

WHITEWATER FALLS

**Cashiers** Pronounced "CASH-ers," this town was until recently little more than a crossroads post office and general store at the intersection of US 64 and NC 107. Since 1845, when South Carolina's Hampton family established their High Hampton hunting lodge there, Cashiers has drawn wealthy South Carolina socialites. In recent decades its popularity with the wealthy has increased. The low hills around High Hampton have become crossed with narrow roads and crusted with hidden mansions, and a downtown area has slowly grown up around the old crossroads. You will now find Cashiers a full-service town, although you might have to ask where to find something. There's an Ingles Supermarket a mile east of town on US 64, the only chain supermarket in this chapter's area.

**Lake Toxaway** Founded in 1903 as a resort for the ultra-wealthy, the town's fortunes collapsed when its dam broke in 1916. With the dam rebuilt in 1961 the settlement has come back to life, but remains mostly a crossroads community at the intersection of US 64 and NC 281, east of Cashiers.

## ✷ Wild Places

**THE GREAT FORESTS** **Panthertown Valley** Panthertown Valley (locals say "Painter-town") is a classic Blue Ridge perched valley, a wide, flat-bottomed bowl sitting just below the crest, between Cashiers and Lake Toxaway. Part of the Nantahala National Forest since 1989, it is noted for its high cliffs, waterfalls, sandy-beached swimming holes, and incredible biological diversity. The valley has two access points, one on each side. The western gate is reached from Cashiers, an interesting and beautiful drive that crosses the Blue Ridge Crest twice: take US 64

**THE BLUE RIDGE IN ITS GLORY**

Three of the Blue Ridge's most characteristic and beautiful features reach their finest expression along the 56 miles it spends within this chapter's area. While you can find these features almost anywhere along the Blue Ridge, from Maryland to Georgia, it is in the Cashiers-Highlands area that they are at their largest, most dramatic, most frequent, and easiest to reach.

WHITESIDE MOUNTAIN

*Perched valleys* form along the Blue Ridge Crest where an unusually hard rock layer resists erosion, forcing rainwater to carve a bowl before it finally finds a place to run off its edge. They typically range from a dozen to a hundred acres—but here you'll find four of them that are a square mile or more in size, lined up along US 64. The first of these bowls (east to west) is **Panthertown Valley**, a wild area owned by the Nantahala National Forest, located behind the Blue Ridge to the north of the highway. Next comes **Cashiers** itself, occupying a lozenge-shaped bowl directly under the Blue Ridge. The next bowl is the biggest, a 3-square-mile double bowl containing the town of **Highlands**. The

west 1.8 miles to a left on Cedar Creek Road (SSR 1120), then climb 2.1 miles to a right on Breedlove Road (SSR 1121), which you follow to its end in 3.5 miles. The eastern gate is reached from Lake Toxaway: take NC 281 north from US 64 0.8 mile to Cold Mountain Road (SSR 1301), which you follow to its end in 5.5 miles. The valley stretches between these two gates, closed to motor vehicles but easily traversed by foot or mountain bike.

Panthertown has been gaining a reputation among local outdoors enthusiasts for its amazing scenery and wide choice of recreational opportunities. **Salt Rock** offers great views from an exposed clifftop a short stroll from the western parking lot. From the eastern parking lot, a gravel road heads a mile downhill to **Schoolhouse Falls**, a popular swimming hole with its 20-foot cascade and sandy beach. From the same lot, a stepped footpath travels nearly 2 miles to the top of the granite dome named **Little Green Mountain**, with fine views over the entire valley. Experienced off-trail hikers will want to explore the **Devil's Elbow**, a rock-hop down the Tuckaseegee River headwaters whose little-explored scenery includes an unnamed 25-foot waterfall. Panthertown's granite cliffs are becoming popular with **rock climbers**, with Black Rock Mountain, Big Green Mountain, and Laurel Knob being among the favorites.

last of the great perched valleys, 7 miles west of Highlands straddling NC 106, is known simply as The Flats, a long, remarkably level valley largely given over to farming.

*Granite cliffs* on the Blue Ridge have a characteristically rounded shape, and are known as **rocky balds**. Their odd shape, nearly flat at the top curving with deceptive gentleness into vertical drops, results from the Blue Ridge's unique geology (foliation features of granitic schists and gneisses, if you must ask). They form walls around all of our perched valleys, as well as on slopes below them. Panthertown Valley is ringed by them, including the readily accessible **Salt Rock**. Cashier's bowl ends at the remarkable dual cliffs of **Rocky Mountain and Chimneytops**, which so dramatically frame the High Hampton golf course. On the far eastern edge of the large Highlands bowl sits the tallest cliff in the East, **Whiteside Mountain**. Several more cliffs follow before reaching **Sunrise and Sunset Rocks**, which flank the east and west sides of the Blue Ridge. Lastly, **Scaly Mountain** sits on the northern edge of The Flats.

*Waterfalls* form as rivers encounter the edges of hard rock layers—including, but by no means limited to, these perched valleys and granite cliffs. The Tuckasegee River carves several waterfalls as it drops out of Panthertown Valley, of which **Schoolhouse Falls** is only the first. Cashier's waterfalls are not publicly accessible, but lesser-perched valleys nearby give us the **Falls of the Horsepasture River** and **Silver Run Falls**. The **Cullasaja Gorge,** with its series of falls, carries water out of the Highlands bowls, and **Glen Falls** drops off its flanks.

**Jocassee Gorges** In this area the Blue Ridge shifts north, leaving a maze of hard rock side ridges and outliers extending south into South Carolina. While this terrain stretches throughout this chapter's area, the eastern half (between Lake Toxaway and Cashiers) is the rougher—a land of narrow, cliff-sided gorges and tall waterfalls. Duke Power acquired most of this area for its hydroelectric potential during the 1960s, building Lake Jocassee in the 1970s and the Bad Creek Project in the 1980s. In the 1990s Duke negotiated with a group of governments and conservation organizations to convert most of its undeveloped land into public conservation areas, with the remaining Duke properties having conservation easements and public access via wildlife management programs. By 2001 the conversion was complete, and the 60,000-acre Jocassee Gorges Tract had been created.

The tract possesses immense value for its biological diversity, rugged scenery, and many waterfalls. However, it is now split between six different entities (North Carolina State Parks, South Carolina State Parks, North Carolina Wildlife Resources, Nantahala National Forest, Sumter National Forest, and Duke Power), and cooperation is less than perfect. For instance, the North Carolina Division of Parks and Recreation announced plans to manage 7,000 acres as a biodiversity preserve—only to have the South Carolina Department of Natural Resources declare that they would exercise what they claim is their legal right to build a public road through the middle of it. Meanwhile, existing recreational facilities at Horsepasture River and Whitewater Falls give some taste of the wonders to come.

By the time you read this more facilities may be available, particularly in North Carolina's **Gorges State Park**. At press time, this 7,100-acre park consists only of two trailheads with picnic areas, plus a whole lot of backcountry. The backcountry, a series of gorges formed by the Toxaway River and its tributaries, is reached from Auger Hole Trail, a former wagon road that cuts diagonally across the gorges, and the **Foothills Trail**; a third path, Canebrake Trail, allows backpackers to loop back to their cars. No paths explore the park's half-dozen gorges themselves. An ambitious new park center is currently under development, reached from NC 281, about a mile south of its intersection with US 64 between Cashiers and Lake Toxaway. It will feature a 2.3-mile scenic loop road with pull-outs and overlooks, a family campground nestled in a tiny perched valley, and a 7,500-foot visitor's center.

**Ellicott Rock Wilderness** This wilderness, created by Congress in 1975, contains nearly 13 square miles of tough mountain terrain flanking a 3.2-mile stretch of the upper Chattooga River Gorge. It is named for the Chattooga river boulder, carved in 1811 by surveyor Andrew Ellicott, that marked the common boundary between North Carolina, South Carolina, and Georgia and sits in the center of the wilderness.

The wilderness boundary follows the gorge's ridgelines fairly closely, so that its slopes drop very steeply toward the river at the center, and elevations decline steadily from north to south. The entire area had been logged during the early 20th century, but has since grown back into a fine second-growth stand, with the handsomest forests closest to the river. Access is from roads that cross the Chattooga at the wilderness's northern and southern boundary. The northern (North Carolina) boundary follows Bull Pen Road (SSR 1100); from Cashiers go south on NC 108 for 6.8 miles, then right for 1.2 miles to the start of the wilderness boundary on your left. Trailheads are farther on, at 2.6 miles and 6.4 miles, and both of these trails drop steadily, and sometimes steeply, down the gorge side for some distance. The southern access is from Burrells Ford Road in South Carolina, 13 miles south of Cashiers via NC/SC 107, then right for 2.5 miles to **Burrells Ford Bridge**, with three fine **waterfalls** nearby. From here, the Chatooga River Trail follows the river's left bank upstream for 3.8 miles, reaching Ellicotts Rock just before it ends at its intersection with the two North Carolina trails. This is by far the easier walk, very scenic and heavily used, particularly by fishermen.

There are actually two "Ellicott Rocks," the result of conflicting surveys, and both can be easily viewed from the Chattooga River Trail, on the left, 0.1 mile from its end. You will first come up on what is properly known as "Commissioners Rock," carved in 1813 with the inscription "Lat 35 AD 1813 NC + SC." Ellicott Rock is 500 feet upstream and much harder to find; it's carved simply with "NC-GA." After a great deal of dispute the states agreed on Commissioners Rock as the official three state corner, a victory for North Carolina which gained 500 feet of territory from its two neighbors.

**Scaly Mountain and Lickskillit** This side ridge extends north from the Blue Ridge for 7.5 miles, staying above 4,000 feet the entire way. It has handsome forests and more than its share of cliffs and rocky balds, and access is easy via the Bartram Trail, which traverses the entire ridge. Wholly within national forest-lands, this impressive and little-visited tract starts at Scaly Mountain, about 5 miles west of Highlands via NC 106. There's a good trailhead at Lickskillit; from US 64 in Highlands take NC 106 west for 4 miles to a right onto Turtle Pond Road (SSR 1620), then 0.2 mile to a left fork onto Lickskillit Road (SSR 1621), then 0.9 mile to a gated Forest Service road on your left—a side trail leading to the Bartram Trail in 1 miles.

FARMLAND AT NORTON

**RIVERS The Chattooga Wild and Scenic River** The Chattooga River rises from waters that flow off the cliffs of Whiteside Mountain, then southward through deep, boulder-strewn gorges. It became notorious as the model for the 1970 book and 1972 movie, Deliverance. However, when Congress declared it a Wild and Scenic River in 1974, they were more concerned with the four separate proposals to destroy this 57 miles of free-flowing wilderness river for hydropower. Today, the U.S. Forest

Service holds 15,432 acres along its banks, very nearly its entire length. All but about 3 miles of this is paralleled by a footpath, the Chattooga River Trail.

The U.S. Forest Service divides the river into five sections, The uppermost two sections, upstream from US 28, have been closed to boaters since 1976, much to the consternation of whitewater enthusiasts, who have launched a lawsuit. For bankside travelers this is the most scenic section, moving through a deep mountain gorge with numerous waterfalls, including the glorious swimming hole at **Norton Mill Creek Falls** and three different waterfalls at **Burrells Ford**. Several Class V+ rapids are on this closed section, including Big Bend Falls, a single 25-foot drop stretching across the entire river.

Floating starts at the GA 28 bridge, on the GA/SC line. Here the West Fork flows into the Chattooga, and the boating ban is lifted. Upstream on the West Fork is 4 miles of easy Class I–II canoe stream, with a put-in at FS 86 (Overflow Creek Road). Up from FS 86, however, the stream is 5 miles of Class IV–V+, noted for its beautiful scenery. The Chattooga proper starts with Section 2, 7 miles of Class II—as you might expect, as you are entering the foothills now, and the ridges that line the river rise only to 2,500 feet. Surprisingly, this mildness ends in Section III, which starts as the long-distance **Bartram Trail** wanders down from the Blue Ridge on the last 2,500-foot ridge. For the next 13 miles the river cuts downward by 300 feet even as the ridgelines become large hills; the many rapids in this stretch are Class II–IV. The final section, from US 76 to Tugaloo Lake, is known as the Five Falls of the Chattooga, Class III–V.

**WATERFALL COUNTRY** This 55-mile stretch of the Blue Ridge, with its rough, broken gorge country to its south, may be one of the best places for waterfalls anywhere. This list, running from east to west, is far from complete.

**Schoolhouse Falls** This Panthertown Valley waterfall forms where the headwaters of the Tuckaseegee River plunge over an overhanging 20-foot ledge into a large pool, not a half-mile from the crest of the Blue Ridge; like many such waterfalls, it has formed a grotto which protects a variety of rare ferns and other plants. The large pool is a popular swimming hole, complete with sandy beach. Schoolhouse Falls is reached from the east gate of Panthertown Valley, from the trailhead at the end of Cold Mountain Road (SSR 1301). The round-trip walk is 2 miles, with a return climb of 250 feet.

**Falls of the Horsepasture Wild & Scenic River** In 1986 the U.S. Congress acted to stop a California carpetbagger from destroying the little Horsepasture River in a hydroelectric scheme, by declaring it a Wild and Scenic River, the result of an extraordinary campaign by local residents. Waterfalls were the reason for this unusual congressional action—five of them. Three are easily accessible from NC 281 a mile south of Sapphire, then left into the Gorges State Park trailhead parking lot; an excellent, newly constructed path leads out of the park, into the adjacent Nantahala National Forest, and then down the river. First up is Drift Falls, a 30-foot slide rock with a large swimming hole at the bottom. Ten minutes farther down the path is Turtle Back Falls, which looks like water rolling over a turtle's back, with a 15-foot drop into the pool beneath. Some of the foolhardy (and one may doubt the "hardy" part) use this as a slide rock as well. Nobody uses the next waterfall as a slide rock. Rainbow Falls drops 150 feet straight down in a roar of water that puts up a perpetual mist in which rainbows form. Farther downstream the path becomes much steeper and quite difficult as it enters the State of North Carolina's Toxaway Game Lands, where the adventuresome will find Stairstep Falls and Windy Falls.

**Whitewater Falls** One of several waterfalls claimed as the "tallest in the East," Whitewater Falls is an impressive sight. Located in the Nantahala National Forest, off NC 281 near the state line, it carries a huge flow of water 450 feet straight down in three great jumps. It has carved a great bowl for itself, and a projecting ledge (a short, flat walk from the parking lot) gives an unobstructed view of its entire length. The old pioneer-era road ran right by this waterfall, and its roadbed can be walked to its top. Downstream, Lower Whitewater Falls can be reached from Duke Power's Bad Creek facility, just south of the state line; just drive right up and ask the guard at the gate.

**Falls of the Jocassee Gorges** (e-mail: gorg@citcom.net; 828-966-9099; P.O. Box 100, Sapphire, NC 28774). In a very real sense, the previous two waterfall entries are classic Jocassee Gorge waterfalls, fortunate enough to have public protection for many years. North and South Carolina are still making plans on how they intend to develop the remaining 53,000 acres of the Jocassee Gorges, purchased in 1999 from Duke Power. Neither state has designed a trail network, much less started construction. A pity—the 7,100-acre Gorges State Park in North Carolina has inventoried 13 major waterfalls on only 14 percent of the land, and this may be an undercount.

**Falls of the Chattooga at Burrells Ford** The rough side mountains of the Blue Ridge extend deep into South Carolina. Three attractive waterfalls can be found grouped around the Burrells Ford Bridge over the Chattooga River. (You'll find Burrells Ford Road 13 miles south of Cashiers on NC/SC 107, on the right.) Burrells Ford forms a sort of minirecreation area along a smooth stretch of the Chattooga River, in South Carolina's Sumter National Forest; it has many good places to fish, a primitive camping area that can double as a picnic area, and a network of trails that leads to (among other things) three waterfalls. You will find trailhead parking a bit uphill from the bridge. For Spoonauger Falls, go to your right up the Chattooga River Trail for a short half-mile; this small stream stair-steps 40 feet down a cliff on your left. Straight ahead, the path continues to the Ellicott Rock Wilderness, following the Chattooga. However, for more waterfalls, return to Burrells Ford and continue across the road on the Chattooga River Trail. Very shortly (inside the camping area) a side trail will lead 0.3 mile uphill to Kings Creek Falls, another 40-foot drop but much more violent than Spoonauger. Return to the Chattooga River Trail and continue downstream for another 3 miles to reach Big Bend Falls, down a fisherman's path on your right (listen for the noise of the waterfall). This is a 25-foot waterfall stretching the width of the Chattooga, with a 12-foot plummet over an overhang onto an equally large cascade. The trail doesn't end here—it continues another 4 miles, following the Chattooga through a deep gorge, reaching SC 28 in 10.5 miles from Burrells Ford.

**Glen Falls** Just west of Highlands, a violent little stream called the East Fork throws itself straight down the Blue Ridge escarpment, dropping 800 feet in a half-mile. On the way down it forms three impressive waterfalls, each one bigger than the last. The Nantahala National Forest path goes straight down as well, using interminable steps to drop through old-growth forest to views of the waterfalls.

**SWIMMING HOLES** **Silver Run Falls** The only difficulty in exploring this isolated piece of the Nantahala National Forest is finding the parking area. It's on NC 107, 3.92 miles south of US 64, near Cashiers, a wide gravel area on the left; and, if its summer, there are cars parked there. This is a justifiably popular swimming hole. The falls are lovely, one of those active little rivers that throws itself over a 15-foot ledge.

**Norton Mill Creek Falls** One of the finest swimming holes in the mountains, this gem is little known and little visited—possibly because it's a bit of a walk. (Directions: from US 64 in Cashiers go south on NC 107 for 6.9 miles to Bull Pen Road, SSR 1603, then west 5.1 miles to the spectacular steel truss bridge with wonderful views of the Chattooga River far below; park where you can.) From the steel bridge, the Chattooga River Trail leads upstream 3 miles through a lovely riverside forest in a deep gorge, to this small, beautifully formed waterfall with a large, deep pool and sand beach. There's a steel foot bridge over it, which the Forest Service helicoptered in.

**RECREATION AREAS** **Cliffside Lake Recreation Area** This Nantahala National Forest recreation area, inside the Cullasaja Gorge, has a lovely little lake underneath cliffs. Paths lead around the lake shore and up the cliffs for some really excellent views. The park features classic CCC architecture from the 1930s, including a gazebo at the top of the cliff and a number of picnic shelters. The picnic area sits by the lake, under a canopy of tall old trees.

**Oconee State Park** (864-638-5353; 624 State Park Rd., Mountain Rest, SC 29664). Located at the far southern end of the Blue Ridge's craggy outliers, just off SC 107, this South Carolina state park offers lakeside recreation as well as picnicking. The CCC built most of this lovely little park's buildings in the 1930s, including 19 rental cabins. Footpaths lead to a variety of worthwhile sites, including a 50-foot waterfall on Hidden Falls Trail and a spectacular clifftop viewpoint on Tamassee Trail.

In addition to Oconee State Park, there are several Sumter National Forest picnic areas along SC 107, starting just below the state line.

**Bad Creek Power Station** You don't normally think of a power station as a recreation area. However, Bad Creek is a different type of hydropower station. This Duke Power–pumped storage facility floods a bowl-shaped valley perched high in the mountains near the South Carolina–North Carolina border, just south of Whitewater Falls. Its purpose is to create extra hydropower during peak demand periods; Duke actually pumps water up to this reservoir during slack times, then runs it through the Lake Jocassee turbines when its needed. Duke occasionally opens it for tours. More to the point, they always allow recreationists to enter the site during daylight hours (you can leave, but not enter, after dusk), to use the network of hiking trails. The most prominent feature is Lower Whitewater Falls, over 300 feet high and every bit as beautiful as the more famous waterfall upstream. As the lands are closed to hunting, this is a good place for October backcountry walking. You will find it just inside South Carolina on NC 281/SC 130; you will need to sign in at the visitors' gate.

**PICNIC AREAS** **Ravenel Park** Adjacent to the Highlands Botanical Gardens, this town park follows a narrow, winding lakeshore through a residential area. Such lakes are a typical and charming feature of Highlands neighborhoods, and Ravenel makes for a good picnic spot.

**Devils Fork State Park** (e-mail: devilsfork@scprt.com; 866-345-7275, 864-944-2639; fax: 864-944-8777; southcarolinaparks.com) 16 Holcome Circle, Salem, SC 29676). This attractive South Carolina park, at the far southern edge of this chapter's area, gives access to giant Jocassee Lake. It has a lakeside picnic area, boat ramps, family camping, and rental cottages.

## ✷ To See

### *Along the Blue Ridge*

The Blue Wall (see "The Blue Ridge: Chimney Rock & Saluda," Wild Places) section of the Blue Ridge ends suddenly. The crestline of the Blue Ridge sweeps backwards, well into North Carolina, and the space between the retreating crest and the line of the Blue Wall is filled with a jumble of hard rock ridges. Those jumbled ridges are separated by spectacular gorges, with an incredible concentration of waterfalls. Back at the crest—now running from Lake Toxaway through Cashiers and into Highlands—the Blue Ridge is up to its old tricks, with great gray cliffs plunging down its south face, and gentle slopes leading to high valley bowls on its north face. This makes for a unique treat: wide views from the highest cliffs in the East, over a massive jumble of deep gorges and craggy mountains—and all of it easy to reach from those gentle north slopes. Here are a few of the best spots, from east to west.

**Salt Rock** Naturalist and biographer George Ellison has called this "one of the most delightful views in the southern highlands." Salt Rock sits above the western end of Panthertown Valley in the Nantahala National Forest. It is a large rocky bald, decorated with moss and wind-dwarfed trees, that gives a wide panorama of the cliff face of the Blue Ridge rising straight up from Panthertown Valley. You will find it a very easy 0.2-mile walk down the gravel road from the gated end of Breedlove Road (SSR 1121), with the bald on the left through a tree belt.

**Chimneytop Mountain and Rocky Mountain** Cashiers sits at the feet of these two craggy outliers of the Blue Ridge. Rocky Mountain, on the north, provides a long, smooth, gray cliff that serves as backdrop to Cashiers and the High Hampton golf course. To its immediate south, Chimneytop pokes a tall, narrow, black crag up through the trees. The High Hampton Inn includes both peaks in their 1,400-acre resort, and maintains exciting (and none too easy) hiking trails to the tops of both. These trails lead to breathtaking views over Cashiers, along the cliff-sided Blue Ridge, and toward Whiteside Mountain.

**Cowee Gap** Here's one you can drive to. When US 64 crosses the Blue Ridge Crest between Cashiers and Highlands, it opens up a broad panorama over the headwaters of the Chattooga River. Rocky and Chimneytop Mountains are ahead of you; the part of Whiteside Mountain known as the Devils Courthouse is to your right. This overlook comes up quickly on a very sharp bend, 4.5 miles east of Highlands, so be alert.

**Whiteside Mountain** Reputed to be the highest continuous cliff in the East, Whiteside projects a mile out into the valley of the Chattooga River from the Blue Ridge Crest. Its gentle north slope, typical of the Blue Ridge, makes for a moderate walk to the clifftop. The view must be seen to be believed—and the loop path follows this clifftop for a mile, opening up new vistas at every turn. Like most Blue Ridge cliffs, these start off as a gentle rock slope that gets gradually steeper; a foolhardy hiker can get quite a ways down before noticing the extraordinary danger. A failed tourist attraction in the 1950s, the attraction's old tram bed makes for an easy but viewless walk to the top, where a loop trail follows the cliff line back to the parking lot. Whiteside is part of the Nantahala National Forest, which may charge a parking fee.

**Sunset Rock** Part of the town of Highlands' Ravenel Park, Sunset Rock is a large bald overlooking Highlands. It sits on one side of the Blue Ridge Crest, here an unimpressive little ridgeline. From Sunset Rock this little mountaintop town looks particularly quaint and attractive, its downtown surrounded by forests and framed by mountain ridges. On the other side of the ridge, Sunrise Rock gives more limited views over the face of the Blue Ridge. You can walk up to Sunrise Rock from the Highlands' Nature Center, or drive up a rough gravel road that goes right from Horse Cove Road (SSR 1603) to follow the Blue Ridge.

**Scaly Mountain** Scaly Mountain anchors the western end of this segment of the Blue Ridge. It has a large, south-facing rocky bald that gives broad views over the low ridges that drop into Georgia. Access is by the Bartram Trail, a long-distance path that retraces the steps of 18th-century naturalist William Bartram. From NC 106 south of Highlands, turn right on Turtle Pond Road (SSR 1620), then left onto gravel Lickskillit Road (SSR 1621); as you top a gap, look for a place to park. The Bartram Trail goes left 1 mile to Scaly Mountain, a 500-foot climb.

**BIG DAMMED LAKES** **Glenville Lake** This large lake, 3,500 feet in elevation, sends out long, thin arms into many former valleys in the Glenville area, north of Cashiers on NC 107. The highway skirts the lake for some distance before swerving away as it reaches what passes for central Glenville (still a dispersed mountain community).Lakeside scenery is very mixed, with much forest, a number of farms and meadows, and a slowly but steadily increasing number of subdivisions. A winding narrow lane (SSR 1157) turns left off NC 107 on the north end of Glenville, first reaching a nice county park with picnicking and a boat ramp, then crossing the impressive World War II–era dam (with a free boat launch on the other side). The lake is owned by Duke Power; water from the lake flows through a giant pipeline to a hydropower station at Tuckaseegee. By the way, it's officially known as "Thorpe Reservoir," but if you call it that no one will know what you are talking about.

**Lake Toxaway** (laketoxaway.com; 800-443-0694; 100 Waterfall Cir., Lake Toxaway, NC 28747). This is the lake that would not die. The Toxaway Company, established in 1896, aggressively developed Sapphire and Toxaway as resorts for the rich. In 1903 they built Lake Toxaway and placed a giant luxury hotel on its shore. It seemed to be a roaring success, filling with millionaires who would park their private railroad cars on a special siding built for that purpose. However, the Toxaway Company flared out in 1911, going into bankruptcy. In 1916 the Lake Toxaway Dam failed, sending a wall of 5.4 billion gallons of water straight down the mountainside; you can still see the scoured-out trail it left just below the US 64 bridge. The grand inn was abandoned then dismantled for scrap in 1947. In 1961 a group of investors purchased the dried-up lakebed and rebuilt the dam, selling lots once again around the lakeside. Only a few of the original mansions remain along the rebuilt Lake Toxaway, the most remarkable being the Moltz Mansion, now the Greystone Inn. The lake itself is private, closed to the public.

**Lake Jocassee** Lake Jocassee floods 7,600 acres of Blue Ridge valleys in South Carolina, just below the state line. It's part of a massive hydropower operation by Duke Power, in combination with Lake Keowee to the south and the Bad Creek Project to its north. Most of the lands to the north of Jocassee have been owned by Duke Power since the 1960s, protecting them from development; now they are in public ownership as the 53,000-acre Jocassee Gorge area. Lake Jocassee sends long, thin arms deep into this wilderness, allowing easy access to some remarkably remote areas. There are boat ramps at Devils Fork State Park, on SC 11 east of SC 107.

**HISTORICAL SITES** **Stumphouse Tunnel** This local park, at the far southern edge of the Blue Ridge's outliers, preserves the mortal remains of an extraordinarily overambitious antebellum railroad project. In 1850—a time when no accurate maps existed of the Blue Ridge and Smoky Mountains—the Blue Ridge Railway made a serious attempt to run a road straight across the southern Appalachians. At Stumphouse Tunnel, the railroad tried to breach the first rock face of the Blue Ridge and failed. The tunnel was to be well over a mile long, and was mainly completed when the venture collapsed in 1859. Today, a local park keeps the south end of the tunnel open for 500 feet, with a nice picnic area nearby. (Up to 1994 you could go 1,600 feet into the tunnel, viewing a giant air shaft at midway, but a roof collapse has closed that part of the tunnel.)

Elsewhere in the park, a short, easy trail leads to the top Issaqueena Falls, a 200 foot cascade, with excellent views.

**Oconee Station State Historic Site** (864-638-0079; 500 Oconee Station Rd., Walhalla, SC 29691). Open for tours on weekends This stone-built 1792 Cherokee trading post sits in grassy fields at the bottom of the Blue Ridge's last outlier. The adjacent Richards House dates from the same era. Now a South Carolina state park, you will find it 2 miles off SC 11 north of Walhalla—by coincidence, just downhill from Oconee State Park, with which it is linked by a 3.2-mile segment of the Palmetto Trail. A side trail leads 1 mile to 60-foot Station Cove Falls.

**The Church of the Good Shepherd** This lovely little Episcopalian church, located off NC 107 in Cashiers, was

THE VILLAGE GREEN AT CASHIERS

built in 1896 to serve Cashier's summer colony. Listed in the National Register, it's a particularly handsome example of the rustic Gothic style then favored by the Episcopal and Catholic churches. It is still in use, the center of a year-round parish since 1982.

**GARDENS AND PARKS** **Highlands Botanical Garden** (www.wcu.edu/hbs/Garden.htm; e-mail: pbrannon@email.wcu.edu; 828-526-2602; fax: 828-526-2797; 930 Horse Cove Rd., P.O. Box 580, Highlands, NC 28714). Open all year, daily. At the center of Highlands sits a very special botanical garden. Run by Western Carolina University, the 30-acre Highlands Botanical Garden is a biological reservoir of native species and a serious research station for mountain botany, ecology, and biology. The garden is highly informal in its design and layout, a skillful modification of the found environments that safeguards and showcases the specimens. Paths loop around a lakeshore thick with lily pads, climbs along sheltered stream banks, and breaks into old cove forests. The gardens were established in 1962, but the research station has been there since the 1930s, and has the look and feel of an old-time ranger station. New additions include a Cherokee Garden and the William Bartram Trail, an interpretive trail that features 30 mountain species connected with the great early botanist. On-site, facing Horse Cove Road, is the Highland Nature Center, a nature museum open seasonally. Ravenel Park is adjacent, and Sunset Rock is an easy walk up a footpath.

## ✷ To Do

**WHITEWATER ADVENTURES** **Rafting the Chattooga River** The Chattooga River does not become floatable until it has put the high cliffs of the Blue Ridge well behind. The National Forest Service, which owns nearly all of the river, sets the upper limit of the floatable river at the SC 28 highway bridge—the southern end of this chapter. Two large regional float companies are licensedd by the Forest Service to run trips on the Chattooga below SC 28: the Nantahala Outdoor Center and Wildwater Rafting.

**HORSEBACK RIDING** **Arrowmont Stables and Cabins** (www.arrowmont.com; 800-682-1092, 828-743-2762; 276 Arrowmont Trail, Cullowhee, NC 28723). Open all year, Mon.–Sat., 8 AM–5 PM. Arrowmont provides horses for guided trail rides on 6 miles of trail on their remote 200-acre property in the high mountains north of Cashiers, near Glenville. They also have two cabins, older but clean and well kept, as well as group camping in bunk cabins left over from when the property was a boy's camp.

**GOLF** **High Hampton** (www.highhamptoninn.com; e-mail: info@highhamptoninn.com; 800-334-2551, 828-743-2450; 1525 Hwy. 107 S., P.O. Box 338, Cashiers, NC 28717). Designed by George Cobb in 1956, this 18-hole course is noted for its outstanding beauty, including wide views of the cliffs of the Blue Ridge reflecting in the glassy surface of Hampton Lake.

**Trillium Links** (trilliumnc.com/amenities/trillium-golfing; e-mail: info@trilliumnc.com; 888-909-7171, 828-743-4251; 1 Trillium Ctr., Cashiers, NC 28717). Designed by Morris Hatalsky in 1998, this 4,000-foot high course is part of a land development project in the Glenville Lake area north of Cashiers.

**Sapphire Mountain Golf Club** (828-743-1174; 50 Slicers Ave., Sapphire, NC 28774). This 1982 Ron Garl course, part of a large modern resort and subdivision development east of Cashiers on US 64, features mountain scenery from its narrow and undulating fairways (including a hole that plays over a waterfall).

## ✷ Lodging

### COUNTRY INNS AND HOTELS

**Olde Edwards Inn** (oldedwardsinn.com; 866-526-8008, 828-526-8008; 445 Main St., Highlands, NC 28741). Open all year. The oldest building in downtown Highlands, the 1878 Old Edwards Inn is a distinctive three-story brick building with a stone entrance (an early owner ran a rock quarry), plus a long wooden annex with a second-story verandah, almost as old as the main building. All 20 rooms have 19th-century style wall stenciling; most rooms have balconies, and some have sitting areas.

**The Highlands Inn** (www.highlandsinn-nc.com; e-mail: stay@highlandsinn-nc.com; 800-964-6955, 828-526-9380; P.O. Box 1030, 420 Main St., Highlands, NC 28741). This classic wood coaching inn, listed on the National Register, has dominated downtown Highlands since 1880. A long, low three-story building, its second-story verandah covers the sidewalk for most of a block. Completely renovated in 1989, its 31 rooms range from cozy to large in size, and some have separate sitting areas. The tariff includes an extended continental breakfast.

✐ 🐾 **The Lodge at Olde Edwards Inn** (oldedwardsinn.com; 866-526-8008, 828-526-8008; 445 Main St., Highlands, NC 28741). Formerly the Kelsey and Hutchenson Lodge, it is now the Old Edwards Inn and Spa. A 1997 reconstruction of the 1883 Lees Inn, the 3.5 acres of land include several surviving outbuildings of the Lee's Inn, two of which have been restored for additional rooms. More business-friendly than many historic inns, there are meeting rooms, concierge services, a gift shop, data ports in every room, and 24-hour voice-mail service.

**The Main Street Inn** (www.mainstreet-inn.com; e-mail: info@mainstreet-inn.com; 800-213-9142, 828-526-2590; fax: 828-787-1142; 270 Main St., Highlands, NC 28741). Built in 1885 and restored in 1998, this farmhouse sits in the middle of Highlands' Main Street shopping district, surrounded by its own oak-shaded lawns. The 20 guest rooms vary greatly in size; some are small while others have individual sitting areas or balconies. A large country breakfast is served, as well as afternoon tea.

**The Chandler Inn** (www.thechandlerinn.com/index.html; e-mail: thechandlerinnc@yahoo.com; 888-378-6300, 828-526-5992; 790 N. Fourth Street, Highlands, NC 28741). Open all year. This unusual inn, located on the east side of town on US 64, consists of several wooden buildings grouped tightly around a central garden area, linked by decks and walkways. A modern complex, it has a rustic look and feel, with well-tended gardens; although convenient to the main highway, it's very quiet. All 15 oversized rooms have private entrances onto the interconnecting decks. A hospitality room has morning coffee and home-baked goods, with a sitting area by a fireplace.

**The Inn at Half Mile Farm** (www.halfmilefarm.com; e-mail: mail@halfmilefarm.com; 800-946-6822, 828-526-8170; fax: 828-526-2625; 214 Half-Mile Dr., P.O. Box 2769, Highlands,

NC 28741). This 14-acre landscaped property in Highlands, North Carolina, has a large, traditional lodge overlooking a pond with 23 rooms and a restaurant, plus eight cabins. The tariff includes a full breakfast and evening hor d'oeuvres with wine.

**RESORTS** **High Hampton Inn and Country Club** (www.highhampton inn.com; e-mail: Info@HighHampton Inn.com; 800-334-2551, 828-743-2411; 1525 Highway 107 South/P.O. Box 338, Cashiers, NC 28717). Located in Cashiers, this 1,400-acre resort has been run by the McKee family since 1922. However, it's older than that—Wade Hampton, a South Carolina planter, established the High Hampton estate as the family summer home in 1845, and the entire resort is a National Historic District. Most of these buildings date from the 1920s and '30s, built as part of the resort. The main inn is a classic rustic lodge built in 1933, noted for its walls clad in chestnut bark, and for the wide views from its wraparound verandah. The large Hampton Lake, beside the main building, opens up vistas to the wide front of the Blue Ridge, which flanks the lake with great gray escarpments and granite crags. The 117 rooms are rustic, with board-and-batten paneling from wood logged on the estate and simple, country furniture. The tariff includes three meals a day, plus afternoon tea on the verandah; meals are hearty country fare, prepared fresh from scratch, and served buffet style.

**The Greystone Inn** (www.greystone inn.com; e-mail: info@greystoneinn .com; 800-824-5766, 828-966-4700; fax: 828-862-5689; Greystone Ln., Lake Toxaway, NC 28747). This resort complex centers on a six-level Alpine-style 1915 mansion, built by local heroine Lucy Moltz (who lived there until her death in 1970). Since becoming a resort in 1985, the 13 guest rooms and suites in the Moltz Mansion have been supplemented by 4 suites in two new buildings. The resort strives to present gourmet meals to its guests, all included in the tariff—a full breakfast, an afternoon tea on the sun porch, wine and hor d'oeuvres before dinner, and a formal dinner with menu choices and dessert by the inn's pastry chef. An evening champagne cruise is offered free to guests, as is canoeing, kayaking, powerboating, waterskiing, tennis, and lawn games. Golf privileges are available at nearby Lake Toxaway Country Club.

🐾 **Fire Mountain** (firemt.com; e-mail: reservations@firemt.com; 800-775-4446, 828-526-4446; fax: 828-526-5518; P.O. Box 2772). This remote resort, located 6 miles west of Highlands in the large perched valley known as The Flats, emphasizes seclusion and unplugging. Its large tract sits astride the Blue Ridge, with elevations above 4,000 feet and excellent views. It has a six-room inn, a separate three-room building called The Treehouse that offers additional privacy, and six cabins. There are no phones in the rooms, but there is a phone room in the lodge with free local calls.

**BED & BREAKFAST INNS**

**Colonial Pines Inn** (www.colonial pinesinn.com/home.htm; e-mail: sleeptight@colonialpinesinn.com; 866-526-2060, 828-526-2060; 541 Hickory St., Highlands, NC 28741). Located in a residential neighborhood not far from downtown Highlands, the Colonial Pines occupies a large mid-20th-century plantation-style house on 2 acres. Common rooms have a cozy, 1940s look with country furniture, red-brick fireplace and knotty pine paneling. The knotty pine carries throughout the six rooms and one kitchenette apartment, which range in size from cozy to large. The tariff includes a full breakfast.

**4 Street Inn** (www.4andahalfstinn.com; e-mail: Relax@4andaHalfStInn.com; 888-799-4464, 828-526-4464; 55 4 St., Highlands, NC 28741). Located in a residential neighborhood a few blocks from downtown Highlands, the 4 Street Inn has 10 rooms in an historic farmhouse with a wraparound porch and a large back deck. The tariff includes a full breakfast, fresh homemade cookies, and an afternoon wine hour with hors d'oeuvres.

**MOTELS Laurelwood Mountain Inn** (www.laurelwoodmountaininn.com; 800-346-6846, 828-743-9939; Hwy. 107 N./P.O. Box 196; center of town, Cashiers, NC 28717). This attractive modern facility in the heart of Cashiers has motel-style rooms in a pleasantly rustic building, surrounded by well-landscaped grounds. They also have three lofted efficiency suites in a separate log-built building, and a traditional mountain-style log cabin.

**CABINS The Cabins at Seven Foxes** (www.sevenfoxes.com; e-mail: reservations@sevenfoxes.com; 828-877-6333; fax: 828-862-4132; 7 Foxes Ln./P.O. Box 123, Slick Fisher Rd., Lake Toxaway, NC 28747). Located 4 miles north of Lake Toxaway on the Blue Ridge, this group of 5 new cabins sits on 6 wooded acres. These one- and two-bedroom cabins, modestly styled on the outside, are comfortably furnished with antiques and reproductions, each with its own theme. All cabins have porches, gas fireplaces, fully equipped kitchens, and quilts.

**Cabins in the Laurel** (nc-cabins.com; e-mail: info@cashierscabins.com; 828-743-2621; P.O. Box 2475, Cashiers, NC 28717). Five modern-built rustic cabins are each the size of a small house, with either shingle or log exteriors, porches, fireplaces, and lots of interior wood. The heavily wooded site is very close to the center of Cashiers.

♿ **Devils Fork State Park, South Carolina** (discoversouthcarolina.com; e-mail: devilsfork@scprt.com; 866-345-7275, 864-944-2639; fax: 864-944-8777; 161 Holcombe Cir., Salem, SC 29676). This South Carolina state park, located on the western shore of Lake Jocassee, has 20 large modern cabins in a contemporary/rustic style, with a large screened porch. Each has a living room with a fireplace, a kitchen, and either two or three bedrooms, and 11 have lake views.

**Oconee State Park, South Carolina** (southcarolinaparks.com/park-finder/state-park/750864-638-5353; e-mail: oconee@scprt.com; fax: 888-803-0844; 624 State Park Rd., Mountain Rest, SC 29664). These 19 rustic cabins were built by the CCC in the 1930s, with 13 overlooking the park's tiny lake, and six in an isolated forest. All have stone fireplaces, heating and air-conditioning, and well-equipped kitchens.

## ✷ Where to Eat

**EATING OUT Carolina Smokehouse** (thecarolinasmokehouse.com; e-mail: info@thecarolinasmokehouse.com; 828-743-3200; 281 Highway 64 West, Cashiers, NC 28717). If you find yourself looking for a good, simple roadside eatery, this is your place. It occupies a plain little building with a covered deck, west of Cashiers on US 64. Inside it's just as plain, but clean and with a decor centering on old automobile tags. The barbeque is fresh and tasty, with a sweet tomato-based sauce, served up with the classic sides, and reasonably priced.

**Pescado's Highland Burrito** (pescados-highlands.us; e-mail: pescadoshighlands@yahoo.com; 828-526-9313; 226 S. Fourth St., Highlands,

NC 28741). Lunch and dinner This downtown Highlands Mexican eatery prepares its food from scratch using fresh ingredients. Their specialty is large California-style burritos, tacos, quesadillas and salads, with plenty of fresh-made salsa.

**DINING OUT On the Verandah** (ontheverandah.com; 828-526-2338; 1536 Highlands Rd., Highlands, NC 28741). Dinner daily; Sunday brunch. Located west of Highlands on US 64, this family-owned restaurant occupies an old 1920's speakeasy overlooking Lake Sequoyah, with lovely views over the lake from its deck or enclosed verandah dining areas. Inside, the bright and attractive dining room is dominated by founding owner Alan Figel's collection of over 1,300 bottles of chile sauce (any one of which diners are welcome to try). The menu features a fusion of Caribbean, South American, and Asian approaches, always with fresh, local ingredients emphasized. As you might expect from someone with 1,300 bottles of hot sauce, at least a couple of items will feature fresh, unusual chile peppers, and the mild dishes tend to be richly flavored. This restaurant has a 200-bottle wine list, and a wine bar with an extensive choice of wines by the glass.

**Ristorante Paoletti** (paolettis.com; 828-526-4906; 440 Main St., Highlands, NC 28741). Open for dinner, June–October, Mon.–Sat. This downtown Highlands storefront restaurant offers fine Italian dining with a rich choice of foods that go well beyond red sauce on pasta. The Paoletti has a long menu of gourmet pastas with a wide variety of treatments, any of which may be ordered as a main dish or as a side to one of their entrées—veal, lamb, fish, chicken, and filet mignon. Their wine list includes over 800 bottles.

**Madison's** (800-230-4134, 828-526-8008; 445 Main St., Highlands, NC 28741). Located in the center of downtown Highlands, in the Old Edwards Inn, Madison's offers gourmet breakfasts, lunches and dinners, as well as a Sunday brunch, all prepared by a professional culinary team. Recipes are unique and memorable, merging fresh flavors in imaginative ways.

## ✷ Entertainment

### *Highlands*

**Highlands Playhouse** (www.highlandsplayhouse.org; 828-526-2695; fax: 828-526-0761; 2 Oak St., Highlands, NC, 28741). This respected summer theater performs plays and musicals in its shingle-clad playhouse behind downtown Highlands.

**Highlands Chamber Music Festival** (828-526-9060; P.O. Box 1702, Highlands, NC 28741). This summer series of chamber music performances is held at the Episcopal Church of the Incarnation in July and August.

## ✷ Selective Shopping

### *Highlands*

Highlands's large concentration of million-dollar vacation cottages insures that it has an equally large concentration of antique shops and art galleries. In fact, Highlands has had a first-class collection of antique shops for a number of decades, about half in its quaint downtown and the other half scattered about town. The chamber of commerce lists 16 antique shops and art galleries, with five more craft galleries and shops, 14 gift shops, and two book stores.

**Scudders Gallery** (scuddersgalleries.com; e-mail: info@scuddersgalleries.com; 828-526-4111; fax: 828-526-5355; 352 Main St., Highlands, NC 28741). Open all year. Established in

1925 (in Silver Springs, Forida), Scudder's has antique auctions every night at 7:30 pm. During the off-season it can be the town's primary form of evening entertainment. Definitely a high-end antique dealer, its stocks include oriental carpets, estate jewelry, furniture, silver, paintings, and other art. Catalog sales are held the second and fourth Saturday, June–November, at 11 am. You will find it in downtown Highlands.

**The Christmas Tree** (828-526-3687; P.O. Box 1196, Highlands, NC 28741). In downtown Highlands, for over a quarter of a century, the Christmas Tree offers just about everything you could put on, under, or near a tree. It has a particularly large selection of miniatures, and is a Department 56 Gold Key Dealer.

### *Cashiers*

**Basketworks** (828-743-5052; NC 107 South, Cashiers, NC 28717). Located south of Cashiers' center on NC 107, this shop features locally made smoke vine baskets, as well as Shenandoah Valley antiques, 18th-century antique botanicals, dried and handmade silk flowers, and a range of gift items.

## ✷ Special Events

**SUMMER Symphony Under the Stars** (828-743-9941). Fourth of July. The Charleston Symphony Orchestra performs on the banks of Lake Sapphire, east of Cashiers.

**AUTUMN Cashiers Annual Chili Cook-off** Mid-September. This annual chili cook-off, sponsored by the Cashiers Chamber of Commerce, has live music.

# FRANKLIN & THE NANTAHALA MOUNTAINS

Franklin. The headwaters of the Little Tennessee River carve out two of the southern Appalachian's most impressive ridgelines: the Cowee Mountains and the Nantahala Mountains. Between the two lies the deep, flat valley of the Little Tennessee, and the little gem-mining town of Franklin.

The Nantahala Mountains (pronounced Nanna-HAY-luh) dominate this area, with their stunning waterfalls, spectacular cliff views, wilderness rivers, and quaint CCC picnic areas. The Nantahala ridgeline forms a straight, steep edge running north between the Little Tennessee River and its western tributary, the Nantahala River. From its southern end, where it intersects with the Blue Ridge at Big Butt (near Pickens Nose—honestly, no one could make this up), to its northern terminus at Wesser, the Nantahala ridgeline carries the Appalachian Trail through 30 miles of thick, deep forest little disturbed since logging stopped.

East of this mountain system lies the Little Tennessee Valley and the bustling county seat of Franklin. For centuries before the coming of the Europeans, this valley was the center of Cherokee civilization. It supported a chain of settlements known as the Middle Villages, each village ranging from a half-dozen homesteads to groups of 30 or more dwellings. In 1817, the Cherokee Nation ceded the upper Little Tennessee Valley to the government of North Carolina and retreated to the lands west and south of the Nantahalas. Settlers trickled in; after 10 years the valley had enough population to warrant its own county government, with its seat at the Cherokee village of Nikwasi, now named Franklin after a former governor. Another 30 years after that, the valley received its first decent road, a turnpike that linked Franklin with Asheville and Murphy, crossing the Nantahalas at Wayah Gap.

Gem mining started in the upper Little Tennessee Valley in the 1870s. To be more accurate, corundum mining started in the 1870s, and the corundum mines kept kicking up gem-quality rocks. Corundum was (and is) a valuable industrial abrasive, being the second hardest substance found in nature and considerably more plentiful than the first hardest, diamonds. Usually corundum is found as an opaque, milky-white rock, but when crystallized in an exceptionally pure form it becomes either rubies or sapphires (depending on the trace elements that add color). While the quality of the occasional gemstone impressed Tiffany's and

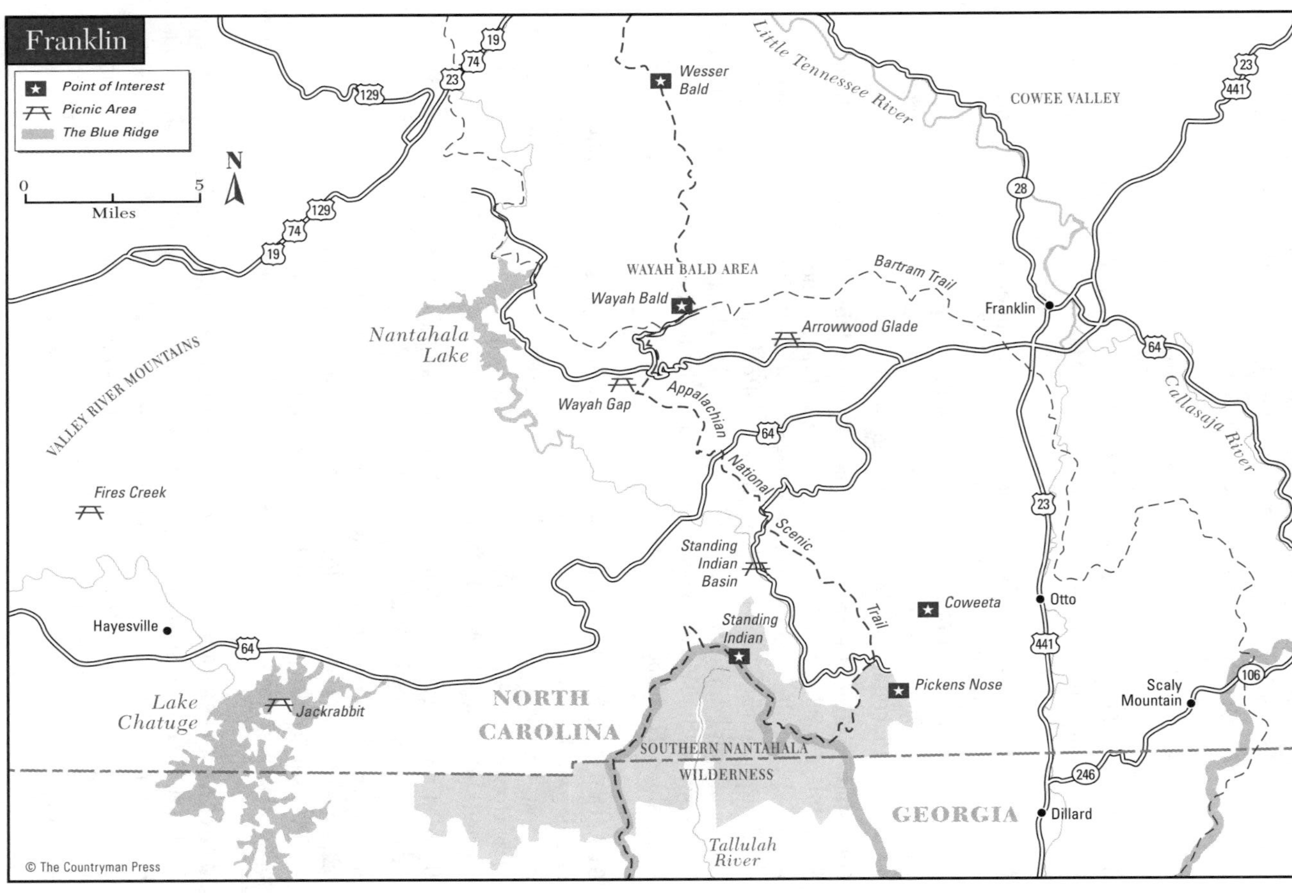
Franklin
Point of Interest
Picnic Area
The Blue Ridge
0
5
Miles
N
COWEE VALLEY
Little Tennessee River
Callasaja River
Franklin
Bartram Trail
Arrowwood Glade
WAYAH BALD AREA
Wesser Bald
Wayah Bald
Wayah Gap
Appalachian
National
Scenic
Trail
Standing Indian Basin
Standing Indian
Coweeta
Pickens Nose
Otto
Scaly Mountain
Dillard
GEORGIA
NORTH CAROLINA
SOUTHERN NANTAHALA
WILDERNESS
Tallulah River
Nantahala Lake
VALLEY RIVER MOUNTAINS
Fires Creek
Hayesville
Lake Chatuge
Jackrabbit
23
441
64
28
106
246
19
74
129
© The Countryman Press

attracted investors in the 1890s, a reliable source for the gemstones was never found. Commercial corundum mining ended with World War II, and today gem stone mining is a popular recreational pursuit.

**GUIDANCE** **Franklin Area Chamber of Commerce** (www.franklin-chamber.com; e-mail: facc@franklin-chamber.com; 866-372-5546, 828-524-3161; fax: 828-369-7516; 425 Porter St., Franklin, NC 28734). The Franklin Chamber handles tourism promotion and visitor relations for all of Macon County. Their visitors center is located south of downtown Franklin on Bus US 441.

**Clay County Chamber of Commerce** (ncmtnchamber.com; e-mail: nfo@ncmtnchamber.com; 828-389-3704; 388 Business Hwy. 64, Hayesville, NC 28904). The Clay County, North Carolina, chamber covers the mountainous area east of Robbinsville, including the county seat of Hayesville, where they operate from an attractive little cottage on the old main highway.

**Nantahala National Forest, Nantahala Ranger District** (828-524-6441; 90 Sloan Rd., Franklin, NC 28734). The ranger station for the Nantahala Mountains is located 1.6 miles west of downtown Franklin, just off Old US 64 (now known as Old Murphy Road, SSR 1442). They have a staffed information desk during business hours, and can help with maps of the Nantahala backcountry. Until 2007, this was known as the Wayah Ranger District; after the name change, it has taken on the Cashiers/Highlands area as well.

**GETTING THERE** **By Car** Franklin has excellent highway connections with the outside world. Its main north-south highway, US 441, is a modern four-lane. From the west, US 64 is modern and well-engineered with gentle curves and wide shoulders. However, US 64 from the east is a mess (albeit a highly scenic one), unmodernized since it was built in 1923; take US 74 to US 441 at Dillsboro instead.

**By Air** Franklin is over an hour from Asheville, and about three hours from Atlanta on good roads. Atlanta is usually cheaper.

**By Bus or Train** (roadrunnerdrivingservice.com; e-mail: nc_driver@mac.com; 828-524-3265; P.O. Box 804, Franklin, NC 28734). Franklin has no bus or passenger train service. Road Runner Driving Services offers shuttle services from all regional airports, as well as driving services within the area.

**MEDICAL EMERGENCIES** **Angel Medical Center** (angelmed.org; 828-524-8411; 120 Riverview St., Franklin, NC 28734). This independent not-for-profit 59-bed hospital has 24/7 emergency room service from its location a few blocks north of downtown Franklin on Riverview Street. It's been in business at this spot since 1923, when it was founded by Dr. Furman Angel; the current campus is quite modern.

## ✷ Exploring the Area

Driving in from the south along the main highway, US 441, your view is so utterly dominated by the wide, flat-bottomed valley of the Little Tennessee River that you may be wondering where the mountains start. They are, in fact, about a mile away on either side of you (such is the distorting power of perspective), and they become very tall, very quickly. To your right, they rise to the 4,500-foot peaks of the Fishhawk Mountains. To your left, the Nantahala Mountains form a jagged mass with mile-high peaks, nearly all of it heavily forested and publicly owned. They are crossed by only two paved roads, and penetrated by only a handful of gravel-surfaced forest roads. Despite this, they offer a wide range of recreational opportunities, particularly camping, short- and long-distance hiking (including the Appalachian Trail), fly-fishing in its wilderness rivers, and still-water boating and fishing in the large and beautiful reservoir, Nantahala Lake. Westward, the mountains become even wilder and less visited, with the narrowest of valleys separating the main ridges. The tiny little courthouse square village of Hayesville is located in these westernmost mountains.

The town of Franklin is in the middle of this chapter's area, straddling the Little Tennessee River at a spot where its valley becomes nearly level and 4 miles wide. North of Franklin lie the heavily settled Cowee Mountains, with national forest lands only along the highest and most remote peaks. On its western slopes lies the pastoral Cowee Valley, the home of the authentic gem mines. The Little Tennessee River runs along the western base of Cowee Mountain, separating it from the Nantahala Mountains to the west. Large areas of the Little Tennessee are public lands, as part of the State of North Carolina's Needmore Game Lands.

**EXPLORING BY CAR** **The Nantahala Mountains** Leg #1 (16.9 miles, one way): US 64 west from Franklin 3.8 miles; right on Old Murphy Road (SSR 1442), then 0.2 mile; left on Wayah Road (SSR 1310), 8.7 miles; right on Wayah Bald Road (FS 69) 4.2 miles. Return to US 64. Many curves; steep gravel forest road.

*Leg #2 (19 miles, one way)*: On US 64 westbound, 2.2 miles; left on Old US 64 (SSR 1448), then 6.4 miles to Wallace Gap; left on paved FS 71, then 1.7 miles to end of pavement at national forest campground; continue left uphill on gravel FS 71 for 8.7 miles to Pickens Nose.

*Total return trip: 71.8 miles.*

These two legs use the predecessors to modern US 64 to explore the Nantahala Mountains, topping the crest both times. The first leg follows the 19th-century coach road, while the second follows the early 20th century's first attempt at a paved auto road.

The first leg follows the handsome, pastoral valley of Wayah Creek upstream, at 7.2 miles passing **Arrowwood Glade**, a national forest picnic area with a swimming hole and some nice **CCC architecture**. From there the road continues along Wayah Creek as it enters deep woods; at 10.4 miles it reaches the side road to **Rufus Morgan Falls** (FS 388), then climbs straight up to 4,180-foot-high **Wayah Gap** in a series of five steep, tight switchbacks, reaching it at 13 miles. It's amazing that the 1850 coach road chose this route; only ignorance of the mountain's true layout could be responsible for climbing up to this high, cold gap. Look for **Bertie's Falls** on the left as you switch upward. Once in Wayah Gap, you turn off the main road steeply uphill to the right, to follow gravel FS 69 for over 4 miles, mostly along the Nantahala Crest, with the **Appalachian Trail** nearby the entire way. Be sure to stop for the **Wilson Lick Ranger Station** on your left, an attractive historic site preserving what may be the oldest ranger station in the East. The road ends at **Wayah Bald**, with good views from the picnic area parking lot; be sure, however, to walk up the quarter-mile to the stone **Wayah Bald Tower** for some remarkable panoramas. The **Bartram Trail**, this region's other long-distance footpath, crosses the Appalachian Trail at this spot. Go back the way you came.

The second leg leaves modern US 64 to the left, to follow the original US 64 auto road that was designed and constructed in the 1920s, and replaced only in the late 1970s. It's a dramatic climb; try to picture a fully loaded semi, circa 1975, coming downhill toward you with smoking brakes. When you top out, leave the old highway to take the paved Forest Service road into the **Standing Indian Basin**. This is a beautiful forest drive along a lovely wild river, then uphill on a good gravel road. The pavement ends at **Standing Indian Area Recreation Area**, a national forest picnic and camping area with multiple trailheads—several of which lead to the 5,500-foot rock-bound peak of **Standing Indian**, another spot crossed by the Appalachian Trail. The gravel road continues gently up the headwaters of the Nantahala River, giving easy access to the **waterfalls of Standing Indian**. The road's good maintenance ends at a parking area for the short, easy trail that leads to stunning clifftop views from **Pickens Nose**. A high-clearance four-wheel-drive vehicle can (except in winter) continue downhill through the **Coweeta Hydrologic Laboratory**, eventually emerging onto US 441 a half-dozen miles south of Franklin. Otherwise, return the way you came.

FOOTPATH IN STANDING INDIAN

**EXPLORING ON FOOT** **Standing Indian** The Standing Indian Basin is an outstanding hiking area, with varied and interesting scenery easily reached by a variety of loop trails. For an easy leg stretcher that samples the best of Standing Indian, take in the two waterfalls, then follow up with a walk out to Pickens Nose.

**LONG-DISTANCE PATHS** **The Appalachian Trail** The Appalachian Trail has already wandered for more than 72 miles through the mountains of North Georgia before entering the Southern Nantahala Wilderness at Blue Ridge Gap, Georgia—but nowhere yet as high as now. In the next 62 miles that it spends in this chapter's area, it will be above 4,000 feet for 49 miles.

The trail starts by making a giant, leisurely S-curve as it follows the Blue Ridge Crest around the Upper Tullulah River, then reverses itself to loop around **Standing Indian Basin** before climbing onto Nantahala Mountain. More than 25 miles of this section are continuously above 4,000 feet, with some peaks more than a mile high—including wide views from 5,500-foot **Standing Indian**, the trail's high point in this area. It drops to Old US 64 at 3,740-foot Wallace Gap after 31.5 miles.

Climbing up from Wallace Gap, the trail quickly regains 4,000 feet, and stays there (except for two brief flirtations with 3,900 feet at Winding Stairs Gap and Tellico Gap) for the next 25 miles, generally huging the Nantahala crest northward for 80 miles through mountaintop forests, with several opportunities for wide views. There are trailheads at US 64/74 and at **Wayah Gap**, where the trail passes through Wayah Crest Picnic Area. From there the trail roughly parallels gravel FS 69 to the old stone tower atop **Wayah Bald**, for panoramic views and an intersection with the **Bartram Trail**. In this area the trail spends a number of miles above 5,000 feet, before reaching the end of its high-altitude section at **Wesser Bald**, whose old fire tower has been converted into a viewing platform with a 360-degree view that includes the **Nantahala Gorge**. From here the trail drops nearly 3,000 feet down to the mouth of the Nantahala Gorge at **Nantahala Outdoor Center**.

**The Bartram Trail** The Bartram Trail spends 41 miles going east-west within this chapter's area, crossing the Appalachian Trail at Wayah Bald. It starts at the remote Jones Knob trailhead (see "The Blue Ridge: Cashiers & Highlands") then follows the 4,000-foot ridgeline, with its remarkable cliff views, until it runs out of national forest land . From there it's a 14-mile ramble down country lanes to Franklin, where it once again regains public lands and ascends remote Trimont Ridge, using it to climb the 3,000 feet in elevation to the peak of Wayah Bald, with its panoramic views. Here it crosses the Appalachian Trail, and continues to head west while the Appalachian Trail heads north. Now it drops 2,400 feet down a side ridge to the shores of Nantahala Lake, for a 1-mile road walk with good views of the lake. It leaves this chapter's area by slabbing a ridge above the Nantahala Dam, then dropping down to follow the Nantahala River into its gorge.

**EXPLORING BY BICYCLE** **Little Tennessee River Greenway** (www.littletennessee.org; e-mail: frogquarters@verizon.net; 828-369-8488; fax: 828-349-4119; 573 E. Main St., Franklin, NC 28734). This paved 4-mile walk/bike path follows the Little Tennessee River from one end of Franklin to another. Apart from many views of this lovely river, it has four major bridges over the Little Tennessee (including one historic steel structure), canoe launch points, picnic areas, and a nice, large playground with water features. Its monarch butterfly garden is certified as a monarch waystation by the University of Kansas's Monarch Watch program (www.monarchwatch.org), a protected place for monarchs to regain their strength on their long migration to Mexico.

## ✷ Villages

**Franklin** An early pioneer town, Franklin has been a major market center for the surrounding mountains since stage coach roads converged here in the 1850s. Today it has a handsome and shopable downtown of three square blocks, with lots of businesses sprawling outward along its U.S. highways, US 441 Bypass, US 441 Business, and US 64. It sits in the middle of a broad flat valley, straddling the Little Tennessee River with low hills that wouldn't look out of place in the Piedmont. However, when the mountains get started they kick in with a vengeance, with all local ridgelines surpassing 4,000 feet and the Nantahalas reaching a mile high.

**Hayesville** The tiny seat of Clay County (population just 350), Hayesville sits 2 miles off the main highway, US 64, between Franklin and Murphy. Isolated by the rugged Valley River Mountains on its west and the Nantahala Mountains on its east, Hayesville remains nearly unchanged, a 50-year step back in time. It has a wonderfully beautiful Town Square—a 19th-century red-brick courthouse, framed by azaleas and rhododendrons, shaded by oaks, and with a little gazebo in front. The square is surrounded by tiny shops, forming Hayesville's downtown. East of town, US 64 gives excellent views as it climbs out of Clay County.

**Cowee Valley** This remote and pastoral valley is dotted with so many old farmhouses and barns that it has been declared a National Historic District. Its rolling farmlands are framed by the tall-forested peaks of the Cowee Mountains, and easily visited from a network of country lanes. But that's not why it's famous. No, it's the rubies. Cowee Valley has been a source of rubies since the 1870s. Not crummy, cloudy little industrial corundum specks either, but big star rubies and sapphires, gem quality and weighing hundreds of carats. Gem-quality rubies are found in other mountain valleys as well. Be aware, however, that the large majority of the local "gem mines" salt their dirt with foreign corundum, the cheap industrial abrasive you get when the stones aren't gem quality. This guide lists only those mines that provide unsalted pay dirt from their own property.

**Otto** South of Franklin, the Little Tennessee River drains a wide, flat-bottomed valley that stretches to the state line and beyond. US 441 follows this valley south into Georgia, and on to Atlanta and Florida. Somewhere along this valley, between Franklin and the state line, Franklin ends and Otto begins. Otto is a broad rural community with no town center. For practical purposes, places in Otto are places that are way south of Franklin but still in North Carolina.

## ✷ Wild Places

**THE GREAT FORESTS** **The Southern Nantahala Wilderness** Congress created this 24,500-acre wilderness to protect the great knot of mountains at the juncture of the Blue Ridge and the Nantahalas. Although only the northern slopes of the Blue Ridge are easily reached from Franklin, the wilderness extends a great distance over the southern slopes as well, including large tracts in Georgia's Chattahoochee National Forest. The Appalachian Trail follows the crest of the Blue Ridge through this wilderness from Georgia to the Nantahala Mountains, then follows the Nantahalas north.

These lands are extremely rugged, with knotted ridgelines, steep slopes, and peaks that push above 5,000 feet. Nearly all of the forests are second-growth hardwoods, as the entire area was logged between 1910 and 1940. The logging camp was located at the modern **Standing Indian Recreation Area**, and logging railroads were built up the stream valleys. Some of these old railroad grades now make for attractive walking through nicely recovered riverine and cove hardwood forests.

The National Forest Service owns perhaps twice as much land in the immediate area that is not included in the wilderness but remains open to public recreation. This includes the entire Standing Indian Basin, adjacent to the wilderness on its north. Many good-quality trails start in the Standing Indian area, with easy trailheads on its gravel access road, and extend into the wilderness; by connecting these trails, hikers and backpackers can make a wide variety of loops. One ambitious loop day hike (or good overnighter) starts at the Standing Indian Campground trailhead, hikes up the railroad grade along Kimsey Creek to the Appalachian Trail, then climbs **Standing Indian** on the Appalachian Trail for wonderful views; hikers can return to their cars by a half-dozen different alternative paths.

While Standing Indian and its main road, FS 67, supply the most popular trailheads, two remote trailheads give access to the less visited parts of the wilderness. In North Carolina, the Deep Gap trailhead lets you drive up to the Appalachian Trail in a 4,340-foot-high gap, the easiest way to reach the wide views from **the peak of Standing Indian**; from Franklin, go 14.4 miles west on US 64 to a left onto good gravel FS 71, then go 5.7 miles to its end at Deep Gap. Until the 1970s this road continued into Georgia, and what remains of it on the other side of the mountain creates a second, little used, trailhead. It's a long drive, though; from Franklin take US 23/441 south for 20.6 miles to Clayton, Georgia, then turn right onto US 76 and go 8 miles to a right on Persimmon Road, then go 4.2 miles to a right onto Tallulah River Road (becoming good gravel FS 70 in 0.8 mile), which ends at the wilderness trailhead after 8.9 miles. These last 9 miles follow the extremely scenic **Upper Tallulah River**, with many excellent river views along the way.

**The Wayah Bald Area** The highest peak in the northern Nantahalas is not Wayah Bald; it is Wine Springs Bald, a mile to the south and a good 100 feet higher. No one cares. Everything in this area is named after Wayah Bald, including (until 2007) the Nantahala National Forest's ranger district. The bald has its own gravel road, 4.5 miles long, climbing 1,100 up from Wayah Gap just to reach it. It has one of the oldest ranger stations in the East on its slopes, preserved as the Wilson Lick Historic Site. It has a stone lookout tower that's been there since 1912 and is simply beautiful. And it has 360-degree panoramic views that just won't quit.

HISTORIC RANGER STATION ON WAYAH BALD

Wayah Bald marks a rough halfway point in the northward march of the Nantahala Mountains. It's surrounded by huge expanses of the Nantahala National Forest, a lot of it purchased as soon as the Weeks Act established the national forest system in 1911. (That's why it has such an old ranger station.) Nearly all of the recreational development has centered on the Nantahala Crest, traversed by the **Appalachian Trail** from one end to the other. Downslope, the public lands roll on and on, cut by logging roads and open to those who don't mind entering trailless areas armed only with 50-year-old USGS maps.

**The Valley River Mountains** This tall ridgeline runs along the far western boundary of this area, isolating Hayesville, North Carolina, from nearby Murphy and Andrews. Here two gapless ridges run southwest, surrounding Fires Creek with two walls that never sink below 4,000 feet and rise above 5,000 feet on its east. Most access is by the good gravel Fires Creek Road, FS 340, which is motorable nearly to its end 7 miles above the point it enters the national forest. A series of hiking paths radiate uphill from Fires Creek, and are linked together by the ridgetop Rim Trail (FT 72), which forms a giant 30-mile circle around the Fires Creek watershed. Backpackers should note that this long trail links with the Chunky Gal Mountain Trail (FT 77), which heads southeast for 22 miles through some of the forest's most remote and beautiful tracts to intersect with the Appalachian Trail within the Southern Nantahala Wilderness.

**Needmore State Game Lands** Purchased by the State of North Carolina in 2004, this 4,500-acre tract protects 26 miles of the Little Tennessee River downstream (that's north) from Franklin. This section curves through valley lands, and is paralleled by NC 28 and crossed by many side roads—so access is excellent. This is just the sort of cultivated valley land that National Forest Service has always ignored, and until recently could only be admired from a distance. North Carolina's state government has stepped up to the plate not only here, but along Asheville's Sandymush River (see "The City of Asheville," Wild Places).

FOOTBRIDGE OVER THE LITTLE TENNESSEE RIVER AT NEEDMORE

**RIVERS The Little Tennessee River** The Little Tennessee is wide, smooth, and beautiful, passing through handsome farmland with wide views toward the Nantahala and Cowee Mountains. This Class I and II stream is popular with local canoeists, particularly now that 26 miles of it are state-owned downstream from Franklin. It is, however, an uncontrolled stream and subject to the vagaries of flood and drought. At this time, no raft-trip operators offer tours along it, but the Smoky Mountain Fish Camp, on the river's banks near Cowee Valley, offers canoeing, kayaking, and tubing.

**The Nantahala River** The Nantahala River flows north from Standing

Indian into Nantahala Lake; from there it flows through a penstock to a power generator, then back again into its bed to be come the famous whitewater destination, the Nantahala Gorge. This chapter, however, covers only its headwaters, above the lake—from a recreationalist's standpoint, a disappointing section. Upstream (south) from Standing Indian the river is easily reached from FS 67, and popular with fishermen, although too small to kayak. It continues to be accessible downstream from the Standing Indian campground via Park Creek Trail (FT 33), an old logging railway bed that follows its left bank for 1.4 miles before turning up Park Creek. At this point the river enters private lands and stays there until it flows into the slack water of the lake, 11 miles later. Kayakers who have done this stretch report it to be Class I–II, much choked with laurels, and with many NO TRESPASSING signs strung across it.

**The Upper Tallulah River, Georgia** The Tallulah River rises along the south-facing slopes of the Southern Nantahala Wilderness to flow southward into Georgia, leaving this book to empty into Lake Burton after 15 miles. Its uppermost 9 miles are closely paralleled by an old logging railroad that's been converted into a narrow mountain lane—a spectacular drive that gives ready access and wide views over this rough, rocky, and beautiful stream. To reach it from Franklin (a 32.8-mile drive), take US 23/441 south for 20.6 miles to Clayton, Georgia, then turn right onto US 76 and go 8 miles to a right on Persimmon Road, then go 4.2 miles to a right onto Tallulah River Road, marked by a brown recreation sign. The road enters national forest land in 0.8 mile and becomes FS 70, then turns into a well-surfaced, narrow gravel road at 1.5 miles. From here it hugs the river until its end, with many wide views and opportunities to park, including three National Forest Service campgrounds. As a kayaking stream, this section is Class V and quite dangerous, partly from logs choking the run; but as a fishing stream it can't be beat. At 4.8 miles, after the third campground (Tate Branch Campground), national forest-lands end and the gorge suddenly opens up into a wide, grassy-floored cove known as Tate City, now given over to second homes but beautifully kept nonetheless. This section of river is Class I and II, and is said to be good canoeing so long as you get out at Tate Branch Campground. At 7 miles the road crosses into the State of North Carolina, becoming FS 56; from here its mainly national forest land again, but now a gentle and forested hollow with several places to pitch an informal roadside camp. The road ends after 8.9 miles, at the boundary of the Southern Nantahala Wilderness; its bed, however, continues as a wilderness path that hugs the river for the next mile, before heading uphill to Deep Gap and the Appalachian Trail.

**WATERFALLS** **Waterfalls of Standing Indian** Two worthwhile waterfalls can be easily reached from the gravel road through the Standing Indian area. At Big Laurel Falls, 4.9 miles up from the campground, a large stream makes a 20-foot plunge over a ledge; the trail to it is a half-mile long. At 5.6 miles past the campground, Moony Falls is just off the road to the right.

**Leatherwood Falls** This waterfall is the main feature of Fires Creek Picnic Area, north of Hayesville in the Valley River Mountains. It's an impressive 20-foot cataract explored top and bottom by a nature trail; views, however, are surprisingly limited.

**RECREATION AREAS** **Standing Indian Basin** Established as a Nantahala National Forest campground in the 1950s, on the site of a logging camp from the 1940s, the Standing Indian Basin has evolved into a major outdoor destination. It encompasses the headwaters of the Nantahala River, surrounded by the 5,000-foot peaks of the Blue Ridge and the Nantahala Mountains. The highest peaks on its south are protected in the Southern Nantahala Wilderness. Lower down, the lands are open to logging and other such operations.

No doubt much of the interest in this area comes from the fact that the **Appalachian Trail** makes a three-quarters circle around the Standing Indian Campground, allowing weekenders to do a two-night backpack on the Appalachian Trail and return to their car. There are a large number of trails that loop down and up, allowing any number of different routes from a single camping space at the center. For the auto-bound hiker, this is a unique place.

The scenery is worth the attention it gets. The Nantahala River runs merrily through a narrow flat-bottomed valley, lined with meadows. The trout fishing is said to be excellent, and there are lots of places to pitch a tent. While all of the upstream slopes were logged in the early 20th century, they were selectively cut and recovered quickly to form impressive forests. The side streams are violent and lovely, and higher streams have mighty **waterfalls**. The high ridgeline of the Blue Ridge and the Nantahalas has wide views from grassy balds at **Standing Indian**, and from sheer crags at **Pickens Nose**.

A gravel road, FS 71, cuts southward to the heart of this district. From it most of the paths radiate. It is a worthy drive, passable by all but the wimpiest automobiles all the way to Pickens Nose; SUVs can continue down it into Coweeta Hydrologic Laboratory without difficulty.

**Chatuge Dam (TVA)** This earth dam is nearly 3,000 feet long and just shy of 150 feet high, an impressive structure easily visited from the Tennessee Valley Authority's (TVA) picnic and boat launch area on its eastern side. This recreation area has two sites, with different approaches, one for the dam and the other for the picnic area. To reach the dam from the intersection of US 64 and NC 69 at Hayesville, go east on US 64 for 0.6 mile to a right on Myers Chapel Road (SSR 1140), then go 0.6 mile to a left fork onto Chatuge Dam Road (SSR 1146), which ends at the dam in 1.2 miles. From the dam-side parking lot there are great views over Lake Chatuge and the large overflow structure built to handle extreme floods. To the right a paved hike/bike path leads over the 0.5-mile-long dam top itself with great views, then continues another mile along the lake side to a county park. You can see the picnic area on the other side of the overflow chute, with plenty of tree-shaded tables widely spaced along the lakeshore. To get there, go back to US 64 and turn right, then go 0.7 mile (1.3 miles from the NC 69 intersection) to a right turn onto Hinton Center Road (SSR 1148), then go 1.7 miles to a right fork into the picnic area.

**PICNIC AREAS** **Arrowwood Glade Picnic Area** Located on the road to Wayah Gap (Wayah Road, SSR 1310), this is a classic CCC picnic area, little changed since the 1930s and simply beautiful. If you miss it, there is another nice national forest picnic area in Wayah Gap (on the left as you crest out), named Wayah Crest.

**Standing Indian Picnic Area** Yes, you can picnic at Standing Indian. The picnic area, by the Nantahala River, is very beautiful and makes a great starting (or ending) place for further exploration.

**Jackrabbit Recreation Area** Jackrabbit is a large and handsome Nantahala National Forest site on the shores of Lake Chatuge, south of Hayesville. It occupies a pine-covered peninsula extending far out into the lake. Its pine-shaded picnic area has excellent views over the lake toward the Valley River Mountains.

**Fires Creek Picnic Area** Located in the Valley River Mountains north of Hayesville, North Carolina, this small national forest picnic area has tables by the stream, shaded by a deep forest. The base of Leatherwood Falls is visible from the picnic area, and a short path leads to the top. The good forest road that leads to the picnic area, Fires Creek Road, continues on to explore Forest Service lands in the Valley River Mountains, with many trailheads. To reach the picnic area from the Hayesville Town Square, go north on Anderson Street (SSR 1307) 0.4 mile; then left on Mission Dam Road (SSR 1300) for 4.5 miles; then right on Fires Creek Road for about 2 miles.

## ✷ To See

**BIG DAMMED LAKES Chatuge Lake** This large lake, built by the TVA in 1942 for wartime power production, sprawls over 11 square miles of surface, extending from Hayesville south to the Georgia town of Hiawassee (not to be confused with Lake Hiwassee near Ducktown, Tennessee). Unlike the other lakes in this area, Lake Chatuge has a broad open central area from which many arms extend deep into mountain valleys. This is a prime recreation lake, with private marinas and the excellent Jackrabbit Recreation Area. It is particularly noted for its beautiful views toward the Valley River Mountains to its north. There is a large amount of privately owned land along its 128 miles of shoreline, and many second homes.

CHATUGE LAKE AT JACKRABBIT MOUNTAIN PICNIC AREA

**Nantahala Lake** One of the most remote and beautiful hydropower lakes in the region, Nantahala was built in the 1940s by this region's local power company, Nantahala Power and Light (now Duke Power). It floods a rugged mountain valley 17 miles west of Franklin via Wayah Road/SSR 1310 (which crosses 4,200-foot Wayah Gap on the way). Nantahala Lake is T-shaped, with each of its arms 2–3 miles long and 0.25–0.5 mile wide. It's surrounded by 4,000-foot and 5,000-foot peaks on all sides, which rise straight up out of the water; the west side, and nearly all of the surrounding mountains are primitive national forestlands. This makes the lakeside scenery very wild and remote, particularly when viewed from SSR 1310, which follows it for some length.

Release water from Nantahala Lake provides the dependable, high-quality whitewater sports in the downstream **Nantahala Gorge**. Like several other hydropower sites in these mountains, Nantahala's power station is located some miles from the dam; the river water is carried to it through pipes, leaving the channel "dewatered" for some distance below the dam.

**IN THE MOUNTAINS** The Nantahala Mountains dominate the Franklin area. Running almost due north from the Blue Ridge, the Nantahalas have always been a great green barrier, with more than a dozen peaks over 5,000 feet and only three gaps that barely dip below 4,000 feet. The Blue Ridge, running east and west, merges with the southern end of the Nantahalas to form the backbone of the Southern Nantahala Wilderness, and to wall off the Standing Indian Recreation Area. There are many things worth exploring in these mountains, all of them in the Nantahala National Forest; a few of them are listed below, from south to north.

**Standing Indian—The Mountain** Well over a mile high, Standing Indian dominates the Southern Nantahala Wilderness. It's also one of the tallest peaks on the Blue Ridge, just a foot shy of 5,500 feet. Known as "the grandstand of the southern Appalachians," it has wide rocky balds with 180-degree views over the headwaters of the Nantahala River, framed by the 5,000-foot wall of the Nantahala Mountains. Reaching it is a bit of an adventure; paths up from Standing Indian Recreation Area are good, but climb a whopping 2,100 feet before reaching the top. However, there's an easier way up—a passable Forest Service road, FS 71, leads 6 miles to the Appalachian Trail at Deep Gap, reducing the hike to a short, steep 1100-foot climb. You will find FS 71 on the left, 14.4 miles west of Franklin on US 64.

**Pickens Nose** This easily reached high bald has wide and wonderful views over the much lower Georgia mountains to the south, and over the rich valley of the Little Tennessee River. A side ridge of the Nantahalas, it forms the eastern edge of the Southern Nantahala Wilderness. The path to it leaves the Standing Indian gravel road on the right, 8.7 miles from the campground, then follows a ridgeline for 0.75 mile, climbing 200 feet.

**Coweeta Hydrologic Laboratory** The National Forest Service established this forest in 1933 to perform a series of in-depth, long-term experiments that would map out the precise relationship between forest cover and stream flow—at the time a hotly controversial subject on which there was almost no data. This involved altering the forest cover in a number of small stream basins, setting up a dense network of rain gauges and ground water wells to measure water flowing into a basin, then measuring the water flowing over a weir at the bottom. These experiments have been crucial in improving land conservation practices on public and private lands throughout the South. Today's Coweeta continues these long-term experiments, using a multi-disciplinary approach that includes detailed ecological studies, yielding data capable of addressing such questions as the effects of controlled burning on climate change. This is a serious research program, very active throughout its almost 6,000 acres. While there are no recreational opportunities,

Coweeta is happy to answer questions and give tours. The main Forest Service road through the center of Coweeta, FS 83, is easily passable by SUV (though steep, rough, twisty, and ill-marked), and your author has been known to drive it with a Ford Escort; it connects with the road through Standing Indian, FS 71, at Pickens Nose.

**Wayah Bald** The 5,350-foot peak of Wayah Bald is crowned by a two-story stone tower that gives a full-circle panorama. There are more views from the nearby picnic area. This area's long-distance footpaths, the Appalachian Trail and the Bartram Trail, intersect just 500 feet north of the tower. The gravel Forest Service road to Wayah Bald (FS 69) climbs 1,100 feet in 4.5 miles, from its start in 4,200-foot Wayah Gap; on the way it passes Wilson Lick, one of the first National Forest Service ranger stations ever built, now preserved as an historic site.

Dedicated explorers might want to stop for **Shot Pouch Trail**, 0.9 mile up FS 69. It leads 0.75 mile (one way) across a grassy meadow (maintained by the U.S. Forest Service for wildlife), then past a small waterfall to a good view south and east.

**Wesser Bald** The last and the lowest of the Nantahala's major peaks, Wesser Bald (4,630 feet) may well have the best views. A viewing platform built on top of its old fire tower gives a complete circular panorama whose views down into the valleys below are unobstructed. It requires a 2-mile round trip hike on the Appalachian Trail with an 800-foot climb; the trailhead, at Tellico Gap, is a 30-mile drive from Franklin. (Directions: Go as to Wayah Gap, then continue straight ahead on paved SSR 1310 for 13.4 miles; then go right on gravel Otter Creek Road (SSR 1365) 3.9 miles to the Forest Service parking lot in Tellico Gap.)

**CULTURAL SITES** **Macon County Historical Museum** (www.maconnchistorical.org; 828-524-9758; 36 W. Main St., Franklin, NC 28734). Open Mon.–Fri., 10 AM–4 PM; Sat., 1 PM–4 PM. Free. Downtown Franklin's 1904 Pendergrass Store still has the appearance of a turn-of-the-century small rural department store, with its wood paneling and central stairs to a mezzanine balcony. However, it's now filled with historical artifacts and displays about the Franklin area, as part of a local history museum and research center run by the Macon County Historical Society.

TOWER ON WAYAH BALD

**The Franklin Gem and Mineral Museum** (www.fgmm.org; e-mail: franklingemsociety@fastmail.fm; 828-369-7831; 25 Phillips St., Franklin, NC 28734). Open May–October; Monday–Friday, noon–4 PM; Saturday, 11 AM–3 PM. Free. The old Macon County Jail in downtown Franklin housed prisoners from 1850 until 1970. In 1976 it became the site of the Franklin Gem and Mineral Museum, run by the local rockhound club, the very active Franklin Gem and Mineral Society. The building remains very much an old jail, with gem and mineral exhibits in the cells. One such exhibit contains gems and minerals from North Carolina, including a most rare and valuable piece—an 18th-century Wedgewood porcelain made from clay taken from Franklin (then a Cherokee village). Another exhibit has minerals from every state in the Union. There are displays of wire-wrapped jewelry, of fluorescent minerals, of Native American artifacts, and of fossils.

**Scottish Tartans Museum** (www.scottishtartans.org; e-mail: tartans@scottish tartans.org; 828-524-7472; 86 E. Main St., Franklin, NC 28734). Open Mon.–Sat., 10 AM–5 PM. The official North American museum of the Scottish Tartan Society—the governing society for all tartans worldwide, located in Pitlochry, Scotland—occupies a storefront in downtown Franklin. Its museum displays Scottish tartans, and relates the tartans to Scottish history and culture. It has facilities for looking up family tartans, and a really great gift shop. The Scottish Tartans Museum sponsors the annual Taste of Scotland Festival.

**PARKS AND GARDENS** **Perry's Water Gardens** (www.perryswatergarden .net; e-mail:perrywat@dnet.net. 828-524-3264; fax: 828-524-0963; 136 Gibson Aquatic Farms Rd., Franklin, NC 28734). Open April to Labor Day; Mon.–Sat., 9 AM–5 PM; Sun., 1 PM–5 PM. Free. Located in Cowee Valley, these extensive water gardens are part of a large commercial aquatic nursery, founded by the noted water lily breeder Perry D. Slocum in 1986. Here you will see every conceivable type of water plant, but most especially water lilies, lotuses, and irises. Every pond has its own population of giant goldfish, who keep the area mosquito free.

## ✷ To Do

**STILL-WATER ADVENTURES** **Great Smokey Mountain Fish Camp & Safaris** (www.fishcamp.biz; 828-369-5295; 81 Bennett Rd., Franklin, NC 28734).

COWEE VALLEY

This Little Tennessee River outfitter, just north of Franklin on NC 28 (near Cowee Valley), offers guided fishing trips, canoeing and kayaking, biking (including rentals), and a gourmet food store, in addition to its campground.

**BICYCLING** **Smoky Mountain Bicycles** (828-369-2881; smokymtnbikes.com; e-mail: info@smokymtnbikes.com; 179 Highlands Rd., Franklin, NC 28734). Located next to the Little Tennessee River Greenway, this bicycle shop rents bikes by the hour, day, or week, and sponsers road and mountain rides.

**GEM MINING** **Mason's Ruby and Sapphire Mine** (masonsmine.com; 828-369-9742; 6961 Upper Burningtown Rd., Franklin, NC 28734). Open April–October, daily, 8 PM–5 PM. This ruby mine in the Nantahala Mountains west of Franklin allows miners to dig their own dirt, and does not practice salting. This mine is different from, and unconnected with, Mason Mountain Mine (which is near Cowee Valley and salts its dirt with foreign stones).

**Sheffield Mine** (www.sheffieldmine.com; e-mail: sheffieldmine@yahoo.com; 828-369-8383; 385 Sheffield Farms Rd., Franklin, NC 28734). Open April–October, daily, 9 AM–5 PM (admissions close earlier). This long-established Cowee Valley mine—open to the public since the 1940s but in existence before then—features unsalted dirt from its own property. It is one of the few places in the world where star rubies (purple-red rubies that form a star when cabochoned) can be mined. They also sell salted dirt, clearly labeled as such; they do not salt rubies or sapphires. Their website has good information on ruby mining.

**Cherokee Ruby and Sapphire Mine** (cherokeerubymine.com; 828-349-2941; 41 Cherokee Mine Rd., Franklin, NC 28734). Open April–October. This mine, located in Cowee Valley, uses only unsalted dirt off their own property, and has produced some notable gem-quality stones since it opened in 1993.

**GOLF** **Mill Creek Country Club** (millcreekcountryclub.com; E-mail: rentals@millcreekcountryclub.com; 828-524-6458; Mill Creek Rd., Franklin, NC 28734). This 18-hole course, located on the west side of Franklin adjacent to Nantahala National Forest lands, offers very scenic play with wide mountain views.

**Mountain Harbour Golf & Yacht Club** (828-389-4111; 100 Mountain Harbour Dr., Hayesville, NC 28904). This 18-hole course in Hayesville, North Carolina, was built on rolling terrain in the early 1990s as part of a housing subdivision.

**Chatuge Shores Golf Course** (828-389-8940; 260 Golf Course Rd., Hayesville, NC 28904). This 18-hole course was built in 1972 as part of a lakeside subdivision on Lake Chatuge near Hayesville, North Carolina. It features scenic views over the lake toward the mountains.

**Franklin Golf Course** (828-524-2288; 255 First Fairway Dr., Franklin, NC 28734). This nine-hole course was built in 1929 as part of a subdivision just south of downtown Franklin. It offers convenient in-town play.

**Holly Springs Golf Course** (828-369-8711; 115 Holly Springs Golf Village, Franklin, NC 28734). This nine-hole golf course near Franklin was built in 1976 as part of a housing subdivision.

## ✷ Lodging

**BED & BREAKFAST INNS** ✐ **Buttonwood Inn** (buttonwoodbb.com; 828-369-8985; 50 Admiral Dr., Franklin, NC 28734). This historic (1920s) board-and-batten lodge sits between the fifth and seventh greens of Franklin's golf course. It has a fire-engine red exterior; its three attractive, full-size rooms are en suite. A full breakfast is included.

**Blaine House Bed & Breakfast** (www.blainehouse.com; 828-524-3633; 661 Harrison Ave., Franklin, NC 28734). This 1910 cottage sits on lightly traveled NC 28 on the north end of Franklin. With elaborate gables and dormers, its entrances framed with neoclassical columns and pediments, it has a lot of personality. Inside, it's carefully decorated with family antiques and heirlooms. Two cozy rooms are decorated in a simple, country style with quilts on the beds; the two large suites, with separate sitting areas, are more formally decorated. Gourmet breakfasts are served in a bright and airy sunroom.

## ✷ Where to Eat

**EATING OUT The Frog & Owl Kitchen** (frogandowl.com; e-mail: scott@frogandowl.com; 828-349-4112; 46 E. Main St., Franklin, NC 28734). Open Mon.–Sat., 11 AM–3 PM. This downtown Franklin storefront café serves American fusion cuisine for the casual lunch crowd. It's a rare small-town treat, when you are looking for a lunch that's light and sophisticated. Wine is available.

**Fat Buddies Ribs and BBQ** (www.fatbuddiesribsandbbq.com; 828-349-4743; 311 Westgate Plaza, Franklin, NC 28734). Open Mon.–Sat., 11 AM–2:30 PM, and 5 PM–9 PM. You will find this authentic pit barbeque in a suburban shopping plaza off the freeway portion of US 64 west. Meats are slow cooked over a blend of hardwoods, and basted with their own recipe of sauce. They smoke pork, beef, chicken, and baby back ribs, and serve it as a sandwich with fries, or as a platter with two sides. They also have a good choice of well-thought-out salads for the barbeque impaired, as well as Brunswick stew and black-eye pea stew. They make four different barbeque sauces and five salad dressings, all from their own recipes.

## ✷ Entertainment

### *Franklin*

**Pickin' on the Square** (828-349-1212). There's free music and dancing every Saturday night at the gazebo on the square in downtown Franklin, in front of the County Courthouse. It starts with an open mike at 7 pm, with the main band—either bluegrass or gospel—coming on at 8 pm.

**The Licklog Players** (www.licklogplayers.org; 877-691-9906, 828-389-8632; 301 Church St., P.O. Box 223, Hayesville, NC 28904). Organized in 1977, the Licklog Players are named for the notched log used to hold salt for grazing livestock (and a common place-name in the mountains). They are a community theater, presenting amateur productions from Hayesville's Peacock Playhouse.

## ✷ Selective Shopping

### *Franklin*

Franklin is an important market center for its surrounding region, and so takes on more of the look of a contemporary southern town than many of its peers in the mountains. Its three-block downtown is definitely worth a stroll, with gift, antique, and gem shops as well as two museums and a nice town square. Beyond that, a large number of shops string out for 2–3 miles along all of the main highway: at the exits along US 441 Bypass, US 441 south of town (the biggest concentration), US Bus 441 north and south of downtown, and US 64 east and west of downtown.

**Michael M. Rogers Gallery** (sharethebeauty.com; 828-524-6709; 1511 Highlands Rd., Franklin, NC, 28734). This well-known watercolor artist lives in Franklin and maintains a gallery, formerly downtown now in a new location 3 miles down the road. He paints highly detailed and accurate scenes of nature in the Blue Ridge, the Nantahalas, and the Smokies, showing how weather highlights seasonal changes. His website is worth a visit.

**FROG Quarters** (littletennessee.org /frogquarters; e-mail: frogquarters@ frontier.com; 828-369-8488; fax: 828-349-4119; 523 East Main St., Franklin, NC, 28734). Headquarters of Franklin's Friends of the Greenway, this offers visitor information, a coffeeshop, and a gift shop featuring local crafters.

*Otto*

**Spring Ridge Creamery** (828-369-2958; inthesmokymountains.com /springridgecreamery; e-mail: jmmooresr@msn.com; 11856 Georgia Hwy. [US 441 South]—2 miles north of Dillard, Georgia—Otto, NC 28763). The small dairy selling its fresh products by the highway—this once-common sight has all but disappeared from the South. So it's a surprise to see exactly that, sitting by US 441 north of the state line (about 10 miles south of Franklin). The Spring Ridge Dairy's Jersey cows graze in the meadows beside their shop. They stock the products of their dairy: milk, butter, and ice cream. Ice cream! Real ice cream made from cream. You may have noticed that all the ice cream shops and restaurants throughout the mountains stock the same brand of ice cream, one manufactured by a giant regional dairy using the latest technology from Modern Food Science. Stop by Spring Ridge and get the real stuff.

COWEE VALLEY

*Cowee Valley*

**Rickman's General Store** (828-524-2223; 259 Cowee Creek Rd, Franklin, NC 28734). This traditional general store has stood at the entrance to Cowee Valley, north of Franklin off NC 28, since time out of mind. It beckons to visitors with its doorside collection of flags, stuffed bear, and whatnot; inside you will find gift items as well as the stock of a functioning general store.

**Cowee Creek Pottery** (828-524-3324; 20 West Mills Rd., Franklin, NC 28734). Located a few blocks from Rickman's General Store, the former West Mills General Store is now a gallery of handmade pottery, made in a studio in the back of the old store.

## ✱ Special Events

**SUMMER Taste of Scotland Festival** (828-524-7472). Mid-June. Scottish food and Scottish music—what could be better? In this downtown Franklin festival people eat their haggis with a bagpipe accompaniment, and call it good. There's dancing, sheep dog demonstrations, and lots of Scottish stuff to buy at this annual event, sponsored by the Scottish Tartan Museum.

**Fourth of July Celebration** The Chamber of Commerce sponsors Franklin's annual Independence Day parade at the Macon County Recreation Park. Athletic competitions include a rubber ducky derby, a horseshoe tourney, a watermelon roll, a plunger toss, cow pattie bingo, and—for the under five set—a tricycle race. There's plenty of food, and fireworks begin at dark.

**Macon County Gemboree** Last week in July. This annual rock show brings in gem and mineral dealers from all over, as well as custom jewelers. Sponsored by the Gem & Mineral Society of Franklin, its been running every year since 1965.

**Folkmoot** (828-452-2997). Last week in July. This major gathering of international folk dancing troupes, headquartered out of Waynesville, uses Franklin as one of its venues.

**Gem Capital Auto Club Antique Auto Show** (828-369-0557). Labor Day weekend. This annual auto show, held at the Macon County fairgrounds, features a wide assortment of antique automobiles and trucks.

**AUTUMN Macon County Fair** Free Mid-September. This classic county fair features livestock shows and sales, agriculture displays, food, crafts, and entertainment.

**Pumpkin Fest** Last Saturday in October. This downtown Franklin street fair has food, entertainment, crafts, games, a costume parade and contest, a pumpkin cook-off, a pumpkin rolling contest, and trick-or-treating for kids.

# THE NORTHERN UNICOIS: ROBBINSVILLE & TELLICO PLAINS

South of the Great Smoky Mountains National Park, the Little Tennessee River cuts a deep gorge through the mountains, marking the end of the Smokies. The mountain range picks up again on the other side of the gorge, however, under a new name—the Unicoi Mountains. As with the Smokies to the north, the Unicois mark the line between North Carolina and Tennessee, and between the Nantahala and the Cherokee National Forests. The eastern side of the mountains, in North Carolina, looks to the tiny county seat of Robbinsville for shopping and services. The western side, in Tennessee, relies on the remote village of Tellico Plains.

Between these two small towns lies 40 miles of nearly unpopulated forestland. These huge, empty stretches of public land include 35,000 acres of congressionally declared wilderness, and another 20,000 acres of roadless and primitive areas—a wonderful, and little-visited, recreational opportunity. Here you will find huge waterfalls, wide mountaintop meadows, thousands of acres of virgin and old-growth forest, and incredible views from high crags. You will also find long lakes that send thin arms of still water deep into this wilderness, impounded behind four hydropower dams.

Until recently these two sides of the mountain could have been on different continents for all the interaction between them. There wasn't even a road between them until 1931—and that highway, US 129, has never been modernized. However, in 1997 the stunning recreational parkway known as the **Cherohala Skyway** finally opened after 20 years of construction. The Cherohala flies high above the valleys in broad sweeps along the crest of the Unicois, with constantly changing panoramas along its 25-mile length. It now links Robbinsville directly with Tellico Plains, bringing these two areas very close together and opening their huge wilderness to the outside.

**GUIDANCE—TOWNS AND COUNTRYSIDE** **Graham County Travel and Tourism Authority** (www.grahamcountytravel.com; 800-470-3790, 828-479-3790; 12 N. Main St., Robbinsville, NC 28771). Located in central Robbinsville, the Travel and Tourism Commission is the county's official tourism promoter. They have a detailed website with many accommodations listed.

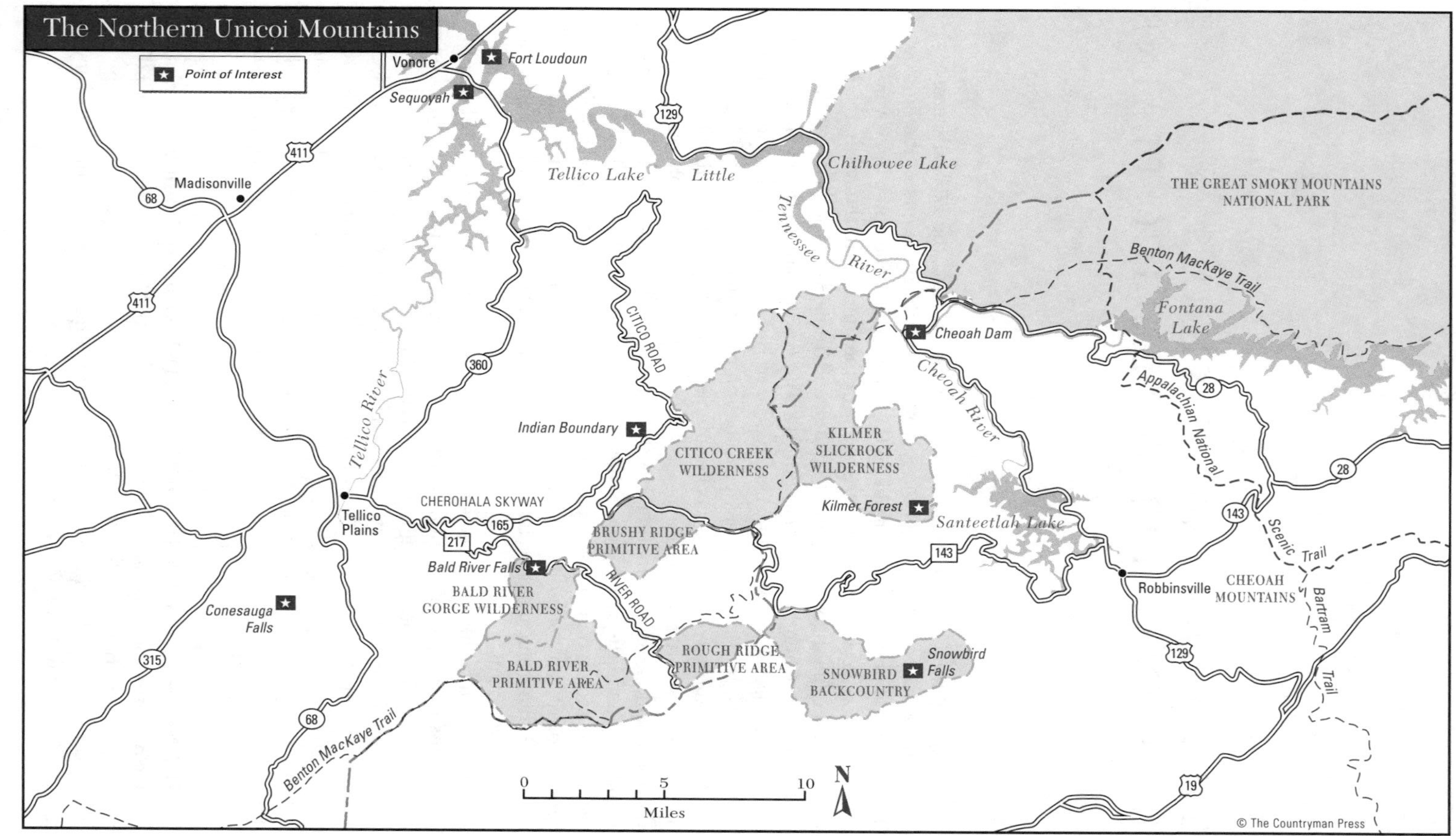
The Northern Unicoi Mountains
Point of Interest
Vonore
Fort Loudoun
Sequoyah
Madisonville
Tellico Lake
Little
Tennessee River
Chilhowee Lake
THE GREAT SMOKY MOUNTAINS NATIONAL PARK
Benton MacKaye Trail
Fontana Lake
Cheoah Dam
Cheoah River
Appalachian National Scenic Trail
Bartram Trail
CITICO ROAD
Tellico River
Indian Boundary
CITICO CREEK WILDERNESS
KILMER SLICKROCK WILDERNESS
Kilmer Forest
Santeetlah Lake
Tellico Plains
CHEROHALA SKYWAY
BRUSHY RIDGE PRIMITIVE AREA
Bald River Falls
BALD RIVER GORGE WILDERNESS
RIVER ROAD
ROUGH RIDGE PRIMITIVE AREA
BALD RIVER PRIMITIVE AREA
SNOWBIRD BACKCOUNTRY
Snowbird Falls
Robbinsville
CHEOAH MOUNTAINS
Conesauga Falls
Benton MacKaye Trail
411
68
129
360
165
217
143
28
315
19
0
5
10
Miles
N
© The Countryman Press

♿ **Cherohala Skyway Visitors Center** (cherohala.org/visitorcenter; 800-245-5428, 423-253-8010; 225 Cherohala Skyway, Tellico Plains, TN 37385). Open daily, 9 AM–5 PM. This large new structure, operated by the Monroe County Department of Tourism, sits at the beginning of the Cherohala Skyway in the town of Tellico Plains. It is immediately adjacent to the Charles Hall Museum.

**Tennessee Overhill Heritage Association** (www.tennesseeoverhill.com; e-mail: info@tennesseeoverhill.com; 877-510-5765, 423-263-7232; P.O. Box 143, L&N Depot, Etowah, TN 37331). This private not-for-profit promotes tourism development in the southern Tennessee Mountains.

**GUIDANCE—PARKS AND FORESTS** ♿ **Nantahala National Forest, Cheoah Ranger District** (828-479-6431; fax: 828-479-6784; Route 1, Box 16-A, Robbinsville, NC 28771). The ranger station for the eastern side of the Unicoi Mountains, including all national forest land around Robbinsville, is located on NC 143 northwest of Robbinsville, near Santeetlah Lake. This station is on the site of an historic CCC camp, and has some interesting exhibits and a nature trail on the subject.

♿ **Cherokee National Forest, Tellico Plains Ranger Station** (www.fs.fed.us/r8/cherokee; e-mail: mailroom_r8_cherokee@fs.fed.us; e-mail: mailroom_r8_cherokee @fs.fed.us; 423-253-8400; 250 Ranger Station Rd., Tellico Plains, TN 37385). This ranger station, set in a lovely little cove off the Tellico River, has an information desk and a bookstore, with a staff that is eager to answer your questions. It's also a fascinating and beautiful historic site in its own right.

THE CHEROHALA SKYWAY IN NORTH CAROLINA

**GUIDANCE—WEBSITES** **Welcome to Graham County** (main.nc.us/graham) This independent website by a local enthusiast is a cornucopia of information and photographs of this remote, mountainous place.

**GETTING THERE** **By Car** The Tennessee area around Tellico Plains is easily reached from I-75; take the TN 68 exit, and follow TN 68 east to the town. At anytime other than winter, this is the best approach to Robbinsville from the west as well, following the Cherohala Skyway eastward from Tellico Plains. From any other direction (and from the west in winter), approach Robbinsville from US 129 via US 19.

**By Air** Knoxville and Chattanooga are the two closest airports.

**By Bus or Train** There is no bus or train service to this area.

**MEDICAL EMERGENCIES** **Medical Emergencies in Tennessee: Woods Memorial Hospital, Etowah** (www.woodshospital.org; e-mail: woods@woodshospital.org; 423-263-3600; 886 Hwy. 411 N., Etowah, TN 37331). Etowah's hospital is a dozen miles from Tellico Plains, making it the closest hospital for the Tennessee side of this chapter.

**Medical Emergencies in North Carolina: Murphy Medical Center** (www.murphymedical.org; 828-837-8161; 4130 US Hwy. 64 E., Murphy, NC 28906). There is no hospital in Robbinsville or Graham County, North Carolina. A call to 911 will bring the Robbinsville Rescue Squad. The nearest hospital is in Murphy, 36 miles away via US 129 and US 19 south.

## ✷ Exploring the Area

The great twisted massif of the Unicoi Mountains covers almost the entire center area of this chapter, with the state line running down its spine. You have to look at the east and west edges of this region for human settlement. On the east, the tiny county seat of Robbinsville, North Carolina, occupies the center of a good-sized valley. On the west, Tellico Plains, Tennessee, straddles the lower end of a river gorge. These are linked by the Cherohala Skyway, one of the great scenic drives of the Blue Ridge, curving for miles along the top of a mile-high ridgeline. A second scenic drive explores the gorge of the Tellico River along a paved recreation road, from Tellico Plains almost to its headwaters. Footpaths explore the virgin forests of Joyce Kilmer, and the 35,000 acres of the Citico and Kilmer-Slickrock Wildernesses. As you might expect, waterfalls are plentiful on both sides of the state line.

Two long-distance paths traverse this area. The **Benton MacKaye Trail** follows the crest of the Unicois through the middle of this region. On the far eastern edge, the **Appalachian Trail** explores the **Cheoah Mountains**, with famously spectacular views from 5,062-foot Cheoah Bald.

**EXPLORING BY CAR** **The Cherohala Skyway** Total length: 57.6 miles, on paved state highways.

*Leg #1* (*17.9 miles*): Start on NC 143 at Stecoah Gap (off NC 28 between Fontana and Bryson City). Take NC 143 west to the start of the Cherohala Skyway.

*Leg #2 (39.7 miles)*: Continue on NC 143 uphill, now known as the Cherohala Skyway; however, as the highway crosses into Tennessee its designation changes to TN 165. End at the village of Tellico Plains. No services available.

This drive enters the area as would a traveler from the Great Smoky Mountains, crossing the **Cheoah Mountains** at Stecoah Gap. Here the **Appalachian Trail** crosses the highway as it follows the crest of the Cheoahs. The parking lot gives views back toward the Smokies, while the road ahead gives a broad view over Robbinsville toward the Unicoi Mountains—our destination, 35 miles away. The highway drops into **Robbinsville**, using a nondescript bypass to go around it; the three-block drive downtown is worthwhile. At **Santeetlah Lake**, NC 143 turns off the main highway to follow the south side of the lake, passing the Forest Service headquarters and some attractive views over pastoral scenery. On this stretch the state highway is a twisting, intimate lane through remote countryside.

The start of the **Cherohala Skyway** is obvious, not only because of its sign, but also because of NC 143's sudden return to full modern width and shoulders. Right at the start you'll find a first-rate view, with a 180-degree panorama northward toward the **Joyce Kilmer-Slickrock Wilderness**. With a design patterned after the Blue Ridge Parkway, the next 26 miles feature sweeping and ever-changing views. The Cherohala slabs and switches up a major side ridge of the Unicois, reaches the top, then runs from gap to gap along the crest of the Unicois. After 9.2 miles of steady climbing you'll reach 5,200 feet in elevation, with two scenic sites nearby. The first, on your right, is a trailhead for an easy walk of up to 3 miles (round-trip) to mile-high meadows on **Huckleberry Knob**, covered in wildflowers and berries. A short distance later on your left is a parking lot for trails to the top of **Hooper Bald**, with cliff views over the parkway and eastward toward the Smoky Mountains. You'll reach the **Unicoi Mountains** at 11.6 miles, then turn north to follow the high ridge that carries the state line. At 14.2 miles you will reach Mud Gap and intersect with this region's second long-distance footpath, **The Benton MacKaye Trail**, following the originally planned route of the Appalachian Trail. At 17.6 miles the parkway swerves west again and enters Tennessee for good, becoming TN 165. At this point the Benton MacKaye Trail continues north along the Unicoi

TELLICO RIVER SCENIC DRIVE

SLICKROCK CREEK, IN THE KILMER-SLICKROCK WILDERNESS

Mountains, exploring the highest points of the **Citico and Kilmer-Slickrock Wildernesses**. From here the parkway follows **Sassafras Ridge** slowly downward. At 19.1 miles, a parking lot on your right is the trailhead for lovely **Falls Creek Falls**.

At the bottom of the mountain a right turn will take you to **Indian Boundary Lake** as well as trailheads for Citico Creek Wilderness. Our route, however, continues left on TN 165 for a long, easy 12-mile ramble. The first 9 miles wander through the Unicoi foothills, an easy forest drive. Then the parkway meets the Tellico River, with **Tellico River Road** heading upstream to the left. TN 165 now follows the river closely for 3 miles, along the bottom of its gorge, ending at the attractive village of **Tellico Plains**, a fine little museum and visitors center marking its western end.

OLD RANGER'S CABIN IN THE FORESTS SOUTH OF KILMER-SLICKROCK

**Tellico River Road (FS 210)** Total length: 22.9 miles (one way). From Tellico Plains, take TN 165 (the Cherohala Skyway) east for 4.8 miles to a right on paved Tellico River Road (FS 210). Continue on FS 210 for 18.1 miles (which becomes a good gravel road), to the end of its motorable section at the Tennessee–North Carolina state line. Return the way you came.

This route follows a classic **Shay railroad grade** (see "Townsend, Cades Cove, and the Northwest Quadrant,"

*Exploring the Area*) from the pretty little village of **Tellico Plains**, Tennessee, to the crest of the Unicoi Mountains at the North Carolina state line. Along the way you will climb from 860 feet above sea level to 2,580 feet, a vertical distance of 0.33 mile, and you'll get to see the Tellico River change from a wide river in a hot valley, to a river roaring over waterfalls in a deep gorge, to a creek in a high cove forest.

The Baldwin Lumber Company built this road in 1905 in order to open up the Upper Tellico River to clear-cut logging, completing this by 1933 and selling the devastated land to the U.S. Forest Service. It's a typical logging railbed, constructed specifically for the powerful little logging steam engines called Shay locomotives, with characteristic multiple sharp curves, grades up to 6 percent, and many river crossings. The forests have long since recovered, particularly near the river, and present a fine mixture of mature trees. The road follows the river very closely along its entire length, with many fine views.

From Tellico Plains this route follows the **Cherohala Skyway** for its first few miles, passing the Telliqhah Preserve's decorative covered bridge and Saturday **Traders Row Marketplace** at 1.3 miles. When the parkway turns left to climb out of the gorge, this route continues on the old rail bed along the river, now a paved Forest Service recreation road. Views are wide across the river to your right as you pass the turnoff (to your left, 0.4 miles after the turnoff) to the **historic CCC complex** that holds the Cherokee National Forest ranger station and information desk. You cross the river at 5.2 miles from the turnoff, and pick up the lower boundary of the **Bald River Gorge Wilderness** on your right. At 6.2 miles giant **Bald River Falls** are hard on your right, as the road arches over them on a high bridge; parking is ahead on your left. As you walk back to view the waterfall you'll pass a trailhead on your left for the Bald River Trail (FT 88) that climbs to the top of the waterfall, then follows the Bald River Gorge through the wilderness

CITICO CREEK, IN THE CITICO CREEK WILDERNESS

area (4.2 miles one way). Back at the parking lot, look down toward **Baby Falls** on the Tellico River, a 14-foot undercut waterfall that kayakers love. In fact, this is a good place to watch for **kayakers**, as the Tellico at high water is one of the finest whitewater streams in the area. This is the visual high point of this drive, and if you are lacking for time, a good place to turn around.

Counting mileage from Bald River Falls, you'll cross the river again at 0.9 mile, then pass gravel road FS 217 (North River Road) on your right, a pleasant forest drive that leads 11.8 miles to the Cherohala Skyway at its **Stratton Ridge Picnic Area** on the crest of the Unicois. This makes for a good way to prolong the drive and turn it into a loop with high mountain views (although the final 2 miles climb very steeply). Our route, however, continues straight on FS 210. You cross the river again at 7.4 miles after Bald River Falls. At 7.6 miles on your right, gravel FS 126 (Bald River Road) leads to the upper trailhead for the Bald River Trail (6.3 miles), then to the trail to the **Waucheesi Mountain Lookout** (8.1 miles), and finally to TN 68 south of Tellico Plains (14.1 miles). At 8.5 miles you pass a bridge on your left that leads to the Pheasant Fields Fish Hatchery, run by the National Forest Service and worth a stop. The **Benton MacKaye Trail** crosses here on a long meander down from the Unicoi ridgeline to explore these beautiful forests.

The road now turns into a good gravel surface, and reaches the state line in 3.3 miles. Across the state line is North Carolina's Nantahala Forest, and an 8,000-acre tract known as the Upper Tellico. You are not on the crest of the Unicois here, but rather on the edge of a high perched valley, and these 8,000 acres serve as the Tellico's headwaters. Heavily logged as private lands until 1969, it has already become popular with off-road vehicle (ORV) drivers when the Forest Service acquired it in 1980. They continued to manage it for for off-roaders for 29 years, but closed it permanently in 2009.

**EXPLORING ON FOOT** **A Slickrock Wilderness Walk** Slickrock's isolation adds to its charm. Cut off from the rest of the world when Calderwood Lake flooded its entrance in 1928, Slickrock Creek has always been a difficult area to penetrate. Although a national forest wilderness area since 1975, the Forest Service has long had the policy of doing nothing to improve its network of rough hunters' paths beyond assigning them numbers and showing them on a map. Even a level hike is tiring and difficult, because of the rough trail. It's incredibly scenic, though, and the very roughness makes the track more memorable.

This walk takes the only reasonably level path into Slickrock, starting at US 129 at the **Cheoah Dam**. From the south side of the highway bridge, a Forest Service trail heads west along the steep slopes above Calderwood Lake, hugging the top of the Little Tennessee River's drowned gorge. After a half-mile the trail climbs to an intersection; continue straight. When the trail starts to fall it is turning the bend to enter the Slickrock Creek basin; a sign marks the wilderness boundary. From here the trail follows the old lumber railroad along the creek, very rough from long abandonment, and a mere ledge in some places. Nevertheless, the forests are handsome and the stream is very beautiful. At 2.6 miles from the trailhead the path reaches **Lower Falls**, an attractive 20-foot waterfall with a high volume. This is a good destination for a 5-mile return trip. However, the creek-side trail continues another 6 miles past a gorge and two more waterfalls. The many side trails lead high into the Unicoi Mountains, over into **Joyce Kilmer Forest** or the **Citico Wilderness**.

**LONG-DISTANCE PATHS** **The Appalachian Trail** The Appalachian Trail (AT) runs along the northern edge of this chapter's area, following the high barrier ridge that divides this chapter from the previous one. It starts in the Nantahala Gorge at 1,700 feet, passes through the Nantahala Outdoor Center, then starts a long, hard slog up Cheoah Mountain, a 6.7-mile climb that reaches 5,062 feet, with wide views over mountaintop meadows. Here the Bartram Trail meets the AT for its second and last time, forming a 50-mile-long backpacking loop. From here the AT drops northeastward down the mountain's shoulder for 3.6 miles to 3,200-foot Stecoah Gap, a good trailhead for exploring Cheoah Mountain on a day hike. From here the trail follows a long, low ridgeline with unusually little elevation change, staying at about 3,800 feet to reach another trailhead at Yellow Creek Road (SR 1242), then continues northward to Fontana Village—a 12.3-mile stretch that may possibly be the least traveled section in North Carolina.

**The Bartram Trail** The northernmost 5.4 miles of the Bartram Trail climb out of the Nantahala Gorge (see "Bryson City and the Southwest Quadrant," Villages) to meet the Appalachian Trail just below the wide meadow views of Cheoah Bald, climbing nearly 3,000 feet. Its southern trailhead, within the Nantahala Gorge, is opposite the old road known as "The Winding Stairs," now a bicycle path. From here it's the only trail that lets you climb the gorge wall, then follows a mountain creek to its source, and spends its last mile along the top of a 4,800-foot ridge. Its northern terminus is only 0.25 mile, and a 200-foot climb, to Cheoah Bald, taking the Appalachian Trail to the right. The nearest trailhead is Stecoah Gap, 3.6 miles to the left (west) along the Appalachian Trail, and a 1,800-foot drop.

**The Benton MacKaye Trail** The Benton MacKaye Trail traverses this chapter's area for 53 miles, for the most part following the crest of the Unicoi Mountains. To the south, a trailhead on TN 68 (16 miles north of Ducktown, Tennessee), starts a long ridgeline climb from 1,800 feet, reaching only 3,600 feet after 8.3 miles; from here, the wide views from Waucheesee Knob are 2 miles ahead (including a half-mile up a side path). At 11.1 miles is the next trailhead, North Carolina's SSR 1327 (Shuler Creek Road, FS 50), motorable last time I checked; consult a detailed map for directions. The ridgewalk continues for another 5.5 miles, generally staying around 3,600 feet, and finally breaking the 4,000-foot mark at Rocky Top. (The Rocky Top is, of course, found elsewhere (see "North of Asheville: The Bald Mountains," To See).

Here the trail turns downhill for a 14.5-mile run through the forests of the Upper Tellico River, dropping down to the Bald River's headwaters, then climbing a small side ridge, then dropping even farther to the **Tellico River Road**, with a trailhead at the Pheasant Fields Fish Hatchery at 2,000 feet in elevation. Climbing up from this trailhead it passes the 4,000-foot elevation mark in only 4.6 miles, and will stay above 4,000 feet for the next 14 miles. It hits the 5,000-foot mark at the wide views from mountaintop meadows at Whigg Meadows (7.6 miles from the trailhead)—the high point of the entire Benton MacKaye Trail. It reaches the **Cherohala Skyway** at Mud Gap in 1.3 more miles, making for a good day hike back from the parkway to Whigg Meadows. It intersects the parkway a second time near Stratton Ridge Picnic Area, and for a third time at Unicoi Crest Picnic Area.

Here the trail follows the Unicoi Crest northward as the Cherohala turns away. This is the border between the Citico and the Kilmer-Slickrock Wildernesses, as well as the state line; the Benton Mackaye stays either within the Citico Wilderness or on the ridge crest for the next 11.3 miles. At Farr Gap (there may be a motorable trailhead here; enquire at the ranger station) the trail turns eastward off the ridgeline to descend to the **Kilmer-Slickrock Wilderness**, following Little Slickrock and Slickrock Creeks before turning away. It reaches the paved road at a trailhead parking area shared with the **Slickrock Creek Trail**.

## ✷ Villages

**Robbinsville** The county seat of Graham County, North Carolina, Robbinsville is a tiny (2000 pop: 747), down-at-the-heels town where life centers on the hardwood lumber mill and the small string of new franchise restaurants along the US 129 bypass. It's Main Street, one block off US 129, has a one-block downtown next to the handsome 1942 Courthouse, clad in local stone. Downtown Robbinsville was the location for the small-town shots for the 1994 movie ***Nell*** (staring Jodie Foster and Liam Neeson), playing itself; interiors depicting local stores (including 80-year-old Sniders Department Store, the local pool hall, and the local café), were shot in the actual businesses, sometimes with the employees as extras.

**Tellico Plains** This small town sits at the feet of the Unicoi Mountains in Tennessee, tucked among low ridges and drained by the Tellico River. Farther west the mountains yield to flat lands, but here they remain in control. For many years Tellico Plains was a small industrial town, appealing to businesses that needed to reach mountain resources with a railroad. In the last few decades, tourism has grown as industry retreated, as visitors learn about the huge tracts of Cherokee National Forest wilderness and recreation lands that extend for dozens of miles from the town center. Today's Tellico Plains has a small, handsome downtown with antique and art galleries, as well as some good places to eat and stay. The beautiful Cherohala Skyway starts (or ends) here on its long run along the Unicoi Crest, and the county is anchoring this scenic highway with a visitors center and museum. A colony of fine artists and crafters has been growing in the surrounding valleys, with the downtown Tellico Arts Center putting the spotlight on their work.

## ✷ Wild Places

**THE GREAT FORESTS** The Northern Unicoi Mountains are the only range in the southern Appalachians that can match the Great Smoky Mountains for twisted, knotted ruggedness. This is not surprising; like the Great Balsam Mountains far to the east, the Unicois are a southward extension of the Smokies, separated from them by the water gap of the Tennessee River. This area is covered in dense forests that are preserved in a series of wilderness and primitive areas, accessible by hiking trail and the remarkable Cherohala Skyway. Here the long-distance Benton MacKaye Trail follows the high ridge through the adjacent Citico Wilderness and Kilmer-Slickrock Wilderness. On the eastern, North Carolina side sits the scenic Snowbird Creek Area as well as the virgin Joyce Kilmer Memorial Forest. On the western, Tennessee side you'll find the Upper Tellico River, with several primitive areas and the Bald River Gorge Wilderness.

**Joyce Kilmer Memorial Forest** In the 1930s the National Forest Service decided to dedicate a large, virgin forest to the poet Joyce Kilmer, author of "Trees," who was killed in World War I. They chose the forests of Little Santeetlah

Creek, northwest of Robbinsville, calling them "some of the finest original growth in the Appalachians." Today this watershed contains thousands of acres of never-cut old-growth forest, with trees reaching 20 feet in diameter. A 2-mile loop trail leads through some of the most dramatic forest, climaxing in a grove of champion trees that include 165-foot tall tulip trees (once known as "yellow poplars"). A separate trail, Naked Ground Trail (NFT 55), follows the valley uphill to its end, reaching the Unicoi ridgeline in 5 miles after a 2,700-foot climb; at the crest, the path to the right leads another 2 miles to stunning views from Hangover Lead. The original "Memorial Forest" has now become part of the much larger Kilmer-Slickrock Wilderness, which extends into Tennessee and combines with the Citico Creek Wilderness to protect 33,600 acres. With all this wilderness surrounding it, the original Joyce Kilmer Memorial Forest remains one of the best places to see the forests of the Appalachians as they appeared to Cherokee hunters and European settlers.

**Kilmer-Slickrock Wilderness** This 17,400-acre wilderness, created in 1975, combined the Joyce Kilmer Memorial Forest with the adjacent stream basin drained by Slickrock Creek. The Slickrock Creek basin had been partially logged in the mid-1920s, but the 1928 impoundment of Calderwood Lake had drowned the loggers' railroad; after that, logging was abandoned, the land visited only by hunters and fishers. Today the Slickrock trails remain unimproved, and the Slickrock experience remains one of deep and difficult backcountry. Trails interconnect between Slickrock, Kilmer, and the adjacent Citico Creek Wilderness, creating a large number of possible ridge and valley trips that combine old-growth forests with waterfalls and mountaintop meadows.

**The Snowbird Creek Forests** Snowbird Creek drains the uppermost heights of the Cherohala Skyway, west of Robbinsville in the Unicoi Mountains. The Nantahala National Forest owns all of the Snowbird drainage, and protects it as a backcountry primitive area. A network of good-quality Forest Service trails follow the main creek (actually a tumultuous little river), its major side creek, and several nearby ridgelines. A 3-mile walk into the area brings you to a whole series of lovely

SASSAFRAS FALLS ON SNOWBIRD CREEK

waterfalls, including the beautiful Sassafras Falls on NFT 65 along Sassafras Creek. (Directions: Follow NC 143 west of Robbinsville toward the Cherohala Skyway for 5.4 miles; turn left on Snowbird River Road, SSR 1115, and go 3.1 miles; turn left on SSR 1120 to its end at a Forest Service parking lot.)

**The Cheoah Mountains** The Cheoah Mountains form an east-west barrier between Robbinsville and the Great Smoky Mountains, with peaks as high as 5,000 feet and gaps above 3,000 feet. The Appalachian Trail runs along its crest, after first climbing 3,300 feet in elevation from the bottom of the Nantahala Gorge (see "Bryson City and the Southwest Quadrant," Wild Places). The slopes of the Cheoahs have been subjected to logging by the Nantahala National Forest over the years, so that the Appalachian Trail remains the prime recreational resource of these mountains. It is most easily reached from NC 143 as it crosses the Cheoahs at Stecoah Gap, between Robbinsville and Fontana. A 3.6-mile hike eastward (with 1,800 feet of climbing) leads to Cheoah Bald with a famous panoramic view.

**Citico Creek Wilderness** Created in 1984, this 16,200-acre wilderness protects the western slopes of the Unicoi Mountains as they extend into Tennessee. The eastern slopes had already been protected by the 1936 Joyce Kilmer Memorial Forest and the 1975 Kilmer-Slickrock Wilderness; together, these areas protect 33,600 contiguous acres of mountain wilderness, the second largest area in the East. Citico is noted for its deep stream valleys and violent little rivers, most with extraordinarily clean water. Its lower slopes were extensively and destructively logged in the 1920s, but a huge forest fire in 1926 destroyed the logging operation so thoroughly that it was abandoned, leaving the upper slopes untouched. Today's hiking trails follow the old lumber trams up the streams, past rapids and waterfalls, to enter the old-growth forest, and eventually reach the crest of the Unicois. The Cherohala Skyway follows a side ridge along the southern edge of the wilderness, creating additional trailheads into the Citico's 57-mile trail system. If you have time for only a brief taste of this large area, take the short Fall Creek Falls Trail from the Skyway's Rattlesnake Rock parking lot.

**The Bald River Gorge Wilderness and the Forests of the Tellico River** The upper reaches of the Tellico River are almost entirely owned and controlled by the National Forest Service, mostly within Tennessee's Cherokee National Forest and easily reached from Tellico Springs. A paved scenic road, the Tellico River Road (FS 210), runs along the river's bank, frequently flanked by gray cliffs as the Tellico digs its way deep into a gorge. At one point, FS 210 passes immediately by a huge waterfall, 100 feet tall and carrying a huge volume of water. This is Bald Creek Falls, and behind it is the 3,700-acre Bald Creek Gorge Wilderness. Here you'll find a 4.3-mile trail that follows the gorge bottom upstream, gaining 500 feet in elevation before it reaches Bald Creek Road (FS 216), a good gravel road that forms the wilderness's upper boundary. Arrange a car shuttle, and enjoy the many views of rapids and waterfalls on a downhill walk. The nearby Waucheesi Mountain Tower gives good views over the gorge.

The Bald River Gorge makes up only a third of the protected forests of the Tellico. Another 10,000 acres upstream from the Bald Creek Gorge Wilderness have received administrative protection as a series of **primitive areas** and provide some more remote opportunities for hiking, camping, and fishing. The **Benton MacKaye Trail** runs along through these protected areas, first following the Unicoi Mountain ridge, then descends to the remote upper reaches of the Bald River before climbing back up to the crest of the Unicois.

**RIVERS** **The Tellico River** One of the most beautiful streams in this book's area, the upper Tellico River is paralleled by FS 210 and lined with picnic and camping areas. It is noted for its fly-fishing, as well as for its many swimming holes. Water levels are unregulated, leaving kayakers at the mercy of recent weather; in general, water levels need to be above average to be run. The 2-mile stretch downstream from Bald River (with its stunning waterfall visible from the road) is known as "The Ledges," and filled with Class III and IV rapids, including 15-foot Baby Falls. No rafting outfitters run this river, so kayakers and fishers have it all to themselves.

**The Cheoah River** Since 1926 ALCOA's Santeetlah Dam has dewatered the Cheoah River, leaving it a dry ribbon of boulders. No longer; starting in 2007, ALCOA now schedules 18 recreational water releases each year, with a commitment to continue these releases through 2047 at a minimum. And how good is it? The Cheoah offers a steep, unchanging gradient where Class IV and V rapids abut each other almost continuously, with nearly no room for a breather between them. One section of Class V rapids lasts for 1.5 miles!

**WATERFALLS** **Falls Branch Falls** This lacy waterfall dances over an 80-foot cliff very close to the top of a mountain, easily reached from the Cherohala Skyway. The 2.6-mile (round-trip) walk starts at the Rattlesnake Rock Parking Area, 20.6 miles from Tellico Plains. It starts as a pleasant stroll along the abandoned bed of the Cherohala's predecessor road for 0.9 miles, then turns right and downhill to the waterfall, dropping 400 feet in all.

**Bald River Falls and Baby Falls** Magnificent Bald River Falls may well be the easiest waterfall to see in this entire book; the Tellico River Road crosses right in front of it on a high bridge. The view is dramatic. Here the Bald River pours out of its high gorge through a narrow slot of superhardened Blue Ridge rock, dropping 100 feet to the Tellico River below. The Tellico has its own waterfalls, and the best of these is slightly upstream. Baby Falls completely spans the Tellico with a single 14-foot drop, straight down and undercut. If you're lucky you'll be here when the water is high. Not only are the two waterfalls at their noisy dramatic peak then, but kayakers will be on the river and going over the Class IV–V Baby Falls.

**Conasauga Falls** This exceptionally beautiful set of falls is worth the work it takes to reach them. This is a double set of large waterfalls, beautiful at low water and overwhelming at high water. The foot trail will let you down at the bottom of the upper set, an 80-foot-tall horseshoe across the river with smaller, but still impressive, falls below it. Be sure to rock hop a short distance downstream to catch the second set, not obvious from the trail.

The approach is a bit of an adventure in itself. From Tellico Plains, go south on TN 68 for 2.3 miles to a right onto a minor side road marked by a large brown recreation sign as the road to Conasauga Falls. The next 1.1 miles follow the abandoned bed of old TN 68 and, although paved, are not maintained by anyone; parts are a mess. Then it enters Cherokee National Forestlands and becomes FS 341, a good gravel road through attractive young forests. At 2.3 miles from the main highway, take the right fork, FS 341A to its end in another 0.6 mile. The trail, FT 170, is easily followed. Ignore all temptations to shortcut steeply downhill, and follow it to its end in 0.8 mile, dropping 500 feet.

Conasauga Creek has been conquered by kayakers, who rate it as continuous Class III–IV—except for the falls, which are optimistically rated as V+.

**Falls of Snowbird Creek** North Carolina's 10,000-acre Snowbird Creek area is popular for its remote beauty, its 37 miles of looping hiking trails, its fine fishing, but most of all for its waterfalls. Directions for the trailhead are given above; from there you can hike into four major waterfalls. Heading up Snowbird Creek along the old logging railroad grade that serves as the trail, the 10-foot double cascade misnamed Big Falls comes first at 3.9 miles. Then comes the most impressive of the four main falls, 20-foot Middle Falls, at 5.1 miles. After 6.3 miles you reach Upper Falls, and your reward is a ten-foot slide rock into a large swimming hole. Go ahead and jump in; you are probably already wet, as the trail crosses Snowbird Creek seven times to get here. The fourth waterfall, Sassafras Falls, is a dramatic 50-foot plummet over hard gray rock on a side stream, Sassafras Creek. An ambitious day hike goes up Big Snowbird Trail (FT 64) to Big Falls and Middle Falls, then goes left on Burntrock Ridge Trail (FT 65A, with 400 feet of climb and descent) to Sassafras Creek Trail, then left, passing Sassafras Falls to complete a 12-mile loop.

**RECREATION AREAS** **Indian Boundary Recreation Area** This small man-made lake nestles at the base of the Unicoi Mountains in Tennessee, 2 miles from the place where the Cherohala Skyway finishes its descent. A recreation area of the Cherokee National Forest, it has a picnic area by a sandy swimming beach, with impressive views over the lake toward the Unicoi Mountains. Take the easy loop path around this lake for more views and some pleasant woods walking. There's also a fairly large campground in this area.

**Calderwood Village Recreation Area** This remote, lovely recreation area off US 129 is owned by the ALCOA Corporation and is open to the public daily from 8 am to 4 pm. The ALCOA road goes south from the highway to a lakeside fork; the right fork follows the lake through grassy meadows then swerves left onto a short causeway pier out into Chilhowee Reservoir. Here you'll find a few picnic tables and a portable toilet—and views, a full circle of views over the lake to the surrounding mountains, from this quiet and serene spot well out into the lake. When returning, be sure to take the left fork 0.75 mile to admire Calderwood Power Station, a handsome industrial Gothic structure inred-brick, built by ALCOA in 1928 and still used by them to help power their aluminum smelters in nearby Maryville.

**PICNIC AREAS** **Joyce Kilmer and Vicinity** Joyce Kilmer Memorial Forest has a very nice picnic area at its trailhead parking lot; however, it does tend to fill up during the busy season. Heading back toward the nearby Cherohala Skyway, you will find a table with a fabulous view toward the Unicois 2 miles from the Kilmer entrance road. Another 5.3 miles down NC 143 toward Robbinsville, a small national forest picnic area with a nature trail sits beside Lake Santeetlah.

**Cheoah Point** This Nantahala National Forest recreation area sits on the shore of Santeetlah Lake, 7 miles north of Robbinsville off US 129. It has a nice picnic area and a sandy swimming beach on the lake, with views over the lake to the mountains beyond.

**Along the Tellico River** Northeast of Tellico Plains, the Tellico River forms a recreation corridor within the Cherokee National Forest. Because of the steady tourist use along its scenic road, FS 217, the Forest Service has developed several picnic areas along it, as well as creating parking for fishermen and trail users, and designating several small primitive camping areas.

**Picnicking along the Cherohala Skyway** The people who designed the Cherohala Skyway managed to improve upon its more famous model, the Blue Ridge Parkway, in at least one respect: the Cherohala has plenty of picnic sites. You'll find seven picnic spots on the North Carolina side, and two on the Tennessee side.

## ✷ To See

**BIG DAMMED LAKES** People frequently assume that the lakes that stretch through this area are part of the Tennessee Valley Authority (TVA), a Great Depression hydropower project (still going strong). Not so. Only the huge Tellico Lake, completed in 1979, was a TVA project (along with Fontana Lake, upstream, completed in 1943; see "Bryson City and the Southwest Quadrant," To See). The four other lakes in this area are part of a project that long predated TVA, a completely private initiative of the ALCOA Corporation that's still known as Tapoco. Tapoco (which stands for "Tallassee Power Company") is a division of APGI ("ALCOA Power Generating, Inc."), a wholly owned subsidiary of ALCOA. Tapoco owns and runs four major dams and the lakes behind them: Chilhowee, Calderwood, Cheoah, and Santeetlah. Built between 1917 and 1957, these four dams supply about half the power sucked down by the giant ALCOA smelter at nearby Maryville, Tennessee, outside Knoxville. Although privately owned, all four lakes are open to recreational boating.

Dam enthusiasts will want to supplement the detailed information from ALCOA's Tapoco pages with the photos and descriptions from dam baggers Jan and Pat.

**Chilhowee Lake** The newest of the four Tapoco projects, the 1957 Chilhowee Dam is just up the Little Tennessee River from the TVA's new Tellico Lake. It floods a deep gorge, providing a long, serpentine lake that extends 8.5 miles upstream but covers less than 3 square miles. The lower parts of the lake are hugged by US 129, with picnic tables and a boat launch. The upper half of the lake is remote from roads, accessible only from Alcoa's Calderwood Recreation Area, open to the public.

**Calderwood Lake** The ALCOA Corporation built Calderwood Dam in 1928, the third of its four Tapoco Dams. It's located a mile upstream from the end of their Chilhowee Lake—a mile that's typically dry, as ALCOA reroutes the river water through a large pipe to the downstream power plant. The narrow lake backs up into a deep gorge for 7 miles, lined by wilderness its entire length. No roads follow it, but US 129, meandering along a ridgeline high above it, gives a spectacular bird's-eye view. The long lake finally ends at the base of the next dam, Cheoah, where US 129 gives access to it. The dam itself is a classic arch structure, unfortunately not accessible to the public.

**Santeetlah Lake** ALCOA added Santeetlah to its Tapoco project in 1926. Its big dam blocks the Cheoah River, turning it dry for 9 miles as it sends its waters through a pipeline to a power station on Cheoah Lake, far below and far away. Santeetlah Lake has the best-developed recreational opportunities of all the lakes in this area, with two private marinas and a Nantahala National Forest boat ramp at Cheoah Point. Santeetlah has a long and highly convoluted shoreline, most of it owned by the Nantahala National Forest; there are many shoreline camping spots within the national forest, and views are spectacular.

**Tellico Lake** (www.tva.com/sites/tellico.htm). Tellico Dam, located deep in the Great Valley, backs up a huge reservoir that reaches deep into the Unicoi Mountains. Within the mountains, the impoundment includes 12 square miles of surface and 128 miles of shoreline—yet this is less than half of the lake's total area. If you started boating down the lake from its extreme upper end at the base of Chilhowee Dam, you'd have to go 15 miles before you left the mountains, and would still have another 19 miles to go before you reached Tellico Dam.

Started in 1967, Tellico Dam and its reservoir became a symbol to environmentalists of development out of control, and a symbol to developers of environmentalism out of control. At one point the U.S. Supreme Court stopped the entire dam project to save an endangered species known as the "snail darter." Congress sided with developers and amended the law to allow the dam to be completed, snail darters or not, and the giant Tellico Lake started backing up in 1979.

The entire lake is public land, as is much of its shore. Within the mountains, US 129 closely hugs its northern shore with many wide views and several boat ramps. Its southern shore wraps itself through remote and mountainous countryside, with several more boat ramps.

**HISTORIC SITES** **Fort Loudoun State Historic Area** (423-884-6217; 338 Fort Loudoun Rd., Vonore, TN 37885). This very scenic state park occupies part of a forested island within the large Tellico Lake. Its centerpiece is a careful reconstruction of Fort Loudoun, a large British fortification that figured prominently in the conflicts between the Cherokee, the British, and the colonials. This palisaded fort, with formidable walls overhanging any attacking force, encloses a variety of military log structures furnished according to their original uses. Views from the fort are impressive, sweeping over the length of the large Tellico impoundment to the great wall of the Smokies and the Unicois. This is a favorite place for reenactment encampments, and the white tents and colorful uniforms add great charm to the scenery. A small museum sits near the fort, with exhibits interpreting life in the fort using archeological finds, as well as a 15-minute video. Elsewhere on the grounds are walking paths and a very nice picnic area. (To find Fort Loudoun State Park, follow the brown signs south off US 411 at Vonore, just south of the bridge over the Tellico Lake. Don't be confused by signs north of the bridge pointing to Fort Loudoun Reservoir; that's a different place altogether, and in the wrong direction to boot.).

**Sequoyah Birthplace Museum** (423-884-6246; Citico Rd., P.O. Box 69, Vonore, TN 37885). Open Mon.–Sat., 9 AM–5 PM; Sun., noon–5 PM. In 1821 Sequoyah, a nonliterate Cherokee silversmith, living in northern Alabama, introduced a Cherokee syllabary—an alphabet in which each symbol represents a syllable rather than a sound. This astonishing feat made him the first, last, and only historic figure to invent a writing system from scratch, having no previous knowledge of the concept of reading or writing. The Sequoyah Birthplace Museum, operated by the Eastern Band of the Cherokee Nation, presents exhibits on Sequoyah's life and accomplishments, as well as a full presentation of the succession of native peoples in the Tennessee Valley along with the archeological artifacts through which we know them.

It also features a small exhibit area of Native American art, and a very nice gift shop with a good selection of Cherokee and other Native American arts and crafts. To find the Sequoyah Museum, follow the brown signs south off US 411 at Vonore, just south of the bridge over Tellico Lake. It's only a short distance beyond Fort Loudoun State Park, on the right.

**The Charles Hall Museum** (www.charleshallmuseum.com; 423-253-8000; 229 Cherohala Skyway, Tellico Plains, TN 37385). Open every day, 9 AM–5 PM. This mammoth hall is the centerpiece of the visitors center complex that anchors the Tellico Plains end of the Cherohala Skyway. It presents artifacts gathered by enthusiastic local collector Charles Hall, including several older collections that he saved from destruction. The arrangement is logical and fascinating, giving a good clear overview of Hall's favorite subjects, then letting you home in on favorites: local Cherokee artifact, telephones, record players, typewriters, and automatic weapons from the two World Wars. The gift shop supports this free museum, and both are worth seeing.

**Tellico Plains Ranger Station** (423-253-2520; 250 Ranger Station Rd., Tellico Plains, TN 37385). Open Mon.–Sat., 7 AM–5 PM. Free. The earliest Civilian Conservation Corp (CCC) camp in Tennessee, still in pristine condition, houses the offices of the Tellico Ranger District of the Cherokee National Forest. It's a nice place to drop by—scenic, historic, and friendly. You'll find it off the Tellico River Road (FS 210, about 5 miles north of Tellico Plains via the Cherohala Skyway), down a scenic little drive that winds along a mountain stream through a lovely old forest. The station is a collection of white clapboard buildings, built in 1937, centered on a small white-columned headquarters building. It's the administrative headquarters for about a sixth of the 633,000-acre Cherokee National Forest, and forest crews frequently come and go from its large, neat maintenance yard. The pine-paneled headquarters building welcomes visitors with an information desk with books and maps, as well as exhibits on the CCC at Tellico, including a 1931 map of the Cherokee National Forest and 19th-century geological maps of the area.

**The Stewart Cabin** This minor site is a fun side trip from the Joyce Kilmer Memorial Forest or the Cherohala Skyway. From the start of the Skyway, 2 miles south of Kilmer, FSR 81 drops down to the right to cross Santeetlah Creek in a mile, with good views over this handsome creek (and good access for fishermen) from the bridge. Another 2 miles farther, the Stewart Cabin sits in riverside meadows by the gravel road. It's a modest, handsome log cabin, framed by wildflowers and a split-rail fence. The Nantahala National Forest restored it, and preserves it as an historic site. Return the way you came.

**Cheoah Dam** This is the most easily viewed of the Tapoco dams, built by ALCOA to supply electricity to their aluminum smelter in Maryville, Tennessee. Built in 1919, Cheoah was the tallest dam in the world at the time (at 225 feet) and had the largest turbines. The dam remains impressive nearly a century later, and gives you a good idea of the scale of ALCOA's early electrical project, very successful and still going full tilt. It is now best known, however, as the site of Harrison Ford's famous dam jump in the movie *The Fugitive*—accomplished by tossing a dummy off the dam, combined with a matte to add the appropriate background. US 129 crosses the river just in front of the dam with wonderful views of it, and more views from the side of the road. Take a gander at the industrial Gothic turbine station in the gorge under the dam, a beautiful piece of architecture instantly recognizable in the movie. Incidently, this section of highway is historic in itself—essentially unchanged since it was built in 1931, the first paved road into this remote corner of the mountains. The trailhead for the Slickrock Wilderness Walk is downstream on the left.

**Junaluska's Grave** Chief Junaluska was a respected Cherokee warrior who fought with General Andrew Jackson against the Creeks at the Battle of Horseshoe Bend (in Alabama). Junaluska and his warriors saved Jackson's European troops from near-certain defeat, and turned the battle. The victory opened Alabama to European settlement. Years later, President Andrew Jackson betrayed the Cherokee who saved him; Jackson signed the order that expelled Junaluska from his home near Robbinsville, North Carolina, sending him with his tribesmen on the Trail of Tears to Oklahoma. In old age, Junaluska was given permission to return to Robbinsville, and his grave, immediately outside town, is a sacred site of the Cherokee Nation.

**CULTURAL SITES** **Snowbird Indian Trading Post & Gallery** (snowbirdindian.com; e-mail: gc@snowbirdindian.com; 828-479-2330; Cornsilk Branch Rd., Robbinsville, NC 28771). Open normal business hours in season; call for appointment in winter. This modest building at the heart of the Snowbird Cherokee community has been a trading post since the early 20th century. Now it houses a craft cooperative for the Snowbird community, featuring the work of local Native American artisans. (Directions: Follow NC 143 west of Robbinsville toward the Cherohala Skyway for 5.4 miles; turn left on Snowbird River Road, SSR 1115, and go 1.8 miles; then turn left on Cornsilk Branch Road, SSR 1119, and go 0.7 mile.)

**Tellico Arts Center** (423-253-2253; 113 Scott St., P.O. Box 906, Tellico Plains, TN 37385). Open 12 PM– 6 PM. Closed Wednesdays and the whole month of January. Open Saturdays February and March. Tellico Plains's craft colony continues to grow, and this excellent not-for-profit gallery is at its center. Located a block off the village's Town Square on Scott Street, the Tellico Art Center hosts the work of 74 artists, all from the immediate area. The center occupies a large, handsome old red-brick building, filling the large loft-like space with a wide variety of fine art and craft art, from the traditional to the contemporary. The Tellico Art Center sponsors eight or so events a year, centering on mountain music and story telling.

**SCENIC PLACES** **Waucheesi Mountain** This remote 3,690-foot mountain sits just off the main crest of the Unicois, allowing fantastic views along the Unicoi Crest and back toward the foothills as they fall off into the flat lands to the west. Once crowned by a lookout tower, it is now given over to the usual assortment of antennae and (for the time being at least) kept clear of view-encroaching vegetation for their benefit. For directions from Tellico Plains see the Tellico River Road description, above. Its 1.5-mile access road (climbing 860 feet) may be motorable, but a high-clearance four-wheel-drive vehicle is strongly recommended.

**Pheasant Fields Fish Rearing Pools** (twra4streams.org/tellicohatchery; 423-253-2661; P.O. Box 265, Tellico Plains, TN 37385). Most days during business hours. Free. This remote hatchery, run by the Tennessee Wildlife Resources Commission, sits on the banks of the Tellico River along the Tellico River Road Drive. Long concrete troughs are filled to bursting with giant trout, waiting to be released into local streams.

## ✷ To Do

**STILL-WATER ADVENTURES** **Santeetlah Marina** (www.santeetlahmarina.com; e-mail: santeetlahmarina@gmail.com; 828-479-8180; 1 Marina Dr., Robbinsville, NC 28771). Open daily April–October. This full-service marina is located on Lake Santeetlah, 5.2 miles north of Robbinsville just off US 129. They rent canoes, ski boats, and pontoon boats, as well as slips by the night and overnight vehicle and RV storage.

**Deyton Camp Boat Rentals** (828-479-7422; Hwy. 143, 1 mile north of Robbinsville, Robbinsville, NC 28771). Open daily, spring through fall. Located on the south shore of Lake Santeetlah, on NC 143 near Robbinsville, Deyton Camp rents canoes, john boats, ski boats, and pontoon boats.

**Ron's Bait and Tackle** (www.graham.main.nc.us/~rlofty; e-mail: rlofty@graham.main.nc.us; 828-479-4467; fax: 828-479-4617; Hwy. 129 N., Robbinsville, NC 28771). Open daily, 8 AM–8 PM. This small but well-equipped bait shop, located on US 129 north of Robbinsville, North Carolina, has house boats for rent on Lake Santeetlah, as well as pontoon boats and bass boats.

**WHITEWATER ADVENTURES** **Nantahala Outdoor Center (NOC)** (www.noc.com/river_cheoah.html; 888-905-7238, 828-488-2176; 13077 Hwy. 19 W., Bryson City, NC 28713). NOC offers guided rafting trips on the Cheoah River 16 times a year. With continuous Class IV–V rapids, this is one of the East's premiere runs, and prior rafting experience is required.

**FISHING** **Cherohala Outfitters** (www.cherohalaoutfitters.com; e-mail: cherohalaoutfitters@brmemc.net; 828-479-9399; 260 Snowbird Rd., Robbinsville, NC, 28771). Open all year. This guide and outfitting service, headquartered north of Robbinsville near Lake Santeetlah, offers guided trips for both fly-fishing and lake fishing, as well as hunting trips for the Russian blue boar found in this area, and backcountry backpacking (including equipment rentals).

**Telliquah Outfitters** (www.telliquahoutfitters.com; e-mail: gage@fusemail.com; 423-253-3081; 1650 Cherohala Skyway [Hwy. 165], Tellico Plains, TN 37385). This fly-fishing store offers a variety of guided fishing excursions from their attractive, modern store in the Telliquah Preserve community, 1.3 miles east of Tellico Plains on TN 165, the Cherohala Skyway.

## ✷ Lodging

**COUNTRY INNS AND HOTELS**
**Snowbird Mountain Lodge** (www.snowbirdlodge.com; e-mail: innkeeper@snowbirdlodge.com; 800-941-9290, 828-479-3433; 4633 Santeetlah Rd., Robbins-ville, NC 28771). Open April–November. This 1941 rustic-style lodge sits high in the mountains above Lake Santeetlah, very near the Cherohala Skyway and Joyce Kilmer Forest. Built by a Chicago tour operator as a place to pamper guests, it features wide views from its native stone terrace. The lodge's rooms all have en suite private baths and are paneled in a variety of local hardwoods. The room tariff includes a full breakfast buffet, a picnic lunch, and a gourmet dinner.

✐ **The Blue Boar Inn** (www.blueboarinn.com; e-mail: innkeeper@blueboarinn.com; 828-479-8126; 1283 Blue

Boar Rd., Robbinsville, NC 28771). Built in 1950 as a hunting lodge by Cincinnati's Bruckmann Brewery, the Blue Boar has been completely renovated into an elegant little bed & breakfast inn. The eight guest rooms all have outside private entrances with private porches. A full breakfast, included in the tariff, is served in the dining room, as is lunch (open to the public), and dinner by reservation. The Blue Boar is located on Lake Santeetlah, just off NC 143.

**Blue Waters Mountain Lodge** (www.bluewatersmtnl.com; e-mail: info@bluewatersmtnl.com; 888-828-3978, 828-479-8888; fax: 828-479-9558; 292 Pine Ridge Rd., Robbinsville, NC 28771). This modern, wood-built lodge sits by Lake Santeetlah with its own 10-boat slip and lakeside deck. It serves lunch and dinner; a full, traditional breakfast is included in the tariff.

**RESORTS** **Tapoco Lodge Resort** (www.tapocolodge.com; e-mail: info@tapocolodge.com; 800-822-5083, 828-498-2435; 14981 Tapoco Rd., Robbinsville, NC 28771). ALCOA constructed Tapoco Lodge in 1930, using it as a corporate retreat center until 1997, located north of Robbinsville off US 129. The main lodge is an ivy-covered Georgian structure, simple and elegant in red-brick. The second story contains rooms, as do a series of classic 1930s white clapboard cottages wandering up the hill. Between the lodge and the cottages are the 1930s-era swimming pool and tennis courts, fully restored. The tariff includes a full breakfast, a light lunch, and a hearty southern-style dinner. The resort has 150 acres of property and adjoins the Nantahala National Forest; hiking trails extend from the lodge deep into the Kilmer-Slickrock Wilderness.

**BED & BREAKFAST INNS**

**Appalachian Inn B&B** (appalachianinn.com; e-mail: Info@Appalachianinn.com; 828-479-8450; 300 Knoll Top, Robbinsville, NC 28771). This modern-built log home is located north of Robbinsville, in the Cheoah Mountains' Stecoah Gap on NC 143, a short distance from the Appalachian Trail. It has five en-suite guest rooms, individually decorated and medium to large in size. The common area has a large stone fireplace and great views. A full breakfast is included.

**CABIN RENTALS** **Tellico Vacation Rentals** (www.tellicovacations.com; e-mail: tvr@tellicovacations.com; 866-253-2254, 423-253-2253; 113 Scott St., P.O. Box 906, Tellico Plains, TN 37385). These private cabins, scattered around Tellico Plains countryside, offer the comfort of an immaculately kept and handsomely furnished private house. Owned by Sandra Pyron of the Tellico Arts Center, this rental service has offerings that range from small and simple rustic structures to luxurious chalets.

**Mountain View Cabin Rentals** (tellicologcabins.com; e-mail: reservations@tellicologcabins.com; 423-519-2000; 133 Rafter Rd., Tellico Plains, TN 37385).This varied collection of 19 cabins faces the Tellico River a short distance east of Tellico Plains. The remarkable price range reflects a wide choice of amenities and sizes. Some of the small cabins do not have full kitchens, although all have at least a microwave and a refrigerator.

**Telliquah Falls Log Cabins** (telliquahfalls.com; e-mail: stay@telliquahfalls.com; 800-919-3137, 423-253-6378; 825 Steer Creek Rd., Tellico Plains, TN 37385). These four recently constucted log homes are full sized, and come with an excellent set of amenities—satellite TV, telephone, master bath Jacuzzi, fireplace with wood supplied, washer and dryer, outdoor hot tub, and a game room on the property with pool table and air hockey. Located on 75 wooded acres near Tellico Plains.

**The Historic Donley Cabin** (423-253-8400; fax: 423-253-2804; 250 Ranger Station Rd., Tellico Plains, TN, 37385). Of all the lodgings listed in this guide, the Donley Cabin comes closest to an authentic pioneer experience. Owned and operated by the Cherokee National Forest, the cabin is located in the Tellico River area, 20 miles from Tellico Plains by gravel road—and a quarter-mile walk into the forest. A two-crib cabin dating from the 1860s and '70s, the earlier and cruder crib is said to have been built by a Civil War draft dodger who was hiding out, while the later, much more sophisticated crib was added by Jack Donley, a prominent local settler. Donley's descendants owned and used the cabin until selling it to the Forest Service in 1994. The Forest Service has since restored the cabin to its 1880 condition, as a typical example of a log farmstead that has grown organically through multiple ownerships and generations. It's a beautiful little cabin, sitting in a little wildflower meadow with a nice front porch. Guest accommodations are in period as well: two slab beds without mattresses, a table with chairs, and a fireplace. That's it. No bedding; no shower; no water; no toilet. There's a stream and an outhouse nearby. Despite the less-than-luxurious conditions, it stays booked up, and reservations are required.

## ✷ Where to Eat

EATING OUT **Tellahala Cafe** (423-253-2880; 228 Bank St., Tellico Plains, TN 37385). Open Sun.–Thurs., 11 AM–8:30 PM; Fri.–Sat., 11 AM–9:30 PM. Don't be deceived by the modest appearance of the Tellahala Cafe, in a converted fast-food building near some edge-of-town strip shopping plazas. Inside is a warm, inviting place, with soft, rich colors and solid oak furnishings. The menu is imaginative and ambitious—and food is made from scratch on the premises by a staff of experienced, trained chefs.

**Town Square Cafe & Bakery** (423-253-2200; 704 Hwy. 165, Tellico Plains, TN 37385). Open Mon.–Thurs., 6 AM–8 PM; Fri.–Sat., 6 AM–9 AM; Sun., 7 AM–7 PM. Years ago, nearly every town in the South had a friendly little storefront café like this on its square. This spotlessly clean eatery is paneled with warm pine planks and matching pine tables, for a real homey feel. The fresh food, prepared to your order, concentrates on traditional southern favorites, and will serve you up a fresh breakfast anytime of the day. They also serve a full range of salads, sandwiches, and burgers.

DINING OUT **The Blue Boar Inn at Lake Santeetlah** (www.blueboarinn.com/home.html; e-mail: Innkeeper@BlueBoarInn.com; 828-479-8126; 1283 Blue Boar Rd., Robbinsville, NC 28771). The first-rate restaurant of this elegant little bed & breakfast opens to the public for lunch, and for dinner by reservation only. The lunch menu focuses on sandwiches and salads, made with a flare. The Blue Boar is located near Joyce Kilmer and the Cherohala Skyway, off NC 143.

## ✷ Entertainment

### *Tellico Plains*

**The Tellico Arts Center** (tellicoplains.com/tellico-arts-center; e-mail: tvr@tellicovacations.com; 866-253-2254, 423-253-2253; 113 Scott St./P.O. Box 906, Tellico Plains, TN 37385).

The Tellico Art Center sponsors eight or so events a year, centering on mountain music and story telling.

## ✷ Selective Shopping

### *Coker Creek*

**Coker Creek Gallery** (tnvacation .com/vendors/coker_creek_gallery; e-mail: gallery@cokercreekgallery.com; 423-261-2157; 206 Hot Water Rd., Coker Creek, TN 37314). Open April 1–December 21, Tues.—Sat., 10 AM–5 PM; all other times and dates by appointment. Owners Bill and Laura Hodge have assembled a fine collection of craft art from 30 local and regional artists. Their large selection of pieces, jammed into a building the size of a small house, includes photography, pottery, basketry, jewelry, forged metal, stained and blown glass, candles, woodcarving, sculpture, weaving, copper, painting and furniture, and some pieces that are just plain eccentric.

COKER CREEK GALLERY

While styles range from traditionalist to abstract, all their pieces are united by a high degree of technical competence and originality. Prices are nearly always under $1,000, with a wide selection of pieces under $60. (Coker Creek Gallery is 9 miles south of Tellico Plains via TN 68, to Hot Water Road, then a short distance west; the turn-off is well sign-posted.)

### *Vonore*

**Sequoyah Birthplace Museum Gift Shop** (www.sequoyahmuseum.org; e-mail: seqmus@tds.net; 423-884-6246; fax: 423-884-2102; 576 Hwy. 360, P.O. Box 69, Vonore, TN 37885). Open Mon.–Sat., 9 AM–5 PM; Sunday, noon–5 PM. Concentrating on Native American art, with a special emphasis on Eastern Cherokee artists, this museum gift shop offers a wide variety of jewelry, pottery, sculpture, and other items. The gourd pots are particularly remarkable and attractive. Book lovers will enjoy browsing the small but extremely well-selected collection of Cherokee titles.

## ✷ Special Events

**SPRING The Telliquah Native American Gathering** (monroe countychamber.org; e-mail: info@ monroecountychamber.org; 423-442-4588; fax: 423-442-9016; 520 Cook St., Ste. A, Madisonville, TN 37354). Mid-April. This annual gathering of tribes features Native American ceremonies and crafts. Contact the Tellico Plains Chamber of Commerce, who sponsors the event.

**SUMMER Cherokee Arts & Crafts Festival and the 18th Century Trade Faire** (fortloudoun.com/special -events/18th-century-trade-faire; e-mail: fortloudoun@tds.net; 423-884-6217; fax: 423-884-2287; 338 Fort Loudoun Rd., Vonore, TN 37885). Sec-

**GRAHAM COUNTY RAMP FESTIVAL**

(www.main.nc.us/grahamcoems/index.html; e-mail: terry.slaughter@ncmail.net; 828-479-7971; 49 S. Main St., Robbinsville, NC 28771). Last Sunday in April. Small communities throughout the North Carolina mountains traditionally support their volunteer fire departments and rescue squads with a ramp dinner. A ramp is a broadleaf wild leek with a strong onion-garlic flavor, one of the first plants to poke through the snow in the mountain forests. In the bad old days, people who were at the end of their winter food supplies would go into the forests and gather ramps as a healthy and hearty food until the crops came in. Ramps meant hope, and better things to come. And they taste good too—both the greens and the bulbs are edible, and delicious. The Graham County Ramp Festival is just such a traditional community get-together at the Rescue Squad building on Moose Branch Road in Robbinsville. They want everyone to come in and enjoy ramps cooked with mountain trout, chicken, baked beans, hushpuppies, cornbread, potato salad, and dessert.

ond weekend in September. The Sequoyah Birthplace Museum sponsors an annual celebration that mixes Native American handmade crafts with Cherokee dancing, stickball, games, artists, reenactments, and story tellers. Meanwhile, the European settlers are whooping it up at the 18th Century Trade Faire, a few blocks down the road at Fort Loudoun State Historic Site. Hundreds of reenactors attract thousands of visitors to an authentic 18th-century trade fair at the gates of the fort, with period wares, food, and entertainment from music to fire eaters.

**Graham County Heritage Festival** (grahamcountytravel.com; 800-470-3790, 828-479-3790; 837 Rodney Orr Bypass, Robinsville, NC 28771. July Fourth Weekend. This Independence Day festival opens the last weekend in June and continues through July 4, culminating in a Veteran's parade.

**Traders Row Marketplace** (telliquah.net/traders; 423-253-3081). Open June–October, every Sat., 11 AM–4 PM. Free. This crafters market is held every Saturday at the Telliquah Preserve development, 1.3 miles east of Tellico Springs, Tennessee, on the Cherohala Skyway (TN 165).

REVOLUTIONARY WAR RE-ENACTORS AT FORT LOUDOUN

# THE SOUTHERN UNICOIS: MURPHY & THE COPPER BASIN

The great massed knot of mile-high mountains that characterize the Smokies start to slowly drop away as their ridgelines head south to the Georgia border. While the area remains ruggedly mountainous, 4,000 feet becomes a high peak instead of a low one, and valley widths start being measured in miles instead of yards.

An exceptionally long, wide valley unifies this area, even as three state lines divide it. This valley runs for 22 miles east and west, reaching up to 10 miles wide, and bordered on all sides by large, tangled mountain ranges and huge tracts of public lands. To the north lie the Unicoi Mountains, a southern extension of the Great Smoky Mountains, while our old friend the Blue Ridge enters from the south to end on Big Frog Mountain, deep in a wilderness area. The attractive county seat of Murphy, North Carolina, holds down the valley's eastern end, while the two Tennessee towns of Ducktown and Copperhill sit in its center.

Here tourism turns from the mountain summits to the rivers beneath them. The Ocoee River, site of the 1996 Olympic whitewater competitions, furnishes nearly continuous Class III to V rapids, its flow regulated to perfection by upstream dams. The Hiwassee River in Tennessee, noted for its exceptional beauty, is popular with fishermen, canoeists (rapids are Class I and II), and hikers. A series of four major TVA lakes (two on each major river) give a wide choice of stillwater boating; this definitely includes wilderness exploration, as several of these lakes extend long, narrow arms for dozens of miles into unsettled national forestlands.

There are plenty of opportunities for mountain recreation as well. On the south side of this valley, the mountains rise again as the Unicoi/Smoky Range meets the western end of the Blue Ridge. This point is preserved within Georgia's giant Cohutta Wilderness, one of the great untrammeled sites of the South, as well as North Carolina's Big Frog and Little Frog Wildernesses on related ridges of these mountains in collision. Nor is this all. The western edge of this massif forms a continuous linear mountain, 25 miles of near cliff face looking out over the flat valley lands that stretch to the Mississippi. Known variously as Chilhowee Mountain, Chestnut Mountain, and Starr Mountain, this remarkable feature offers a wide variety of choices, from sophisticated recreation areas to the nearly impenetrable Gee Creek Wilderness.

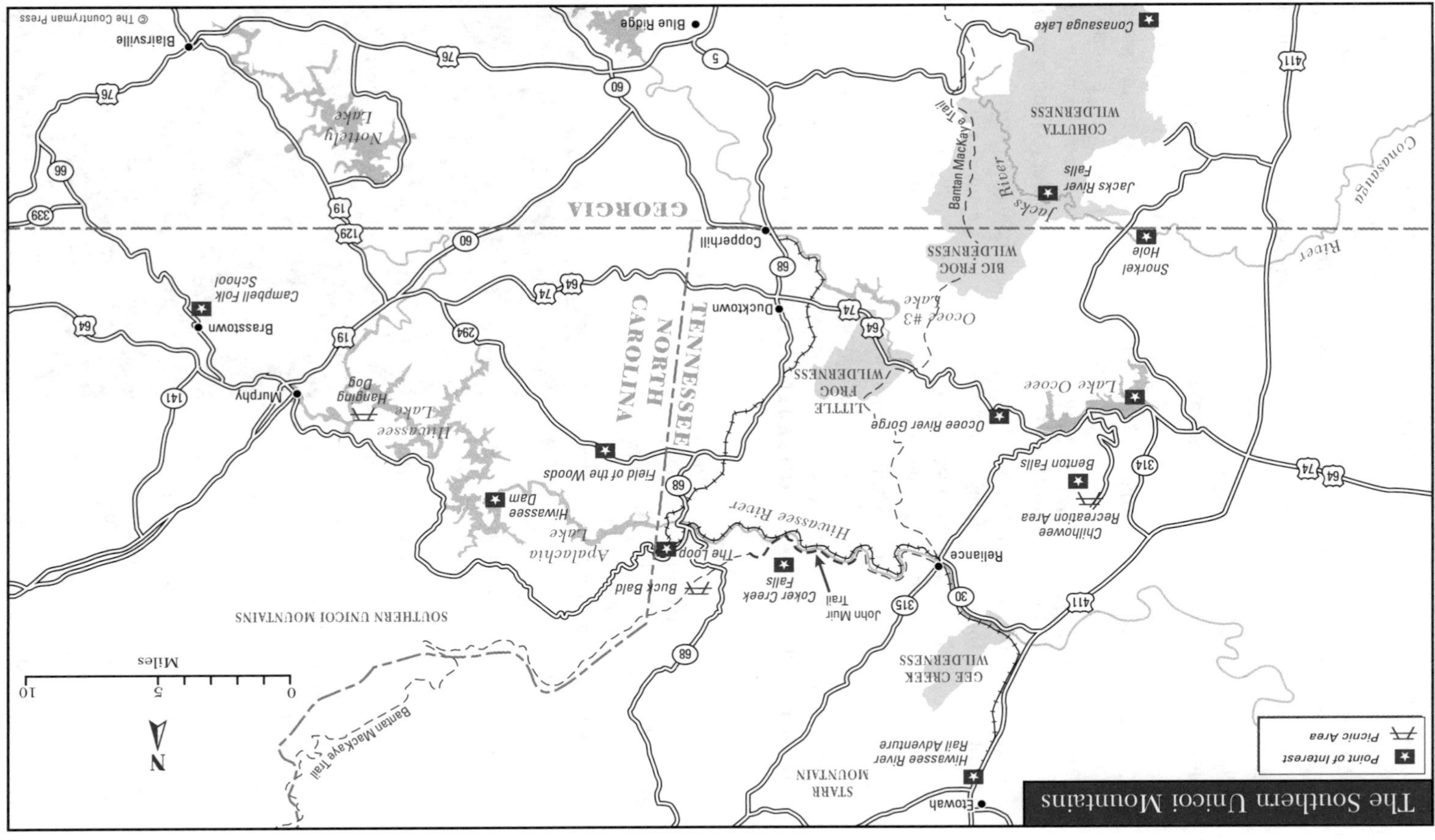
The Southern Unicoi Mountains
Point of Interest
Picnic Area
N
0
5
10
Miles
SOUTHERN UNICOI MOUNTAINS
Bantan MacKaye Trail
STARR MOUNTAIN
Hiwassee River Rail Adventure
Etowah
GEE CREEK WILDERNESS
Reliance
John Muir Trail
Coker Creek Falls
Hiwassee River
The Loop
Buck Bald
Apalachia Lake
Hiwassee Dam
Field of the Woods
Hiwassee Lake
Hanging Dog
Murphy
Brasstown
Campbell Folk School
Nottely Lake
Blairsville
Blue Ridge
TENNESSEE
NORTH CAROLINA
GEORGIA
Ducktown
Copperhill
LITTLE FROG WILDERNESS
Ocoee River Gorge
Ocoee #3 Lake
BIG FROG WILDERNESS
Bantan MacKaye Trail
Jacks River
Jacks River Falls
COHUTTA WILDERNESS
Conasauga Lake
Snorkel Hole
Conasauga River
Lake Ocoee
Benton Falls
Chilhowee Recreation Area
411
314
64
74
30
315
68
294
19
129
60
76
66
339
141
5
© The Countryman Press

ANDREWS

Although this area is a coherent whole, easily toured from a base in Ducktown, Copperhill, or Murphy, our Founding Fathers nevertheless saw fit to split it between three states. Tennessee and North Carolina split the valley in half, while Georgia takes the mountains to the south of the valley, including part of the Town of Copperhill. This is little more than a curiosity—until you try to get information on National Forest Service sites and trails. Then you will find yourself dealing with three different national forests. The Nantahala National Forest handles the forestlands within North Carolina in the eastern third of the region, from their ranger station in Murphy. The Cherokee National Forest takes charge of the Tennessee lands in the western part of the region from the small Town of Benton on the western edge of this region. And the Chattahoochee National Forest handles Georgia's Cohutta Wilderness from a station 20 miles south, in Chatsworth.

**GUIDANCE—TOWNS AND COUNTRYSIDE** **Cherokee County Chamber of Commerce** (cherokeecountychamber.com; 828-837-2242; fax: 828-837-6012; 805 West US 64, Murphy, NC 28906). The Cherokee County, North Carolina, chamber covers Robbinsville and the surrounding countryside.

**Andrews Chamber of Commerce** (andrewschambercommerce.com; e-mail: info@AndrewsChamber.com; 828-321-3584; 345 Locust St./P.O. Box 800, Andrews, NC 28901). The small town of Andrews, North Carolina, 16 miles north of Murphy on US 19, has its own chamber, with a visitors center in the center of town.

**Polk County-Copper Basin Chamber of Commerce** (ocoeetn.org; e-mail: eastoffice@ocoeecountry.com; 877-790-2157, 423-496-9000; 111 Ocoee St., Copperhill, TN 37317). The Polk County, Tennessee, chamber covers all of the Tennessee mountains in this chapter, including Ducktown and the Copper Basin. They maintain a visitors center in Copperhill.

**Etowah Area Chamber of Commerce** (etowahcoc.org; e-mail: info@etowahcoc.org; 423-263-2228; fax: 423-263-1670; L&N Railroad Depot, P.O. Box 458, Etowah, TN 37331). This chamber operates a visitors center inside Etowah's beautiful, fully restored L&N Depot.

**Tennessee Overhill Heritage Association** (tennesseeoverhill.com; e-mail: info@tennesseeoverhill.com; 877-510-5765, 423-263-7232; fax: 423-263-1670; 727 Tennessee Ave./P.O. Box 143, Etowah, TN 37331). This private, not-for-profit organization promotes nature and heritage tourism in Tennessee's three southeastern mountain counties. Its website is an excellent source of information.

**GUIDANCE—FORESTS AND PARKS** **Cherokee National Forest, Tennessee—Ocoee Ranger District** (423-338-5201; Rte. 1, Box 348D, Benton, TN 37307). The national forest ranger station for this part of the Tennessee Mountains is located on US 64 by Lake Ocoee. They have an information desk and bookstore.

**Nantahala National Forest, North Carolina—Tusquitee Ranger District** (828-837-5152; 201 Woodland Dr., Murphy, NC 28906). This ranger station covers all of the Nantahala National Forest around Murphy and Hayesville. Located off US 64 east of Murphy, it has a staffed information desk and sells maps of the forest.

**Chattanooga National Forest, Georgia—Conasauga District** (706-695-6736; 3941 Hwy. 76, Chatsworth, GA 30705). The Conasauga Ranger District covers the Cohutta Wilderness as part of its extensive and mountainous area in northern Georgia. Its headquarters lie 20 miles southwest of the Cohutta, between Dalton, Georgia, and Chatsworth, Georgia, on US 76.

**GETTING THERE** **By Car** This region's modern four-lane highway still follows (at least roughly) the tracks of the 1850s wagon road that crossed through this area from Asheville to the rich farmlands of Tennessee. Whether you approach from Asheville and I-40, or from Chattanooga and I-75, you need to take US 74.

*By Air* **Chattanooga Metropolitan Airport** (www.chattairport.com; e-mail: csiebold@chattairport.com; 423-855-2200; 1001 Airport Rd., Ste. 14, Chattanooga, TN 37421). Chattanooga Metropolitan Airport is the closest, being only 80 miles away from Murphy via US 74. Knoxville's airport is an extra 20-mile journey, at 100 miles away via I-75 and US 74. Asheville's is 35 miles farther, and Atlanta (which may be cheapest) is 50 miles farther than Chattanooga. You will have to rent a car in any case; none of the towns in this chapter has bus or train service.

**By Bus or Train** This region has no scheduled train or bus service.

**MEDICAL EMERGENCIES** **Murphy Medical Center** (www.murphymedical.org; 828-837-8161; 3990 E. US Hwy. 64 Alt., Murphy, NC 28906). This 57-bed local hospital, renovated in 2002, is the closest 24/7 emergency facility for the Murphy area. It's a short distance east of town on US 64.

**Copper Basin Medical Center** (www.copperbasin.org; 423-496-5511; 144 Medical Center Dr., Copperhill, TN 37317). This 44-bed local hospital has 24/7 emergency-room service from its facility on TN 68 near Copperhill.

**Woods Memorial Hospital in Etowah, Tennessee** (woodshospital.com; e-mail: woods@woodshospital.com; 423-263-3600; 886 Hwy. 411 North, Etowah, TN 37331). This 46-bed county-owned hospital, 3.3 miles north of Etowah on US 411, operates a 24/7 emergency room.

## ✷ Exploring the Area

This chapter covers the point, at the extreme southwest corner of this book's region, where the Blue Ridge terminates at the Great Valley of the Tennessee River. Not surprisingly, it has more scenic variety than any other chapter in this book.

The main central feature of this area is a rugged-floored valley, typically 8 to 10 miles wide, stretching east–west from **Murphy, North Carolina,** to **Ducktown, Tennessee**, a distance of 22 miles. Within this valley, rich farmland lines bottomland at or below 1,600 feet in elevation, while hills climb 500 feet to 1,500 feet upward from the valleys into a region of barren soils and dry pine forests. A great deal of the valley bottomland lies covered by **Hiwassee Lake** in North Carolina. North of this lake, mountains slowly rise to the 4,500-foot peaks of the **Unicoi Mountains**.

West of Ducktown and Copperhill, Tennessee, the valley ends in a tight jumble of low mountains mainly owned by the Cherokee National Forest, with the **Little Frog Wilderness** preserving an environment otherwise given over to logging. Two recreation streams cut east–west gorges straight through this jumble: the mild **Hiwassee River** and the wild **Ocoee River**.

On the far western edge of this chapter lies a single, massive mountain, 23 mile long and several miles wide, rising more than 2,000 feet above the valley floor. On its top is a west-facing ridge where, if you can find a break in the forest, you can gaze over the Great Valley stretching for miles before you. Behind that lie a series of oval perched valleys; then a long, slow drop to the smaller jumbled mountains below. This mountain is split by the water gap of the Hiwassee River; to the south it's called **Chilhowee Mountain**, while its northern half is known as **Starr Mountain**.

And finally, to the south of Chilhowee Mountain, the **Blue Ridge ends**. Here the East's mightiest ridge turns northward to meet the last low tail of the Smoky/Unaka/Unicoi complex in a final glorious tangle of high, hard mountains and deep gorges at the **Cohutta Wilderness** and the adjacent **Big Frog Wilderness**, straddling the Tennessee and Georgia state lines.

## EXPLORING BY CAR

### *Driving the Southern Unicois*

**The Cohutta Circle** This 50.1-mile drive on gravel forest service roads forms a half-loop around the Cohutta Wilderness, with several spectacular views along the way. To reach the start, take US 64/74 westward from Sugarloaf State Recreation Area at the foot of Ocoee Dam for 4.4 miles to US 411, then south on US 411 for 6.7 miles to a left (east) onto Willis Springs Road. Unlike the previous drive, these roads are neither particularly good nor easy to follow.

*Leg #1—Approaching the Cohutta (17.3 miles)*: Follow Willis Springs Road, becoming gravel FS 221 (Peavine-Sheeds Creek Road), for 8.7 miles, to a right over Jacks River; then go 5.2 miles on gravel FS 16 (Cable Rd, becoming Old Highway 2) to a left onto narrow gravel FS 17 (West Cowpens Road), reaching the ridge top in 3.4 miles.

*Leg #2—The Cohutta Circle (14.8 miles)*: Continue on rough, steep, narrow gravel FS 17 for 7 miles to its end at gravel FS 68 (Lake Conasauga Road); take FS 68 right for 3.8 to its intersection with gravel FS 64, and continue straight ahead on FS 64 for 4 miles, where it swerves right away from the Cohutta Wilderness.

*Leg #3—Leaving the Cohutta (18 miles)*: Continue on narrow gravel FS 64 (now Old Highway 2) for 7.9 miles to Watson Gap; then go right, still on gravel FS 64 (Old Highway 2), reaching pavement in 1.2 miles and GA 5 in another 8.9 miles.

*To return:* Turn right onto GA 5, reaching Copperhill in 6.4 miles. Turn left onto TN 68 to reach Ducktown and US 64/74 in 3.5 miles.

You could, if you wanted, drive completely around the Big Frog-Cohutta Wildernesses in a giant 90-mile circle, using an ordinary passenger car. Your author has

ORIGINAL 1911 SLUICE FROM OCOEE DAM

done it, and found much of it very rough, and some of it less than compelling. Parts of it are worthwhile, however, and this drive explores the best of it. As a bonus, this drive also leads you to the Cohutta's many trailheads.

The first leg starts out a bit suburban in character, but loses both its cityness and its pavement as it enters Cherokee National Forest lands, zigzagging through pleasant forests. After 8.1 miles you'll reach the Conasauga River, with a trailhead for **Snorkeling Hole**, a superb swimming hole, sharp on your right. The road parallels the river for the next half-mile, with a few campsites and some fishing access. At the intersection (8.9 miles) the Cohutta Wilderness is straight ahead, with a large trailhead for **Jacks River**, a beautiful gorge with a very popular path to **Jacks River Falls** along it. Your route goes right over the river, crossing on a modern steel truss arch bridge—an indication of how fierce this river gets during high flood.

You have now entered Georgia, and the **Chattahoochee National Forest**. The next 5 miles follow Alaculsy Valley, where mountains rise steeply from hay meadows with many beautiful views; much of this land is private. At 0.75 mile after the bridge, a forest road (FS 51) forks steeply upward and left; this is **Old Highway 2**, a former Georgia state highway that once traversed what is now the Cohutta Wilderness, and whose roadbed still functions as a wilderness trail. A turn onto FS 16 brings you to the border of the Cohutta Wilderness, after a long drive through an attractive forest. The trailhead for Cohutta's Conesauga River Trail is here.

From this point, Leg #2 circles the wilderness on a high ridge, for the most part forming the wilderness boundary. In many places the road marks the border between the two forest types, mature hardwoods in the wilderness on your left and post-clear-cut thickets in the ordinary national forest lands on your right—a sharp division between two types of national forest management. At 3.8 miles, FS 630 (Mills Creek Road) comes in from your right, with another Cohutta trailhead down a short spur road on your left. Now your road enters its worst section. Continue straight and, at 5.1 miles, your perseverance is rewarded by a wide **view** over Mills Creek to the Alaculsy Valley, from a formal lookout platform. From here it's 2 more miles to the Lake Conasauga Recreation Area, and the resumption of comparatively decent gravel roads.

**Lake Conasauga** is a mile to your right and worth a detour, a lovely mountaintop pond that's particularly nice in the spring and early summer when the rhododendrons bloom. The through road continues to your left, still following the ridge and passing two more trailheads (Bald Mountain and Chestnut Lead). After 3.7 miles, gravel FS 68 turns right to drop off the mountain and, while this is not your route, it is nevertheless worth detouring down it for 1.5 miles for a 180-degree **panorama** over the end of the Georgia mountains. Returning to the intersection, FS 64 becomes your ridgetop route, and passes two excellent overlooks and a trailhead in the next 4 miles.

Here, at the end of Leg #2, you will note an unusually large trailhead parking area as FS 64 suddenly swerves hard right and down the mountain. This is none other than **Old Highway 2** emerging from the wilderness on your left, and your road has swerved to follow it as it meanders away from the Cohutta. Here, Old Highway 2 is a one-lane gravel road, and it's amazing to contemplate that the 1972 Rand McNally map shows this as *better* than the section that then ran through the Cohutta. The forest here is mature and attractive. You cross the **Pinhoti Trail** at 2.4 miles, pass a nice picnic/camp area named **Jacks River Fields** (as well as the Jacks River) at 4.2 miles, and pass the **Benton Mackaye Trail** at 4.9 miles. From here you start climbing again, but now you are climbing something famous: the **Blue Ridge**, in its penultimate section. The next 3.8 miles follow the crest of the Blue Ridge, frequently narrowing to a one-lane ledge with some stunning views. This ends at Watson Gap, where the Blue Ridge heads straight, followed by narrow gravel FS 22 (Tumbling Creek Road), leading to the final Cohutta trailhead at Dally Gap in about 3 miles; the Benton MacKaye Trail crosses here as well. Your route, however, turns right and downhill, continuing on Old Highway 2, as it becomes a paved road through a lovely farming valley, ending at the main highway to Copperhill, GA 5.

**EXPLORING ON FOOT Hiking the Hiwassee River on the John Muir Trail** The two great rivers of Tennessee's Unicoi Foothills, the Hiwassee and the Ocoee, are both completely controlled by upstream dams. Despite that, the two are a study in contrasts; the Hiwassee River is as mild and beautiful as the Ocoee River is rugged and violent. The Ocoee is best explored by raft or kayak; but the Hiwassee can be fully enjoyed on foot. The 19-mile John Muir National Recreation Trail follows the north bank of the river.

The most popular section of the John Muir is its western end, reached from FS 108, off TN 315 just north of Reliance. This level section follows the river, with wide views of its rapids and rock formations; tall gray river bluffs tower on the left.

At the trail's halfway point, a remote and difficult trailhead gives access to its most remarkable area. (To the trailhead: From Ducktown go 19.2 miles north on TN 68 to a left onto Bailey Road, then 0.7 mile to a left onto Duckett Ridge Road [FS

22], then left onto FS 228 to its end in 1.6 miles.) From this trailhead, follow the John Muir Trail right (west) to switchback up to the top of one of those river bluffs, with broad views over the river south. At the base of this climb, a short, hard side trail leads right to the bluff's foot for a close view of a riverine cliffside. Also from this remote trailhead, Coker Creek Trail goes uphill through a deep defile along a raucous stream to reach **Coker Creek Falls**; this entire walk has been declared a National Scenic Area.

**Exploring the Unicoi Foothills** Despite their low size, the Unicoi Foothills are true mountains with rugged terrain, cliff-like slopes, turbulent streams, and rich environments. Much of this land is either privately owned, or national forestlands dedicated to timbering. The Little Frog Wilderness, however, protects a range of 2,000-foot and 3,000-foot peaks just west of Ducktown. Despite being adjacent to the Copper Basin areas devastated by acid rains in the 1860s and '70s, this rugged range now shows little obvious damage; before the restoration of the Copper Basin's vegetation in the 1980s, the contrast was very dramatic. Although logged in the early 20th century, the Little Frog's hardwood and pine forests are lush and beautiful, with a large number of wildflowers.

Two trails penetrate the wilderness from US 64/74 west of Ducktown. The first climbs a mountain ridge uphill from the #3 Powerhouse on US 64, for varied ridgeline forests and occasional views; if you stay on it to its end, you'll travel 5.5 miles and climb 900 feet to a trailhead on the remote gravel forest road known as the **Kimsey Highway**. A few miles closer to Ducktown, a second trail starts on US 64/74 to climb through the center of the wilderness. This is a more difficult hike, crossing several creek valleys as it climbs into a gap, then descends to lovely little Pressley Cove.

North of the Little Frog stretches a large area of rugged and remote Cherokee National Forest land, now actively logged. Here the **Benton MacKaye Trail** lets you explore this otherwise trailless area.

**Trails of the Big Frog and Cohutta Wilderness** These adjacent wildernesses, straddling the Tennessee/Georgia state line, protect more than 45,000 acres of steep mountains and deep gorges along the southern end of the Blue Ridge. Together, they make up a coherent mountain region of 3,500- to 4,000-foot ridges trending north-south, an area 16 miles long and typically 6 miles wide shaped a little like Greenland. Nevertheless, the hiking is distinctly different.

Tennessee's Big Frog envelops the northern end of this unusual range, a radial tangle of ridges running from this chapter's tallest mountain, the 4,200-foot Big Frog Mountain at the end of the Blue Ridge. Trails mainly run along ridges, or follow old lumber railways at even elevations. The **Big Frog Trail** is particularly recommended, and has the added advantage of climbing to the Big Frog summit. Big Frog trailheads are all well marked with large signs, and all can be reached by passenger autos (in good weather) from the narrow and ocassionally rough gravel FS 211. To reach FS 211, take US 64/74 west from Ducktown for 7.6 miles to a left across the Ocoee at **TVA Powerhouse #3**, then go uphill on gravel FS 45 about 3 miles to its end at FS 211; trailheads are in both directions.

The Cohutta is reputed to be the most popular wilderness in the south, and its major trails are a social experience on most days. The most famous of these follows Jacks River to **Jacks Falls**, a beautiful waterfall set in river meadows with a fine swimming hole. This is a fine through-hike, from the Dally Gap trailhead upstream to the downstream trailhead at the bridge in Alaculsy Valley. The abandoned roadbed of **Old Highway 2**, an unpaved state "highway" decertified to make way for the wilderness, gives easy access to the interior and some good views as well; it's called the East Cowpens Trail, another name for this old road. A third popular trail follows the Conasauga River. Away from these big three, and a few spurs that feed them, a number of trails offer solitude rather than society, chief among these are Hickory Creek Trail (reached from the Consauga River trailhead) and the Benton MacKaye Trail as it follows the Blue Ridge north from Dally Gap.

**LONG-DISTANCE PATHS The Benton MacKaye Trail** (www.bmta.org). The Benton MacKaye Trail (BMT) wanders through this area for 58 miles, hitting much of this chapter's best scenery and giving access to some of its least visited areas. When it enters this area from the south, it has already traveled 67 miles from Georgia's Springer Mountain, where it shares a terminus with the Appalachian Trail (AT). From there, however, the BMT zigs where the AT zags; more specifically, the BMT heads northwest to the Cohutta Wilderness while the AT heads northeast to the Southern Nantahala Wilderness (see "Franklin and the Nantahala Mountains," Wild Places). This, in fact, is the main point of the BMT when it was started in 1980—to follow MacKaye's original route for the Appalachian Trail, proposed in 1925.

This section of the BMT is unusually varied. From its southern trailhead on Old Highway 2 just east of the Cohutta (on the **Cohutta Wilderness Drive**), it follows the Jacks River headwaters where it meets the northern end of the **Pinhoti Trail**. From here it climbs to the crest of the Blue Ridge, and follows it into the Cohutta Wilderness and on into Tennessee and the **Big Frog Wilderness**. From there it drops down to the **Ocoee River** at **Ocoee Powerhouse #3**, then passes through the **Little Frog Wilderness** before traversing an otherwise pathless tract of heavily wooded national forest land. It then reaches **Reliance** and crosses the **Hiwassee River**, then parallels it using the **John Muir Trail**, passing the **Coker Creek Falls** trail on the way. After swerving northward away from the Hiwassee, the BMT finally leaves this area at **Buck Bald**.

**The Pinhoti Trail** (www.pinhotitrailalliance.org). The 236-mile-long Pinhoti Trail links the rugged Blue Ridge Mountains of northern Georgia with the low, long mountains farther south, in Georgia and Alabama, that make up the tail end of the Appalachians. It starts just outside the eastern boundary of the Cohutta Wilderness, then quickly leaves this book's area to enter the lower mountains and wide valleys the extend southwest beyond the Blue Ridge and Smoky Mountains. It's important to afficianados of the long-distance hike, as a major link in the Eastern Continental Trail, at 5,400 miles the longest foot path in North America, stretching from Key West, Florida to the northern tip of Newfoundland.

## ✷ Villages

**Murphy** The largest town of this area, Murphy is a good-size, somewhat sprawling place at the center of a very large valley. It has a lovely, well-developed old downtown that climbs a hill, making for interesting strolling. Within North Carolina it is famous for its early-20th-century courthouse, reputed to be the most beautiful in the state—a large and stately neoclassical structure completely clad in locally quarried marble. Hiwassee Lake, which starts 10 miles east of town, backs up into the village's downtown.

**Andrews** The small town of Andrews sits at the dead end of a wide, flat-bottomed river valley stretching northeast from Murphy to the Nantahala Gorge (see "Bryson City and the Southwest Quadrant," Villages). The first large piece of flat land on the far side of the gorge, it was a natural location for a major railroad siding. Like many railroad towns, Andrews declined for decades along with its line. In the last few years its fortunes have been reviving, and its small but well-formed downtown of old brick storefronts is beginning to attract new businesses. Andrews is the closest town to the isolated and beautiful Nantahala Lake; the road from Andrews to the lake, Junaluska Road, follows the 1855 stagecoach turnpike.

DOWNTOWN MURPHY

**Ducktown and Copperhill** Ducktown is a small, compact hilltop village just off US 64/74. Reliant on copper mining from 1850 to 1987, it's a neat, whitewashed town dominated by modest workers housing and a few small stores. Five miles south, Copperhill is considerably larger, with a well-formed downtown of brick storefronts facing the Ocoee River. The area between Ducktown and Copperhill, known as the Copper Basin, was utterly stripped of vegetation by acid rain during the 1860s and '70s, a byproduct of the crude copper smelting methods then in use. The worst of the pollution ended in the 1880s, when local mines started recovering and selling the acidifying sulphur instead of spewing it into the air. However, the vegetation did not start to grow back until a revegetation effort in the late 20th century, and rural landscapes remain immature. Ironically, the sulphur extraction outlasted the copper mining by almost two decades, the last sulphur plant closing in 2001.

**Reliance** This rural community sits in the gorge of the Hiwassee River,

MARBLE MINE BETWEEN MURPHY AND ANDREWS

tightly hugging TN 30. Noted for its concentration of old-fashioned small-town buildings, it's now a National Historic District. Look for the L&N Watchman's House, the Vaughn-Webb Homeplace, the Hiwassee Union Church/Masonic Lodge, Higdon Hotel, and Webb Brother's General Store—all listed on the National Register. Just over the river north of the village, the John Muir National Recreation Trail gives an easy walk along the beautiful Hiwassee River.

**Etowah** Founded in 1906 to support a railroad repair yard, Etowah sits at the base of Starr Mountain, at the far western edge of this chapter. Its old brick downtown lines US 411—on one side only, the other side being a strip of mainly vacant land, up to 100 yards wide, between US 411 and the large, and very active, railroad yard. An old photo in its railroad museum, located in the large and beautiful Louisville & Nashville passenger depot, shows the town built this way from the first. The L&N Depot also hosts the new and wonderful rail excursion trip, the Hiwassee River Rail Adventure. The downtown buildings across from the L&N Depot house a number of antique shops, as well as a couple of decent cafés.

## ✷ Wild Places

**THE GREAT FORESTS** **The Southern Unicoi Mountains** The Unicoi Mountains end north of Murphy and Ducktown in a series of 4000-foot ridgelines. Heavily logged in the early 20th century, it's now covered in second-growth hardwoods. Most of these mountains are in public ownership within the Nantahala and Cherokee National Forests. Nevertheless, recreational opportunities are few, and these peaks remain remote and little visited. The most prominent recreation site is Buck Bald, a grassy-topped knob with picnic tables and a full 360-degree view. Walkers can either day-trip or backpack along the newly opened Benton MacKaye Trail following its highest ridgeline. Other than that, the area lacks formal trails; hunters, hikers, and mountain bikers must use Forest Service logging roads and other old tracks, poorly documented on topographic maps.

**The Unicoi Foothills** The Unicois do not end suddenly and dramatically. Instead, they decline into smaller ridges and wider valleys. These foothills remain mountainous in character, but with only 1,000 feet or less local relief they lack the drama found only a few miles farther north. This is a land of wide valleys filled with attractive farms, with meadow views toward low mountains. It has a surprising amount of Cherokee and Nantahala National Forest land, including the Little Frog Wilderness west of Ducktown. Outside the Little Frog, the Benton MacKaye Trail furnishes the best opportunity for exploration as it crosses little-visited terrain between the wilderness area and the village of Reliance.

**Chilhowee and Starr Mountains** This 23-mile long mountain marks the westernmost edge of the Blue Ridge and Smoky Mountains in this chapter. It is a continuous linear mountain broken in the middle by the Hiwassee River, with its northern half named "Starr Mountain" and its southern half named "Chilhowee Mountain." As the last of the mountains, it offers some spectacular views from cliffs as much as 2,000 feet above the flatlands that stretch westward. Most of this large feature is publicly owned, part of the Cherokee National Forest, and managed for recreation, preservation and hunting, although its northernmost point has seen much timbering activity.

**Chilhowee Mountain** is the taller of the two, with peaks as high as 2,800 feet above sea level, and Tennessee River flatlands only 800 feet in elevation less than 2 miles west. Its most notable feature is a series of large mountaintop basins, and the largest of these contains the **Chilhowee Recreation Area**, whose paved scenic drive leads to views, hiking and biking trails, camping and picnicking by a small lake, and a notable waterfall, **Benton Falls**.

Starr Mountain is much less developed, with recreation centering on the tiny **Gee Creek Wilderness** and the larger, surrounding Gee Creek Primitive Area. Gee Creek itself is a deep gorge carved into the west side of the mountain, with ancient forests and several waterfalls, explored by a fisherman's trail that eventually ends at a beautiful glade underneath a 150-foot cliff. Oddly enough, most of this gorge parallels the steep western edge of Starr Mountain, carving it into a dramatic razor edge with a number of remarkable views both west over the flatlands and east over the gorge; the trail to it climbs 1,400 feet to a ridgetop intersection, where the cross-trail leads to views in either direction. To reach the Gee Creek trailhead, take US 411 2 miles north of its intersection with TN 30 between Etowah and Benton, then right onto Gee Creek Road for another 2.5 miles.

North of Gee Creek, Starr Mountain's top holds a series of shallow basins nearly 2 miles wide, ringed by sharp-edged peaks. It is easily reached by ordinary autos on a network of good gravel forest roads. Unfortunately, this area has been much logged over the last couple of decades, and the roadside scenery is nearly all the sort of thick, scrubby second-growth characteristic of recent clear-cut. There is a large network of horse trails exploring the lands away from the roads. Starr Mountain's narrow western ridge, noted for its wide views, is traversed by a good hiking trail, nearly level along its length, and easily reached from FS 44.

For impressive views of Starr Mountain from the valley below, try driving down TN 310 from Etowah to Tellico Plains.

**The Cohutta and Big Frog Wilderness** Located at the southwest corner of this area, straddling the Tennessee–Georgia state line, this is one the East's largest congressionally declared wildernesses, at 45,000 combined acres. It encompasses a wild and rugged zone of 3,500-foot ridges, separated by violent rivers in steep defiles. It can be a real surprise; the approaches to it are through the much lower relief of the Unicoi Foothills, or the nearly level Great Valley. Although heavily logged in the early 20th century, this area has rested for decades and now is covered by lush and attractive forests. The extensive trail network leads through every sort of mountain scenery imaginable, and the large size allows multi-day backpacking loops. Like all national forest wilderness areas, it's open to those remaining hunters who still wish to confront the wilds without their pickup trucks and ORVs; game is plentiful and wildlife observation is excellent.

It is here that the **Blue Ridge ends**—or begins, depending on which way you look at it. The last (or first) section of the Blue Ridge runs through the northeastern part of the Cohutta Wilderness and into the Big Frog, where it terminates at the 4,200-foot-tall **Big Frog Mountain**, to drop down to the Ocoee River Valley in a tangle of descending ridges. Back in the Cohutta, the Blue Ridge throws off a series of 3,500-foot side ridges, cut by the Jacks River into steep, gorge-like valleys. This area is easier to explore than you might expect; it's **surrounded by motorable gravel roads** leading to eight different trailheads; a lumber railroad parallels Jacks River for its entire length; and the closed roadbed of a former state highway, the never-improved GA 2, crosses its interior widthwise.

**RIVERS The Ocoee River** The Ocoee River gained fame with whitewater enthusiasts as the site of the 1996 Olympic Games' whitewater competition. The river drains northward out of Georgia (where it is named the Taccoa River), through the center of downtown Copperhill, and then down the mountains into Tennessee's Great Valley. In that final downhill stretch the Ocoee is controlled by three dams: Ocoee #3 Dam on the uphill end, then tiny Ocoee #2 Dam in the middle, and finally the large Ocoee #1 Dam at the downstream end. Below the Ocoee #3 Dam is a long dewatered stretch of river, as the river is piped from the dam to a downstream power station. This forms the "Upper River Section," the site of the Olympics, bone dry unless Ocoee #3 releases water. Downstream, between Ocoee #2 Dam and Ocoee Lake, is the "Middle River Section," which receives regular water releases from Ocoee #2 specifically for whitewater sports, a practice that started in 1976. Both of these sections offer nearly continuous Class III and IV rapids, with predictably optimal water flows because of the dam controls. Trips that combine the two sections typically run the Upper Section, paddle into #2 Lake, have lunch on the lakeshore, and then portage around #2 Dam to start the Middle Section. Downstream from Ocoee #1 the river enters the Great Valley, becoming much calmer; this is where tubing trips are held.

**The Hiwassee River** The Hiwassee forms a peaceful counterpoint to the violent Ocoee River. It's a broad, sparkling river, flowing over many Class II rapids, beloved of fishermen, canoeists, and campers. It flows through rugged and remote scenery, with many miles of cliffs along one bank or another, and many miles of Cherokee National Forestlands. Its north bank is followed by the John Muir National Recreation Trail. Like the Ocoee, the Hiwassee's water flows are completely controlled by upstream dams, in this case Apalachia Dam and Hiwassee Dam (see Big Dammed Lakes). The shrunken village of Reliance sits on its south bank.

COPPERHILL

**Jacks River** This lively little river forms a twisting gorge that runs for 17 miles through the heart of Georgia's Cohutta Wilderness. This is a surprisingly wide and full river, with dramatic scenery and a well-known waterfall. Logged in the early 20th century, access is via an old railroad grade that closely follows the river. None of the bridges has survived, however, so that a through-hike requires 42 fords, some of them waist deep in normal water. Despite this, it's a popular route for hikers, and you are apt to meet several other parties on any day during the season. The river can be kayaked when water levels are high, but with rapids ranging up to Class V and no maps available, this one is for the experts. Trout fishing is said to be excellent.

**WATERFALLS** **Jacks River Falls** Located deep in the Cohutta Wilderness, this waterfall drops the Jacks River by 60 feet in three big steps. Upriver from the falls is the large, level glade known as Beech Bottoms, now closed to camping; downriver is a deep gorge. This extremely popular hike has several approach trails, with the Beech Bottoms Trail being the easiest, shortest (at 7.7 miles round-trip), and most popular. From the Jacks River Bridge on the western edge of the wilderness go north (away from the river) on gravel FS 221 (Sheeds Creek Road) to a very sharp right onto winding gravel FS 62 (Big Frog Loop Road), then go 4.1 miles to the Beech Bottoms Trailhead on your right.

**Benton Falls** Benton Falls is a dramatic 65-foot drop within the Chilhowee Mountain Recreation Area. You'll find the trailhead well marked at the lakeside parking area at the center of the recreation area. From there, the good-quality trail leads over the tiny dam, then 1.4 miles through the mostly level mountaintop basin before dropping a hundred feet to the waterfall. The falls occur where three creeks flow together and drop into a gorge, protected as the Rock Creek Scenic Area.

**Coker Creek Falls** This very wide, 20-foot waterfall is the main attraction of the Coker Creek Scenic Area, protecting this lovely little gorge carved into the northern bank of the Hiwassee River. The waterfall is at the northern end of the 3.1-mile trail down this heavily forested gorge; the John Muir Trail is at the other end. From the Hiwassee River Bridge at Reliance, take TN 315 north for 4.2 miles to a right on CR 22 (Towee Pike), then go 7 miles to a right onto FS 2138, which leads to the trailhead.

**North Shoal Creek Falls** Little visited although easily reached (its approach path is a half-mile round-trip with a hundred feet of elevation change), this waterfall on a small creek drops straight down a 20-foot cliff into the calm waters of Apalachia Lake. It is well positioned for a side trip from two more spectacular sites, being 4.4 miles from Hiwassee Dam and 11.4 miles from the stunning panoramic views of Buck Bald. From the Buck Bald and Ducktown direction, take TN 68 to the Hiwassee River Bridge, then take River Road along the north side of the Hiwassee River (becoming SR 1322 at the state line) for 3.7 miles to a right on SR 1323, then go 2.8 miles to a right on SR 1324; the trailhead is 0.7 mile ahead. From Hiwassee Dam, go 0.6 mile north on SR 1314 to a left onto SR 1324; the trailhead is 3.8 miles ahead.

**SWIMMING HOLES** **Snorkeling Hole on the Conasauga River** This long, wide pool on the Conasauga River is a favored spot for snorkelers, noted for its clear, cold waters and more than 35 species of fish. Early summer is the best time for snorkeling, as the fish are still in their mating colors but the water is a bit warmer (still cold, though). Wear wading shoes instead of fins, and don't disturb the bottom, where the fish hide and spawn. To get there, follow the first 8 miles of the Cohutta Wilderness Drive, park, and walk a short distance down the path.

**RECREATION AREAS** **Ocoee Whitewater Center** (877-692-6050, 423-496-0100; fax: 423-496-0115; 3970 Hwy. 64, Copperhill, TN 37317). Built by the Cherokee National Forest for the 1996 Olympic Whitewater Slalom Races, this whitewater racing channel looks like an accidental product of nature. Not true—this course is completely man-made, carefully designed to test the skills of the world's top athletes. This stretch of the Ocoee appealed to Olympic officials precisely because it was (and is) dewatered by its upstream dam. This allowed large-scale manipulation of the Ocoee's dry riverbed, and carefully planned water releases put just the right amount of water into the course. Apart from its large visitors center, the main feature is the beautifully constructed pedestrian bridge over the Ocoee River, giving great access and excellent views of the whitewater course underneath. On the opposite side of the river is a large, well-maintained network of mountain bike trails known as the Tanasi System, with easy-going uphills and a steep downhill known as the Thunder Rock Express. The greatest crowds, however, come on warm days to swim in the many pools formed by the course, and to admire the kayakers. The center also includes a native plant garden, paved walkways with interpretive signs and a 2.3-mile (one-way) hiking and biking trail on the historic Old Copper Road along the bank of the Ocoee.

FOREST ROAD TO THE COHUTTA WILDERNESS

**Chilhowee Mountain Recreation Area** Chilhowee Mountain forms a 1,000-foot high barrier on the far western edge of this district. Oval-shaped, its sides are even and cliff-like, but its top is a broad, gently sloping basin. The Cherokee National Forest's Chilhowee Mountain Recreation Area occupies that mountaintop basin. Its access road, FS 77, makes a dramatic climb straight up from Lake Ocoee, with wide panoramas toward the Unicoi Mountains, over the Ocoee Gorge, and over the Great Valley of Tennessee. Recreation facilities center on a lovely little lake, and include a fine picnic area. An extensive trail system allows walkers and mountain bikers to explore the entire mountaintop basin, including 65-foot Benton Falls, declared a Scenic Area. To reach it, take US 64/74 west from Ducktown to Lake Ocoee, where FS 77 is on your right.

**PICNIC AREAS** **Hanging Dog Recreation Area** Three miles east of Murphy, this attractive Nantahala National Forest recreation site gives access to Hiwassee Lake. It has a lovely picnic area, nice walking paths, a little pioneer cemetery, and lake views. It also has a good quality public boat ramp and a camping area. A good-sized network of mountain bike trails uses Hanging Dog as its trailhead, exploring a number of former ridgetops, now peninsulas in Hiwassee Lake. You will find Hanging off the Joe Brown Highway, heading west from the Murphy town center.

**Buck Bald** The site of an old fire tower, this conical 2,350-foot mountain is crowned with open grassy lawns and a handful of picnic tables. Remarkable views in all directions make this a popular spot despite its remoteness. It's located in the Cherokee National Forest north of Ducktown, Tennessee; go north on TN 68 for 18.2 miles; then go right on gravel FS 311, following the signs on this rough but passable road for about 2 miles.

## ✷ To See

**BIG DAMMED LAKES** The Tennessee Valley Authority (TVA) owns and operates four hydropower dams in this area, two on the Hiwassee River and two on the Ocoee River. On the Hiwassee River in North Carolina Hiwassee Dam backs water up as far as Murphy, and Appalachia Dam produces additional power near the state line. On the Ocoee River in Tennessee, the unimaginatively named Ocoee #1 Lake (mostly known as Lake Ocoee) and Ocoee #3 Lake break this fierce river to harness. The TVA, "a corporation clothed with the power of government" as Franklin Roosevelt described it, uses these and 45 other hydropower dams to produce much of Tennessee's electrical power. North Carolina, whose valleys have been flooded by several of these TVA dams, gets no TVA power.

**Lake Ocoee** Sometimes known as "Ocoee #1 Lake" and officially dubbed "Parksville Reservoir," this large lake was built in 1910 by a local power company and purchased by the TVA, who now runs it. It's a long, thin lake that floods the lowermost (western) section of the Ocoee Gorge, with a main pool over 7 miles long and with over 100 miles of shoreline—but with only 3 square miles of water surface. US 64/74 follows Ocoee Lake for its entire 7-mile length, giving continuous views and many recreational opportunities, ending with a good view of the old dam. The dam itself is a massive concrete structure, 135 feet high and 800 feet long, one of the biggest in the world in its day. Needless to say, this lake is a popular spot.

Upstream is **Ocoee #2 Dam**, built in 1913 and later purchased by the TVA. It serves merely to divert the river into a wooden flume that carries it to a downstream power plant, so that its impoundment is tiny. If you are interested in this old complex, you can see it from US 64/74. As you drive west from the Ocoee Whitewater Center, look for the #2 Dam on your left at 2.3 miles; watch for its flume on the other side of the Ocoee River for the next 4 miles; then look for the #2 Powerhouse.

**Ocoee #3 Lake** Built by the TVA during World War II, this small, narrow lake covers a bit more than 4 miles of the Ocoee River downstream from Copperhill, Tennessee. Recreational access is from US 64/74, 3.1 miles west of the TN 68 intersection. The #3 Dam controls the flow of the Ocoee River's Upper Section, the site of the 1996 Olympics.

**Apalachia Lake** TVA's Apalachia Lake (yes, it's spelled with only one p) covers 9 miles of narrow Hiwassee River gorge within the State of North Carolina, between the state line and Hiwassee Dam. It's little used by fishermen and other boaters, probably because it has no marinas and its only boat ramp is in an isolated location. In recent years it has gained a number of second-home subdivisions on its shores, but for the most part it remains a remote wilderness experience, and most of its shoreline is national forest land. You will find the single boat ramp a short distance from the Hiwassee Dam.

**Hiwassee Lake** Water from the TVA's Hiwassee Dam backs up into the town of Murphy, 10 miles away. This long, skinny lake with many arms floods a long gorge of the Hiwassee River, with steep-sided hills rising out of the water, and the tall Unicoi Mountains visible to the north. Its main channel takes 20 miles to travel the 10 miles from the dam to Murphy, and its largest side channels extend another 10 miles—and nearly all of this 163 miles of shoreline are national forestlands, wild and open to the public. Recreational access is provided by the National Forest Service at Hanging Dog Recreation Area, and by TVA at the dam—a worthwhile site in itself.

**HISTORIC SITES** **Ducktown Basin Museum and Burra Burra Mine Site** (www.gamineral.org/commercial-burra-burra.htm; 423-496-5778; 212 Burra Burra Hill [off TN Hwy. 68], Ducktown, TN 37236). Open Mon.–Sat., 10 AM–4 PM. When copper mining came to Ducktown in the 1850s, it was a remote and inaccessible mountain community. The ore was mined in the crudest way possible, using techniques already long abandoned in most of the industrialized world. These mining methods, practiced by dozens of independent miners scattered throughout the valley, pumped so much sulphur into the air that the mountain rains turned into a sulfuric acid bath, killing all the vegetation for miles around. This high a degree of acid rain ended in the 1880s when more modern facilities recovered and sold the sulphur, but by then it was too late. A hundred years later the Copper Basin was still stripped bare of vegetation, restored only in the late 20th century at great effort and expense.

The Ducktown Basin Museum tells the story of the copper mines from the site of the 1899 Burra Burra Mine. Here the desolate ochre landscape survives, preserved as a National Historic District. Owned and operated by the Tennessee State Parks system, the museum sits above the mine, with exhibits (redesigned in 1996) that tell the story of the Cherokee expulsion from this valley, the subsequent European settlement, and the devastating copper mining. An overlook gives impressive views over the mine's flooded pit, and guided tours visit the mine's buildings.

♿ **Cherokee County Historical Museum** (cherokeecounty-nc.gov; e-mail: cchm@webworkz.com; 828-837-6792; 87 Peachtree St., Murphy, NC 28906). This local museum, owned and operated by Cherokee County, is located in downtown Murphy's handsome old police station, just behind their giant, white marble courthouse. The museum concentrates on the Cherokee Indians at the time before their expulsion from this area to Oklahoma, known as the Trail of Tears; Murphy's founding dates from that episode, having been built as a holding camp. The museum also has displays of local geology, and a collection of over 500 dolls.

**Hiwassee Dam** The TVA built this massive concrete structure in 1940, as part of their efforts to bring economic development to the poorest areas of the South by providing them with cheap and plentiful electricity. Today, paved SSR 1314 uses its top as a 0.25-mile-long bridge, with clear and somewhat disturbing views over the 300-foot vertical drop of the dam's downriver face. An excellent TVA picnic area sits on a grassy hill, shaded by large old trees, with sweeping views over Hiwassee Lake and Dam. From Murphy, take US 64/74 west 7.6 miles to a right on NC 294; then north for 8.6 miles to a right on SSR 1314; then north for 5.2 miles to the dam.

**Ocoee Powerhouse #3** (www.tva.com/sites/ocoee3.htm). More than any other TVA site in this area, the Ocoee #3 Powerhouse gives the feel of the massive scale of the war effort during World War II, and the excuberant optimism of the era. Built in 1942 to supply power to wartime industry, this handsome collection of structures sits in a deep gorge 4.1 miles below Ocoee #3 Lake, from where it gets its water. The massive aquaduct that links the lake with its powerhouse is mainly underground, but emerges as a highway-sized cylinder as it approaches the powerhouse. The powerhouse itself is a pleasant surprise a simple and elegant structure in the art deco style reached by a long, narrow bridge from US 64/74. It has a number of cast bronze interpretive plaques, and plenty of places to park a car and walk around. (The interior is closed to the public.) From here a hiking trail (the Rhododendron Trail, FT 337) follows the left bank of the Ocoee upstream 1.2 miles to the Ocoee Whitewater Center, with many good river views along the way.

**Sugarloaf Area, Ocoee State Scenic and Recreation River** (tnvacation.com/vendors/hiwassee_ocoee_scenic_river_state_park/; 423-263-0050; 404 Spring Creek Rd., Delano, TN 37325). Formerly Sugarloaf Mountain State Park, this state recreation area sits at the base of Ocoee #1 Dam, giving access to the calm Lower Section of the Ocoee River as it flows out of the mountains and into the Great Valley. In the early 1990s, TVA engineers constructed a fully functional scale model of the upcoming 1996 Olympic Whitewater Slalom Race Channel, later built upstream at the Ocoee Whitewater Center, in order to test and refine its water flows. This model is still there, as is the remains of the 1910 aqueduct that was part of the original dam project, now long abandoned. The views upstream to the dam are excellent, and there's a monument to those killed in its recent renovation, as well as a small interpretive pavilion and an excellent picnic area.

**CULTURAL SITES** **Fields of the Wood** (fieldsofthewoodbiblepark.com; e-mail: FOTW@cogop.org; 828-494-7855; 10000 Hwy. 249, Murphy, NC 28906). This "biblical theme park," run by the Church of God of Prophecy, commemorates its founding with monumental art deco sculptures in poured concrete, including the world's largest Ten Commandments. It occupies the spot where A. J. Tomlinson professed to have received the revelation (in 1903) which led to the founding of the Church of God. (Tomlinson led a split from the Church of God in 1923, his group becoming the Church of God of Prophecy. Both groups are now major Pentecostal denominations.) It's a remarkable place. It's white arched entrance leads into a landscaped valley filled with Christian monuments. The most striking date from the park's founding in the 1940s, and show a brilliant vernacular use of art deco elements in their curved, whitewashed concrete. The enormous Ten Commandments are the most famous, covering a grassy hillside with 7-foot-tall concrete letters. However, the most impressive monument is the Place of Prayer, a 320-step landscaped path lined with gigantic concrete tablets engraved with biblical verses, leading to a prayer garden with wide views. Other monuments include a reconstruction of Golgotha and the tomb in which Jesus was buried, and a hilltop garden displaying the flags of all nations where the Church of God has congregations. There is also a large gift shop. Field of the Woods is 18 miles west of Murphy; take US 64/74 west for 10 miles, then go right on NC 294 for 8 miles.

♿ **John C. Campbell Folk School** (www.folkschool.org; 800-365-5724; fax: 828-837-8637; 1 Folk School Rd., Brasstown, NC 28902). Founded in 1925 by New England social worker Olive Campbell and named for her late husband, the Campbell School occupies 380 acres in the rural community of Brasstown, 7 miles east of Murphy. The beautiful and well-kept campus looks like a large and prosperous farmstead, complete with barn and farmhouse; but these buildings hold studios and classrooms. The school sponsors an incredible list of six-day courses, with a large number going on at once and the courses changing every week. While every aspect of folk and fine art crafts are covered, the school is particularly strong in wood, textiles, and baskets. They run a first-rate craft store and sponsor weekly concerts as well as bimonthly dances. From Murphy, go east on US 64 for 4.6 miles, to a right turn onto Settawig Road, and look for the signs.

**RAILROADS** ♿ **Hiwassee River Rail Adventure** (hiwassee.tvrail.com; 423-894-8028; fax: 423-894-8029; 4119 Cromwell Rd., Chattanooga, TN 37421). Open April–November, most days. The Louisville & Nashville Railroad's "Old Line" runs diagonally through the center of this region, from Etowah to Copperhill. Built in 1890 to serve the copper and sulphur mines of Ducktown and Copperhill to markets in Atlanta and Knoxville, this spur died when the last major plant closed, in 2002.

It is dead no longer. Chattanooga's Tennessee Valley Railroad Museum, one of the largest railroad museums in America, has collaborated with the **Tennessee Overhill Association** to create an excursion line on this incredibly scenic railroad. Its standard trip, 50 miles there and back, traverses the entire length of the wild Hiwassee River Gorge, then climbs out of it on a 360-degree pigtail loop, called the "Hook & Eye" by the L&N railroaders. Three to four times a month it offers an extended trip, nearly doubling the length by continuing on past Ducktown to historic Copperhill before returning. Rolling stock consists of mid-20th-century passenger cars pulled by modern diesel-electric engines. All trains depart from Etowah; the schedule is irregular, so check its website.

♿ **The L&N Railroad Museum** (www.etowahcoc.org/qualityoflife/lndepot.asp; e-mail: info@etowahcoc.org; 423-263-2228; fax: 423-263-1670; P.O. Box 458, Etowah, TN 37331). The Louiville & Nashville Railroad built the town of Etowah when they acquired the "Old Line," constructed 12 years earlier by the Marietta and North Georgia Railway. Founded in 1850, the L&N was one of the nation's most powerful railroads, having sailed through the Civil War behind Union lines and entered reconstruction with great sackfuls of Federal greenbacks earned from hauling Federal troops and supplies. They quickly replaced the twisty mountainous Old Line as a through route, but kept it active to service the mines and towns of the mountains. They built Etowah at the intersection, as a repair yard, and created a grand passenger station to serve it.

Modern rolling stock made the Etowah repair yard redundant by the end of the 1920s, and the depot became useless when the last passenger train rolled out in 1971. It didn't stay abandoned long; by 1981 it was fully restored, and occupied by a museum commemorating Etowah's brief glory as a railroad town. It wanders through several rooms, with a wealth of artifacts, photos, and maps telling the story. Also in the building is the Visitors Information Center for Etowah, and the meeting place for the Hiwassee River Rail Adventure.

## ✷ To Do

**WHITEWATER ADVENTURE** **Ocoee Outdoors** (www.ocoee-outdoors.com; e-mail: info@ocoee-outdoors.com; 800-533-7767; P.O. Box 72, Ocoee, TN 37361). Rafting trips on the Ocoee and Hiwassee.

**Outdoor Adventure Rafting** (www.raft.com; e-mail: oar@raft.com; 800-627-7636; P.O. Box 109, Ocoee, TN 37361). Rafting, tubing, and rock climbing instruction from a 20-acre site on the Ocoee.

**Ocoee Adventure Center** (www.ocoeeadventurecenter.com; e-mail: info@ocoee adventurecenter.com; 888-723-8622; fax: 423-338-5086; 4651 Hwy. 64, Copperhill, TN 37317). Rafting and kayaking on the Ocoee, as well as mountain bike tours and rentals.

**High Country Outfitters** (www.hcrivers.com; 800-233-8594; 430 Hwy. 64 E., Ocoee, TN 37361). Kayaking and rafting on both the Ocoee and the Hiwassee from a 30-acre compound on the Hiwassee, as well as rock climbing instruction and backpacking trips. They have rental cabins and a campground on their compound.

**Nantahala Outdoor Center** (www.noc.com; 888-905-7238, 828-488-2176; 13077 Hwy. 19W, Bryson City, NC 28713). This large outfitter, headquartered in Bryson City, leads whitewater rafting trips on seven Southeastern rivers, including the Chattooga, Cheoah, French Broad, Nantahala, Nolichucky, Ocoee, and Pigeon.

**Wildwater, Ltd** (www.wildwaterrafting.com; 866-319-8870; fax: 864-647-5361; P.O. Box 309, Long Creek, SC 29658). This South Carolina company maintains an outpost for Ocoee River rafting.

**STILL-WATER ADVENTURES** **Lake Ocoee Inn Marina** (423-338-5591; www.ocoeeinn.com/Marina/Marina.html; Benton, TN 37307). This marina on Lake Ocoee rents pontoon boats, fishing boats, and canoes.

**GOLF** **Cherokee Hills Golf & Country Club** (800-334-3905, 828-837-5853; Harshaw Rd., Murphy, NC 28906). Located east of Murphy, North Carolina, this 18-hole, 1969 course has a reputation for difficulty, with hilly terrain and water hazards.

**GLIDING** **Chilhowee Gliderport** (www.chilhowee.com; 423-338-2000; P.O. Box 53, Benton, TN 37307). Open weekends; weekdays by appointment. This full-service glider aircraft operation offers 20 and 30 minute rides from the foot of Chilhowee Mountain, just outside Benton on US 411.

## ✷ Lodging

### BED & BREAKFAST INNS

**The White House Bed & Breakfast** (ocoee-whitehousebb.com; e-mail: mardan@etcmail.com; 800-775-4166, 423-496-4166; 104 Main St., Ducktown, TN 37326). This National Register listed bed & breakfast sits within the Ducktown Historic District, in a residential area a block from the town center. It's a large white clapboard house with a wide wraparound porch, shaded by large trees. A classic bed & breakfast, it has three guest rooms, all with private baths and furnished with antiques. A full breakfast is included.

**The Company House B&B** (www.companyhousebandb.com; e-mail: companyhousemt@tds.net; 800-343-2909, 423-496-5634; 125 Main St./P.O. Box 154, Ducktown, TN 37326). This 1850 white clapboard house has wraparound porches that overlook the center of Ducktown's Historic District. Listed in the National Register, it was built by the local doctor, remembered for his service to the copper miners in those rough early years. The lovely water garden in the back has the biggest goldfish I have ever seen. The six guest rooms, comfortable and furnished in antiques, are named after local mines. A full breakfast is provided.

✐ 🐾 **The Hawkesdene House** (www.hawkesdene.com; e-mail: Innkeeper@Hawkesdene.com; 800-447-9549, 828-321-6027; 381 Phillips Creek Rd., P.O. Box 670, Andrews, NC 28901). This is a modern-built house, looking like a large old farmhouse with dormers, sitting in broad meadows in a cove above Andrews, North Carolina. The interior is furnished in antiques, with a stone fireplace in its great room. The five private-bath guest rooms (one has its private bath across the hall) are all large enough for sitting areas. A set of two-bedroom cabins is also on the property, and a three-bedroom cabin is off the site. Young children are welcome in the cabins only.

**Huntington Hall Bed & Breakfast** (828-837-9567; bed-breakfast-inn.com; e-mail: info@huntingtonhall.com; 272 Valley River Ave., Murphy, NC 28906). Huntington Hall, furnished with period antiques, is a 19th-century lawyer's house two blocks from downtown Murphy. For business travelers, a fax machine/copier is available. Telephones are located in the common areas. Wireless internet is throughout the house. The full breakfast is served weekdays as early as 6 am and as late as 9 am.

**CABIN RENTALS** **Stone Creek Cabins** (www.sccabins.com; e-mail: steve@sccabins.com; 800-780-3459, 423-338-2674; 662 Mountain View Rd., Benton, TN 37307). Open all year. These five rustic cabins sit at the base of Chilhowee Mountain, on 20 acres adjacent to Cherokee National Forestlands. The recently built cabins are sided with stained logs or clapboards; furnishings are country style with wood paneling and floors. There's a volleyball court and fishing pond (catch and release) on site.

**Welcome Valley Village** (www.welcomevalleyvillage.com; e-mail: WelcomeValley@BellSouth.net; 800-542-8567, 423-338-9499; P.O. Box 577, Benton, TN 37307). This 17-acre property fronts the Ocoee River, just under Chilhowee Mountain and a short distance from US 64/74. It has four modern log cabins, spaced apart for privacy, each with its own design and decor. All cabins have full kitchens and porches, wood floors and exposed log walls. Guests have a choice of cabins with river views, whirlpool tubs, and/or wood-burning fireplaces.

🐾 ♿ **Cobb Creek Cabins** (www.cobbcreekcabins.com; e-mail: cobbcreekcabins@yahoo.com; 828-837-0270; 106 Cobb Circle, Murphy, NC 28906). The collection of seven cabins occupies a quiet, rural site just off US 19, southwest of Murphy. Each cabin is an individual (one is an apartment in the owner's 140-year-old farmhouse), but all share a high level of comfort. The site has a fishing pond, volleyball, and a horseshoe pitch.

🐾 **Copperhill Country Cabins** (www.copperhillcabins.com; 423-496-5225; 496 Deal Rd., Copperhill, TN 37317). Four modern-built log cabins sit in an 8-acre grassy glade, well off the main highway yet with easy access to Copperhill, the Ocoee River, and the Big Frog Wilderness. All have rocking porches, air-conditioning, gas barbeques, gas fireplaces, and sattelite TV. Three have full kitchens, while the smallest has only a fridge and microwave. They accept small dogs only.

**Apalachia Lake Wilderness Vacations** (wlvcabins.com; e-mail: jacook@wlvcabins.com; 888-865-2537; 36 Lake Point Dr., Murphy, NC 28906). These large, modern cabins, built in a rustic style, sit either on, or with views of, Lake Apalachia. Boat rentals are available.

## ✷ Where to Eat

EATING OUT **El Rio Authentic Mexican Restaurant and Cantina** (423-496-1826; 113 Ocoee St., Copperhill, TN 37317). This downtown Copperhill Mexican restaurant occupies a large and attractive two-story storefront, nicely decorated, with mezzanine seating and a tin ceiling. The menu includes the old favorites, then adds some old family recipes, topping it off with some vegetarian specialties. All food is made fresh from fresh ingredients.

**ShoeBooties Cafe** (shoebootiescafe.com; e-mail: info@shoebootiescafe.com; 828-837-4589; 25 Peachtree St., Murphy, NC 28906). Open Tues.–Sat., 11 AM–3 PM and 5 PM–9 PM. This downtown Murphy storefront eatery has deli sandwiches and salads for lunch, and steak, seafood, chicken, pasta, and chef specialties for dinner. Wine is available.

**Talk of the Town Ice Cream and Eatery** (423-263-6600; 804 S. Tennessee Ave [US 411], Etowah, TN 37331). Lunch and dinner, every day. This friendly, local café, located in a brick storefront directly across from the L&N Depot, and as the name implies, features traditional diner fare with 1950s decor. It's a good choice when you're in town for the excursion railroad, Hiwassee River Rail Adventure.

## ✷ Entertainment

### *Murphy*

**Friday Night Concerts at the Campbell Folk School** (www.folkschool.org; 800-365-5724; fax: 828-837-8637). Free. Most Friday nights the Campbell Folk School sponsors a showing of student work at 6:40 pm, followed by a music concert at 7:30 pm, featuring old-time mountain instruments and music. When weather permits concerts are held in the Festival Barn, so bring a lawn chair or be prepared to sit on a hay bale.

**Saturday Night Dances at the Campbell Folk School** (www.folkschool.org; 800-365-5724; fax: 828-837-8637). Twice a month on Saturdays, 8 PM–11 PM. These community square and contra dances, with live music, welcome couples, singles, and beginners.

### *Etowah*

♿ **The Gem Theater** (gemplayers.com; e-mail: gem_players@bellsouth.net; 423-263-3270; fax: 423-263-3223;

P.O. Box 486, Etowah, TN 37331). This restored 1927 movie theater hosts the Gem Theater Players, and has a regular series of other scheduled events throughout the year. No movies are shown—live plays and events only. It's located across the street from the L&N Depot.

## ✷ Selective Shopping

### *Murphy Area*

**John C. Campbell Folk School Craft Store** (www.folkschool.org; 800-365-5724; fax: 828-837-8637; 1 Folk School Road, Brasstown, NC 28902). Located on the beautiful campus of the Campbell Folk School east of Murphy, this craft shop has a juried selection of folk and fine arts by Campbell School students, faculty, and alumni.

### *Reliance*

**Webb Brothers General Store** (webbbros.com; e-mail: info@webbbros.com; 877-932-7238, 423-338-2373; Hiwassee River/Box 61, 3708 Hwy. 30/Hiwassee River Box, Reliance, TN 37369). This general store has been serving Reliance, Tennessee, since 1936, from its store on the banks of the Hiwassee River on TN 30. The store stocks food and supplies for camping or picnicking and has gas pumps. They also rent rafts for rafting the Hiwassee and provide lodging in their guesthouse. Artifacts from the Reliance Historic District are displayed in glass showcases.

## ✷ Special Events

**SPRING Murphy Spring Festival** (cherokeecountychamber.com; 828-837-2242; fax: 828-837-6012; 805 West U.S. Hwy. 64, Murphy, NC 28906). First weekend in May. This downtown Murphy Street festival features crafts, fun, food, and music.

**Polk County Ramp Tramp Festival** (423-338-4503). Fourth weekend in April, 10 AM–2 PM. This annual event near Copperhill, Tennessee, begins with a trip to Big Frog Mountain to gather ramps, the pungent and delicious wild leek that heralds the coming of spring. When a bountiful ramp har-

MURPHY STREET SCENE

vest has been assured, the bluegrass music and eating begin. A mountain tradition, the Ramp Tramp has been held every year since 1958 at the McCroy 4-H Camp, located 2.5 miles off Hwy. 64 on Hwy. 30 between Ocoee and Ducktown.

**AUTUMN Fall Festival at the Campbell Folk School** (www.folkschool.org; 800-365-5724; fax: 828-837-8637). First weekend in October. Held annually since 1973, this festival at the famous folk school features crafts, food, live music, dance, children's activities, and live demonstrations.

**WINTER Christmas Celebrations in Murphy and Andrews** (cherokeecountychamber.com; 828-837-2242; fax: 828-837-6012; 805 West U.S. Hwy. 64, Murphy, NC 28906). Murphy has a downtown Christmas street festival on the first weekend in December, with a Christmas parade, arts, crafts, food, and entertainment. A week later, nearby Andrews has its nighttime Christmas Parade.

**Annual Possum Drop at Clay's Corner** (www.clayscorner.com; e-mail: info@clayscorner.com; 828-837-3797; 11005 Old Hwy. 64 W., Brasstown, NC 28902). Every New Year's Eve the good people of Brasstown, 7 miles east of Murphy down a back road, gather at Clay's Corner (that's the general store) and bring in the new year with a ceremonial Lowering of the Possum. There's a Miss Possum contest, a possum song contest, bluegrass music, and the Little Brasstown Church Choir. You can even buy a can of USDA-approved possum from Clay's Corner.

# INDEX

## A

## G

## H

## M

## N

## Q



## R

## S